THE COMPLETE GUIDE TO THE
BIRDLIFE
OF BRITAIN & EUROPE

THE COMPLETE GUIDE TO THE
BIRDLIFE
OF BRITAIN & EUROPE

Peter Hayman & Rob Hume

MITCHELL BEAZLEY

To Henry Birch, the Thorogoods, and my
parents for their generous encouragement
from the beginning
RH

The Complete Guide to the Birdlife of Britain & Europe
Peter Hayman and Rob Hume

Published in 2001 by Mitchell Beazley,
an imprint of Octopus Publishing Group Ltd
2–4 Heron Quays, London, E14 4JP

ISBN 1 85732 795 0

A CIP catalogue copy of this book is available from the British Library.

Commissioning Editors   Vivien Antwi, Lindsay Porter
Executive Art Editor   Christine Keilty
Project Editor   Chloë Garrow
Editor   John Woodward
Production   Alexandra McCulloch
Proofreader   Jane Gilbert
Indexer   Diana le Core

Illustrations
Page 1 Great Spotted Woodpecker
Page 3 Golden Oriole
Page 4 Kittiwake
Page 5 Osprey
Page 6 Olive-tree Warbler

Printed and bound by Toppan Printing Company, China
Typeset in Garamond, GillSans, and Life

Contents

Introduction

This book is about the fascination of birds as much as how to tell them apart. If it conveys our own enthusiasm for discovering birds, and our enjoyment of their behaviour, then it will, we hope, inspire a similar excitement in our readers.

We cover all the birds that breed in Europe, as well as all the regular visitors. So many changes are taking place in bird distribution that detailed maps in each entry would have been out of date within a few months of publication, but the map below shows the total range of the book. We have avoided taking on the whole of the Western Palearctic – a zone that includes north Africa and the Middle East – yet we wanted to include some of the many rarities that visit Europe, some of which are more easily seen than some European breeders. We would have liked to include even more: we were sometimes tempted to write 'compare with…' only to remember that the other bird was not in the book. In the event we have omitted the really rare species, allowing us to do full justice to the non-European breeders that we have included.

An increasingly obvious challenge was to meet the needs of readers new to the joys of watching and identifying birds – in itself a challenge, but a richly rewarding one – while at the same time ensuring that the new information we had was communicated to the experienced birdwatcher. Even the most experienced enthusiast, however, enjoys a new book with new illustrations to pore over, and the size and scope of the book, and its wealth of illustrations will, we trust, appeal to anyone wishing to learn more.

We found, and indeed have long known, that there is much to learn about even the most familiar species. Much of the new information comes from a detailed study of specimens, mostly from the unrivalled collection of The Natural History Museum at Tring, Hertfordshire. Such study can never replace knowledge of the living bird, and we do not suggest that it should, but it adds an altogether different dimension. In fact, problems encountered in the field and explored in the museum often set us off on another line of enquiry in the field.

The birds in this book are all the regular breeders and visitors that can be found in the area shown on this map

For most of us, for example, a Garden Warbler is just that (if we can identify it at all). If it sings, we assume it is a male. Measurements, however, reveal differences between the sexes that can be seen if you get a good enough view and try hard enough. Species after species showed the same distinctions, which were frequently defined by variations in the length of the bird's body: a measurement rarely taken, even by the specialists who catch birds for ringing and measure their wings, tails, claws, bills, and weight, and even record their state of moult. In the spirit of presenting new information where we have it, we have included as much of this material as possible in the available space. It may seem a little esoteric to the beginner, but gives the expert something extra to find within these pages, and explains the subtle and sometimes not so subtle differences within many species.

Expert or beginner, we hope you enjoy this book. More importantly, we hope it encourages you to get out and watch the birds themselves, and share our enthusiasm for some of the most attractive, intriguing, and inspiring of creatures.

Peter Hayman and Rob Hume

How to use this book

The pages of this book work on several levels. The illustrations provide an instant visual impression of each bird for quick identification. The text provides vital facts to check this visual judgement, and also gives a wealth of extra information on behaviour and habitat. Yet both the illustrations and text go much deeper, exploring subtle distinctions of age, sex, and populations in enough detail to intrigue and inform the most advanced birdwatcher.

MAIN TEXT
The main text panel includes information on habitat, food and feeding techniques, displays and calls (where appropriate), breeding details, migration (if relevant), and length. The breeding details have been omitted for some species that do not nest in Europe.

HABITAT AND RANGE
In the coloured box at the foot of the column are brief details of the seasonal presence or absence of the bird within Europe (When to See) and its habitat and range (Where Found). These are vital when you try to identify a bird: it is highly unlikely that you will see one outside its usual range, or at the wrong time of year. Some species are remarkably restricted: you are unlikely to see a Stonechat in a wood, a Dipper in a garden, or a Tawny Owl on an open moor. Nor will you see a Willow Warbler in northwest Europe in January. Others, however, such as the Dunnock, can be found in many habitats throughout the year.

INTRODUCTION
An introduction in bold type within the illustration panel provides a general impression of the bird, often invaluable in identification. If you know a species well, such as the House Sparrow, you can often identify it at a glance. You don't have to check the details one by one. It may be the way the bird stands, or flicks its wings, or bobs its head; the general pattern of its head or back, or some other part of its 'character' that catches your eye. It is rather like picking out a good friend in a crowd of people: you may not be able to explain why, but you can do it, instantly.

COLOUR-CODING
Each species is colour-coded, so you can see at a glance to which group of birds it belongs. If you know which group you want, use the colour to turn quickly to the right pages.

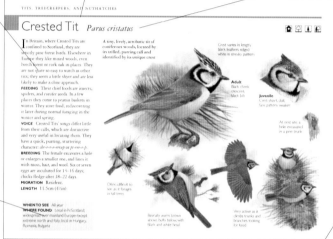

SCIENTIFIC NAME
The heading strip includes the scientific name of the species in italics. Scientific names convey a lot of information. Each has two words. The first word indicates the genus. All species in the same genus are closely related: something that is not always apparent from their English names. The Blackcap and Garden Warbler, for example, are near relatives, and this is made plain by their scientific names: they are both in the genus *Sylvia*. The second word is the specific name. Together with the genus, this gives every species its own 'label', so the Blackcap is *Sylvia atricapilla*, while the Garden Warbler is *Sylvia borin*.

ICONS
The symbols in the heading strip indicate the status of the species in Britain and its preferred habitat. The meaning of each symbol is given in the key below.

ILLUSTRATIONS
The accurate, yet evocative illustrations show as much information about each species as possible, with several different views of the bird in a variety of postures. They show all the common plumage variations, as well as some rarer forms, and include many details derived from careful research and measurement.

CAPTIONS
The captions to the illustrations pick out points that you will need to check if you cannot quickly identify a bird. They also reveal much more, such as differences in plumage or structure between the sexes or individuals at different times of year, or different parts of Europe.

■ KEY TO SYMBOLS

not recorded in Britain		town and built-up areas		mountains, moorlands, and crags	
rare vagrant in Britain		freshwater marsh		rivers and streams	
resident in Britain		coast and sea		cliffs and islands	
rare, but annual, visitor to Britain		farmland		broadleaved woods	
summer visitor to Britain		low scrub		pine woods	
winter visitor to Britain		high scrub		mixed woods	
passage migrant to Britain		lakes and reservoirs			

The parts of a bird

Throughout this book we have tried to avoid technical terms as far as possible, but some of the more precise details cannot be effectively described in any other way. So it is worth taking the time to study the basic anatomy of a typical bird, and becoming familiar with the names of all the main feather groups and facial markings. These terms are shown on the diagrams below, which will also provide a useful reference when reading the main species descriptions.

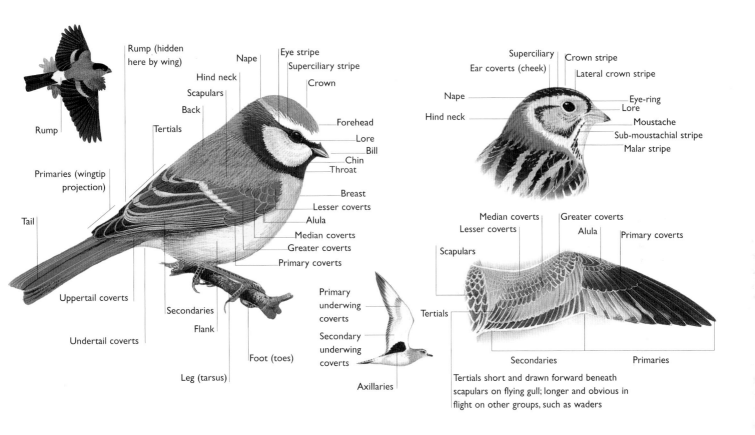

The patterns and colours of a bird's plumage are important clues to its identity, but they can be surprisingly easy to forget. This is partly because most people are not familiar with bird anatomy, so they cannot define the actual positions of colour patches or markings. Learning the parts of a bird, and especially the wing feathers, enables you to name the details you see through your binoculars. Even if you do this only mentally it makes the details much easier to check later.

Memory can play tricks, though, so one of the best ways to ensure you can identify a bird is to write a description in a notebook as you watch it. Better still, make a drawing, even the roughest sketch, with the various parts labelled. It may sound laborious, but making a fully annotated drawing requires that you look at all the parts of a bird, or at least as much as you can see while you are watching it. It is not easy, but practice makes perfect – and writing down such things as leg colour, bill colour, eye colour, and all the feather patterns reinforces your observation and helps you to memorize what you see. Once you have seen, described, and identified something in this way, you are much more likely to remember the bird in future.

The shapes and proportions of the various feather tracts vary greatly between the bird families. On a perched finch or bunting, for example, all the wing feathers – the lesser, median, and greater coverts, the tertials, secondaries, and primaries, and even the primary coverts and alula – are often clearly visible. On a swimming duck, however, the bird's scapulars often droop down to overlie its flanks, covering its wing feathers so that none of them can be seen except for the tertials, which are often prominent, and the tips of the primaries. It is only when the duck stretches, rises up, and flaps its wings, or actually takes flight, that you get to see its various wing feathers.

The measured drawings in this book allow detailed comparison of the exact proportions of the most prominent feathers, such as the main wing and tail feathers. This can be very helpful when you are trying to identify a bird with confusing plumage. A perched falcon such as a Kestrel, for example, will typically show long, slim wingtips because it has long primaries, but a Sparrowhawk in the same situation will show almost no exposed primary tips. Such distinctions may provide the only sure way of identifying birds such as larks, which are often indistinguishable at a glance.

How this book was created

The illustrations for this book are the culmination of several years' research based on the experience of a lifetime studying birds. They not only capture the essential character of each species, but are highly accurate and detailed.

Each illustration in these pages has been created after many years spent watching birds out in the field. In addition, museum specimens have been painstakingly studied – in particular those preserved in spirit, rather than skins or stuffed birds which are fixed rigidly in position. Countless photographs have also been examined and scores of books and identification papers read. The combination of expertise in the museum, field experience, and field notes and sketches has produced vivid, accurate illustrations with a wealth of useful detail.

Many of the details concern lengths and proportions. Most books give a simple measure of bill tip to tail tip for each species. More specialized works add the length of the folded wing, from the bend to the tip, and sometimes the lengths of the tail and bill. These are useful in some circumstances, but they are of limited value in judging the shape of a living bird.

Body length, for example, is never given, yet it is fundamental to a bird's proportions. It determines the extent to which the tip of the tail extends beyond the tips of the folded wings when perched. Measuring the wings and tail may not give this information, but a measure of body length does. When folded, the wings are more or less fixed in position relative to the body. A long body makes the tail project farther beyond the wingtips, while a short body reduces the projection or eliminates it altogether. This can be a valuable means of identifying species with nondescript plumage.

The research for the book has also revealed that body size frequently varies from male to female within a species. Consequently many of the illustrations show the wing-to-tail proportions of males and females, allowing the sexes to be distinguished even when their plumage is identical. This reveals why, for example, some gulls have long wingtips reaching well beyond their tails, but others do not. The difference is not random variation between individuals, but sexual dimorphism, and often adds to the complexity of identification.

The detailed measurements used as a basis for the illustrations have also revealed some surprising differences in other proportions, such as the length and breadth of the open wing. In some species a different ratio of wing length to breadth can make a flying male look quite different from a female. People who have studied a species for years often find they are able to tell the males and females apart at a glance, yet they do not know why. As a result they may even doubt their own judgement. The subtle differences in proportion explain how they do it. The ability of the human eye and brain to judge such subtleties is remarkable.

In most cases these distinctions are not necessary for simple identification of a species, but they take us a step further towards understanding the birds we are watching. In other cases such details can be critical to identification: there are some extremely difficult species among European birds that challenge even the experts, and the more information we have, the better. You only have to look at some of the streaky brown larks, pipits, and plain brown warblers to appreciate this. It is also amazing how much you can discern in the field once you know the difference is there.

TAXONOMIC TANGLES

Taxonomy is the study of classification, of relationships in the natural world. It sounds dull, but it isn't: it creates a great deal of heated debate.

The classification of a species may change as our knowledge increases and our interpretation of the data alters. Such changes are often based upon the views of very few influential people. The research for this book has raised a number of queries over thorny issues, in some cases revealing facts that suggest that a new classification is desirable. These are noted on the appropriate pages. For examples, see the 'Mediterranean' shearwaters, the White-backed Woodpecker, the Rock and Water Pipit complex, Booted and Olivaceous Warblers, and redpolls and crossbills. Such changes may already have been made by the time you read these words, but they will not alter the nature of the birds themselves.

The measurements
Each scale drawing of a standing or flying bird requires about 70 measurements of the wings, tail, wing bones, individual feathers, bill, legs, and feet. Male, female, and juvenile may be different. Whole birds are the most useful, but skins are used if necessary. The measurements enable a grid to be built up showing the main proportions of the bird.

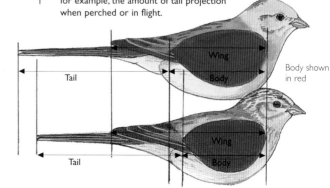

Primaries

Secondaries

A typical songbird has seven secondaries and nine primaries

The illustrations
The measurements and scale drawing form the basis for five or more drawings on tracing paper showing the bird's shape and character. When this is right the final drawing is rubbed down onto the paper to be worked up into the finished illustration.

Wing, tail, and body length
Birds of equal wing and tail length may be different shapes because their body length varies: usually males have a longer body than females, more rarely the reverse is the case. The difference affects, for example, the amount of tail projection when perched or in flight.

Wing

Body

Tail

Body shown in red

Wing

Body

Tail

How to identify birds

There is no quick way to learn your birds – but that means you have years of enjoyment ahead of you. Much of the appeal of birdwatching is discovering species that are new to you, and when you are starting out, they are all new.

Identifying birds takes practise. It isn't reasonable to dabble once or twice a year while on holiday and expect to become really proficient. But so what? It doesn't matter how good you are, you can still enjoy watching the birds around you. Even so, knowing more about them and being able to tell one from another adds to the enjoyment; it certainly doesn't reduce it.

As well as practise, identifying birds requires careful observation. First of all, when you see an unfamiliar bird, try to get an idea of its size. This may not always be easy: if it flies overhead against a plain sky, you have nothing to go on. But there is usually some sort of reference – foliage, grass, other birds – that allows you to make a judgement. Compare it to something familiar: 'about the size of a pigeon', 'smaller than a sparrow', and so on. For more advanced cases, such as the rarer warblers, your judgement of size may have to be more subtle than this!

Check the shape. Is the bird basically long and slim, or round and dumpy? Is it squat or elegant, tall or short? Is it heavy or light in its actions? A Grey Partridge, for example, might be about the size of a pigeon, but it is short-legged, short-billed, and round-bodied, with a small head and short tail. A Jackdaw, on the other hand, although also about the size of a pigeon, has a longer tail, longer wings, and a longer bill, creating a quite different general effect. When you start looking at birds like this you will soon learn the overall appearance of major groups such as the wildfowl, birds of prey, gamebirds, waders, gulls, pigeons, owls, thrushes, and finches, and begin to fit what you see into some sort of order, to give you a clue where to start. This is one of the main steps to identifying birds: getting a clue, rather than being altogether lost.

GETTING DOWN TO DETAIL

Once you have an idea of size and general shape, try to make a note (mental, or in a notebook) of any details that strike you about the bird's form. If you have decided it is a wader, you might be looking at things such as bill length and shape, and leg length.

Colours and patterns are next. If your wader flies away, does it have a wingbar? Or a white rump? Did it have black or pale legs? Do your best to make a note of as much as you can, because once it has gone, you will not be able to check again. If the bird really has flown, and you are none the wiser but you want to find out what it was, scribble down all you saw right away. It is extremely important to put down what you actually saw, before you look at a book. Once you start flicking through pages, reading bits of text and looking at pictures, then what you saw, what you think you

saw, what you have just read, and what you would like it to have been become so mixed up that any kind of objective identification is no longer possible. We have seen this process many times. We haven't quite seen black called white, but we have been in a hide with people watching a Greenshank (which has a bill that curves slightly upwards) and, on checking a field guide, pronounce 'Ah, it had a curved bill: it must have been a Curlew' (which has a bill that curves markedly down). Confusion sets in, memory plays tricks, the real bird is forgotten…

CALLS AND SONG

The voices of birds are amazingly useful to birdwatchers, for locating birds as much as identifying them. Most birds are first noticed because they make some sort of sound, especially in woodland. You will soon be 'picking up' birds by their calls even though you don't know what they are.

Some bird sounds are only useful for location, but other calls and songs are valuable to identification: indeed, some can be vital. If you see a Marsh Tit or Willow Tit, for example, you may be unable to decide which it is, but if it calls with a clear 'pit-chew!' the answer is easy: Marsh Tit. The song of a Chiffchaff quickly answers a similar identification problem in spring: no Willow Warbler – which looks almost the same – ever produces the sequence of simple, deliberate notes that gives the Chiffchaff its name. Rarer birds may also betray their identity with a call. A 'Greenish or Arctic' Warbler can be a challenge, but should it call 'zik', Greenish is instantly ruled out of the argument.

Calls, then, are important, and you will soon learn many of them, especially if you can watch a bird while it is calling and really make a lasting mental link between the sound and the bird. But how do you describe these sounds? In this book we have tried to do exactly this for the most important calls and songs of vocal species. If you listen closely, you find that birds generally don't have sharp, hard consonants in their calls: something that is written as 'zip' or 'tik' is little more than an emphatic 'i' sound when heard well. But writing down a series of vowels is useless in trying to convey a bird call, and a more imaginative use of letters and combinations such as 'z', 't', 'zzz', or 'tikitiki-tik' can give the right impressions of buzzy, sharp, slurred, or rattled notes.

Despite this the transcriptions in the book are really *aide mémoires* at best. Usually you have little idea what the bird really sounds like until you hear it: then 'zit-zit-chew' becomes clear! If you like, remember it as 'zit-zit-chew' from then on; but the chances are you will hear it as 'zap-zap-sue' and if so, think of it like that. Or maybe 'what's up, you?' might suit the purpose. But do try to get the best impression you can of inflexion and character: descriptions such as 'plaintive', 'sweet', 'rasping', 'nasal', 'emphatic', and 'explosive' are common in bird books, and they are all attempts to give information that really does help separate one bird from another. It is, anyway, all part of the fun.

The living bird

The illustrations in this book show birds in all their plumage variations and in a wide variety of poses. Yet a living bird can look quite unlike any picture. Its behaviour, the state of its feathers, and even the weather conditions can give it a unique appearance for the few minutes that you have it in view, and you need to allow for this.

The basic shape of a bird is defined by its skeleton, its bill, and its feathers. These help give a bird of a particular species, sex, age, and season an overall appearance that is usually remarkably stable. A juvenile Robin looks like any other juvenile Robin; a first-winter Common Gull looks like hundreds of thousands, indeed millions, of other first-winter Common Gulls. Yet other factors can change them, and you must remember these when looking at birds in the wild – or 'in the field' as biologists say.

The stability of basic structure can be seen on the wing of a small warbler. The lengths of the outer feathers, the primaries, may not be precisely identical in every individual, but they nevertheless conform to a distinctive pattern, just like the fingers of your hand. On a Willow Warbler this pattern is recognizably different from that of the very similar Chiffchaff. It is a function of the fact that the Willow Warbler is a long-distance migrant that winters in Africa, so it needs a longer, stronger wing for such epic flights; the Chiffchaff is a short-distance migrant, so it can make do with a shorter, rounder wing.

Close examination of the wing structure also reveals a tapered outer edge (emargination), and a more sharply stepped or notched inner web on some, but not all, of the feathers. The combination of the relative lengths of the feathers and their emarginations and notches is unique to each species. On millions of individuals this structural difference proves to be the same: a constant element that, if necessary, can be used to separate one species from another.

PATTERN AND COLOUR

Similarly, the pattern on some feathers can often be used to identify a bird with equal certainty. This is more useful to most of us than detailed structure, if only because it can be seen at a distance. You can see, for example, that a Mistle Thrush has white outer tail feathers while a Song Thrush does not; a Brambling has a white rump while a Chaffinch's rump is green. More subtly, there are a few broad dark bars on a Green Sandpiper's tail, while a Wood Sandpiper has several narrower ones. An adult Knot in winter has plain feathers on its back while each back feather of a juvenile is delicately fringed with dark and light lines. Such consistency of pattern, repeated millions of times within a species, allows us to tell species apart and often to separate the different sexes and ages.

The actual colours of feathers are also remarkably consistent. Tens of thousands of Black-headed Gulls show precisely the same shade of pale grey on their backs, and it is exceptional to see one that is paler or darker than its fellows. So if you see a darker grey back within a flock of Black-headed Gulls it is worth a second look, because it may belong to a different species. In the same way the precise shade of green on the back of a Blue Tit, or of pink on the breast of a Bullfinch, is repeated again and again.

WEAR AND TEAR

If birds are characterized by such striking consistency of structure, pattern, and colour, how is it that a living bird can look so unlike 'the bird in the book'?

Superimposed upon these consistent patterns are the effects of wear and tear. Feathers, after all, have a rough time over the course of many months, since they are subject to knocks, abrasion, and bleaching by the sun or, in seabirds, by salt. Dark areas in feathers are coloured by pigments that contain melanin, which adds strength to a feather. White areas, on the other hand, have no melanin; they are therefore weaker, so they wear more quickly. If you find an old feather from a bird such as a Curlew, with pale spots along its edge, you may see that the pale parts are actually worn right away, giving a saw-tooth edge. The white spots on the wingtip of a gull can wear off, leaving a solid patch of dull black (gull feathers can often be picked up on a beach, and are worth a close look). Patterns can and do change with time as the feathers are physically altered.

The other factor that modifies a bird's appearance over time is the effects of moult: the regular replacement of old feathers by new ones. This also proceeds with a marked regularity, and in most species there is a precise 'programme' of feather replacement. During moult a wingtip, for example, may have a very old, battered outermost feather, a gap where the adjacent feather is completely missing, and alongside that a pristine new feather, still only half grown. The wingtip pattern (and indeed shape) will therefore be a little unlike that shown in the book. Moult also affects a bird's colour. A Robin in fresh plumage looks immaculate, but after a hard breeding season it is pale and dowdy, bleached and tattered; when it moults in late summer it renews its plumage, and after a short time when it is inconspicuous, it reappears as fresh and bright as ever.

CHANGING POSTURE

The Robin also illustrates another factor that affects a bird's appearance. On a hot day it is positively skinny: taut and tight-feathered, standing upright on long, fully exposed legs. On a cold day in winter, as every Christmas card shows, it will be as round as a tennis ball, its legs all but hidden within loose, fluffed-out belly feathers that retain a layer of warm air as insulation against the frost. A Crested Lark can look equally round and dumpy on a cold morning, but in the semi-desert of southern Spain at midday it might appear as thin as a stick.

The posture of a bird is also influenced by what it is doing. A resting Grey Heron usually looks dumpy, its head withdrawn into rounded shoulders. When searching out a fish, though, it can look extraordinarily long and thin, tall, and forward-leaning, its head and neck stretched to their full extent: the very essence of concentration. Another familiar example is the Mallard, so round, squat, and pot-bellied as it sleeps beside a park pond, but slender and alert when feeding in a saltmarsh where it faces the dangers of predators or wildfowlers hidden in the creeks.

Birds also use posture to deliberately change their appearance. A displaying male Chaffinch spreads its wing feathers in such a way that the broad white wingbars show to greatest advantage. Yet the same Chaffinch, feeding quietly beneath a shady tree, cleverly covers its white feathers by tucking them under darker ones, so it is much harder to see – and therefore less vulnerable to attack.

TRICKS OF THE LIGHT

Light has a huge influence on the way we see things. Everyone knows this, but we sometimes forget. A white bird silhouetted against a bright, white sky can look dark grey; similarly a dark bird, moving against a shaded background but lit by a strong, low sun, can look misleadingly pale. A female Hen Harrier against a pale green field looks dark, but it may look surprisingly pale against a dark brown heather moor in bright sunshine.

A warbler in the dappled light of sun-washed leaves in spring may look green and yellow, yet the same bird in a bare bush of grey and brown twigs on a dull day looks grey. Gulls standing on white snow in dull weather look beautifully clear in their various shades of grey and white, but low sun turns the snow blue and the gulls orange. Conversely strong sun at noon makes the gulls dazzling white and the subtle variations of their pale greys are invisible.

Strong light can shine through feathers and change their appearance. Viewed against the sun, a slightly spread outer tail feather may seem to have a white edge that does not really exist.

Reflected light can be particularly misleading because it is often coloured. A bright blue bird once seen flying over a hotel swimming pool proved to be a House Sparrow, illuminated from below by blue light. That is an extreme example, but the influence of light reflected off snow is familiar enough: it produces a marvellous effect, projecting a ghostly, or sometimes remarkably solid whiteness onto the underside of a bird flying above. A Common Gull over snow, for example, has a wonderful whiteness with most strikingly contrasted inky black wingtips.

A bird in a tree against the sky is always likely to create identification problems. Even the brightest colours and strongest contrasts can be elusive in such circumstances. In late evening birds can look surprisingly orange: we usually compensate for this without thinking about it, because the birds surroundings are washed with orange light too, but published photographs taken in evening light may be misleading.

Tricks of the light also affect our impressions of size and sometimes shape. A distant pale bird may look bigger than it really is, while a dark bird may appear smaller.

The infinite variety of such effects can be confusing, but it also adds to the appeal of living, moving birds. Just bear in mind that, while all birds are essentially constant in their structure, pattern, and colour, the appearance of an individual bird can and does vary greatly, almost from moment to moment.

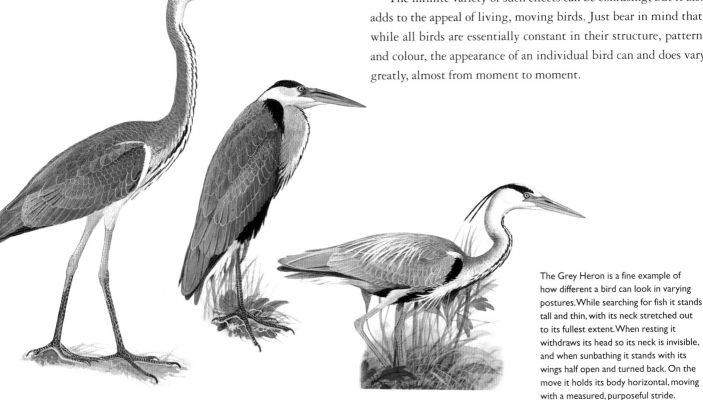

The Grey Heron is a fine example of how different a bird can look in varying postures. While searching for fish it stands tall and thin, with its neck stretched out to its fullest extent. When resting it withdraws its head so its neck is invisible, and when sunbathing it stands with its wings half open and turned back. On the move it holds its body horizontal, moving with a measured, purposeful stride.

The families of birds

With a very few exceptions the sequence of birds in this book follows the widely accepted 'scientific' order of birds, and their position in the order indicates the closeness of their relationships. The species are arranged in colour-coded groups, most of which consist of species from several families. This introduction to the various groups follows the sequence used in the book, but the different families within the groups are indicated in bold type.

The scientific classification of birds into families was originally achieved by comparing their appearance, anatomy, and behaviour. In general the classification reflects their true relationships, but the status of some species is still debated, as are the links between some families. Species that seem very different may actually be close relatives, while others that look similar are not closely related at all, but examples of 'convergent evolution' by which species that live in similar ways have evolved to resemble each other. Swifts, swallows, and martins, for example, all feed on flying insects and have evolved much the same look and habits, but the swifts are not closely related to the others. Zoologists are now able to establish these relationships by studying the DNA of contentious species and families, and ultimately this will clarify the relationships of the different families of birds beyond all doubt.

DIVERS AND GREBES

The divers and grebes are two small families of aquatic birds, rarely seen on land except when on the nest. Perfectly adapted for life on water, they are remarkably capable swimmers both on and beneath the surface. Yet their legs are set so far back on their bodies – for efficiency while swimming – that they are virtually useless on land, forcing the birds to slide on their bellies. Their long, slim, pointed bills are ideal for seizing slippery fish.

SHEARWATERS, CORMORANTS, AND GANNETS

The shearwaters and petrels are weak-legged ocean birds that live at sea but come to land to nest in burrows. Unable to walk well, many visit the shore under cover of darkness to avoid predators, making a loud, unearthly cacophony of calls as they do so. They are superb fliers and travel vast distances at sea. Storm petrels are small, delicate-looking relatives of the petrels that live in a similar way, spending most of their lives at sea. The gannets and cormorants appear very different, but share several structural features including having all four toes joined by webbing. Their wings also reveal a remarkably similar basic structure when spread wide. Gannets are huge birds that fly superbly well and feed by plunge-diving; cormorants are adapted for swimming underwater and are less efficient in the air.

HERONS AND PELICANS

The herons, bitterns, and egrets are long-billed, long-necked, long-legged birds of the waterside. They are all slender-bodied birds that move easily through vegetation. Some inhabit open shores, while others live a secretive life in heavily overgrown marshes, but they all require access to water for catching fish (with the exception of the Cattle Egret which feeds largely on insects in drier places and even forages on refuse tips). Several species nest colonially in trees, building large and obvious nests. Cranes are large birds resembling herons, but they are heavy-bodied and have smaller bills. Cranes require large areas of undisturbed land both in winter and in summer, and such shy, large birds find life increasingly difficult in the busy, heavily-populated Europe of today. The large, long-legged, long-billed storks look stately on the ground and magnificent in the air, travelling great distances by gliding. They are long-distance migrants, wintering in Africa. The spoonbills and ibises are closely allied to the storks, and also to the extraordinary flamingos which, like the spoonbills, are highly adapted for feeding in shallow water. Pelicans are actually related to the gannets and cormorants, and have the same type of feet with all four toes webbed. In their way pelicans are among the world's finest flying birds, able to exploit rising air currents to perfection, but they are better known for their capacious throat pouches which they use to scoop fish from the water.

WILDFOWL

This single family includes all the swans, geese, and ducks, and displays a wide variety of adaptations. Swans are large, short-legged, long-necked birds that feed in water or on land. Geese are stockier than swans but larger than most ducks, with longer legs which make them more mobile on land. They feed in large flocks and fly in wonderful V-formations, lines, and chevrons. They form two basic groups, the 'grey geese' (grey-brown and white with variously coloured legs and bills) and the 'black geese' (grey or dark brown with a lot of black, and black legs and bills). The shelducks are more or less intermediate between geese and true ducks. Dabbling or surface-feeding ducks feed by filtering water through fine 'combs' in their bills to extract food; they also feed underwater by 'up-ending' but rarely diving, and graze or pick up grain on land. They have short legs but walk moderately well, and long wings which, despite their heavy bodies, allow fast and powerful flight. Diving ducks feed underwater, diving from the surface. Some species live at sea, others mostly on freshwater or both; the sea ducks include maritime species such as eiders and scoters. Finally the sawbills are fish-catching species whose bills have toothed edges for gripping slippery prey.

BIRDS OF PREY

Well known for their hooked bills and often their sharp, curved claws, the birds of prey catch live food or forage for dead animals (carrion) or refuse. Many are superb in the air, but spend long periods inactive on perches. The vultures, kites, harriers, hawks, buzzards, and eagles all belong to the same family, the Accipitridae. Vultures are carrion-eaters that exploit air currents to stay aloft as they search the ground for food; however repellent their eating habits, they are sensational in the sky. The kites are elegant fliers that both kill live prey and eat dead meat and rubbish of all kinds. Harriers are long-winged birds with sharp claws and a long reach, adapted for snatching prey while hunting at low level over grassy or reed-covered areas and open moors. Bird-eating hawks such as the sparrowhawk also have a long reach, with long needle-sharp claws; they are short-winged, long-tailed, fast, agile hunters of woods and gardens. The buzzards both soar and hover; they catch live food and eat a lot of carrion, and even plod about in fields in search of earthworms and beetles. The biggest members of the family, the eagles, vary from medium-sized to very large; most are powerful hunters and expert fliers that kill much of their food, but they often survive winters by scavenging meat from dead animals. The **falcons** belong to a different family; long-winged and long-tailed, they range from hunters of insects and small birds to powerful predators of larger birds and mammals.

GAMEBIRDS, CRAKES, AND RAILS

The gamebirds are a small but diverse group of seed-eating species with short, curved bills, longish legs with sharp 'spurs', and a low, fast, whirring flight. They include the various types of **grouse** which are mainly upland or northern birds adapted to

harsh climates, and the partridges, pheasants, and quails. Partridges are squat, short-tailed birds but pheasants are larger, with long or very long tails. Quails are tiny and secretive, living in dense crops. The crakes and rails are waterside birds with long toes, sometimes lobed, that allow them to walk over waterlogged ground and floating weed; some are common and obvious, often on open water, while others are rare and secretive, living in dense vegetation. All are rather round-looking birds from the side, but their bodies are extremely slim for slipping through the dense vertical stems of reedbeds. The bustards combine some of the features of the gamebirds with those of waders; they are rare and restricted, having declined as a result of hunting, disturbance, and loss of habitat.

WADERS

This is a very large, mixed, complex group of families. In North America they are usually termed 'shorebirds', but neither term fully describes all the species. Many live far from any shore and rarely wade; some breed in dry areas but spend the winter on shorelines. The strangest waders are the stone-curlews, with just one European species: a big-eyed, partly nocturnal ground bird of dry, open terrain. The pratincoles are quite different, with a somewhat swallow-like form, although much larger; they share with swallows and some terns an aerial, insectivorous lifestyle. The stilts and avocets are true wading birds that exploit shallow water. Stilts wade deeply and snatch insects from the surface with needle-like bills, while avocets sweep their upturned bills sideways through shallow watery mud to catch tiny shrimps and other small animals. Oystercatchers eat shellfish when they can, smashing or prising them open with their strong red bills, but when food is short they are forced into fields to look for worms. They are noisy, eyecatching birds, and often highly gregarious. The plovers include the widespread but declining Lapwing that breeds and spends the winter on arable land and marshes, the 'ringed' plovers that nest on beaches, and the Dotterel that breeds on mountain grasslands and the northern tundra. The sandpipers include some very numerous and gregarious species such as the Knot, which flies in huge, spectacular, highly coordinated flocks. Many species breed far to the north and winter far to the south (the Sanderling, for example, migrates from the Arctic almost to the Antarctic). The Dunlin is one of the most widespread and familiar of the sandpipers, and a 'standard' by which others are judged and identified. The 'shanks' are larger and have longer legs than typical sandpipers; the *Tringa* sandpipers – which include the Green Sandpiper and Wood Sandpiper – are medium-small, and the 'stints' are tiny and small-billed. Some species mix together freely. The sandpiper family also includes specialized waders like the very long-billed, short-legged, large-eyed Snipe which needs soft, oozy, wet ground, and the cryptically coloured Woodcock: a woodland wader that emerges at dusk to feed in wet places with thick layers of soft leaf-mould. Finally the phalaropes are remarkable for their sexual role reversal, the female being more brightly coloured than the male and taking the dominant role in courtship. Unlike most waders they feed while swimming and spend the winter at sea, often far from land.

GULLS, TERNS, AND AUKS

This group includes the skuas: long-winged, elegant fliers that are both predatory and piratical, stealing much of their food from other species. The more abundant and widespread **gulls** range from small and neat to very large and aggressive, with several 'generalist' and opportunist species such as the Black-headed Gull and some very specialized ones, such as Audouin's Gull. The rather similar **terns** include pale-plumaged 'sea terns' that plunge-dive for prey, and 'marsh terns' that dip the surface for food while flying and have a good deal of black on their plumage in summer. The **auks** are a small group of seabirds that spend most of their life well out at sea and come to land only to nest, rather like the shearwaters. Unlike the shearwaters, however, they spend their time swimming rather than flying, being heavy-bodied and short-winged. They are capable of riding out most storms so long as they are not driven close against a shore, when they may be found washed up in an exhausted 'wreck'. They are also susceptible to oil pollution. They are highly gregarious when breeding, gathering in spectacular nesting colonies on sea cliffs and islands.

SANDGROUSE, PIGEONS, AND CUCKOOS

The sandgrouse are seed-eating ground birds that live in arid terrain. They resemble gamebirds, which explains their name, but they are actually close relatives of the pigeons and doves. These are common and successful birds of woods, farmland, and suburbs: small-billed, round-headed, and rather long-tailed, with soft, dense plumage. They have familiar cooing songs but no obvious flight-calls; to some extent their sharp, loud 'wing claps' in display and clattering wing noise in alarm replace calls. The **cuckoos** are superficially hawk-like birds, well known for placing their eggs in the nests of other birds, who then rear the cuckoo chicks as their own. The Cuckoo is celebrated for its unmistakable two-note song, but few people would recognize it on sight.

OWLS

These round-headed, mostly nocturnal predators have large, forward-facing eyes and large ears to help them locate prey at night, and most have soft plumage that is silent in flight. There are two families: the barn and bay owls, which in Europe consists of just the Barn Owl, and the typical owls. Larger species eat mammals and birds, smaller ones mostly insects. Some species are nomadic, opportunist breeders that rear large families when food is abundant, but few or no chicks at all in poorer years.

SWIFTS, WOODPECKERS, AND ALLIES

The swifts are almost exclusively aerial birds: unable to perch or walk, they spend years aloft, catching flying insects, and come to land only to nest. They are long-range migrants, spending very little time in Europe. The nightjars are similar but larger; they hunt at night for moths and flying beetles, and are known for their strange, mechanical, churring songs. Of more than 90 species of kingfishers found worldwide only one breeds in Europe, but it is widespread and surprisingly common. Brilliantly coloured, it is closely related to three other families with glorious plumage: the bee-eaters, which really do eat bees, the larger but otherwise similar rollers, and the unmistakable, high-crested Hoopoe which is the only species in the hoopoe family. This collection of small, unrelated families also includes the woodpeckers: stout-billed, sharp-clawed, stiff-tailed birds that excavate tree holes for nesting. Some woodpeckers extract prey from tree bark and rotten wood, but the various 'green' woodpeckers and Wryneck eat ants. They have loud calls and some also 'drum' on resonant, dead timber in spring.

LARKS, SWALLOWS, AND PIPITS

The larks are short-billed birds that perform extended song flights in the breeding season. They have long hind claws for walking through short vegetation, and anonymous streaky brown plumages that make some species difficult to tell apart. Swallows and martins are long-winged, fork-tailed, swift-like birds that catch insects in flight with their wide-open mouths.

They have tiny feet, but unlike the swifts they are well able to perch; they are often seen gathering on overhead wires before undertaking their long-range migrations. The pipits and wagtails are ground-feeding birds with long legs, long hind claws, and short bills. Wagtails have striking plumage patterns or colours, while most pipits are duller, streaky, and brown. They have an undulating flight and launch themselves into song flights from trees or from the ground.

WRENS AND ALLIES

This selection of birds consists of the few European representatives of four families: the waxwings, dippers, wrens, and accentors. The Waxwing is a plump tree-dwelling bird usually seen feeding on berries in small flocks. The Dipper is very different: a songbird that, uniquely for its kind, specializes in feeding underwater in fast-flowing streams. The Wren is a tiny, noisy insect-eater, common and widespread throughout much of the Northern Hemisphere. The accentors, which include the familiar Dunnock, are small, rather secretive birds, some of which breed at very high altitudes.

CHATS AND THRUSHES

A single, large, varied family, this includes such familiar species as the Robin, rarer ones such as the Rufous Bush-robin, and the striking wheatears of more open habitats. These smaller species are collectively known as chats. Thrushes are mostly rather larger, with stout bills and legs, and feed on fruit and berries or specialize in catching earthworms or snails. Many of this family are exceptionally fine songsters. Some, such as the Blackbird and Robin, have become familiar garden birds. Gardens can provide a reasonable replacement for a woodland glade or edge, although the food supply is usually poorer.

WARBLERS AND FLYCATCHERS

The small, slim, but varied warblers include some widespread, common, and easily-identified birds, as well as a few rare and local ones, rare visitors, and many that are very hard to identify. They fall into several distinct generic groups. The secretive *Locustella* warblers have prolonged reeling or trilling songs, round tails, curved wings, and long undertail coverts. *Acrocephalus* warblers are streaked or plain birds with distinctive song patterns that live in reeds or marsh vegetation. *Hippolais* warblers are small or medium-large, stocky, large-billed, strong-legged, and square-tailed. *Phylloscopus* leaf warblers are small, sleek, mostly greenish, and rather weak-looking birds of leafy trees

and bushes, with distinctive songs. *Sylvia* warblers are heavier in their movements, generally more colourful and well-marked, but with scratchy songs; they are often found in scrub or low bushes. 'Crests' such as the Goldcrest are minute warblers with striped crowns and needle-sharp calls that test our high-frequency hearing. The flycatchers are a family of rather upright, short-legged, specialist insect-eaters, which typically catch prey in short flights from a perch.

TITS, TREECREEPERS, AND NUTHATCHES

Stout, small, fast-moving, with strong feet and short, thick bills, the **tits** are acrobatic birds well equipped for foraging in the trees; they are also familiar visitors to bird feeders in gardens. The treecreepers and nuthatches are mostly specialized for picking food from tree bark: the treecreepers use their tails for support as they creep over bark, while nuthatches use their strong feet. The Wallcreeper is an exception, living on cliffs and crags in mountain regions.

SHRIKES, STARLINGS, AND CROWS

The shrikes are medium-small birds with hooked bills and strong, sharp claws, capable of catching small birds and large insects which they often impale on thorns. The starlings are sharp-billed, stocky birds with strong legs and a fast walk. They fly straight and fast, and form large, coordinated flocks. Gregarious and often associated with people, they are found in woodland, farmland, and suburbs. The rather larger crows are stout-billed birds with nostrils covered by dense bristly feathers; most are good fliers, the choughs especially so. They are typically black, but magpies and jays are boldly patterned.

SPARROWS, FINCHES, AND BUNTINGS

Small birds with short, stout, or sharply triangular bills and short legs, the sparrows are drab brown at a glance but actually strongly patterned, some with marked differences between the sexes. The finches are very varied, ranging from cross-billed pine cone specialists to stout-billed seed crackers. Some breed semi-colonially, sharing sources of abundant food, while others are territorial and defend scarcer, more dispersed food supplies. Finally the **buntings** have slightly differently shaped bills, mostly longer tails, and live in a variety of open places from moors and fields to marshland.

Bird habitats of Europe

Europe has a rich variety of bird habitats, extending as it does from the Arctic to the Mediterranean, and from the mild Atlantic to the harsh extremes of the continental heartland. Each habitat has its own characteristic bird species, including many breeding or wintering migrants that come and go with the seasons.

The largest numbers of oceanic birds are to be seen from western headlands and on cliffs and islands, mostly in the northwest. The western shores of Britain and Ireland, especially, support huge colonies of breeding Gannets, Manx Shearwaters, Storm Petrels, Guillemots, Puffins, Kittiwakes, and Fulmars. These seabird colonies are among Europe's most exciting birdwatching sites.

The Mediterranean has its own shearwaters, gulls, and terns, but it is more often associated with waders, especially where the coast is backed with lagoons or salt pans. Some of these have big flocks of Greater Flamingos and rare ducks. Migrant waders can be numerous on the lagoons, but as the sea is essentially non-tidal its beaches are rather disappointing.

ESTUARIES AND BAYS

The North Sea and Irish Sea coasts, by contrast, have large tidal ranges that create big, muddy estuaries and bays. These shallows teem with waders and wildfowl feeding on mud, sand, and marshes that are enriched twice a day by the incoming tide. In winter they attract great flocks of migrants escaping the harsh climates of the far north and east, and some also come from the northwest, from Greenland and beyond. Wigeon, Pintails, Teal, and Brent Geese feed on the marshes and mudflats, along with great gatherings of Knots, Oystercatchers, Dunlins, and Bar-tailed Godwits. The smaller, more sheltered estuaries may harbour Black-tailed Godwits and Avocets, while Redshanks, Grey and Ringed Plovers, Curlews, and Turnstones are widespread. Estuaries also provide opportunities to watch Black-necked and Slavonian Grebes, Red-throated Divers and other marine birds that drift in with the tide.

WETLANDS AND LAKES

Freshwater wetlands often have extensive reedbeds that may support Bitterns, Bearded Tits, and Marsh Harriers. Lagoons in the north may have Avocets, while farther south you can expect Kentish Plovers, Black-winged Stilts, and Little Egrets. In winter marshy places near the coast may attract groups of Snow Buntings, Lapland Buntings, and Shore Larks, as well as larger numbers of Twites, Greenfinches, and Chaffinches feeding on seeds washed up on the strandline and caught up in the marsh vegetation.

Lakes and reservoirs vary greatly in their bird life. Lowland waters are usually richer than the cold, acid pools of the uplands.

They may attract ducks such as Mallards, Shovelers, Gadwalls, Tufted Ducks, and Pochards, as well as Goosanders, Goldeneyes and others locally in winter. Larger reservoirs are often used as secure roosts by gulls almost all year round. On far northern pools you may find Red-throated and Black-throated Divers, Whooper Swans, and Slavonian Grebes. Ospreys fish in all kinds of water in summer and can be widespread on migration in spring and autumn. Reedy freshwater margins are good for Reed and Sedge Warblers; in eastern Europe you may see Penduline Tits and Purple Herons. In the Low Countries and Scandinavia the reeds may be enlivened in summer by the stunning song of the Bluethroat.

Flocks of Arctic Terns sometimes fly over land in spring, stopping off at reservoirs for an hour or two, and Black Terns may appear in spring and autumn. The autumn gales are likely to bring rare seabirds inland: waifs and strays such as Grey Phalaropes, Leach's Petrels, and Little Auks. If the water level of a reservoir falls in late summer it could be excellent for migrant waders in autumn.

Low-lying marshland and seasonally-flooded pastures have special birds too, but such habitats are becoming hard to find. Ruffs and Black-tailed Godwits, Snipe, Redshanks, Lapwings, Yellow Wagtails, and Reed Buntings breed in such places, while Wigeon, Bewick's Swans, White-fronted Geese, and Golden Plovers arrive in winter.

FIELDS AND PASTURES

Farmland used to be rich in birds, but the intensification of farming has caused massive declines throughout Europe. Corn Buntings, Tree Sparrows, Skylarks, Grey Partridges, Turtle Doves, and many others are becoming rare, and breeding Lapwings and Curlews have vanished from vast areas. Hay meadows used to be found everywhere and were full of Corncrakes: both are now practically extinct in many regions, although for the time being Corncrakes survive in surprising numbers in eastern Europe.

Changing patterns of farming have a huge influence on birds. Quails may be abundant in less-intensively farmed cereal fields in southern Europe, but disappear when the fields are planted with oilseed rape. Black Kites are everywhere along the coast of Spain, but intensive olive cultivation gives them little chance to thrive inland. Rice fields can be marvellous for Whiskered and Gull-billed Terns, Black-winged Stilts, and other species, but plans to intensify rice cultivation threaten to drive them out for good.

Grassy pastures used to support an abundance of wagtails, Swallows, Starlings, and Jackdaws, but many are now almost deserted. It is not always clear why, although pesticides may be to blame. Many small, seed-eating birds of arable land also seem to be suffering from a lack of food in winter, primarily because the adoption of autumn-sown cereals eliminates the winter stubbles with their spilt grain and seed-bearing weeds. Nevertheless, some farmland can still be excellent for birds. Old-fashioned fields in the south and east have White Storks, Red-backed and Woodchat

Shrikes, and even, in places, Great and Little Bustards. Winter farmland in the Low Countries can be stunningly rich in geese of several species, wild swans, and wintering birds of prey, including Common and Rough-legged Buzzards, Merlins, Sparrowhawks, and the occasional Goshawk and White-tailed Eagle.

FORESTS, WOODLANDS, AND GARDENS

Forests and woodlands vary greatly in their bird populations. There are some special woodland types, often shaped by human influence: the Spanish cork oak forests, for example, are splendid places, with Hoopoes, Orphean Warblers, Imperial Eagles, and a host of common species such as Serins and Greenfinches. Holm oak forests produce great crops of acorns that are harvested by Common Cranes and vast numbers of Woodpigeons all winter.

Magnificent conifer woodlands grow high on the shoulders of the Alps, the Pyrenees, and other mountain ranges throughout Europe. These remote, wild woods may support Capercaillies, Crossbills, elusive Hazel Hens, and Tengmalm's Owls. Other exciting owls live in the great conifer forests of the north.

Beech woods cast deep shade and have little growing beneath them, yet this is much to the liking of Wood Warblers and Nuthatches. Their crops of beech mast also attract some of Europe's largest bird flocks: the great concentrations of Bramblings that, in parts of central Europe, occasionally number in their millions. Old oak woods with tangles of holly, cherry, elder, hawthorn, and many other shrubs can boast a range of birds including Blackcaps, Garden Warblers, Lesser Whitethroats, Marsh Tits, Great Spotted Woodpeckers, Woodpigeons, Stock Doves, Jackdaws, Song Thrushes, Blackbirds, and Dunnocks. Nightingales make the air throb with their songs in many Mediterranean areas; in southeast England they largely rely on woods and thickets managed by people, especially coppices that produce dense growths of stems almost from ground level. Nightingales are showing disturbing signs of decline in Britain, but Woodlarks, which like felled plantations rather than woods, are doing well and spreading.

Robins, Chaffinches, Blue Tits, and Great Tits are often abundant in woods. In rural and suburban areas they also spill out into gardens, finding them good substitutes in the main. But tits, especially, require endless supplies of caterpillars to feed their chicks, and sometimes cannot breed very successfully in gardens because they are too poor in insect life. Sparrowhawks are the typical avian predators of most woods, and they too have learned to exploit gardens, often raiding bird tables in winter.

HEATHLANDS, MOORS, AND MOUNTAINS

Mediterranean heaths – variously called *garrigue* or *maquis* – support a whole suite of warblers. Some are common almost everywhere, such as the Sardinian Warbler, while others are locally frequent like the Subalpine Warbler. A few are rather scarce like the Dartford Warbler, and some are decidedly rare and very local, such as the Spectacled and Marmora's Warblers. Woodlarks and Tawny Pipits sing overhead, Ortolan and Cirl Buntings sing repetitively from bush tops, while high above soar Short-toed Eagles, Booted Eagles, Black and Red Kites, and Griffon Vultures.

Dartford Warblers are also found on southern heaths in England, where they are doing well and spreading. British heaths may also have Linnets, Stonechats, Yellowhammers, and Hobbies, and Nightjars often appear at dusk in summer.

In winter there are few birds up on the moors of the north and west, but in summer Meadow Pipits, Whinchats, and Wheatears join the resident Red Grouse, while Curlews and Golden Plovers breed among the heather. On lower ground farther north the rich pickings of summer attract a variety of waders including Whimbrels, Dunlins, Oystercatchers, and Ringed Plovers.

The habitat of the far north is more or less replicated on higher hills farther south, and both share such birds as Ptarmigan, Dotterels, Ring Ouzels, and Shore Larks. Mountain peaks in southern and central Europe, however, boast birds that do not extend to the north, such as the incomparably beautiful Wallcreeper and the stunning Lammergeier.

■ SPECIALISTS AND GENERALISTS

Some species have adapted along such specialist lines that they are tied strictly to a particular habitat, or a particular situation. Others are 'generalists' and occupy a variety of landscapes. The 'specialists' include the Dipper, which spends its life by a clean, tumbling river, the Treecreeper, whose day is entirely devoted to probing tree bark with its slim, curved bill, and the Bittern, found throughout the year in wet reedbeds. Only unusual circumstances, such as a hard frost that exiles the Dipper to the coast, drives such birds from their usual habitats.

Many other birds are not so exacting, but still have special requirements. They include birds such as the Grey Heron: this feeds by hunting fish in shallow water, but it can do so in a river, beside a lake, in a saltmarsh creek, or from seaweedy rocks on the shore. Similarly the Wood Warbler can occupy beech woods, oak woods, or even larch plantations, so long as they have a dense canopy high up and open space beneath, with a ground layer of dead leaves.

The generalists include such birds as the Black-headed Gull, which breeds near water – on a coastal marsh, an inland lake, or even a peaty pool high on a moor – but might feed anywhere from the beach to a ploughed field, a garden, a town park lake, or even a mountain top.

Most birds are not quite so adaptable, but they still enjoy a little variety. Often the 'edge' of a habitat, or where two or three habitat types meet, is a very good place to see birds since it offers a range of feeding opportunities and brings several kinds of birds together. It is worth getting into the habit of recognizing such places: looking carefully along hedgerows, walking quietly up to bridges to glance quickly each way along streams, treading softly as you enter woodland clearings, or checking the edges of a ploughed field for feeding finches or buntings. You will also soon realize that water is usually a magnet to birds, and since there is always some sort of 'dry' habitat alongside, this doubles the chances of seeing something interesting.

What you need to watch birds

All you need to watch birds is a pair of eyes, but anyone really interested in watching birds will want a closer view. The best way to achieve that is to obtain a good pair of binoculars.

Binoculars are near-essential equipment for every birdwatcher. A telescope may come later, or not at all. Looking through binoculars does not allow you to see farther than you can without them, but it enlarges what you can see so that the detail becomes clear.

The size of the enlarged image depends on the magnification, and this is shown in the figures that are used to describe the binoculars. These might be 8x30, 10x50, or perhaps 10x42. The first of the two figures is the magnification: the number of times an object is increased in size. A figure of 8x simply means that a bird you see with the naked eye will be increased in apparent size by eight times. Eight to ten is the range to consider. Don't be tempted by offers of binoculars that allow you to 'see craters on the Moon', with magnifications of 12, 15, or 20. The bigger the magnification, the duller the image, the narrower the field of view, and the more problems you have keeping them still. A large magnification magnifies 'handshake' too, and the image dances about in front of your eyes unless you are able to steady the binoculars against a solid support. The higher the magnification, the worse the effect.

So forget high magnification. What you really need is a bright image: plenty of light. This means one (or both) of two things. The first is large 'object lenses': the bigger lenses at the far end of the binoculars. Their diameter in millimetres is the second of those two figures: 8x30 means your binoculars magnify eight times and have 30mm diameter object lenses. The bigger the lenses the more light they let in, but after 50mm they get too big, too heavy, and difficult to handle. The other option is to go for the best possible quality, with special coatings and special glass that increase light transmission. This means that a really top-class pair of 10x40s can be as bright or brighter than modest 10x50s. Quality costs money, though, and the best binoculars can be very expensive.

You also need a good field of view, meaning that you see a reasonably wide picture and not just a tiny part of the landscape. Typically the larger the magnification, the narrower the field of view. This makes it hard to locate a bird that you have spotted with your naked eye, and may mean you miss other birds just out of view. Miniature binoculars also tend to suffer in this way. Close focus is useful too: sometimes it is wonderful to focus on a bird perched nearby so that you can see every detail. Binoculars of lower magnification tend to be better in this respect.

So binocular choice is a compromise between good magnification (higher than six), a stable image (magnification no more than ten), plenty of light (bigger object lenses), light weight and ease of use (smaller object lenses), a wide field of view (lower magnification), close focus (lower magnification), good quality (high cost) and something you can afford (low cost). Not easy! Also, you need something you feel comfortable with. You could pay a small fortune for 'the best that money can buy' and find that they don't fit comfortably in your hands, or the eyecups don't feel comfortable around your eyes. You must try them out first.

You must also learn how to focus properly. Most important, you have to set the right-hand eyepiece to balance any difference between your eyes, or the best binoculars available will produce only blurred images. Aim the binoculars at something with sharp detail like a wire fence, shut your right eye and focus using the centre focus wheel. Then shut your left eye and adjust the individual eyepiece on the right until the image is sharp. Open both eyes, and you should have perfect stereoscopic image. Memorize the setting and check it regularly.

A telescope adds greater magnification: perhaps 30x or even higher, up to 60x. It will have a smaller field of view and be much less easy to handle: you might take several seconds to locate a bird. It will also need a rigid support like a tripod. So a telescope is not for ordinary, everyday birdwatching, and certainly not in a wood or other confined space, and you might do without one altogether. Yet if you regularly watch birds on an estuary or reservoir, you may need the extra power. The considerations listed for binoculars apply here too: you must compromise between power, light-gathering performance (big lens, heavy glass), weight, quality, and cost. Telescopes do not come cheap. You will also need a big, solid (and therefore heavy) tripod to mount it on.

Both binoculars and telescopes should last a lifetime if you look after them. Don't drop them, don't scratch the lenses, don't smear your fingers over the glass, and don't scrub them with coarse cloths. They should be treated as delicate instruments.

You may be tempted into bird photography or even recording birdsong. These are really specialist activities, although you can achieve quite a lot in the garden with modest equipment. Out in the field the birds are much more wary and further away, so the problems tend to escalate, expensively. You may need to build a hide, and you will certainly be spending a lot of time waiting for that elusive critical moment. If you have the money, time, and dedication, good luck – but be warned!

Once you have your optics sorted, you need a good field guide: perhaps the pocket version of this one. And a notebook. You don't have to draw or describe everything you see, but it is great fun and teaches you a lot about birds. It makes you look more carefully at each bird and helps fix the details in your head. It is hopeless trying to remember everything, then looking through a book and trying to decide whether the bird really had red legs or brown legs – or were they green? A notebook also allows you to describe the bird as *you* see it, instead of getting your descriptions second-hand. Once you start doing that, you are well on the way to becoming not just a birdwatcher, but an ornithologist.

■ USEFUL CONTACTS IN BRITAIN AND IRELAND

Britain and Ireland are well served with a network of amateur bird and wildlife clubs. The bird club network in particular is remarkably good, with many expert people involved.

A typical bird club will have regular indoor meetings and monthly outings to see birds. You can meet other birdwatchers at all levels of experience and ability; in particular, you can pick the brains of the experts and learn from them. The club will probably produce a bulletin or newsletter that gives invaluable details of local birds, and an annual report that brings together the year's records and relates them to the experience gained over past decades. These are enormously helpful in telling you what to expect and where. You can see where other people are going birdwatching and find out the best places to see many species – where to see winter wildfowl or migrant waders, for example. The reports help you to put your own experiences into context: have you seen a rare or unexpected species, or something quite common?

In Scotland, the Scottish Ornithologists' Club is the national body, playing in part the role of regional and county bird clubs in England. The Welsh Ornithological Society has a similar role in Wales.

Local members' groups of the Royal Society for the Protection of Birds (RSPB) also perfom some of the functions of bird clubs, but are essentially a means to promote and support the society locally. The RSPB is probably the largest bird conservation body in the world; it has more than a million members, and owns or manages more than 160 nature reserves. It organizes research into the needs of birds and threats to their survival, and plays an important role in promoting legislation favouring wildlife, as well as policies such as the agricultural schemes that help farmers conserve wildlife on their land.

The RSPB is the UK partner of BirdLife International, a global federation of similar organizations that has its base in England. The RSPB's increasing international work is largely focused through BirdLife International projects, including the training of conservation staff from all over the world, while BirdLife International also has partners worldwide working to improve prospects for birds and people.

The British Trust for Ornithology (BTO) is another national organization, which mobilizes amateur (but often expert) birdwatchers in projects and monitoring schemes such as the Breeding Bird Survey. It also oversees activities such as bird ringing in the UK. Much of its work provides crucial data that enables government agencies and the RSPB to promote conservation policies: it provides many of the facts and figures that back up their arguments.

Specializing in wetlands and their birds, particularly ducks, geese, and swans worldwide, the Wildfowl & Wetlands Trust is an organization with worldwide responsibilities and involvement in conservation issues. Its British centres include its famous headquarters at Slimbridge, which attracts many wild ducks, geese, and swans in winter.

There are also the county wildlife trusts, which have a broader interest in wildlife of all kinds and perhaps do more conservation work than the organizations that concentrate on birds: they often own or manage several nature reserves. Each county in England has its own trust with its own headquarters, but they are supervised by an umbrella body known as The Wildlife Trusts.

All of these and more deserve the support of birdwatchers who gain so much from their hobby and naturally wish to help to ensure that birds have a place in the future in our increasingly hostile world.

There are also several magazines and journals for birdwatchers: monthlies include the long-established *British Birds*, the younger *Birding World*, and even more recent *Birding Scotland*, all available on subscription only, while the bookstalls and newsagents offer *Bird Watching* and *Birdwatch*. BBC *Wildlife* has some bird content, too. The RSPB magazine, *Birds*, which is concerned with bird conservation issues as well as RSPB nature reserves and other bird material, is a members-only publication, not available from shops or independent of RSPB membership. Details of nature reserves, bird clubs, RSPB members' groups, wildlife trusts, and other relevant bodies are published annually in *The Birdwatcher's Yearbook*, which may be available in your local library or can be ordered through any good bookshop.

■ USEFUL ADDRESSES

Royal Society for the Protection of Birds (RSPB), The Lodge, Sandy, Bedfordshire SG19 2DL. Tel: 01767 680 551 http://www.rspb.org.uk

British Trust for Ornithology (BTO), The Nunnery, Thetford, Norfolk IP24 2PU. Tel: 01842 750 050 http://www.bto.org

Birdwatch Ireland, Rutledge House, 8 Longford Place, Monkstown, Co Dublin. Tel: 00 353 1 2804322 http://www.birdwatchireland.ie

Scottish Ornithologists' Club, 21 Regent Terrace, Edinburgh EH7 5BT. Tel: 0131 556 6042 http://www.the-soc.org.uk

Welsh Ornithological Society, 196 Chester Road, Hartford, Northwich CW8 1LG. http://members.aol.com/welshos/cac

Society of Wildlife Artists, 17 Carlton House Terrace, London SW1Y 5BD. Tel: 0207 930 6844

Wildfowl & Wetlands Trust, Slimbridge, Gloucestershire GL2 7BT. Tel: 01453 890 333 http://www.wwt.org.uk

Wildlife Sound Recording Society, 36 Wenton Close, Cottesmore, Oakham, Rutland LE15 7DR

The Wildlife Trusts, The Kiln, Waterside, Mather Road, Newark NG24 1WT. Tel: 01636 677711 http://www.wildlifetrusts.org

British Birds, The Banks, Mountfield, Robertsbridge, East Sussex TN32 5JY. Tel: 01580 882039 http://www.britishbirds.co.uk

Birding Scotland, 51 Charlton Crescent, Aboyne, Aberdeenshire AB34 5GN. Tel: 013398 86450 http://www.birdingscotland.ic24.net

Birding World, Stonerunner, Coast Road, Cley next the Sea, Norfolk NR25 7RZ. Tel: 01263 740 913 http://www.birdingworld.freeserve.co.uk

Birdwatch, 17 College Road, Brigg, Lincolnshire DN20 8JL. Tel: 020 7704 9495 http://www.birdwatch.co.uk

Bird Watching, Bretton Court, Peterborough PE3 8DZ. Tel: 01733 264 666

Great Northern Diver *Gavia immer*

The Great Northern and White-billed are the biggest divers. Both have chequerboard plumage and black heads in summer, but their winter colours are dull. In winter Great Northerns range from wide, sandy bays and sheltered estuaries to the wilder coasts of northwest Scotland, and may appear on large inland lakes. The White-billed is more elusive, and rarely nests outside the Arctic.

FEEDING These divers capture fish and crabs in long, deep dives from the surface, often bringing larger prey back to the surface to deal with.

VOICE All divers are silent in winter, but the Great Northern's loud, evocative wails and bubbling, laughing calls may occasionally be heard before it leaves in spring.

BREEDING Both species lay two large, dark eggs at the edge of a lake.

MIGRATION Autumn movements take Great Northerns south into the North Sea and along west European coasts; the White-billed is much rarer.

LENGTH 70–80cm (28–32in)

WHEN TO SEE A few immatures all year in non-breeding areas; most September to April
WHERE FOUND Great Northern Diver breeds on large lakes in Iceland; winters on coasts from Scandinavia to France

A goose-sized diver with a massive, dagger bill and a very broad body with bulging 'shoulders' often obvious when viewed end-on

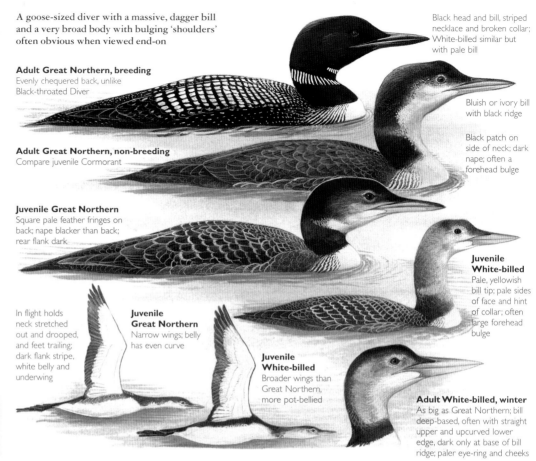

Adult Great Northern, breeding
Evenly chequered back, unlike Black-throated Diver

Adult Great Northern, non-breeding
Compare juvenile Cormorant

Juvenile Great Northern
Square pale feather fringes on back; nape blacker than back; rear flank dark

In flight holds neck stretched out and drooped, and feet trailing; dark flank stripe, white belly and underwing

Juvenile Great Northern
Narrow wings; belly has even curve

Juvenile White-billed
Broader wings than Great Northern, more pot-bellied

Black head and bill, striped necklace and broken collar; White-billed similar but with pale bill

Bluish or ivory bill with black ridge

Black patch on side of neck; dark nape; often a forehead bulge

Juvenile White-billed
Pale, yellowish bill tip; pale sides of face and hint of collar; often large forehead bulge

Adult White-billed, winter
As big as Great Northern; bill deep-based, often with straight upper and upcurved lower edge, dark only at base of bill ridge; paler eye-ring and cheeks

Black-throated Diver *Gavia arctica*

Of all the divers a Black-throat in full breeding plumage is arguably the most beautiful. It lacks the impact of the huge Great Northern, but makes up for it with the most delicate of plumage patterns, almost too perfect to be true. Yet most people see it, if at all, in winter or immature plumage, which is much duller but still highlights the perfect form of this superb bird.

FEEDING It takes fish, frogs, and a few aquatic invertebrates, hunting underwater in long dives.

VOICE Silent in winter, the Black-throated Diver has wonderful howling or wailing calls in summer and a deep, short *kwok* in flight.

BREEDING It lays two dark eggs at the water's edge on an islet, or on an artificial raft in some Scottish lochs.

MIGRATION Breeding birds move to the sea in late summer and are thinly scattered southwards in winter, mostly in broad, sandy bays. They are rare inland but sometimes stay for weeks on larger reservoirs or lakes.

LENGTH 60–70cm (24–28in)

WHEN TO SEE In the south, mostly November to March or April
WHERE FOUND Breeds on large lakes in Norway, Sweden, Scotland; winters in estuaries and sandy bays south to Biscay coasts

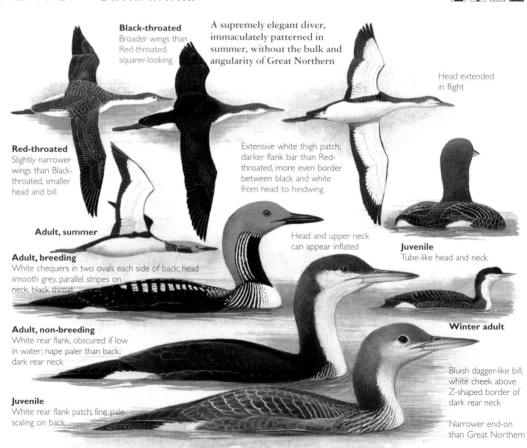

Black-throated
Broader wings than Red-throated, squarer-looking

A supremely elegant diver, immaculately patterned in summer, without the bulk and angularity of Great Northern

Head extended in flight

Red-throated
Slightly narrower wings than Black-throated, smaller head and bill

Extensive white thigh patch; darker flank bar than Red-throated, more even border between black and white from head to hindwing

Adult, summer

Adult, breeding
White chequers in two ovals each side of back; head smooth grey, parallel stripes on neck; black throat

Adult, non-breeding
White rear flank, obscured if low in water; nape paler than back; dark rear neck

Juvenile
White rear flank patch; fine pale scaling on back

Head and upper neck can appear inflated

Juvenile
Tube-like head and neck

Winter adult

Bluish dagger-like bill; white cheek above Z-shaped border of dark rear neck

Narrower end-on than Great Northern

Red-throated Diver *Gavia stellata*

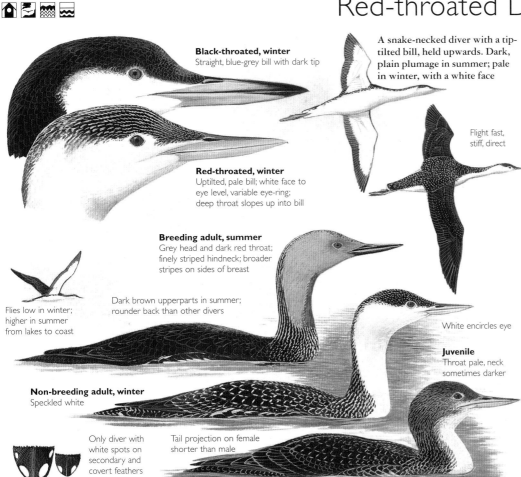

Black-throated, winter
Straight, blue-grey bill with dark tip

A snake-necked diver with a tip-tilted bill, held upwards. Dark, plain plumage in summer; pale in winter, with a white face

Flight fast, stiff, direct

Red-throated, winter
Uptilted, pale bill; white face to eye level, variable eye-ring; deep throat slopes up into bill

Breeding adult, summer
Grey head and dark red throat; finely striped hindneck; broader stripes on sides of breast

Dark brown upperparts in summer; rounder back than other divers

White encircles eye

Flies low in winter; higher in summer from lakes to coast

Juvenile
Throat pale, neck sometimes darker

Non-breeding adult, winter
Speckled white

Only diver with white spots on secondary and covert feathers

Tail projection on female shorter than male

The smallest diver, about the size of a Mallard, the Red-throated Diver is best distinguished by its slender bill which it holds tilted slightly upwards. It sits low in the water, rolling forwards to dive and often reappearing far away. It only comes to land to breed, but it flies frequently, especially in summer, making regular trips from the small lakes on which it nests to hunt for food at sea.

FEEDING It catches small fish during lengthy dives, but feeds its small young on insects and crustaceans.

DISPLAY & VOICE Although silent in winter, it makes loud, quacking flight notes in summer and produces weird, far-carrying, syncopated wailing and rattling sounds during its strange, ritualized courtship displays.

BREEDING Nests are simple scrapes on lake shores in northern Europe. Pairs rear one or two young each summer.

MIGRATION In autumn, Red-throats move south around the coasts as far as the Mediterranean but are rare inland.

LENGTH 55–69cm (22–27in)

WHEN TO SEE All year; on breeding lakes April to August, otherwise at sea
WHERE FOUND Breeds on small lakes from Scotland and S Sweden northwards; in winter widespread on coasts

Great Crested Grebe *Podiceps cristatus*

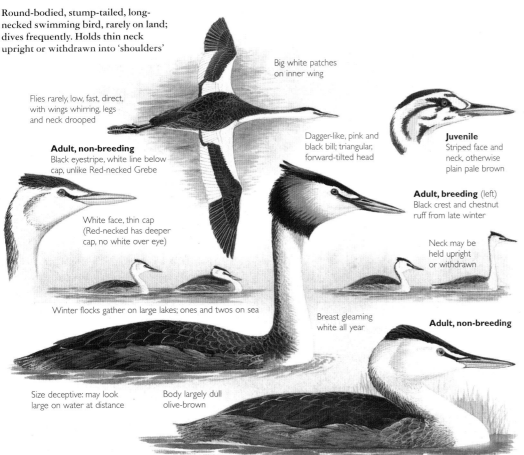

Round-bodied, stump-tailed, long-necked swimming bird, rarely on land; dives frequently. Holds thin neck upright or withdrawn into 'shoulders'

Big white patches on inner wing

Flies rarely, low, fast, direct, with wings whirring, legs and neck drooped

Dagger-like, pink and black bill; triangular, forward-tilted head

Juvenile
Striped face and neck, otherwise plain pale brown

Adult, non-breeding
Black eyestripe, white line below cap, unlike Red-necked Grebe

Adult, breeding (left)
Black crest and chestnut ruff from late winter

White face, thin cap (Red-necked has deeper cap, no white over eye)

Neck may be held upright or withdrawn

Winter flocks gather on large lakes; ones and twos on sea

Breast gleaming white all year

Adult, non-breeding

Size deceptive: may look large on water at distance

Body largely dull olive-brown

Unmistakable facial adornments make the Great Crested Grebe a distinctive bird in spring and summer. The colourful ruffs are absent in winter, when it looks very white-faced and white-breasted, with a slender neck and dagger bill.

DISPLAY & VOICE During courtship pairs rise breast-to-breast and face each other with their crests and ruffs spread wide, wagging their heads in a ritual display and offering rags of waterweed to each other. The voice is a loud quacking and growling.

BREEDING They nest at the water's edge, laying up to six eggs on floating heaps of dank weed. The chicks quickly leave the nest and make loud, whistling calls during the summer.

FEEDING These grebes eat small fish and other aquatic creatures, caught during lengthy underwater dives.

MIGRATION After nesting many move to the coast, or gather on reservoirs that are free from ice; those from northern and eastern Europe move to the North Sea or Mediterranean coasts.

LENGTH 46–51cm (18–20in)

WHEN TO SEE All year in south and west, April to October in north and east
WHERE FOUND Freshwater lakes, large rivers, coasts; locally in all Europe except N Scandinavia

Red-necked Grebe *Podiceps grisegena*

While not so large as the Great Crested Grebe, the Red-necked Grebe is stocky, thick-necked and big-headed, with a heavy bill, and it can look deceptively big out on the water. Like other grebes it dives easily and often, flies with some difficulty, and almost never comes onto dry land.

FEEDING Red-necked Grebes eat more insects and crustaceans than fish.

DISPLAY Their black and white faces, contrasted bills and deep red necks are important in displays that involve much bill-to-bill 'dancing' on water.

BREEDING They nest among reeds or rushes, laying four or five eggs on a sodden mass of weed. The young fly after 10 weeks and do not breed until they are two years old.

MIGRATION After breeding on inland lakes, mostly in eastern Europe, many move to the coast or larger lakes in winter to avoid ice; only then are they frequent around the North Sea and Adriatic coasts.

LENGTH 40–50cm (16–20in)

WHEN TO SEE Mostly August to May in west; from March or April onwards on breeding territories

WHERE FOUND Breeds on lakes from Denmark eastwards; in winter on S Scandinavian and North Sea coasts; E Britain, where scarce inland

A chunky grebe, with a large, round head and a thick bill. Body lies low in water and often looks short, exaggerating size of head and thickness of neck. May dive deep with a leap from the surface like a Shag

White inner wing patches smaller than on Great Crested Grebe

Adult
Bill black, small yellow base; eye blackish; face white to dusky grey

Immature
Eye yellow (red on Great Crested)

Trailing legs and feet in flight

Non-breeding adult, winter (below)
Head round; black surrounds eye, no white stripe above, unlike Great Crested Grebe

Double 'bump' on rear crown in summer

Breeding adult, summer (left) Neck and breast deep rusty-red

Foreneck grey in winter (bright white on Great Crested). Often a flash of white on upper flank

Juvenile
Dark head stripes

Lacks snaky elegance of Great Crested Grebe; at long range in winter more like Slavonian Grebe

Slavonian Grebe *Podiceps auritus*

The middle-sized grebe of northern waters, the Slavonian is a glorious bird in summer when it prefers cold, shallow lakes with shoreline vegetation. It is more familiar, however, in its neat, clean-cut black and white winter plumage, when it is usually seen on the coast.

FEEDING Dives underwater to find aquatic insects and their larvae, and various species of small fish.

BREEDING Nests among reeds and rushes in shallow water. The nest is a typical grebe heap of dank weed, nearly always floating but anchored to a stem, holding four or five eggs. The young fly after 45 days and return to breed when two years old.

MIGRATION After nesting all Slavonian Grebes move south and west to the coast, becoming widespread but scarce around Scandinavia, Britain and the North Sea. Some arrive in autumn in full breeding colours and look equally colourful again before moving north in spring.

LENGTH 31–38cm (12–15in)

WHEN TO SEE August to May on coasts

WHERE FOUND Remote breeding lakes in Iceland, N Scotland, Scandinavia; on coasts in winter, especially estuaries

A well-proportioned, round-headed grebe, with a lower forehead profile and straighter bill than Black-necked. Colourful in breeding plumage; very black and white in winter

White cheeks almost meet at back

Slavonian, winter
Black cap contrasts sharply with white face; flattish head

Bill blackish, pale tip

Black-necked Grebe
Uptilted bill, darker cheeks, peaked head

Red eye, unlike Red-necked

Back tapers to tail, less blunt than Black-necked

White inner forewing patches vary, presumably a sex difference

Legs trail in flight

Usually pale spot in front of eye

Non-breeding, winter
Black and white

Beware spring birds in transitional plumage

Breeding adult, summer
Flanks and neck all rusty-red

Black head, wedge-shaped golden tufts

Little Grebe *Tachybaptus ruficollis*

A squat water bird with a peaked, rounded head and a short, fairly thick bill with a pale spot at base. Body very rounded. Often heard calling in spring: a sudden, loud, whinnying sound

Breeding, summer
Blackish with rufous cheeks, pale bill spot

Non-breeding, winter
Head buff with darker cap, pale spot near bill still there but less contrasted

Breeding, summer
No sign of ear tufts. Flanks reveal bright orange-buff when feathers fluffed out

Rufous cheeks may look sharply-defined or blend into black in strong light and shade

Shy and easily disturbed

Non-breeding adult

Legs trail in flight

No white on upperwing

Frequently dives, hides in weeds

Fluffs out rear flanks: whitish in winter, rufous in summer

Non-breeding, winter
Brown and buff: face contrasts less with cap than on Black-necked

This smallest and dumpiest of grebes lives on small freshwater pools and even quite narrow rivers, although many move to larger lakes or the coast in winter. Its short bill, round head, tailless appearance and constant diving habit make it impossible to confuse with other waterbirds. It is not often seen in flight, which is hurried, low and weak.

FEEDING Little Grebes eat molluscs, insects and their larvae, caught underwater; they also catch small fish.

DISPLAY & VOICE Posturing is less extravagant than in larger grebes, but involves head-shaking and swimming together side by side, with frequent loud calls. Little Grebes are often heard more than seen, giving sudden loud, whinnying trills in summer.

BREEDING The nest is a floating heap of weed, and the parent bird covers the clutch of 4–6 eggs with weed if it leaves them unattended. The chicks can fly after 45 days.

LENGTH 25–29cm (10–11in)

WHEN TO SEE All year
WHERE FOUND UK, central and S Europe

Black-necked Grebe *Podiceps nigricollis*

A round, tailless grebe with a steep forehead and peaked crown; bill uptilted. Dives constantly; swims very buoyantly even on rough seas

No forewing white patch

Extensive white only on trailing edge of wing

Slavonian   Black-necked
Winter birds are confusing; bill and head shape are best clues

Black cap to below eye in winter, but pattern varies; sunlight increases contrast

Pale 'hook' on ear coverts typical

Slavonian (right)
Flatter head, narrower cap, whiter foreneck, pale bill tip

Non-breeding adult, winter

Uptilted bill tip

Dusky sides of neck may meet under throat

Juvenile, autumn
Drab, often trace of buff on ear coverts

Breeding adult, summer
Black head with drooped fan of coppery-gold or yellow; coppery-red on flanks

Although colourful in summer, the Black-necked Grebe becomes a dusky grey, black and white in winter, less spick-and-span than the slightly larger Slavonian. It is distinguished by its peaked head and thin, slightly uptilted bill. It prefers freshwater lakes with plenty of bankside vegetation in summer; in winter many move to estuaries and other sheltered coasts.

FEEDING It feeds on insects and tiny fish caught during frequent dives.

DISPLAY & VOICE Courtship displays involve head-wagging with golden ear-tufts fanned, synchronized dives and rapid dashes across the water accompanied by shrill, trilling calls.

BREEDING Three or four eggs are laid in a typical grebe nest of damp weed anchored to vegetation. The young are independent after just three weeks.

MIGRATION After breeding, those from eastern Europe, Denmark and the Low Countries move west and south, mostly to the sea. Scattered sites in southern Europe are occupied all year.

LENGTH 28–34cm (11–13½in)

WHEN TO SEE All year; on southern and western coasts August to May
WHERE FOUND Breeds on reedy lakes, mainly E Europe; scarce and scattered west to UK; winters on lakes and estuaries

25

Cory's Shearwater *Calonectris diomedea*

Large, brown, lazy-looking shearwaters of the Mediterranean and mid Atlantic, Cory's Shearwaters usually fly in small groups but occasionally in large flocks. They may be seen drifting by headlands in southern Spain or Majorca in small, unhurried parties all day long.

FEEDING They catch fish, squid and other marine creatures, mostly at night, and scavenge from trawlers.

VOICE Sobbing, rasping *kaa-ough* notes repeated several times at the breeding colony at night, creating an unearthly cacophony. Silent at sea.

BREEDING Breed in colonies on rocky islands, using rock cavities or burrows which they visit only at night. The single egg hatches after 53 days. The young bird wanders at sea for some years before returning to breed.

MIGRATION After breeding, many move west and north, appearing close to the coasts of Ireland, more rarely the UK, in July, August, and September.

LENGTH 45–55cm (18–22in)

WHEN TO SEE March to October
WHERE FOUND Breeds on rocky islands throughout Mediterranean, Portugal, Canaries; winters far offshore in open Atlantic; rare SW Britain and Ireland

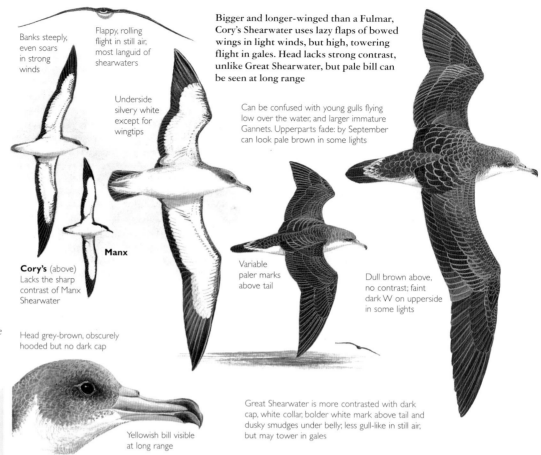

Banks steeply, even soars in strong winds

Flappy, rolling flight in still air; most languid of shearwaters

Underside silvery white except for wingtips

Bigger and longer-winged than a Fulmar, Cory's Shearwater uses lazy flaps of bowed wings in light winds, but high, towering flight in gales. Head lacks strong contrast, unlike Great Shearwater, but pale bill can be seen at long range

Can be confused with young gulls flying low over the water, and larger immature Gannets. Upperparts fade: by September can look pale brown in some lights

Variable paler marks above tail

Dull brown above, no contrast; faint dark W on upperside in some lights

Manx

Cory's (above) Lacks the sharp contrast of Manx Shearwater

Head grey-brown, obscurely hooded but no dark cap

Yellowish bill visible at long range

Great Shearwater is more contrasted with dark cap, white collar, bolder white mark above tail and dusky smudges under belly; less gull-like in still air; but may tower in gales

Manx Shearwater *Puffinus puffinus*

This is the common North Atlantic shearwater: a small, fast-moving, black and white bird of the open ocean. Long, straggling lines fly low over the waves, their wingtips almost 'shearing' the water, while resting flocks sit on the sea in elongated rafts.

FEEDING Manx Shearwaters dive from the surface or just above to snatch small fish, sometimes in excited groups.

VOICE Noisy at the colony, they create a unique, maniacal chorus as they return to their nesting burrows at night. At sea they are silent.

BREEDING Nests in colonies on offshore islands and remote mainland cliffs, in burrows dug in turf or among rocks on high, barren hills. The single chick does not return to breed until five to eight years old.

MIGRATION After breeding they move to the mid Atlantic, far offshore. Many pass by headlands in summer and autumn, especially in onshore winds, all around the UK but most commonly in the north and west, and around Ireland.

LENGTH 35cm (14in)

WHEN TO SEE Mostly April to October
WHERE FOUND Islands from S Iceland to N France; frequent in offshore waters, but oceanic in winter

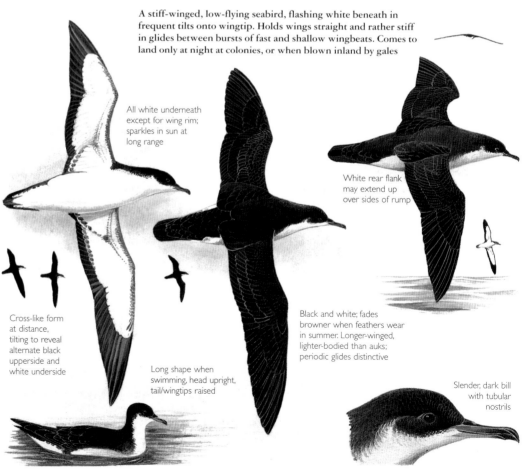

A stiff-winged, low-flying seabird, flashing white beneath in frequent tilts onto wingtip. Holds wings straight and rather stiff in glides between bursts of fast and shallow wingbeats. Comes to land only at night at colonies, or when blown inland by gales

All white underneath except for wing rim; sparkles in sun at long range

White rear flank may extend up over sides of rump

Cross-like form at distance, tilting to reveal alternate black upperside and white underside

Black and white; fades browner when feathers wear in summer. Longer-winged, lighter-bodied than auks; periodic glides distinctive

Long shape when swimming, head upright, tail/wingtips raised

Slender, dark bill with tubular nostrils

26

Levantine Shearwater *Puffinus yelkouan*

Broad dark wingtip below; variable diagonal bar aross base of underwing

A relatively short-headed, short-tailed, Manx-type shearwater, looking fairly compact, with slim wings but a chunky body, and with a rather fast, low, scurrying flight. Feet project beyond tail – a diagnostic feature separating it from the Manx Shearwater

Dark brown above, pale feather edgings only at very close range

White patch on flank, as on Manx, never on Balearic

Upperparts fade to a much warmer pale brown than Balearic Shearwater

Pale form pure white below; typically found in eastern Mediterranean and Black Sea, but also ranges west to Balearics and Gibraltar

Dusky forms are seen in western Mediterranean, including southern France and Balearics; variable degree of brown on underside, unlike Manx

Foot projection beyond tail is short (compare with Balearic)

White vent on pale birds

Traditionally all European 'Manx' shearwaters have been treated as one species. Now it is clear that the Mediterranean birds deserve specific status, and must be split further into the Levantine Shearwater in the east and the Balearic Shearwater in the west. The Levantine is closest to the Manx in its clean brown-and-white appearance. It is the species often glimpsed speeding through the straits at Istanbul, or seen floating in rafts off Greek beaches or from ferries passing between the Greek islands.

FEEDING Catches fish in shallow plunges from the surface.

VOICE A nocturnal visitor to its nest, where noisy; silent at sea.

BREEDING Nests in a deep burrow, laying a single egg that hatches after 48–52 days.

MIGRATION Probably remains in the Mediterranean and Black Sea all year.

LENGTH 30–36cm (12–14in)

WHEN TO SEE All year
WHERE FOUND Breeds very locally in S France, Sardinia, Italy, Balkans, Greek Islands, Crete; widespread in E Mediterranean and Black Sea

---

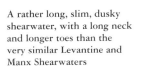

Balearic Shearwater *Puffinus mauretanicus*

A rather long, slim, dusky shearwater, with a long neck and longer toes than the very similar Levantine and Manx Shearwaters

Balearic Long rear body/tail/foot

Levantine Short rear body/tail/foot

Feet projecting well beyond tail identify species if close enough, and separate it from Levantine; this feature adds to elongated profile

Variable below, usually dusky, unlike Manx; dark wingpit patch; bigger, sharper, paler patch on coverts than Sooty Shearwater

Dark brown above, but may fade paler; underside dusky; no pale flank patch

Generally appears much darker than Levantine Shearwater

Dark vent on paler birds

Closely resembling the Manx and Levantine Shearwaters, this is a rare bird of the western Mediterranean, with only a few thousand pairs known. It moves out into the Atlantic and North Sea after breeding, so despite its rarity it may be seen by seabird watchers in northwest Europe.

FEEDING Catches fish and squid by plunging from the air and surface; large flocks gather over shoals and follow fishing boats.

VOICE Like the Manx and Levantine Shearwaters it makes noisy visits to its nesting colonies at night, but at sea it is quiet.

BREEDING One egg is incubated for 52 days and the chick does not fly for a further 72 days.

MIGRATION Breeding is very early and most leave the Mediterranean from May onwards, moulting off western France in late summer and autumn.

LENGTH 34–38cm (13–15in)

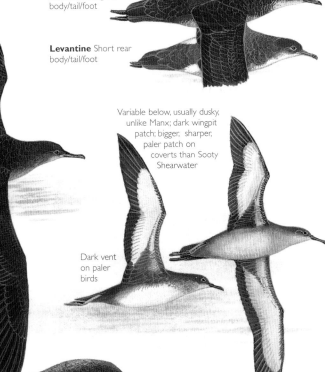

Levantine Grey bill; black tip may be regular feature

Balearic Longer, all-dark bill

WHEN TO SEE All year; off Britain and France mostly June to October
WHERE FOUND Breeds Balearics

Great Shearwater *Puffinus gravis* Sooty Shearwater *P. griseus*

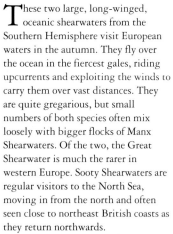

These two large, long-winged, oceanic shearwaters from the Southern Hemisphere visit European waters in the autumn. They fly over the ocean in the fiercest gales, riding upcurrents and exploiting the winds to carry them over vast distances. They are quite gregarious, but small numbers of both species often mix loosely with bigger flocks of Manx Shearwaters. Of the two, the Great Shearwater is much the rarer in western Europe. Sooty Shearwaters are regular visitors to the North Sea, moving in from the north and often seen close to northeast British coasts as they return northwards.

FEEDING They eat small fish and squid, caught in shallow dives.

BREEDING Great Shearwaters breed in burrows on the South Atlantic island of Tristan da Cunha, while Sooty Shearwaters breed in the Falklands.

MIGRATION Both species migrate in a loop around the North Atlantic from their southern breeding grounds.

LENGTH Great 43–51cm (17–20in); Sooty 40–51cm (16–20in)

WHEN TO SEE July to September
WHERE FOUND Offshore, open ocean; Sooty frequent UK; Great rare British Isles

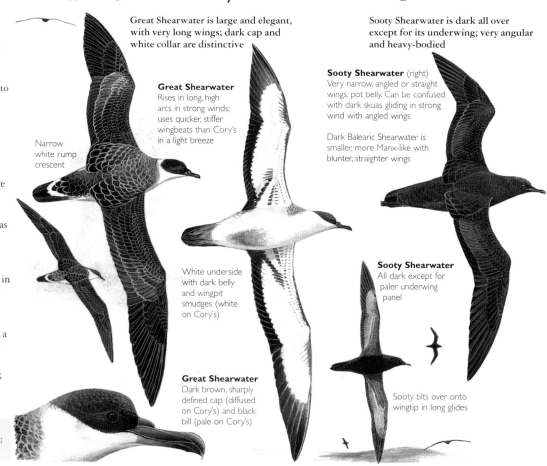

Great Shearwater is large and elegant, with very long wings; dark cap and white collar are distinctive

Sooty Shearwater is dark all over except for its underwing; very angular and heavy-bodied

Great Shearwater
Rises in long, high arcs in strong winds; uses quicker, stiffer wingbeats than Cory's in a light breeze

Sooty Shearwater (right)
Very narrow, angled or straight wings, pot belly. Can be confused with dark skuas gliding in strong wind with angled wings

Dark Balearic Shearwater is smaller, more Manx-like with blunter, straighter wings

Narrow white rump crescent

White underside with dark belly and wingpit smudges (white on Cory's)

Sooty Shearwater
All dark except for paler underwing panel

Great Shearwater
Dark brown, sharply defined cap (diffused on Cory's) and black bill (pale on Cory's)

Sooty tilts over onto wingtip in long glides

Leach's Petrel *Oceanodroma leucorhoa* Storm Petrel *Hydrobates pelagicus*

These two tiny, dark seabirds look ill-suited to life at sea. They are delicately built, barely bigger than sparrows and the most appealing creatures. Yet they are oceanic for most of the year, coming to land only to nest – and then only in darkness.

FEEDING They fly low over the waves seeking tiny crustacea, fish, jellyfish and squid: pattering, hovering and dipping to the surface to snatch food without alighting and never diving.

VOICE They are silent at sea but have soft, purring calls at the nest.

BREEDING Storm Petrels breed on many western islands, but Leach's Petrel is found on only a handful of remote islets between northern Scotland and Iceland. Both birds nest in crevices in walls or broken rocks. The single egg does not hatch for more than 40 days, and juveniles will not breed for four or five years, spending their time over the mid Atlantic.

MIGRATION Both move out to sea in autumn; Leach's is more prone to be blown in to coasts or even inland.

LENGTH Leach's 19–22cm (7½–9in); Storm 14–18cm (5½–7in)

WHEN TO SEE Mostly April to October
WHERE FOUND Breeds on a few islands in NW Europe; at sea; offshore in autumn storms

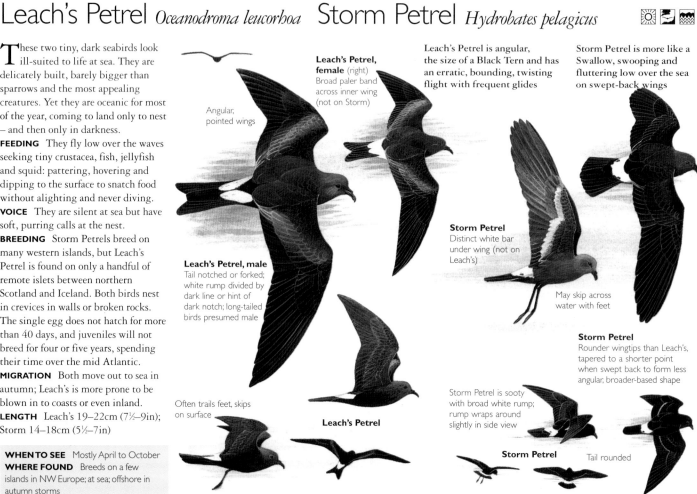

Leach's Petrel is angular, the size of a Black Tern and has an erratic, bounding, twisting flight with frequent glides

Storm Petrel is more like a Swallow, swooping and fluttering low over the sea on swept-back wings

Leach's Petrel, female (right)
Broad paler band across inner wing (not on Storm)

Angular, pointed wings

Storm Petrel
Distinct white bar under wing (not on Leach's)

Leach's Petrel, male
Tail notched or forked; white rump divided by dark line or hint of dark notch; long-tailed birds presumed male

May skip across water with feet

Storm Petrel
Rounder wingtips than Leach's, tapered to a shorter point when swept back to form less angular, broader-based shape

Often trails feet, skips on surface

Leach's Petrel

Storm Petrel is sooty with broad white rump; rump wraps around slightly in side view

Storm Petrel

Tail rounded

28

Gannet *Morus bassana*

Powerful seabird with long, narrow wings held out straight, and pointed head protruding on thick neck. Adults gleaming white; immatures dark or piebald. Distinctive dive from height into sea

Black wingtips

Older juvenile
Whiter on body; wings become chequered

Juvenile
Dusky grey with fine white speckling

Adult
Against a dark sea, adult looks sparkling white and jet black. Headlong plunges from a height with great splash diagnostic, but may dive from low level at shallow angle

Yellow-buff head
fades in winter

Pointed tail

Juvenile

Beware similarity with immature gulls, especially Great Black-backed, which can approach sub-adult Gannet pattern but have blunter head and tail

Looks slender-bodied at long range but really quite deep-chested and solidly built; a powerful flier

Flight direct, with slow, steady rhythm in calm air; in wind, frequent glides; in gales, rises high over waves on wingtip in fast, powerful action

Near-adult
Yellow head, wings spotted black

Adult, breeding
All white except for rich buff head and black wingtips

Black facial skin

Eyes face forwards, set in broad, round head

Juvenile

Striped toes of adult
visible at close range

The juvenile grows quickly at the nest, eventually refusing food when it is already too fat and heavy to fly; it flops into the sea and swims away, starving until it is light enough to take off again

All four toes joined by web (like cormorants but unlike gulls)

The Gannet is the most dramatic and impressive North Atlantic seabird simply because of its size and power: it has a charismatic presence that smaller birds lack. A Gannet at sea looks dynamic and elegant; a closer view at the colony reveals a fascinating bird, with its dagger-like bill, forward-facing eyes, fluttering gular (throat) pouch, its strange, striped, completely-webbed feet and peculiarly stereotyped communication postures. In normal flight in still air a Gannet moves steadily over the open sea, its wings held out straight and beating with a regular, shallow action, flexing at the tip. Given a good wind, however, the Gannet shows itself a master of its element, soaring on upcurrents over the waves, frequently banking onto one wingtip and travelling for miles with scarcely a wingbeat.

FEEDING Gannets eat fish: usually fast muscular fish such as mackerel and herring, which are difficult to catch and subdue. To do so they fly over the sea, using their sharp eyes to spot the fish, then dive headlong from the air – either from a great height with a loud splash, or from low level spearing into the water at an angle – to reach deep down to the shoals of potential prey.

DISPLAY & VOICE Loud, rhythmic, repetitive calls create an almost mechanical chorus at the colony. The displays are ritualized communications between paired birds and with other pairs nearby. Males advertise nest sites with a headshaking action, but attack approaching females with a bite to the nape. Reunited pairs greet each other standing breast-to-breast, shaking their heads and fencing with their bills; each will preen the head and neck of the other. When one of the pair is about to fly off, leaving the other to protect the nest, it points its head skywards to make its intention clear.

BREEDING A breeding colony in full swing is a vibrant, noisy scene, full of action. The nests are built of seaweed, discarded netting and twine on broad ledges, usually on islands but increasingly on mainland cliffs. A single chick fledges after 90 days. It will not breed for five or six years, although it may survive to 15 or 20 years of age.

MIGRATION A fledged Gannet flies south to the ocean off the west African coast for its first year of life. Mature birds spend the winter in the North Sea and North Atlantic.

LENGTH 90–100cm (35–39in)

WHEN TO SEE All year; at colonies March to October
WHERE FOUND Breeds in isolated colonies from N France, UK to Iceland; widespread off coasts

Cormorant *Phalacrocorax carbo*

Cormorants eat fish, and although there is no evidence that they cause lasting damage to fish stocks they have been vilified by anglers; hundreds are shot under licence, even though there is no apparent benefit to the fisheries as a result. Yet to others Cormorants are a welcome sight, especially in Britain where such large, dramatic birds are uncommon. Some colonies have developed inland, in the tops of trees beside lakes, reservoirs, and gravel pits. These are spectacular places, especially when groups of birds return from fishing trips, flying in at a height and spiralling or twisting down in aerobatic dives.

On the water, Cormorants are goose-sized but much flatter, with lower backs and slender bills. A close view of the bill reveals a sturdy hooked tip, ideal for handling slippery, muscular fish. After feeding, Cormorants often stand on the shore, on buoys or in tree tops with their wings half outspread; birds adopting this attitude have always been assumed to be 'drying their wings', but it may have more to do with the digestion of a good meal.

FEEDING They take fish of many kinds, from both fresh- and saltwater. In lakes and rivers they prefer eels, but they may catch almost anything that is available and of suitable size.

DISPLAY & VOICE At the nest they are noisy and display with fanned tails and half-open wings raised up from the body; the white face patches, long white nape plumes, and white thigh patches are all shown off to advantage by the display. Their calls are deep, croaking notes, while young in the nest make a higher, chattering chorus.

BREEDING Cormorants nest in colonies that may be from a few to hundreds of nests strong. The nest is a great heap of sticks or, at the coast, of seaweed, piled up in the fork of a tree or on a broad cliff ledge. The area around each nest soon becomes liberally splashed with white droppings, and trees may eventually die from the effects. The clutch of 3–4 eggs hatches within 30–31 days; it is a further 50 days before the young first fly.

MIGRATION Some Cormorants that breed on the Continent reach the UK, and UK breeders (and especially immatures) move south to Spain. Even those living inland make long and irregular movements.

LENGTH 80–100cm (32–39in)

WHEN TO SEE All year
WHERE FOUND Breeds locally around the coasts of UK and Ireland, and a few places inland; also breeds around the coasts of NW Europe, rivers of E Europe. The Cormorant is more widespread in winter on large lakes, estuaries, and sheltered coastal waters

Cormorant is goose-sized but more slender, with longer tail and slim, hook-tipped bill. Often found in small, loose flocks or at nesting colonies on cliffs or in tall trees. Flies well, often in lines or V-formation at moderate height, or in ones and twos at much greater heights on long fishing trips

Cormorant
Extended neck; long, broad wings with slight S-shape to trailing edge; longer tail than goose; characteristic habit of gliding between bouts of flapping

Tree colony

Shag
Smaller, with slightly narrower wings and tail

Cormorant
Note flat belly

Shag
Pot-bellied shape

Typical 'wing-drying' pose

Juvenile
Browner than adult

Breeding adult
White thigh patch never seen on Shag

Adult
Race *sinensis*; some British birds have as much white; face patterns variable

Juvenile

Adult, winter

Swims low in water, back sometimes awash; typically holds head and bill slightly uptilted

White cheek patch unlike Shag; bill thicker; forehead lower and flatter

Sub-adult

Breeding adult

Winter adult

Juvenile
dark type

Shag

Juveniles

White thigh patch develops in late winter

Short, thick, dark legs; all toes joined by webs like Gannet

Shag *Phalacrocorax aristotelis*

Shag is slightly smaller, rounder-headed than Cormorant, with slimmer bill, steeper forehead and more snaky neck. Generally flies low over water in small, irregular groups; large flocks may gather in good fishing areas. Often seen on rocks and cliffs but not in trees inland

Adult, winter
Glossy green and purplish with black feather edgings creating neat, scaly pattern on back; yellow gape

Juvenile
Compare face and head shape with Cormorant; white chin spot, dark underside

Juvenile
Upperwing quickly wears paler in midwing panel

Immature
Gaining adult colours in second year

Juvenile, Mediterranean
Southern race has white underparts, dark thighs

Breeding adult, spring
(above) Upstanding crest unlike any Cormorant

Juvenile (above)
Wing panel distinctive: whiter on Mediterranean race

Mediterranean
Adult has short crest in spring

Swims low in water

Flies low over sea with rapid wingbeats

Note uptilted head, steep forehead, thin bill

Shags are more strictly marine than Cormorants. They are scarce inland, and even at the coast they rarely fly over headlands. Small groups are seen flying low over the sea, looking much quicker in their actions than heavier Cormorants. They may concentrate in bigger flocks to feed in shallow bays and tide races, and they are equally at home in the roughest seas just off fearsome rocks.

FEEDING Fish form their staple food: mostly quite small fish, especially sandeels taken at a considerable depth.

DISPLAY & VOICE Shags indulge in various head-wagging and aggressive displays at the nest, producing raucous calls and harsh, rattling notes both in alarm or to threaten intruders.

BREEDING They nest on cliff ledges. These are usually well-sheltered, often just inside caves; some are low down but they may be up to 100m above the waves. Up to eight eggs are laid, and take 28–31 days to hatch; usually two chicks fledge, after about 53 days.

MIGRATION There is some dispersal along coasts after the breeding season; far northern birds and immatures move farthest south.

LENGTH 65–80cm (25½–31½in)

WHEN TO SEE All year
WHERE FOUND Appears on the coasts of NW and W Europe, and around the Mediterranean

---

Pygmy Cormorant *Phalacrocorax pygmeus*

A small, handsome, but stub-billed freshwater cormorant with bronze or chestnut brown on the head and long, fine, whitish plumes on the head and breast in spring

Adult, breeding
Gains bronze or brown head and fine white plumes

Flight quicker than Cormorant, with glides on bowed wings

Adult
Dark breast

Juvenile
Pale breast

Adult, non-breeding
Duller brown head loses white plumes; some have white on chin

Rounded head, steep forehead

Adult, breeding

Long tail and heavy body

Adult, non-breeding
Short, thick bill

This small, chunky cormorant is a freshwater species, restricted to reed-fringed lakes and rivers in southeast Europe. It is often found in mixed colonies with egrets and herons, but is rare and declining, and may even be threatened.

FEEDING It eats mainly fish, which it catches by diving in shallow water. It is usually solitary when fishing.

DISPLAY & VOICE Posturing in spring reveals fine, spiky, hair-like crest feathers. Breeding birds give deep, guttural calls at the nest.

BREEDING Nests in reeds and waterside bushes, often over water; 4–6 eggs hatch in 27–30 days, but the young do not fly until 70 days old.

MIGRATION Breeders from the Balkans move towards coastal lagoons and marshes in winter. Black Sea birds make longer southward migrations.

LENGTH 45–55cm (18–22in)

WHEN TO SEE All year
WHERE FOUND On reed-fringed rivers and lagoons in SE Europe; rare on coast

Bittern *Botaurus stellaris*

Restricted as it is to dense reedbeds, the Bittern is a rarely-seen, mysterious bird of the marshes. If it appears close to the water's edge it is still difficult to spot, because its camouflage is remarkably effective against golden reed stems. In flight it is an odd, unlikely-looking bird: vaguely owl-like with bowed wings, trailing feet, and a long, thickly-feathered, half-withdrawn neck.

FEEDING It stands still or strides slowly forward looking for fish, which it catches with a typically heron-like strike, grabbing its prey in its bill.

VOICE Males produce a deep, booming *whoomp*, as if blowing across the wide neck of a large bottle. The calls carry for miles, and can be analyzed to identify individual males.

BREEDING The nest is a large heap of reeds; 5–6 eggs hatch in 25–26 days.

MIGRATION In winter many fly west to avoid frost on the European mainland, some to regular wintering sites in quite small marshes.

LENGTH 70–80cm (28–32in)

WHEN TO SEE All year, but more widely in winter
WHERE FOUND Reedbeds; rarely other waterside places; very local, all Europe

A richly marked, golden-buff, heron-like bird, with a thick neck and big, green feet, broad wings and a dagger bill

Flies high over breeding areas in spring

Eyes face forward; blackish moustache

Striped foreneck

Neck much thicker than that of immature Purple Heron

Upperparts have complex blotches and bars, usually looking pale at a distance

Arched wings show it is a heron, but looks more compact; otherwise resembles a huge owl in flight

Black crown

Pale forewing shows as broad band in flight

Thick feathers conceal kinked neck in flight

Long toes provide support when body tilts forward, and help grasp reed stems above water level

Leans forward when fishing; may shake body from side to side

Squacco Heron *Ardeola ralloides*

A beautiful little heron, pinkish-buff or sandy at rest, the Squacco reveals startlingly white wings when it flies. It is usually seen in waterside vegetation or on floating weed, either on or beside rivers and still lakes.

FEEDING It catches small aquatic creatures in its bill after long, patient waiting and watching. It is much less active in its feeding than the egrets, preferring to wait for prey to come within range.

DISPLAY & VOICE Usually silent except for an occasional harsh *karr* at dusk, or during a pairing display which involves leaning forward with outstretched neck, passing sticks from bill to bill and temporary 'blushing' of face and bill colours.

BREEDING It nests in a thicket of willows or dense reeds, in a loose colony or with other herons and egrets; 4–6 eggs hatch after 22–24 days.

MIGRATION In autumn Squacco Herons move south to Africa, returning in late March and April.

LENGTH 44–47cm (17–18½in)

WHEN TO SEE March to September
WHERE FOUND Reedy marshes, swamps, richly vegetated rivers; scattered in S Europe; very rare in the UK

A squat, well-camouflaged heron, often hard to spot; in summer quite pink, in winter much duller

Breeding adult
Black-edged head plumes

Bill blue and black in spring

White wings contrast with dark back, unlike all-white egrets: sudden 'shock' of white as bird takes flight

Juvenile
Darkest, most streaked plumage

First winter

Non-breeding adult
No head plumes; bill yellow and black

Shows little white when standing, but reveals eyecatching white wings in flight

Typically stands leaning forwards, head and neck withdrawn into shoulders in tapered oval shape; lunge for fish reveals startlingly long neck

Immature
Broad, soft neck streaks

Little Bittern *Ixobrychus minutus*

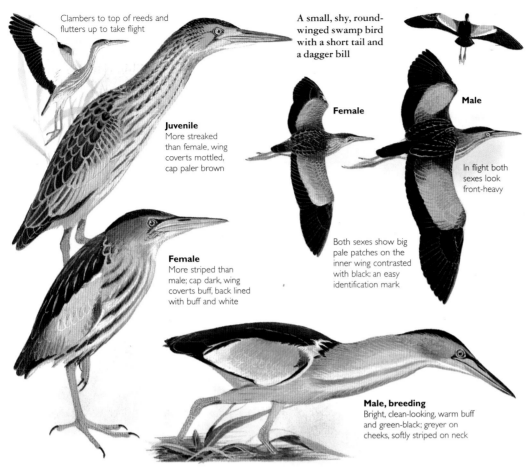

Clambers to top of reeds and flutters up to take flight

A small, shy, round-winged swamp bird with a short tail and a dagger bill

Juvenile
More streaked than female, wing coverts mottled, cap paler brown

Female

Male

In flight both sexes look front-heavy

Female
More striped than male; cap dark, wing coverts buff, back lined with buff and white

Both sexes show big pale patches on the inner wing contrasted with black: an easy identification mark

Male, breeding
Bright, clean-looking, warm buff and green-black; greyer on cheeks, softly striped on neck

This tiny, colourful heron is very secretive and hard to see, which is a pity for such a handsome species. It is often glimpsed as a Moorhen-sized bird with big, pale wing patches, flying low and flat over a reedbed or riverside marsh before dropping out of sight into the reeds.

FEEDING It is most active around dusk, moving to good feeding sites at the water's edge where it catches small fish, frogs, newts, and large insects.

VOICE During courtship the male produces a monotonous 'song': a hollow *kok* repeated every two seconds mostly at dusk.

BREEDING The nest is a pile of reed stems built in willows or reeds over shallow water. Five or six eggs hatch after an incubation of 17–19 days.

MIGRATION Little Bitterns leave Europe between August and October, spending the winter south of the Sahara; they return from Africa in March and April.

LENGTH 33–38cm (13–15in)

WHEN TO SEE Late March to October; vagrants to UK mostly in spring
WHERE FOUND Reedbeds, reed-fringed rivers; locally through S Europe and north to the Baltic states

Night Heron *Nycticorax nycticorax*

A thickset, sociable heron of well-wooded watersides. Active at twilight and at night, it often flies in small groups that rise and scatter if disturbed at the roost

Juvenile
Brown, spotted with white

Adult, breeding
Looks pale except for a black 'saddle'; the wings are uniform, unlike Grey Heron's

Typical hunched pose

Adult **Juvenile**
Short-necked, bow-winged in flight

Adult, breeding (left)
Spring adults have two long white plumes from the nape

Juvenile
Brown with white, drop-shaped spots above

Immature, first year
Loses pale spots

Immature, second year
More or less mottled above, streaked on breast

Legs pink-red in spring

A handsome, medium-sized heron, most active at dusk and dawn, the Night Heron is widespread in five continents but has a restricted distribution in Europe, where suitable wet habitats are few and far between. It spends the day in a willow thicket or waterside tree and moves at dusk to find good feeding beside a lake or river.

FEEDING Usually active after dark, it catches fish, frogs, insects, small mammals, and small birds.

DISPLAY & VOICE Males display by stretching erect, swaying from one foot to the other, then gradually 'subsiding' into the usual hunched pose. The usual call is a crow-like *quok*.

BREEDING Night Heron nests are fragile but become increasingly robust after several years' use. Small colonies nest in reeds, bushes or tall trees, often with other species. The 3–5 eggs hatch after 21–22 days.

MIGRATION Night Herons migrate to Africa in October and return in March and April.

LENGTH 58–65cm (23–26in)

WHEN TO SEE Late March to October; vagrants to UK mostly in spring
WHERE FOUND Rivers, lakes, fishponds and adjacent thickets; locally through Europe north to Netherlands; rare in UK

Great White Heron *Ardea alba*

Also known as the Great White Egret, this large, dramatic bird has the white plumage of a Little Egret but the size and dagger bill of a Grey Heron. It is a particularly angular bird, with a long, slim, kinked neck which makes a deep bulge when its head is withdrawn in flight.

FEEDING It searches for fish to snatch up in its bill, using the patient, waterside wait-and-see or more active hunting methods typical of herons.

DISPLAY & VOICE The courtship and territorial displays involve ritual postures that show off the elongated plumes to best effect in beautiful and dramatic performances. Calls are short, low, harsh monosyllables.

BREEDING Nests are usually in trees, made of sticks and lined with finer stems. The clutch varies from two to five eggs which hatch after 25 days.

MIGRATION Most move south in winter, but some wander erratically into western Europe.

LENGTH 85–102cm (33–40in)

WHEN TO SEE All year, but mostly March to October
WHERE FOUND Very localized in SE Europe, increasingly in the Netherlands, S France and as a vagrant to Britain

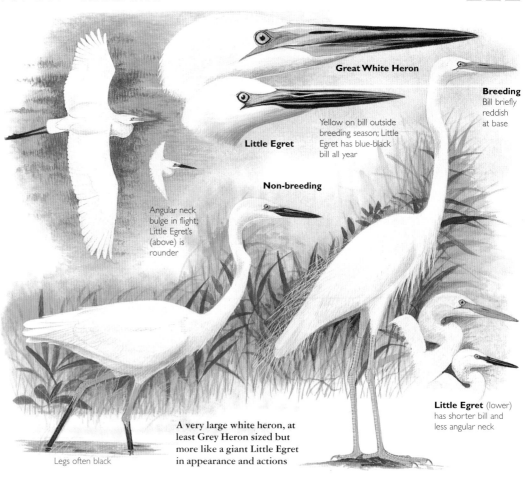

Great White Heron

Little Egret

Yellow on bill outside breeding season; Little Egret has blue-black bill all year

Breeding Bill briefly reddish at base

Non-breeding

Angular neck bulge in flight; Little Egret's (above) is rounder

Little Egret (lower) has shorter bill and less angular neck

A very large white heron, at least Grey Heron sized but more like a giant Little Egret in appearance and actions

Legs often black

Little Egret *Egretta garzetta*

Little Egrets are superb, lively, elegant white herons, always fun to watch. They are showing signs of spreading in northwest Europe but are most familiar in the warmer south.

FEEDING Little Egrets wade in shallow water, sometimes belly-deep, often running to and fro to stir fish and other prey into tell-tale action and grasping them with their long, sharp beaks. They have a habit of perching on floating weed, flapping their half-open wings for balance.

DISPLAY & VOICE In display Little Egrets make full use of their nuptial plumes: long, wispy, white back feathers and two slender head plumes. The voice is a nasal croak, not at all fitting for such a beautiful bird.

BREEDING They nest in tree colonies, often with other herons and egrets. Each pair incubates three to five eggs in a stick nest for 25 days.

MIGRATION In winter most move south to the Mediterranean area or into north Africa, but some stay as far north as southern Britain.

LENGTH 55–65cm (22–26in)

WHEN TO SEE All year, but mostly March to October
WHERE FOUND Southern and central Europe, increasingly in S Britain, with a few breeding since 1996

Flight is heron-like with bowed wings, withdrawn neck, and trailing legs, but quite quick wingbeats

A small, startlingly-white heron-like bird of both fresh- and saltwater margins, that nests in colonies in trees, often with other herons

Non-breeding

Breeding Spreads plumes of head, back and breast in courtship display; bill grey-black, never yellow

Yellow feet rule out other European egrets and herons

Yellow feet distinctive, but beware muddy feet looking dark

Feeds in shallows, from rocks, or from floating vegetation; often dashes jerkily sideways with raised head and open wings

Non-breeding

Cattle Egret *Bubulcus ibis*

Adult, breeding
Bill becomes red in spring; face flushes red and green

Adult, non-breeding

Flies fast, with head withdrawn and legs trailing; usually in flocks

Immature
Dark bill turns yellow

Small, gregarious egret, far less tied to watersides than Little Egret, but usually nesting and roosting in trees near water

Non-breeding (left)
Yellow bill, dark legs (Little Egret has dark bill, yellow feet)

Breeding (left and right)
Buff plumes and cap, yellow to red bill, yellow or reddish legs; the only white egret with buff patches

In parts of Iberia, and also far more commonly in Africa and the Middle East, Cattle Egrets are a familiar sight along watersides, in fields with livestock or recently-tilled earth, on roadside verges, and even in town parks and rubbish tips. Adaptable, successful birds, they bring a touch of elegance to some of the world's poorest regions.

FEEDING They often feed around the feet of cattle and horses (or take ticks from their backs), or follow the plough to snatch worms and grubs. They also eat frogs, lizards, insects, and offal.

DISPLAY & VOICE Most displays are at the nest, exploiting the birds' elegant, elongated plumes. Calls include hoarse, short notes and a rapid quack.

BREEDING They nest in trees, in sizeable colonies, often with other egrets, ibises, and herons. Four or five eggs hatch after 22–26 days.

MIGRATION Many move south in winter into Africa. A rare vagrant in northwest Europe, including Britain.

LENGTH 48–53cm (19–21in)

WHEN TO SEE All year
WHERE FOUND Wetlands and adjacent fields and trees, refuse tips. Very local in Europe, mostly SW Spain; a few elsewhere in Iberia and extreme S France

Spoonbill *Platalea leucorodia*

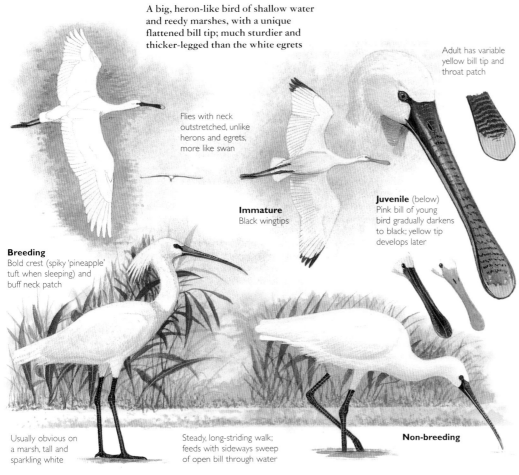

A big, heron-like bird of shallow water and reedy marshes, with a unique flattened bill tip; much sturdier and thicker-legged than the white egrets

Adult has variable yellow bill tip and throat patch

Flies with neck outstretched, unlike herons and egrets, more like swan

Immature
Black wingtips

Juvenile (below)
Pink bill of young bird gradually darkens to black; yellow tip develops later

Breeding
Bold crest (spiky 'pineapple' tuft when sleeping) and buff neck patch

Usually obvious on a marsh, tall and sparkling white

Steady, long-striding walk; feeds with sideways sweep of open bill through water

Non-breeding

Although white like an egret, the Spoonbill is a quite different bird, identifiable at great range. Its thick legs, solid build and almost human walk (and its habit of feeding in small, tight groups) create a much more stable and sedate impression, although it can become quite agitated and move fast when chasing prey.

FEEDING It typically walks slowly forwards through shallow water, its bill half open and immersed, detecting prey by touch: it eats small fish, tadpoles, and other aquatic creatures.

DISPLAY & VOICE Pairs preen each other at the nest, stretch up their heads and bills to display the coloured skin beneath their throats, and spread their peculiar, spiky 'pineapple' crests. They are usually silent birds.

BREEDING They nest in colonies in reeds and tall trees, often with herons. The bulky stick nests hold three or four eggs that hatch in 24–25 days.

MIGRATION Moves south into Africa in the autumn; scarce in Britain.

LENGTH 80–90cm (32–36in)

WHEN TO SEE March to October
WHERE FOUND Freshwater lakes and reedbeds, brackish lagoons; extremely local: Netherlands, Spain, E Europe

Purple Heron *Ardea purpurea*

This is a slender, snaky-necked southern heron of reedbeds and dense marshes. It is often hard to see well, preferring to hide in reeds more like a Bittern than a Grey Heron, although from time to time it appears on the edge of the marsh beside open water, perches in a low tree or flies overhead on its way to a new feeding place. Whatever it is doing it is an elegant bird: more finely-drawn than a Grey Heron, slightly longer and more slender in the bill, head, neck, and legs, and narrower in the wing.

Compared to the Grey Heron it is much more restricted to extensive wetlands with clean water invading tall marshland vegetation: it cannot make do with wet ditches, reservoir edges, or sea coasts like the more adaptable Grey. Nor does it use nesting platforms or nest in tall trees, and it is far less tolerant of human disturbance.

FEEDING The Purple Heron usually feeds alone, mostly in the cover of waterside vegetation and typically in the early morning and evening. It stands silently, then swiftly darts out its long neck to snatch small fish or large aquatic insects; more rarely it takes small snakes, birds, and voles. Fish prey includes bream, carp, perch, roach, sticklebacks, rudd, and eels.

DISPLAY & VOICE Rather quiet compared with the Grey Heron, the Purple Heron has a rough, rasping note, especially as it flies up when disturbed. It produces various raucous calls at the nest, and the male makes rhythmic rattles with his bill. Displays include a rather exaggerated 'stretch display' compared with the Grey Heron's version, pointing its head and neck vertically upwards for a moment before making a sudden deep bowing movement with back plumes raised; the male clatters his bill.

BREEDING Most nests are built of dead reed stems among reeds, some of twigs in low bushes. The birds make new nests each year, often in small colonies. The four or five eggs are laid in May or June and incubated for 26 days by both parents. The chicks fly after about seven weeks; they are ready to breed themselves at one year old.

MIGRATION European Purple Herons move south to Africa, south of the Sahara, in September and October, returning in March. A few reach Britain each spring but do not breed. Juveniles tend to be more nomadic in late summer and reach areas well outside the usual breeding range.

LENGTH 78–90cm (31–35in)

WHEN TO SEE March to October
WHERE FOUND S and central European swamps and marshes, north to the Low Countries; rare visitor to UK

Adult
Dark rufous under forewing

Juvenile
Paler sandy colour under forewing

A large, elegant, snaky-headed heron with a long, slim bill. In flight it reveals rather narrow wings and the curved neck makes a deep, narrow bulge; the long legs and toes trail noticeably far beyond the tail

Juvenile
Almost uniform pale rufous neck; pale buff 'landing lights' on leading edge of wing

Adult male
Forewing clear zinc grey; often more buff on female; white 'landing lights'; coiled neck striped black and chestnut

Sometimes flies in small flocks on passage, over land and at sea in the Mediterranean

Flight silhouettes reveal long wings with often prominent secondary bulge and narrow base; very deep neck; long legs

Adult female
Tendency to have more buff, less clear grey, on wing coverts than male. Raised head and neck extremely long and slim; very long bill

Juvenile
Rufous when first fledged, gradually becomes duller; browner or tawny; can look very pale

Looks much darker than Grey Heron, more steely-grey, with sandy-buff plumes. Chestnut flanks and thighs diagnostic

Legs vivid orange-yellow with black front in spring

Remarkably long toes

Juvenile (below)
No black crown; much browner than Grey Heron

Immature
Second-year bird looks dark; plumage variable as adult colours gradually assumed

Grey Heron *Ardea cinerea*

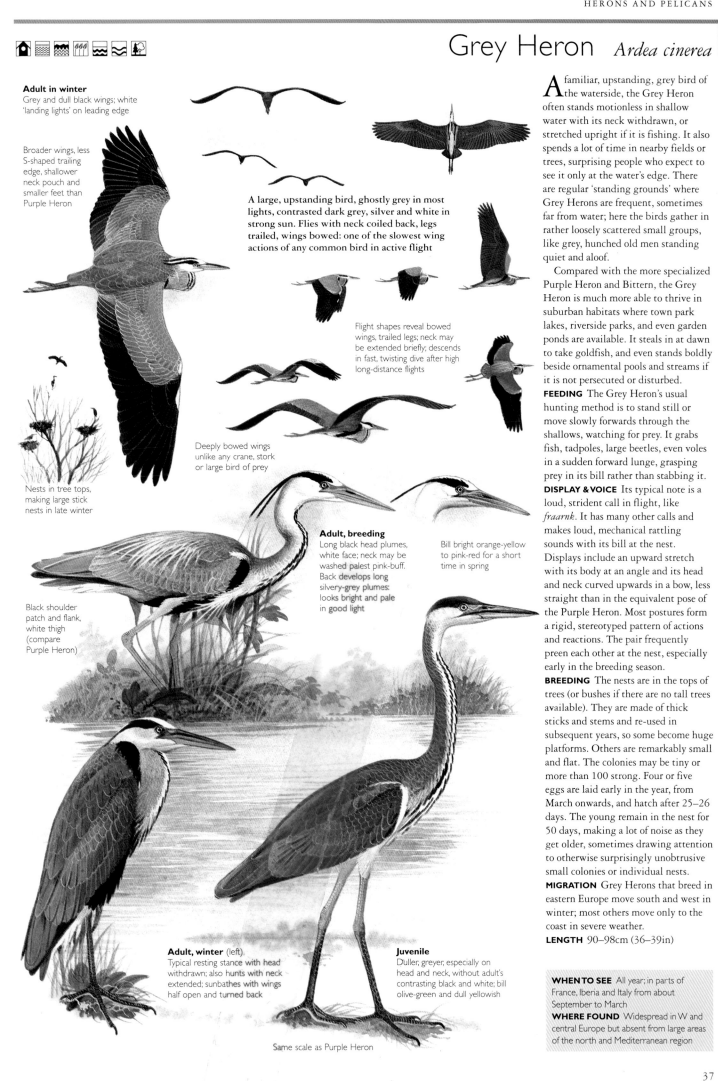

A familiar, upstanding, grey bird of the waterside, the Grey Heron often stands motionless in shallow water with its neck withdrawn, or stretched upright if it is fishing. It also spends a lot of time in nearby fields or trees, surprising people who expect to see it only at the water's edge. There are regular 'standing grounds' where Grey Herons are frequent, sometimes far from water; here the birds gather in rather loosely scattered small groups, like grey, hunched old men standing quiet and aloof.

Compared with the more specialized Purple Heron and Bittern, the Grey Heron is much more able to thrive in suburban habitats where town park lakes, riverside parks, and even garden ponds are available. It steals in at dawn to take goldfish, and even stands boldly beside ornamental pools and streams if it is not persecuted or disturbed.

FEEDING The Grey Heron's usual hunting method is to stand still or move slowly forwards through the shallows, watching for prey. It grabs fish, tadpoles, large beetles, even voles in a sudden forward lunge, grasping prey in its bill rather than stabbing it.

DISPLAY & VOICE Its typical note is a loud, strident call in flight, like *fraarnk*. It has many other calls and makes loud, mechanical rattling sounds with its bill at the nest. Displays include an upward stretch with its body at an angle and its head and neck curved upwards in a bow, less straight than in the equivalent pose of the Purple Heron. Most postures form a rigid, stereotyped pattern of actions and reactions. The pair frequently preen each other at the nest, especially early in the breeding season.

BREEDING The nests are in the tops of trees (or bushes if there are no tall trees available). They are made of thick sticks and stems and re-used in subsequent years, so some become huge platforms. Others are remarkably small and flat. The colonies may be tiny or more than 100 strong. Four or five eggs are laid early in the year, from March onwards, and hatch after 25–26 days. The young remain in the nest for 50 days, making a lot of noise as they get older, sometimes drawing attention to otherwise surprisingly unobtrusive small colonies or individual nests.

MIGRATION Grey Herons that breed in eastern Europe move south and west in winter; most others move only to the coast in severe weather.

LENGTH 90–98cm (36–39in)

Adult in winter
Grey and dull black wings; white 'landing lights' on leading edge

Broader wings, less S-shaped trailing edge, shallower neck pouch and smaller feet than Purple Heron

A large, upstanding bird, ghostly grey in most lights, contrasted dark grey, silver and white in strong sun. Flies with neck coiled back, legs trailed, wings bowed: one of the slowest wing actions of any common bird in active flight

Flight shapes reveal bowed wings, trailed legs; neck may be extended briefly; descends in fast, twisting dive after high long-distance flights

Deeply bowed wings unlike any crane, stork or large bird of prey

Nests in tree tops, making large stick nests in late winter

Adult, breeding
Long black head plumes, white face; neck may be washed palest pink-buff. Back develops long silvery-grey plumes: looks bright and pale in good light

Bill bright orange-yellow to pink-red for a short time in spring

Black shoulder patch and flank, white thigh (compare Purple Heron)

Adult, winter (left)
Typical resting stance with head withdrawn; also hunts with neck extended; sunbathes with wings half open and turned back

Juvenile
Duller, greyer, especially on head and neck, without adult's contrasting black and white; bill olive-green and dull yellowish

Same scale as Purple Heron

WHEN TO SEE All year; in parts of France, Iberia and Italy from about September to March
WHERE FOUND Widespread in W and central Europe but absent from large areas of the north and Mediterranean region

Crane *Grus grus* Demoiselle Crane *Anthropoides virgo*

Cranes are superb, giant birds, best known for their spectacular courtship dances involving lovely, rhythmic posturing. In the far north their noisy, migrating flocks are symbols of the changing seasons.

FEEDING Although Cranes eat insects, voles, frogs, and some young birds, they feed mainly on roots, leaves, seeds, and fruits picked from the ground.

DISPLAY & VOICE In courtship each bird performs a deep bow followed by an elegant upward stretch and a leap into the air with raised wings. The calls include a duetting *krruee-krruee* and trumpeting notes in flight.

BREEDING Crane nests are mounds of vegetation on the ground, in open areas of bog or marshland. Cranes are very shy at the nest and require large areas of undisturbed 'wilderness'. The two eggs hatch after a 30-day incubation.

MIGRATION A very few may spend the winter in Britain and elsewhere; most fly south to Iberia and Africa.

LENGTH 115–130cm (45–51in); wingspan 233cm (92in)

> **WHEN TO SEE** All year; March to September in north
> **WHERE FOUND** Breeds on bogs and marshes from Scandinavia and N Germany eastwards; winters in Spain, France

The Demoiselle Crane is a slightly smaller, more tapered bird than the Crane, much rarer in Europe (but occasionally encountered as an 'escape' from captivity). It is really a bird of the central Asian steppe, with a very few found in eastern Turkey and Cyprus.

FEEDING Its food is similar to that of the Crane and taken in the same way, in the bill, from damp ground or short vegetation.

DISPLAY & VOICE The Demoiselle's displays include typical crane dances, but it performs these with its bushy 'tail' flat rather than raised. Its movements are more balletic than those of the Crane, with less leaping. Its calls are rather like the Crane's but usually higher-pitched.

BREEDING The Demoiselle incubates two eggs for 27–29 days.

MIGRATION In Europe Demoiselle Cranes are usually vagrants or escapes, and it is only in Cyprus that they can be seen at all regularly; breeding birds migrate to Africa each winter.

LENGTH 90–100cm (36–39in); wingspan 203cm (80in)

> **WHEN TO SEE** April to October
> **WHERE FOUND** Extensive lakes and marshes around Black Sea

Juvenile crane (above) Dull grey-brown, with unmarked browner head

Crane, non-breeding (above) Blue-grey with black forehead and throat, white neck stripe

Red on rear of crown difficult to see unless at close range

Crane is a large, erect, grey bird with white head stripes, dark wingtips and bushy secondaries over tail when standing. Walks with a long, elegant stride

Crane, breeding Drooping black secondaries create bushy 'tail'. Variable dark spots on coverts. Long, slender black legs

Crane Flies with head and neck outstretched, unlike herons; flocks fly in long lines and V-formations, with loud, clanging calls

Crane Black throat stripe stops short of breast; otherwise hard to tell from Demoiselle from below

Demoiselle Black throat stripe extends onto upper breast; smaller than Crane but very similar

Demoiselle Shorter bill and steeper forehead than Crane

Demoiselle Crane is smaller, slimmer, more elegant than Crane, with a long white neck stripe. Black on foreneck extends lower down as wispy plumes, and greyer secondaries create a longer, paler, bushy 'tail'

Upperparts paler, more uniform than Crane's

Demoiselle Shorter bill, rounder head, shorter neck than Crane, black extends to breast

Demoiselle Shorter legs than Crane

Crane Larger, darker, broader-winged than Demoiselle; upperwing has more black, extending onto primary coverts, inner primaries and secondaries, but can be hard to confirm

Crane **Demoiselle**

Grey bloom on fresh wing plumage of Demoiselle (far right) wears to black by breeding season

White Stork *Ciconia ciconia*

A huge, stately, long-legged black and white bird with a deliberate, long-striding walk. In flight, wingbeats deep and slow; soars on flat wings with neck outstretched

Wings broad, deeply-fingered

White with black flight feathers from below

Birds in flocks circle independently, crossing and recrossing as they rise; pelicans usually more coordinated, whole flock circling as one

Fresh flight feathers edged whitish; all-black when worn

Adult
Bill red, dagger-like

Soars to great heights, often in tight flocks

Walks with long, slow, elegant strides

Juvenile
Blackish bill

Red legs often chalky-white with droppings

A popular bird in European villages, the White Stork builds huge stick nests on rooftops, church towers, special man-made poles, and less often in trees. It has declined in many regions, possibly because of problems in Africa as well as wetland drainage and pesticide use in Europe.

FEEDING It feeds on farmland and around lakes, eating grasshoppers, beetles, frogs, and voles. Land drainage and intensive cultivation drives storks away from traditional feeding sites.

DISPLAY & VOICE Courtship displays at the nest include noisy bill-rattling with heads bent back, and rhythmic, ritualized bowing with spread wings. Otherwise, storks are silent.

BREEDING The 3–5 eggs hatch in 30 days. Young birds migrate with adults but do not breed until 3–7 years old.

MIGRATION In August, White Storks form huge flocks and cross the Mediterranean at its narrowest points, bound for the east African plains where they feed on insects disturbed by grazing herds. They return in March.

LENGTH 100–115cm (39–45in)

WHEN TO SEE March to September
WHERE FOUND Open farmland, wet pastures, marshes; Iberia and eastwards from the Low Countries; rarely UK

Black Stork *Ciconia nigra*

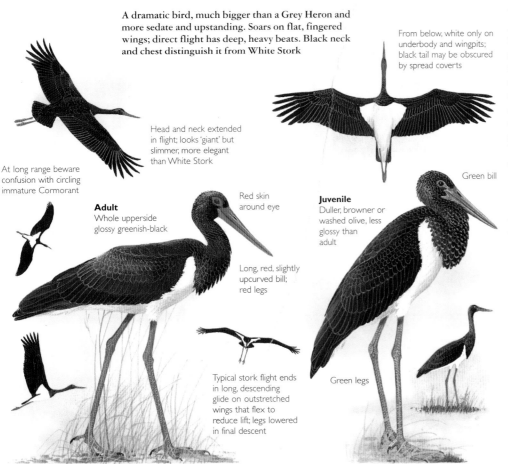

A dramatic bird, much bigger than a Grey Heron and more sedate and upstanding. Soars on flat, fingered wings; direct flight has deep, heavy beats. Black neck and chest distinguish it from White Stork

From below, white only on underbody and wingpits; black tail may be obscured by spread coverts

Head and neck extended in flight; looks 'giant' but slimmer, more elegant than White Stork

At long range beware confusion with circling immature Cormorant

Green bill

Adult
Whole upperside glossy greenish-black

Red skin around eye

Juvenile
Duller, browner or washed olive, less glossy than adult

Long, red, slightly upcurved bill; red legs

Typical stork flight ends in long, descending glide on outstretched wings that flex to reduce lift; legs lowered in final descent

Green legs

More a bird of forests and wooded gorges than the White Stork, the Black Stork is almost as large but more slender, with a longer bill. It is by no means so closely linked with human settlements and is rather shy and elusive. In flight it is as grand and expert as the White Stork, but rarely forms large flocks. In spring it may be seen spiralling upwards to gain height before crossing mountain ranges such as the Pyrenees on its way north.

FEEDING It eats mainly fish, hunting in shallow water and wet pastures.

DISPLAY & VOICE Like the White Stork, the Black Stork rarely calls. Its displays are mostly confined to bill-clattering and posturing at the nest.

BREEDING Its nest is large yet well hidden, in a tree or on a cliff ledge. It does not nest on buildings like the White Stork. It lays 3–5 eggs; the young fly when 35 days old.

MIGRATION After breeding, all but a few Iberian pairs migrate to southern Africa. Some of the few breeding birds in central Spain remain all year.

LENGTH 95–100cm (37½–39in)

WHEN TO SEE March to September
WHERE FOUND Forests, cliffs, open areas, Spain, Belgium, central and N Europe; rarely UK

Dalmatian Pelican *Pelecanus crispus*

This magnificent bird is virtually restricted to Europe, where it is dangerously threatened by persecution, disturbance and drainage of its wetland habitats. It breeds around the Black Sea and very locally in the Balkans.

FEEDING Dalmatians feed sociably like other pelicans, often gathering to drive shoals of fish into the shallows where they can scoop them up in their grotesque, fleshy bill pouches. Only rich, shallow, warm waters with thriving fish populations can support large numbers of these pelicans.

DISPLAY & VOICE The males display in groups; the voice is a quiet croak.

BREEDING The nests are huge heaps of vegetation, built in reedbeds and on semi-floating islands. There are usually 2–3 (rarely 5–6) eggs, incubated for 30–32 days; the chicks fly at 85 days.

MIGRATION Most remain in southeast Europe and Turkey in winter; a few non-breeding sub-adults may be found with breeding White Pelicans and on other lakes in summer.

LENGTH 160–180cm (63–72in); wingspan 295cm (116in)

| WHEN TO SEE | All year |
| WHERE FOUND | Black and Caspian Seas, Balkans, Turkey |

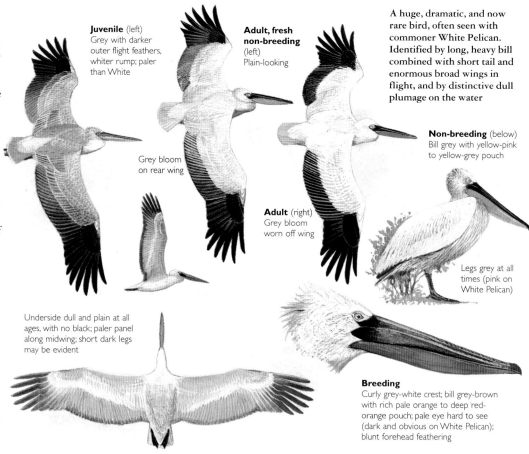

Juvenile (left) Grey with darker outer flight feathers, whiter rump; paler than White

Adult, fresh non-breeding (left) Plain-looking

Grey bloom on rear wing

Adult (right) Grey bloom worn off wing

A huge, dramatic, and now rare bird, often seen with commoner White Pelican. Identified by long, heavy bill combined with short tail and enormous broad wings in flight, and by distinctive dull plumage on the water

Non-breeding (below) Bill grey with yellow-pink to yellow-grey pouch

Legs grey at all times (pink on White Pelican)

Underside dull and plain at all ages, with no black; paler panel along midwing; short dark legs may be evident

Breeding Curly grey-white crest; bill grey-brown with rich pale orange to deep red-orange pouch; pale eye hard to see (dark and obvious on White Pelican); blunt forehead feathering

White Pelican *Pelecanus onocrotalus*

White Pelicans are massive and solid on water, swimming like battleships, and huge and upstanding on land. Yet it is in flight that they reveal their true majesty, soaring to great heights, circling in synchrony (much more coordinated than storks) or forming long lines and chevrons.

FEEDING Their staple diet is fish, taken in warm, rich, shallow lakes and deltas. Large flocks sometimes form horseshoes that gradually drive fish towards the shore and entrap them. In many areas pelicans fly long distances each day to and from feeding areas.

DISPLAY & VOICE Males display to females in groups, croaking quietly.

BREEDING They build their nests within reedbeds and on more open islands, often in large colonies. The two eggs hatch after 29–30 days, and the chicks fly at 65–70 days.

MIGRATION Large flocks move south in autumn, soaring on thermals to save energy, like storks and large birds of prey. They pass through the Middle East where many remain all winter, others moving on into Africa.

LENGTH 140–175cm (55–69in)

| WHEN TO SEE | All year |
| WHERE FOUND | Balkans, Turkey, Black Sea |

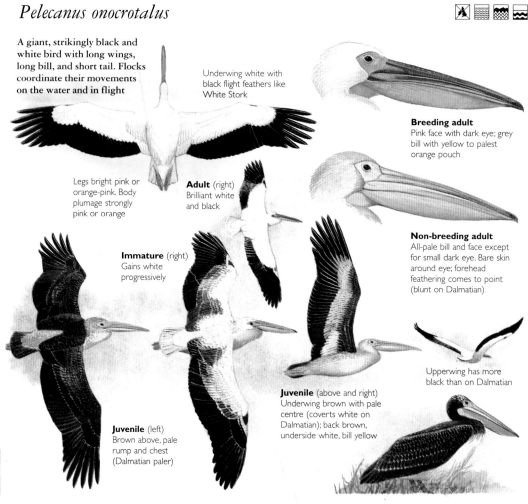

A giant, strikingly black and white bird with long wings, long bill, and short tail. Flocks coordinate their movements on the water and in flight

Underwing white with black flight feathers like White Stork

Legs bright pink or orange-pink. Body plumage strongly pink or orange

Adult (right) Brilliant white and black

Immature (right) Gains white progressively

Juvenile (left) Brown above, pale rump and chest (Dalmatian paler)

Juvenile (above and right) Underwing brown with pale centre (coverts white on Dalmatian); back brown, underside white, bill yellow

Breeding adult Pink face with dark eye; grey bill with yellow to palest orange pouch

Non-breeding adult All-pale bill and face except for small dark eye. Bare skin around eye; forehead feathering comes to point (blunt on Dalmatian)

Upperwing has more black than on Dalmatian

Greater Flamingo *Phoenicopterus ruber*

A tall, long-necked, long-legged bird with downcurved bill, unique in Europe except for escaped individuals of other species

Adults
Reveal glorious crimson and black wings in flight

Bright pink and black bill

Breeding

Flies with amazing extension of neck and legs

Non-breeding

Immature
Lacks red in wings

Adult, breeding
Pale pink or whitish with a hint of crimson visible at rest

Non-breeding
Duller, less pink

Immature
Dull, browner, with darker bill, grey legs

Feed by sweeping bills through shallow water; may also wade much more deeply or swim, swan-like, on lakes. Dense flocks look pale pink; smaller flocks like scattered pink/white spots

Adult
Bright pink legs; escaped Chilean race has grey legs with pink joints

Juvenile

Flamingos are familiar from their many stylized representations, as well as captive flocks in ornamental collections and wildlife parks. Wild flamingos are superb, but in Europe they are almost confined to the far south. They are worth going a long way to see, being among the most spectacular wildlife sights in Europe.

FEEDING A flamingo feeds on tiny invertebrates and algae, sweeping its head sideways through the water to trap them in a complex mesh of fine structures within its specialized bill.

DISPLAY & VOICE Displays include remarkable coordinated marching and head-waving by tightly packed flocks. Most calls are loud, clanging, goose-like notes, especially a double, grunting *gagg-agg* or *gegg-egg*.

BREEDING Large colonies move between several traditional sites around the Mediterranean, settling wherever conditions are best. Sometimes they do not breed at all, but occasional bumper years produce thousands of young.

LENGTH 125–145cm (49–57in)

WHEN TO SEE All year
WHERE FOUND Saline lakes, lagoons and salt pans in France, S and E Spain, Balearics, Corsica, Sardinia, Sicily, Balkans

Glossy Ibis *Plegadis falcinellus*

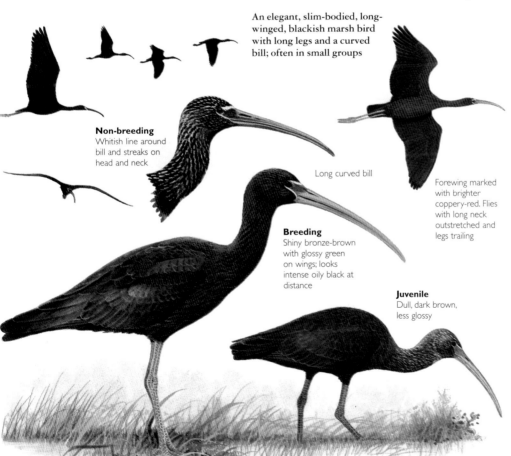

An elegant, slim-bodied, long-winged, blackish marsh bird with long legs and a curved bill; often in small groups

Non-breeding
Whitish line around bill and streaks on head and neck

Long curved bill

Forewing marked with brighter coppery-red. Flies with long neck outstretched and legs trailing

Breeding
Shiny bronze-brown with glossy green on wings; looks intense oily black at distance

Juvenile
Dull, dark brown, less glossy

A bird of lakesides, deltas, and rivers flanked with quagmires and swamps of wet vegetation, the Glossy Ibis is chiefly found in southeast Europe. Its habitat is often destroyed or fragmented, so its numbers and distribution fluctuate considerably. The birds often fly between feeding and roosting areas at dawn and dusk, frequently in mixed flocks with egrets.

FEEDING The Glossy Ibis uses its long, curved bill to probe into shallow water, wet mud and ooze to detect and seize worms and other invertebrates.

VOICE The usual call is a throaty, crow-like grunting *kraa kra kra*.

BREEDING Ibises breed in colonies, with each pair building a nest of thin twigs and sticks among reeds, bushes or taller trees. They often nest and feed alongside various herons and egrets.

MIGRATION Some European breeders remain in the Mediterranean area all winter, wandering widely, but most migrate south to central Africa. A few reach western Europe, at almost any time of year.

LENGTH 55–65cm (22–26in)

WHEN TO SEE Mostly March to October
WHERE FOUND Marshes and lakes, mainly SE Europe, occasionally UK

Mute Swan *Cygnus olor*

Few birds are so visible at such great range, and that may be part of the reason why swans are so large and white. No need for a song: visibility acts as a territorial statement in itself. Mutes are the largest swans, but also the most approachable, in many areas effectively semi-domesticated.

FEEDING Mute Swans graze freely on short grass or cereals, but they mostly feed in shallow water, up-ending to reach down for the shoots and roots of aquatic plants with their long necks.

DISPLAY & VOICE Far from mute, a Mute Swan uses a range of hisses, snorts and strangled trumpetings. Displays include elegant posturing with entwined necks, and an aggressive territorial display with arched wings and an S-shaped neck that often leads to violent battles with intruders.

BREEDING Swan nests are huge piles of reeds and stems at the water's edge; the usual clutch is of 5–8 eggs.

MIGRATION Most long-distance flights are connected with migrations to safe places to moult in the late summer.

LENGTH 145–160cm (57–63in)

WHEN TO SEE All year
WHERE FOUND Britain, Ireland, S Scandinavia, France and Germany, locally in E Europe including N Greece

Huge, white, long-necked, short-legged, water bird. Elegant on water, heavy and waddling on land. Flight powerful and direct, with loud humming or throbbing sound from wings

Adult female
Orange-red bill; black basal knob larger on male

Immature
Grey bill at first, later dull orange with black base

Long neck obvious; wing noise much louder than anything from Whooper or Bewick's Swan

Occasionally spend time on the sea

Wings arched during display and territorial disputes

Pointed tail, often raised above water. Neck often slightly curved, head and bill usually angled down

Juvenile

Bewick's Swan *Cygnus columbianus*

A breeding bird of the High Arctic tundra that winters in Europe, Bewick's Swan is a most romantic, inspiring species, even though it is easy to see at close range at a handful of nature reserves where flocks are fed and overlooked by public hides. At other places it is always an exciting bird to find, wild and wary of people.

FEEDING Bewick's usually feed on land, grazing or eating potatoes, waste carrots, spilt grain, or other crops. Their feet often become caked with mud after feeding on wet ploughed fields.

DISPLAY & VOICE Like larger Whooper Swans, Bewick's have elaborate greeting and triumph ceremonies and whole groups (often in family parties) may be watched bobbing their outstretched heads, spreading their wings, and calling loudly. Their calls are less ringing than a Whooper's: a softer bugling honk. Flocks have a musical babble, audible at long range.

MIGRATION Bewick's reach western Europe in October or November, leaving in February or March.

LENGTH 115–130cm (45–51in)

WHEN TO SEE Mostly November to March; not found in Europe in summer
WHERE FOUND Baltic, Low Countries, locally Britain and Ireland, N France

A smaller swan than Mute or Whooper, often more goose-like and chunky, but neck can look equally long and slim. Compact shape, with square tail

Powerful flight, but no heavy, rhythmic wing noise

Frequent noisy displays with wing flapping and forward-thrusting head. Musical calls frequent

Adult
Bill has rounded yellow patch each side, very variable central black stripe, often broken

Short-tailed, thick-necked on water

More agile, flatter-backed than Mute Swan on land

Juvenile
Dull grey-fawn

Adult
White overall

Juvenile
Pink, black and whitish bill

Canada Goose *Branta canadensis* Egyptian Goose *Alopochen aegyptiacus*

Canada is large, heavy, long-necked goose, boldly patterned

Egyptian is stocky, rufous, or greyish, with bold white forewing

Canada
Unique black neck 'stocking' with white chinstrap, white breast

Egyptian (right)
White underwing, compare Ruddy Shelduck

Grey Egyptian

Rufous Egyptian

Juvenile

Long red-pink legs

Typically raised tail reveals white stern

Generally brown appearance

Egyptian
Brown eye patch, short pink bill; rufous and grey forms, both with long, red-pink legs

Both of these geese were introduced into Britain as ornamental birds. The Canada Goose has now spread to adjacent parts of Europe and is abundant in many places, especially around gravel pits, reservoirs, and park lakes. The Egyptian Goose, however, remains scarce.

FEEDING Both feed on grassland near water, or in the shallows, taking shoots, roots, grasses, and seeds.

VOICE Canada Geese have the deepest, throatiest honk of any goose: a penetrating *ah-honk*. Egyptian Geese have a shorter, wheezing, chuffing bark or cackle.

BREEDING Canadas nest mostly on small, sandy islands, laying 5–6 eggs on a thick pad of downy feathers. The eggs hatch after 28–30 days.

MIGRATION Although they are mostly resident, Canadas have developed some regular movements to safe areas in which to moult. Rarely, genuine vagrants from North America reach western Europe in autumn.

LENGTH Canada Goose 90–110cm (35–43in); Egyptian 66–72cm (26–28in)

WHEN TO SEE All year
WHERE FOUND Canada Goose in Britain and Ireland, Low Countries, S Scandinavia; Egyptian mostly in E England

Whooper Swan *Cygnus cygnus*

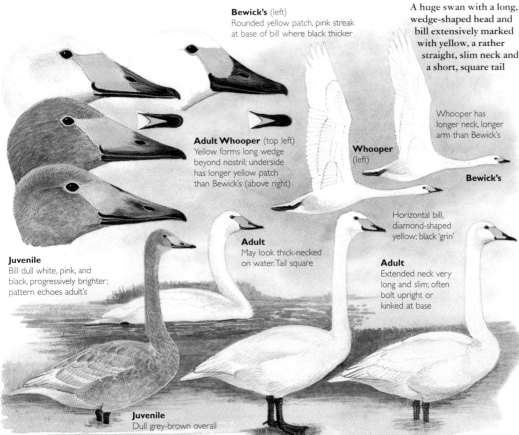

Bewick's (left)
Rounded yellow patch, pink streak at base of bill where black thicker

A huge swan with a long, wedge-shaped head and bill extensively marked with yellow, a rather straight, slim neck and a short, square tail

Adult Whooper (top left)
Yellow forms long wedge beyond nostril; underside has longer yellow patch than Bewick's (above right)

Whooper has longer neck, longer arm than Bewick's

Whooper (left)

Bewick's

Horizontal bill, diamond-shaped yellow; black 'grin'

Juvenile
Bill dull white, pink, and black, progressively brighter; pattern echoes adult's

Adult
May look thick-necked on water. Tail square

Adult
Extended neck very long and slim; often bolt upright or kinked at base

Juvenile
Dull grey-brown overall

Compared with Mute Swans, Whoopers are much wilder, far less approachable, and not very familiar to most people. Their range is much more restricted, but in many traditional wintering sites they mix with Mutes and Bewick's Swans.

FEEDING Whoopers feed in water like Mutes, but they spend more time on dry land grazing on grasses and eating grain and roots, including potatoes.

DISPLAY & VOICE Whoopers use a variety of calls based on a trumpeting, slightly yodelling *whoop-whoop*. They do not arch their wings in display but have noisy greeting and dominance displays with wings half-open and head and neck thrust forward.

BREEDING They nest beside northern lakes and in remote marshes, laying 3–5 eggs in a mound of vegetation.

MIGRATION Icelandic Whooper Swans move south in winter to Britain and Ireland; Scandinavian birds move mostly to the Low Countries and the southern Baltic area.

LENGTH 145–160cm (57–63in)

WHEN TO SEE In W Europe mostly September to March, a few remain all year
WHERE FOUND Breeds Iceland, N and E Scandinavia; winters Baltic, North Sea, locally Britain and Ireland

Greylag Goose *Anser anser*

Familiar as a semi-tame introduced species in some areas, the Greylag is genuinely wild in most of its range. It is a rather heavy-bodied goose, less elegant and romantic than most.

FEEDING Flocks feed on meadows and arable land in winter, eating grass, grain, root crops, and cereals.

DISPLAY & VOICE Its posturing with outstretched head and neck is familiar from the similar actions of farmyard geese, which are descended from Greylags. The calls are similar, based on a loud, hard, rattling repetition of nasal *krang-ang-ang* notes.

BREEDING Pairs nest on the ground in heather (in the north) or among rushes and other waterside vegetation. Up to six eggs take 27–28 days to hatch; the goslings fly at 50–60 days.

MIGRATION Wild Greylags from Iceland move to Britain and Ireland in winter; those from Scandinavia and eastern Europe move south and west.

LENGTH 75–90cm (30–35in)

WHEN TO SEE All year in Britain, migrants September to April; mostly summer in N and E Europe; winter Spain, Greece

WHERE FOUND Breeds Iceland, locally N and E Europe, Britain (most introduced, but native in N Scotland); large numbers winter locally S Europe and Low Countries

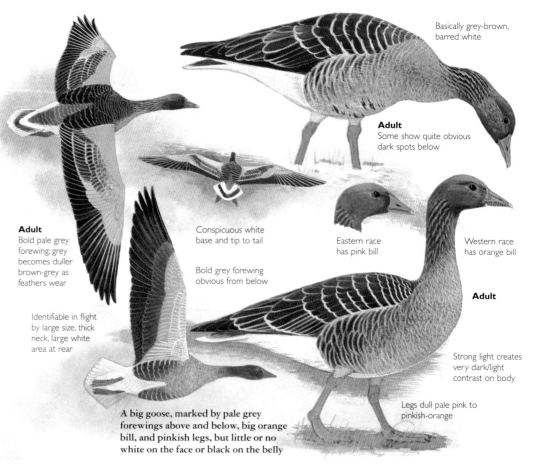

Basically grey-brown, barred white

Adult
Some show quite obvious dark spots below

Adult
Bold pale grey forewing; grey becomes duller brown-grey as feathers wear

Conspicuous white base and tip to tail

Bold grey forewing obvious from below

Eastern race has pink bill

Western race has orange bill

Adult

Identifiable in flight by large size, thick neck, large white area at rear

Strong light creates very dark/light contrast on body

Legs dull pale pink to pinkish-orange

A big goose, marked by pale grey forewings above and below, big orange bill, and pinkish legs, but little or no white on the face or black on the belly

Bean Goose *Anser fabalis*

These large, dark, handsome geese gather for the winter in traditional areas – in Britain they use just two or three specific sites – but one or two often turn up in flocks of other species and always a challenge for the keen goose-watcher. There are several forms; currently regarded as races, these may actually represent separate species.

FEEDING Bean Geese feed in flocks, often mixed with Pink-footed and White-fronted Geese. They eat grass, sedges, grain, and root crops.

VOICE The call is a noisy, cackling, bass note: *kayakak* or *kay-ak*.

BREEDING Their nests are simple depressions on the ground, in tundra, peat bogs, and open river deltas.

MIGRATION Breeding birds from north Scandinavia and Siberia move west and south in the autumn. Very few reach England and Scotland, but large numbers stay in the Low Countries, parts of central Europe and Spain.

LENGTH 66–88cm (26–35in)

WHEN TO SEE Mostly September or October to April or early May

WHERE FOUND Breeds in the far north, from N Scandinavia eastwards. Migrates to Denmark, Germany, the Netherlands, Belgium, France, and Spain; rare in Britain, N Italy, Balkans

Tail has narrow white base, mostly streaked grey (compare Pink-footed and White-fronted geese)

A large, long-necked, long-legged, elegant goose, individuals in mixed flocks picked out by size, shape, dark brown head and neck, and bold upperpart bars

Adult
Race *rossicus*: shorter neck and shorter, broader wings than *fabalis*

Adult
Race *rossicus*: dumpier, shorter rear, shorter neck than *fabalis*

Adult
Race *fabalis*: long neck; long, narrow wings

Forewings quite dark brown, grey only on primaries; long, dark, slender neck

Both races have very dark head, dark neck, dull chest (unlike Pink-footed), orange bill band, orange legs

Dark back with neat, parallel white bars

Adult
Race *fabalis*: white flank stripe often striking

Race *fabalis* (left) has straight cutting edge to long bill; *rossicus* (right) has shorter bill with less orange, and open 'grin' effect

White-fronted Goose   *Anser albifrons*

A pale brown goose, adults with white forehead blaze and black belly bars, juveniles plainer; only moderately pale grey patch on upperwing

Adult
Greenland race: orange bill; may be solidly black below

Adult
Russian race: mostly pink bill; typically paler overall, less boldly marked below than Greenland race

Juvenile
Scaly pattern; no white on forehead or black on belly, but pale bill unlike Pink-footed; wings darker than Greylag

Vivid orange legs (both races)

White forehead usually obvious even in side view

Dark upperwing with fine white bar and small grey patch

Adult

Black belly bars much bolder than on Greylag

Adult has broad dark tail band; helps separate from Pink-foot in flight

Juvenile

Of the grey geese, this is the most colourful and often the most lively and nervous. Flocks winter in well-defined, traditional localities, although in Britain several sites have been abandoned in recent decades; meanwhile numbers have increased in the Low Countries.

FEEDING Fields and grazing marshes supply a diet of grass, cereals, potatoes, and grain; the Greenland race also feeds in boggy moorland areas, plucking the leaves and roots of sedges.

DISPLAY & VOICE Lively dominance and threat displays are a feature of winter flocks. The high, laughing calls have a 'catch' in the middle, giving a yodelling quality: *lyo-lyok*, or *kow-yow*, like a pack of dogs at a distance.

BREEDING White-fronts nest on the ground in the northern tundra.

MIGRATION Greenland breeders move to Scotland and Ireland in winter; most Siberian birds go to the Netherlands, but some winter in northern France, England, and southeast Europe.

LENGTH 65–78cm (26–31in)

WHEN TO SEE October to March
WHERE FOUND Greenland race in S Scotland, Hebrides, Ireland; Russian race in the Low Countries, France, very locally S and E England and SE Europe

Pink-footed Goose   *Anser brachyrhynchus*

Juvenile

Adult
White tail band much broader than White-fronted; juvenile slightly narrower than adult

Round head, delicate bill, short, 'waisted' neck

A grey and buff-brown goose with a round, dark head, short neck, stubby bill and extensive mid-grey on the upperwing; distinctive calls help identify flocks; pale chest and very dark head visible at long range

Adult
Grey of forewing can be very pale in some lights. Grey of upperwing more obvious than on White-front, darker than Greylag

A dark adult resembles a Bean Goose but has pink legs and bill band

Adult
Grey upperparts with fine white bars, bluish and pale in strong light. Head and bill look all-dark; pink bill band in good view; chest pale fawn

Adult's legs pale pink to deep cerise-pink

Juvenile
Browner than adult, scaly, no white flank line, dull legs; dark bill unlike White-fronted

Perhaps the most attractive of the grey geese, this is a neatly turned-out, subtly beautiful bird. Its large flocks are the essence of 'wild geese' – hard to approach but familiar in many regions where migrating flocks are symbols of the passing seasons.

FEEDING These geese are attracted to saltmarshes, wet grazing meadows, stubbles, and ploughed fields, where they eat a variety of grasses, cereals, carrots, potatoes, and waste sugar beet roots and leaves.

VOICE While the flock chorus is generally quite deep and nasal, based on cackling *unk-unk* sounds, frequent high-pitched, quick *wink-wink* notes make Pink-feet easy to identify by call.

BREEDING This goose breeds in eastern Greenland, small parts of Iceland, and in Svalbard, nesting on the ground in quite barren regions.

MIGRATION Svalbard geese move to the Low Countries bordering the North Sea in winter; Iceland and Greenland populations winter in Britain.

LENGTH 60–75cm (24–30in)

WHEN TO SEE September to April in wintering areas
WHERE FOUND Breeds Iceland; winters Denmark to Belgium, locally E England and S and central Scotland

Lesser White-fronted Goose *Anser erythropus*

Sadly diminished in Scandinavia, the Lesser White-front is most often seen in western Europe as a result of reintroduction schemes. It is a neat, delicate goose, but when in company with White-fronts – as it usually is – it can be extremely difficult to pick out. In Britain it is most regularly seen at Slimbridge in Gloucestershire.

FEEDING Although they feed on grass and other vegetation like White-fronts, smaller individuals at least have a faster pecking rate and move forward at a quicker pace.

VOICE The call is noticeably higher-pitched and more ringing than a White-front's, like *dyee-yeek* or *dyee-yik*.

BREEDING Very few breed in open birch and willow woodland in north Scandinavian mountains, and on more open tundra farther east.

MIGRATION Most move south or southeast, but a few wild birds get 'caught up' in flocks of White-fronted Geese moving west in the autumn.

LENGTH 53–66cm (21–26in)

WHEN TO SEE In western Europe, November to March
WHERE FOUND Breeds N Scandinavia; in winter very rare in Netherlands, rare and decreasing in Britain, SE Europe

Adult Dark forewing, white bar: see White-front

Juvenile

A small, neat, round-headed, short-billed goose with long wingtips, a yellow eye-ring and high-pitched calls. Usually found in ones and twos among flocks of White-fronted Geese

Juvenile Yellow eye-ring thin but clear; white may be more extensive

Head neat, round, or flat-topped, or with high, vertical forehead; bill triangular, bright shocking pink

Short neck

Adults White extends back in V onto crown; bright yellow eye-ring

Wings longer in proportion and narrower than White-front's

Adult

Juvenile Rear flanks often dark

Wingtips project beyond tail (equal in White-front). Feeding action quicker

Orange legs

Adult Upperparts plainer than White-front, underparts less barred

Barnacle Goose *Branta leucopsis*

While many wildfowl are very attractive birds, few geese are so immaculately turned out as the Barnacle Goose. It is a highly social species that uses traditional migration routes and wintering areas. Here it may be seen in large flocks, although these are often restricted to nature reserves until after the shooting season when they move onto nearby farmland.

FEEDING Dense flocks graze fields and saltmarsh for grass, clover, and seeds.

VOICE Individually, the call is a sharp, yapping, or barking note, but flocks produce a noisy and more rhythmic chorus like the barking of dogs.

BREEDING Barnacles breed far to the north, on open tundra and cliffs.

MIGRATION Breeding birds from Greenland fly to western Scotland in autumn, and some move on to Ireland; those from Svalbard move to the Solway Firth, mostly on the Scottish side; from farther east, many thousands fly to the Netherlands each winter.

LENGTH 58–70cm (23–28in)

WHEN TO SEE In W Europe, September to April; some feral birds outside usual range all year
WHERE FOUND W and SW Scotland, Ireland, E England, Netherlands, and Belgium and some feral breeders in Baltic

A handsome grey, black, and white goose, often pale bluish at long range with a bold black chest and pale face. Flocks fly in shapeless groups, with loud, yapping barks

Long wings give easy, relaxed flight

Grey on wings lost by spring, so looks quite dark

Juvenile Markings on back more diffuse than adult

Face varies from dead white to yellow-buff

Adult Immaculate; some more solidly black on upper back (far right)

White belly, sharp contrast with black breast, and bold white face unique

Brent Goose *Branta bernicla* Red-breasted Goose *B. ruficollis*

Adult
Upperwing all dark.
Uppertail coverts all
white, covering tail

Juvenile
Pale bars
across inner
wing reveal age

Dark-bellied

Light-bellied

**Brent is small, chunky,
dark goose, with black
breast, all-dark head,
and small neck patches**

Adult
Dark-bellied

Adult
Light-bellied

Juvenile (right)
Light-bellied

Juvenile (right)
Dark-bellied

Juvenile (above)
White on dull black
neck develops only
in spring

Adult
Dark-bellied

**Red-breasted is a strikingly
marked goose, yet easy to
miss when individuals
are grazing among
flocks of Brent or
Barnacle Geese**

**Red-breasted
Goose**

Adult (above)
Black underwing
and belly, striking
white band along
flank to vent

Adult 'Black Brant'
N American race, vagrant
in Europe; white neck
patch complete across
throat, white flank above
black belly

Adult
Two white
wing stripes

**First
winter**

Adult Red-breasted
Red areas may shine in sun, but
very dark and dull in poor light;
remarkably elusive with Brent or
slightly larger Barnacle Geese

First winter has small cheek patch, or none
at all; looks scruffier and duller than adult and
has pale tips across smaller wing coverts

On a muddy estuary in winter the deep, rolling calls of Brent Geese make pleasant background music. Although scarcely longer than Mallards, Brents look bigger and heavier and a big flock makes a fine sight. In recent decades they have increased and have also taken much more to feeding on farmland adjacent to the estuaries.

FEEDING Flocks tend to feed in dense, irregular packs, so they 'puddle' the ground beneath their feet when it is wet and damage crops. They eat eelgrass and algae on the mudflats, and grasses, cereals, linseed, and other crops.
VOICE Flocks make a grunting chorus of nasal *krronk-krronk* calls.
BREEDING Brents breed in the extreme north, on open tundra.
MIGRATION Flocks move faster than Barnacles, flying in shapeless packs rather than lines. Greenland breeders (pale-bellied) winter in Ireland and NE England, Siberian ones in southern Britain, the Low Countries, and France.
LENGTH 56–61cm (22–24in)

WHEN TO SEE September to May
WHERE FOUND Pale-bellied in Ireland, Northumberland; dark-bellied in S Wales, S and E England, NW France and S North Sea; migrates through Baltic

Extraordinary in its appearance, yet surprisingly easy to overlook when a single bird is feeding with Brent or Barnacle Geese, the Red-breasted Goose is a prized find in western Europe. Its status as a wild bird is, however, blurred by the presence of small numbers of 'escapes' from captivity, for it is highly-rated as an ornamental goose.

FEEDING Grazes on grass and other short vegetation, or on eelgrass on estuary mud.
VOICE A sharp, high, staccato *pik-wik!* becoming a loud, jumbled chatter from flying flocks.
BREEDING Its nesting areas are in the extreme north on the tundra, often in the company of Peregrines or Rough-legged Buzzards which provide a measure of protection against Arctic Foxes and other predators.
MIGRATION Most Red-breasted Geese move south to the Danube area of eastern Europe each winter, but as if by mistake a few associate with Brent Geese, and turn up among flocks of Brents in western Europe.
LENGTH 53–56cm (21–22in)

WHEN TO SEE October to April
WHERE FOUND E Europe bordering the Black Sea; rare in flocks of other geese in Baltic, Netherlands, S Britain

Shelduck *Tadorna tadorna*

A link between ducks and geese, the Shelduck has some of the terrestrial character of grazing geese, including an easy walk on relatively long legs. It is among the more arresting birds to be seen on an estuary or marsh, easily identified at very long range. This visibility might leave it vulnerable to predation, but perhaps aids its territorial defence in spring and summer.

FEEDING It takes tiny snails from estuarine mud with a side-to-side sweep of its bill, which filters food from soft mud and water. Various other crustacea and insects are also eaten.

DISPLAY & VOICE Displays involve much head-bobbing and also gentle aerial chasing; calls include a squeaky whistle and a deep, rhythmic, cackling *ga-ga-ga-ga-ga* from the female.

BREEDING Pairs nest under brambles, in rabbit holes, and in many artifical situations, lining them with down; 8–10 eggs hatch after 29–31 days.

MIGRATION Most western European Shelducks go to the Waddenzee in late summer to moult; some UK birds go to the south side of the Severn estuary.

LENGTH 58–71cm (23–28in)

WHEN TO SEE All year
WHERE FOUND Breeds on Scandinavian coast, UK and Ireland (sparse inland); in winter to Biscay coasts, Mediterranean

A boldly-pied, large, somewhat goose-like duck, often terrestrial; juvenile unexpectedly different

Male has broader breast band and black belly patch

Male

Female

Sparkling white in flight, black patterns stand out well; heavy, direct action

Very bow-winged on short flights

Male Bold red knob on bill

Female Whitish face marks, duller bill

Juvenile White face

Juvenile Drab white body with dark brown bands and cap; pale pink legs

Ruddy Shelduck *Tadorna ferruginea*

A clear view of the Ruddy Shelduck reveals a handsome bird, with rich rusty-orange plumage and sharp black features. It is a surprise in flight, with eyecatching black and white wings dominating the rusty body. Sadly its ability to escape from ornamental collections makes its status in western Europe difficult to ascertain.

FEEDING Its diet and feeding habits are much like those of the Shelduck, but Ruddy Shelducks also feed on wet grassland and swamps around lakes and estuaries.

VOICE Various calls include a goose-like *gag-ag* or *pok-pok-pok* and a rolling, growling *porr porr porr* in flight.

MIGRATION There is some limited dispersal in late summer and autumn and stragglers occasionally fly north and west. When the European population was larger a century or more ago, such movements occasionally amounted to sizeable 'invasions' of western Europe.

LENGTH 61–67cm (24–26in)

WHEN TO SEE All year; most likely in early autumn in W Europe
WHERE FOUND Only about 200 pairs breed in E Europe (Romania, Bulgaria, Greece) after serious decline; rare vagrant elsewhere but frequent 'escape'

Large and goose-like, very like Shelduck, but rusty body colour instantly obvious

Male, winter

Bold white wing patches striking, but compare Egyptian Goose

Female

Winter male lacks collar; female has duller head

Rich orange-buff to coppery body, black bill and legs: beware escaped near-relatives with different head patterns

Male, summer Black collar

Female Paler face than male

Juvenile Greyer head than adult

Wigeon *Anas penelope*

A gregarious, short-legged, short-billed, long-winged duck, on sea or freshwater, typically grazing on wet fields or marsh in tight groups; often very noisy, drakes' clear whistles unique

Flight swift and agile on long, swept-back wings; pointed tail but short neck and blunt-faced look

Adult female
Wing dark; forewing slightly greyer, hindwing dull green/black, thin white midwing bar and white line on outer tertial (Gadwall has bigger white patch and no wingbar)

Adult male, breeding
Big white wing patch striking; hindwing dull green/black, back pale grey

Immature male similar but white wing patch mostly obscured

Juvenile
Like dull female but hindwing brown

Adult female
Clearly defined white belly and dark underwing unlike Mallard; chunky head shape unlike Gadwall

Adult male
Bright white belly, black under tail

Juvenile
Typical head shape, short bill; bright orange-brown flanks, chestnut edges on back; lacks white tertial streak of adult

Male, breeding
Creamy-yellow crown striking

Male, breeding
Pale body, dark head (Teal darker), broad white bar along wing (Teal's narrower); grey legs, blue-grey bill

Crops grass in forward-leaning posture; very short legs; often in tight-packed flocks

Male, breeding
Grey body, pink chest, red-brown head, yellow forehead, variable dark behind eye

Male, summer
Head and breast chestnut to dark red-brown

Female (right)
Variable from grey-brown to red-brown, greyer types with pale heads, often pale forehead; white streak on wing; grey bill with black tip, grey legs

Most ducks are beautiful, but there is little to compare with the sight of a densely-packed flock of Wigeon grazing on an emerald-green saltmarsh with deeply-incised, silver creeks in low winter sunshine. They have a perfection of form combined with an elegance of colour and pattern that elevates them to a level above that of many other common birds. Added to this perfection in appearance, they are lively and interesting to watch. The males also have lovely calls, making a Wigeon flock one of the delights of winter birdwatching. In the air, Wigeon tend to form long lines, chevrons, and V-shapes as they fly high up, moving very fast, although they do not have the Teal's aerial agility in confined spaces.

FEEDING Wigeon have short legs and short, deep, wide bills that are perfect for nipping short stems of grass and other vegetation: they are grazers, the avian equivalent of sheep. In winter they eat eelgrass on estuarine mud, but chiefly grass, sedge, and rush stems and roots from wet pastures and coastal grazing marshes. They are typical birds of open spaces with big skies, flat ground, and stretches of water to which they can withdraw for resting, bathing, or to escape danger on the land.

DISPLAY & VOICE Female Wigeon make a deep, rather angry-sounding growl, often a double *grr-rrrr*. It penetrates the winter gloom across a reservoir or flooded marsh surprisingly well. Males, in sharp contrast, provide a high counterpoint, making loud, pure whistling sounds with a distinct emphasis on the first syllable: *whee-oooo*. Displays are relatively inconspicuous except for aerial chases; most pairs are formed in late winter when the males are still in full plumage. In summer, as with most ducks, they have a duller, less eyecatching 'eclipse' plumage.

BREEDING Unlike the wintering grounds, the breeding areas used by Wigeon tend to be near remote moorland pools and peat bogs, far from the green swards that the flocks graze so effectively. Pairs breed in isolation, or at best in loose groups. The nest is made in a tussock of rushes or sedge, lined with a mixture of vegetation and down from the female. Up to nine eggs are laid; they hatch after 24–25 days.

MIGRATION Most Wigeon from northern Europe move southwest in autumn, returning in April. Icelandic breeders move to Scotland and Ireland.

LENGTH 45–51cm (18–20in)

WHEN TO SEE In N Europe, mostly April to September; the converse in W and S Europe
WHERE FOUND Breeds Iceland, Scandinavia, N Scotland; in winter scattered south to Iberia and Mediterranean coast

49

Mallard *Anas platyrhynchos*

There are Mallards on most town and village ponds, although many are of various colour forms that are not found in the wild. Dark brown ones with white bibs, 'khaki' birds with dull brown heads, and white ones with yellow bills all betray the influence of centuries of domestication. Yet truly wild Mallards remain among the most beautiful of all ducks. The drakes have extraordinary glossy green heads that are shot with blue, lovely purple-blue patches on each wing, and the typical curly black tail feathers that often remain even in domestic forms. Wild Mallards are often unapproachable and nervous, with good reason as so many are shot. The species is almost too familiar in its duckpond persona, but should not be overlooked as a handsome, wild bird in its own right.

FEEDING Many Mallards feed at night, when they are safer on dry land. They glean grain from harvested fields, search out acorns from among fallen leaves at woodland edges, and dabble in shallow water for seeds that have fallen onto lakes and rivers and been washed up on the shore. They often up-end, and sometimes dive, to reach shoots, roots, aquatic insects, and shellfish.

DISPLAY & VOICE Most courtship takes place in late autumn and through the winter, when the drakes are in immaculate plumage. They get together around a female, bobbing their heads and calling with low whistling sounds. They force their attentions on the females, often chasing them in the air and forcing them to the ground. Only the ducks quack, making the familiar loud, descending series of vulgar *quaarrk quarrk quark quack* notes.

BREEDING Drakes take no part in rearing the ducklings, moving away to moult into dark, dull 'eclipse' plumage while the ducks hide themselves away on nests in dense vegetation, often under brambles or in tussocks of sedge. Some nest in artificial sites, especially near town park lakes. The usual clutch is 9–13 eggs; they hatch after 27–28 days and the ducklings are led to the nearest water (often crossing busy roads) where they remain for 50–60 days before their first flight.

MIGRATION Mallards from northern and eastern Europe move south and west in autumn, so Scandinavia and areas east of the Baltic have Mallards only as summer visitors while much of western Europe has residents, migrants, and winter visitors, too.

LENGTH 51–62cm (20–24in)

WHEN TO SEE All year except in N and E Europe
WHERE FOUND Almost throughout Europe except in the most barren and mountainous regions

The common wild duck, one of the largest ducks with a loud quack, sometimes shows features and varied patterns of semi-domestic ducks, but always has a blue wing patch. Drakes retain curly central tail feathers

Male, autumn to spring

Heavy in flight, head well forward, tail short, wings beat below body level; several males chase each female in spring

Broad purple-blue panel, edged black and white both front and back

Female

Male
White tail obvious

Females

Males, autumn to spring

Up-ends in shallow water; female shows whitish tail, shorter wingtips than Shoveler; male reveals white-edged curly tail

Striking white underwing

Male

Female
Dark belly, unlike Wigeon or Gadwall

Adult female (above)
Bill has different orange pattern from Gadwall; legs vivid orange like Shoveler (Gadwall's yellower)

Male in summer resembles female, but darker, more rufous, blotched, dark crown and stripe through eye separated by pale band; retains yellow bill

Adult male, autumn to spring (right)
Grey with dusky dark brown band along body; chocolate breast; white neck ring, glossy head, legs brilliant orange, bill green-yellow

Gadwall *Anas strepera*

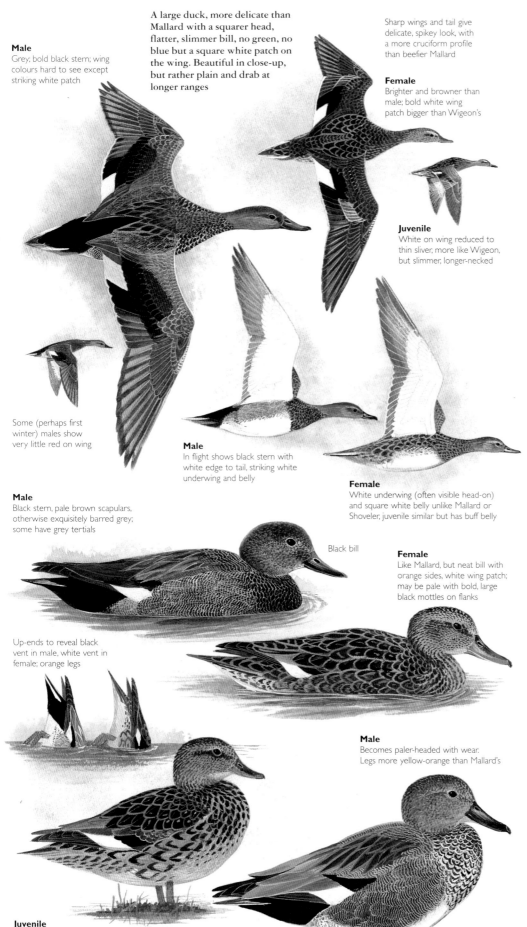

Male
Grey; bold black stern; wing colours hard to see except striking white patch

A large duck, more delicate than Mallard with a squarer head, flatter, slimmer bill, no green, no blue but a square white patch on the wing. Beautiful in close-up, but rather plain and drab at longer ranges

Sharp wings and tail give delicate, spikey look, with a more cruciform profile than beefier Mallard

Female
Brighter and browner than male; bold white wing patch bigger than Wigeon's

Juvenile
White on wing reduced to thin sliver, more like Wigeon, but slimmer, longer-necked

Some (perhaps first winter) males show very little red on wing

Male
In flight shows black stern with white edge to tail, striking white underwing and belly

Female
White underwing (often visible head-on) and square white belly unlike Mallard or Shoveler; juvenile similar but has buff belly

Male
Black stern, pale brown scapulars, otherwise exquisitely barred grey; some have grey tertials

Black bill

Female
Like Mallard, but neat bill with orange sides, white wing patch; may be pale with bold, large black mottles on flanks

Up-ends to reveal black vent in male, white vent in female; orange legs

Male
Becomes paler-headed with wear. Legs more yellow-orange than Mallard's

Juvenile
Bright, orange-buff with bold dark streaks and V-shapes, buff belly unlike adult

Tertials sometimes reflect light, creating pale patch above black

This is a large duck, but noticeably smaller, neater, and more finely built than the Mallard. It is a delicately-patterned, rather handsome bird, but at long range it tends to look quite dull compared with some more vividly patterned waterfowl. In some ways it is a connoisseur's bird: one to pick out, not too easily, from a flock of Mallards, and to appreciate for its subtlety. It is nothing like so widespread as the Mallard: its range is wide, but peculiarly patchy. In some areas Gadwall populations have been increased by past introduction schemes. It is not usually found on saltwater but may feed in brackish areas at the edges of saltmarsh and coastal grazing marsh.

FEEDING Gadwalls frequently swim close to Coots, waiting until a Coot dives and brings up a beakful of weed, then moving in. They don't appear to steal food from the Coots, but snatch up scraps that would otherwise float away. They are dabblers, like Mallards: they filter food from the water with filaments in their bills, 'dibbling' or 'dabbling' by rapidly opening and closing the bill while holding it almost along the water surface. They up-end, too, to reach food below the surface. They eat a variety of aquatic plants, seeds, and insects.

DISPLAY & VOICE Gadwall displays are quite subdued and include aerial chases with nasal calls from the drakes, and a variety of postures on water. They make short croaks and whistles, including a nasal *ehk ehk*; females have a more refined version of a Mallard's quack, the call being quieter, more even, and slightly higher in pitch.

BREEDING The female finds a nesting site on the ground at the edge of a pool, usually well hidden in tall grass, sedge, or rushes. She makes the nest using grass stems and leaves, and lines it with down from her breast. She lays up to 12 eggs and incubates them for 24–26 days. She also takes sole charge of caring for the ducklings, which fly when they are about seven weeks old.

MIGRATION Gadwalls breeding in eastern Europe head west and south in autumn. Those in the west disperse more randomly, often simply gathering in large groups on broad expanses of freshwater such as lakes, reservoirs, and large complexes of flooded gravel pits.

LENGTH 46–56cm (18–22in)

WHEN TO SEE Mostly summer in E Europe, from April to August; all year but most widespread in winter in W Europe
WHERE FOUND Breeds in parts of Spain, France, UK, S Scandinavia, NE Europe; in winter scattered locally but more widely south to Mediterranean

Shoveler *Anas clypeata*

There are times when a female Shoveler at moderate range is not immediately obvious, looking rather like a female Mallard. At close range, however, it seems almost inconceivable that such a huge bill could be overlooked: it makes the Shoveler look uniquely front-heavy. A drake in full plumage is unmistakable even at a distance, with its richly coloured and boldly contrasted pattern, Compared with the Mallard, which seems to be almost everywhere, the Shoveler is more sporadically distributed: over much of its range it is a scarce breeding bird. In winter, in places where other wildfowl gather in hundreds or thousands, there may be fewer than 20 Shovelers to be seen except in the most favoured spots. They prefer rich, lowland lakes with plenty of shoreline vegetation, but they can also be found on saltmarsh and sometimes quite open reservoirs and flooded pits in autumn and winter.

FEEDING The Shoveler uses its long, broad bill to filter food from the water. Plankton, floating seeds, insects, crustaceans, and molluscs are caught in fine filaments called lamellae along each side of the bill as the bird squeezes water out with its tongue. As they feed, Shovelers swim slowly forward, their shoulders almost awash; sometimes they gather in dense groups which may spin like a huge wheel. Shovelers also up-end to feed, showing off their particularly long wingtips crossed over a short tail.

DISPLAY & VOICE Pairs and small parties fly over breeding areas in spring, often performing rapid twists and turns as several males pursue a single female. Males make a short, double note while the female calls with a short, low quack. At other times Shovelers are fairly quiet birds, but their wings make a loud 'whoofing' noise, especially on take-off.

BREEDING The Shoveler nests near water, in a hollow in thick vegetation, lined with leaves and grass stems and the duck's own down. Up to 12 eggs are incubated solely by the female for 22–23 days. The ducklings fly at 40–45 days old.

MIGRATION Eastern European birds move south and west in autumn, replacing many western European breeders that move south to the Mediterranean from late summer to early spring.

LENGTH 49–52cm (19–20in)

WHEN TO SEE In E Europe mostly March to September; in W Europe all year, but breeders move south in winter, replaced by visitors from the east
WHERE FOUND Britain and Ireland, locally North Sea coasts, W France, E Europe; in winter south to Mediterranean coasts, Italy, and Spain

A large duck with a long, heavy bill, usually held low on the water as it swims with shoulders almost awash; in flight grotesque bill obvious. Much quieter than the larger Mallard, but wings noisy on take-off

Adult males
Striking combination of blue forewing above, green-black head, broad white band around chest, deep rufous body

In summer male is heavily blotched rusty-brown with grey head, dark forehead and crescent of white curving up in front of eye

Head blacker than Mallard's, bill black, eye yellow

Adult females
Like Mallard but blue-grey forewing, green hindwing without white bars; similar dark body, white underwing

Juvenile female (above)
More regular dark spots along flanks than on adult female (below)

Breeding males
Large white patch on rear flank between black stern and chestnut body; vivid orange legs

Female
Head plainer than Mallard's, bill longer, broad-tipped, orange near base

Female
Note low shape, long wingtips, obvious when up-ending, no white on greenish wing panel

Pintail *Anas acuta*

An elegant surface-feeding duck with a slender bill, slim, often raised neck, narrow wings, and pointed tail. Males in winter are strikingly patterned while females are pale and rather plain-faced

Flight swift and direct

Female
Less extreme than male but still slim, with long neck and pointed tail

Male
Long tail point, yellow-buff vent against black undertail, white trailing edge to wing and orange-buff wingbar; bright white breast

Narrow white trailing edge to inner wing catches the eye.

Buff wingbar browner on juvenile

Resting male shows white breast, both sexes have dark legs (Shoveler has orange legs); female shows pale tail sides

Graceful profile makes Pintails easy to pick out in flight

Male
Preparing to land

Black 'shoulder'

Female
Note grey bill, grey legs, pale, plain head; shape best clue at distance

Male
Unique shape and pattern, with long white neck stripe

Tail tip curls up in breeze

Male
Bill striped grey and black; eyecatching white breast

No duck has a greater elegance of form and plumage pattern than the Pintail, although its subtle plumage lacks the vivid colours of some other species. Females have a typical female Mallard streaky-brown pattern, but are more neatly marked with more uniform, paler heads and necks. They are a test for the keen duck watcher, for along with eclipse males in late summer and early autumn they can be hard to pick out from among scores or hundreds of Mallards. In winter, however, the startling white breasts of adult drakes are obvious at great range, making them hard to miss on the marsh or mudflat. Pintails are unusually local in occurrence: some traditional sites attract hundreds or thousands of them, but in most areas a handful, at best, might be found on a few occasions each winter. They are rather wild and elusive, rarely allowing a close approach in the wide open spaces that they prefer.

FEEDING On estuaries Pintails take tiny snails from mud. On lakes and freshwater floods they are able to reach food in deeper water than other dabbling ducks by up-ending and using their particularly long necks. They take seeds, berries, shoots, and roots and a variety of aquatic insects and crustaceans. Many also move onto fields to feed on spilled grain and root crops such as potatoes and sugar-beet.

DISPLAY & VOICE The white breast and long white neck stripes of males are shown off to advantage in their head-bobbing and stretching postures. During these displays the males call with a nasal *wheee*. Normally Pintails are quite quiet: females have a low quack and a Wigeon-like growl, while males make a quiet whistle.

BREEDING Few breed in western Europe: in Britain only a handful at most. The nest is typical of dabbling ducks, made in a waterside hollow among tall grasses or sedge, lined with leaves, stems, and some down from the duck. Up to nine eggs are incubated by the female for 22–24 days and the ducklings fly at 40–45 days old. Males take no part in rearing the family.

MIGRATION Pintails from Iceland, Scandinavia, and northeast Europe move south and west in autumn. They reach the western coasts of France, much of Spain and Portugal, and most of Britain and Ireland, but most concentrate on a handful of favoured estuaries and flooded grasslands inland.

LENGTH Male 61–76cm (24–30in); female 51–57cm (20–22in)

WHEN TO SEE In W Europe mostly September to April
WHERE FOUND Breeds Scandinavia, NE Europe, Iceland; in winter W and S locally to Ireland and Mediterranean

Teal *Anas crecca*

The smallest and most agile of surface-feeding ducks, the Teal could almost be taken for a wader at times, especially if a small group flies up from a muddy pond, twisting and turning before getting underway at top speed. Teal are lovely ducks, but a close view is needed to appreciate their dark, varied colours fully; even then, a little bright sunlight is best for all the highlights to show well. It is worth trying to get close, but unless they are watched from a hide Teal tend to be suspicious, easily alarmed, and difficult to approach.

FEEDING Teal can be found on both salt- and freshwater, but they are most common on shallow lakes and winter floods. They eat all kinds of seeds, roots, and shoots, along with some aquatic insects. In the late summer and autumn they can gather in hundreds, especially at reservoirs where the level has fallen to expose areas of mud well-stocked with freshly-ripened seeds of waterside plants. Often they stay half-hidden in the vegetation, and their numbers might not be apparent unless something disturbs them and they fly off or swim out onto open water. Flocks often feed on marshes and around estuaries at night. In summer they feed in the *Sphagnum* and deep, peaty creeks of upland bogs and moors.

DISPLAY & VOICE Pairs chase each other over breeding pools and marshes. The male has a wonderful ringing call, far-carrying in still winter air, a bell-like or piping, cricket-like *krik* or *kreek*. Females make a high quack and a lower growling sound.

BREEDING Most Teal breed in the north, around moorland pools or lakes within areas of forest. They nest on the ground in thick vegetation near water, lining the nest with down from the female's breast. She lays 8–11 eggs and incubates them alone for 21–23 days. The ducklings soon leave the nest but cannot fly until 25–30 days old. Males take no part in rearing the family.

MIGRATION Large numbers of Teal from western Asia and northern Europe move south and west in autumn, to spend the winter scattered locally over much of Europe. Others join them from Iceland and a handful of North American 'green-winged' Teal arrive in western Europe each autumn. Some go as far as north Africa, and part of the breeding population of western Europe moves south.

LENGTH 34–38cm (13–15in)

WHEN TO SEE All year; in non-breeding areas, mostly August to April. In N and E Europe, only in summer
WHERE FOUND Breeds Iceland, locally Britain and Ireland, France, N and E throughout Scandinavia into Asia. In winter, also in SE Europe, Italy, S France, and Iberia

Small, quick, and agile in flight, more like wader than duck; flocks often tight and coordinated

Female
Wing like male, duller brown body with no white lines

Juvenile has narrower wingbar than adult female

Male, breeding
Dark; pale line along midwing, green and black hindwing patch

Female or juvenile
Whitish underwing, forewing grey, not dark as on Garganey

Common, widespread duck in marshes, around the edges of pools and floods. Small and dark; often revealed by the drakes' sharp, whistling calls. Male has dark head, long white stripe along side; female has bright green wing patch

Male, breeding
Dark head, brown with broad dark green stripe; dark bill

Rich cream triangle undertail; white stripe along body; short dark legs

Female
Pale stripe along tail side; bright green wing patch; dark legs

Male
Pale undertail, divided by central black line

Female or juvenile

Female, juvenile, and eclipse male all have dull plumage relieved by green wing patch, pale streak by tail; head often dark-capped, pale-cheeked

Garganey *Anas querquedula*

A small, fast-flying, elegant duck, with dark legs and bill and typically a rather striped head pattern

Juvenile (right)
Brown wing patch, lacks black of Teal; two equal wingbars

Outer wing grey

Flight shapes as Teal, but bill longer

Plain rump, no white V like Teal

Darker beneath forewing than Teal

Male, spring
Forewing bluish, gets duller grey before July moult

Female
Dull wing; greyish wing patch, two prominent white bars of equal width, unlike Teal

Midwing bar on male is broader than hindwing bar

Distinctive grey on primaries as if light reflects from outer wing

Juvenile male
Dark crown, pale stripe over eye and on upper cheek, pale spot by bill, white chin

Male, spring
Striking head stripe; drooped, spiky scapulars

Female
Large spots, thin pale edges, more 'solid' than Teal

In a way this species reverses the usual duck pattern, as it is a summer visitor to Europe. It is not much bigger than a Teal and found in similar places with shallow water, often temporary floods, and plenty of vegetation.

FEEDING It eats small beetles, snails and other aquatic creatures, along with a variety of plant material.

VOICE Males in spring have a strange, dry, rattling note, a short crackling *crrrk*. Females quack quietly.

BREEDING Nests are near water, often in grass tussocks, and lined with down. The 8–11 eggs hatch after 21–23 days. The male ignores the ducklings, which fly when 35–40 days old.

MIGRATION The winter months are spent in tropical Africa. In the Middle East and southeast Europe large migrant flocks reappear in spring, but in western Europe it is much scarcer and very local, most places seeing only a pair or two in spring and up to a dozen or so on their return in autumn.

LENGTH 37–41cm (14½–16in)

WHEN TO SEE Mostly early March to late September
WHERE FOUND E Europe, E Scandinavia, Baltic area; locally and irregularly scattered farther west to England

---

Marbled Duck *Marmaronetta angustirostris*

A rare duck of southern Europe, looking pale and poorly-marked at any distance except for a dark eye smudge and, in flight, a white underwing

Pale tail

Largely white underwing; dark leading edge varies; dark primary coverts above may catch the eye

Rather squat and dumpy in flight despite long neck

Male

Female

Adult male

Washed-out look, but a smart bird; paleness makes it stand out well on water at long range

Overall pale, neat brown with diffuse spots; pale tail

Pale grey hindwing; no upperwing contrast, unlike other ducks

Unique pale-spotted flanks; usually white-edged tail

Adult male
Crest, dark face smudge

Female
Duller than male; face almost plain or with obvious dark patch; pale spots when fresh, fades plainer

This rare and threatened bird has disappeared from many of its former breeding sites across southern Europe, although in some places in southwest Spain its numbers have recently shown signs of increasing. It prefers shallow lakes with plenty of waterside vegetation, flooded salt pans and, in winter, the margins of undisturbed estuaries.

FEEDING Unless disturbed it usually keeps well within areas of vegetation where it feeds on shoots and stems, dabbling in the shallows, up-ending and occasionally diving.

VOICE This is a quiet bird. Males call in spring with a squeaky *eeeeep*. Ducks have a similar call and a weaker, high *pleep pleep*.

BREEDING It nests on the ground under bushes or in dense, low thickets. Up to 14 eggs are incubated for 25–27 days; other details are little known.

MIGRATION Spanish breeding birds move out of their nesting areas in late summer, mainly to nearby coasts.

LENGTH 39–42cm (15½–17in)

WHEN TO SEE All year
WHERE FOUND Very local near southern and eastern coasts of Spain

Pochard *Aythya ferina*

Typically Pochards spend much of the day asleep, drifting in flocks, often mixed with Tufted Ducks. They are common and widespread except in summer when they are local and scarce breeders in much of Europe.

FEEDING Pochards dive underwater to find seeds, shoots, and roots, taking only a small amount of animal food. They tend to be most active at night.

DISPLAY & VOICE Displays are subdued, including various head-stretching postures with wheezy, rising double *aawoo* notes from the male and quiet whistles from the female. Otherwise the most usual call is a low, gruff, short growl.

BREEDING Pochards nest near water in reeds, laying 8–10 eggs on a thick pad of waterweed and down; they hatch after 25 days.

MIGRATION Large numbers reach western Europe from eastern Europe and Asia; in the UK there is a marked autumn migration in most areas with large flocks in October and November.

LENGTH 42–49cm (16½–19in)

WHEN TO SEE All year, but increased numbers in W Europe October–March
WHERE FOUND Widespread from UK, Ireland, and Iceland east through central and NE Europe; locally S Scandinavia; in winter also Iberia, S France, Italy, Balkans

Larger, broader than Tufted; rufous head, grey sides distinguish from Scaup

A gregarious, freshwater diving duck; often sleeps by day in tight flocks with Tufted Ducks on lakes and reservoirs. Dark front and back, pale middle helps to identify males; females much dowdier

Male, non-breeding

Female

Male
Broad midwing panel paler than forewing but no white

Female

Immature male
Plumage of immatures and females variable and confusing

Red eye; blue band on bill

Male

Pale bill band

Female, winter

Male, breeding
Handsome winter drake pale with black breast and stern

Red-crested Pochard *Netta rufina*

One of the more flamboyant European ducks, this rare and local species combines characteristics of both diving and surface-feeding ducks. In places 'escapes' can be seen outside the usual range and some of these birds regularly nest successfully.

FEEDING Although capable of diving well, Red-crested Pochards often feed at the surface, dabbling and even up-ending like Mallards as they search for seeds, shoots, and leaves of water plants.

DISPLAY & VOICE Males pursue females in flight over nesting areas in spring, like most dabbling ducks, showing their big white wingbars. The males often raise their bushy orange crown feathers and call with a nasal, sneezing *keuvik*. The usual call is a short *gik*.

BREEDING Nests are hidden in dense vegetation beside reedy lakes and swamps and overgrown saltpans. The 8–10 eggs hatch after 26–28 days.

MIGRATION In Spain most are resident; some from NE Europe move south in autumn, mostly to Greece and Turkey; in most places they occur irregularly.

LENGTH 53–57cm (21–22½in)

WHEN TO SEE All year; in UK most are semi-resident feral birds, very few wild ones in autumn; in N Europe April to October
WHERE FOUND Central and S Europe, very local and scattered, most in S Spain

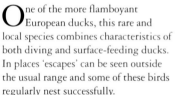

A bulky duck that feeds by dabbling as well as diving; extraordinary male easy to identify, but female can be confused with maritime Common Scoter

Male

Female

Male
Broad white wingbar and leading edge may have pinkish flush

Male, summer
Retains red bill

Female
Broad white wingbar

Juvenile
No pink on bill

Male, breeding
Fuzzy ginger crown, red bill, black breast, ragged white sides

Female (right)
Brown cap and dull white cheeks; dark bill

Ferruginous Duck *Aythya nyroca*

Very broad white panel under wing, sharp white belly patch on male; female has blurred belly; juvenile dusky belly until September

Female
Inner wingbar narrower than male's; outer part duller

Male

Female

Male
Broad white bar on blackish wing extends to wingtip

Small white stern shows in flight

White leading edge to wing

A dark, richly-coloured duck with white beneath the tail and broad white wingbars revealed in flight or when flapping wings. Head peaked, forehead slopes into bill profile

No greyer scaling on back; no contrast between breast and flanks: these would indicate a hybrid

Adult male
Bluish bill with tiny black nail; white eye; dark neck ring hard to see

Pale band on bill of female, behind black tip

Female
Duller than male; darker eye; bill may have duskier area at tip

Adult male (right)
Deep mahogany over breast and flanks, no hint of barring; white stern edged black

The Ferruginous Duck has suffered a rapid decline in recent years: it evidently has specialized needs which it finds more difficult to meet as the shallow, rich lakes that it favours are drained, disturbed, or polluted. At first glance it seems a plain bird, but a close view reveals a finely-built, elegant duck with great depth of colour.

FEEDING It dives underwater for seeds and plant matter, and a much smaller proportion of animal food.

DISPLAY & VOICE Small groups display unobtrusively on the water. Males have short *chuk* notes; females give a loud, frequent, grating *err err err* in flight.

BREEDING They breed in the marshy fringes of lowland lakes with plenty of aquatic plants, hiding their nests in the reeds; fish ponds are used in the east. The 8–10 eggs hatch in 25–27 days.

MIGRATION Those from far eastern Europe move south through the Middle East in autumn into Africa; a few move west or remain in the Balkans in winter.

LENGTH 38–42cm (15–16½in)

WHEN TO SEE Mostly September to April in W Europe; all year in Greece
WHERE FOUND Very local; in UK now only rare vagrant; in winter locally Spain, France, Italy, Balkans, more regular on reedy lakes in Greece

White-headed Duck *Oxyura leucocephala*

A stiff-tailed, dumpy-bodied, large-headed diving duck with a distinctive swollen bill base. In Europe only the Ruddy Duck resembles it, but hybrids between the two may cause identification problems – and the possible extinction of the White-headed Duck

Male
Very broad-bodied end-on

Juvenile
Short bar across pale face; bill shape unlike Ruddy Duck; dark undertail

Male

Female (below)
Bold black and white face marks; bill grey in winter, bluer in spring; dark undertail

Heavy-bodied and short-winged in flight; dark except for belly and paler underwing

First-summer male
Not all have black heads

Male
Pale, gingery, very finely barred; lacks broad black nape of Ruddy Duck; bill swollen

Male, eclipse
Variable dark head mottles

Rare and declining for several decades, the White-headed Duck has made a welcome comeback in Spain but its future is far from secure. Possibly genuine vagrants have turned up in England, but it is difficult to prove their origin.

FEEDING It finds its food underwater in frequent dives: insect larvae, other aquatic invertebrates, and some seeds.

DISPLAY & VOICE The male raises its peculiar stiff tail as it bobs its head up and down, showing off its head pattern and swollen bill to the female. It is generally a silent species.

BREEDING These ducks prefer shallow lakes with open water but a broad fringe of vegetation. Their nests are large structures hidden in dense reeds. Up to 10 eggs are incubated by the female for about 25 days.

MIGRATION Most are more or less resident, with local movements to open lakes and salt pans in winter. In Turkey large numbers concentrate outside the breeding season on a few lakes.

LENGTH 43–48cm (17–19in)

WHEN TO SEE All year
WHERE FOUND S Spain; Turkey

Ruddy Duck *Oxyura jamaicensis*

The Ruddy Duck established itself in Europe after a few escaped in Britain in the 1950s. It is harmless in most places, but in Spain it interbreeds with the endangered White-headed Duck, prompting real concern for the rarer bird. Less controversial 'escapes' include the dazzling Mandarin and the similar North American Wood Duck, both of which now breed in the wild.

FEEDING Ruddies dive for food, eating small insects, crustaceans, and seeds.

DISPLAY & VOICE Male Ruddies raise their tails, draw back their heads and rattle their bills against fluffed-out breast feathers, forcing out a flow of bubbles. They also make low, deep, grunting noises.

BREEDING Ruddy Duck nests are platforms of stems, sometimes domed, in reeds, often beside very small pools. Up to 10 eggs hatch after 25–26 days; the ducklings fly at 50–55 days old.

MIGRATION Most Ruddies move short distances to gather on large lakes and reservoirs for the winter; some move further to Spain and central Europe.

LENGTH 35–43cm (14–17in)

WHEN TO SEE All year
WHERE FOUND S Britain, rare Ireland; locally in small numbers in NW Europe and south to Spain

Male Ruddy Duck, spring Bold white face, black cap and neck; body rich rufous

Ruddy Duck is round-backed, big-headed, stiff-tailed, bobs like a cork; in winter often in flocks

Mandarin is stocky, small-billed; male is exotically multicoloured; male Wood Duck less flamboyant

Female Ruddy Duck (left) Darker face crossed by dark bar, bill dark; tail often flat on water

Male Ruddy Duck, winter Cold white face; dark brown body

Ruddy Duck Wings plain, dark; flight low, fast, almost whirring

Female Mandarin Thin white spectacle; frosted white below

Mandarin Duck (right and left) Occurs in local feral groups

Male Mandarin (above) Chestnut and green crest; bright orange sails

Mandarin (above) has dark underwing; **Wood Duck** (below) paler

Female Wood Duck Broad white spectacle; dull below; yellow eye-ring

Male Wood Duck Occasionally escapes from waterfowl collections

Scaup *Aythya marila*

Scaup may turn up in many different situations: in lively, buoyant flocks on choppy seas, large rafts drifting sleepily on smooth, sheltered estuaries, or as isolated individuals among dense flocks of Tufted Ducks and Pochards on inland lakes. However, most spend winter on traditional coastal feeding sites.

FEEDING Scaup dive for molluscs and invertebrates, but also eat waste grain and other food discharged into the sea.

DISPLAY & VOICE Males can be seen courting females in winter, gathering in groups around them and calling with deep whistles. The usual call is a low, short growling note.

BREEDING In northern Europe Scaup breed near the coast and beside remote upland lakes with sparse vegetation, laying 8–11 eggs in a ground nest.

MIGRATION Breeding birds from Iceland, northern Scandinavia, and Siberia move southwest, with large numbers in the Baltic region and parts of northern and eastern Britain.

LENGTH 42–51cm (16½–20in)

WHEN TO SEE In W Europe mostly September–April; in north only in summer
WHERE FOUND Breeds Iceland, N and central highland Scandinavia; in winter Britain and Ireland, Baltic and North Sea coasts, scarce south to Mediterranean

A large, thickset but elegant diving duck, in flocks on the sea, small numbers on freshwater; combines features of Pochard and Tufted Duck

Long, broad white wing stripe shows in flight

Male White wing stripe and belly like Tufted, grey back like Pochard

Distinctly more elongated than Tufted Duck in all features

Female Longer-winged than Tufted; note larger bill, white facial blaze

Juvenile Dull, small facial spot; pale ear crescent; dusky bill tip

Underwing lacks dark front edge of Tufted Duck

Long-necked in alarm

Female, breeding (right) Broad blaze; pale ear crescent

Female, breeding (above) Broader beam than Tufted, noticeable in mixed group

Female, non-breeding Grey bars wear off; round, dark head with white face; broader, paler than Tufted

Male, non-breeding Large body; large high-crowned head sweeps into long, heavy bill; sides pure white, 'black at both ends'

Tufted Duck *Aythya fuligula*

Stocky, round-headed and buoyant, a common freshwater duck, often in flocks with pochards and coots. Dives frequently

Female
Dark brown; belly may be darker

Male, winter
Striking black and white, drooped crest, bright yellow eye

Flight fast, wings rather straight, rapid beats

Female
Long white wing stripe, like flattened M

Male, winter
Pure white side panel striking

Female
Greyer variant

Male, summer
Brownish above, flanks smudged warm brown; immature male is the same

Female, winter
All dark, but some have small dull or bright white patch under tail; pale mark by bill

Male
Note broad black bill tip

Female, breeding
Very dark overall; slight crest; often pale face but dark cheeks

Female
May show white blaze, less extensive than Scaup (below); note head shape and slimmer; upcurved bill with more black at tip

Female, winter
Dumpy shape on land; dark legs

Scaup

Scaup female (below)
Broader crown, wider bill with small black tip, often pale ear patch

Tufted female
Narrower bill with more black

This is one of the most familiar ducks in Europe, for while entirely wild and highly migratory, many Tufteds have taken advantage of park lakes and other areas of water in and around cities. They may even come to be fed bread with the local Mallards and Coots. Yet they are equally likely to be seen on sheltered estuaries and coastal bays, or on remote pools and marshes. Tufteds are frequently found with Pochards and these mixed flocks may attract a variety of rarer birds inland, such as Scaup, vagrant Ring-necked Ducks and Ferruginous Ducks. There are natural variations in appearance according to age, sex, and season in all these species, but the possibility of escapes from waterfowl collections and even hybrids with intermediate features make these mixed flocks quite fascinating to determined wildfowl-watchers.

FEEDING Tufteds dive, bouncing back to the surface like corks. They are much more active by day than Pochards and eat different food, so the mixed flocks do not compete too much. Tufteds eat more animals, taking a variety of molluscs, crustaceans, and insects as well as some plant matter.

DISPLAY & VOICE Males swim quite quietly around females, bobbing their heads and calling with pleasant, low whistling sounds. The most usual call at other times is the female's deep growl, most often heard from a bird as it takes flight.

BREEDING Tufteds use a variety of sites, usually in lowland areas, from broad rivers and town lakes to reservoirs and flooded gravel pits. Nests are lined with vegetation and down from the duck's own breast. The female incubates 8–11 eggs for about 25 days. The young are typically lively, engaging, inquisitive ducklings which begin to fly at about seven weeks old.

MIGRATION Their movements are complicated, but most Tufted Ducks winter in big flocks on larger waters, or move to sheltered coasts such as the IJsselmeer where they gather in huge numbers. In Iceland, northern Europe, and eastwards from Germany and Scandinavia they are summer visitors, flying south and west to escape the hard winters. These birds move into central Europe and as far as Spain, Italy, and Greece, and many supplement the mostly resident breeding population of Britain and Ireland.

LENGTH 40–47cm (16–18½in)

WHEN TO SEE All year; April to October in NE Europe, mostly September to April in SW and S Europe
WHERE FOUND Breeds Iceland, Britain, and Ireland, locally France and Sweden eastwards; in winter also farther southwest and south to Mediterranean

Red-breasted Merganser *Mergus serrator*

The fine lines typical of sawbills combine with the Red-breasted Merganser's rich colour and pattern to create a supremely elegant bird. Unlike many diving ducks it is also lively and active: a fascinating bird to watch.

FEEDING Like all sawbills it is a fish-eater, diving energetically and staying submerged for long periods as it drives itself along underwater with its feet.

DISPLAY & VOICE Displays involve dramatic posturing by the males: their tails down, backs arched, heads thrown back, and bills jerked upwards and open. They use a low, purring call during courtship. Females make a low, harsh *krr* call as they fly.

BREEDING The nests are on the ground in tall grass or among rocks or roots, close to the shore. Up to 11 eggs are incubated by the female alone for 31–32 days; the chicks fly after nine weeks.

MIGRATION Breeding birds from northern Europe move south in winter to North Sea and Atlantic coasts.

LENGTH 51–62cm (20–24in)

WHEN TO SEE Summer in N Europe; all year in Britain; winter in S and SW Europe
WHERE FOUND Breeds Scandinavia, Iceland, N Britain and Ireland, winters south to Mediterranean, locally central Europe

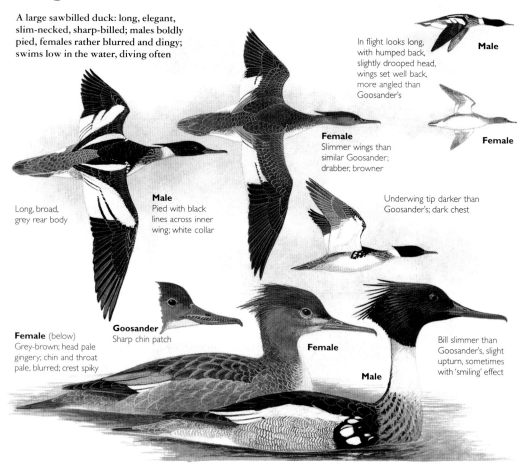

A large sawbilled duck: long, elegant, slim-necked, sharp-billed; males boldly pied, females rather blurred and dingy; swims low in the water, diving often

In flight looks long, with humped back, slightly drooped head, wings set well back, more angled than Goosander's

Male

Female

Female Slimmer wings than similar Goosander; drabber, browner

Underwing tip darker than Goosander's; dark chest

Long, broad, grey rear body

Male Pied with black lines across inner wing; white collar

Goosander Sharp chin patch

Female

Male

Bill slimmer than Goosander's, slight upturn, sometimes with 'smiling' effect

Female (below) Grey-brown; head pale gingery; chin and throat pale, blurred; crest spiky

Goosander *Mergus merganser*

A big, fish-eating, sawbilled duck, the Goosander is one of the most impressive of Europe's wildfowl. It can be seen on the sea, but is more of a freshwater bird than the Red-breasted Merganser, both when breeding and in winter. Both are persecuted because of their fish-eating habits, although there is no proof that they affect the numbers of fish in the rivers they occupy.

FEEDING They dive underwater from the surface to catch a variety of fish, including small trout and salmon parr.

DISPLAY & VOICE Males posture in much the same way as Red-breasted Mergansers, with quiet croaks. Otherwise this is a very quiet species.

BREEDING Goosanders nest in holes in riverside trees, and less often in banks or among tree roots. Up to 11 eggs hatch after 30–34 days; the chicks soon drop from the nest hole and make their way to water. They fly after 10 weeks.

MIGRATION Northern breeding birds migrate to central and western Europe to spend the winter.

LENGTH 58–66cm (23–26in)

WHEN TO SEE Summer only in N Europe; September to April in C Europe and S Britain; all year in N and W Britain
WHERE FOUND Breeds Scandinavia, Iceland, Britain; winters south to France

Large, elongated, heavy sawbilled duck with a big head; males very striking, females clean-cut grey, white and red-brown

Female Crisp grey; square white wing patch

Long grey rear body

Long neck, sharp white throat and chin patch

Straight-winged in flight; adult and juvenile female alike under wing, young male like adult male

Male Long white neck; unmarked white inner wing

Spindle-shaped body

Female Dark shaggy crest; white chin, dark foreneck

Rich salmon-pink of breeding male fades in late winter

Male

Hooked, deep plum-red bill

Smew *Mergus albellus*

A beautiful duck, small-headed except when crest erected in display; lively, often flying, diving out of sight for long periods; usually adult males in minority

Male, winter
Piebald in flight with obvious white foreparts (compare Shoveler) and wing patches

Adult females
Juvenile has brown lores through first autumn/winter

Smaller than Goosander and merganser, with faster flight action

Female, summer
Quite small but bright white cheek patch; face becomes blacker in winter

Male, winter Stunning, often yellowish-white with striking black patterns and grey flanks (appears white mostly at front)

The smallest of the sawbills, the stockily-built Smew is one of the liveliest ducks, especially where it is common and found in flocks of scores or hundreds together. These are scenes of constant activity, with Smews always diving, chasing, or flying swiftly back and forth in small parties. Even when wintering in ones and twos with large numbers of commoner ducks, Smews often move about restlessly and are sometimes very elusive.

FEEDING Smews dive for fish but take a variety of other aquatic creatures such as insect larvae and crustaceans.

DISPLAY & VOICE Males often display in winter, sometimes alongside displaying Goldeneyes, drawing back their heads and bobbing up and down. They are generally silent birds.

BREEDING Nests are in tree holes near lakes in forested northern regions.

MIGRATION In autumn Smews move southwest to the Baltic and North Sea regions, especially the Low Countries.

LENGTH 38–44cm (15–17in)

WHEN TO SEE In W Europe mostly November to April
WHERE FOUND Breeds N Scandinavia and east into Russia; in winter sparsely in Britain, France, central Europe; commonest in IJsselmeer and S Baltic area

Goldeneye *Bucephala clangula*

A round-backed, round-headed duck with a stubby bill, typically with dark grey females and immatures far outnumbering adult males

Juvenile (right) has less white on wing than adult female (below)

Juvenile

Round-bodied, rather short-winged in flight; wings make loud whistle

Female

Note high crown, steep forehead, low, round nape and triangular bill

White collar on adult female; white wing patch often hidden on water; immature looks dark and dull

Males
Green-glossed head and large white spot. Juvenile males develop white patch in winter

Females

Long tail, cocked at rest but inconspicuous when feeding

Although not a sawbill, the Goldeneye is similar in many ways to the scarcer Smew; indeed the two occasionally hybridize. Goldeneyes tend to keep apart from other ducks such as Tufted Ducks in winter, forming separate feeding and roosting groups. It may seem that only a few are present, as they dive so constantly, but if disturbed they gather together and may fly off in surprising numbers. They are usually nervous and quite difficult to approach.

FEEDING They gather molluscs, crustaceans, and insect larvae from the bottom in lengthy dives.

DISPLAY & VOICE Males display to females in late winter, raising their heads and suddenly arching them back over their rumps. The courtship call is a nasal, slightly grating or creaking *ay-eeek*. Females make quick croaks.

BREEDING Nests are in holes in trees or nest boxes; up to 11 ducklings take to the water as soon as they hatch.

MIGRATION Breeding populations move south and west in winter.

LENGTH 42–50cm (16½–20in)

WHEN TO SEE In south mostly October to April; summer visitor in N and E Europe
WHERE FOUND Breeds Scandinavia, Scotland; winters Britain, North Sea and Baltic coasts, locally in central Europe

Common Scoter *Melanitta nigra*

A true sea-duck, the highly sociable Common Scoter lives in dense flocks in sandy bays and firths, often associating with Eiders, smaller numbers of Velvet Scoters, and Long-tailed Ducks. Often they are far offshore and not easy to see well.

FEEDING Common Scoters dive deep for their food, taking a variety of shellfish, worms, and other aquatic life.

DISPLAY & VOICE Displays are quite subdued, but the males' soft whistling or piping calls can be heard on calm days. Females have a deeper growl.

BREEDING They nest on the ground, on islands or the shores of moorland lakes. Six or eight eggs hatch after 30–31 days' incubation by the female.

MIGRATION Movements are complex: breeding birds move south in winter, and large moulting flocks appear in traditional areas offshore in July and August. In spring and late summer small parties often appear briefly on inland lakes and reservoirs.

LENGTH 45–54cm (18–21in)

WHEN TO SEE All year; in south mostly July to April
WHERE FOUND Breeds in Iceland, N Scandinavia, rarely N Scotland and Ireland; winter south to Portugal, scarce E Spain, numerous Baltic and North Sea

A heavy-bodied but elegant sea-duck, with a large head, very slim neck, and pointed tail; often in long flocks well offshore

Adult female

Adult male All black except bill patch

Adult female All-dark above, pale cheek

Adult male Pale beneath outer wing

Immature Pale belly

Immature

Neck-stretch and wing-flap, head down, shows dark wing

Very thin outer primary on adult male

Thin tail often cocked

Typical flock flying low over sea

Immature male, spring

Adult female (left) Pale greyish face; 'double' patch at first (above left)

Adult male

Adult male All black except for yellow bill patch; sometimes thin line extends over basal knob

Velvet Scoter *Melanitta fusca*

Always scarcer than Common Scoters, Velvet Scoters are best found by visually searching through flocks of more numerous species. At long range they are hard to spot, but if they fly the problem is resolved. It is worth getting a close view, for they are big, handsome, and impressive ducks.

FEEDING Like other scoters and eiders, Velvet Scoters dive for their food: mostly mussels, shrimps, crabs, and other small marine creatures which they crush with their stout bills.

VOICE Males make a whistling call and females a gruff croak or growl, but these are rarely heard in winter.

BREEDING Nests are often far from water, near northern lakes and coasts. Up to nine eggs hatch within 28 days.

MIGRATION The breeding season is late, but males move in summer to moulting areas while the females incubate their eggs and rear their young; these then move south from September, returning in April and May.

LENGTH 51–58cm (20–23in)

WHEN TO SEE All year; in north mostly April to October; in North Sea often July onwards, mostly November to March
WHERE FOUND Breeds Norway, Baltic coasts; winters in S Baltic, North Sea including E Scotland and NE England; some south to Spain, a few to S France

Adult male

Adult female

Adult male

Adult female

All have broad white hindwing patch; most have red legs

Immature male White belly, black legs

Wing-flap, head up, reveals white: a clinching feature at long range

Adult female Two pale spots on face below blacker cap become brighter white with wear

Juvenile Dark face at first; dark wedge bill

Adult male White under eye; yellow bill panel

A big, eider-like sea-duck, usually seen with more numerous Common Scoters, and most readily identified by white wing patches

Surf Scoter *Melanitta perspicillata*

A large, eider-like scoter with a wedge-shaped bill, recalling the Velvet Scoter but with all-dark wings; adult drakes have obvious head and bill patterns

Bill shape obvious in side view but less so from other angles

Males with female (centre)
Adults all dark below

Adult female (below)
Two face spots; compare Velvet

Juvenile (left)
Wing-flapping posture reveals young bird's pale belly

Adult female (right)
Dark wings unlike Velvet; big bill hard to confirm in flight

Distant sleeping male may resemble Coot

First-winter female (right)

Adult male
All-dark except for bold white head patches

First-winter male (above)
Small white nape but black forehead, dark-tipped bill

Adult male (right)
Glossy black with bold white forehead and nape patches; bright bill, red legs

Although little more than a rare vagrant from North America, the Surf Scoter is nevertheless discovered in mixed scoter flocks somewhere in the North Sea each year. The males are relatively easy to identify, as their white nape patches stand out well even when they are very far offshore, but the females require a closer view that is rarely forthcoming.

FEEDING Like the other scoters with which it associates, the Surf Scoter dives to find molluscs, crabs, starfish, and similar prey, mostly in sandy bays or over offshore mussel-scarps. As its name implies it is quite at home in the rough and tumble of a sandy bay with enormous breakers rolling onshore.

MIGRATION A few individuals appear to be regularly associating with Common Scoters, and move around with them in northern Europe. One or two 'new' birds probably reach western European coasts each autumn. Very rarely one appears inland.

LENGTH 45–56cm (18–22in)

WHEN TO SEE Mostly October to March
WHERE FOUND Very rare except in a few places in NE Britain where one or two are seen each year

Steller's Eider *Polysticta stelleri* King Eider *Somateria spectabilis*

Steller's is small and unlike other eiders; King is a distinctive and obvious eider, but females are easily overlooked

Steller's, adult male
Unique white head, buff body, black patches

Steller's, juvenile (above)
White wingbar narrower than adult female's

Steller's, female
Dark red-brown; two broad white bars frame blue wing patch; squarish head, 'stuck-on' grey bill

Males

Steller's (left and right)
Smallish size, pointed tail

Female

King, male
White forewing patch and crescent each side of rump; unique orange facial shield

King, female (below)
Rufous-brown, head plain, long facial wedge, 'smiling' gape; may have tiny 'wings' on back like male

King, male

King, male

King, juvenile
Bright flanks with sparse bars; whitish around eye and bill

Steller's Eider is an extremely rare vagrant in Europe away from the extreme north of Scandinavia; it breeds farther east in Siberia. The King Eider breeds in Siberia and Greenland, and appears rarely but more regularly in northwest Europe, typically with large flocks of Eiders. In both species the adult male is distinctive but other plumages are much more difficult to pick out, especially out at sea.

FEEDING Both are diving ducks that feed on shellfish and other marine creatures in sheltered, shallow seas.

MIGRATION Steller's Eiders are regular visitors to the extreme north of Europe and move into the Baltic at times. King Eiders may sometimes be seen consorting with Eiders in summer, but they are chiefly winter visitors. Some individuals return to the same places regularly for several years.

LENGTH Steller's 42–48cm (17–19in); King 55–63cm (22–25in)

WHEN TO SEE Steller's all year; King mostly October to April or May
WHERE FOUND Steller's mostly extreme N Norway, rare in Baltic; King mostly NW Scandinavia, Iceland, Scotland, on sandy coasts and estuaries

Eider *Somateria mollissima*

Like the scoters, Eiders are often
found in flocks well offshore, yet
they are much more likely to be seen
pottering about in harbours, at the
mouths of estuaries, or around the
myriad rocky islets, headlands, and
weedy bays that characterize so many
north European coastlines. They are
sociable, unhurried, unflappable. Their
plumage variations are complicated
and there are several racial varieties, so
they are always interesting to look at,
but it is the colours and calls of the
drakes and confiding behaviour of the
ducks that makes them such enjoyable
birds to watch.

FEEDING Eiders find their food
underwater, diving from the surface
with a forward roll and half-opened
wings. They eat mussels and other
molluscs, crabs which they bring to
the surface to dismember, starfish, and
other invertebrates. Sometimes they
up-end in shallow water, or simply dip
their heads into the shallows or among
drifts of seaweed between the rocks.

DISPLAY & VOICE Males have a typical
head-throwing display, pulling their
heads well back with their bills
pointing upward. During this display
whole groups of males make highly
distinctive loud, deep, crooning calls
sounding like *ah-aaooh!* Females have a
low, guttural *kok-ok-ok*.

BREEDING Individual pairs or small,
loose groups nest close to the shore in
rocky places, or on rocky islands. The
nests are in hollows, under driftwood
or sometimes exposed, lined with the
prized down from the female's body.
Just four to six eggs are incubated by
the female for 25–28 days, and the
ducklings do not fly until about 10
weeks old. Incubating females sit tight
when approached. They rely on their
excellent camouflage, but often do not
move even when it is obvious that they
have been discovered. The ducklings
gather together in large groups, or
crèches, to seek safety in numbers from
predators, but they are still vulnerable,
especially to large gulls.

MIGRATION Northern breeders move
south along Scandinavian coasts,
including the Baltic, reaching
northern France. In Britain breeding
birds gather in large flocks, making
local movements, but relatively few
continental birds arrive in winter.
Non-breeding groups are regularly
seen in isolated but traditional spots
around the coasts of southern Britain.
LENGTH 50–71cm (20–28in)

WHEN TO SEE All year; in N Baltic in
summer; in much of S Baltic and southern
North Sea mostly September to May
WHERE FOUND Breeds Iceland, all
coasts of Scandinavia, Scotland, and NE
England; non-breeders S Britain; winter
south to Biscay coasts

A large, powerful, fast-flying diving
duck of coastal waters. Females dark and
closely barred all over, males strikingly
contrasted, beautifully clean and neat;
the wedge-shaped face is distinctive

Females
Small pale areas
under the wings, but
may look all dark.

Common Scoter has
shorter, rounder head,
thinner neck, paler
flight feathers

Female
Dark bars over upperparts;
typically (but not always)
finely barred white on wing

Males
Eyecatching in flight with
complicated chequered
patterns

Flight direct, strong, low
over water; head held
low, often forms lines

Often swims low, head
sunk in but short tail
cocked; dives with slightly
open wings. Sometimes
in very large, elongated
flocks; may stand out on
rocks or sandbars

Male, eclipse
Young or moulting males
have complex plumage
variations

Male, breeding

Male, first summer

Female
Looks dark
when worn

Juvenile
Dark, bars
diffuse; pale
over eye

Female

Female
Plumage quite pale and bright
when fresh; sharp bars

Male
Breast yellowish
or white when
worn, strong pink
when fresh

Male (right)
Green nape patches,
unique bill structure;
white rear flank patch

Long-tailed Duck *Clangula hyemalis*

A chunky, short-billed, buoyant sea duck; dark-winged, blunt-tailed except in adult male, with a confusing variety of patterns. Typically has round head with pale eye patch, dark cheeks; dives constantly. Social, often with scoters, but stray individuals turn up inland and in estuaries

Female, winter
Unique head pattern

Dark tail and white sides to rump recall Guillemot

All dark wing; white flank/vent, unlike scoters

Male, winter

Male, winter
White on head and foreparts shows at great range

Male, summer

Pot-bellied, squat appearance, but flight fast, low, rocking sideways

Female

Females, summer (below)
Some have white faces; bill band may be grey, usually pink

Female, winter

Males look spectacled from front

Male, summer

Male, winter

Dives with open wings, like bigger Eider and smaller Little Auk

Male, summer

Male's tail is longer and more flexible than Pintail's

Females, breeding
Head pattern varies with wear (left)

Male, winter (above)
At distance a confusing jumble of white and dark brown, white areas striking in good light; grey face patch fades browner

Juvenile, first winter
Dark cheeks, pale collar, eye-ring

Steep forehead, round nape, thick, triangular bill always distinctive

White sides or rear flank patch obvious

Females, winter

Male, spring
Pink on bill

This is one of several sea-ducks that live in flocks, often far offshore and frequently associated with scoters and Eiders. The flocks are very active, often flying fast over the sea, and can resemble auks as they whirr along, flashing black and white and rolling between the wavetops. In a few areas they move close inshore, especially at the mouths of estuaries where they are brought in by the tides, but on more exposed coasts they tend to be harder to see at close range. This is a pity, because they are among the most attractive of the sea-ducks, full of vigour and lively interaction. All sea-ducks have their charms, but the stub-billed, round-headed profile and wispy central tail feathers of the drakes add extra character and individuality to the Long-tailed Duck.

FEEDING They feed mainly on small molluscs and crustaceans such as crabs, taken from the sea floor in deep dives. In summer they also eat insects and their larvae, and these form the main diet of the ducklings.

DISPLAY & VOICE Drakes bob their heads and raise their long tails to impress the ducks. They create a loud, attractive chorus of soft, cooing *ow-owdl-ow* or *owdl-ee* calls. In courtship chases, sometimes far out at sea, several drakes pursue single females in fast flights with abrupt, splashing descents to the water before flying up again in a constant whirl of activity.

BREEDING Small numbers breed in Scandinavia, many more in Iceland and arctic Russia. They nest near small pools on the tundra, or in mountain areas farther south. In Iceland they nest around lakes with an abundance of insect life in summer. Often several pairs cluster on small islands out of reach of foxes and other predatory mammals. The nest is a hollow, lined with down, sometimes well-hidden but often quite exposed. The 5–7 eggs are incubated by the female only and take 24–29 days to hatch; the ducklings soon move to the nearest water where several broods may group together. They fly at about 40 days old, by which time the female may have moved away to moult.

MIGRATION After breeding Long-tailed Ducks move out to sea and then south, often through the Baltic. In spring many pass north through the Baltic and the Gulf of Finland in late May, often arriving on the tundra well before the lakes are free from ice.

LENGTH Male 58–60cm (23–24in); female 37–41cm (14½–16in)

WHEN TO SEE In W Europe mostly October to May
WHERE FOUND Breeds Iceland, N and central Scandinavia; winter Britain and Ireland, S Baltic, S North Sea coasts

Griffon Vulture *Gyps fulvus*

One of Europe's great birds, both in terms of size and sheer presence, the Griffon is glorious in the air. Early on cold days Griffons use updraughts where the wind meets steep slopes. On hot days they appear later, riding the rising masses of warm air (thermals) over cliffs and hillsides. Both techniques show their skill at manoeuvring to gain height for long-distance gliding with little expenditure of energy.

FEEDING Griffons eat dead animals; rarely in Spain they attack live lambs where the population is too big for the amount of carrion available. In places they are fed offal and carcasses.

DISPLAY & VOICE Other than angry hissing sounds Griffons are silent. They display chiefly in the air; where close formation flying in groups clearly has an important social function.

BREEDING The stick nests are on cliff ledges, usually in small colonies. A single egg hatches after 52 days; the chick flies when about 16 weeks old.

MIGRATION Most are resident.

LENGTH 95–105cm (38–42in); wingspan up to 275cm (108in)

WHEN TO SEE All year
WHERE FOUND Spain, Portugal, S France, Sardinia, sparsely in Balkans

An immense, impressive bird, capable of fast glides and dives around colony (often three to five in tight formation); typically soars in wide, rising circles or takes long, direct glides towards feeding site or roost

Adults Two-tone pattern above and below

Complex 'warped' and bowed wing creates very different shapes as bird circles, much more curved than Black Vulture

Juvenile Longer tail than adult, fresh flight feathers neater, browner

Adult Typical V-shape when soaring; contrasted pattern below

Adult female Heavier, broader than male

Wings drawn in during fast descent or glide in strong wind; pale ruff obvious

Adult Tips of flight feathers rounded; on juvenile (left) saw-toothed

Black Vulture *Aegypius monachus*

Less elegant and shapely than a Griffon, the Black Vulture is bigger and its spread wings are more 'plank-like': a mightily impressive bird in the air. It is less a bird of cliffs, although it does search for food over mountain ranges; it is more typical of undulating wooded areas. Central Spain, with rolling landscapes dotted by cork oaks and open woodland, suits it perfectly.

FEEDING Like Griffons, Black Vultures eat dead animals: they dominate Griffons at carcasses and are able to rip into thicker hides with their huge bills.

DISPLAY & VOICE Display flights include impressive tumbling by pairs with feet interlocked, and high circling over the nest site. Black Vultures are practically silent birds.

BREEDING Pairs breed when five or six years old, making a bulky nest of sticks in a tree, and only exceptionally on a cliff. Both sexes incubate a single egg for 50–55 days; the chick flies when around 15 weeks old.

MIGRATION Resident.

LENGTH 100–110cm (39–43in); wingspan up to 280cm (110in)

WHEN TO SEE All year
WHERE FOUND Central Spain, rare Majorca, very rare in SE Europe

The biggest, heaviest, squarest-looking of all the great birds of prey: the most like a 'flying door'

Always looks very dark: contrasts in wing subtle at best

Soars on flat wings; pale feet

Griffon soaring

Griffon soars on raised wings and glides on bent wings, while Black Vulture keeps its wings flat

Griffon gliding

Griffon soaring

Only tips of wings curve up

Black soaring

Stands with body more horizontal than Griffon

Bill and facial colour vary, perhaps with age, from blue to pink or white

Griffon Stands upright

Lammergeier *Gypaetus barbatus*

A spectacular, long-tailed vulture with a slow, sailing flight, occasional very deep, languid wingbeats. Looks smaller beside Griffon Vulture in the air

Adult
Gliding; when soaring it holds wings straighter

Gliding with head down, searching for food

Immature
Pale head, dark chest, streaked wings

Juvenile (above)
Very dark at first, head goes whitish, body pale grey, upperwing streaked; some very variegated with bleached feathers

Adult
Long-tailed individual

Adults
Pale head obvious at great range

Adult
Red eye may be visible at reasonable range; 'beards' easier to see; some much whiter-headed

Adults
Long, bow-winged shape in 'everlasting' glide; charcoal upperwings

Also known as the Bearded Vulture, the Lammergeier is a magnificent bird. Seen with Griffons it looks less bulky, sometimes obviously smaller, but its huge wingspan, long tail, white head and orange breast give it a superior air. It looks the part: one of Europe's rarest, biggest, and most legendary birds.

FEEDING Although capable of killing prey, Lammergeiers typically feed on large carcasses, including the marrow bones which they drop from a height to break them against rocks.

DISPLAY & VOICE In winter, pairs chase each other near the nest site, sometimes linking talons and falling towards the ground. They may then make oddly thin, squeaky calls. They often patrol the cliff face in long, slow glides.

BREEDING Nests are on cliff ledges, especially in caves. One or two eggs are laid in midwinter and incubated by both parents for 55–60 days; usually only one chick flies after 110 days.

MIGRATION Resident.

LENGTH 100–115cm (39–45in); wingspan up to 240cm (94in)

WHEN TO SEE	All year
WHERE FOUN	Pyrenees; Corsica (very rare), Alps (reintroduced), Greece, Crete

Egyptian Vulture *Neophron percnopterus*

A small yet impressive vulture; soars on flat wings with few wingbeats, over cliffs or near rubbish tips

Adult
Pale grey bloom on new flight feathers gradually wears off

Adult
Pattern like larger White Stork, White Pelican, or smaller Booted Eagle, but note white, wedge-shaped tail, thin yellow head

Sub-adult
Two years old

Immatures
Dark brown; juvenile in Europe up to September, but most older immatures remain in Africa

Adult
Unique thin bill, yellow face; may look pristine white or very dirty

Immature
Adults far outnumber dark immatures in Europe

Its unspeakable habits mean that the Egyptian Vulture is not everyone's favourite bird of prey. Yet it is a most impressive sight as it sails through the air, especially when seen against a bright blue sky when its plumage may look almost translucent.

FEEDING Although most famous for using stones to break Ostrich eggs in Africa, Egyptian Vultures often feed at refuse tips and relish the most awful rubbish and excrement. They also feed in proper vulture fashion, at carcasses, as well as taking insects, eggs, and sometimes even nestling birds.

DISPLAY & VOICE On arrival at a nesting area in spring, pairs perform energetic diving display flights with high-speed, acrobatic manoeuvres. They are, however, usually silent.

BREEDING Nests are typically on cliffs, less often in trees; pairs breed at 4–5 years old. Two eggs are usual; they hatch after 42 days and the chicks fly when about 10 or 11 weeks old.

MIGRATION Adults fly south in August, juveniles later, to Africa, where juveniles remain for a few years.

LENGTH 60–70cm (24–28in)

WHEN TO SEE	March to September
WHERE FOUND	Iberia, S France, S Italy, SE Europe; migrants over Gibraltar, Istanbul

Red Kite *Milvus milvus*

While predominantly a scavenger, the Red Kite has a brightness of colour, strength of pattern, elegance of form, and mastery of flight that make it a star in the bird world. In Britain it is a symbol of conservation: a truly rare bird, once on the edge of extermination, that is now on the verge of a remarkable comeback. Elsewhere in Europe it is now not so rare as was recently thought: in Spain, especially, it has staged a fine recovery.

FEEDING Kites search for food from the air, dropping down to pick up worms and scraps but also catching birds as large as crows and Black-headed Gulls in short, swift chases.

DISPLAY & VOICE Display flights over territories are frequent in spring. Kites make loud, wavering squeals, less powerful or emphatic than a Buzzard.

BREEDING Large nests of sticks, leaves, earth, scraps of paper, and cloth are built in trees. Two to four eggs hatch after 31–32 days' incubation.

MIGRATION Many north European birds move south and west in autumn.

LENGTH 60–65m (24–26in)

WHEN TO SEE All year; March or April to October only in central and E Europe
WHERE FOUND Locally UK; common Iberia, SE France, Balearics; scarcer N and E Europe, N Balkans

The most elegant of large raptors, with long, angled wings, a forked tail, and fluent flight

Adults Narrow wings; white patch on underwing; dark upperwing (right); forked tail

Juvenile

Black Kite

Juvenile

Juvenile

Juvenile Tail less forked

Juvenile (left) Secondaries and greater coverts have white tips; adult (below) lacks these

Juvenile

Adult Grey-white head with neat fine streaks, bright yellow eye

Black Kite

Red Kite

Black Kite *Milvus migrans*

Black Kites are common in parts of Europe, but they are less able to cope in areas of intensive farming or modern urban development. In coastal areas of southern Spain and parts of the Pyrenees they are still numerous, but as the traditional landscapes are threatened, so too are the kites.

FEEDING They eat all kinds of offal, scraps, and refuse, along with insects, small mammals, and fish; Black Kites are often found close to water. They are remarkably agile in the air.

DISPLAY & VOICE Courtship consists largely of flights over the nest site. Calls are mostly gull-like, vibrant, or whining notes like *kueee-ee-ee-eee*.

BREEDING Nests are made in tree tops, well-hidden in foliage although quite large, and made of sticks and debris. Two to four eggs hatch in 31–32 days.

MIGRATION Black Kites head south in autumn, crossing the Mediterranean in thousands at Gibraltar in August and September, with fewer passing through Sicily, Malta, and over the Bosphorus at Istanbul; most return in April.

LENGTH 55–60cm (22–24in)

WHEN TO SEE March/April to October
WHERE FOUND S and central Europe, to Finland; rare Scandinavia, UK, Low Countries

Adult Muddy brown with little pattern below

Slightly chunkier, less rangy than Red Kite, but also exceptionally agile in flight; note generally duller underwing, shorter tail

Adult Wings angled, tail notched when closed

Compare angled and bowed wings, tail twisting, hint of wing patch and especially broad pale band across inner wing with Marsh Harrier

Juvenile May show strong whitish wing patch

Juvenile (above) Broad, pale buff feather edges wear off to leave whitish spots by September

Juvenile Rusty with marked pale feather edges

Adult By contrast, Red Kite has paler head, whiter wing patch, brighter tail and underbody

Red Kite

Marsh Harrier *Circus aeruginosus*

Male
When soaring, shows longer, less broad tail than Buzzard

Gliding, hunting, sailing profile with raised wings, unlike Black Kite

The largest, heaviest harrier with the shortest tail. Male distinctive; female usually obvious but needs care at long range or high up, when may resemble Black Kite, Buzzard or even Booted Eagle

Juveniles have narrower wings than adults, males narrower than females

Juvenile male

Juvenile female

Sub-adult male

Juvenile male
Dark chocolate, paler edges to wing coverts

Adult female
Some have clear cream forewing patch

Sub-adult male
Breeds in this plumage with dark trailing edge to wing

Adult male
Trailing edge and forewing all pale

Adult male

Adult female
Some are more marked on breast

Floats low over reeds and open, damp ground

Adult male
Head may be very pale or streaked; tail pale grey or faintly barred on sides; solid rufous underbody

Adult female
Cream crown and throat; cream wing patches can be much bigger; juvenile plumage varies greatly, can be difficult to age, usually pale edges to wing coverts visible close up

Juvenile
Typical pale crown and throat; paler on face

This bird of prey is usually instantly recognizable as a harrier, despite being rather larger and bulkier than other harriers. It tends to fly low, flapping gently between wavering glides on slightly raised wings. Yet it is also capable of high soaring flights, and can be taken for a Buzzard or a Black Kite if its plumage details cannot be seen against a bright sky. Marsh Harriers are often associated with marshes, but they travel widely when hunting over adjacent farmland and sometimes turn up in very dry areas while on migration.

FEEDING The Marsh Harrier eats a variety of small waterside birds and animals such as voles, moles, and young rabbits, as well as birds of drier places near the nesting marsh. It hunts with a low, floating flight, switching instantly to a fast dive as it targets a frog, Coot, or duckling, often with a sideways twist or turn back onto its course.

DISPLAY & VOICE The display flights follow a typical harrier pattern, with the male swooping and climbing high over the nesting territory. He brings food to the female, and gives it to her in a thrilling mid-air pass from foot to foot as she rolls beneath him. This continues when the male hunts for food to feed the growing chicks and calls the hen from the nest to receive it. Calls are a loud, nasal, Lapwing-like *way-oo* from the male, a harsher chattering rattle and various mewing notes or whistles. Often a male pairs with two or three females; it seems to be a matter of chance whether he mates with a particular female in successive years.

BREEDING The female builds a bulky nest of reeds and twigs in reeds, on the ground, or over shallow water. She lays four or five (sometimes up to eight) eggs, which are often quickly stained by the damp. They hatch after 31–38 days' incubation solely by the female. The chicks fly when about 35–40 days old; the youngest often die when food is short and many clutches fail completely, succumbing to flooding or predators. The young are fed by their parents for another two or three weeks after they leave the nest.

MIGRATION Marsh Harriers breeding in northern and eastern Europe move to the Mediterranean area in winter, or even along the Nile valley into central and eastern Africa. Those from western Europe may go to west Africa, but some remain in eastern England and the Low Countries.

LENGTH 48–55cm (19–22in); females larger than males

WHEN TO SEE Mostly April to October; a few in winter in W Europe
WHERE FOUND E Britain, locally most of Europe except extreme north and mountain ranges

Hen Harrier *Circus cyaneus*

For centuries the males and females of the three smaller harriers were thought to be different species, because while the adult males are grey the females and immatures are brown with white rumps and barred or 'ringed' tails. These harriers can be difficult to distinguish; all prefer hunting over open ground, heaths, marshes, and extensive areas of cultivation. They use a low, often slightly wavering flight with relaxed wingbeats between glides on slightly raised wings. It looks slow, but they cover a lot of ground quickly. Of the three, Hen Harriers are by far the most likely to be found on higher ground, typically with heathery slopes and rushy valleys, in summer.

FEEDING Hen Harriers eat rodents and small birds, or the chicks of ground-nesting birds. They catch them on the ground, often with a sudden, twisting pounce. Harriers have long, bare legs, ideal for snatching prey from tall vegetation. They often carry their prey to a small hummock, rock, or fence post to pluck and eat it at leisure.

DISPLAY & VOICE In spring, males perform an exciting 'sky dance'. They fly over the territory in a deeply undulating flight, 'bouncing' at the bottom of each dive and rolling or tumbling as if out of control at the top of each climb. They call with a hard, even, quick *chuk-uk-uk-uk*, while females make a less even, higher, whickering *chek-ek-ek-ek-ek-ek*.

BREEDING Males may pair with two or three females and supply them all with food while they incubate eggs and brood young. The grass-lined stick nests are built on the ground, often in heather or rushes on a slope with a wide view. Each female lays three to six eggs, incubating them until they hatch after 29–31 days. The last eggs may hatch some days after the first, and these later, smaller chicks die if food is short. Surviving chicks fly when 32–42 days old. Intruders at the nest are often attacked by females and some bold males: they may strike people on the head with their feet.

MIGRATION Northern and eastern breeders move south and west; in western Europe they may move shorter distances, perhaps to low ground or coastal marshes. In much of southern and southeastern Europe Hen Harriers are seen only as winter visitors.

LENGTH 43–50cm (17–20in); females larger than males

WHEN TO SEE In UK and Ireland all year, but mostly winter in south and east; in much of NW, W, and central Europe, September to April but some resident; in Scandinavia and E Europe, only in summer
WHERE FOUND N Scandinavia, N Europe, and locally E Europe, UK and Ireland, locally Denmark to France and Spain; locally in SE Europe in winter

Adult male
Faint dark hindwing bar becomes darker with wear

Male pale and gull-like against dark moorland or ploughed field

Juvenile female
Typical raised-wing profile

A large, long-winged, white-rumped bird of prey, flying low and apparently slowly on raised wings; sexes entirely different in colour but need careful observation to distinguish from other harriers

Adult female

Adult male
Grey chest; white underwing with dark trailing edge; secondaries sometimes faintly barred

Juvenile male
Narrower wings than adult

Juvenile male (above)
Rich, dark brown, paler forewing panel; has white rump and banded tail like adult female; male has narrower wings than female

Compare four-fingered long primaries with narrow-winged Pallid and Montagu's Harriers

Juvenile female
Some have lighter primary barring

Adult female
Some have lighter barring on flight feathers

Adult male (above)
Pale grey; sub-adults look dingy, marked browner, less pearly-grey. Dark band on tips of secondaries, not across base as on Montagu's Harrier

Adult female
Facial disc gives slightly owl-like effect; older females greyer when fresh, wear browner; some have paler shoulder area

Long legs and toes

Montagu's Harrier *Circus pygargus*

A graceful, slender-winged harrier with typical strong sexual differences; adult males easiest to identify

Adult male

Black cross-bar on wing, rufous streaks

Compare diffuse paler area on wing coverts with juvenile Pallid Harrier

Juvenile female
Wingtips fall short of tail (equal on male)

Adult female
Three quite narrow bars plus dark terminal band

Juvenile
Two narrow bars; narrow pale tip

Adult male
(right) Dark upperwing bar; often dark forewing, pale hindwing

Juvenile female
Dark bars on dark ground; rusty coverts and body; broader wings than adult

Adult female
Small white rump; long, slender wingtips sweep back

Adult female
Dark bars on pale ground; underwing barring hits primary coverts (Pallid has pale band around coverts)

Adult male
All-black wingtip; two secondary bars; rusty flecks on coverts; dark chest

Perhaps the most elegant of the harriers, Montagu's is a bird of warm, open landscapes with rolling cereal fields and grassy steppe. Changing agricultural practices have made life more difficult for nesting harriers in many parts of Europe. Very few Montagu's Harriers now breed in semi-natural grassland habitats.

FEEDING They eat lizards, mice and voles, small birds and nestlings, caught on or near the ground in a sudden pounce from a low, wavering flight.

DISPLAY & VOICE Males perform an undulating 'sky dance' over the nesting territory. They call with a very high, staccato *kyek-kyek-kyek*. Otherwise this is a rather silent bird.

BREEDING Twig nests are built on the ground in grass, crops, or reeds. Four to five eggs hatch after 27–30 days. The male delivers food to the female and young in a dramatic mid-air food pass.

MIGRATION All Montagu's Harriers move to Africa in winter, most leaving by September and returning in April.

LENGTH 43–50cm (17–20in)

WHEN TO SEE Mostly mid April to late September
WHERE FOUND Iberia, E Europe; very local in between from Italy north to Denmark, E England

Pallid Harrier *Circus macrourus*

A striking harrier; male small and elegant, but female much larger than Montagu's Harrier

Primary bars clear of primary coverts, leaving wide pale band

Adult female (left)
Two broad central bars, three narrow outer ones; very broad pale tip

Male, second year
Ghost of black wingtip; seven tail bars

Broader wing than Montagu's

Male
Black wingtip wedge; white underparts gull-like; barred outer tail

Juvenile female
Male same but smaller. Dark shawl, pale collar unlike Montagu's. Bold pale upperwing patch

Adult female

Adult female

Juvenile female
Wingtips well short of tail

Tail has two centre bars, plain sides below, broad pale tip

Dark cheek; pale edge unlike Montagu's

Adult female

Adult male
Underwing white (grey wash may indicate sub-adult); white breast

Adult male
Wingtips equal or exceed tail tip; shorter on female

A very rare and much-prized bird in most of Europe, the Pallid Harrier is small and slight and lives in dry, open steppes and extensive cereal fields.

FEEDING It eats mainly lemmings, wood mice, voles, and a few small birds. It pounces upon prey from a low hunting flight like other harriers, but it often moves more quickly than other harriers when hunting. Its numbers vary locally with fluctuations in small rodent populations.

DISPLAY & VOICE The bouncing display flight is accompanied by a sharp, high *kek-kek-kek-kek* chatter. Otherwise this species is very quiet.

MIGRATION In autumn Pallid Harriers move to India and Africa where they hunt over the open savannah, often close to large herds of grazing animals. In spring they return, taking a more westerly route, but in both seasons most of them pass through the Middle East. Small numbers travel through Turkey. In most years a few are seen much farther west in Europe.

LENGTH 40–48cm (16–19in)

WHEN TO SEE Most April–May and August–October; very few in winter
WHERE FOUND Rare in SE Europe; very rare vagrant elsewhere

Sparrowhawk *Accipiter nisus*

This is the main predator of small woodland birds such as tits and finches, although it is also quick to take advantage of concentrations of prey on fields, in gardens, and even on saltmarshes or other open places. It suffered particularly badly in the pesticide era of the 1960s, being completely wiped out in many places where it had been common. Changes in the pesticides used on farmland have allowed it to regain most of its lost ground, but ironically it has declined again in many places because of a reduction in numbers of prey, also thought to be caused by changes in farming methods.

FEEDING Males take small prey, especially tits and sparrows, while females, being much bigger and more powerful, are able to take more thrush-sized prey and even birds as large as a Woodpigeon. It is thought that this difference in prey allows a pair to occupy a smaller territory, since they do not compete with each other for food. A Sparrowhawk hunts by flying low and taking prey by surprise: for example, it may dart from one side of a hedge to the other to fall upon an unsuspecting flock of finches. It also hunts by sitting and watching, then chasing prey which flies within range. It may be very determined, chasing birds over long distances, sometimes to quite a height, or even following birds into dense hedges or bushes and continuing the chase 'on foot' through the branches. Some Sparrowhawks may lie in wait inside hedges to ambush foraging tit flocks. Others specialize in raiding garden feeders, snatching Blue Tits from peanut baskets, often hitting windows or fences during the chase.

DISPLAY & VOICE In spring they may be seen flying over the nesting woods with a rather harrier-like action, patrolling their territories. Both sexes also perform remarkable 'bouncing' flights: undulations so fast and steep that, at the bottom of each dive, the bird appears to bounce off some unseen surface. They also perform headlong dives with completely closed wings, plunging at full speed into the woodland canopy. Calls are mostly high, chattering *kyi-kyi-kyi-kyi* sounds.

BREEDING Sparrowhawks nest in trees, often close to the main stem on a flat branch, building a flattish platform of twigs. Up to seven eggs hatch after 33–35 days, and the chicks fly when 24–30 days old.

MIGRATION Many northern breeders move south in winter; in Britain and Ireland most are resident.

LENGTH 28–38cm (11–15in)

WHEN TO SEE All year
WHERE FOUND All of Europe except Iceland; summer only in extreme north

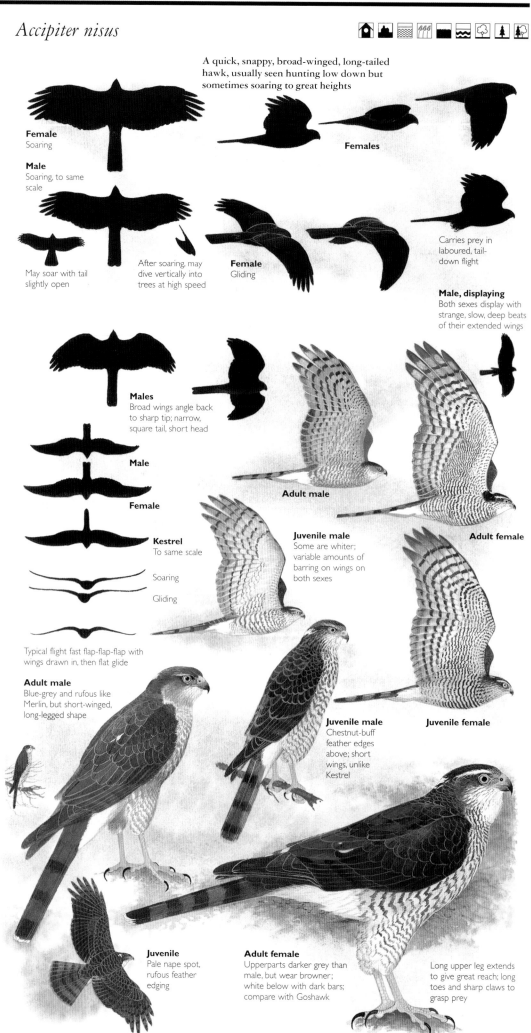

A quick, snappy, broad-winged, long-tailed hawk, usually seen hunting low down but sometimes soaring to great heights

Female Soaring

Male Soaring, to same scale

Females

May soar with tail slightly open

After soaring, may dive vertically into trees at high speed

Female Gliding

Carries prey in laboured, tail-down flight

Male, displaying Both sexes display with strange, slow, deep beats of their extended wings

Males Broad wings angle back to sharp tip; narrow, square tail, short head

Male

Female

Kestrel To same scale

Soaring

Gliding

Typical flight fast flap-flap-flap with wings drawn in, then flat glide

Adult male Blue-grey and rufous like Merlin, but short-winged, long-legged shape

Adult male

Juvenile male Some are whiter; variable amounts of barring on wings on both sexes

Adult female

Juvenile male Chestnut-buff feather edges above; short wings, unlike Kestrel

Juvenile female

Juvenile Pale nape spot, rufous feather edging

Adult female Upperparts darker grey than male, but wear browner; white below with dark bars; compare with Goshawk

Long upper leg extends to give great reach; long toes and sharp claws to grasp prey

Goshawk *Accipiter gentilis*

Essentially a larger version of the Sparrowhawk that takes much bigger prey, the Goshawk is far less familiar than its smaller relative. Even where a pair or two are resident, they may be surprisingly difficult to see for such big birds, except during their spring display flights. Optimistic birdwatchers often misidentify female Sparrowhawks as Goshawks, but on seeing a genuine Goshawk for the first time they wonder at their mistake. A female Goshawk is so big and dramatic that it cannot be taken for the smaller bird: it is more like a Buzzard or even an oversized female Peregrine. The smaller male can be more of a problem, unless seen with other birds for a good size comparison.

FEEDING Male Goshawks take quite small prey, such as thrushes, as well as pigeons, doves, magpies, and other medium-sized birds. Females take many pigeons, but also bigger species including crows, pheasants, grouse, various waders, even smaller hawks and owls. Both also catch many squirrels and some rabbits, even hares. Hunting flights may include steep, fast stoops like a Peregrine, or relatively short, fast, acrobatic chases over open ground or between large trees. Most hunts are low over the ground. They use regular plucking posts in forests, which become surrounded by feathers, uneaten scraps, and white droppings.

DISPLAY & VOICE Males soar with spread tails; both sexes fly over the nest with white undertail coverts fluffed out and prominent. They also perform vertical plunges into the nesting wood. Near the nest their calls include a powerful, Green Woodpecker-like *kyee-kyee-kyee* and a weaker or more melancholy *peee-yeh* from the female.

BREEDING Nests used for several years can become huge, flat platforms of sticks, regularly decorated with green sprays during the season. They are usually in big pines or tall oaks, often close to the main bole of the tree. Some Goshawks breed in immature plumage, but most begin when two or three years old; pairs remain together for life. Two to five eggs are laid, mostly in April; they hatch after 35–38 days. The chicks fledge when 35–42 days old. Some females, especially, may be aggressive to people near the nest.

MIGRATION Young birds move south and west in autumn, but most adults are resident unless forced to move by deep snow or prolonged hard frost.

LENGTH 48–61cm (19–24in); female much bigger and bulkier than male and three or four times as heavy as a female Sparrowhawk.

WHEN TO SEE All year
WHERE FOUND Most of Europe, but very local in most areas

A large, powerful, spectacular woodland predator with rather long, broad wings and a long tail

Glides and soars on flattish, droop-tipped wings

Can look falcon-like when gliding away

Gliding, wings flat at full stretch

Female
Much bigger, heavier, squarer, more robust than Sparrowhawk

Male
Younger adults not so dark-headed as older birds

Female
Note long head

Male

Male Sparrowhawk
To same scale; short head, sharp-cornered tail; quick wingflaps

Female Sparrowhawk
To same scale

Woodpigeon
To same scale

Flap-flap-glide flight flatter than Sparrowhawk, less undulating; wingbeats slower; lack 'snap'

Note longer, rounder tail of female compared with male

Juvenile female
Long streaks and drop-shaped spots on chest, never seen on Sparrowhawk

Adult has plainer rear wing than Sparrowhawk, and longer head

Adult female (left) and male (right) to same scale

Adult male
Pale individual

Adult male, Sardinia
Heavy barring below; striking head pattern

Adult female
Conspicuous white undertail

Male

Woodpigeon

Adult female, Italy
Heavy barring; some immature (browner) plumage in wing coverts

Juvenile female

Worn adult may look very brown

Adult can be grey or blue above

Juvenile female
Compact, dark form found over most of Europe

Juvenile female
Large, pale northern form

Rough-legged Buzzard *Buteo lagopus*

This species replaces the Common Buzzard in the far north. As would be expected for a bird that lives in a colder climate it is slightly larger, so it has less surface area relative to its body size, and therefore loses less heat. In most respects it is very similar to the Buzzard, but it is a little more elegant in flight, with a more elastic, flexible action. It is more accomplished at hovering than the Common Buzzard, but it may also spend long periods perched motionless in a tree, on a post, or even on flat ground. The 'rough legs', or tightly-feathered tarsi, are not at all easy to see.

FEEDING In summer Rough-legged Buzzards feed on small rodents, principally field voles, bank voles, and lemmings. They also kill young hares and even stoats, as well as a few small birds, young ducks, and waders. In winter they still prey mainly on voles, but supplement them with dead meat such as rabbits killed on roads. If voles are scarce, as they are every few years, they eat more birds.

DISPLAY & VOICE Pairing probably takes place in winter, as most birds arrive at breeding sites already paired. Displays include soaring and diving flights over the nest, but these are performed in silence, without the Buzzard's piercing calls. The alarm calls are longer and higher-pitched than the Common Buzzard's, and not usually heard away from the nest.

BREEDING Much depends on the rodent population: in Scandinavia rodent numbers fluctuate on a four-year cycle, and in years with few rodents Rough-legged Buzzards either do not breed or wander far and wide until they find a better food supply and settle to breed there. The nest is built on a cliff or, in wooded areas, in a tree; in open tundra it may simply be on a hummock on the ground. Three or four (sometimes as many as seven) eggs are incubated for 31 days, mostly by the female. The young fly after 34–43 days, but remain dependent on the adults for a few weeks.

MIGRATION All breeding birds and their young leave Norway and Sweden in the autumn, but their wanderings southwards depend largely on the availability of food. Many reach Denmark, Germany, and the Low Countries, but they are much more irregular in Britain. Some travel as far as the Balkans and the Black Sea.

LENGTH 50–60cm (20–24in)

WHEN TO SEE In breeding areas April to October; in S and W Europe mostly October to April
WHERE FOUND Breeds N and central Scandinavia and eastwards; in winter regular from Belgium and Netherlands east to Black Sea, erratic and usually rare E Britain

A big, elegant, long-winged buzzard with a flexible, relaxed flight, frequent hovering and usually a striking plumage pattern; variability in pattern, however, makes structure and flight action a better guide than plumage

Hovers well, but heavily

Sails with wings flat or slightly raised

Adult male (left)
Typical male, with mostly pale belly; contrasting dark forewing and pale hindwing, dark tail band

Adult female
Soaring, with tail well fanned. Broad dark hindwing band indicates adult; black belly typical of species

Adult male (left)
Several bars on tail; dark bars on secondaries; male has shorter tail, narrower wings, and much more elongated profile than female

Juvenile female
Juveniles of both sexes show pale hindwing band and diffuse tail band, but bold black wing patch and wingtips typical at all ages

Juvenile male

Juvenile females

Relaxed wingbeats more kite-like than Buzzard

Males

Male Gliding

Female Gliding

All ages/sexes show broad pale area on upper primaries

Adult (left) has dark eye, juvenile (below) has pale eye

Juvenile

Delicate head, fine bill

Adult female
Female's wingtips very long, equal tail tip

Juvenile
Pale eye

Juvenile male
Male's wingtips are shorter than tail

Adult female
Often only one broad band on tail

Adult male (right)
One broad band on tail, up to three narrow bands

Immature
Diffuse tail pattern, varies greatly

74

Honey Buzzard *Pernis apivorus*

A big, long-winged, supple, buzzard-like bird of prey, with pale eyes, a small head, and a rather long tail with three dark bands; its pattern is highly variable but often strongly barred underneath: identified by distinctive shape and actions

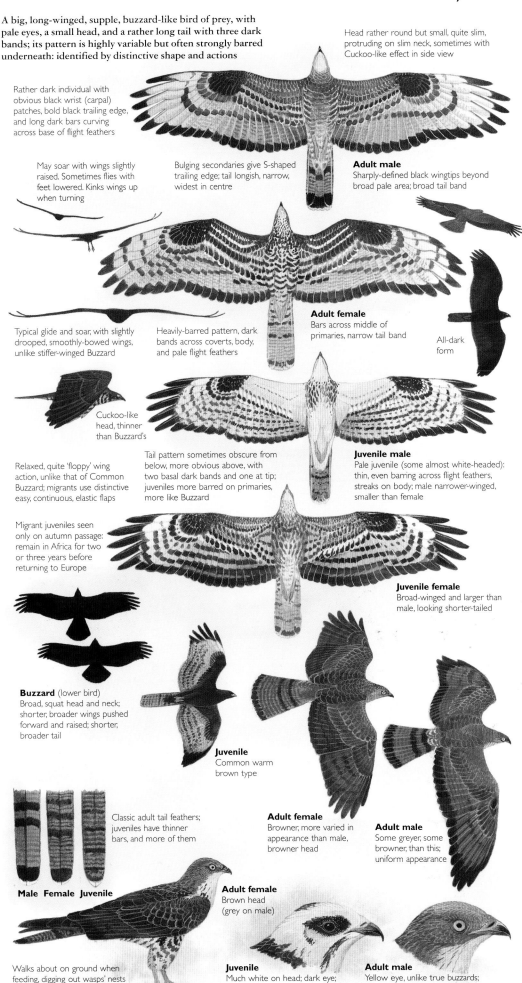

Head rather round but small, quite slim, protruding on slim neck, sometimes with Cuckoo-like effect in side view

Rather dark individual with obvious black wrist (carpal) patches, bold black trailing edge, and long dark bars curving across base of flight feathers

May soar with wings slightly raised. Sometimes flies with feet lowered. Kinks wings up when turning

Bulging secondaries give S-shaped trailing edge; tail longish, narrow, widest in centre

Adult male
Sharply-defined black wingtips beyond broad pale area; broad tail band

Typical glide and soar, with slightly drooped, smoothly-bowed wings, unlike stiffer-winged Buzzard

Heavily-barred pattern, dark bands across coverts, body, and pale flight feathers

Adult female
Bars across middle of primaries, narrow tail band

All-dark form

Cuckoo-like head, thinner than Buzzard's

Relaxed, quite 'floppy' wing action, unlike that of Common Buzzard; migrants use distinctive easy, continuous, elastic flaps

Tail pattern sometimes obscure from below, more obvious above, with two basal dark bands and one at tip; juveniles more barred on primaries, more like Buzzard

Juvenile male
Pale juvenile (some almost white-headed): thin, even barring across flight feathers, streaks on body; male narrower-winged, smaller than female

Migrant juveniles seen only on autumn passage: remain in Africa for two or three years before returning to Europe

Juvenile female
Broad-winged and larger than male, looking shorter-tailed

Buzzard (lower bird)
Broad, squat head and neck; shorter, broader wings pushed forward and raised; shorter, broader tail

Juvenile
Common warm brown type

Classic adult tail feathers; juveniles have thinner bars, and more of them

Male Female Juvenile

Adult female
Brown head (grey on male)

Adult female
Browner, more varied in appearance than male, browner head

Adult male
Some greyer, some browner, than this; uniform appearance

Walks about on ground when feeding, digging out wasps' nests with quite straight claws

Juvenile
Much white on head; dark eye; yellow base to bill

Adult male
Yellow eye, unlike true buzzards; bristly facial feathers, dark bill base

Despite its name this is not a true *Buteo* buzzard. It resembles one superficially, but close views reveal several distinctions; its behaviour and ecology are also quite different. It is particularly variable in its plumage pattern, which makes its distinctive flight shape and the set of its wings all the more vital for identification. Usually seen in flight, Honey Buzzards are secretive when feeding and breeding, and keep within the confines of extensive woodland. They are most easily seen when they concentrate at short sea crossings while on migration, or when displaying over their territories in late spring.

FEEDING A Honey Buzzard spends long periods perched within woodland, watching for wasps and bees. When it sees one it follows it back to its nest, which it then digs out with its feet. Stiff, short feathers on its face probably help protect it from stings. It eats wasp and bee grubs, adults, and honeycomb, as well as ant grubs and various other insects. In early spring it may need to supplement this insectivorous diet with frogs, worms, small birds, and other prey.

DISPLAY & VOICE For a short period in spring Honey Buzzards display over the woodlands where they nest. The male flies upwards, raises its wings over its back and claps them together two or three times; it then rises again and repeats the performance, then rises still higher in a sequence of steep climbs and wing claps. The usual call is a slightly whining, clear *peee-u*.

BREEDING Both sexes build the nest, characteristically of leafy twigs, high in a tree – often a spruce, oak, or beech. Usually two eggs are incubated for 30–35 days; the chicks fly when 33–45 days old.

MIGRATION Honey Buzzards spend the winter in Africa south of the Sahara. Like most birds of prey they find flying over open sea difficult; they prefer to soar on warm, rising air, which occurs only over land. Their migration routes therefore concentrate over short sea crossings. These include the Bosphorus at Istanbul, where large flocks move through in early September and return in April and May, and Gibraltar where even larger numbers pass through. Other good sites include Falsterbo in southern Sweden. Sadly many Honey Buzzards migrating over Sicily and Malta are illegally shot by hunters.
LENGTH 52–60cm (20½–24in)

WHEN TO SEE April to September
WHERE FOUND Extremely rare breeder in UK; local from Spain through France and N Italy north to Baltic, frequent S Scandinavia, Finland, and east into Russia; migrants Gibraltar, Sicily, Malta, Greece, Bosphorus

Long-legged Buzzard *Buteo rufinus*

This is a true buzzard of warm, dry areas, often found on almost semi-desert steppes, but in the Balkans it occurs in more wooded areas in hilly country. It is easily mistaken for a Common Buzzard.

FEEDING It eats small mammals such as voles, rats, and ground squirrels, plus some small birds, lizards, frogs, even snakes. It watches from perches such as telegraph poles, or soars in high circles over open ground. It hovers more often than the Common Buzzard, typically hanging head-to-wind over dry, hot fields or open scrub.

DISPLAY & VOICE Displays include an undulating flight with steep climbs and fast plunges. It is quieter than a Common Buzzard, its higher-pitched calls seldom heard.

BREEDING It nests on cliff ledges, and incubates three or four eggs for 28 days. The young fly after five weeks.

MIGRATION Breeders from north of the Caspian Sea move south in autumn into Africa; some migrate south from Greece, but others remain all winter.

LENGTH 50–65cm (20–26in)

WHEN TO SEE All year
WHERE FOUND E and NE Greece; very rare vagrant NW Europe

A large, agile buzzard with long, rather narrow wings, a pale tail, and a vigorous wing action recalling a small eagle, its character constant despite variable plumage

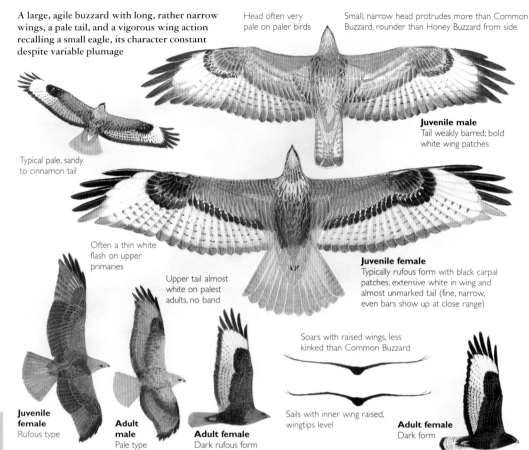

Head often very pale on paler birds

Small, narrow head protrudes more than Common Buzzard, rounder than Honey Buzzard from side

Juvenile male Tail weakly barred; bold white wing patches

Typical pale, sandy to cinnamon tail

Often a thin white flash on upper primaries

Upper tail almost white on palest adults, no band

Juvenile female Typically rufous form with black carpal patches, extensive white in wing and almost unmarked tail (fine, narrow, even bars show up at close range)

Soars with raised wings, less kinked than Common Buzzard

Sails with inner wing raised, wingtips level

Juvenile female Rufous type

Adult male Pale type

Adult female Dark rufous form

Adult female Dark form

Steppe Buzzard *Buteo vulpinus*

Usually treated as a race of the Common Buzzard, this is really a distinct form best separated as a species in its own right. More research into its status and distribution is required, especially in central Europe. It is a common migrant in eastern Europe and the Middle East, crossing the Bosphorus in large flocks between mid September and mid October.

FEEDING Its food and foraging behaviour are much like those of the Common Buzzard, with small mammals forming the bulk of its diet.

DISPLAY & VOICE Displays include soaring and more active flights, with pairs often diving at each other and sometimes grasping each other's feet. Its calls are like a Buzzard's, but rarely heard outside the breeding area.

BREEDING The stick nest is made in a tree. Two to four eggs are incubated for 33–35 days and the chicks fly after about seven weeks.

MIGRATION In autumn they fly south, mostly over narrow sea crossings; rare in NW Europe in late autumn.

LENGTH 50–60cm (20–24in)

WHEN TO SEE April to October
WHERE FOUND Breeds NE Europe through to Russia and into Asia, very few in winter in SE Europe

A possible race of the Common Buzzard, but constant structure from Finland and Poland through Russia to Caspian suggests a separate species; supposed area of hybridization in central Europe needs more research

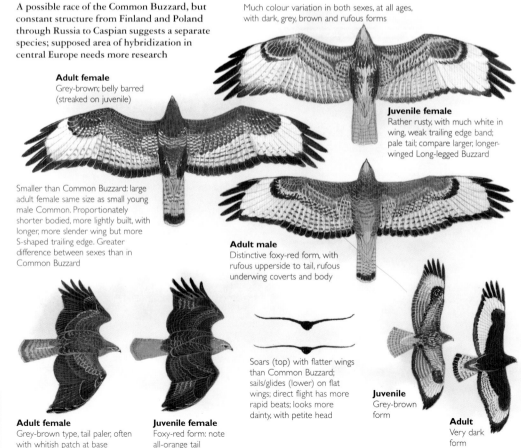

Much colour variation in both sexes, at all ages, with dark, grey, brown and rufous forms

Adult female Grey-brown; belly barred (streaked on juvenile)

Juvenile female Rather rusty, with much white in wing, weak trailing edge band; pale tail; compare larger, longer-winged Long-legged Buzzard

Smaller than Common Buzzard: large adult female same size as small young male Common. Proportionately shorter bodied, more lightly built, with longer, more slender wing but more S-shaped trailing edge. Greater difference between sexes than in Common Buzzard

Adult male Distinctive foxy-red form, with rufous upperside to tail, rufous underwing coverts and body

Soars (top) with flatter wings than Common Buzzard; sails/glides (lower) on flat wings; direct flight has more rapid beats; looks more dainty, with petite head

Adult female Grey-brown type, tail paler; often with whitish patch at base

Juvenile female Foxy-red form: note all-orange tail

Juvenile Grey-brown form

Adult Very dark form

Common Buzzard *Buteo buteo*

In much of western Britain this is the most common and obvious bird of prey, even more numerous than the Kestrel and certainly much easier to see than the secretive Sparrowhawk. It is also common in a variety of habitats over large areas of Europe. It is well able to survive in farmland regions: indeed, a mixture of cultivated fields, permanent pasture, hedges, and woodland makes perfect Buzzard habitat. Ideally it needs undulating or hilly ground, which helps to generate the varied winds and rising air currents that allow it to take full advantage of its skill in the air. It soars on thermals or upcurrents for long periods, but also spends hours perched on telegraph poles, trees, and fence posts, or even standing on the ground. Yet despite its fondness for such mixed, farmed landscapes it is equally a bird of remote moors, bogs, and cliffs, although normally not far from at least some scattered trees or open woodland.

FEEDING Buzzards enjoy a varied diet. They prey mainly on small mammals such as voles, mice, small rabbits, and moles, but also eat a lot of earthworms, big beetles, and grasshoppers. They vary their prey according to location, often taking frogs, toads, slow-worms, lizards, or even fish. In many places dead rabbits and other animals killed on roads make up a large part of their food, especially in winter. Buzzards watch for prey from the air, either soaring in wide arcs or hovering (especially in the wind over steep hillsides). They also use the 'wait and see' technique, simply sitting on high perches and watching for movement.

DISPLAY & VOICE Buzzards perform exciting displays with extravagant switchbacks, steep climbs, and plunges with half-closed wings. A pair will soar and dive together, and sometimes one dives at the other which rolls over and reaches out with its feet.

BREEDING The nest, a bulky structure of sticks, wool, and various scraps, is built in a woodland tree or at the base of a tree sprouting from a cliff face. Incubated by both parents, two to four eggs hatch after 33–38 days. Chicks fly after 50–55 days and are fed by their parents for a further six or seven weeks.

MIGRATION Birds from Scandinavia and the far northeast of Europe move southwest in autumn; thousands pass through southern Sweden; elsewhere they are mostly resident but many cross over Gibraltar. Asian birds migrate south over the Bosphorus in September and October.

LENGTH 51–57cm (20–22½in)

WHEN TO SEE All year; in N and NE Europe, April to October
WHERE FOUND Most of Europe except Iceland and N Scandinavia; absent from most of Ireland and much of E England

Typical profiles (left) and head-on soaring shape with wings in V (right); quite broad, longish wings with bulging rear edge; shortish, round tail

Soars on raised wings in wide, wavering, slow circles

Glides on lower, arched wings

Typically dark with paler tail, barred inner wing and obvious pale patch towards tip

Adult male
Broad dark band shows adult; tail slightly shorter than female

Despite pale underside pattern, usually looks dark

Juvenile
Lacks adult's dark band on edge of wings and tail; white patch restricted to outer feathers

Typical gliding attitudes (above); active flight has slightly jerky wingbeats alternating with glides

Juvenile female

Adult female
Plumage variation is enormous in both sexes, but vast majority show this basic pattern; pale U under chest patch typical

Juvenile
Pale bird: some can be more uniformly cream except for dark wingtips and carpal marks

Juveniles
Pale (left), typical (above right)

Female
Gliding: thickset wings, ample tail, rather rounded, bulging wing shape typical of both sexes

A generally common, widespread, stocky, medium-large bird of prey, often seen perched on poles, wires, or fences, or soaring with wings held up in a V-shape; unremarkable pattern on most individuals

Tail feathers: juvenile (left) has narrow dark bars; adult (right) has broad bar near tip

Juvenile   **Adult**

Juvenile female
Male's wings longer: almost reach tail tip

77

Booted Eagle *Hieraaetus pennatus*

This is the smallest of the eagles, a summer visitor to southern parts of Europe where it is just one of a whole suite of birds of prey. It is more or less buzzard-like, but some features recall a kite or even a harrier at times. It has two forms: pale and dark. Seen against a vivid blue sky in bright sun, the pale type is an extremely handsome bird. It is often harried by other birds of prey, ravens, and crows; it seems to get the worst of it in many aerial battles, although it is usually capable of defending itself well enough by rolling over and presenting its talons. It is found in much the same places as buzzards and kites, especially where open woodland, particularly oak, and aromatic Mediterranean scrub clothe rolling hills and lower mountain slopes. In many areas Booted Eagles have declined in recent decades, largely because of poisoning, shooting, general disturbance, and habitat loss. In particular the destruction of native broadleaved woodland for farming or coniferous plantations usually drives out the eagles.

FEEDING Booted Eagles soar over woods and bushy hillsides, often at a great height, searching for almost anything they can get hold of: lizards, snakes, frogs, small mammals such as voles and young rabbits, small birds, and even large insects. They hang in the wind looking down intently, then stoop dramatically to strike their prey with a killing blow. They also chase birds in fast, low pursuits.

DISPLAY & VOICE Spring and summer display flights are exciting to see: high soaring and steep, fast undulations, with headlong plunges at great speed. The call is a distinctive loud, piping *chi-dee*, often repeated; during display flights more mellow, plover-like *heeup* calls carry far and wide over the hills.

BREEDING The nest is a bulky affair of sticks and roots, built by both sexes in a tree. A dry, warm slope with open oak woods is preferred. Two eggs make up the usual clutch. They hatch after an incubation of 36–38 days, mostly by the female. The young fly when about 50–60 days old, but as a rule only a single chick survives to fledge.

MIGRATION Booted Eagles spend the winter in Africa just south of the Sahara. Small numbers cross the Bosphorus in autumn, but many more move south through Gibraltar in mid September. They return in late March and April. Young, non-breeding birds may disperse more widely to the north, but very few reach areas far outside the breeding range.

LENGTH 45–50cm (18–20in)

WHEN TO SEE March to September
WHERE FOUND Spain and Portugal, S and central France; Balkans

A small eagle with a broad, rounded head, gliding on flat or drooped wings, with a rounded look and longish tail

Head-on glide with slightly bowed, droop-tipped wings

Pale form (about 80 per cent of west European adults); much smaller than Egyptian Vulture, White Stork, which share similar pattern

White 'spotlights' best seen head-on; Honey Buzzard may show similar marks but not such striking white spots

Male

Slightly paler inner primaries; translucent tips to flight feathers and tail

Unusually well marked pale individual

Tail plain, or with slight dark tip or very faint bars

Dark form; paler behind bend of wing; paler tail with hint of dark tip

Female
Slightly longer tail than male

Translucent trailing edge; white 'spotlights' on shoulders

Dives during display or when hunting

Adult
Medium-dark

Juvenile
Pale form

Rufous individual with dark midwing line, like small Bonelli's; round head, white 'spotlights' helpful; upperparts give best clues

Adult
Dark form; pale V above tail, pale band across wing

Juvenile
Pale form; upperwing bands very striking on some birds

Adult (right)
Medium-dark, rufous phase, with heavier bars, commonest E Europe

Adult
Pale form; forehead often white

Feathered legs unlike Buzzard

Dark   Intermediate

Pale phase more constant; darker birds variable

Bonelli's Eagle *Hieraaetus fasciatus*

A big, dramatic, impressive eagle, hunting almost like a huge hawk, but spending long periods perched

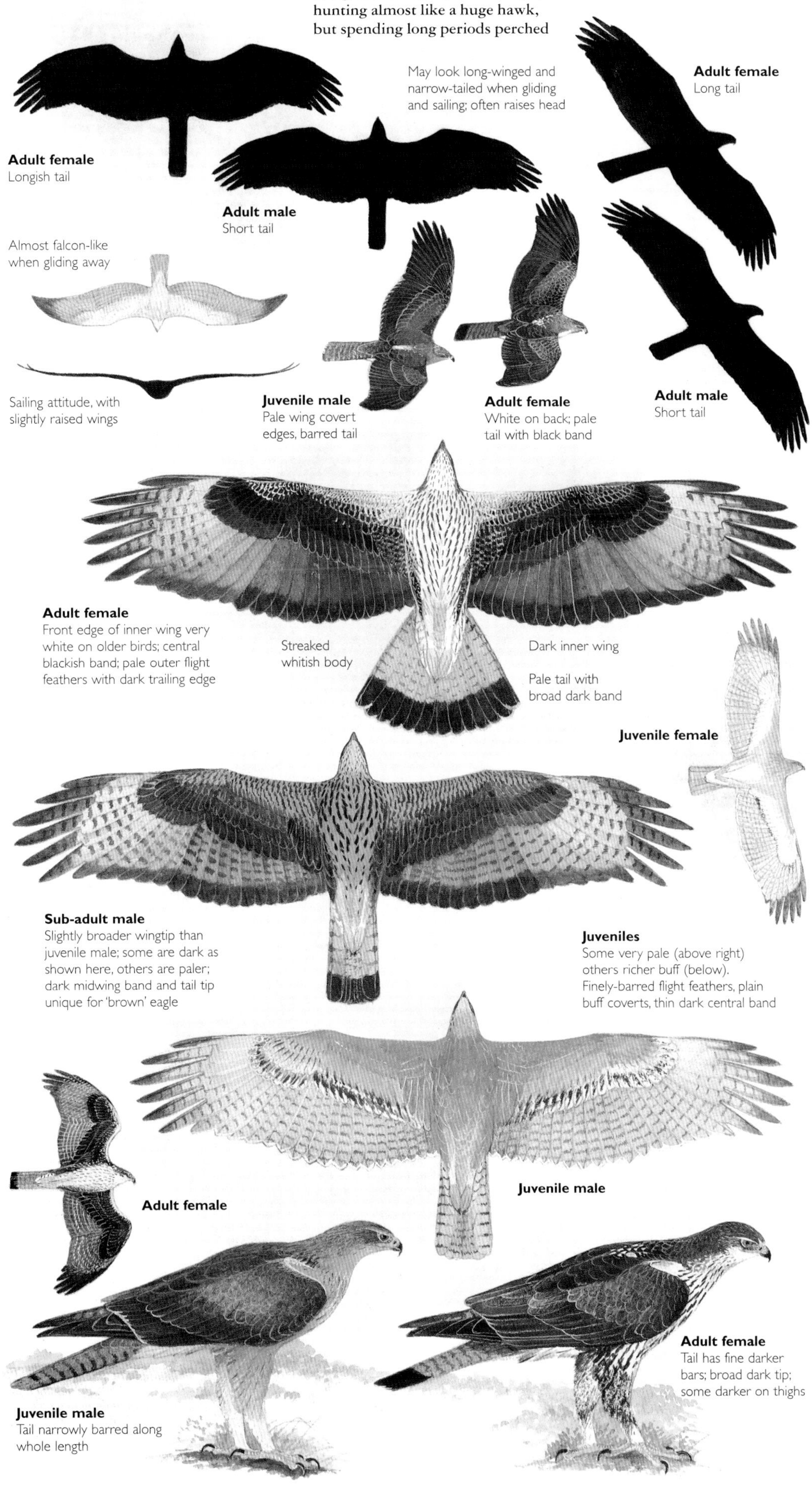

May look long-winged and narrow-tailed when gliding and sailing; often raises head

Adult female
Long tail

Adult female
Longish tail

Adult male
Short tail

Almost falcon-like when gliding away

Sailing attitude, with slightly raised wings

Juvenile male
Pale wing covert edges, barred tail

Adult female
White on back; pale tail with black band

Adult male
Short tail

Adult female
Front edge of inner wing very white on older birds; central blackish band; pale outer flight feathers with dark trailing edge

Streaked whitish body

Dark inner wing

Pale tail with broad dark band

Juvenile female

Sub-adult male
Slightly broader wingtip than juvenile male; some are dark as shown here, others are paler; dark midwing band and tail tip unique for 'brown' eagle

Juveniles
Some very pale (above right) others richer buff (below). Finely-barred flight feathers, plain buff coverts, thin dark central band

Adult female

Juvenile male

Juvenile male
Tail narrowly barred along whole length

Adult female
Tail has fine darker bars; broad dark tip; some darker on thighs

Generally rare and hard to see, this is an exciting bird of prey. It combines the size and power of an eagle with the speed, agility, and impact of a Goshawk. In the unlikely event of a really close view, its whole bearing and facial expression create a wonderfully memorable impression. Sadly, in most areas it is rare and declining owing to continuing persecution, disturbance in once-remote areas, and loss of habitat. Bonelli's Eagles prefer the fringes of mountainous regions, where rocky cliffs and gorges mix with steep wooded slopes and extensive maquis: the bushy scrub so characteristic of the Mediterranean area but now so often replaced by farmland or dense commercial forestry. A pair will often fly at particular times of the day when they can usually be seen over their breeding cliffs, but otherwise they are secretive and easily overlooked.

FEEDING Often hunting in pairs, Bonelli's Eagles patrol the slopes in search of likely quarry, flying low over the ground. Typical prey includes rabbits and medium-sized birds such as jackdaws and partridges. This staple diet is varied by all kinds of birds, from ducks to larks, and other mammals such as hares and rats. It is a dramatic hunter, combining manoeuvrability with the strength and stamina to pursue a chase to its conclusion. Most prey, however, is taken by surprise and quickly caught and killed.

DISPLAY & VOICE Owing to the very early breeding season, display flights may take place well before the turn of the year and continue until February or March when the eggs are laid. They have a typical eagle/buzzard pattern, with soaring developing into steeply undulating displays and plunges. Unlike the Booted Eagle, however, voice does not play any significant part.

BREEDING Pairs form at about three or four years of age and last for life. The nest is a pile of sticks on a ledge or inside a cavity on a sheer cliff face. Two eggs are normal; they hatch after 37–40 days. In two out of three cases, only one chick survives to fledge.

MIGRATION The adults are resident and rarely move far from their breeding territories, but young birds must disperse and sometimes wander a short distance outside the usual breeding range. Very few Bonelli's Eagles cross the Mediterranean into north Africa.

LENGTH 70–74cm (27½–29in)

WHEN TO SEE All year
WHERE FOUND Spain, extreme S France, Sardinia, Sicily, rarely Greece

Osprey *Pandion haliaetus*

Although found worldwide, the Osprey is a rarity in Britain. Persecution and collecting had led to its extinction in Scotland by 1910, but in the 1950s it returned, entirely of its own accord. Since then a long story of protection combined with public viewing at selected nests has made the Osprey a symbol of conservation success in the Highlands, and it has thrived sufficiently well in recent years to reach a total of more than 100 breeding pairs. In spring and autumn they can be seen almost anywhere in Britain as they journey between their northern breeding areas and Africa.

FEEDING What catches the public imagination about the Osprey is its spectacular fishing method. It patrols above the water at a great height until it spots a fish, then hovers like a giant Kestrel. Having judged the position of its next meal it plunges headlong, folding back its wings for speed. Just before striking the water it swings back, thrusting out its feet at full stretch ready to grasp the fish in its long, curved, needle-sharp claws. It can swing its outer toe sideways like an owl to get a secure grip on twisting, muscular, slippery fish, and the soles of its feet are equipped with sharp-edged, roughened scales. As it rises, shaking the water from its feathers, the Osprey often manoeuvres the fish into a more streamlined, head-first position so it is easier to carry back to the nest, or to a perch where it will eat it. Most of its victims are medium-sized fish such as pike, trout, flatfish, and mullet.

DISPLAY & VOICE The early spring displays over the nest involve steeply undulating flights together with loud, high-pitched, shrill whistling calls, *pyew-pyew-pyew*. Ospreys also make a lot of fuss over refurbishing their nest, breaking off dead twigs and green sprays from pine trees or lifting larger branches from the ground.

BREEDING Nests are used year after year, by a succession of different Ospreys, so they soon build up into huge, rounded piles of thick sticks. They are usually on tall pines, often on a broken branch or in a strong fork. Some Ospreys used to nest on ruined buildings in Scotland and elsewhere today they still use a variety of artificial sites. Two or three eggs hatch after 37 days; the young fly when about 44–59 days old. They return to breed on their own account when three years old.

MIGRATION North European Ospreys, including those from Scotland, spend the winter in west Africa.

LENGTH 55–65cm (22–26in)

WHEN TO SEE March to October
WHERE FOUND A migrant through much of England and S Scotland; breeds through N Europe from Scotland through Scandinavia and N Germany, locally in Iberia and Mediterranean islands

Glides and flaps with kinked wings; wingbeats deliberate, long or short glides

Black wingtips, carpal patch, and trailing edge (narrow on some juveniles); barred flight feathers look dull against white coverts at a distance

Hovering: compare with Short-toed Eagle

A big, spectacular bird of prey, with long, angled wings, that feeds on fish caught after a headlong plunge from the air

Hovering: broad-winged, winnowing action

Juvenile

Very white individual with small dark carpal patch at bend of wing

White crown, broad black band across head obvious at long range

Carries fish head-first

Juvenile
Diving for fish; feet brought forward at last moment; shakes off water after dive

Adult
Gliding with typical angled wing; breast band varies; striking white body

Juvenile
Pale patch on lower shoulder obvious on some, but not all

Juvenile (left) has buff feather edges; adult (right) uniform dark brown above

Adult
Wingtips well past tail

Juvenile
Wingtips equal tail

Short-toed Eagle *Circaetus gallicus*

A big, pale, large-headed snake-eagle with bare legs and bright yellow eyes; its pale underwings have no dark wrist patches or tips

Adult
Head/chest can be dark, hooded, or much paler

Pale primary coverts; pale primary tips unusual for bird of prey

Female
Larger tail than male

Adults have dark trailing edge of varying strength

Three dark tail bars

Adult
Gliding on angled wings

Juveniles have pale trailing edge

Male
Smaller tail

Juveniles have ginger on breast, some even more than this

Soaring, wings raised

White underside often has dull or silvery effect at long range, crisp barring shows in close view

Hovers expertly, but looks heavy; wingbeats deep, or may just 'wobble' outer wing

Gliding, wings flat/drooped

Adult
Upperside can look patchy with fading and moult

Pale juvenile
Gliding away

Looks slim- or broad-winged depending on angle and attitude; displays with wings straight and flat, head outstretched

Juvenile
Looks neat, without irregular patchy effect

Variable extent and weight of barring at all ages; some have dark hood, some with white chin

Juvenile

Large, owl-like, loose-feathered head; magnificent yellow eye

Pale, unfeathered legs

Adult

In much of southern Europe this is one of the most conspicuous raptors: a large eagle that spends much of its time in the air. It is a magnificent sight, its pale underside often catching the sunlight as it turns against a bright blue sky. In a close view – which is more likely than with other big eagles – the barring on the underside shows crisp and clear while the large, round, cold, yellow eyes give a piercing, intelligent expression. This is a snake-eagle: a European representative of a group that is more widespread and varied in Africa. They are all distinguished by similarly large, rounded, owl-like heads, yellow eyes and strong, bare-shanked legs.

FEEDING Hunting flights are long, high-level patrols over open ground and warm, bushy hillsides, punctuated by regular periods of hovering. The eagle stares intently at the ground, head-to-wind. With tail fanned and angled downwards, and wings fanned or beating with an almost 'wobbling' action depending on the wind, it pinpoints a snake or lizard, or sometimes in dull or wet weather perhaps a small mammal. Then it drops onto its prey. Sometimes it dives from a great height, plunging at high speed with its feet down, breast pushed forward, and head pulled back in a dramatic stoop. At other times it hunts by watching from a perch, often a tall electricity pylon. Its usual food includes grass snakes, European whip snakes, Montpellier snakes, and less often adders, which it typically grips behind the head and carries off to a perch to eat.

DISPLAY & VOICE Like other eagles and buzzards it displays in flight, performing deep undulations above the breeding territory. Pairs may often be seen flying together, their tails closed, heads thrust forward and wings stretched out flat and straight in a marked cross-shape. The various calls recall the squealing sounds of gulls.

BREEDING In spring the eagles always return to the same place, so pairs form life-long bonds. Together they build a nest of sticks in a tall tree such as an oak. Just one egg is incubated, mostly by the female, for 45–47 days; the chick flies at 10 weeks old. They breed when three or four years old.

MIGRATION In autumn all European Short-toed Eagles migrate to mid-Africa, with concentrated movements over Gibraltar and the Bosphorus in August and September. The adults return in March and April.

LENGTH 62–67cm (24–26cm)

WHEN TO SEE Mostly March or April to September
WHERE FOUND Spain, S France, Italy, and the Balkans; only a rare vagrant outside breeding range

White-tailed Eagle *Haliaeetus albicilla*

Drainage of lakes and marshes, disturbance of previously untouched wildernesses, pollution, and persecution have dealt a succession of severe blows to the White-tailed Eagle. Like many other large European birds of prey it has dwindled in both numbers and range, and in some countries its populations have been reduced to the tiniest remnants. Nevertheless, protection measures have encouraged a small recovery in parts of northern Europe. The Norwegian population is thriving and a concerted effort to reintroduce it to Scotland is, so far, succeeding. So the future of this magnificent bird is, for a time, secure, if only in a small part of its past range. Unlike Golden Eagles, which are typically shy and aloof, White-tailed Eagles may settle close to coastal or lakeside villages, especially where small harbours offer the chance of free handouts of fish and offal.

FEEDING It eats mainly fish, finding most of them dead, washed up onto shores or floating on the surface. It also captures live fish in its feet as it swoops onto lakes or sheltered coastal bays, and may even catch large fish in shallow water by hunting on foot. It kills medium-sized or large birds with a short, surprise stoop, but also takes wildfowl and Coots by forcing them to dive repeatedly until, exhausted, they are no longer able to escape.

DISPLAY & VOICE Pairs remain in their territories all year, but increase their displays in spring. They soar together, sometimes with shallow undulations, and one will dive at the other. Sometimes the lower bird will roll over and the two interlock their feet. Occasionally the two then spin down towards the ground, one upside down beneath the other. They call much more often than Golden Eagles, with various dog-like yapping sounds or screeches, higher-pitched from the male, often in an accelerating sequence of 15–20 calls.

BREEDING The nests are built of thick sticks, on ledges or in particularly large, old, sturdy trees. When close to villages or towns they are always in inaccessible places: in Norway often on small, rocky offshore islands. Up to three eggs hatch after 34–42 days; often only one, sometimes two, very rarely three young fledge after about 10 weeks. They breed at five years old.

MIGRATION Adults are resident but immatures wander quite widely.

LENGTH 77–92cm (30–36in)

WHEN TO SEE All year
WHERE FOUND Breeds NW Iceland, Norway, Baltic coasts, very locally Scotland, NE Europe, Balkans; very rare in winter in N France, Low Countries, and some central European lakes and marshes

Head protrudes well forward, may appear to droop, unlike neater Golden Eagle

One of Europe's giants: a broad, flat-winged bird of prey with a massive yellow bill, bare legs, a protruding head, and a short tail

Huge, square, fingered wings give door-like impression, unlike Golden Eagle. Constant heavy flapping on long flights

Juvenile's pale inner wing patch often conspicuous

Juvenile male
Rear of wing curves forward into body on male; straighter on female (below)

Juveniles have pointed flight feathers, giving 'saw-tooth' trailing edge

Juvenile female
Longer body gives impression of longer tail than male

Adults look magnificent against blue sky in sunshine

Adult female
Wedge-shaped tail; pale head

Adult male
Tail squarer; head even paler

Sailing/gliding, wings arched

Soaring, wings raised, well forward

Gliding away: wingtips look pointed at this angle, as on big vultures

Immature
Second plumage: dark head and chest contrast with boldly-streaked pale belly

Flapping flight – 'all wings'

Upperside of adult varies; often marked pale patch on primaries

Adult male
Old and moulting birds more variegated

Perches very upright in tree; more horizontal on ground

Juvenile shows 'Tear-drop' spots above

Juvenile
Juvenile's dark eye and bill gradually change to pale yellow of oldest birds

Female's wingtips short of tail; male's equal tail

Bare legs separate 'sea-eagles' from true eagles

Upper side of juvenile's tail has whitish feathers edged and tipped dark; feathers become whiter with each succeeding moult

Spotted Eagle *Aquila clanga*

A medium-sized but heavy, square-looking, short-tailed eagle, usually very dark, with a pale crescent more or less obvious towards the wingtip

Pale crescent at all ages, both sexes

Medium head projection; wings pushed well forward when fully spread; note seven separate primary tips in broad wingtip (six on Lesser Spotted Eagle)

Adult male
Smaller, lighter, shorter-tailed than female

Much shorter-tailed, less elegant, than larger Golden Eagle

Juvenile female

Juvenile has very dark wing coverts, paler flight feathers

Fine bars across flight feathers stop short of tip, unlike Lesser Spotted

Juvenile female
Bigger, heavier, longer-tailed, broader-winged than male. Juveniles variably spotted white on purple-brown

Adult female

Adults
Very dark; pale wing crescent; wings slightly drooped, not raised as in Golden Eagle

Sub-adult (below)
Pale rump, pale primary crescent, drooped wings

Juveniles
Male (above) wingtips beyond tail; female (right) wingtips fall short

Both spotted eagle species have long, spindly legs

A very rare bird in Europe, this is smaller than the widespread Golden Eagle but in some ways recalls the large and less closely related White-tailed Eagle. It is usually associated with water, but needs extensive woodlands in summer.
FEEDING Typically a rodent-eater, catching field voles and water voles, the Spotted Eagle may turn to birds in years when voles are scarce. It snatches young herons, gulls, rooks, and doves from nests, but is not agile enough to catch many adult birds such as Coots or ducks on the water.
VOICE Screeching *dip-dip-dip-dip* calls are often heard over breeding sites.
MIGRATION The breeding grounds are occupied in March and April, and vacated in September and October. A few Spotted Eagles winter in southern Europe, but most spend the winter (and their first three years of immaturity) in east Africa.
LENGTH 62–74cm (24–29in)

WHEN TO SEE All year
WHERE FOUND Breeds east of Baltic; in winter, very rare in France, Italy, Greece; only a very rare vagrant elsewhere

Lesser Spotted Eagle *Aquila pomarina*

A medium-sized brown eagle, generally paler than the Spotted Eagle but best identified with experience and care by its shape and often paler wing coverts

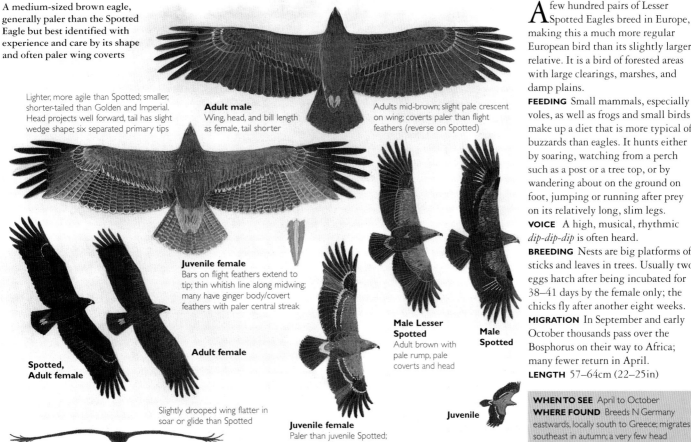

Lighter, more agile than Spotted; smaller, shorter-tailed than Golden and Imperial. Head projects well forward, tail has slight wedge shape; six separated primary tips

Adult male
Wing, head, and bill length as female, tail shorter

Adults mid-brown; slight pale crescent on wing; coverts paler than flight feathers (reverse on Spotted)

Juvenile female
Bars on flight feathers extend to tip; thin whitish line along midwing; many have ginger body/covert feathers with paler central streak

Adult female

Spotted, Adult female

Male Lesser Spotted
Adult brown with pale rump, pale coverts and head

Male Spotted

Juvenile

Slightly drooped wing flatter in soar or glide than Spotted

Juvenile female
Paler than juvenile Spotted; white midwing bar rather than rows of spots

A few hundred pairs of Lesser Spotted Eagles breed in Europe, making this a much more regular European bird than its slightly larger relative. It is a bird of forested areas with large clearings, marshes, and damp plains.
FEEDING Small mammals, especially voles, as well as frogs and small birds make up a diet that is more typical of buzzards than eagles. It hunts either by soaring, watching from a perch such as a post or a tree top, or by wandering about on the ground on foot, jumping or running after prey on its relatively long, slim legs.
VOICE A high, musical, rhythmic *dip-dip-dip* is often heard.
BREEDING Nests are big platforms of sticks and leaves in trees. Usually two eggs hatch after being incubated for 38–41 days by the female only; the chicks fly after another eight weeks.
MIGRATION In September and early October thousands pass over the Bosphorus on their way to Africa; many fewer return in April.
LENGTH 57–64cm (22–25in)

WHEN TO SEE April to October
WHERE FOUND Breeds N Germany eastwards, locally south to Greece; migrates southeast in autumn; a very few head northwest in error and reach Scandinavia

Golden Eagle *Aquila chrysaetos*

Combining great size and power with real grace and poise, the Golden Eagle is one of Europe's most inspirational species. Its expression manages to combine ferocity and purpose with intelligence and a truly regal bearing. Such attributes have not, however, saved it from centuries of persecution, and in common with many other raptors it has also suffered from habitat degradation, disturbance, and pollution. Yet like the Osprey and Peregrine it retains a remarkably wide distribution worldwide, and flourishes in parts of Spain and Scotland. It particularly likes mountainous regions, exploiting both harsh, barren moors and more varied terrain with rocky peaks, extensive crags, and thickly-forested mountainsides.

FEEDING A Golden Eagle finds much of its food already dead: carrion, in the form of sheep and deer that have died of exposure or starvation during the harsh upland winter and early spring. At other times it captures medium-sized mammals and birds, including mountain hares, brown hares, rabbits, grouse, ptarmigan, waders, and gulls. Its is a real opportunist, taking a remarkably wide range of prey: it kills young deer, foxes, and badgers at times, as well as voles, mice, lizards, and even tortoises.

DISPLAY & VOICE In winter and spring a Golden Eagle performs dramatic display flights: diving, climbing, and then half-closing its wings and looking from side to side before tilting over and diving down again. It soars high, then drops in a steep or near-vertical plunge, wingtips held tight over its tail but the front of each wing pushed out from the body to give a broad tear-drop shape. In such dives it probably outpaces almost any other bird. It is not often heard, but has a variety of sharp yelping calls, one sharp *kip* recalling an Oystercatcher call.

BREEDING The nests are rebuilt in late winter and decorated with green sprays during spring, so over many years they become vast piles of sticks, sprays, and bits of earth, sited on inaccessible cliff ledges or in big trees, especially old Scots pines. There may be three, four, or several more alternative nests, of which one or two are particularly favoured depending partly on the snow cover in spring. Two eggs are usual, incubated by the female for 43–45 days. Typically one chick will kill the other before fledging after 65–70 days.

MIGRATION Most are resident, with random dispersal by young birds; in northeastern Europe and Asia there are winter movements to south and west.

LENGTH 76–89cm (30–35in)

WHEN TO SEE All year
WHERE FOUND Breeds Scotland, Scandinavia, Spain, Alps, Italy, Balkans, some Mediterranean islands, and NE Europe

A majestic, elegant, and powerful raptor, that soars on broad wings and mounts spectacular high-speed display flights in winter and spring; one of Europe's most impressive birds

Soars with wings in quite deep V; pale forewing evident

Glides between beats in direct flight on flatter wings

Marked bulge to inner wing in rear view

Adult female
Predominantly dark; underwing faintly barred; weak, dark tail band

Soars with wings at full stretch, pushed well forward, 'fingers' widely spread, tail either fanned or closed

Soaring

Adult male
As female but smaller; with slimmer wings and longer tail

Much bigger, longer-winged, plainer than Buzzard, typically silent and seen at long range; Buzzard often close, perches on posts, calls a lot

Dramatic 'switchback' displays and steep dives at extremely high speed

Juvenile
Can look blackish except for bold white wing patches and white tail base; broad black tail band

Adult male

Adult female

Adult
Paler with wear, especially across upperwing coverts

Juvenile
Fresh plumage rich dark brown; crown and nape pale; white patches on thighs

Gliding fast

Juvenile
Striking wing and tail patches aid instant recognition; white reduces with age

Adult
New feathers black-brown, paler at base; old feathers bleach paler, 'golden', buff or greyish; tail often pale grey at base with thin dark bars

Big bill, flat head; strong feet, thighs heavily-feathered

Imperial Eagle *Aquila heliaca*

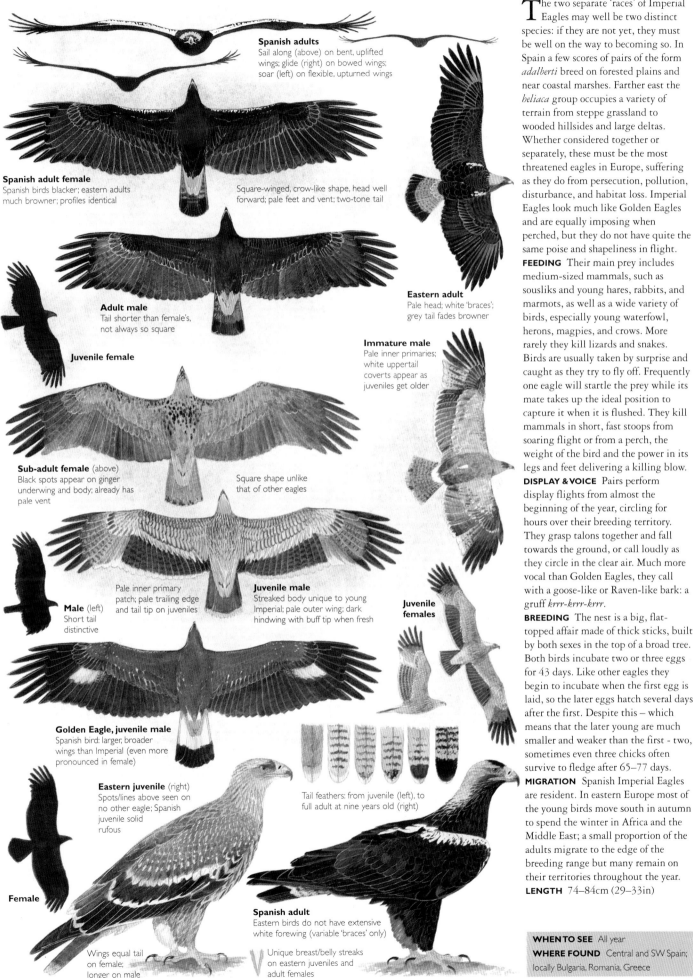

Spanish adults
Sail along (above) on bent, uplifted wings; glide (right) on bowed wings; soar (left) on flexible, upturned wings

Spanish adult female
Spanish birds blacker; eastern adults much browner; profiles identical

Square-winged, crow-like shape, head well forward; pale feet and vent; two-tone tail

Eastern adult
Pale head; white 'braces'; grey tail fades browner

Adult male
Tail shorter than female's, not always so square

Juvenile female

Immature male
Pale inner primaries; white uppertail coverts appear as juveniles get older

Sub-adult female (above)
Black spots appear on ginger underwing and body; already has pale vent

Square shape unlike that of other eagles

Male (left)
Short tail distinctive

Pale inner primary patch; pale trailing edge and tail tip on juveniles

Juvenile male
Streaked body unique to young Imperial; pale outer wing; dark hindwing with buff tip when fresh

Juvenile females

Golden Eagle, juvenile male
Spanish bird: larger, broader wings than Imperial (even more pronounced in female)

Eastern juvenile (right)
Spots/lines above seen on no other eagle; Spanish juvenile solid rufous

Tail feathers: from juvenile (left), to full adult at nine years old (right)

Female

Wings equal tail on female; longer on male

Spanish adult
Eastern birds do not have extensive white forewing (variable 'braces' only)

Unique breast/belly streaks on eastern juveniles and adult females

The two separate 'races' of Imperial Eagles may well be two distinct species: if they are not yet, they must be well on the way to becoming so. In Spain a few scores of pairs of the form *adalberti* breed on forested plains and near coastal marshes. Farther east the *heliaca* group occupies a variety of terrain from steppe grassland to wooded hillsides and large deltas. Whether considered together or separately, these must be the most threatened eagles in Europe, suffering as they do from persecution, pollution, disturbance, and habitat loss. Imperial Eagles look much like Golden Eagles and are equally imposing when perched, but they do not have quite the same poise and shapeliness in flight.

FEEDING Their main prey includes medium-sized mammals, such as sousliks and young hares, rabbits, and marmots, as well as a wide variety of birds, especially young waterfowl, herons, magpies, and crows. More rarely they kill lizards and snakes. Birds are usually taken by surprise and caught as they try to fly off. Frequently one eagle will startle the prey while its mate takes up the ideal position to capture it when it is flushed. They kill mammals in short, fast stoops from soaring flight or from a perch, the weight of the bird and the power in its legs and feet delivering a killing blow.

DISPLAY & VOICE Pairs perform display flights from almost the beginning of the year, circling for hours over their breeding territory. They grasp talons together and fall towards the ground, or call loudly as they circle in the clear air. Much more vocal than Golden Eagles, they call with a goose-like or Raven-like bark: a gruff *krrr-krrr-krrr*.

BREEDING The nest is a big, flat-topped affair made of thick sticks, built by both sexes in the top of a broad tree. Both birds incubate two or three eggs for 43 days. Like other eagles they begin to incubate when the first egg is laid, so the later eggs hatch several days after the first. Despite this – which means that the later young are much smaller and weaker than the first - two, sometimes even three chicks often survive to fledge after 65–77 days.

MIGRATION Spanish Imperial Eagles are resident. In eastern Europe most of the young birds move south in autumn to spend the winter in Africa and the Middle East; a small proportion of the adults migrate to the edge of the breeding range but many remain on their territories throughout the year.

LENGTH 74–84cm (29–33in)

WHEN TO SEE All year
WHERE FOUND Central and SW Spain; locally Bulgaria, Romania, Greece

85

Red-footed Falcon *Falco vespertinus*

Not all falcons are dramatic, fast-flying, solitary bird-eaters: the Red-footed is not, but it is nevertheless a true falcon and it can fly with speed and precision when it needs to. Rather than travelling alone it flies in small flocks; it even breeds in large colonies. In other ways it most closely resembles the Lesser Kestrel, the Hobby, and Eleonora's Falcon.

FEEDING This small falcon likes open areas such as grassy steppes, woodland clearings and the edges of marshes, over which it flies in pursuit of insect prey. It watches from a tree, post, wire, or other suitable perch, rather like a shrike, until it spots a suitable victim and gives chase. It may also hunt from the air, more like a Hobby (indeed, frequently in association with Hobbies). It hunts mainly in the morning and evening: it catches grasshoppers, beetles, caterpillars, ants, and spiders on the ground, and neatly plucks dragonflies, bees, wasps, mayflies, and craneflies from the air with its feet and transfers them to its bill to be eaten in flight.

DISPLAY & VOICE Pairs soar together in spring and the male will dive at the female. The male also flies fast over the territory and dives towards the female on the nest, calling loudly. Calls are typical falcon *kew-kew-kew-kew* notes, fast and rhythmic, but weaker than the calls of a Kestrel or Hobby.

BREEDING Typically Red-footed Falcons take over the nests of Rooks. Several pairs will occupy a colony, from a few to a couple of dozen. Today 50 pairs are considered a large colony, but in the past as many as 500 pairs bred in colonies in eastern Europe. Three or four (rarely as many as six) eggs are incubated by both sexes for 28 days; the chicks fledge after a month.

MIGRATION All Red-footed Falcons migrate in autumn to spend the winter in Angola, Namibia, Zimbabwe, and Botswana. They leave in September and October and return, using a more westerly route, from March onwards. In spring and summer there are sporadic occurrences well to the west of the breeding range, mainly involving immatures, but rarely adult males. These influxes usually occur in May and June, and the birds may range as far west as Britain. In some years they involve so many birds that they amount to small irruptions.

LENGTH 28–31cm (11–12in)

A gentle-looking, small-billed, lightweight falcon, usually seen perched or flying in pursuit of insects, combining some characteristics of the Kestrel and the Hobby; male and female plumages very different but equally distinctive

First-summer male
Strongly chequered underwing

First-year male
Moulting to adult in autumn: new dark flight feathers among old barred ones

Adult female
Unique all-orange underparts and red legs

Hovering

Eating insect in flight

Adult males
All-dark head and breast, rufous beneath tail

Juvenile
Whitish throat and vent; may have pale forehead; dark trailing edge to wing

Glides on slightly drooped wings

First-summer male
Variable barring on underwing, rufous on chest; legs orange, pinkish or pale red

Adult male
Pale on wing shines silvery in good light; dark hood, back, tail

Juvenile
White throat and white spot each side of nape; buff feather edges on upperparts

Adult female
Distinctive rufous cap, barred grey tail

First-summer male
Commoner in western Europe than adults

First-summer male
Rufous collar, brown on wings, rufous beneath tail; all vary in strength

Juvenile (left)
Very white around face and each side of neck, with thin central stripe; tail barred, unlike Hobby

Adult female (right)
Orange crown and nape fade to white; unique grey back and orange breast; barred grey tail

First-summer female
Head gradually fades paler

First-summer female
New, broadly-barred grey feathers and old, browner, narrowly-barred ones on back, wings, and tail

Adult male
Red bill base, eye-ring, and legs; rusty vent

WHEN TO SEE Mostly April to October
WHERE FOUND Breeds Hungary, Romania, Bulgaria, and farther east, rarely and irregularly elsewhere. Sporadic visitor, sometimes rare but widespread, west to Britain, Balearics, Sweden

Hobby *Falco subbuteo*

An elegant, long-winged and short-tailed falcon, with a bold head pattern and dark body; able to accelerate to a great pace from its relaxed patrolling flight

Direct, fast flight very precise, snappy, with deep beats of sharp wings

Pursues large insects with fast chase, then strikes with slow, floating stall

Kestrel
Soaring with wings forward, tail spread

Hobby
More angular, wings sharper

Adult female

Female Kestrel
Can be remarkably like Hobby, but has broader wings, rounder tail tip

Adult female

Adult female
White neck/throat, rufous thighs; rather dark overall

Adult female

Adult male
Longer 'arm', shorter tail than female

Snatches dragonflies, then holds them in feet to eat while flying

Adult male
Dark slaty, fades quite brown, not so pale on rump as Peregrine, narrower body

Black hood, white neck patch striking

Juvenile
White neck side obvious; pale forehead; no rufous; dark underwing and body (compare with juvenile Red-footed Falcon)

Juvenile female
Young birds have pale tail tip, pale trailing edge to wing, browner edges above, duller head

First summer
Worn brown upperparts, develops dark grey on back

Juveniles
Lacy pale feather edges above, but dark in flight; dull below with no rufous, thick stripes; pale tail tip but no other bars

Male's wings extend 25mm beyond tail female's 10mm

Adult male
Striking yellow feet and handsome head pattern

Like the Red-footed Falcon this is largely an insect-eater, but it is faster, slightly more powerful, and also takes a lot of birds in some seasons. Few birds match Hobbies for sheer grace and brilliance of flight: it is a joy to watch them in summer as they cover wide areas using a minimum of energy. Somehow they contrive to fly long distances with scarcely a wingbeat, employing a few flaps every so often to accelerate smoothly, gain height, and snatch an insect from the air with lethal accuracy before moving on as before: fast, smooth, effortless. Close views reveal that they are also beautifully patterned, always well turned out, and extremely handsome.

FEEDING Half the Hobby's diet consists of large flying insects such as dragonflies, wasps, bees, cockchafers, big beetles, and butterflies. It eats flying ants with relish, as well as much bigger termites in winter in Africa. It also catches small birds of many kinds, mostly in the air: swallows, larks, martins, sparrows, and finches. Many are caught at dusk as they go to roost, and mixed swallow, martin and wagtail roosts in reedbeds often attract Hobbies in the autumn. The falcon takes birds to a perch to dismember and eat them, but it eats large insects in mid-air, holding them in its feet as it glides around, head bent down, biting off pieces as it goes.

DISPLAY & VOICE As you might expect from such a fine aerial acrobat, the Hobby displays with vigour and panache: pairs soar together, the male often diving at the slightly larger female or catching prey and passing it to her in the air. The female rolls over beneath him, stretches out a foot and the gift is accepted. They also fly rapidly with deep, fast wingbeats giving a great turn of speed. Calls are loud, nasal, quickly-repeated bursts: *kew-kew-kew-kew*. Yet despite such vocal and aerial activity, Hobbies are notoriously difficult to observe around the nest once their eggs are laid.

BREEDING Three eggs are laid in an old crow's nest or some similar structure in a tree, often a pine. They hatch after 28–31 days, after being incubated almost entirely by the female. The chicks fledge after 28–34 days. The breeding success depends to a large extent on escaping predation by crows, and on the weather: in wet summers they may rear few young.

MIGRATION All Hobbies leave Europe between August and October to winter in southern and western Africa. They return in April and May.

LENGTH 28–35cm (11–14in)

WHEN TO SEE April to October
WHERE FOUND S Britain, S and E Scandinavia, south to Mediterranean

Lesser Kestrel *Falco naumanni*

Although very like the Kestrel in appearance, the Lesser Kestrel is a much rarer bird, far more restricted to the warmer parts of Europe and also a genuine migrant over the whole of its range. Owing to the effects of modern farming in its breeding range, with pesticides eliminating much of its insect food, the Lesser Kestrel is declining fast in Europe; in some areas where once it was common it is now threatened with extinction. It prefers open, often cultivated countryside with scattered trees, old buildings, or cliffs.

FEEDING This species is much more insectivorous than the Kestrel. It eats chiefly grasshoppers, beetles, crickets, and cockchafers; in Africa it preys heavily on termites. It catches a few lizards, far fewer mammals such as voles, and very rarely small birds. It usually hunts from a perch, less often by hovering, and simply drops down to its prey like a shrike. This technique is most effective on very open ground, even places where sparse vegetation exposes a lot of bare earth. Such feeding areas offering an abundance of insect prey must be within easy reach of a town, cliff, or trees where there are safe nest sites.

DISPLAY & VOICE Males reach the breeding territories earlier than females, searching for likely nest sites. When the females arrive, the males display with simple circling flights and dive towards their mates. Much more social than the Kestrel, the Lesser Kestrel is also more vocal, using hoarse *chay-chay-chay* notes and a more musical, wader-like *vivivivi*.

BREEDING They nest in colonies, with as many as 100 or even 200 pairs breeding together in suitable areas. The 3–5 eggs are laid directly on a cliff ledge or in a deeper cleft inside a cave, a niche in a large town building or old ruin, or a cavity in a dead tree. Both sexes incubate for 28–29 days, and the chicks fly when 28 days old. Pairs stay together for just a single season.

MIGRATION A very few adults spend the winter in the extreme south of Europe or in north Africa. The rest of the population moves on south in autumn, to the plains of Africa south of the Sahara and on down the east coast. Large groups forage over the migrating herds of big mammals in east Africa, preying on the many insects they disturb from the grass. Lesser Kestrels from western Asia reach South Africa where many thousands roost together in large trees.

LENGTH 29–32cm (11½–12½in)

WHEN TO SEE March to September
WHERE FOUND Spain and Portugal, where declining fast, rare S France, Sardinia, S Italy, Greece; rare vagrant elsewhere

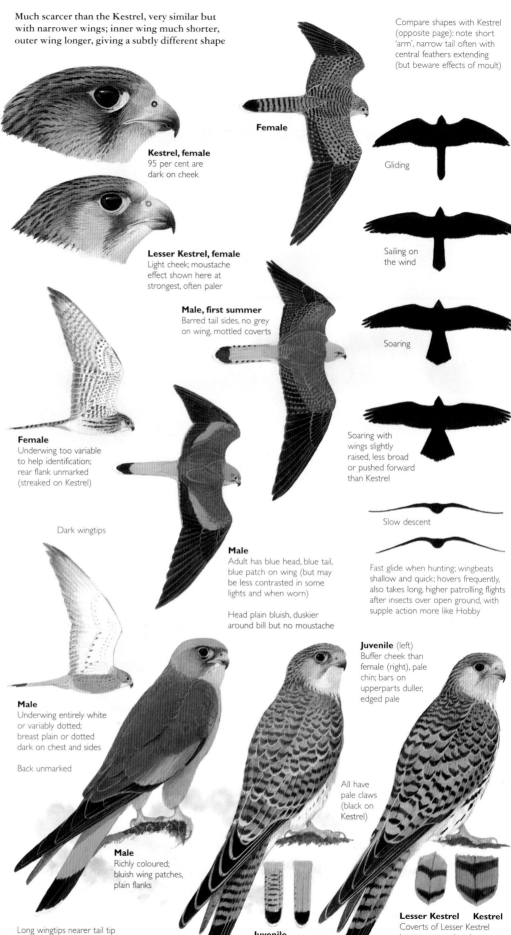

Much scarcer than the Kestrel, very similar but with narrower wings; inner wing much shorter, outer wing longer, giving a subtly different shape

Compare shapes with Kestrel (opposite page): note short 'arm', narrow tail often with central feathers extending (but beware effects of moult)

Female

Gliding

Kestrel, female
95 per cent are dark on cheek

Sailing on the wind

Lesser Kestrel, female
Light cheek; moustache effect shown here at strongest, often paler

Male, first summer
Barred tail sides, no grey on wing, mottled coverts

Soaring

Female
Underwing too variable to help identification; rear flank unmarked (streaked on Kestrel)

Soaring with wings slightly raised, less broad or pushed forward than Kestrel

Dark wingtips

Slow descent

Male
Adult has blue head, blue tail, blue patch on wing (but may be less contrasted in some lights and when worn)

Head plain bluish, duskier around bill but no moustache

Fast glide when hunting; wingbeats shallow and quick; hovers frequently, also takes long, higher patrolling flights after insects over open ground, with supple action more like Hobby

Juvenile (left)
Buffer cheek than female (right), pale chin; bars on upperparts duller, edged pale

Male
Underwing entirely white or variably dotted; breast plain or dotted dark on chest and sides

Back unmarked

All have pale claws (black on Kestrel)

Male
Richly coloured; bluish wing patches, plain flanks

Long wingtips nearer tail tip than on Kestrel: wingtips reach black tailband at all ages and in both sexes

Juvenile
Tail patterns vary in both sexes, as Kestrel; tends to have narrower bars

Female
More often grey on uppertail coverts and rump than Kestrel

Lesser Kestrel **Kestrel**
Coverts of Lesser Kestrel have narrower bands

Kestrel *Falco tinnunculus*

The everyday falcon almost everywhere, typical of farmland and roadsides as well as wilder areas and cliffs; its persistent hovering is highly characteristic

Classic hover, with head stock-still, wings, tail, and body adjusting position

Female
Gliding

Male
Gliding; narrow wings

Male
Gliding fast

Female
Soaring

Gliding

Soaring

Display flight fast, rolling, with very quick, shallow wingbeats

Gliding away: very narrow tail; wings longer-tipped than Sparrowhawk which can look similar in this attitude

Juvenile

Adult male
Grey head, weak moustache, spotted back, blue-grey tail

Male   **Female**

Often watches for prey from post, tree or wire. Active, even hovering, until late dusk

Male (left) has pale underwing, can look very white in sun or reflected light, but more marked than Lesser Kestrel

Adult male

Juvenile female

Adult male
Grey tail with black band

Distinctive pale inner wing and dark outer wing in both sexes

Adult female
Brighter, more barred than Sparrowhawk

Rufous rump, but some females may have barred grey rump

Immature male has unmarked central tail, outer feathers barred

Juvenile male may have barred grey central tail feather, rest rufous

Adult female
Beautifully barred over back and tail

Although it is one of the smaller, less dramatic and less powerful of the falcons, the Kestrel is capable of giving exciting aerial performances, especially given a strong wind swirling against a sheer cliff, in which it can soar and climb and stoop again almost in the manner of a Peregrine. Yet it is as a roadside hunter, perched on trees, wires, or telegraph poles or, most distinctively, hovering head to wind above a grassy road verge, that the Kestrel is most familiar.

FEEDING The Kestrel preys mainly on small mammals: mostly voles and rather fewer mice. It can catch rats, but it usually avoids large prey. If it takes them by surprise a Kestrel can fly fast enough, briefly, to catch small birds including House Sparrows, finches, and starlings. A variety of grasshoppers, beetles, lizards, and the young of larger birds make up a smaller proportion of its varied diet. It has acute eyesight, and it is likely that a Kestrel can see well in a wavelength invisible to people; the prey that remains so well hidden to our eyes probably gives itself away more easily to a hunting falcon. When hovering, the Kestrel is able to keep its head still relative to the ground, absorbing the effects of the wind by moving its body and adjusting its wings and tail. It also detects a lot of prey when watching from a suitable perch, and Kestrels are frequently seen hunting at dusk.

DISPLAY & VOICE The display flights over breeding territories are low, fast, twisting circuits with rapid, almost flickering wingbeats. The male also dives at the female as she perches. The calls used during displays, and often at other times, are high, nasal, rather weak repetitive notes: *kee-kee-kee-kee*.

BREEDING No nest is made; the female lays her eggs on a bare ledge on a cliff, in a quarry, or on a tall building, inside a large cavity in a tree or in an artificial nest box. The usual clutch is from three to six, rarely as many as nine eggs, which hatch after 27–29 days. The chicks fly after about 27–32 days. They remain dependent on their parents for a further month or more.

MIGRATION Kestrels from northeast and northern Europe migrate, escaping the cold winter weather to travel south and west, some of them going as far as central Africa. Most other European Kestrels are more or less resident, but young birds in particular may move generally southwards in winter.

LENGTH 33–39cm (13–15in)

WHEN TO SEE All year except in far north and east where mostly April to October
WHERE FOUND All of Europe except Iceland and bleakest parts of Scandinavia

Eleonora's Falcon *Falco eleonorae*

With its rakish silhouette, exceptional powers of flight, preference for Mediterranean cliffs and coastlines, and frequent occurrence in small groups, Eleonora's Falcon is a particularly exciting and appealing bird. It is a large falcon combining some of the characteristics of smaller species like the Hobby; but as well as being an insect-eater, it is a specialist predator of small birds. It is an unusual species, too, having two distinct colour forms.

FEEDING Outside the breeding season Eleonora's eat insects, often catching them in the air in the manner of a Hobby or Red-footed Falcon. The birds have a particularly elegant, fluent flight, swooping after dragonflies and butterflies as well as tiny fare such as flying ants; they also eat grasshoppers and beetles taken on the ground. In the breeding season they turn to small birds, and their nesting period is delayed into late summer and autumn to ensure that they benefit from the constant supply of tired, night-flying migrant birds along the Mediterranean coasts and islands. Their victims vary from place to place: in one area they may eat chiefly small warblers, in another chats and shrikes: it depends on what is available. Anything from Willow Warblers and Redstarts to Nightingales, Wheatears and Red-backed Shrikes are caught on the wing, often out over the sea as they struggle towards land at dawn. Several falcons hang in the wind, facing the incoming migrants, stooping on them from a height. It is a sad end to the migration, which is over almost before it has begun for some of these songbirds, but a mighty efficient way for the falcons to feed their young.

DISPLAY & VOICE Breeding groups sometimes fly off to feed together, as if this has some special social function. Pairs perform fast, free-flowing aerobatics, playfully diving, soaring, and circling together. They do not call much unless disturbed at the nest, when they make a loud, typically falcon-like chatter, neither so powerful or nasal as a Peregrine nor so musical as a Hobby: *ke-ke-ke-ke*.

BREEDING Always breeding in groups of between 20 to 200 pairs, Eleonora's choose a cliff ledge for their two or three eggs. These hatch after four weeks and the young fly when 35–40 days old.

MIGRATION In autumn Eleonora's Falcons fly east to the Red Sea (even those from north Africa and the Canaries) then down to Madagascar where the whole population spends the winter.

LENGTH 36–42cm (14–16½in)

WHEN TO SEE Late April to November
WHERE FOUND Balearics, Sardinia, islands off Italy, in the Adriatic and the Aegean Seas, Cyprus, vagrant in UK

This large, elegant, long-winged falcon is a Mediterranean coast and island speciality, catching small migrant birds to feed to its young in autumn

Long-winged, long-bodied, rakish shape distinct

Soaring

Sailing

Eleanora's

Hobby

Adult male with male Hobby (left) to same scale

Rufous vent, thin tail bars

Adult male
Light phase

Eleanora's

Hobby

Female with female Hobby (below) to same scale

Adult female
Light phase

Juvenile
Pale; dark trailing edge to wing

Some (probably in second year only) show extended central tail point

Flight dashing, acrobatic; marked changes of pace recall Hobby; wingbeats soft, relaxed, become deep, whippy at speed

Juvenile
Heavily scaled above

Juvenile
Pale feather edges distinct; tail barred beneath

Juvenile
Pale/intermediate phase; unique dark underwing coverts

Adults
Dark phase; pale underwing patch

Adult female
Pale phase; underwing dark, coverts darkest

Female
Mixed grey/brown above, looks quite a brown bird

Juvenile female
Dark individual

Some darker on breast; bill-base, eye-ring and feet grey

Striking moustache, white neck patch on adult

Adult male
Eye-ring yellow (blue on female); wingtips exceed tail (shorter on female)

Adult female
Dark phase; eye-ring blue but feet yellow

Merlin *Falco columbarius*

Juvenile female

Adult female (pale)

Adult male

Juvenile male

Adult male
Worn, darker

A small, thickset, spirited falcon of open spaces, sometimes more like a Sparrowhawk than a Kestrel, swift and agile but without the aerial grace of a Hobby. In summer it frequents moorland, in winter farmland, marshes, and dunes, often sitting on the ground, a low rock, or a post

Male
Tiny, bluish-grey above, orange-buff below, quite vivid at close range in good light but tends to look dark and dull in typical view

Spread tail reveals dark bars; black band

Broad-based wings and short tips tapered to point can recall fast, low-flying Sparrowhawk

Approaches prey fast, with wings withdrawn, tips flicked out in thrush-like action, or with wings below body level as if 'flying on wingtips'

Juvenile female

Spread tail of juvenile female

Breast feather of adult female

Breast feather of juvenile

Flank feather of both

Lacks heavy facial marks of Hobby or Peregrine

Juvenile female

Adult males
Grey (above) and rufous below (right)

Adult female
Earthy-brown, not rufous like Kestrel, tail barred cream

Typical views of passing Merlin (below)

Hunting flight: may stoop, or chase in rapid, level flight, often with tight, acrobatic twists and turns in final moments

Chunkier, shorter-tailed, broader-winged than Kestrel, wingtips sharper than Sparrowhawk

Despite its small size this is a fast-flying, tenacious, gritty little hunter, a bird of open spaces over which it is all too often little more than a fleeting shape, no sooner spotted than disappearing into the distance, low over the ground. This is its winter guise; in summer, it may mob intruders at the nest with great persistence and much noise, or simply slip away until the danger has passed. Those who know it well grow to like the little falcon of the moors for its unique character, no doubt enhanced by the wild environments in which it is usually to be found.

FEEDING Although it eats a good many large moths and a few small mammals, the Merlin chiefly feeds on small birds. It watches from a low perch, then tries to take them by surprise and dash after them, rising above and stooping from a low elevation. If this doesn't succeed, it may simply try to fly them down in a long, tiring chase, but such attempts are generally less successful. If the prey is itself agile and determined to escape, the Merlin is tested to the full and puts on a real show, twisting and turning adroitly in pursuit of its meal. Meadow Pipits are favourite food; also Skylarks, Wheatears, Whinchats, and various tits and finches from the edges of pine plantations. A number of small birds such as young pipits are also taken from nests on the ground.

DISPLAY & VOICE Displays consist of low-level, rather inconspicuous flights and much calling from perches on the ground. Males have a sharp, very fast *ki-ki-ki-ki-ki*, while females have a whinnying, peevish, but slightly fuller *yee-yee-yee-yee*.

BREEDING Many nests are simple scrapes on the ground, in thick heather with a view downhill from a steep slope. Other pairs choose old crows' or Rooks' nests in trees, especially hawthorns, pines, or larches, in isolated spinneys, in long windbreaks, in sheltered gullies, or on the moorland edge. Tree nests are the commonest type in Scandinavia. Three to five eggs are laid; both sexes incubate them for 28–32 days. The chicks are ready to fly after a similar period.

MIGRATION Most Merlins move at least downhill towards the coast in autumn; the majority are true short-distance migrants, going south. A few, even in Scandinavia and Iceland, remain in their breeding areas all year. Most British birds remain within Britain, but a few move to France.

LENGTH 25–30cm (10–12in)

WHEN TO SEE All year; mostly September to March in lowland areas
WHERE FOUND Breeds Iceland, Britain, and Ireland, Scandinavia; widespread in winter but scarce south to Mediterranean

Peregrine *Falco peregrinus*

Wanderer: the name of the most dramatic of the falcons reflects its widespread dispersal outside the breeding season, when it is apt to turn up at a reservoir, lake, marsh, or flood to terrorize the local wildfowl for a few days before moving on. Few birds inspire such admiration as the Peregrine: for those who love wild places and nature in the raw, a Peregrine in full chase pricks up the hairs on the back of the neck. It is certainly a powerful bird, but also a glorious exponent of the art of flying. To many of us, the sight of a Peregrine in the air never palls. Others may not share this adoration of birds of prey, but even they have to agree that this one is a particularly handsome and genuinely impressive example of its kind.

FEEDING This specialist bird hunter virtually ignores insects, mammals, and reptiles. Its preferred prey depends on local circumstances, but pigeons (rock, feral, or racing pigeons, less often Woodpigeons and Stock Doves) often dominate its diet. Thrushes of various kinds, starlings, and waders, including Snipe and Lapwings, make up much of its summer food; in winter it kills more ducks. On moors it regularly takes Red Grouse in small numbers. Many kills are simple chases in level flight; others involve a precise upwards swoop, rolling at the top of the climb to snatch the bird. More dramatic is the classic stoop, the Peregrine often having flown a long distance to get above its prey before diving headlong at great speed. The air rushing over its partly-open wings can be heard easily at quite a distance. Many stoops fail, but a hungry Peregrine will circle, gain height, and stoop again and again if necessary.

DISPLAY & VOICE The displays involve high circling flights; the pair dive and twist together at speed. Calls are loud and raucous: basically a typical falcon chatter, higher-pitched from the male, like *kyee-kyee-kyee-kyee*, and a rougher, lower, rasping and more nasal alarm from the female, *ehk-ehk-airhk-airrhk*.

BREEDING The female lays her eggs on a cliff ledge, often with a bed of earth and some grassy vegetation at its lip, or in a quarry, or on a tall building. The usual clutch is of three or four eggs; they hatch after 29–32 days and the chicks fly at 35–42 days old.

MIGRATION Northern populations move south in winter; southern and western birds are more resident except for wandering immatures.

LENGTH 39–50cm (15–20in)

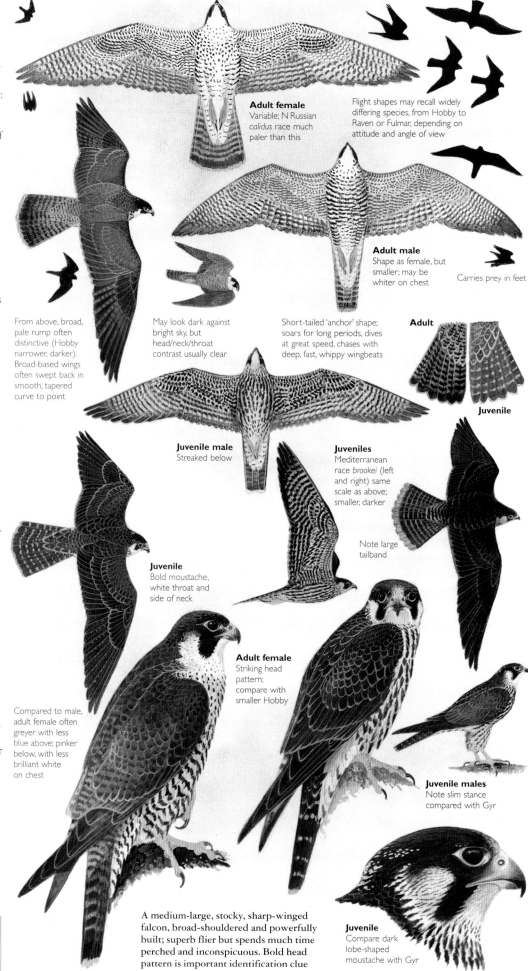

Adult female
Variable; N Russian *calidus* race much paler than this

Flight shapes may recall widely differing species, from Hobby to Raven or Fulmar, depending on attitude and angle of view

Adult male
Shape as female, but smaller; may be whiter on chest

Carries prey in feet

From above, broad, pale rump often distinctive (Hobby narrower, darker). Broad-based wings often swept back in smooth, tapered curve to point

May look dark against bright sky, but head/neck/throat contrast usually clear

Short-tailed 'anchor' shape; soars for long periods, dives at great speed, chases with deep, fast, whippy wingbeats

Adult

Juvenile

Juvenile male
Streaked below

Juveniles
Mediterranean race *brookei* (left and right) same scale as above; smaller, darker

Note large tailband

Juvenile
Bold moustache, white throat and side of neck

Adult female
Striking head pattern; compare with smaller Hobby

Compared to male, adult female often greyer with less blue above; pinker below, with less brilliant white on chest

Juvenile males
Note slim stance compared with Gyr

Juvenile
Compare dark lobe-shaped moustache with Gyr

A medium-large, stocky, sharp-winged falcon, broad-shouldered and powerfully built; superb flier but spends much time perched and inconspicuous. Bold head pattern is important identification clue

Gyr Falcon *Falco rusticolus*

Apart from great size, Gyr has longer 'arm' and body in proportion to Peregrine; wings also broader

Sails on flat wings; powerful and purposeful

Adult female pale type; some (especially males) whiter overall

Female broader-winged, longer-tailed than male; wings of both much broader than Saker's

Male   Female

Adults raise rear body feathers in cold climates, look fat

A big, heavy, broad-winged falcon, with many plumage variations; white individuals easily identified, others require great care: concentrate on the shape of the bird

Juvenile male
Dark midwing band; streaked underbody can be almost solidly dark; feet bluish

Variable tail patterns of juveniles; Peregrine never has such narrowly-barred pattern

Heavier, broader-winged than Peregrine, with bulky belly, more elastic, long-armed wingbeats

Juvenile female

Juvenile male

Males
May be almost entirely white with dark wingtips

Juvenile female

Juvenile male

Juvenile (left) has bluish feet; adult's feet (right) are yellow

Adult female

Juvenile female
Compare stance with Peregrine; Gyr much heavier-footed, thickly-feathered on thighs, more buzzard-like

Juvenile male
'White' type

Juvenile
Cheeks dark, but lacks elongated moustache of young Peregrine

Scapulars of adults ('white' and heavily-spotted types) and juvenile (far right)

Even when compared with most Peregrines, the Gyr Falcon is enormously big and heavy. It is remarkably powerful, but often lacks the elegance and purpose of a Peregrine at its best: it is slower, sometimes even lumbering, and has none of the aerial skill of the smaller falcons. Yet for all that it is a picture of magnificence and a truly charismatic bird. The glorious white phase adults, in particular, are hard to beat. While the Peregrine is a bird of the air – even though it spends long hours perched on cliffs – the Gyr is a bird of the ground, always poised on some rock or mound in the northern tundra, patiently watching for prey.

FEEDING Big birds such as grouse and Ptarmigan form the bulk of its prey in most areas. In some years, when small mammals like lemmings or sousliks are abundant, it eats a great many of these. Gulls, ducks, divers, waders, and auks are all part of its varied diet to a greater or lesser extent; in winter, wildfowl may make up a fair proportion of the kills. The Gyr usually hunts from a perch, with a low chase which may continue over several kilometres until the prey is exhausted. The falcon's quarry may eventually try to gain height to escape, but the Gyr then rises above it in a series of circles and stoops, or sweeps up from beneath to take it with a sudden twist. Although the power and weight of the Gyr may make it look clumsy and even slightly slow, this is deceptive: in level flight a Gyr Falcon is said to be capable of catching a Peregrine.

DISPLAY & VOICE Males begin to defend a territory early in the year and the females soon join them; they rise to a height and dive down noisily towards the nest. They call less often than some falcons; the calls follow a similar pattern but are particularly deep, hoarse, and rhythmic: *krery-krery-krery* or *kerreh-kerreh-kerreh.*

BREEDING The female lays her eggs on a ledge of a sheer cliff, often beneath an overhang which gives shelter and renders it inaccessible. Sometimes the pair use the nest of a Rough-legged Buzzard in a tree. Three to five eggs are incubated for 35 days; the chicks may not fly for about seven or eight weeks.

MIGRATION Western Gyr Falcons are sedentary except for wandering immatures in winter. Russian birds move more regularly to the south and west. Icelandic Gyrs remain in Iceland all year but are joined in winter by more from Greenland.

LENGTH 55–60cm (22–24in)

WHEN TO SEE All year; in W Europe more often early spring
WHERE FOUND Breeds Iceland, N and W Scandinavia; rare vagrant UK and elsewhere

Lanner *Falco biarmicus*

A large and impressive falcon, the Lanner behaves rather like a 'desert Peregrine' – although it is seen perched on top of a post or rock as often as in full flight in pursuit of prey. Rare in Europe, it is largely a bird of Africa, where it inhabits semi-desert plains, savannahs with scattered trees, and the fringes of arid mountain regions. In Sicily it tends to choose steep cliffs overlooking areas of pasture and rough hillsides near the coast.

FEEDING This is essentially a bird-eater: it may take prey as large as a Mallard or Jackdaw, but concentrates on smaller birds such as larks and doves. Small mammals and reptiles are a minor part of its diet. Pairs hunt together, one flushing birds from cover while the other waits to take them by surprise, swooping in as the prey take flight.

VOICE Calls are hoarse cries of varied rhythm and pace: *kyhek-kyhek-kyhek*.

MIGRATION Most Lanners remain in their breeding areas all year. A few descend to lower areas in cold winter weather. Young birds disperse but rarely stray far from the usual range.

LENGTH 43–52cm (17–20in)

WHEN TO SEE All year
WHERE FOUND Rare and threatened in Europe, just a few pairs in Italy (including Sicily), the Balkans, some Aegean islands

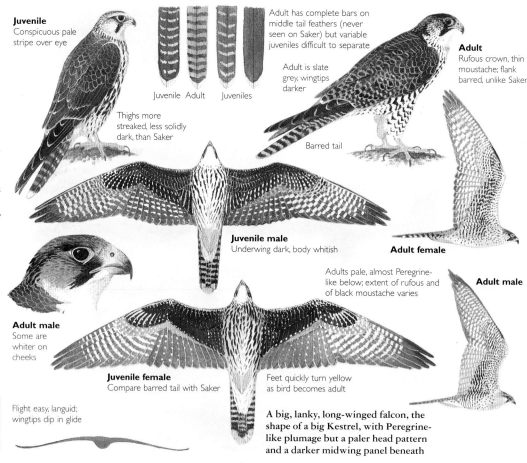

Juvenile Conspicuous pale stripe over eye

Thighs more streaked, less solidly dark, than Saker

Juvenile Adult Juveniles

Adult has complete bars on middle tail feathers (never seen on Saker) but variable juveniles difficult to separate

Adult is slate grey, wingtips darker

Barred tail

Adult Rufous crown, thin moustache; flank barred, unlike Saker

Juvenile male Underwing dark, body whitish

Adult female

Adults pale, almost Peregrine-like below; extent of rufous and of black moustache varies

Adult male

Adult male Some are whiter on cheeks

Juvenile female Compare barred tail with Saker

Feet quickly turn yellow as bird becomes adult

Flight easy, languid; wingtips dip in glide

A big, lanky, long-winged falcon, the shape of a big Kestrel, with Peregrine-like plumage but a paler head pattern and a darker midwing panel beneath

Saker *Falco cherrug*

This is one of the biggest falcons: a massively built and impressive bird. It is extremely rare in Europe, with just a handful of pairs west of the Ukraine. It is a bird of the steppe, inhabiting mixed forest and pasture, uncultivated grasslands and the edges of marshes. It often perches on telegraph poles on plains.

FEEDING Sakers are not bird-eaters like Peregrines or Lanners: they prefer to eat mammals, especially sousliks but also a smaller number of rats, voles, moles, lemmings, marmots, and hares. Medium-sized birds, reptiles, amphibians, and large insects form a minor part of their diet. Sakers watch from a perch and take prey in short, sudden dashes to the ground, although they are powerful birds in flight.

VOICE The hoarse, repetitive screeching calls resemble those of other large falcons and are often used near the nest.

MIGRATION Eastern Sakers move to the Middle East and east Africa in winter; a few remain in the Mediterranean area.

LENGTH 48–57cm (19–22in)

WHEN TO SEE All year
WHERE FOUND Extreme E Europe; rare in winter in Italy, Balkans, Sardinia

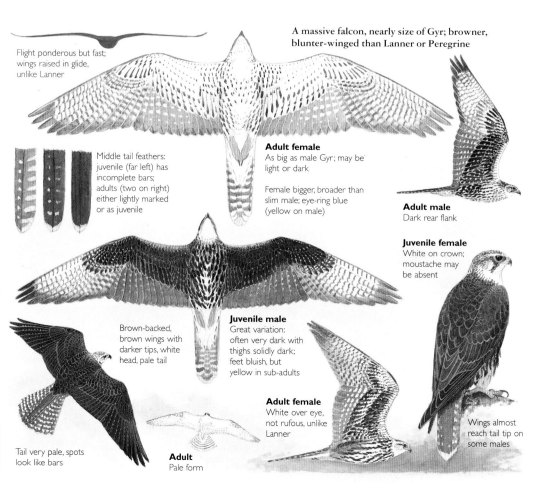

Flight ponderous but fast; wings raised in glide, unlike Lanner

A massive falcon, nearly size of Gyr; browner, blunter-winged than Lanner or Peregrine

Middle tail feathers: juvenile (far left) has incomplete bars; adults (two on right) either lightly marked or as juvenile

Adult female As big as male Gyr; may be light or dark

Female bigger, broader than slim male; eye-ring blue (yellow on male)

Adult male Dark rear flank

Juvenile female White on crown; moustache may be absent

Brown-backed, brown wings with darker tips, white head, pale tail

Juvenile male Great variation: often very dark with thighs solidly dark; feet bluish, but yellow in sub-adults

Adult female White over eye, not rufous, unlike Lanner

Tail very pale, spots look like bars

Adult Pale form

Wings almost reach tail tip on some males

94

Levant Sparrowhawk *Accipiter brevipes*

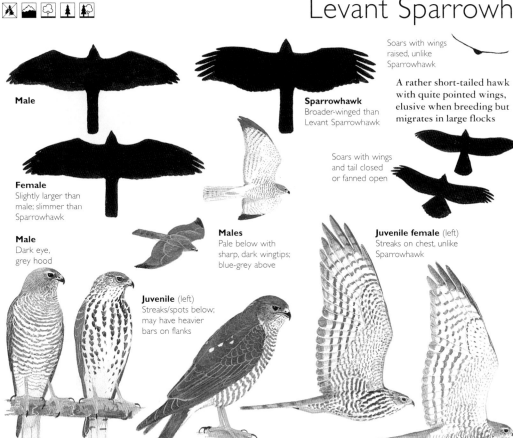

Male

Soars with wings raised, unlike Sparrowhawk

Sparrowhawk
Broader-winged than Levant Sparrowhawk

A rather short-tailed hawk with quite pointed wings, elusive when breeding but migrates in large flocks

Female
Slightly larger than male; slimmer than Sparrowhawk

Soars with wings and tail closed or fanned open

Male
Dark eye, grey hood

Males
Pale below with sharp, dark wingtips; blue-grey above

Juvenile female (left)
Streaks on chest, unlike Sparrowhawk

Juvenile (left)
Streaks/spots below; may have heavier bars on flanks

Female
Dumpy, thick-necked shape; broad rufous bars below; dark head; dark eye, unlike female Sparrowhawk

Sub-adult male
Mixed bars and streaks below; duller wingtips than adult

This large, slim hawk is usually seen in flight over wooded countryside; it is easiest to see on migration, when it forms large flocks. It tends to occupy lowland areas, while in southeast Europe the very similar Sparrowhawk is more commonly found in the mountains.

FEEDING It catches mice, voles, squirrels, and many small birds in low, fast hunting flights, as well as reptiles and insects. Much of the prey is captured after long spells of careful watching from a perch.

BREEDING Nests are usually built in deciduous trees, using slender sticks with a lining of finer material. Three to five eggs are laid; they hatch after about 30–35 days and the young fly when 40–45 days old.

MIGRATION In autumn all Levant Sparrowhawks leave Europe, probably for Ethiopia. They cross the Bosphorus between August and mid October and return in mid April. Large, swirling flocks are seen over a period of just a few days each season.

LENGTH 33–38cm (13–15in)

WHEN TO SEE April to October
WHERE FOUND Breeds sparsely in Albania, Greece, Bulgaria and Ukraine

Black-winged Kite *Elanus caeruleus*

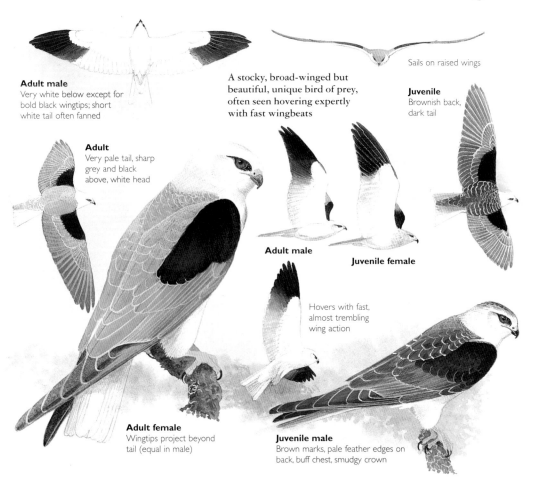

Adult male
Very white below except for bold black wingtips; short white tail often fanned

A stocky, broad-winged but beautiful, unique bird of prey, often seen hovering expertly with fast wingbeats

Sails on raised wings

Juvenile
Brownish back, dark tail

Adult
Very pale tail, sharp grey and black above, white head

Adult male

Juvenile female

Hovers with fast, almost trembling wing action

Adult female
Wingtips project beyond tail (equal in male)

Juvenile male
Brown marks, pale feather edges on back, buff chest, smudgy crown

A small, pale, thickset, but extremely buoyant bird of prey, the Black-winged Kite is more typical of the narrow green strip beside the Nile in Egypt than of Europe, but a small, rather isolated population thrives in Iberia. It is typically seen as a distinctive grey-and-white bird perched in a tree or wire, or hovering like a big, soft-winged, bulky Kestrel over a field or marsh. It favours flat countryside with scattered trees or planted with shelter belts.

FEEDING Most of its prey consists of small animals such as insects, small reptiles, and small rodents, but it also catches some birds.

DISPLAY & VOICE Always elegant in flight, this species becomes a joy to watch in display: it flies up in high spirals, wings beating quickly, then dives or glides down with its wings raised in a V, often with its legs dangling. It calls with whistling notes, like *kyu-it* or *kuee*.

BREEDING It usually nests in flat-topped thorn trees, laying 3–4 eggs.

MIGRATION Resident.

LENGTH 31–34cm (12–13½in)

WHEN TO SEE All year
WHERE FOUND S Portugal and, more rarely, SW Spain

Pheasant *Phasianus colchicus*

Two thousand years ago Pheasants from Asia were introduced to Greece; they were widely introduced to most of northwest Europe only two hundred years ago, but in Britain they have been present since about the 11th century. Bred and released in huge numbers for shooting, they have become widespread and familiar. Many released birds are ridiculously tame, and some enter parks and large gardens where they may survive as ornamental birds. A few, however, live much wilder lives in woodland, on the bushy edges of heathland and, in winter, in and around freshwater marshes with reedbeds, assorted scrub, and mixed woodland. Because of the history of introductions from various parts of Asia, coupled with the effects of breeding and releasing a wide variety of forms, 'wild' Pheasants can be seen in a number of colour variations – but they all have the same basic shape which makes them easy to identify.

FEEDING A Pheasant uses its strong legs and feet to scratch and scrape for earthworms, grubs, and berries in soft earth and thick leaf litter. Its muscular neck gives it a powerful, chicken-like lunge and pecking action. Coupled with its stout, slightly hooked beak, this makes the Pheasant a capable predator, able to kill and eat small creatures from beetles to lizards, and sometimes even small snakes. Much of its food, however, consists of grain, seeds, and berries.

DISPLAY & VOICE A male trying to impress a female uses his colourful plumage and long tail to best effect. He corners the hen, striding around and in front of her, demanding attention as he leans towards her, twisting his tail over and drooping one wing. His territorial call is a loud crow, *korrk-kok*, followed by a burst of rapid wingbeats. Alarm calls are repeated *kok-kok* notes, often becoming a series of calls with a squeaky, hiccuping quality, *kok-kok-i-kok, i-kok, i-kok*. Females are quieter but make a variety of purring and *kia kia* sounds.

BREEDING Females nesting 'wild' rear one brood each year with no help from the male. The nest is on the ground among dead leaves, dense brambles, or other thick plants, with little or no lining. Up to 15 plain olive eggs hatch after 23–28 days. The chicks can fly when still small, just 12 days old, but are not fully grown or properly independent for up to 12 weeks.

MIGRATION Pheasants are sedentary.
LENGTH Males 75–90cm (30–35in); females 52–64cm (21–25in)

WHEN TO SEE All year
WHERE FOUND N and central Europe except N Scandinavia

Female

Male

Males

A striking, long-tailed, heavy-bodied gamebird, often tame where released for shooting but more wary and wild where it has become naturalized

Flies low and straight with bursts of fast wingbeats between flat glides. When disturbed at close range bursts up with startling call and clatter of wings

Male
Variant with no white neck ring

Male
Males variable: most have white neck ring; variants look blacker, creamy-bodied or even brown-headed

Male
Scarce variety, almost wholly glossy green-black

Roosts in trees but otherwise a ground bird

Female
Longer-legged, longer-tailed, more triangular and chicken-like than partridges or grouse

Male
Typical plumage: richly varied with coppery flanks, redder back, and dark brown, creamy or green rump

Juvenile
Smaller, shorter-tailed than female at first, can fly well before fully grown

Capercaillie *Tetrao urogallus*

A giant woodland grouse, rare and elusive, usually seen only at long range flying away from an open area, or at close range flushed from a tree top or dense heather, clattering away in a flurry of powerful wingbeats

Male
Flying away, gliding on stiff, drooped, fingered wings; head outstretched, tail long and rounded

Male
Grey-brown contrast often lost at longer range or in poor light, can look almost black overall

Juvenile female
Richly-coloured, beautifully patterned with inky-black, much white barring on fresh feathers; broad, round tail rufous barred black, contrasts with grey rump

Shown to larger scale than male for clarity of detail

Female (right)
Bright orange-chestnut breastband, much white underneath

Male has bold white underwing patch, round tail held closed in flight

Roosts low in tree with clear escape route

Male
Big, turkey-like, with waxy dark tail feathers barred white, white 'shoulder' spot, green gloss on chest; displays with fanned tail to female, shown to same scale

Female
Grey above with tail and breastband contrastingly rusty; white legs

Juvenile female
Darker above than adult, darker legs

Female is bigger than female Black Grouse, with rounder, redder tail, brighter chest and bolder black flank bars

Male
Brown wings; pale bill; tail feathers large, square-tipped, waxy, with white spots; moulted tail feathers often found in woods

An encounter with a belligerent 'rogue' male Capercaillie in spring is a memorable experience. It might end in tears, with a hefty, vicious peck from that big, hooked bill. A few highly-charged individuals famously attack anything from intruding humans to red Post Office vans, and they are not to be taken lightly. In the main, however, Capercaillies are shy and secretive: so elusive, in fact, that to see one at all is an achievement. Usually the best that can be expected is a distant view of one in flight, retreating from a forest clearing into the depths of the woods, or a brief, close view as one clatters up from the deep heather to disappear almost instantly behind a big pine.

In most parts of their fragmented range, as in the Pyrenees, Capercaillies are so scarce that it is extremely difficult to find one. In northern Scotland they have declined and are restricted to a few extensive tracts of ancient Caledonian pine – some of the most wonderful and attractive forests in the world. They are threatened by the effects of overgrazing by sheep and deer (which reduces the shrub and herb layer and prevents the forest from regenerating) and deer fencing: Capercaillies often fly into these high fences, with fatal results. Predators and cold, wet spring weather also take their toll on one of Europe's most fascinating, unusual birds.

FEEDING Capercaillies eat mainly shoots, seeds, berries, and buds, in particular of bilberry and cowberry, supplemented by pine needles in winter. In summer they feed mainly on the ground; in winter they are more often in the tree tops.

DISPLAY & VOICE A male Capercaillie displays with drooped wings, raised and fanned tail and head erect, his 'beard' of spiky throat feathers puffed out and his bill open, producing a peculiar mixture of crackles and rattling sounds running into loud, hollow 'popping' notes like a series of pulled corks. Where they are still numerous, the males display at forest 'leks', while the females look on from the sidelines to choose the best, fittest males with which to mate. Females make a Pheasant-like *kok-kok*.

BREEDING Nests are on the ground, at the foot of trees. Up to eight eggs are laid; they hatch after 24–26 days and the young flutter when still small at 14 days. They become independent after 10 to 12 weeks. Only the females take an interest in rearing the chicks.

MIGRATION Resident, moving only locally when forced to by bad weather.

LENGTH Males 86cm (34in); females 60cm (24in)

WHEN TO SEE All year
WHERE TO SEE Pine forests, very locally in Scandinavia, E Europe, N Scotland, Alps, Pyrenees

Ptarmigan *Lagopus mutus*

Throughout the year the Ptarmigan thrives in some of the most inhospitable terrain on Earth: the cold, near-barren tundra of the far north. Where tundra conditions prevail on high mountains it occurs further south at increasing altitudes, in the Highlands of Scotland, the Alps, and the Pyrenees. In these regions it lives on the highest ground on gravelly, boulder-strewn ridges and plateaux with short shrubby vegetation, but in Iceland it lives practically at sea level.

FEEDING In summer small insects are its main food, especially for chicks, but otherwise it relies on a dry, tough diet of shoots, buds, berries, and seeds.

DISPLAY & VOICE Males fly up steeply then glide down, calling with deep, throaty croaks: *err-ook-kakakaka, kwa, kwa, kwa*; other calls are hard, cackling notes with an accelerating rhythm.

BREEDING The hen incubates up to nine eggs in a shallow scrape between boulders for 21–26 days; the chicks fly when just two weeks old.

LENGTH 34–36cm (13–14in)

WHEN TO SEE All year
WHERE FOUND Iceland, Faeroes, N and central Scandinavia, Scotland, Alps, Pyrenees

In much of Europe this is a mountain bird; in the far north it lives on lower, exposed ground. White wings separate it from all but similar Willow Grouse in the north; in winter the male's black face patch is distinctive

White in winter except tail; flight fast on stiff wings; fast beats between rocking glides

Adult, winter

Adult, summer

Juvenile

Female, breeding Scotland

Female, breeding Alps/Pyrenees

Male, winter (above)

Female, early spring (above)

Adult male White feathers appear in autumn and may remain in spring to give heavily spotted look

Female, late summer

Black Grouse *Tetrao tetrix*

Sadly this spectacular bird is one of the most threatened in Europe. It is declining fast, and already long gone from many parts of its former range. It requires a mixture of grassland, heather moorland, or rough heath, and damp, rushy hillsides, plus open woodland (for which young plantations are only a poor substitute). Such diversity of habitat is becoming scarce, especially under the pressure of modern farming.

FEEDING The Black Grouse's diet reflects its habitat, as it successively takes buds, shoots, leaves, berries, and fruit from heather, bilberry, and other shrubs and trees. Insects, including caterpillars, are extremely important for young chicks in summer.

DISPLAY & VOICE Males display competitively at traditional 'lek' sites, sparring with fanned tails, fluffed-out body plumage and swollen wattles. The watching females select the fittest mates. Calls include explosive sneezes and a far-carrying, musical cooing.

BREEDING Females incubate 6–10 eggs for 23–27 days in a scrape; the chicks flutter at just 10–14 days old.

LENGTH 40–55cm (16–22in)

WHEN TO SEE All year
WHERE FOUND Rare UK, Alps, more in Scandinavia, rare Germany and E Europe

Juvenile female

Female tail notched (can look square); lacks dark corners of Red Grouse

Fine white wingbar

Northern, greyer Scandinavian and Russian females can have male-type wingbars, centre white spot or none at all. Some females have lyre tails.

Long wings white below

Bold white underwing

Red wattles enlarge in display; neck very blue in good light

Males, breeding Bold white wingbars; curly tail

A beautiful large grouse of the moorland edge. Male unmistakable, female like other grouse or Pheasant, but with notched tail and pale wingbars

Whitish undertail

Adult female Variegated grey-brown, black, buff. Juvenile more rufous, plainer

Willow Grouse *Lagopus lagopus*

Male, summer

Adult, winter

Male, winter
Note heavy bill.
Neither sex has black
face of male Ptarmigan

A thickset, short-legged, round-
headed gamebird of northern
forest and tundra, with white
wings (and white body in winter)
similar to Ptarmigan

Male, spring
Reddish head contrasts
with white body unlike
Ptarmigan

Female, spring

Male, late summer
More rufous than
Ptarmigan, much
less barred

Female, late summer
Slightly larger, thicker-billed
than Ptarmigan, face and
throat more buff, less grey

This is the same species as the Red
Grouse of Britain and Ireland, but
in its mainland continental form. It has
a more striking appearance in spring,
when the males are partly white, and in
winter when they become white all over
like the Ptarmigan. It is more typical
of forest clearings and willow scrub
than the Red Grouse and is generally
found in high, mountainous regions.
FEEDING Like the Ptarmigan, the
Willow Grouse has a diet restricted to
mainly leathery leaves and shoots and
hard, dry seeds. It eats berries in late
summer and insects when they are
available: these are most important to
the development of the chicks.
DISPLAY & VOICE In spring males
stretch upwards, their red wattles
swollen, and call loudly with a series of
accelerating croaks. Startling, nasal
calls, frog-like but very loud, include a
rapid *ke-uk kekekekekekuh-uh-uhk.*
BREEDING Hens incubate 6–9 eggs in
a scrape on the ground for 19–25 days.
MIGRATION Resident.
LENGTH 37–42cm (14½–16½in)

WHEN TO SEE All year
WHERE FOUND Norway, N Sweden,
Finland, Estonia and eastwards into Russia

Red Grouse *Lagopus lagopus scoticus*

The 'Willow Grouse' of Britain and
Ireland, found on heather moorland.
Never has white wings or body
plumage – but darker, redder, more
barred than any partridge

Underwing shows variable
amount of white that may
change with moult, but
usually looks a dark bird

Male
Black tail, dark
outer wing
unlike partridges
or female Black
Grouse

Glides between bursts
of wingbeats

Male
In display flight

Flight fast, direct, on stiff,
arched wings, with long glides

Irish birds greyer
on back

Male, spring
Large red wattle;
some have white
on belly, white
spots on wing

Female
Paler, yellower
than male, less
olive than female
Black Grouse

Unique to Britain and Ireland, the
Red Grouse is now treated as a
race of the Willow Grouse. It lives
mainly on extensive heather moorland,
and it is common only where this
unnatural habitat is maintained and
managed for shooting. A few Red
Grouse live in more natural heathery
clearings in open, upland woods, and
on higher, exposed ground extending
up to the kind of mountain terrain
inhabited by Ptarmigan.
FEEDING It eats a variety of leaves,
shoots, and berries such as bilberry,
crowberry, and cowberry fruits; in
winter it plucks haws from trees at the
edge of the moor. The chicks need
moth caterpillars and other nutritious
invertebrates in summer.
DISPLAY & VOICE In spring displaying
males defy each other with loud,
crowing challenges from prominent
perches. The evocative calls are sudden,
loud outbursts of deep, grating, rapid
notes: *kr-rrrr r r kuk-kuk-ku huk,
go-bak go-bak go-bak, bak, bak.*
BREEDING Females lay 6–9 eggs in a
scrape; incubate them for 19–25 days.
LENGTH 37–42cm (14½–16½in)

WHEN TO SEE All year
WHERE FOUND Scotland, N England,
scarce SW England, Wales; Ireland

Rock Partridge *Alectoris graeca*

This scarce, or even rare and elusive bird lives on rocky or craggy slopes, often high up on mountains, sometimes where there is a scattering of bushes but often in really open, apparently barren locations. It prefers south-facing slopes. Hard to see on the ground, it usually reveals itself when accidentally flushed at close range. Even then it is not easy to distinguish from its relatives, but the range and habitat are useful clues.

FEEDING Like the Chukar the Rock Partridge finds its food on the ground, taking insects when it can but mostly subsisting on seeds and shoots.

VOICE The usual call is a four-syllable phrase, repeated at intervals: *chair tsirit-chee*. Other notes are sharp, clear calls: *vit vit* or *pit-chee pit-chee*.

BREEDING The nest is a simple scrape with a skimpy lining of leaves and stems. The 8–14 eggs are incubated for about 25 days and the chicks are fully grown at about eight weeks.

LENGTH 32–35cm (13–14in)

WHEN TO SEE All year
WHERE FOUND Alps and Balkans including most of Greece; highlands of Italy including Sicily

A boldly-marked partridge of high or barren rocky areas, mostly in southeast Europe, needing close examination for certain identification

Black against base of upper mandible distinctive if present

Head pattern varies; some have black under bill and gape

Brown bloom on back wears off to give greyer colour

Pure white throat, unlike Chukar

Tail feathers all rufous, unlike Chukar

Birds in Swiss Alps have narrow flank bars

Chukar *Alectoris chukar*   Barbary Partridge *Alectoris barbara*

In the extreme southeast of Europe and the Middle East the Chukar is familiar and frequent on warm, open ground and dry farmland, as well as rough, barren slopes to a high altitude in the mountains. It has been widely introduced (belatedly made illegal in the UK) so it occurs – either in 'pure' form or as a hybrid with the Red-legged Partridge – in many areas where it is not native. The Barbary Partridge is a bird of rocky hillsides, found in Gibraltar and Sardinia.

FEEDING Chukars forage like chickens on open ground, sometimes scratching with their feet. In summer insects supplement their vegetarian diet of seeds, shoots, and berries.

VOICE A series of short, loud, abrupt notes sound like a rhythmic *chuk chuk chuk chuk-ke-cher chuk-ke-cher*.

BREEDING Up to 12 eggs are laid in a scrape on the ground, and incubated by the hen for about 25 days. As with other gamebirds, the young can fly moderately well when still only half or three-quarters grown.

LENGTH 32–34cm (13–13½in)

WHEN TO SEE All year
WHERE FOUND Extreme E Europe; widely introduced (but often hybridized) elsewhere; Barbary Gibraltar and Sardinia

Chukar is a large, pale partridge of the warm southeast, scarce in Europe except where introduced. Barbary similar, but has distinctive head and neck

Red-legged × Chukar hybrid
Border of bib spotted beneath

Chukar
Face cream; border of bib neat, black

Chukar

Barbary Partridge
Gibraltar, Sardinia

All-rufous tail

Barbary Partridge
Gibraltar, Sardinia

Chukar
Base of tail feathers grey, unlike Rock and Red-legged Partridge

Grey face, spotted brown gorget, pale stripe beside nape

Red-legged Partridge *Alectoris rufa*

Of the plain-backed, white-faced partridges this is the neatest and most attractive, but it is threatened by interbreeding with released Chukars; compared with Grey Partridge it is larger, heavier, and boldly patterned on the face

Few Red-legged now remain in E England as most are hybrids with Chukars

Long white stripes over eyes almost meet on hindneck

All-rufous tail

Red bill, white face bordered by black, spotted neck and chest

Compared with Grey note plain back, broader flank bars, red legs and bill, white face

Red-legged

Grey

Red-legged   Grey

Larger, often more upright, faster-running, paler than Grey

Perhaps the most beautiful of the partridges, the Red-legged faces an uncertain future since in some places it hybridizes with the irresponsibly introduced Chukars. It is the western representative of the *Alectoris* group.

FEEDING Red-legs share the chicken-like ground-feeding behaviour of other partridges. They find leaves, shoots, roots, and seeds of cereals and grasses as well as tree seeds such as beech mast.

DISPLAY & VOICE Males often call loudly and rhythmically from high perches, including stacks of straw bales and roofs. The song has a 'chuffing' effect, like *kok-chak-kok-chak-kok-chak-chak*. Other calls are short, rather hollow *chuk*, *chuk-ar* or *tschreg* notes.

BREEDING A scrape in the ground, lined with leaves, serves as the nest; 10–16 eggs hatch after 23–24 days' incubation by the female. The male may incubate a second clutch nearby. The young fly after 10 days but are not full-grown for several weeks.

LENGTH 32–34cm (13–13½in)

WHEN TO SEE All year
WHERE FOUND France, N Italy, Spain and Portugal, Balearics, Corsica; also introduced in Britain, mostly England and S and E Scotland

Grey Partridge *Perdix perdix*

The native partridge of northern Europe and Britain, this small, shy, dumpy bird is a subtle beauty compared with the more colourful Red-legged Partridge and bolder Chukar

Grey

Red-legged

Red-legged

Grey flies on bowed wings; Red-legged flies with wings almost flat, slightly raised, before final landing flutter

Sides of tail rufous

Male

Female

Male

Cream underwing coverts, pale vent, dark breast patch distinctive

Some birds have very rufous back feathers

Simple deep brown flank bars; streaked upperparts; pale legs

Female

Dark horseshoe on lower breast most marked on male

The Grey or 'English' Partridge is the only one native to Britain and Ireland. It was once a distinctive feature of arable farmland and hay meadows, especially when calling in spring or in winter coveys, but like many farmland birds it has declined dramatically over most of western Europe in recent decades. Like other partridges it is sociable, often seen in groups of 10 to 20 or so.

FEEDING Chicks require insect larvae in summer; otherwise its diet consists largely of seeds, berries, green leaves, and shoots. It is the loss of insects and weed seeds from intensively cultivated farmland that has caused its decline.

DISPLAY & VOICE Males have a frequent 'song', especially in the evening: a loud, creaky, very pleasant *kee-err-ik*. As the bird takes flight it gives sharp, quick *ker-ik*, *krrip-krrip* and *kit-it* alarm notes.

BREEDING The 10–20 or more eggs are laid in a shallow nest in dense vegetation, and hatch after 23–25 days. Chicks flutter when 10 days old but are not fully grown for about 14 weeks.

LENGTH 29–31cm (11–12in)

WHEN TO SEE All year
WHERE FOUND Sparse and very local in Ireland; more widespread in Britain; widely from N Spain, France, S Norway eastwards

Hazel Grouse *Bonasa bonasia*

Principally a bird of mixed forest, found deep in shady, often damp, luxuriant places, the Hazel Grouse is usually seen when disturbed as it flies a short distance to settle in a tree. It is a wary bird, difficult to approach for a better view. In summer it spends most of its time on the ground, where it is quite agile, but in winter it lives mostly up in the trees.

FEEDING Hazel Grouse eat buds and shoots, leaves, berries, and seeds according to availability, plus ants, beetles, and caterpillars in summer.

DISPLAY & VOICE Males advertise their territories with whirring wings and calls, a sharp whistling song of five to nine notes and a pipit-like *srit-srit*.

BREEDING Pairs are monogamous; nests are well-hidden beneath bushes or tree stumps. Up to 11 eggs hatch after 25 days; the chicks can fly at 15–20 days but are not fully grown until about five weeks old.

MIGRATION Resident apart from short-distance movements in search of food in autumn and winter.

LENGTH 35–37cm (14–14½in)

WHEN TO SEE All year
WHERE FOUND Locally Norway, most of Sweden, Finland, Baltic states, Russia; local in Germany, Alps, Balkans, E Europe

A Woodpigeon-sized gamebird of dark forest with dense undergrowth, flying off early when approached and hard to see

Scandinavian birds tend to be grey (above); those living to south and west are more rufous (right)

Male flies with arched wings; grey tail/rump with black band

Female

Spiky nape

Male
Face pattern distinctive if seen

Loses some of rufous colour with wear; much minor individual variation in detail of pattern

Male
Long tail with black band; many white spots, scapular spots aligned in curved 'braces'; pale shafts and outer webs on primaries

Andalusian Hemipode *Turnix sylvatica*

Although this is a common and quite widespread bird in Africa south of the Sahara, in Europe it is all but extinct (indeed, it may be so) after a drastic decline during the past 150 years. In southern Spain it used to be common in coastal scrub, especially with dwarf palmetto; it was also found rarely in Sicily. It is still to be seen in Morocco, although the population is dwindling. It is very hard to observe in the wild, and therefore little known.

FEEDING It takes seeds and insects from the ground.

DISPLAY & VOICE Females dominate courtship, calling to males with a resonant, slowly repeated call, like wind through a pipe: *hoo, hoo, hoo*.

BREEDING The pattern of 'successive polyandry' is extremely unusual in European birds. The females probably mate with several males in succession. They lay a clutch of eggs for each male to incubate and the males care for the young. Incubation takes 12–14 days.

MIGRATION Probably sedentary in Europe and north Africa.

LENGTH 15–16cm (6–6½in)

WHEN TO SEE All year
WHERE FOUND Uncertain: perhaps a handful of pairs remain in extreme SW Spain but possibly extinct in Europe

A tiny, secretive ground-living bird of dry heathy ground with dwarf palm and similar scrub; exceedingly rare and elusive in Europe, although common in Africa (where known as the Small Button Quail)

Slightly smaller, shorter-winged than Quail, equally difficult to flush; runs fast in horizontal pose

Adult male
Paler, more gingery, than female; bolder black spotting onto flanks

If flushed, reveals broad, diffuse pale area on upperwing, with darker flight feathers

Adult female
Darker, especially on back, than male

May still be present in Spain and Sicily; lack of habitat knowledge may have prevented sightings: waste areas and land near human habitation are possible sites

Corncrake *Crex crex*

Flies low on bowed, rufous wings, with legs trailed

Grey-faced male sings with head raised

Female
More orange than male

A remarkably secretive bird of dense vegetation, rarely seen but often heard on breeding grounds

Male
May look rather dark and grey, with well-barred flanks

Since it spends much of its time concealed in dense, low vegetation the Corncrake is hard to glimpse, but often heard. In spring males may emerge into the open, calling from small clearings and running between iris beds or even along stone walls. But once the grass grows Corncrakes are all but invisible. Early hay cutting has led to a drastic decline almost everywhere, and a huge reduction in range.

FEEDING Corncrakes eat small insects, other invertebrates, and some seeds.

DISPLAY & VOICE Males 'sing' with their heads raised and bills opening with each call, as if 'throwing' the sound across the fields: a loud, hard, rasping *crek-crek*. At a distance the sound has a light, dry quality; close-up, especially at night, it is a loud, ratchet-like, echoing rattle: *brrrp-brrrp*.

BREEDING Laid in dense cover, the 8–12 eggs hatch after 16–19 days.

MIGRATION Most arrive in their breeding areas and leave for Africa in autumn without being seen elsewhere.

LENGTH 27–30cm (10½–12in)

WHEN TO SEE April to October
WHERE FOUND Locally W Ireland, W Scotland, France, W Norway, S Sweden, Russia, Poland, central and E Europe

Quail *Coturnix coturnix*

A small, plump gamebird, rarely seen but frequently heard in breeding areas in summer: liquid triple note repeatedly given from dense cereal crops or hay meadows

Rises at great speed; generally flight is low, fast, with continuous flapping

Migrants have strong, fast, whirring flight

Stocky, sharp-winged, very short-tailed

Call has ventriloquial quality, apparently coming from nearby when bird is too far away to be seen

Male
Striped above, boldly marked head, black throat

Female
Bright with weaker version of male's face pattern

A mysterious voice in the cereal fields, the Quail is easy to hear but hard to see. In many areas it fluctuates, declining locally in years when cereals are replaced by other crops such as rape. It may cope well with clover, however, and still breeds in its natural habitat of extensive grasslands and steppe.

FEEDING Quail pick seeds from the ground; insects are important in summer, especially for the chicks.

DISPLAY & VOICE The male circles the female with his throat feathers puffed out. His far-carrying territorial song is a liquid but abrupt *whit, whit-it*, repeated for long spells throughout the summer. A nasal, doll-like *ma-ma* can sometimes be heard at close range.

BREEDING The clutch is usually 8–13 eggs, but may be as many as 18; laid in thick cover, they hatch in 17–20 days.

MIGRATION Quails once gathered in their thousands on the Mediterranean coast. Now they migrate in smaller numbers, although they can still be abundant, especially in the east.

LENGTH 16–18cm (6½–7in)

WHEN TO SEE March to October
WHERE FOUND Widespread north to North Sea and Baltic; fluctuating numbers, especially in north of range in Britain, Ireland, Scandinavia, W Russia

Water Rail *Rallus aquaticus*

The classic Water Rail habitats are reedbeds and freshwater marshes, but they can be found almost anywhere that is wet: a flooded ditch beneath willows and alders, for example, is good enough for a Water Rail or two to creep about in, quietly, during winter. Here they are elusive but not really shy: with patience it is possible to get superb close-up views. From the side they look round and dumpy, especially in cold weather, but a typical tail-end view shows how remarkably thin and compressed this species is.

FEEDING Water Rails eat a variety of insects, aquatic molluscs, and newts, plus berries, shoots, and even small birds in hard weather.

VOICE Most calls are loud, screaming or whistling, rather pig-like squeals.

BREEDING Nests are neat, just off the ground, in reeds or willows; up to 11 eggs are incubated for 19–22 days.

MIGRATION Northern birds move west and south in autumn, reaching the UK and Ireland from September to April.

LENGTH 22–28cm (9–11in)

WHEN TO SEE All year; in most areas, mainly from August to April
WHERE TO SEE Sparse breeder Iceland, UK and Ireland, much of W, central and E Europe; more widespread in west in winter

Tail often flicked

Low fluttering flight

Juvenile, first winter Flanks blurred with buff, underside finely barred with white feather tips; dark eye

Juvenile

Males often much larger than females, but sizes overlap

Adult Immaculate blue-grey below; sub-adults marked with buff; red on bill varies

White flank bars vary; long, red-pink toes

Not always shy, but stays close to cover and runs into reeds or flooded willows if startled. Looks small, round in side view but very narrow end-on, with spiky bill, long toes. Seen on salt marshes during winter

Underneath tail variable, allowing identification of individuals

Striking pale patch under tail shows as bird runs off

White barring on outer coverts varies with no relation to sex or age

Flight low, quick, tail-heavy, legs trailed

Male Longer, thicker bill

Female

Spotted Crake *Porzana porzana*

This is a remarkably difficult bird to see, but like other crakes and rails it is not so much shy as elusive. At times it appears on open mud or at the edge of a reedbed and trots about in full view, just a few metres away; it will even feed on an angler's stock of worms. A quiet observer can then see the true beauty of its complicated, delicate plumage pattern, and the superb sheeny quality of its feathers. A more typical view is a brief glimpse of the bird in flight, often rising from almost underfoot, before it drops down to be lost for good in dense vegetation.

FEEDING It eats insects, worms, seeds, and berries, mostly picking them from mud beneath reeds or from low stems.

VOICE In spring it repeats a rhythmic, whiplash-like or water-dripping *whit-whit-whit* at dusk; also a hard ticking.

BREEDING Nests in dense, wet vegetation in marshes, incubating two broods of 8–12 eggs for 18–19 days.

MIGRATION In August and September moves south from N and E Europe through W Europe, returning in April.

LENGTH 22–24cm (9–9½in)

WHEN TO SEE Mostly March–April and August–November in W Europe
WHERE TO SEE Sparsely across Europe except extreme N and S; rare in UK

Very dark back; stripy white-edged scapulars

Flight quick, with Snipe-like flurry of wings; sudden 'collapse' into cover

White leading edge to wing visible as bird rises; very obvious in aggressive display

Buff undertail; pale streak on inner edge of tertials

Secretive, shuffling, sometimes almost rat-like bird of water's edge; good views reveal beautiful, richly barred, and spotted plumage. Bill short, pale with orange-red at base, legs green

Broad white fore edge and barred coverts under wing; compare Water Rail (right)

Male, spring Beautifully marked; by August, flank bars and chest spots may wear away. Intense bill colour but dull eye

Female, spring Browner face and chest, less grey than male

Juvenile Paler flanks barred white, white belly

Spotted Crake

Water Rail

Female Worn duller in August, hint of dark chin

Little Crake *Porzana parva*

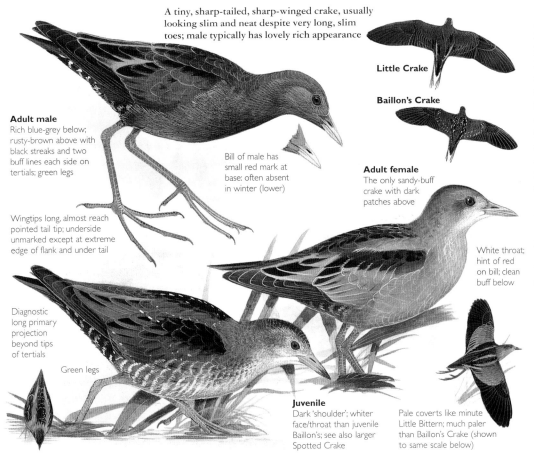

A tiny, sharp-tailed, sharp-winged crake, usually looking slim and neat despite very long, slim toes; male typically has lovely rich appearance

Little Crake

Baillon's Crake

Adult male
Rich blue-grey below; rusty-brown above with black streaks and two buff lines each side on tertials; green legs

Bill of male has small red mark at base: often absent in winter (lower)

Wingtips long, almost reach pointed tail tip; underside unmarked except at extreme edge of flank and under tail

Adult female
The only sandy-buff crake with dark patches above

White throat; hint of red on bill; clean buff below

Diagnostic long primary projection beyond tips of tertials

Green legs

Juvenile
Dark 'shoulder'; whiter face/throat than juvenile Baillon's; see also larger Spotted Crake

Pale coverts like minute Little Bittern; much paler than Baillon's Crake (shown to same scale below)

A patient watcher, concealed in a hide at a nature reserve in eastern Europe or the Middle East, may be lucky enough to see a Little Crake in full view as it forages along the edge of a dyke: a smart little bird, beautifully coloured, with a gloss like polished stone. In western Europe a rare vagrant may provide just the briefest glimpse as it crosses a gap between two clumps of reed, then vanish for good – often leaving the observer wondering if it really was a Little Crake, or something similar but less rare.

FEEDING Like other crakes and rails it creeps about at the edges of reedbeds, reedmace thickets, and reedy ditches or pools, picking tiny insects and molluscs from the mud.

VOICE The song is a low croak accelerating into a hard, staccato trill.

BREEDING Nests irregularly in a few scattered sites in France and Iberia.

MIGRATION A few from eastern Europe move west in autumn, but in western Europe it is a very rare bird everywhere.

LENGTH 18–20cm (7–8in)

WHEN TO SEE Most vagrants in late autumn and early winter in W Europe
WHERE FOUND Breeds in NE Europe and irregularly elsewhere in W Europe; rare vagrant outside breeding range

Baillon's Crake *Porzana pusilla*

A tiny, sparrow-sized, rounded, blunt-ended crake; colours recall Spotted Crake but rich brown back has bold black marks and flecks, splashes and rings of white; green bill has no trace of red

Tail tip well beyond wing point; very short visible primary projection beyond tertials

Adult male
Dark grey face and breast but white-barred flanks; red eye; tertials lack pale streak

Bill pale green (red base on Little and Spotted Crake); red eye often striking (dull on Little Crake); legs pale pinkish to green

Feathers on back have unique long white spots edged black, with black spots in centre

Legs may be pinker than Little Crake

Bill grey-green; eye dull like Little Crake: try to check structure and tertial pattern

Juvenile
Darker than juvenile Little Crake; less boldly patterned above but close flecks of white on black streaks

Adult female
White marks on scapulars form slight zigzag effect not seen on Little Crake; flanks more barred, forward almost to bend of wing. In typical quick glimpse, look for tail/wing position, flank pattern, and spots on back

Of all the crakes this is the tiniest, like a minute ball of animated feathers; quick, elusive, and hard to watch. A sure identification relies on checking a few fine details, but seeing them is a challenge. To most people in Europe, crakes are just impossible. In favoured places in eastern Europe and the Middle East they can be watched at close range, but even vagrants in the west may be remarkably tame, as if totally oblivious to human presence.

FEEDING The bird eats tiny aquatic invertebrates, seeds, and shoots as it forages beneath sedges, rushes, reeds, and other swamp vegetation. Quite small ditches and drainage channels are suitable for it while on migration.

VOICE The song is a dry, rising and falling rattle that lasts two or three seconds, like the 'song' of an Edible Frog. It is quiet, and carries less well than the calls of other crakes and rails.

MIGRATION In autumn breeding birds from central Europe move south into Africa for the winter; they are rare vagrants in western Europe, and very rarely seen in Britain.

LENGTH 17–19cm (7–7½in)

WHEN TO SEE Spring and autumn
WHERE FOUND Extreme E Europe; very sparse in central Europe; vagrant elsewhere

Coot *Fulica atra*

Whether splashing about in quarrelsome groups on a town park lake or large reservoir, or feeding quietly on a grassy bank beside a river or – especially in winter – by the coast, Coots are among the most familiar of water birds. Except for their rather drab young, they are really quite unmistakable.

FEEDING Coots graze on grass but also feed a lot in water, diving under regularly and popping back up like corks. They eat seeds, insects, snails, and tadpoles as well as aquatic plants.

DISPLAY & VOICE Coots often fight like Moorhens, using their feet as they lie back on the water. They make a short, squawking *kowk*, a higher *teuk* and *kt-towk* and a sudden *ptik!*

BREEDING Nests are large affairs at the water's edge, often in overhanging branches or reeds; six to nine eggs hatch after 21–24 days' incubation.

MIGRATION Many move to larger lakes and reservoirs in winter; eastern European birds move west in autumn.

LENGTH 36–38cm (14–15in)

WHEN TO SEE All year; in N and E Europe, mostly March to September
WHERE FOUND Breeds most of Europe except Iceland, N Scandinavia, but only local and widely scattered in much of S Europe

Adults
Flight quick but heavy, little agility; wings paler than body; legs trail

Pale trailing edge obvious; weak in immature birds

Grazing birds flee to water if disturbed

Female   **Male, breeding**

First year has pale chin

A squat, round-backed, low-tailed, duck-like water bird, slaty-black with a bold white facial shield and bill; often in flocks on open water, especially in winter

Large grey-green feet with broadly-lobed toes

Grazing birds walk forwards, pulling head back and sideways to crop grass

Juvenile has white face and chest, dull body: (compare smaller grebes)

Purple Gallinule *Porphyrio porphyrio* Crested Coot *Fulica cristata*

The Purple Gallinule is a truly magnificent bird of dense marsh vegetation. In Europe it is rare and very localized, found beside shallow freshwater pools (but in Africa also beside large rivers). The Crested Coot is confined to marshes in the Seville area of southern Spain.

FEEDING Purple Gallinules eat plant stems and roots (especially the soft pith from rushes), often uprooting and holding them in their huge feet while using their bills to rip them apart. Crested Coots dive for food like Coots.

VOICE Purple Gallinules make many strange noises, including a sharp *chock-chock* and a remarkable booming or mooing. Crested Coots call like Coots, but they also have a 'groaning' or 'moaning' note.

MIGRATION Both are essentially resident; but some wander with changes in temporary wetland habitat.

LENGTH Purple Gallinule 45–50cm (18–20in); Crested Coot 38–42cm (15–16½in)

WHEN TO SEE All year
WHERE FOUND Purple Gallinule in extreme SW Spain, S Portugal, Sardinia; Crested Coot in SW Spain

May swim with tail up

Crested Coot, breeding
Red knobs on forehead, nape low, sloping

Crested Coot resembles Coot but has more prominent hump at rear end, triangular shield and, in breeding season, red knobs. Purple Gallinule is much bigger: a dramatically coloured but secretive bird of tall marsh vegetation

Crested Coot, non-breeding
Lacks red knobs; bluish bill, white shield; shield more triangular than Coot

Coot
Rounder head, less sloping nape

Crested Coot
Unlike Coot, no pale trailing edge nor whitish leading edge to underwing

Purple Gallinule, immature
Dull, greyish beneath

Purple Gallinules
Large, long-legged, long-toed; huge bright red shield and bill, white undertail

Moorhen *Gallinula chloropus*

A familiar riverside, farm pond, and lake bird; shy; quick to run or skitter across water into cover; may even dive and stay underwater with only bill-tip protruding. White flank stripe and patches under tail diagnostic

Flight quite swift and strong despite shallow flaps; usually low over water but may fly from trees or high over meadows

Male
Upperparts rich brown, glossy in good light; immaculate

Constantly flicks tail up to reveal black and white beneath, on land or on water; walks easily, with springy rhythm

Swims with head forward, bobbing rhythmically with tail/wingtips higher than back, unlike Coot

Female
Duller, paler than male, paler on belly

Juvenile
Browner than young Coot, no white on breast but white line along side

Head and bill of juvenile grey by late October

Sub-adult
Black-tipped bill

Chick
Red bill and wing, blue over eye

White flank stripe unmistakable; adult has yellow-green legs with red 'garter' at top; very long, slender toes

Adult male
Thickest bill, gleaming red and yellow

Adult female
Slightly slimmer bill than male

Juvenile
Bill dark, without frontal shield

Often flies about at night, even over towns, calling *kek kek*

Adult male
Broader wings than female; length from rear of wing to tail tip longer than on female

Adult female
Narrower wings than male; rear body/tail length shorter

Sooty grey underwing except for white leading edge; some birds have subtle paler barring

Many people know and admire the Moorhen when they see it on a town park lake or river backwater. Others perhaps wonder what manner of bird it is that skitters across the river with fluttering wings and disappears into the fringing vegetation at the least hint of disturbance. Although it is widespread, the Moorhen has declined where rivers have been straightened, deepened, and 'tidied up' by clearing away the bankside rushes and sedges. Unlike Coots, Moorhens cannot survive in such scoured, open, bleak surroundings: they must have some dense vegetation cover. Yet they also feed out on open fields, often in pastures with horses or sheep, although always just a short, fast run from the nearest hedge. They venture into gardens and orchards and climb old, gnarled apple trees and hawthorns, surprisingly at home high off the ground. Sometimes they even nest in such elevated places. Moorhens are noisy, quite highly-strung birds, very likely to pick fights with intruders of their own kind, especially in spring. It is not easy to overlook them.

FEEDING The Moorhen's diet reflects its habitat: shoots, seeds, buds, and berries from water plants, water beetles and other aquatic invertebrates, snails, tadpoles, worms, and almost any edible bits and pieces gathered from the waterside. Much of its food is found on dry land. The Moorhen does not dive to feed, although it can and does submerge when pressed.

DISPLAY & VOICE Fights and chases are frequent, the birds using their long toes and sharp claws to good effect. The displays exploit the white flank stripes and white patches on each side of the raised tail; these can be expanded and flirted to maximize their impact. Calls include a sharp, sudden, metallic but rather deep *kurruck* or *kittik*; high *kik* or *kek* notes and a rapid, stuttering *kik kik-ikikikik*.

BREEDING Moorhen nests are small and neat; not huge, high platforms like the largest Coot nests. A nest is often made where an overhanging branch brushes the water of a pond or stream. A central cup of fine stems holds up to 11 buff eggs; these hatch after 21–22 days. The chicks are fed for 40–50 days until they can fly; in late summer the young of second broods are often fed by those of earlier broods reared in spring.

MIGRATION Some NW European birds move south to Britain in winter. Most W European Moorhens are resident.

LENGTH 32–35cm (12½–14in)

WHEN TO SEE All year; in Scandinavia and NE Europe, only spring to autumn
WHERE FOUND Lakes, rivers, pools; most of Europe except N Scandinavia, Iceland, high Alps, and other mountainous, bleak, or dry areas

Great Bustard *Otis tarda*

One of the truly great birds of Europe in every sense, this is also one of the most threatened. It is a big bird that needs big spaces, and cannot tolerate modern, intensive farming. That leaves its future deeply uncertain in the face of agricultural pressure throughout its range.

FEEDING Bustards stride open spaces in search of food, which they take from the ground: mostly plants, including seeds, but also insects, small rodents (which they eat in large numbers if they are abundant), and reptiles.

DISPLAY When they display on open ground the males seem to turn themselves inside out as they fan their wings and tails and inflate their necks to reveal large areas of startling white plumage. They are silent birds.

BREEDING Females incubate 2–3 eggs for 21–28 days, in shallow hollows.

MIGRATION In the west they gather into flocks in winter within their usual range; eastern populations move south and west in winter.

LENGTH 75–105cm (29½–41in)

WHEN TO SEE All year; autumn/winter vagrant in NW Europe
WHERE FOUND Breeds Iberia, very locally E Germany, Poland, E Europe

Immense terrestrial bird, but a powerful flier, easily identified by its combination of large size and bold white wing patches

Flight majestic, constant beats of 'fingered' wings

Male much bigger than female; grey head and neck, ginger-brown shawl and back, white belly

Little Bustard (to scale)

Male

Female

Male

Female

Female

Male

Female has narrower wing; immature male (far right) has white as female, wing shape as adult male

Female

Male
Wispy 'moustache' in spring; white often shows on closed wing ;less orange, more buff as plumage fades

Female
Less white on wing. Both sexes can be blacker above when pale tips wear off

Adult females, juveniles, and immatures not distinguishable on ground

Little Bustard *Tetrax tetrax*

Although it is a true bustard, this species is much smaller and much quicker in its actions (especially in flight) than the Great Bustard; it often surprises people on first acquaintance. In winter Little Bustards form flocks and behave more like smaller gamebirds; in flight they are almost pigeon-like, an effect enhanced by their piebald pattern. Although still much more common in places than Great Bustards, Little Bustards are also declining practically everywhere. The males' wing feathers make a loud whistle in flight.

FEEDING It eats small rodents, insects, seeds, shoots, and berries, taking food from the ground or low plants in a slow, statuesque walk.

DISPLAY & VOICE Males inflate their necks and raise their black and white plumage as they give short calls and make quick, vertical leaps into the air.

BREEDING Three to four eggs laid in a scrape are incubated for 20–22 days.

MIGRATION Resident, but from France Little Bustards move south in winter.

LENGTH 40–45cm (16–18in)

WHEN TO SEE All year in south; summer only in central and NE France
WHERE FOUND France, Spain, locally in Sardinia, Balkans

Smallish terrestrial bird, long-legged, long-necked; in flight shows much white and moves surprisingly fast

Spread tail shows white sides, white coverts

Adult male, winter

Adult females

Adult female
Some have two or three dark bars across white

Inner primaries shorter than male's; narrow outer wing shape

Adult male has more white on primary coverts, broader wingtip

Adult male, breeding
Very short fourth primary (fourth equal to third in young males)

Short fourth primary creates high pitched whistling sound in flight

Adult male, breeding
Neck inflated in display; head pattern unique

Winter male resembles female

Displaying males puff out necks, flap and leap

Adult female
Shape and stance of both sexes unlike any other European species

Immature male, winter

Stone-curlew *Burhinus oedicnemus*

A stocky, pale, sandy-brown bird with an obvious pale base to the bill and pale stripe under the eye; boldly marked in flight. Habitat and range are useful clues. Often hard to spot by day, more often heard than seen; calls at night in flight and on the ground

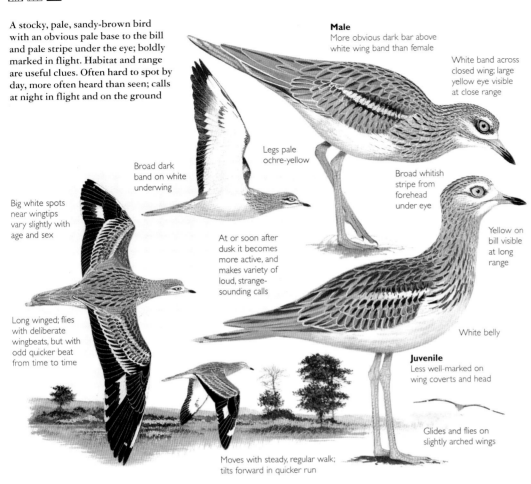

Male
More obvious dark bar above white wing band than female

White band across closed wing; large yellow eye visible at close range

Broad dark band on white underwing

Legs pale ochre-yellow

Broad whitish stripe from forehead under eye

Big white spots near wingtips vary slightly with age and sex

Yellow on bill visible at long range

At or soon after dusk it becomes more active, and makes variety of loud, strange-sounding calls

Long winged; flies with deliberate wingbeats, but with odd quicker beat from time to time

White belly

Juvenile
Less well-marked on wing coverts and head

Glides and flies on slightly arched wings

Moves with steady, regular walk; tilts forward in quicker run

This peculiar, elusive 'wader' of dry, sandy heaths and flinty fields is most active before dawn and at dusk, when its strange wailing and whistling calls, like a mixture of Curlew and Oystercatcher, may betray its presence. By day it stands or crouches near cover or in the shade of a tree, and even in full view it is difficult to spot against pale, dry grassland.

FEEDING It feeds on large insects picked from the ground.

DISPLAY & VOICE Calls play a large part in the courtship displays, as do stiff bowing postures and wings spread to reveal their black and white patterns. The normal calls include a sharp *kit kit kit* and a liquid *cloo-ee*.

BREEDING The nest is a shallow scoop in the soil; the two chicks fly when 36–42 days old and return to breed when three years old.

MIGRATION Flocks form after breeding and fly to Spain and north Africa in October. They return in March or April.

LENGTH 40–44cm (16–17in)

WHEN TO SEE All year in Spain, elsewhere March to October
WHERE FOUND Open farmland, heaths, stony steppe; southern England east to southern Russia and south to the Mediterranean

---

Collared Pratincole *Glareola pratincola*

A large-eyed, small-billed, short-legged wader with a bulky swallow-like form. Elongated when alert; more rounded when resting. Flight buoyant, with frequent twists, climbs, and steep dives; harsh, tern-like, creaking call

Small, scattered groups fly over marsh or dried-up wetland, hawking insects with twisting, elegant action, accelerating into brief chases with quicker wingbeats, like Hobby

Juvenile Collared
Scaly above, dull throat

Adult Collared, summer

Buff throat edged black in summer

Black-winged Pratincole
(left and above)
All-dark underwing, much less contrast above than Collared; no white trailing edge; rare

Adult Collared, winter

Forked black and white tail

Collared
Very long, angular wings show contrast between dark flight feathers and pale coverts

Oriental Pratincole
Very rare; smaller red patch on underwing, no white rear edge, short tail, big white rump

Collared
Underwing rusty-red and black; white rear edge

| Collared | Black-winged | Oriental |

Tail length is useful for identification

Although technically a wader, this elegant bird feeds almost like a big Swallow and calls like a tern. It has a rhythmic, powerful, tern-like action in direct flight. Individuals in small groups often stand a little apart, facing the same way, very inconspicuous on dried earth or grassland; they look much rounder than they do in flight.

FEEDING It glides and weaves in the air, catching insects in its bill.

DISPLAY & VOICE Courtship begins in late winter flocks, and pairs then move to breeding areas where they perform rapid flights overhead and a bowing ceremony on the ground. The voice includes a rolling, vibrating spring song and various rasping calls in flight, like *kik kik* or *kikki-kirrik*.

BREEDING The nest is on the ground near water; the three chicks fly when 25–30 days old. Parent birds draw predators away from nests and chicks with elaborate 'injury-feigning' distraction displays.

MIGRATION In autumn Collared Pratincoles leave Europe for Africa.

LENGTH 23–26cm (9–10½in)

WHEN TO SEE April to October
WHERE FOUND Extensive muddy plains, wetland fringes; Spain, Camargue, Balkans

Black-winged Stilt *Himantopus himantopus*

Grotesquely long legs stamp an unmistakable character on the Stilt and everything it does. It is a slender, elegant bird, with a fine bill that adds a beautifully refined touch to its appearance, yet the length of its legs is evident whether it stands motionless on a sandbank, wades into water, or flies overhead calling noisily, its legs trailing and feet crossed for support.

FEEDING The Stilt picks tiny aquatic invertebrates from the surface of fresh or salty water, bending forwards or wading belly-deep to take food that is out of reach of most shoreline waders.

DISPLAY & VOICE Courtship involves noisy aerial chases, 'butterfly flights' on raised wings and elegant mating rituals with stereotyped preening. Stilts call with a sharp, Coot-like *kek* and longer, harsh, tern-like sounds.

BREEDING The nest is typically a scrape on dried waterside mud. The four chicks fly when 30 days old, and breed at two years old.

MIGRATION Almost all migrate in autumn to central Africa.

LENGTH 35–40cm (14–16in)

WHEN TO SEE Most March to October
WHERE FOUND S Europe, UK, very sporadic on shallow lagoons

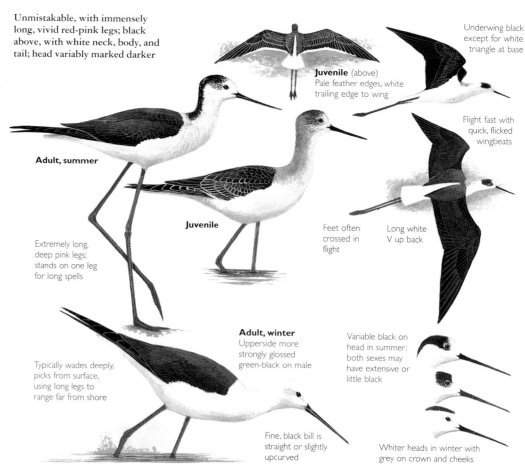

Unmistakable, with immensely long, vivid red-pink legs; black above, with white neck, body, and tail; head variably marked darker

Juvenile (above)
Pale feather edges, white trailing edge to wing

Underwing black except for white triangle at base

Flight fast with quick, flicked wingbeats

Adult, summer

Juvenile

Feet often crossed in flight

Long white V up back

Extremely long, deep pink legs; stands on one leg for long spells

Adult, winter
Upperside more strongly glossed green-black on male

Variable black on head in summer: both sexes may have extensive or little black

Typically wades deeply, picks from surface, using long legs to range far from shore

Fine, black bill is straight or slightly upcurved

Whiter heads in winter with grey on crown and cheeks

Avocet *Recurvirostra avosetta*

An Avocet feeding on a muddy shore among scattered gulls can be overlooked, but a good view reveals its startlingly white body with neat black markings, and its unique upswept bill. In summer Avocets are restricted to areas of shallow, brackish water with islands, often on estuaries.

FEEDING It tilts forwards and sweeps its upcurved bill sideways through water or glistening ooze, to capture tiny shrimps and other invertebrates of saline lagoons and estuarine mud.

DISPLAY & VOICE Courtship involves ritualized displays with rhythmic preening and drinking movements. Avocets are noisy and draw attention by their loud, liquid *quilp* calls.

BREEDING The nest is a mere scrape on mud or sand; four chicks fly when 35–42 days old; they breed at two, sometimes three, years of age.

MIGRATION Most move south and west in winter, to sheltered estuaries of western Europe or even south into Africa. They are then very gregarious, feeding and flying in tight-knit flocks.

LENGTH 42–45cm (16–18in)

WHEN TO SEE All year, March to September at colony
WHERE FOUND Brackish water, estuaries; erratically south from Denmark and the Baltic

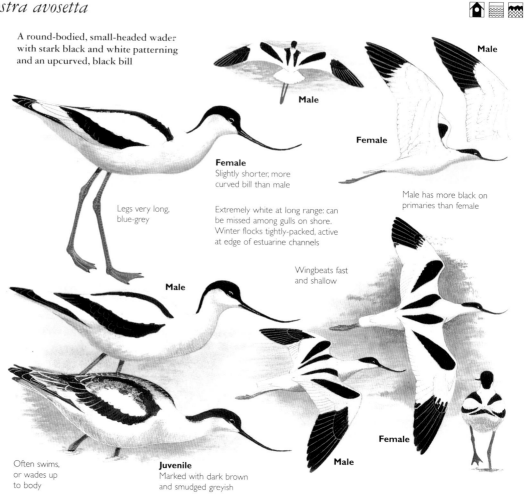

A round-bodied, small-headed wader with stark black and white patterning and an upcurved, black bill

Male

Male

Female

Female
Slightly shorter, more curved bill than male

Male has more black on primaries than female

Legs very long, blue-grey

Extremely white at long range: can be missed among gulls on shore. Winter flocks tightly-packed, active at edge of estuarine channels

Male

Wingbeats fast and shallow

Female

Often swims, or wades up to body

Juvenile
Marked with dark brown and smudged greyish

Male

Oystercatcher *Haematopus ostralegus*

A spectacular, stockily-built, large wader, strikingly pied; adults have an unmistakable vivid orange bill

First winter
White collar

Juvenile
Dull, marked with buff-brown; no white collar at first

Immature
Widest white collar; dull bill

Adult, summer
Striking orange bill; red eye with red ring; no white collar in breeding plumage

Dazzling flight pattern: flocks confuse predators with sudden mass take-off

Broad white wingbar and white V on back, bolder than on Black-tailed Godwit

Legs clear pink on summer adult, dusky on immatures

Small groups bend forward and call in strident, earsplitting piping display with open bills pointing down

Adult, winter
White collar

On northern coasts, along stony rivers and in farmed valleys, Oystercatchers nest in pairs that probably last for life. After breeding, however, they are more familiar in the south and west as birds of estuaries and sandy beaches, or rocky places with an abundance of mussels and limpets.

FEEDING Inland breeders eat mostly caterpillars and earthworms; on the coast they take cockles from soft mud and mussels prised from rocks. Some slip their blade-like bills between the shells to cut the shell-closing muscles; others simply hammer them to pieces.

DISPLAY & VOICE Noisy piping displays in small groups are frequent, often leading to whirring display flights. Calls include loud, strident *kleep*, *kwik* and *k-peep* and variations.

BREEDING Oystercatcher nests are scrapes in the ground, sometimes on stumps or rocks; three eggs are usual, hatching after 24–27 days.

MIGRATION Northern, eastern, and inland breeders all move south and west in winter, some as far as Africa.

LENGTH 40–45cm (16–18in)

WHERE FOUND All UK and NW European coasts; inland in N Britain and Low Countries
WHEN FOUND All year

Dotterel *Charadrius morinellus*

A rounded, long-legged, short-billed terrestrial bird with a striking white V on the head and a white band (sometimes faint) around the breast. Often in small groups, especially on spring migration

Female, winter
Duller, more buff, with 'ghost' of breastband and obvious white V around dark cap

Upperside plain in flight; white vent may catch the eye

Breeding male
Duller, paler than female

Tail of female projects beyond wingtips

Pale ochre-yellow legs

Fine, pointed, black bill

White underwing

Male

Breeding female
Brighter, darker than male with stronger underpart pattern

Juveniles, autumn
Beautifully patterned with lacy feather edgings, breastband and cap

Upright when alert; round and dumpy when resting

Dotterels breed on broad, rolling mountain slopes and northern hills, on the highest tops in the Highlands of Scotland but at lower altitudes farther north. In spring small groups or 'trips' appear on lowland fields in traditional areas, staying for a few days before moving north.

FEEDING Dotterels eat mainly insects and spiders, picking them from the ground or from clumps of moss.

DISPLAY & VOICE In a reversal of the normal roles, females take the initiative and chase individual males from spring groups, forming pairs before arrival on the nesting areas; each female may pair with two or more males. Calls include a soft, penetrating *pweet pweet*.

BREEDING Three eggs are incubated mostly or wholly by the male for 24–28 days, in a hollow on open ground; the chicks fly at 25–30 days. A female may lay more than one clutch to be incubated by several males; females help incubate second clutches.

MIGRATION All breeders move south to north Africa for the winter.

LENGTH 20–22cm (8–9in)

WHEN TO SEE April to September
WHERE FOUND Breeds in Scotland and upland Scandinavia, rarely England, on high moorland; scarce on passage in W Europe

Ringed Plover *Charadrius hiaticula*

The Ringed Plover is often to be seen on a beach of sand, shingle, or mud, running nimbly for a few steps, then stopping – taut, alert – looking around or searching for prey. In summer, pairs are widely spaced along the beaches, or around flooded gravel pits inland. In autumn and winter they join together in flocks, gathering at high tide in their hundreds.

FEEDING The Ringed Plover feeds mainly on tiny beach crustaceans and insects picked from the ground.

DISPLAY & VOICE An aggressive bird runs towards others intruding on its territory in a forward-leaning hunch, its wings slightly open to make itself look larger and show off its bold chest patterning; it may also fan its tail and tilt it towards the adversary. Courtship involves a song flight by the male, using a slow, flicked wing action while tilting side-to-side, singing a rich, fluty *teelew teelew teelew d'loo d'loo d'loo*. Normal calls are bright, mellow, liquid notes emphasizing the second syllable: *toolee* or *keeip*, with variations used to convey alarm, threats, or warnings to young chicks if danger threatens.

BREEDING While most Ringed Plovers in the UK nest on or near the coast, increasing numbers use flooded gravel workings inland, where they may arrive earlier than Little Ringed Plovers and take the best territories. The nest is a shallow dish-shaped hollow scraped in sand or shingle, and lined with tiny shell fragments or stones. Both parents incubate the three or four well-camouflaged eggs, with frequent changes, for 23–25 days. The irresistibly attractive downy chicks are quickly active; they fly after 24 days, soon become independent, and breed when one year old. As so many pairs nest on popular beaches, with considerable human disturbance, failures are frequent. Even inland, or on islands, eggs and chicks are often taken by predators as varied as hedgehogs, gulls, and crows.

MIGRATION Some British birds are resident, but most Ringed Plovers migrate. Those from the far north of Europe, Asia, Greenland, and the Canadian Arctic move farthest south, as far as South Africa, while those breeding farther south in Britain, Ireland, France, and the Low Countries tend to remain in western Europe or the Mediterranean area in winter.

LENGTH 18–20cm (7–8in)

WHEN TO SEE All year in most of NW Europe; March to September in the north and August to May in the southwest
WHERE FOUND Estuaries, exposed beaches of sand, shingle or rock; lakesides and some sandy grassland areas (Breckland) inland

A round-faced, neat, starling-sized shorebird, clean white beneath; adults have crisp black and white head patterns and brightly coloured bill and legs; pleasant, fluty call distinctive

Adult male, summer
Brightly patterned with bold black bands on face and chest, colourful legs and bill

Tail tip of male extends beyond closed wingtips

Some show more white in tail; white sides to rump and tail surround dark central patch

Adult, winter
Note slightly less crisp black band, duller bill, grey eye-ring

Juvenile female
Crown dull brown; white forehead extends as stripe over eye. Breastband narrow, brown, barely complete in centre; back scaly

Adult female, winter
Wingtips and tail tips equal length, unlike male; reduced black on top of head in winter plumage

Typical plover stance: alert 'stop and look', then forward-leaning run and dip to pick food from ground – 'run, stop, tilt'

Juvenile has blackish bill with trace of yellow at base, and dull, yellowish legs

Adult male, summer

Northern populations slightly smaller and darker than in the rest of Europe

Adult female, winter

In flight, reveals bold white stripe along full length of wing and white sides to rump

Juvenile

Adult

Typical flight fast, with shallow wingbeats; display flight slower with slow, deliberate beats of stiffly-straightened wings

Adult   **Juvenile**   **Adult, summer**

112

Kentish Plover *Charadrius alexandrinus*

A small, very pale plover, with dark only at the sides of the breast, slender black legs, and a relatively thick black bill

Long white wingbar and distinctive white sides to tail

Very rarely has paler legs

White sides to tail, unlike other 'ringed' plovers

Male, breeding
Rusty nape in spring

Black marks on head and sides of breast

Cool spring posture (right)

Juvenile
Duller with no black; black/grey legs unlike young Ringed Plover

Nervous and rather shy; wingtips slender, but may look quite dumpy and short-tailed, almost chick-like

Hot summer posture

Legs typically dark grey

Female
Pale sandy, no black on head: the palest of the 'ringed' plovers

In southern Europe may look quite frayed and bleached by mid year

With its long legs, rounded body, and often upright stance, this neat, lively, very pale little plover looks almost like the small chick of a larger species. It is typical of warm, sandy shorelines and saline lagoons, especially on flat areas of hard, salty mud or sand, but sometimes it finds temporary nesting habitats around gravel pits, or even on building sites.

FEEDING It employs the fast run, stop, tilt-over feeding method typical of plovers, using its black bill to pick mainly small crustaceans and molluscs from the sand and shingle.

DISPLAY & VOICE Its display flights over nesting areas are accompanied by grating, trilling calls; more normal calls include a sharp *kip* and a quiet, short, fluty whistle.

BREEDING It nests on the beach in a shallow scrape. The four eggs hatch after an incubation of 24–27 days.

MIGRATION Most leave Europe for Africa in winter. A few reach the UK in spring and autumn.

LENGTH 15–17cm (6–7in)

WHEN TO SEE Mostly March to October, a few in winter
WHERE FOUND Sandy coasts, lagoons, salt pans; mostly S European and S North Sea coasts

Little Ringed Plover *Charadrius dubius*

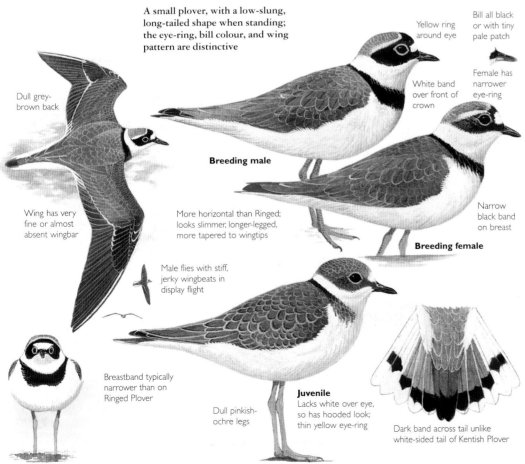

A small plover, with a low-slung, long-tailed shape when standing; the eye-ring, bill colour, and wing pattern are distinctive

Dull grey-brown back

Wing has very fine or almost absent wingbar

Male flies with stiff, jerky wingbeats in display flight

Breeding male

More horizontal than Ringed; looks slimmer, longer-legged, more tapered to wingtips

Yellow ring around eye

Bill all black or with tiny pale patch

White band over front of crown

Female has narrower eye-ring

Narrow black band on breast

Breeding female

Breastband typically narrower than on Ringed Plover

Dull pinkish-ochre legs

Juvenile
Lacks white over eye, so has hooded look; thin yellow eye-ring

Dark band across tail unlike white-sided tail of Kentish Plover

Slender and long-winged, this species looks less dumpy than the bigger Ringed Plover. Its yellow eye-ring is usually conspicuous. Unlike the Ringed Plover it is not a bird of the sea shore, nor is it found in Europe in winter. It prefers drier places, often waste ground or bare earth and gravel, near a lake, river, or flooded pit.

FEEDING It eats mainly small insects, usually picking them from near or just beneath the surface of damp ground or from shallow water.

DISPLAY & VOICE It displays in flight above its territory, rolling on stiff, fully-stretched wings while the male produces a rhythmic, grating song: *grria-grria-grria*. The typical call is an abrupt *piw* or *pew* without the fluty, musical quality of a Ringed Plover.

BREEDING The four remarkably large eggs are laid directly on the ground. Incubated by both parents, they hatch after 24–25 days.

MIGRATION All Little Ringed Plovers leave Europe in autumn, heading for Africa south of the Sahara. They return early, reaching the UK in March.

LENGTH 14–15cm (5½–6in)

WHERE FOUND Scattered throughout Europe in suitable habitat
WHEN FOUND March to October

Sanderling *Calidris alba*

Outside the breeding season the Sanderling is a bird of the open seashore, tripping across sandy beaches, chasing receding waves, or sitting out the high tide in tight-knit, motionless flocks. It is best known as a pearly-grey and white wader, with black legs and bill. In May, small numbers appear beside reservoirs inland, moving on quickly northward.

FEEDING It picks small invertebrates – flies, crustaceans, and occasional small marine worms – from the beach with quick, deft movements and frequent shallow probes of its bill.

DISPLAY & VOICE It makes a peculiar frog-like sound during its song flight over the nesting territory. At other times its usual call is a short, hard, dry *twick*. Flocks twitter when feeding.

BREEDING In summer it breeds on the High Arctic tundra, laying its four eggs on bare earth or stones.

MIGRATION After breeding in the Arctic, winters on suitable beaches as far as the southern tips of Africa and South America, and Australasia.

LENGTH 20–21cm (8in)

WHEN TO SEE Mostly August to May
WHERE FOUND Migrant on all coasts mostly on sandy beaches, scarce inland but regular by some reservoir edges in May

Blackish wings have broad white stripe

A neat wader, just bigger than a Dunlin and with a shorter, straighter bill, black legs, and a gleaming white belly at all times

Adult, breeding Mottled black and rust-red in spring; lacks pale V on back of Little Stint, looks more 'mealy'

Head plain, without strong stripe over eye

Adult, early spring (left) Grey wears off: see bird at far right

Adult, non-breeding (below) Very grey and white, gradually darkens towards spring

Black legs; no hind toe

Upperpart feathers have white tips in spring, giving marbled effect that wears off by late summer

Black bill straighter and shorter than that of Dunlin

Usually runs on clean sand, tripping along water's edge and following waves; may feed on muddier or algae-covered beaches and flat rocks; often inland in May

Juvenile Spotted black above, dark cap

Dark shoulder patch often hidden

Broad-billed Sandpiper *Limicola falcinellus*

Compared with most of the small sandpipers this is a dark, swarthy, almost snipe-like bird. In spring its fresh feathers are pale, giving it a hoary appearance, but the edges wear away to reveal darker centres.

FEEDING It feeds in shallow water with delicate probing and occasional short, quick runs, taking small insects and seeds. It may feed with Dunlins, or in small groups; in the Middle East it often forms much larger flocks.

DISPLAY & VOICE The male gives a rhythmic, buzzing song in flight. If flushed it has a short, rising, dry trill, *chr-e-e-et* or *trrhuit*, more trilling than a Dunlin flight call and less musical than a Curlew Sandpiper's.

BREEDING It breeds in loose colonies; females lay three or four eggs in a grassy cup in a tussock of grass.

MIGRATION It is a rare bird in western Europe, but breeds in Scandinavia and migrates to the Middle East and India in winter. In the UK it appears mostly between May and July.

LENGTH 16–17cm (6½in)

WHEN TO SEE April to September
WHERE FOUND N Scandinavia; on migration very rare elsewhere on coastal lagoons, marshes

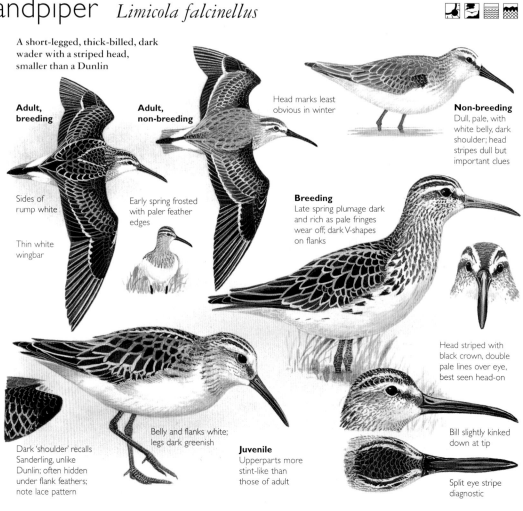

A short-legged, thick-billed, dark wader with a striped head, smaller than a Dunlin

Adult, breeding

Adult, non-breeding

Head marks least obvious in winter

Non-breeding Dull, pale, with white belly, dark shoulder; head stripes dull but important clues

Sides of rump white

Early spring frosted with paler feather edges

Thin white wingbar

Breeding Late spring plumage dark and rich as pale fringes wear off; dark V-shapes on flanks

Head striped with black crown, double pale lines over eye, best seen head-on

Dark 'shoulder' recalls Sanderling, unlike Dunlin; often hidden under flank feathers; note lace pattern

Belly and flanks white; legs dark greenish

Juvenile Upperparts more stint-like than those of adult

Bill slightly kinked down at tip

Split eye stripe diagnostic

114

Temminck's Stint *Calidris temminckii*

A short-legged, small-billed, dull grey-brown sandpiper with pale legs, white sides to tail and short, trilling call; a freshwater bird, with a slow, deliberate walking action when feeding, distinctive at long range

Male, non-breeding

Towers up in erratic flight when flushed, often calling

Greyish; white belly, grey breastband

Wingtips equal tail on male

Tail projects on female

Male, breeding
Irregular dark blotches on back; these appear slowly in spring

Juvenile female
Upperpart feathers edged with yellow-buff and thin dark crescent; white mark between wing and breast recalls Common Sandpiper

Legs pale yellow-ochre to greenish-yellow

Thin white wingbar, white sides to tail. Broader, less angled wings than Little Stint in typical flight

Underwing distinctive in flight or wing stretching

Wide white sides to tail unlike other small sandpipers

This is a rather rare bird in western Europe: a scarce passage migrant. In the UK it occurs in threes and fours in May. It breeds in Scandinavia (with a very few in Scotland) and northern Asia, and moves to Africa and southern Asia in winter.

FEEDING It feeds less actively than most small sandpipers, creeping and shuffling over wet grass or mud to pick up insects, worms, and molluscs.

DISPLAY & VOICE The song is a rising and falling trill, *sirrrrr* or *kilililililili* given in flight; the usual call when flushed is a valuable clue: a short, hard *tr-r-r-r*.

BREEDING The nest is built on the ground in low vegetation, often near willow scrub, or in an open space near water, close to Arctic inlets, deltas, and rivers. The four eggs hatch after 21–22 days; sometimes one parent incubates a clutch each, or two males and one female may incubate three clutches.

LENGTH 13–15cm (5–6in)

WHEN TO SEE May to September; some winter in Italy, Greece
WHERE FOUND Breeds along Scandinavian spine and extreme north coast of Europe; scarce migrant elsewhere on muddy lake edges and coastal lagoons but not on estuary mud or beaches

Little Stint *Calidris minuta*

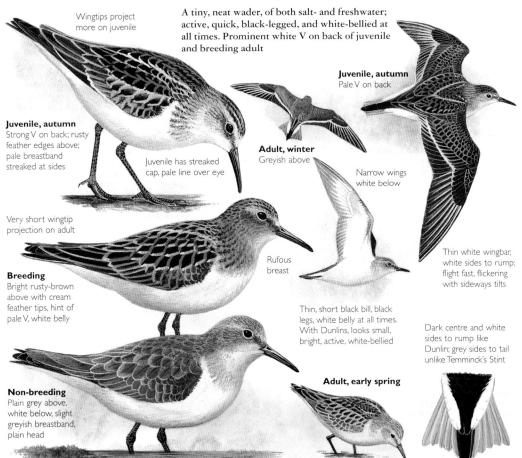

A tiny, neat wader, of both salt- and freshwater; active, quick, black-legged, and white-bellied at all times. Prominent white V on back of juvenile and breeding adult

Wingtips project more on juvenile

Juvenile, autumn
Strong V on back; rusty feather edges above; pale breastband streaked at sides

Juvenile has streaked cap, pale line over eye

Adult, winter
Greyish above

Very short wingtip projection on adult

Breeding
Bright rusty-brown above with cream feather tips, hint of pale V, white belly

Non-breeding
Plain grey above, white below, slight greyish breastband, plain head

Juvenile, autumn
Pale V on back

Narrow wings white below

Rufous breast

Thin, short black bill, black legs, white belly at all times. With Dunlins, looks small, bright, active, white-bellied

Adult, early spring

Thin white wingbar, white sides to rump; flight fast, flickering with sideways tilts

Dark centre and white sides to rump like Dunlin; grey sides to tail unlike Temminck's Stint

In most of western Europe Little Stints are usually seen in late summer and autumn, with a small number of migrating adults followed by larger numbers of juveniles. There are far fewer seen in spring. They usually travel and feed with Dunlins and sometimes Curlew Sandpipers, and often they are absurdly tame.

FEEDING A Little Stint usually feeds at the water's edge, using short runs and quick-picking from the surface with its bill.

DISPLAY & VOICE Little Stints have a typical sandpiper/stint song flight; autumn migrants twitter in flocks and call with a short, sharp *pit*, *chit* or *pit-it*.

BREEDING Nesting areas are in High Arctic tundra and islands.

MIGRATION Each autumn they move south to spend the winter in Africa and India, visiting many west European coasts and inland waters, but they are much more frequently seen in southeast Europe in spring.

LENGTH 12–14cm (5–5½in)

WHEN TO SEE May to October, mostly August-September in NW Europe
WHERE FOUND Breeds in extreme N Norway and Siberia; widespread on migration, especially in coastal areas

Dunlin *Calidris alpina*

On almost any smooth coastline, whether of mud or sand, there will be small, short-legged waders scuttling about at low tide. They will usually be Dunlins, for these are by far the most widespread and numerous of the smaller seashore waders. They are also often seen inland in spring and autumn, beside muddy lakes and reservoirs – and should the water levels remain low and shores stay muddy, groups of Dunlins may stay around reservoirs all winter. This frequency makes the Dunlin the 'benchmark' against which to judge scarcer waders such as the Little Stint or Curlew Sandpiper, as well as more local coastal species such as the Knot.

The Dunlin is a small wader, with a medium-length bill and rather short legs, and a broad-bodied, round-shouldered shape. It is neither so elegant and long-legged as a Curlew Sandpiper, nor so quick and nimble as a Little Stint. Yet it is certainly not unattractive: Dunlins are enchanting little birds in their own right, and in full breeding plumage they can be really handsome creatures.

Dunlins illustrate the plumage sequences shown by all the *Calidris* sandpipers, which are typical small waders. In early spring they moult into new body plumage with broad, pale feather edges; these pale edges then wear away to reveal the brighter, darker colours beneath, creating a rich breeding plumage. The extent of the moult and abrasion varies somewhat; one bird's upperparts may retain some grey winter feathers, while another still has pale edges on its bright summer feathers; this creates a lot of individual variation that can be often be seen in close views.

The birds moult their larger wing and tail feathers in late autumn, so by spring these are only slightly worn; by late summer they are faded and abraded at the tips.

The breeding plumage of different races varies too, as shown opposite. British breeders have big black feather centres creating a boldly mottled upperpart pattern, while northern birds have smaller black spots in more extensive chestnut, once the broad pale grey fringes have worn away.

FEEDING In summer, on bogs and moors, Dunlins eat insects. At other times they eat a variety of tiny worms and molluscs. They are equally at home feeding on soft mud and weed-covered rocks. On soft mud they probe quickly with a 'stitching' action, but on harder ground they locate more prey by sight and pick it up with more precision.

DISPLAY & VOICE Outside the breeding season Dunlins are sociable and may feed in groups of hundreds, roosting in flocks of several thousands.

(continued opposite)

Winter adults and juveniles

Typical 'small sandpiper' thin white wingbar and white sides to dark-centred rump and tail

Adult, winter

Adult, winter

Juvenile (right)
Shares basic flight pattern but much brighter above; hint of pale V on back

Adult, autumn
Transitional plumage shows scattered remaining dark chestnut summer feathers among winter grey

Adult, autumn
Transitional plumage

Juvenile

Adult, summer

Juvenile
Rich chestnut with black and cream on back, scaly on wings; flanks streaked and blotched

Little Stint, winter
Shorter, straighter bill

Juvenile
Moulting into winter plumage with scattered, very dark summer feathers and old, brown tertials

Tail length varies with individuals and discrete populations within Europe

A small, short-legged, medium-billed, hunch-backed wader; grey-brown in winter, chestnut in summer with distinctive black belly; sometimes in huge flocks

Adult, winter
Complete non-breeding plumage, wholly pale brownish-grey above with dark shaft-streaks

Dunlin *Calidris alpina*

Greenland breeder
Small, short bill, fades to yellowish above; migrates along western coasts of France and Britain, but not common: most in late spring

Males in breeding plumage

Breeding male, Britain
Large black feather centres on back

Slightly curved bill, long, tapered rear, thickset shape, rather plodding feeding action; roosts in dense flocks at high tide; breeding plumage often seen on coasts in spring

Square-fronted black belly patch and streaked grey breast unique to breeding Dunlin

North European breeders
Long bill; wide grey feather edges in spring (above) wear off to produce extensive rich chestnut brown (right)

In spring the Dunlin flocks separate into pairs, and the males advertise their territories in display flights. These begin with a fast, steep rise, followed by a hovering or switchback flight into the wind, with a prolonged, whinnying trill: *chrrii-i-i-i-i-ri-ri-ri-ri*. This can often be heard from roosting flocks on beaches in spring. The typical call is a low, drawn out, slightly grating, reedy *tr-reeee* or slurred *treep*.

BREEDING Dunlin nests are slight scrapes on the ground, usually concealed in tussocks of vegetation. The four eggs are incubated by both parents, and hatch after 21–22 days. The chicks leave the nest quickly, and are able to fly at 19–21 days old.

MIGRATION Breeders from the north and inland move to the coast and head south to spend the winter throughout Europe to north and west Africa. Small parties often appear inland.

LENGTH 16–20cm (6½–8in)

WHEN TO SEE All year; in N Europe mostly April to September
WHERE FOUND Breeds Iceland, Scotland, N England, scarce Wales and Ireland; Norway, locally Sweden and Finland, Baltic states and Germany. Widespread at other times

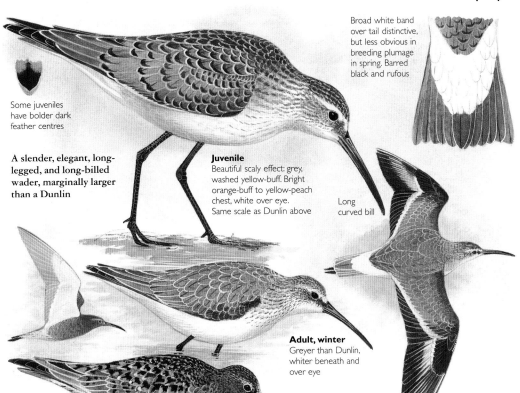

Curlew Sandpiper *Calidris ferruginea*

Broad white band over tail distinctive, but less obvious in breeding plumage in spring. Barred black and rufous

Some juveniles have bolder dark feather centres

A slender, elegant, long-legged, and long-billed wader, marginally larger than a Dunlin

Juvenile
Beautiful scaly effect: grey, washed yellow-buff. Bright orange-buff to yellow-peach chest, white over eye. Same scale as Dunlin above

Long curved bill

Adult, winter
Greyer than Dunlin, whiter beneath and over eye

Male has long, projecting wingtips

Breeding female duller and paler

Adult, breeding
Hoary white feather edges wear away to reveal rich chestnut

White rump and wingbar; projecting feet

Of the several sandpipers with a general resemblance to the Dunlin, this is the most elegant. Like larger species such as the Knot it sports rich red breeding plumage in spring, but at that time it is common only in southeast Europe. Small numbers appear in the west in autumn, with Little Stints and Dunlins.

FEEDING It wades in water, probing for small molluscs and crustaceans.

VOICE Although it lacks the vibrant effect of the Dunlin's, the flight call is distinctive: a soft, chirruping or slightly rippling *chirrrip* or *kil-l-lee*.

BREEDING Breeds in extreme north of Siberia. Four eggs are incubated for 21 days.

MIGRATION In spring large flocks occur in eastern Europe. In autumn a few scores to thousands stop off in Britain and the Low Countries, on estuaries or shallow coastal lagoons, or beside lakes inland. Adults move in July and early August, juveniles in August and September. Good years for autumn migration occur when lemming numbers are high, as predators eat them in preference to Curlews.

LENGTH 18–23cm (7–9in)

WHEN TO SEE March to May; July to October or November; rare in winter
WHERE FOUND Most of Europe on migration

117

Turnstone *Arenaria interpres*

Always close to the water's edge, Turnstones search busily for food among rocks, seaweed, and the strandline of debris thrown up by the tides on sandy or shingle beaches. At high tide they fly to secluded places to roost with other waders, often mixing with Ringed Plovers and Dunlins.

FEEDING Turnstones search for small crustaceans and molluscs by riffling through (and really turning over) stones, shells, and bits of weed, or poking about at the edges of rock pools. In the breeding season they eat insects, spiders, and some seeds.

DISPLAY & VOICE Calls are quick, staccato repetitions: *kitititit*, *tuk-i-tuk* or a rolling *titwoootitwooorit-it-itititit*. These birds may chase each other while calling loudly, and posture with hunched backs and spread tails.

BREEDING Breeds in the far north on coasts and islands, laying four eggs in a simple scrape on the ground.

MIGRATION Moves south to North Sea and Atlantic coasts in autumn.

LENGTH 22–24cm (9–9½in)

> **WHEN TO SEE** Almost all year in non-breeding areas; May to September in north
> **WHERE FOUND** Coasts of Scandinavia; migrates to NW European and African shores; scarce inland

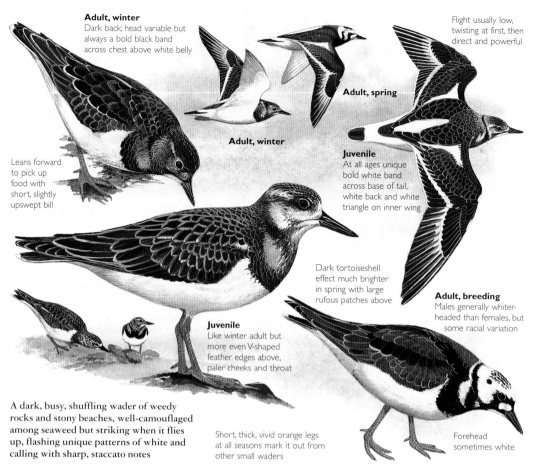

Adult, winter
Dark back; head variable but always a bold black band across chest above white belly

Flight usually low, twisting at first, then direct and powerful

Adult, winter

Adult, spring

Juvenile
At all ages unique bold white band across base of tail, white back and white triangle on inner wing

Leans forward to pick up food with short, slightly upswept bill

Dark tortoiseshell effect much brighter in spring with large rufous patches above

Adult, breeding
Males generally whiter-headed than females, but some racial variation

Juvenile
Like winter adult but more even V-shaped feather edges above, paler cheeks and throat

A dark, busy, shuffling wader of weedy rocks and stony beaches, well-camouflaged among seaweed but striking when it flies up, flashing unique patterns of white and calling with sharp, staccato notes

Short, thick, vivid orange legs at all seasons mark it out from other small waders

Forehead sometimes white

Purple Sandpiper *Calidris maritima*

Purple Sandpipers live at the very edge of the sea, where they often have to leap clear of breaking waves. They are typical of really rocky shores, where they feed among the barnacles and seaweeds. They often occur with Turnstones, when they are less easy to approach than when alone.

FEEDING They feed where the sea is in constant motion, using their slim bills to pick up invertebrates momentarily exposed by the waves.

DISPLAY & VOICE Typical winter calls are short and sharp, such as *pwit* or *wit*; the song is a series of fast trills. Pairs seem to form in the winter flock, without obvious displays on the breeding areas. The white underwing is important in communication.

BREEDING They nest from about mid-May, the female selecting one of several scrapes made by the male; four eggs hatch after 21 days.

MIGRATION In autumn, after the breeding season, birds move to adjacent coasts or farther south to Britain, France, and northern Spain.

LENGTH 20–22cm (8–9in)

> **WHEN TO SEE** August to May in south
> **WHERE FOUND** Breeds Iceland; central spine of Scandinavia; winters on nearby coasts and south to Spain; rare inland

Breeding adult, August
Bright feather edges wearing thin; very streaked below, streaked rusty cap, but face pattern varies; some paler, more buff above

A small, neat, round-bodied wader, looking dark unless seen against very dark seaweed of typical rocky shore habitat; subtly beautiful plumage combined with yellow bill and orange-yellow legs

Adult, winter (below)
Dark greyish-brown, with white eye-ring and chin, pale scallops on coverts

Legs often darker, greenish-yellow

Immature, first winter
Like dull adult with more pale scalloping on back; white eye-ring may be striking

Adults, winter
Dark, with broad dark rump edged white, thin white wingbar

Often hard to spot on rocks, but very tame unless with more nervous Turnstones

Juvenile
Paler than adult; bright feather edges on head and back; no pale stripe over eye; note bill and leg colour; neat scales of white on coverts. In flight shows narrow wingbar, broad black centre to rump

Stockier than Dunlin; no black belly patch; in summer, more streaked onto belly, in winter darker; pale-legged

Knot *Calidris canutus*

A dumpy, medium-sized wader with a medium-short bill and legs; typically very gregarious; distinctive grey rump; very quiet for a wader, lacking loud alarm calls; individuals can be extraordinarily tame

Winter
Pale rump (dark bars hard to see), thin white wingbar, square grey tail

Shortish, thick black bill

Huge flocks in distance look like smoke

Winter
Dull, grey, pale, lacks striking features

Breeding
Underside pale to deep rufous, white vent

Adult, winter
Grey above; pale line over eye

Breeding

Clean grey in autumn, fading duller and browner by spring

Legs short, pale, grey-green

Juvenile (right)
Grey with neat, lacy, scalloped feather edges above; breast flushed pale orange-buff. Greyer; dumpier than Ruff, bigger than Dunlin, paler than Redshank

Wingtip equal to tail (above) on Siberian breeders.

Wingtip beyond tail (below) on North American breeders

Adults moulting to winter plumage look particoloured in autumn

Winter

Both godwits are much bigger, Curlew Sandpiper smaller, slimmer; all have longer bills

Adult, spring
Deep rufous, dark legs

Even among the waders – a group that boasts many long-distance travellers – the Knot is a remarkable globetrotter, flying vast distances each spring and autumn. Knots have been intensively studied because of this hugely demanding way of life, which must bring great benefits to offset its stresses. The 24-hour daylight and abundant food of the Arctic summer clearly outweigh the problem of escaping the dark, cold Arctic winter by undertaking long, dangerous flights over the sea. Knots are especially sociable, feeding in dense flocks on open mudflats. They advance like a grey carpet: even if there are only a hundred or so they jostle almost shoulder-to-shoulder. When disturbed, or moving to their roosts as the tide rises, airborne flocks are wonderfully impressive as they twist and turn like columns of smoke in turbulent air.

FEEDING In the Arctic Knots feed on insects and seeds. On coasts outside the breeding season they prefer muddy, or less often sandy or shingly areas, where they pick small molluscs from the surface or just below.

DISPLAY & VOICE Many Knots return to their breeding areas already paired. Other males and females arrive singly, but ready to court and claim a territory as soon as the ground thaws in the summer sun. The male flies slowly over the territory, circling on rapidly vibrating wings, then glides down on wings held stiffly in a V, levels out on flat wings, and rises again with wings quivering. During this display he sings: *whip-poo-mee* and *poo-mee*, the song changing with his style of flight. At other times the usual call is a low, hoarse note, often from feeding flocks, creating a jumbled, unmusical chorus. A liquid double note is occasionally used in flight.

BREEDING The three or four eggs are laid on the ground in a slight hollow with a flimsy lining of leaves, stems, and lichen. They hatch after 21–22 days, and the chicks quickly move to feed beside nearby stretches of water. They fly after just 18–20 days.

MIGRATION Knots from the extreme north of Canada and Greenland winter in western Europe (from farther south in Canada, they go to South America). Those from central Siberia migrate through Europe to west and south Africa, while Knots from farther east go to Australia and New Zealand. They can lose as much as 80 per cent of their body weight during these long flights.

LENGTH 23–25cm (9–10in)

WHEN TO SEE All year; in W Europe, most late July or August to early May
WHERE FOUND Winters mostly on a few estuaries around North Sea, Irish Sea, English Channel, and Biscay coasts; widespread on migration

Terek Sandpiper *Xenus cinereus*

Its curious dumpy body, short legs, and long, upswept bill make this smallish sandpiper quite unique. It has a peculiar, almost 'drunken' action at times, dashing to and fro or twisting from side to side with sudden stops and starts, its head pushed forward and breast held low. It is a rarity in Europe, and always an exciting find.

FEEDING It uses its long bill to probe for invertebrates in exposed mud, often washing its food before swallowing it. It also eats seeds and even insects caught in the air.

DISPLAY & VOICE Little is known about its breeding displays, but it has a rich, melodious, whistling song. The flight call is a soft, rippling trill, like a shorter, softer, more melodious version of the Whimbrel's call.

BREEDING It breeds in northern marshy valleys, laying four eggs on the ground. They hatch after 23 days.

MIGRATION The Terek Sandpiper's wintering grounds are on the coasts of Africa, Asia, and Australasia; very few migrants reach western Europe.

LENGTH 22–24cm (9–9½in)

WHEN TO SEE May to August
WHERE FOUND East from Finland; rare migrant, chiefly on muddy or sandy coasts and shallow water at lake edges

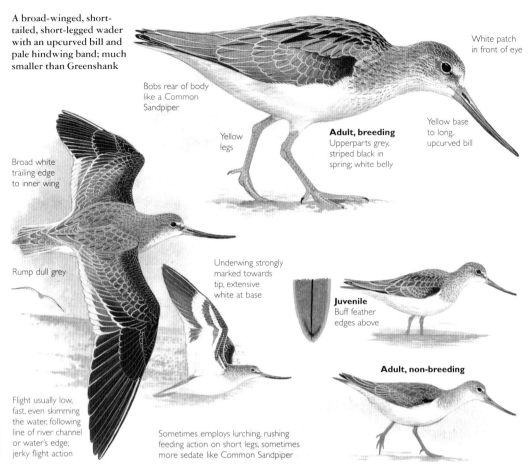

A broad-winged, short-tailed, short-legged wader with an upcurved bill and pale hindwing band; much smaller than Greenshank

Bobs rear of body like a Common Sandpiper

Yellow legs

Adult, breeding
Upperparts grey, striped black in spring; white belly

White patch in front of eye

Yellow base to long, upcurved bill

Broad white trailing edge to inner wing

Rump dull grey

Underwing strongly marked towards tip, extensive white at base

Juvenile
Buff feather edges above

Adult, non-breeding

Flight usually low, fast, even skimming the water, following line of river channel or water's edge; jerky flight action

Sometimes employs lurching, rushing feeding action on short legs, sometimes more sedate like Common Sandpiper

Common Sandpiper *Actitis hypoleucos*

This wader is easily identified by the constant up-and-down, rhythmic swing of its rear body and bobbing head. In flight it is equally distinctive, keeping low and using a stiff, bow-winged, flickering action.

FEEDING It feeds along streams and the edges of lakes, picking insects from mud, stones, and the water surface. It rarely probes in mud or wades deeply.

DISPLAY & VOICE Its display involves rapid flights above clear, stony streams, making good use of the white underwing pattern, as well as frequent vocal contact with loud trilling and rhythmic songs. The normal call is a high, ringing *tswee-wee-wee*.

BREEDING It lays four large eggs on the ground, usually on a bank near a stony river or shingly lakeside. They hatch in 21–22 days, and the chicks fly after 28 days.

MIGRATION Most spend the winter in Africa, but a tiny number remain in western Europe, usually on sheltered estuaries or lakesides.

LENGTH 19–21cm (7½–8½in)

WHEN TO SEE Mostly April to October
WHERE FOUND All Europe, scarce in south; breeds beside small rivers and shingly lakes but visits all kinds of watersides when on migration

Upperside marked blackish in summer

White patch in front of eye

Leans forward, constantly bobs tail in rhythmic up-and-down swinging motion

Obvious white 'peak' in front of closed wing

Broad white wingbar

Bowed, stiff wings flicker in flight in shallow downbeats

Legs blue-grey to dull yellowish, not conspicuously bright

Adult, breeding
Chest pale-centred, greyer on sides with short, fine streaks

Underwing well-marked but usually hard to see

An olive-brown and bright white wader with short, dull legs and a medium length, straight bill; flight and feeding action distinctive

Sides of tail white; centre creates dark 'blob'

Juvenile
Pale feather edges on back, barred wing coverts

Sides of breast streaked, centre paler, belly bright, eyecatching white

Wings held stiff, arched, and rather straight

Wood Sandpiper *Tringa glareola*

A neat, pretty wader with medium-length bill, long legs, and a distinctly spotted pattern on upperparts; has a white rump but plain wings

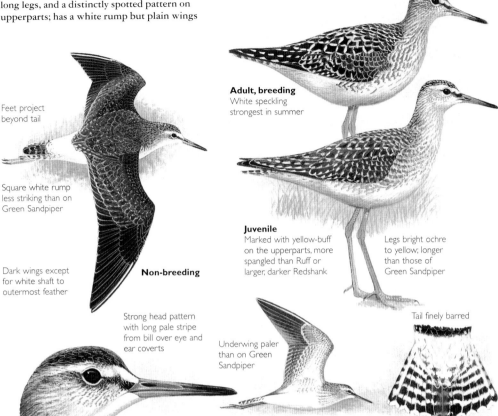

Feet project beyond tail

Square white rump less striking than on Green Sandpiper

Dark wings except for white shaft to outermost feather

Non-breeding

Strong head pattern with long pale stripe from bill over eye and ear coverts

Adult, breeding
White speckling strongest in summer

Juvenile
Marked with yellow-buff on the upperparts, more spangled than Ruff or larger, darker Redshank

Legs bright ochre to yellow; longer than those of Green Sandpiper

Underwing paler than on Green Sandpiper

Tail finely barred

Aflighty, noisy wader, the Wood Sandpiper has a round body, slim neck, long legs, and a high-stepping, elegant appearance. Like other sandpipers it bobs its head and tail, but less obviously than the Common Sandpiper. It tends to fly erratically and fast to a great height, giving sharp calls that are unlike the more liquid notes of a Green Sandpiper.

FEEDING It feeds on the edge of shallow, fresh water or in marshes, taking small worms and insects. It likes marshes and patches of wet mud, and is rarely seen far out on open mud or on beaches.

DISPLAY & VOICE Both sexes circle over their nesting area with rhythmic, whistling songs. The normal call is a loud, thin *chiff chiff chiff*.

BREEDING Nests are on the ground among scattered trees or on open bogs, often on a slight rise. The usual clutch of four eggs hatches in 22–23 days.

MIGRATION In autumn it moves south to Africa, appearing in most of Europe on passage. It is scarcer in spring, but seen in western Europe in May.

LENGTH 19–21cm (7½–8½in)

WHEN TO SEE April to October
WHERE FOUND Breeds north and east from Denmark; widespread on migration but scarce by freshwater lakes and marshes

Green Sandpiper *Tringa ochropus*

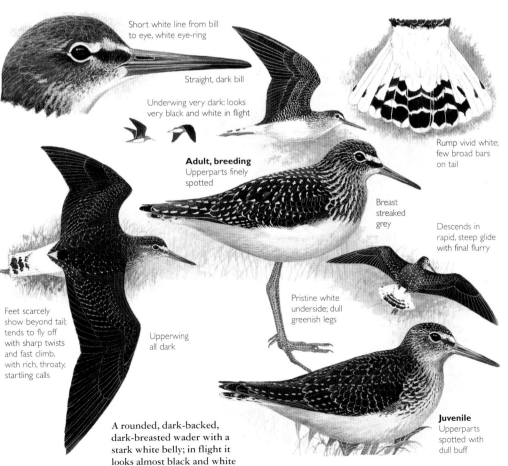

Short white line from bill to eye, white eye-ring

Straight, dark bill

Underwing very dark: looks very black and white in flight

Adult, breeding
Upperparts finely spotted

Rump vivid white; few broad bars on tail

Breast streaked grey

Descends in rapid, steep glide with final flurry

Feet scarcely show beyond tail; tends to fly off with sharp twists and fast climb, with rich, throaty, startling calls

Upperwing all dark

Pristine white underside; dull greenish legs

A rounded, dark-backed, dark-breasted wader with a stark white belly; in flight it looks almost black and white

Juvenile
Upperparts spotted with dull buff

This small sandpiper looks dark on the ground, yet boldly pied in flight as it displays its blackish underwing and striking white rump patch. As it walks it bobs its head and swings its rear up and down. When disturbed it tends to rise high and flies far away before settling again.

FEEDING It pecks tiny items of food from mud or shallow water, often wading but rarely venturing far out onto open mud. It is often to be seen feeding in small ditches or muddy creeks at the edge of saltmarsh.

DISPLAY & VOICE Display flights are accompanied by rich, rippling songs; the normal call is full, throaty, and liquid, a slurred *kluw-w-it-wit-wit*.

BREEDING It breeds in swampy places with scattered pines and birches, laying its eggs in old nests of pigeons or thrushes, or even in squirrel dreys.

MIGRATION Most move south to Africa but some regularly spend the winter in Britain and France.

LENGTH 21–24cm (8½–9½in)

WHEN TO SEE Mostly April to October
WHERE FOUND Breeds from Scandinavia eastwards; throughout Europe on migration, in marsh creeks, by lakes, even small wet ditches and ponds

121

Redshank *Tringa totanus*

On beaches of rocks, shingle, sand, or mud, around reservoir edges and beside winter floods or freshwater marsh, there will likely be Redshanks probing in wet mud and shallow water for food. At the merest hint of danger they raise their voices in almost hysterical, wild yelping whistles.

FEEDING Redshanks delve rather sluggishly for worms, crustaceans, and other small invertebrates.

DISPLAY & VOICE Displays include wing-raising to reveal sparkling white undersides and stiff-winged flights with yodelling *tyoo* notes that become excited *tuleeu tuleeu tuleeu* choruses on landing. Usual calls are a mournful, squealing or yelping *tyuuuuu*, and a quick, 'bouncy' *teu-huhu*, *tyu* and *tui*.

BREEDING Nests on the ground, by a grassy tussock or under a canopy of long grass. Four eggs hatch after 24 days; chicks fly 25–35 days later.

MIGRATION After breeding, Redshanks move to coastal areas of the British Isles, western Europe, and the Mediterranean.

LENGTH 27–29cm (11–11½in)

WHEN TO SEE All year in Britain, Ireland, France; April to October N & C Europe
WHERE TO SEE Widespread in N Europe, British Isles; sparse, localized in central and SW Europe

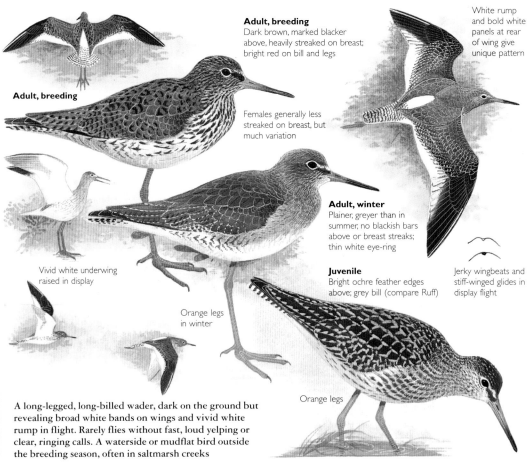

Adult, breeding

Adult, breeding
Dark brown, marked blacker above, heavily streaked on breast; bright red on bill and legs

White rump and bold white panels at rear of wing give unique pattern

Females generally less streaked on breast, but much variation

Adult, winter
Plainer, greyer than in summer; no blackish bars above or breast streaks; thin white eye-ring

Vivid white underwing raised in display

Orange legs in winter

Juvenile
Bright ochre feather edges above; grey bill (compare Ruff)

Jerky wingbeats and stiff-winged glides in display flight

Orange legs

A long-legged, long-billed wader, dark on the ground but revealing broad white bands on wings and vivid white rump in flight. Rarely flies without fast, loud yelping or clear, ringing calls. A waterside or mudflat bird outside the breeding season, often in saltmarsh creeks

Greenshank *Tringa nebularia*

Unlike the Redshank this is a breeding bird of wild moors and boggy clearings in northern forests. On migration it appears beside freshwater almost anywhere, staying for a few days in autumn in favoured spots with soft mud and shallow lagoons. Most are rather wild and unapproachable.

FEEDING Catches small fish and tiny crabs; probes for worms and molluscs. Sometimes very quick in its actions.

DISPLAY & VOICE Display flights over moorland territories are long and high, with quick, liquid *too-hoo-too-hoo* notes. Typical clear, ringing, three-syllable *tew tew tew* calls have a more even emphasis than the Redshank's call.

BREEDING Nests on the ground, often beside an old stump or rock; the four eggs hatch within 24–25 days.

MIGRATION All breeding birds move south in autumn, mostly to Africa; a few spend the winter in southwest England, southern Ireland, western France, and Iberia. They return north in April and May.

LENGTH 30–33cm (12–13in)

WHEN TO SEE Mostly April to October, fewer winter in W Europe
WHERE FOUND Breeds on remote moors and bogs of Scotland, Scandinavia; widespread on migration, local on estuaries in winter in UK, Ireland, France, Iberia

A supremely elegant, long-legged wader with a faintly upswept bill; in flight, dark wings contrast with a white V on its back

Female, breeding
Irregular black-centred feathers on back and scapulars; pearly-white spots on feather edges.

Finely streaked greyish head and neck; grey deep-based bill, with fine, dark, slightly uptilted tip

Adult, winter (right)
Paler, greyer than in summer with whiter breast, often much paler head with trace of white line up back of neck. Legs rarely yellow

Wingtips of female longer than on male

Legs olive-green to grey-green

Male
Short wingtips

In flight wings look all-dark, but long, narrow white V on rump and back (compare with Spotted Redshank)

Juvenile
Speckled head greyer than winter adult

Juvenile
Some individuals are more spotted than shown

Spotted Redshank *Tringa erythropus*

Spring adult
Early breeding plumage has broad white feather tips, which wear off to produce blacker appearance (with a few white spots mostly on wings) by midsummer

A lively feeder, often wading deeply, up-ending or swimming, snatching food with its straight, fine bill. In flight its call and the white patch on its back are distinctive

Bill needle-fine with a faint hint of downcurve

Summer

Blood-red legs; go black on breeding grounds

Dark wings and tail surround narrow oval or oblong of white on back

Long, trailing legs and feet: occasionally tucked forwards out of sight in cold weather

Winter adult
Pale, grey, with spotted white feather fringes above; distinctive black line from bill to eye, with thin white stripe above it. Bright red legs and base to bill

Moulting adult

Juvenile
Often seen on migration in autumn. Quite brown with barred underparts which wear much whiter with fainter bars by September; head pattern like winter adult

In its breeding plumage a Spotted Redshank is a spectacular bird. Such adults may be seen far south of their nesting areas in mid or late summer, but most birds seen in western Europe are paler winter birds or dull juveniles, identifiable by their lively feeding action, thin bills, long legs, and calls.

FEEDING Typically fast and energetic, they chase fish or probe underwater, often in small groups.

DISPLAY & VOICE Circling, dipping, or diving display flights are accompanied by creaky, whistling calls: *kurrevi-kurrevi-kurrevi*. The usual call is a very clear, sharp, loud *chew-it* or *tee-veet* lacking the ringing quality of Redshank or Greenshank.

BREEDING Nests are on the ground in wooded tundra; the three or four eggs may be incubated wholly by the male.

MIGRATION Arctic breeders migrate to Africa just south of the Sahara; a few winter in western Europe, including southern Britain and Ireland.

LENGTH 29–31cm (11½–12in)

WHEN TO SEE Mostly April to October in UK, a few in winter; some remain all summer in southern England
WHERE FOUND Shallow freshwater lagoons, coastal marshes, muddy estuary creeks of W Europe; breeds N Scandinavia

Marsh Sandpiper *Tringa stagnatilis*

Adult, breeding
Long white V like Greenshank, but whiter tail; long legs trail beyond tail

Juvenile wing covert

Head of adult often white by July

Needle-like bill diagnostic

Summer   **Winter**

Fresh juvenile (above)
By July, buff/brown patterning often lost to give adult grey on back, but pale-edged wing feathers remain

Some have more barring on tertials

Adult, winter
Upperparts pale grey, becoming browner with wear; very white below, on forehead, and over eye

A rather small-bodied but long-legged, upstanding waterside bird with a thin, straight bill, dull legs, dark wings, and a Greenshank-like white V on its back

Adult, breeding
Full breeding plumage: many retain some grey winter feathers, with fewer black diamonds on back. Some, probably female, are less marked on chest

Bill fine, straight, rather long. Legs long, slender, dark or pale olive-green (compare with heavier, thicker-billed, larger Greenshank)

A rarity in Europe, this is a bird of central Asia that sometimes strays westwards on migration. It resembles a smaller, more dainty Greenshank but its very thin, straight bill identifies it at once. It is often unusually tame.

FEEDING It picks worms and insects from shallow water in ditches or pools.

DISPLAY & VOICE Breeding behaviour is little known, but it produces a melodious, far-carrying song. The usual calls from migrants are short, sharp and metallic, such as *kew* or *tew*.

BREEDING Pairs or small groups nest on the ground in wet river valleys, flooded meadows, or shallow marshes. The usual clutch is of four eggs.

MIGRATION Marsh sandpipers move south from eastern Europe and central Asia through the Middle East; a few winter in Egypt and the Arabian Gulf but most go to Africa and India. In spring some straggle west as far as Britain and the Netherlands.

LENGTH 22–24cm (9–9½in)

WHEN TO SEE Mostly May to August in W Europe, but sporadic breeders in north and east. A few regularly winter in Spain
WHERE FOUND Rare in shallow lagoons and freshwater marshes of S and W Europe

Grey Phalarope *Phalaropus fulicarius*

Such a tiny, dainty bird seems ill-fitted to a life at sea, yet for much of the year it rides the waves in mid ocean, buoyant as a cork and as resilient as a bird several times its size.

FEEDING Phalaropes mostly eat small invertebrates, but they also take seeds, especially in the breeding season. They pick most of their food from the water while swimming. In winter they eat crustaceans, gathering them from mats of floating weed and even from the backs of whales, or from the disturbed water around pods of whales.

DISPLAY & VOICE The usual sex roles are reversed, with females being larger and brighter and making circling display flights. Calls are short, shrill and clipped monosyllables: *pit* or *wit*.

BREEDING Nests are shallow cups of plant material on the ground, in small, loose colonies. Males incubate the eggs and care for the young.

MIGRATION Most spend the winter at sea off the coasts of west Africa. Some are blown ashore by gales in autumn.

LENGTH 20–22cm (8–9in)

> **WHEN TO SEE** Mostly late autumn in W Europe
> **WHERE FOUND** Breeds in Iceland and the Arctic; migrants scarce off W European seaboard, sometimes blown into coastal lagoons or lakes inland

A small, long-billed, swimming bird, normally seen in non-breeding grey, white, and black plumage; looks gleaming white underneath, with contrasted dark mask and wingtips. Usually at sea, but storm-blown onto shore or far inland

Female, breeding
Bright with mostly yellow bill, crisp white face patch

Male is duller, with more black on bill

Grey
Bill relatively thick and blunt-tipped

Red-necked
Bill finer, more pointed

Red-necked, bill from above

Juvenile, summer
(Rarely seen in Europe)

Grey, bill from above

Adult, autumn

Adult, winter

Juvenile, autumn

In autumn, buff-edged black-brown back and wing feathers of juvenile are replaced by grey more quickly than on Red-necked Phalarope

Juvenile, late autumn

Red-necked Phalarope *Phalaropus lobatus*

Red-necked Phalaropes are slightly less northerly breeders than Grey Phalaropes, but scarcely more familiar to European birdwatchers: of the two, the Grey is more frequently seen ashore in autumn. However, Red-necked Phalaropes can be found in remote parts of northwest Europe in summer.

FEEDING Typically for a phalarope the Red-necked swims while searching for food, often spinning on one spot to pick tiny insects and other creatures from the water.

DISPLAY & VOICE As with other phalaropes the female takes the lead, flying over the territory, calling and whirring her wings. Calls are mostly short, sharp *kirk* or *cherrp* notes.

BREEDING Nesting areas are wet marshes beside lakes, where single pairs or small groups nest on the ground. The male incubates three or four eggs for 17–21 days.

MIGRATION Most Red-necked Phalaropes winter at sea off Arabia; rare migrants reach western Europe.

LENGTH 18–19cm (7–7½in)

> **WHEN TO SEE** May to September
> **WHERE FOUND** Breeds in Iceland, Faeroes, Scandinavia, N Scotland (rare); on migration rare on coasts

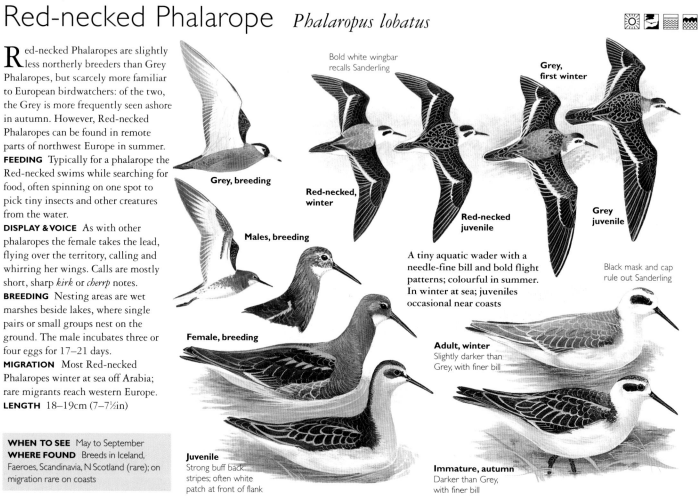

Bold white wingbar recalls Sanderling

Grey, first winter

Grey, breeding

Red-necked, winter

Red-necked juvenile

Grey juvenile

Males, breeding

A tiny aquatic wader with a needle-fine bill and bold flight patterns; colourful in summer. In winter at sea; juveniles occasional near coasts

Black mask and cap rule out Sanderling

Female, breeding

Adult, winter
Slightly darker than Grey, with finer bill

Juvenile
Strong buff back stripes; often white patch at front of flank

Immature, autumn
Darker than Grey, with finer bill

Ruff *Philomachus pugnax*

Ruffs are medium-sized, round-bodied waders with shortish bills and long legs, typically buff with scaly feather edges; males in spring are extraordinarily ornamented

Juvenile male
Large wings of male give powerful impression in flight

Juvenile female
Note feet project beyond tail in both sexes

White underwing

Narrow wingbar; long, broad wings give slow, gentle flight action over short distance

Juvenile
Buff breast

Plain head; thick, shortish, slightly curved bill

Juvenile female
Small; greenish legs

White sides to rump meet in long U-shape or create separate ovals

Males look masculine, slightly brutal; females look more delicate

Back feathers are variable

Juvenile male (left)
Large; bright buff V-shapes on back feathers; greenish legs

Feathers vary on upperparts

Mantle feathers lift in wind like a shield

Breeding female
Heavily blotched

Male
Moulting ruff in late spring

Male

Winter female
Much plainer than breeding bird. Winter males larger, often red-legged, whitish around head and neck

Breeding males, spring
Extraordinary variety in colours of ruff, tippets, and legs

Male

Male

Male

Female

In its spring plumage the male Ruff is one of the most remarkable and eyecatching of all European birds, yet it is best known as a relatively dull, brown bird of the autumn. Most Ruffs seen in Britain are juveniles on autumn migration: not so dramatic as their fathers, but subtly beautiful and exceptionally neat. Ruffs are variable in all other plumages, and also in their size: adult females are much smaller than males, and juveniles smaller still. They occupy a place between 'small waders' such as sandpipers and 'large waders' like godwits – and to match their medium size they have medium-length bills and legs. This gives them an ordinariness – outside the breeding season – that is in itself characteristic, lacking extremes of shape or structure.

FEEDING Ruffs like freshwater, not saltwater, and feed in muddy places at the edges of reservoirs, on flooded fields, or on damp grass in the kind of old-fashioned, rough, poorly-drained meadowland that has become a rarity in western Europe. Occasionally they join plovers on ploughed fields. They pick small worms and insects from the surface, occasionally taking frogs or small fish and sometimes seeds.

DISPLAY & VOICE No two males are quite alike in their spring adornments. Those with white ruffs help to attract others to a display ground, or lek, but it is often the dark-ruffed birds that are chosen as mates by watching females. The males spar and chase, performing mock fights intended to show off their fitness rather than to do real damage. Each female mates with a chosen male which then plays no further part in family matters. Ruffs are strangely silent birds. They occasionally make a low *wek* call, but unlike most waders they have no distinctive flight note.

BREEDING Once mated, the female leaves the lek and the posturing males and moves off to a secluded area, making a well-hidden nest in long grass and laying four eggs. These hatch after 20–21 days' incubation; the chicks soon leave the nest and fledge after 25–28 days. Each female rears one brood, but males may father several.

MIGRATION Most European Ruffs move to Africa in winter, but there are a number of places on the coast (and a few inland) where groups remain all winter in western Europe, including Britain and Ireland.

LENGTH Males 26–32cm (10–13in); females 20–25cm (8–10in)

WHEN TO SEE All year, mostly in non-breeding areas from July to October
WHERE FOUND Breeds Scandinavia, NE Europe and very locally Netherlands, Denmark, Germany, sporadic France and Britain; widespread migrant; winters Britain, North Sea coast, locally France, Iberia, Italy

Bar-tailed Godwit *Limosa lapponica*

This is one of a number of wading birds that have predominantly coppery-red plumage in summer, when they breed in the Arctic; they become essentially dull brown birds outside the breeding season, but the juveniles show a warmth of plumage colour that echoes the breeding adults. Unlike the Black-tailed Godwit of more temperate regions the Bar-tailed Godwit migrates far to the north in late spring, although most breed in the Low Arctic rather than High Arctic. The birds do not need to move north early, despite the length of the journey, because only in June do conditions on the tundra become feasible for nesting and rearing chicks. In winter Bar-tailed Godwits like muddy estuaries, often mixing with other waders such as Redshanks and Curlews when feeding. They fly to their high-tide roosts, often with exciting, aerobatic manoeuvres and sudden, twisting dives to the roost from a great height. At the roost they tend to form dense groups a little aside from the smaller Redshanks and Knots and the larger Curlews.

FEEDING Bar-tailed Godwits are typically active feeders, using their long, sensitive bills to probe into wet sand and soft mud in search of lugworms, molluscs, and crustaceans. They rotate their heads slightly during shallow or full-depth probes, often immersing them in shallow water.

DISPLAY & VOICE Males fly high over territories, using a range of calls. Away from the breeding area the usual call is a rather sharp, low *kirruk* or nasal *yak*.

BREEDING The nest is a scrape on a slightly raised, and therefore drier, ridge surrounded by swampy ground. Typical breeding habitat is damp, peaty terrain close to the coast, although the adults perch freely on scattered trees. Three or four eggs are incubated for three weeks and the chicks fly when around four weeks old, although the exact period is uncertain.

MIGRATION Bar-tailed Godwits breeding in northern Europe and western Siberia move to the estuaries of western Europe and down to west Africa in autumn, fewer reaching Mediterranean shores, the Red Sea, and the Arabian Gulf. The great majority winter in Mauretania. A few find their way far inland into mainland Europe, or even inland Britain. There is a marked migratory movement along the southern side of the North Sea and through the Baltic in spring.

LENGTH 37–39cm (14½–15½in)

WHEN TO SEE All year; in W Europe mostly September to May

WHERE FOUND Breeds extreme N Norway, Sweden, Finland, and Russia. Most in winter in Low Countries, Britain and Ireland, France, and W Iberia

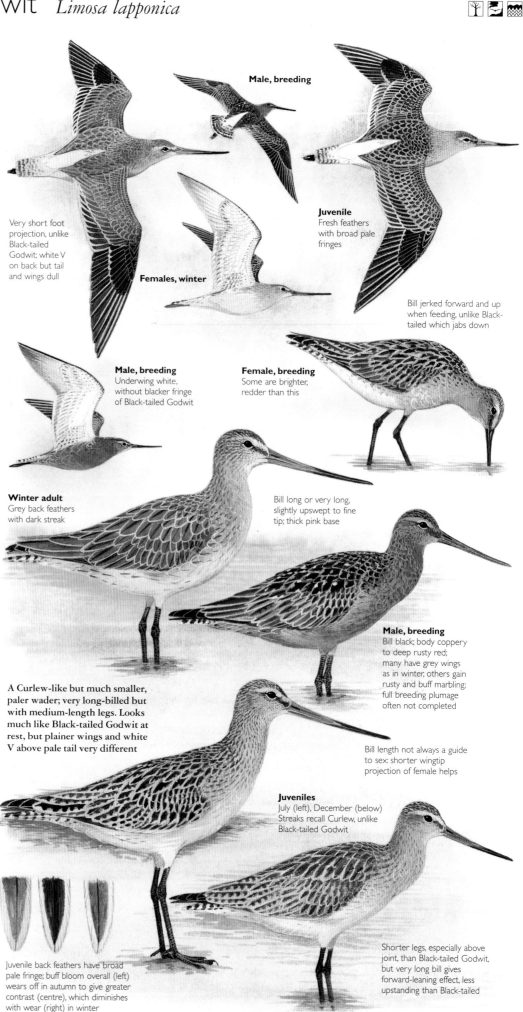

Male, breeding

Very short foot projection, unlike Black-tailed Godwit; white V on back but tail and wings dull

Females, winter

Juvenile
Fresh feathers with broad pale fringes

Bill jerked forward and up when feeding, unlike Black-tailed which jabs down

Male, breeding
Underwing white, without blacker fringe of Black-tailed Godwit

Female, breeding
Some are brighter, redder than this

Winter adult
Grey back feathers with dark streak

Bill long or very long, slightly upswept to fine tip; thick pink base

A Curlew-like but much smaller, paler wader; very long-billed but with medium-length legs. Looks much like Black-tailed Godwit at rest, but plainer wings and white V above pale tail very different

Male, breeding
Bill black; body coppery to deep rusty red; many have grey wings as in winter, others gain rusty and buff marbling; full breeding plumage often not completed

Bill length not always a guide to sex: shorter wingtip projection of female helps

Juveniles
July (left), December (below)
Streaks recall Curlew, unlike Black-tailed Godwit

Juvenile back feathers have broad pale fringe; buff bloom overall (left) wears off in autumn to give greater contrast (centre), which diminishes with wear (right) in winter

Shorter legs, especially above joint, than Black-tailed Godwit, but very long bill gives forward-leaning effect, less upstanding than Black-tailed

126

Black-tailed Godwit *Limosa limosa*

Large, but much smaller than a Curlew, elegant and upstanding; particularly long-legged and long-billed, even for a wader. Essentially dark at rest, it reveals a dramatic pattern of white when it spreads its wings

White patch above black tail; long leg projection unlike Bar-tailed Godwit

Broad wingbar less extensive than Oystercatcher's, quite unlike Bar-tailed Godwit

Adult, breeding
Extensive white underwing

Adult, winter

First winter

Icelandic race (right)
Shorter bill; breeding plumage very deep red, more complete than southern birds

Adult female, winter
Very plain grey-brown; large pink area on bill

Tail and wingtips of adult barely project beyond tertials

Female (above) has longer bill than male (below)

Breeding plumage rusty-red; white on belly and dark flank bars unlike Bar-tailed Godwit

Male, first winter
Tail and wingtips well beyond tertials

First year
From about December, more barred on tertials than winter adult, more pale buff feather edges and more spotted look than plain adult

Male, breeding, southern bird
Often greyer on wings and tertials through summer

Juvenile
Fresh plumage warm orange-buff, with large buff feather edges on upperparts; much bigger than young Ruff, with longer and blacker legs

Typical feeding pose, with bill vertical, tail up, mantle feathers lifted in wind; jabs bill down when feeding

Female, breeding
Often paler, more buff

Bill often as long, but straighter, than that of Bar-tailed Godwit; legs longer, especially above the joint

In a bird family marked by elegance and grace the Black-tailed Godwit stands out as a particularly upstanding, long-legged and long-billed bird, although it does not have quite the sinuous ease of movement displayed by some of its smaller relatives. In flight its legs trail well beyond its tail; on the ground it tends to feed with its bill pointing vertically down to probe close to its toes. It has declined substantially over much of its former breeding range in western Europe because of changes in agriculture, especially the drainage and 'improvement' of wet pasture. In most countries it is most familiar as a wintering species, on sheltered, muddy, mild estuaries.

FEEDING It locates prey by sight and by touch, immersing the sensitive tip of its long bill into shallow water or soft mud. The bird probes almost vertically and quite vigorously, with sudden rapid, deep probes once it has detected prey. The unfortunate worm or mollusc is then hauled out and usually swallowed instantly.

DISPLAY & VOICE The display flights by the male are varied, rising and falling and often employing half-rolls onto one side before the bird nose-dives steeply to the ground. The display shows off the bold white wing stripes and bold contrast between the white underwings and dark belly. The song during these flights is far-carrying, high-pitched, and ringing, although with a Lapwing-like nasal quality. Other calls are a strident *weeka-weeka-weeka*, *kip kip* and *chut*.

BREEDING In Iceland Black-tailed Godwits occupy vast areas of marshy moorland, drier hummocks, and damp meadows. Elsewhere some use moorland sites and even heathland, but most breed on farmland, particularly in waterlogged areas which may be prone to flooding. This can cause a failure to rear chicks in some years. Three or four eggs are laid in a shallow hollow in the ground, either exposed or more hidden in short vegetation, and incubated for 22–24 days. The chicks leave the nest soon after hatching, like those of other waders; they feed easily from the start and fly after 25–30 days.

MIGRATION Many breed in Iceland and spend the winter in western Europe. Others breed in Denmark, the Netherlands, and across northeastern Europe, then migrate in autumn to southern Europe and the Middle East and on into west Africa along the southern edge of the Sahara.

LENGTH 40–44cm (16–17in)

WHEN TO SEE All year
WHERE FOUND Breeds Iceland, very locally Norway and Sweden, Britain and France, more widely Denmark and the Netherlands, Germany, Poland, and scattered across E Europe

127

Golden Plover *Pluvialis apricaria*

In summer this is a colourful bird of upland moors and mountains, but in winter it becomes much more subdued and lives in flocks in the lowlands. In its breeding areas it is a wild, solitary bird with far-carrying calls that make it difficult to locate, but on its wintering grounds it is often mixed with Lapwings and Black-headed Gulls on pastures or ploughed fields.

FEEDING It has a run-and-tilt action, picking worms and insects from the ground; it is often robbed by gulls.

DISPLAY & VOICE Breeding males fly over their territories with a slow, butterfly-like wing action and a plaintive, wailing song. Flight calls are liquid *too-ee* and *tloo* notes.

BREEDING Nests are shallow scrapes on the ground, on limestone grassland, heathery moors, or low tundra in the far north. Four eggs hatch after 28–31 days; the young fly 30 days later.

MIGRATION A general movement to the south and west in winter.

LENGTH 26–29cm (10–11in)

WHEN TO SEE All year; March to August on breeding areas
WHERE FOUND Iceland, Britain, Scandinavia; in winter NW France, Low Countries, locally south to Mediterranean

A short-billed, round-headed terrestrial bird, inconspicuous on ground; yellow spangled upperparts clear at close range but uniform golden-brown at distance

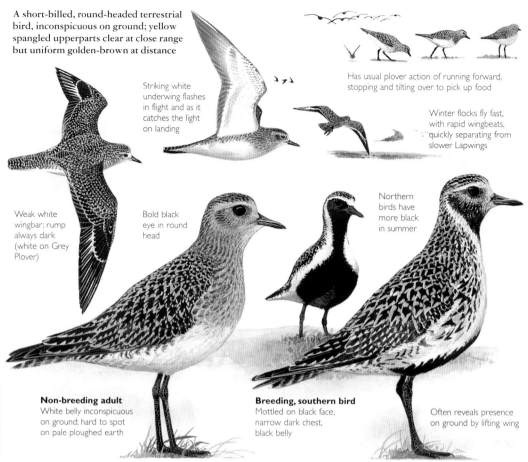

Has usual plover action of running forward, stopping and tilting over to pick up food

Winter flocks fly fast, with rapid wingbeats, quickly separating from slower Lapwings

Striking white underwing flashes in flight and as it catches the light on landing

Weak white wingbar; rump always dark (white on Grey Plover)

Bold black eye in round head

Northern birds have more black in summer

Non-breeding adult White belly inconspicuous on ground; hard to spot on pale ploughed earth

Breeding, southern bird Mottled on black face, narrow dark chest, black belly

Often reveals presence on ground by lifting wing

Grey Plover *Pluvialis squatarola*

A larger, more northerly counterpart of the Golden Plover, the Grey Plover is a bird of High Arctic tundra in the brief northern summer, and of estuaries for the rest of the year. It is a coastal wader in winter, not usually found inland or on farmland habitats used by Golden Plovers and Lapwings.

FEEDING In winter it pulls most of its food from soft mud: small worms, crustaceans, and molluscs. It usually pecks from the surface, stands still for several seconds, then moves to a new spot and repeats the process.

VOICE Grey Plovers are easily detected on estuaries by their far-carrying boyish whistle, a three-note *tlee-oo-ee*, the middle note lower.

BREEDING This is a bird of the northern tundra, beyond the tree limit, nesting on drier, stony ridges above rolling ground with patches of snow. The four eggs hatch after 26–27 days.

MIGRATION Many spend the winter in northwest Europe; others fly to southern Africa and Australia.

LENGTH 27–30cm (11–12in)

WHEN TO SEE All year; only a few remain in Europe in summer
WHERE FOUND Most W European coasts, locally in Mediterranean

A stocky, thick-billed, large-eyed wader; usually looks rather dark out on an estuary but close views reveal spangling; unique black 'armpits' in flight

Adult, autumn Moulting

Stronger wingbar than Golden Plover; white rump

Non-breeding Large, heavy bill for a plover; bold black eye; rather dull, plain brownish-grey in winter

Breeding Stunning silver and black from late spring to early autumn

Adult, winter No other wader has black underwing patches

Juvenile Spangled black and yellowish-buff through first winter

Adult, breeding From below

Lapwing *Vanellus vanellus*

Despite a widespread decline with changing farming practices, the Lapwing remains a familiar and much-loved bird in Europe. In spring males perform exciting display flights, while in winter Lapwings gather into large flocks, often of hundreds and sometimes thousands, in lowland fields and flooded pastures. In the past its eggs were gathered as a spring delicacy: today, though, so few remain in most areas that it would be difficult to find them.

FEEDING Lapwings frequently feed sociably, even in summer, but they inevitably compete for food with each other and face competition from Golden Plovers and gulls in winter. They eat small invertebrates and worms, sometimes pulling them from the ground with much effort. Lapwings are often seen pattering the ground with their feet, to soften it and gain access to buried prey. Occasionally they feed on moonlit nights.

DISPLAY & VOICE The song flight of the Lapwing is a memorable feature of the countryside in early spring: males fly up, twist and tumble and dive apparently out of control towards the ground, only to rise again with loudly-beating wings. The throb of the wing feathers combines with a loud, nasal, rhythmic song: *airr, willuch-o-weep*. Other calls include notes that give rise to several local names, such as peewit: *peer-wit, pee-wee, weep* and similar variants on the theme.

BREEDING The nest is little more than a shallow scrape on the ground, in an open space with a good view of potential dangers. Lapwings like a patchwork of bare earth and short grass: the change to autumn-sown cereals has made life difficult for them, as the crop is usually too tall and dense for small chicks by the time the Lapwing eggs hatch. Four eggs are laid, hatching after 28 days; the chicks fly when they are about 35–40 days old.

MIGRATION Lapwings are present all year in parts of southern and western Europe, but even there they make local movements, or leave the hills and gather on lowland farmland. They are joined by many more from northern and eastern Europe, which move west and south each autumn to escape the icy winters. Cold spells and especially snow in winter frequently cause mass movements to the south and west of Britain and Ireland, and into France and Spain.

LENGTH 28–31cm (11–12in)

WHEN TO SEE All year
WHERE FOUND Almost all of Europe in summer, on farmland and moors; south from Britain and Low Countries in winter, chiefly on pastures, ploughed land, and also coastal grazing marshes

---

Distinctive jerky action in flight, recognizable at great distance

White rump contrasts with black tailband

Male **Female**

Male has broader, rounder outer wing than female; flight often highly aerobatic when coming in to land

Striking white underwing coverts contrast with black quills

Raises wings as it settles and also to ward off intruders at nest

Juvenile
Pale-edged upperpart feathers and short crest; non-breeding adult similar but crest longer

Male, breeding
Black throat; female's throat has small white mottles

A sociable, short-billed, thickset black and white bird with a unique wispy crest. Black breastband contrasts with white belly and underwing, while green upperside looks dark at long range or in flight. Unmistakable broad-winged shape in the air; solitary birds not infrequent

Juvenile

Non-breeding
White throat; pale buff tips to upperpart feathers

Female **Male**

Winter male has broader, blacker breastband, blacker face patch, longer crest than female

Spur-winged Plover *Hoplopterus spinosus*

This splendid 'lapwing' is found in the Middle East and Africa in a broad band from west Africa to Kenya, and only just makes Europe with a sparse population in Greece. Where it is common it forms large, loose parties; everywhere the pairs are eyecatching, bold, and noisy.

FEEDING Mostly insects, picked from the ground in areas with dried mud or bare patches on grassy banks.

DISPLAY & VOICE The birds typically display on the ground, showing off the head and breast pattern in forward-leaning runs; they also stand upright with opened wings to reveal their vivid undersides. Calls include a strident, screeching *did-he do-it* and sharp, metallic *hik* or *zik zik* alarm notes.

BREEDING Four eggs are laid on the ground; incubation lasts 22–24 days.

MIGRATION The small numbers breeding in Greece and Turkey move south to northern Africa in September, returning in March and April.

LENGTH 25–27cm (10–10½in)

WHEN TO SEE Mid March to late September
WHERE FOUND Sandbanks, grassy flats, and embankments beside lagoons, marshes, and rivers; in Europe only in Greece

White beneath wing contrasting with black belly and white band on upperwing unique in Europe

Adult male (left) Feet project farther beyond tail than on female. Spurs on forewing rarely visible

Adult female (right) Shorter foot projection and narrower tail band than on adult male

Adult female Shorter wingtip than on male (shown beneath)

Broad wings reveal affinity to Lapwing

Juvenile has barred upperpart feathers, brown bars on crown

A strikingly contrasted wader of rather dry, open, waterside habitats; the bold black cap, white neck patch and broad white band along the upperwing are diagnostic; sharp, agitated calls draw attention to its presence

Whimbrel *Numenius phaeopus*

While Curlews are present in Europe all year round, Whimbrels are welcome visitors in spring, sometimes moving north in flocks of several dozen together. In autumn they make a more leisurely return southwards, their frequent flight calls drawing attention to small parties flying high overhead.

FEEDING Whimbrels probe for worms and take various insects and molluscs.

DISPLAY & VOICE The song is a beautiful repetition of low, fluty notes, accelerating into a more rapid trill than the very similar Curlew song. The call is a quick series of sharp notes in an evenly-pitched trill: *pip ip ip ip ip ip ip*.

BREEDING Whimbrels breed on northern moors and wild heath, from sea level to high tundra and hills above the tree-line, nesting on the ground. The three or four large eggs hatch after 27–28 days.

MIGRATION European populations migrate south to the coasts of Africa each winter.

LENGTH 40–42cm (16–16½in)

WHEN TO SEE Mostly April to October
WHERE FOUND Moors and islands of Iceland, N Scotland, Scandinavia; widespread on migration on W European coasts

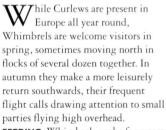

Adult Long, dark wings and clean white V on lower back and rump. Long, flat crown, shortish bill

Slightly darker, quicker, chunkier and deeper-chested than Curlew in flight

Adult On average, bill longer on female, but some overlap

Note head stripes

Both sexes deep pink on bill outside breeding season

Female

Wingtips equal tail tip on female (top), shorter on male

Male, breeding

Juvenile Fresh feathers have neat buff edges

Breeding birds have pale notches on fresh feathers

Upperparts look darker by midsummer as pale spots wear away

Very Curlew-like, the Whimbrel is smaller, darker, more stripey-headed, with a slightly shorter bill; in flight it is more compact, quick, and dark-looking

Curlew *Numenius arquata*

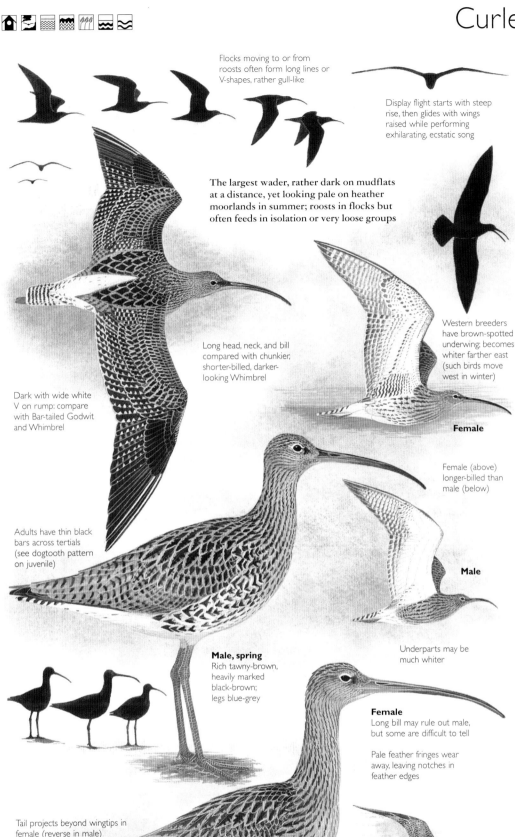

Flocks moving to or from roosts often form long lines or V-shapes, rather gull-like

Display flight starts with steep rise, then glides with wings raised while performing exhilarating, ecstatic song

The largest wader, rather dark on mudflats at a distance, yet looking pale on heather moorlands in summer; roosts in flocks but often feeds in isolation or very loose groups

Western breeders have brown-spotted underwing; becomes whiter farther east (such birds move west in winter)

Female

Long head, neck, and bill compared with chunkier, shorter-billed, darker-looking Whimbrel

Dark with wide white V on rump: compare with Bar-tailed Godwit and Whimbrel

Female (above) longer-billed than male (below)

Adults have thin black bars across tertials (see dogtooth pattern on juvenile)

Male

Male, spring
Rich tawny-brown, heavily marked black-brown; legs blue-grey

Underparts may be much whiter

Female
Long bill may rule out male, but some are difficult to tell

Pale feather fringes wear away, leaving notches in feather edges

Tail projects beyond wingtips in female (reverse in male)

Juvenile
Note dogtooth dark barring at rear

Large, stately and blessed with a wonderful voice, the Curlew is also remarkable for its long, smoothly-downcurved bill. It is a widespread bird with a range of habitats, familiar both inland and on the coast, on remote hills and in grassy meadows, on wild marshes and beside busy seaside promenades. Throughout most of the year it is the distinctive voice of the saltmarsh and muddy estuary, and in spring it is the chief glory of the heather moor and blanket bog. Curlews are sociable outside the breeding season and form large flocks at high tide. Yet they often keep separate from the godwits, Redshanks, Grey Plovers, and smaller waders that roost nearby, forming long lines of bigger, hunched, dark-looking birds that might almost be taken for young gulls.

FEEDING The benefit of the Curlew's curved bill is still debated. It may give the bird a better view of its bill-tip for more precise probing. It probably allows easier withdrawal of worms from deep within sand and mud in one long, backward-leaning pull. If it can be rotated in wet mud or sand it could also let the Curlew detect prey in a wider area than a simple probe with a straight bill. It is certainly sensitive at the tip and can both feel and grasp worms, crabs, shellfish, and similar prey hidden in mud or sand, beneath seaweed, in rock pools, or under clumps of heather, grasses, or rushes. The bird shakes crabs to break off their legs, and usually washes lugworms before swallowing them whole.

DISPLAY & VOICE In spring Curlews fly over their breeding territories, rising with slow wingbeats and then gliding slowly down, with a song that begins with long, slow, melancholy notes and develops into a fast, liquid, throbbing or bubbling ecstatic trill. The song may be heard at other times of the year in a more or less developed form, with a variety of loud calls: a hoarse, throaty *whaup*, a repeated *lee lee lee* and a liquid, sad *cour-li*. These calls echo around saltmarsh creeks and estuaries, and are an essential part of their atmosphere.

BREEDING The nest is a grass-lined hollow in heather, grass, or rushes, on a quiet moor or in a rough field. Four eggs hatch after 27–29 days; the chicks fly when about five weeks old.

MIGRATION Many Curlews simply move to the coast in autumn, but some western European breeders go south to Iberia; northern and eastern European nesters move south and west.

LENGTH 50–60cm (20–24in)

WHEN TO SEE All year
WHERE FOUND Breeds Ireland, Britain, NW France east across Europe to Siberia, north to N Norway, south to S France and parts of S Germany; widespread migrant

131

Woodcock *Scolopax rusticola*

Unusually for a wading bird the Woodcock is active between dusk and dawn and lives in woodland, not on the shore. More heavily built than a Snipe, with broader wings and a thicker bill, it is associated with deep leaf mould on the forest floor, beneath brambles, or sometimes under thick bracken on open slopes.

FEEDING It probes for earthworms in soft earth, its flexible bill detecting and grasping them deep underground.

DISPLAY & VOICE Males display at dusk, flying at treetop height and alternating sharp whistles with throaty croaks. Some people hear the high *tswik* more easily than the deep, double *grrk grrk;* others find the opposite.

BREEDING Four eggs are laid on the ground; the chicks fly when just 15–20 days old. Females breed at one year old, males at two.

MIGRATION Most birds breeding in continental Europe migrate west or south in winter to areas bordering the North Sea and Mediterranean.

LENGTH 33–35cm (13–14in)

WHEN TO SEE Breeds March to August
WHERE FOUND Mixed and deciduous woods, meadows and field edges in winter; Ireland eastwards to Russia, sparse in south

A stocky, long-billed, barrel-chested bird with complex patterns; rarely seen on the ground. If disturbed, flies off fast and low with noisy wingbeats

Dark silhouette over woods at dusk

Many shorter-billed birds now found; the reason is not known

Wings angled back to short point

Fast, noisy take-off if disturbed

Back of head has broad black bars

Eyes far back on head

Rich brown, buff, and grey mottling above

Bill points down in flight

Note white tail band

Whole underside narrowly barred

Sometimes feeds in the open by day in hard winter weather

At dusk watch for birds moving to feeding areas at treetop height

Great Snipe *Gallinago media*

A heavy-bodied snipe with a rather thick bill, this rare bird should not be confused with the common Snipe; it is much heavier, has broader wings and a slower, more Woodcock-like flight. Usually seen in the air, its bold wing pattern and white tail sides are its most distinctive features. If flushed at close range its flight is low and straight, lacking the fast zigzags of the Snipe.

FEEDING It feeds in typical snipe fashion, probing for worms in soft earth and wet mud.

DISPLAY & VOICE Groups gather on the ground where males puff out their plumage and perform low, fluttering leaps and complex posturings, along with gurgling and rasping sounds.

BREEDING It breeds in areas of mixed bog and open woodland: marshy mountain slopes and drier places in the north; extensive marshes in the east. The four eggs hatch in 22–24 days.

MIGRATION The whole population migrates to Africa for the winter.

LENGTH 27–29cm (10½–11½in)

WHEN TO SEE April to October
WHERE FOUND Wild and remote marshes in central Scandinavia, NE Europe; on migration very rare in rough, often drier ground in W Europe

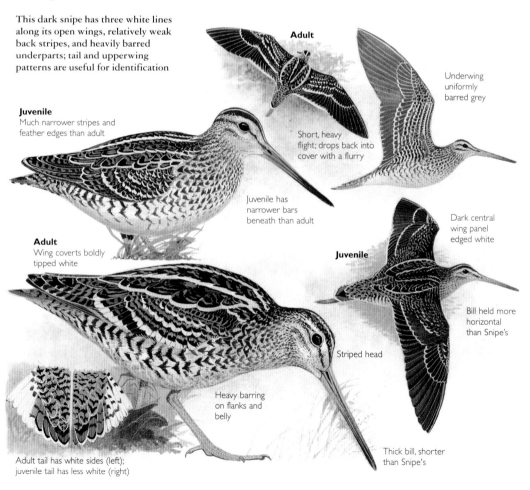

This dark snipe has three white lines along its open wings, relatively weak back stripes, and heavily barred underparts; tail and upperwing patterns are useful for identification

Adult

Juvenile Much narrower stripes and feather edges than adult

Underwing uniformly barred grey

Short, heavy flight; drops back into cover with a flurry

Juvenile has narrower bars beneath than adult

Adult Wing coverts boldly tipped white

Dark central wing panel edged white

Juvenile

Bill held more horizontal than Snipe's

Striped head

Heavy barring on flanks and belly

Thick bill, shorter than Snipe's

Adult tail has white sides (left); juvenile tail has less white (right)

Snipe *Gallinago gallinago*

A marshland wader that flies up almost underfoot with a loud rasping call; striped back and dark wings distinctive but hard to see in sudden, fast zigzag take-off

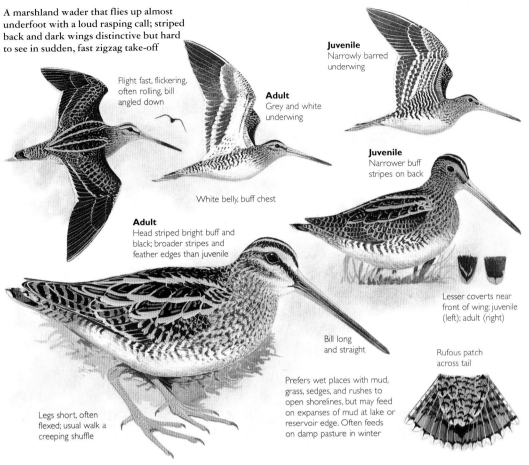

Flight fast, flickering, often rolling, bill angled down

Adult
Grey and white underwing

Juvenile
Narrowly barred underwing

Juvenile
Narrower buff stripes on back

White belly, buff chest

Adult
Head striped bright buff and black; broader stripes and feather edges than juvenile

Bill long and straight

Lesser coverts near front of wing: juvenile (left); adult (right)

Rufous patch across tail

Legs short, often flexed; usual walk a creeping shuffle

Prefers wet places with mud, grass, sedges, and rushes to open shorelines, but may feed on expanses of mud at lake or reservoir edge. Often feeds on damp pasture in winter

Favouring overgrown mud and shallow water, the Snipe is hard to see when on the ground. It flies away high and fast if disturbed, sometimes in small groups or 'wisps'. Unlike most waders it does not normally associate with other species.

FEEDING It needs soft ground so it can probe for earthworms with its sensitive bill; hard frost is a threat.

DISPLAY & VOICE Snipe are easiest to see in spring when the males display in high switchback flights, producing a buzzing whirr (known as 'drumming') from their stiff tail feathers. They also stand on wires or telegraph poles calling with repetitive *chip-per* notes. When flushed from cover they call with a hard tearing or rasping note.

BREEDING Snipe typically breed on wet meadows or moors; four eggs laid on the ground hatch in 18–20 days.

MIGRATION Most European Snipe move west or south in winter to Britain and Ireland, France, Spain, Greece, and Turkey.

LENGTH 25–27cm (10–10½in)

WHEN TO SEE All year; March to August in north and east of range
WHERE FOUND Breeds Iceland, Britain, Netherlands eastwards, in marshes and on upland moors; scattered farther south

Jack Snipe *Lymnocryptes minimus*

A small, short-billed, dark-backed snipe, restricted to grassy or rushy vegetation in wet places; typically seen only when put up at very close range

Looks dumpy, with short rear body, triangular head, and shortish bill. White belly contrasts with dark underwing

Shows strong back stripes and a dark central crown

Rather dull, poorly marked underwing

Flies up in sudden flutter, half-circles then drops down

Dark, dull, pointed tail

Long cream stripes contrast with green-glossed blackish back

Central crown stripe dark (pale on Snipe)

Dark wing with pale trailing edge

Bill shorter than Snipe's

Wedge-shaped tail has no rufous

A skulking bird of dense marsh vegetation, the Jack Snipe is even more secretive than the Snipe and extremely hard to spot on the ground. It is usually seen as it flies up when almost trodden on, quickly dropping back into the marsh. Even if there are several in a small marsh they usually rise singly and rarely join up in the air, unlike common Snipe.

FEEDING The typical snipe probing for worms is accompanied by a characteristic springy bobbing action.

DISPLAY & VOICE When flushed it is usually silent, unlike the Snipe, but in display it produces muffled sounds like a distant cantering horse.

BREEDING Jack Snipe breed in open spaces in northern forests, laying four eggs in a nest on the ground and incubating them for 17–24 days.

MIGRATION The species winters in Britain and Ireland, the Low Countries, and parts of southern Europe, arriving there in September and October and leaving in late March.

LENGTH 17–19cm (7–7½in)

WHEN TO SEE April to September in north; September to May in west
WHERE FOUND Densely vegetated muddy or waterlogged marshes; breeds NE Scandinavia, winters in W Europe

Great Skua *Stercorarius skua*

The largest and heaviest of the skuas, with the broadest wings and slowest direct flight, the Great Skua can be powerful and fast when necessary; it is able to tip a Gannet into the sea by grabbing its wing in flight. It is often an exciting bird to watch.

FEEDING This big skua is a pirate, chasing gulls, terns, Fulmars, and Gannets to steal fish; it also kills many auks, Kittiwakes, and other birds.

DISPLAY & VOICE Its displays include raising its wings while on the ground to show off the big white patches to best effect. Its vocal repertoire is restricted to short, low, gruff notes and deep *tuk tuk* calls.

BREEDING Nests are shallow scrapes in loose colonies on remote islands and coastal moors. The birds are fiercely protective of their eggs and chicks.

MIGRATION In autumn all Great Skuas move south, many through the North Sea and English Channel, to winter at sea in the South Atlantic.

LENGTH 53–58cm (21–23in)

WHEN TO SEE Mostly March to October, rare in winter
WHERE FOUND Breeds on peaty and moorland hills and islands from N Scotland north to Faeroes, Iceland. On migration, seen off many western headlands

Adults often streaked pale gingery-buff; some juveniles very dark, with smaller wing patches

Capable of killing gulls and auks on water with hammer blows of bill

Thick, hooked, dark bill

A dark, powerful, gull-like bird with large white wing patches. Looks heavy-bodied and broad-winged; usually flies low over the sea singly or in pairs. Size, bulky body, and long, ample wings (especially 'arm' length) distinguish it from other skuas

Can accelerate dramatically when chasing a gull or Gannet, showing power and agility in short chase

Tail is short, square, or slightly wedge-shaped with only very short central projection

Clear white patches on the outer wing, especially beneath, show at great range

Rare individuals look bleached creamy-buff, especially around head and neck

Long 'arm'

Plumage (including wing patches) too variable to be reliable; best to go by size and shape

Arctic Skua **Pomarine Skua** **Great Skua**

Pomarine Skua *Stercorarius pomarinus*

A big skua, the Pomarine has the variable colour phases of the Arctic Skua but almost matches the Great Skua in bulk and power. It is generally the scarcest of the three, although it can be seen from many headlands in May and may be relatively numerous in late autumn.

FEEDING Like other skuas it harries seabirds until they drop fish, and also kills a number of gulls and auks; on the tundra it eats mainly lemmings.

DISPLAY & VOICE Exciting aerial displays take place over breeding sites. It is silent at sea.

BREEDING It nests on northern tundra and lays two eggs in June. Like other skuas it attacks intruders – animal or human – at the nest.

MIGRATION Spring movement to the north is often concentrated in May, through the English Channel and North Sea or around western Scotland. Return movements take place from August to November; a few spend the winter in western Europe, but most move far south.

LENGTH 46–51cm (18–20in)

WHEN TO SEE In W Europe mostly May to November
WHERE FOUND Off headlands, in northern estuaries.

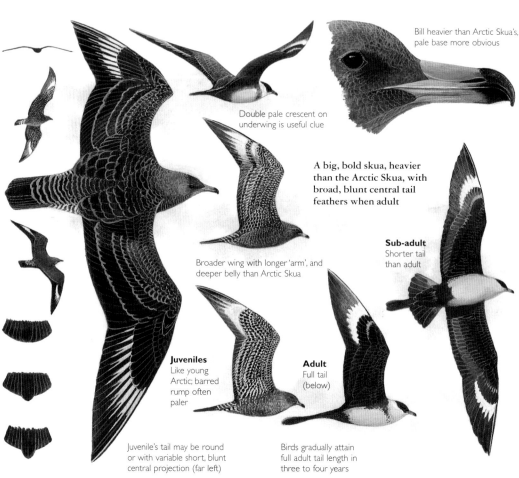

Bill heavier than Arctic Skua's, pale base more obvious

Double pale crescent on underwing is useful clue

A big, bold skua, heavier than the Arctic Skua, with broad, blunt central tail feathers when adult

Sub-adult Shorter tail than adult

Broader wing with longer 'arm', and deeper belly than Arctic Skua

Juveniles Like young Arctic; barred rump often paler

Adult Full tail (below)

Juvenile's tail may be round or with variable short, blunt central projection (far left)

Birds gradually attain full adult tail length in three to four years

Arctic Skua *Stercorarius parasiticus*

An exciting, ocean-going buccaneer with long, slim, pointed wings and a pointed tail spike when adult. Flies low over the sea in a steady, relaxed flight, accelerating to chase terns or gulls in acrobatic attack

An agile, elegant, fast-flying pirate of the seas, the Arctic Skua lives by forcing other birds to give up the prey they have caught. On migration it flies low over the ocean, moving easily in relaxed, supple flight. It is unusual in that it can be seen in two or three different colour varieties.

FEEDING Arctic Skuas chase gulls, terns, and auks until they disgorge fish; they often harry their victims in pairs.

DISPLAY & VOICE At the breeding grounds loud, nasal, wailing *ya-woh* or *gee-ah* calls accompany wild, dashing display flights which include steep climbs and fast, roaring dives.

BREEDING Nests are on the ground on wild coastal moorland, close to other seabird colonies.

MIGRATION Arctic Skuas move south in autumn, passing most European coasts on their way to the South Atlantic. They are less commonly seen on their return in spring.

LENGTH 41–46cm (16–18in)

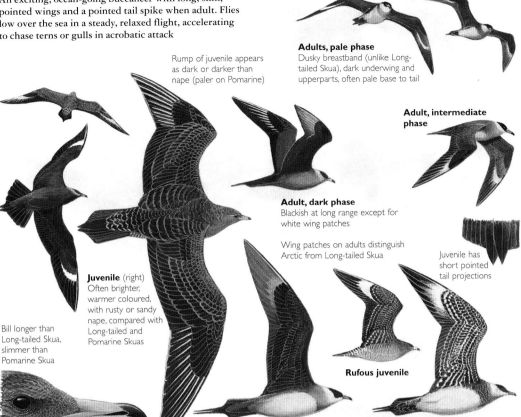

Rump of juvenile appears as dark or darker than nape (paler on Pomarine)

Adults, pale phase
Dusky breastband (unlike Long-tailed Skua), dark underwing and upperparts, often pale base to tail

Adult, intermediate phase

Adult, dark phase
Blackish at long range except for white wing patches

Wing patches on adults distinguish Arctic from Long-tailed Skua

Juvenile has short pointed tail projections

Juvenile (right)
Often brighter, warmer coloured, with rusty or sandy nape, compared with Long-tailed and Pomarine Skuas

Bill longer than Long-tailed Skua, slimmer than Pomarine Skua

All primary shafts white

Rufous juvenile

Pale adult

Pale sub-adult

Long-tailed Skua *Stercorarius longicaudus*

A small, tern-like skua with a short bill and long narrow wings that make it look larger in flight; adults have long, whippy tail projections. Flight easy at sea: light body gives it a more floating action than the heavily laden Arctic Skua. They can look similar to brown terns

Long-winged, slender, and distinctly tern-like, with exceptionally long tail streamers on adults, this is a predatory bird in summer and less piratical than the Arctic Skua. Of all the European skuas it is the least common off western European headlands in spring and autumn, although in some years large numbers are seen at favoured sites.

FEEDING It preys upon lemmings and other small mammals, small birds, eggs, and fish. It rears more young in good lemming years than in poor years, when many pairs fail to breed.

VOICE It calls with high-pitched squeals near the nest; otherwise silent.

BREEDING The Long-tailed Skua nests on the ground, on high arctic-alpine hills and coastal tundra. It lays two eggs which hatch after 23–25 days.

MIGRATION Long-tailed Skuas move south in autumn, but are scarce off most coasts; they winter in the South Atlantic. In some years there is a marked spring movement off the Western Isles of Scotland.

LENGTH 35–58cm (14–23in)

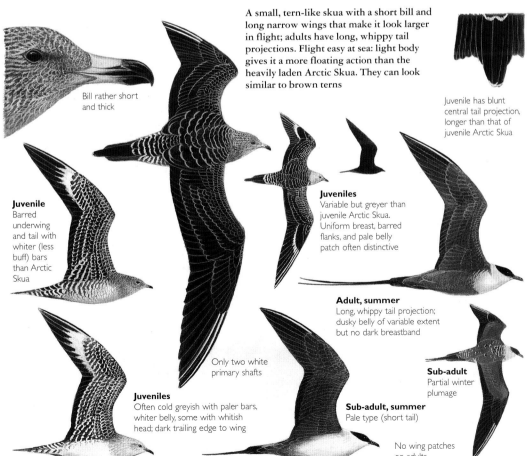

Juvenile has blunt central tail projection, longer than that of juvenile Arctic Skua

Bill rather short and thick

Juvenile
Barred underwing and tail with whiter (less buff) bars than Arctic Skua

Juveniles
Variable but greyer than juvenile Arctic Skua. Uniform breast, barred flanks, and pale belly patch often distinctive

Only two white primary shafts

Juveniles
Often cold greyish with paler bars, whiter belly, some with whitish head; dark trailing edge to wing

Adult, summer
Long, whippy tail projection; dusky belly of variable extent but no dark breastband

Sub-adult, summer
Pale type (short tail)

Sub-adult
Partial winter plumage

No wing patches on adults

135

Black-headed Gull *Larus ridibundus*

Few gulls are really restricted to the sea. The Black-headed Gull never has been, and flocks of these gulls seen inland are no indication of conditions at sea. They breed inland as often as they breed near the coast, favouring sites beside lakes both in the lowlands and on hills and moors. In autumn they follow the plough, gleaming white against the dark, freshly turned earth. In winter they are still on the fields, finding worms or chasing Lapwings to steal theirs. Flocks forage along riversides even in city centres, while groups stand around on shop roofs or dive briefly into gardens to pick up scraps. In short, they are everywhere: easy to see, easy to learn, and thoroughly enjoyable. They squabble and scrap, adding life and movement wherever they are. If your interest lies in more unusual species Black-headed Gulls still have appeal, because their flocks are likely to attract wandering rarities such as a Mediterranean Gull.

FEEDING They catch insects and other small invertebrates, including a great many earthworms, on grass or ploughed land. They snatch insects from the air, especially flying ants, and pick caterpillars and even fruit from leafy trees. They also capture small fish and other aquatic creatures, picking them from the surface in flight or grabbing them in shallow plunges.

DISPLAY & VOICE In summer the birds use their dark hoods as signals of aggression or dominance, showing their pale napes as they turn their heads in a head-flagging display. Calls are equally important in displays: most have a high-pitched, squealing or grating quality: *kwarrr*, an angry, emphatic *kee-earr*, *kwuk*, *kuk-uk*, *orr* and variations. Feeding groups make a quiet, babbling, yapping chorus.

BREEDING They nest in colonies of anything from two pairs to several hundred. The nests vary from small scrapes in mud or peat to substantial structures in reeds and rushes. Two or three eggs hatch after 23–26 days; the chicks fly when about 35 days old.

MIGRATION Many move inland to exploit feeding areas and safe roosts on reservoirs in winter; northern European breeders move south and west in autumn. The adults move back to their breeding colonies suddenly and quickly in early spring; immatures remain on their wintering grounds later into spring and summer.

LENGTH 34–37cm (13–14½in)

WHEN TO SEE All year; mostly April to September in north and east
WHERE FOUND Breeds Iceland, Britain, and Ireland, France eastwards, local in extreme north and absent from most of S Europe; widespread in winter, mostly coastal in Mediterranean region

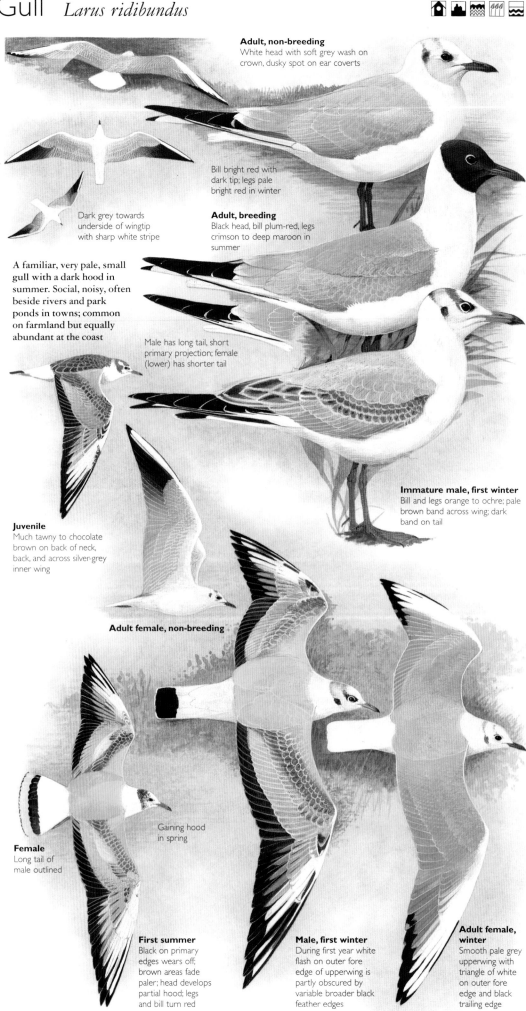

Adult, non-breeding
White head with soft grey wash on crown, dusky spot on ear coverts

Bill bright red with dark tip; legs pale bright red in winter

Dark grey towards underside of wingtip with sharp white stripe

Adult, breeding
Black head, bill plum-red, legs crimson to deep maroon in summer

A familiar, very pale, small gull with a dark hood in summer. Social, noisy, often beside rivers and park ponds in towns; common on farmland but equally abundant at the coast

Male has long tail, short primary projection; female (lower) has shorter tail

Immature male, first winter
Bill and legs orange to ochre; pale brown band across wing; dark band on tail

Juvenile
Much tawny to chocolate brown on back of neck, back, and across silver-grey inner wing

Adult female, non-breeding

Female
Long tail of male outlined

Gaining hood in spring

First summer
Black on primary edges wears off; brown areas fade paler; head develops partial hood; legs and bill turn red

Male, first winter
During first year white flash on outer fore edge of upperwing is partly obscured by variable broader black feather edges

Adult female, winter
Smooth pale grey upperwing with triangle of white on outer fore edge and black trailing edge

Mediterranean Gull *Larus melanocephalus*

Stocky in build, with a heavy bill and frowning expression, long legs and a strutting walk; rather straight, stiff, blunt wings in flight; beautifully ghostly, pearly-white plumage makes it an exceptionally handsome gull

Males

Tail of female shorter

Male

Female, first winter
Outer primaries show white lines when fully spread; pale midwing panel blends into patch behind bend of wing; narrow dark trailing edge and tail band

Second year

Adult, breeding

Second year
Adult and second year have clean white underwing, unlike Black-headed Gull

First winter
Pale, pearly-grey back and panel across midwing (darker on Common); outer primaries blackish, inner ones pale

Variable amount of black across outer primary tips in second year; probably in evolutionary process of losing black in wings

Both first and second years can look like this; much individual variation

First winter (right)
Head rounded or angular with peaked crown; black smudge through eye curves up into grey nape; white eyelids obvious; grey of back cold, hard, silvery, not bluish

During first winter bill varies from ochre-buff to dull red with black tip

Juvenile (below)
Pale head, gingery neck, black bill, bold black marks on back

Adult, non-breeding
Variable black on head may form 'mask' and turn up into grey wash across nape; bill red or black; legs red, purple-red, or black

Male (upper) longer-tailed than female (lower)

Wingtip of adult pure white: may contrast with grey back, or blend in according to light; thin black outer line at close range; underwing spotless white

Adult, breeding
Jet black hood extends over nape; big white eyelids; scarlet bill with variable black band and yellow tip

With its inky-black hood, big white eyelids, vivid red bill, pearly upperwings, and spotless white underwings, a Mediterranean Gull in breeding plumage is a stunningly beautiful bird. Even those who maintain that 'gulls are boring' cannot fail to be impressed. At other times this is a bird with real character: a bully, aggressive and confident in a mixed flock, its 'pirate patch' often completing the impression. Mediterranean Gulls were once thought to be declining in a sorry spiral towards extinction, but in recent years they have increased and spread. Before their numbers built up sufficiently to establish a small, pure population, they were so scarce in parts of western Europe that single birds sometimes formed mixed pairs with Black-headed Gulls. Now there are substantial numbers in autumn and winter at some coastal locations along both sides of the English Channel, although nesting pairs remain few and erratic over much of the species' range.

FEEDING Less likely to turn up on fields and tips inland than other gulls (although it sometimes does so) the Mediterranean Gull feeds chiefly on beaches, at sewage outfalls and over the sea, finding all kinds of offal and scraps, invertebrates, small fish, and molluscs. On its summer breeding grounds it feeds mainly on insects, snails, and earthworms.

DISPLAY & VOICE Like other hooded gulls the Mediterranean uses its bold black hood in courtship and territorial displays. It is mostly silent in winter, but in spring its calls have a nasal, throttled quality, with a piercing *whaa-whaa-whaa-whaa-oo-ah* and a more tern-like *kee-er*.

BREEDING Isolated pairs nest among Black-headed Gulls, but larger colonies in eastern Europe are usually pure. Three eggs are laid in a grassy nest on the ground; they hatch after 23–25 days, and the young fledge after another 35–40 days.

MIGRATION Black Sea breeders mostly move to the Mediterranean in winter. Increasing numbers move west to the North Sea and Atlantic coasts and some remain to breed in these regions. Most adults return east in March while immatures remain in the west all year.

LENGTH 36–38cm (14–15in)

WHEN TO SEE All year; in northwest, adults typically winter and spring; immatures spring to autumn. Small breeding population in W Europe
WHERE FOUND Breeds very locally, often erratically, in Greece, central Europe, Baltic and North Sea coasts, rarely England, France, E Spain; in winter more widespread on coasts

Slender-billed Gull *Larus genei*

This is effectively a 'hooded gull' without a hood: in other respects its plumage looks very like that of a Black-headed Gull. It is very much rarer, though, being restricted to Mediterranean lagoons, salt pans, and marshes in summer; even in winter it remains scarce and essentially coastal.

FEEDING It catches fish and insects by plunge-diving, up-ending, surface-dipping from the air, picking from the surface while swimming, or by foot-paddling and probing on the shore.

DISPLAY & VOICE A sociable breeder, its behaviour resembles that of the Black-headed Gull; its calls are deeper, and more nasal.

BREEDING Most colonies are small, on the ground in open places near lagoons or on low islands. Two or three eggs hatch after 22 days' incubation.

MIGRATION Mostly resident, moving within the Mediterranean or to west Africa. Eastern breeders move to the Red Sea in winter.

LENGTH 42–44cm (16–17in)

WHEN TO SEE At breeding sites spring to autumn; in Mediterranean sparsely all year
WHERE FOUND Breeds S Spain, S France, Sardinia, N Italy, N Greece; scarce in Mediterranean and very rare farther north

An elegant, forward-leaning, long-necked gull with a pattern like Black-headed, but with no dark hood in summer

Black-headed

Black-headed Gull (left) has smaller, rounder head, shorter bill, thinner, shorter neck, white tips to shorter tertials

Slender-billed

Adult, breeding

Longer tail, longer neck than Black-headed Gull; longer inner wing gives less snappy flight action

Adults, breeding Summer adult flushed pink; with white head; winter adult may have pale grey ear spot

Bill red in summer but often looks black, even at moderate range; eye can be pale

Possible to see right through nostrils

Broad white forewing wedge above and below wing like Black-headed Gull; long-bodied shape in flight

Juvenile and first winter Duller than Black-headed Gull, less contrasted, with grey ear spot, plain dull orange bill

Fulmar *Fulmarus glacialis*

Fulmars have increased hugely in the 20th century, thanks to the vast amount of dead fish and offal thrown overboard by bigger trawler fleets. Nesting colonies have spread to quite low cliffs and, in the north, even grass banks and ruined buildings. Fulmars are otherwise entirely sea birds.

FEEDING Fulmars eat fish, crustaceans, and all kinds of floating waste and offal from ships; they always feed at sea.

DISPLAY & VOICE Pairs and immature birds visit potential nesting cliffs and soar to and fro along them. The pairs are noisy at the nest, making a hoarse, throaty, rapid cackling. Quiet at sea.

BREEDING Fulmar pairs breed from seven years old, choosing a broad ledge or an earth scrape on a sea cliff. Some colonies are well inland where there are few cliffs. Each pair incubates a single egg for 52–53 days and the chick flies when seven weeks old.

MIGRATION Most Fulmars disperse widely in the Atlantic after breeding, but a few remain inshore all year; immatures remain at sea all year.

LENGTH 45–50cm (18–20in)

WHEN TO SEE All year; fewest inshore in late autumn
WHERE FOUND Breeds Iceland, Britain and Ireland, N France, locally to N Norway; widespread in North Sea and N Atlantic

Gull-like but really a petrel, the Fulmar is heavy-bodied, with large white head but grey tail, unlike gull; glides and soars on stiff, almost straight wings

Typical pale form mostly white below with grey wingtips

Dark forms blue-grey to dull brownish; (compare Sooty Shearwater)

Thick white head and neck visible at very long range

Pale inner primaries make obvious patch; no black on wingtips; often uneven, blotchy effect on upperwing

Flies low and heavily in calm weather; glides masterfully in wind, rising high and banking over in gales

Tubenosed bill obvious at close range

Unique appearance when squatting on cliff ledge; unable to stand, and merely shuffles; loud cackling distinctive

Little Gull *Larus minutus*

A delicate gull; rather tern-like , but adults blunt-winged, short-tailed and short-billed; juveniles have sharper wings but similar gentle-faced character. Flies head-to-wind low over water, dipping to take food from surface

First summer
Like first winter but variable dark hood; wing markings gradually fade paler and browner; often more obvious white streaks along inner webs of outer primaries

Second year
Some look adult; others have variable amount of black on outer primaries (often less than shown), more rarely on primary coverts

Second summer
Dark underwing may be similar to adult, but coverts often much paler

First winter
Black zigzag above, black on tail; dark cap and ear spot

First autumn (right)
Juvenile plumage replaced by first winter feathers, giving clear grey back; dark wing bars often joined across rump at this stage, never seen on young Kittiwake; also darker marks on hindwing

Adult, winter (left)
Clean grey above with even, broad white rim around hindwing to small 'spot' at tip; no black on upperwing at all

Adult, summer
At all seasons shows very dark underwing with white rear edge broader at tip; unique dark-light twinkling contrast as it flies low over water visible at great range

Closed wingtips white, but dark underside of far wing often shows

Adult, summer
Jet black hood, bill dark or bright red

Adult, winter
Grey cap, blacker ear spot, black bill

Late juvenile (below)
During transition to first winter dark upper back extends as lobe onto sides of breast

Second year
In early spring hood develops quickly from rear edge forwards; may be complete in summer; dark wingtips on perched or swimming bird may confuse identification

Juvenile (left)
Dark brown above at first; quickly loses brown on hind neck and sides of breast; gains grey on back during autumn as first winter plumage develops; pale pink legs

This is the smallest and most tern-like gull: an elegant, light, airy creature that seems to be at the mercy of the winds and waves. Yet it is quite capable of riding out storms on the open sea and is often to be seen at the coast – dipping, twisting, and turning over surf crashing against a breakwater, or in the melée of assorted gulls fighting for scraps at a sewage outfall. Flocks migrate along coasts, but small groups are equally likely to be seen over large reservoirs inland where they behave quite like Black Terns, beating into the wind, low over the surface, and dipping, rather than diving, to pick morsels from the water.

FEEDING Most of the Little Gull's diet consists of insects and other aquatic invertebrates, especially in summer when it takes flies in the air and from the surface of shallow floods and lakes. It also catches small fish, chiefly tiny fry from the surface, particularly when wintering at sea. It searches by flying low, head to wind, its bill angled downwards. When it dips it usually makes a clean snatch with its bill, but it may settle for a moment, submerge its head, or patter along the surface with its feet before rising steeply again. This feeding behaviour helps to identify Little Gulls even at very long range. When feeding they often mix with small groups of terns.

DISPLAY & VOICE Compared to most gulls Little Gulls are relatively quiet birds, except near the nesting colony. The usual call is a low *kek-kek-kek*; in alarm this develops into a harsher, tern-like or squeaky chatter. Territorial calls also have a chattering, squeaky quality. The courtship displays are like those of the Black-headed Gull: the birds show off their jet black hoods by posturing with their heads stretched forward or raised; a pair will walk side by side and tilt their heads away from each other to reduce the amount of black visible; this seems to be a way of reducing the 'threat' posed by the dark hood. The birds also threaten intruders by raising their heads vertically to show off their hoods.

BREEDING They nest colonially, in hollows in wet vegetation beside freshwater lakes and close to water in marshes. Pairs incubate two or three eggs for 23–25 days and the chicks fly after about three weeks.

MIGRATION Movements are complicated, but most eastern European breeders move west to the North Sea and Atlantic or south into the Mediterranean in winter.

LENGTH 25–27cm (10–11in)

WHEN TO SEE Mostly August to May in W Europe, a few in summer
WHERE FOUND Breeds from Finland eastwards; a few scattered in W Europe

Kittiwake *Rissa tridactyla*

In winter Kittiwakes forage around fish docks and ferry terminals, and in spring and autumn they are not infrequent over inland waters. Yet the Kittiwake is most at home far offshore, over the open ocean, for of all the gulls the Kittiwake is the most truly marine. Its mastery of the elements, even in a North Atlantic gale, matches that of large shearwaters and petrels: it rides the wind in a series of high, bounding arcs, now on one wingtip, now on the other, travelling effortlessly over huge distances. Few people get to see it at sea, though, and to most of us it is best known as a bird of sheer, rocky sea cliffs, where it forms summer nesting colonies along with Guillemots and Razorbills. The massed Kittiwakes make the cliffs ring to their clamour as they endlessly call their name from the ledges. They can be seen at close range at the nest, revealing that they are delightful creatures, immaculate in full breeding plumage, and with a gentle, dove-like facial expression.

FEEDING The bulk of a Kittiwake's food is fish, especially sandeels in summer, supplemented by a variety of marine invertebrates caught at sea. Kittiwakes do not scavenge at tips or feed on the shore: they dip to the surface of the open sea, or plunge from a low height to reach deeper-swimming fish, or join in the general melée around trawlers, snapping up whatever bits of offal they can reach. They also forage at sewage outflows, although rarely form more than a small minority of the gull flocks at such sites. In the Arctic upwelling water masses bring enormous quantities of shrimps to the surface (as do feeding whales in places) and huge flocks of Kittiwakes take advantage of the abundance of food.

DISPLAY & VOICE Kittiwakes call repeatedly at their breeding colonies: a loud, ringing, nasal *kitt-i-awa-ake* or *k-wake*. They also make quieter, whining, mewing, or wailing sounds. Away from the colony they are silent. Displays involve posturing on the nest, head-bobbing, 'choking' motions, and feeding of the female by the male.

BREEDING Nests are small masses of weed, grass, and mud on minute cliff ledges. Two eggs hatch after 27 days and the young fly when 42 days old.

MIGRATION Most move far into the North Atlantic in winter; small groups cross inland Britain in spring but rarely stay long at reservoirs or lakes. A few penetrate into the Mediterranean but they do not enter the Baltic Sea.

LENGTH 38–40cm (15–16in)

WHEN TO SEE All year, but most March to September on coasts
WHERE FOUND Breeds NW European coasts from N Scandinavia and Iceland to Portugal; widespread at sea in winter

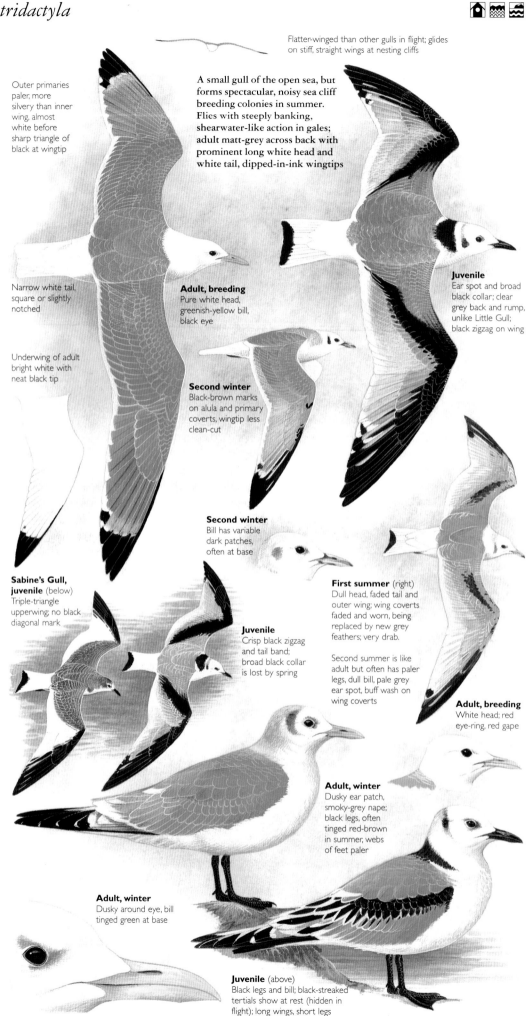

Flatter-winged than other gulls in flight; glides on stiff, straight wings at nesting cliffs

Outer primaries paler, more silvery than inner wing, almost white before sharp triangle of black at wingtip

A small gull of the open sea, but forms spectacular, noisy sea cliff breeding colonies in summer. Flies with steeply banking, shearwater-like action in gales; adult matt-grey across back with prominent long white head and white tail, dipped-in-ink wingtips

Narrow white tail, square or slightly notched

Adult, breeding
Pure white head, greenish-yellow bill, black eye

Juvenile
Ear spot and broad black collar; clear grey back and rump, unlike Little Gull; black zigzag on wing

Underwing of adult bright white with neat black tip

Second winter
Black-brown marks on alula and primary coverts, wingtip less clean-cut

Second winter
Bill has variable dark patches, often at base

Sabine's Gull, juvenile (below)
Triple-triangle upperwing; no black diagonal mark

Juvenile
Crisp black zigzag and tail band; broad black collar is lost by spring

First summer (right)
Dull head, faded tail and outer wing; wing coverts faded and worn, being replaced by new grey feathers; very drab.

Second summer is like adult but often has paler legs, dull bill, pale grey ear spot, buff wash on wing coverts

Adult, breeding
White head; red eye-ring, red gape

Adult, winter
Dusky ear patch, smoky-grey nape; black legs, often tinged red-brown in summer, webs of feet paler

Adult, winter
Dusky around eye, bill tinged green at base

Juvenile (above)
Black legs and bill; black-streaked tertials show at rest (hidden in flight); long wings, short legs

Glaucous Gull *Larus hyperboreus*

A big, heavy-billed, pale gull with no black on the wingtips, secondaries or tail band at any age

Bill may be heavy, or rather slim but long; small eyes; head quite round or flat-topped

First winter
Beautifully patterned with pale flight feathers; underwing coverts and belly often quite dark; tail barred but no very dark band

Third/fourth year

Adult
White and silvery-grey; broad secondary and primary tips make bold white triangle at rear; head pure white in summer, streaked autumn to spring

First summer

First winter

Primary tips extend beyond tail, but less so than on Iceland Gull; legs longer; bill longer and pale pink with small, sharp, black tip; despite size and bulk, can be shapely and elegant

Beware confusion with 'shiny' pale underwing tips of some young Herring Gulls

First winter
Some first winters much darker below; juvenile darker; first summer blotched and faded much paler

Older immatures become more uniformly pale, gain grey on back; bill has narrower dark band near tip

Adult, summer

Iceland Gull
To same scale as Glaucous above: dark bill; paler underwing; slimmer rear body; shorter-tailed effect

Breeding around the Arctic, this is a charismatic, scarce winter visitor to northwest Europe. It is a large, powerful bird between a Herring Gull and Great Black-backed Gull in size: a handsome bird with a suitably frosty, Arctic look. It forages at refuse tips, outfalls, and fish quays, and often roosts on reservoirs inland with other gulls.

FEEDING It eats mostly fish, some birds, and offal or refuse at tips. It finds dead animal matter on the tideline and steals food from other birds.

DISPLAY & VOICE Displays are much like those of other large gulls, with long calls with head raised. Calls are like a Herring Gull's, but hoarser.

BREEDING A shallow grassy nest is made on a rocky pinnacle, cliff ledge or bank. Three eggs are incubated for 27–28 days; chicks fly in seven weeks.

MIGRATION East Greenland birds reach Iceland in winter; variable numbers reach Britain and Ireland. Iceland breeders are resident. North European birds move south with the winter ice; some reach the North Sea.

LENGTH 63–68cm (25–27in)

WHEN TO SEE In Iceland all year; Faeroes and NW Europe mostly October to April
WHERE FOUND Breeds Iceland, Spitsbergen, extreme N Russia; winters Atlantic and North Sea S to France

---

Iceland Gull *Larus glaucoides*

A large gull with long wingtips, a rounded head and a short bill; no black on wingtips

First winter

Iceland (top) has slimmer belly, shorter 'arm' than Glaucous

Short body of Iceland gives short-tailed look in flight

Gentler, more dove-like, with larger, more central eye than Glaucous Gull; lacks brutal look

Male

Female

Inner wing proportionately shorter than on Glaucous, giving broad-winged effect

First winter
Long pale primaries extend well past tail; small, thick or slender bill less hooked than Glaucous; steep forehead, rounded crown and nape; shortish legs rather dark pink; underparts never very dark

Male's bill (inset above) heavier than female's. Juvenile has dark bill with dark tip extending back as wedge; loses dark with age

Adult, winter

Second winter

Adult, summer

Glaucous
same scale

Wingtip projection variable: can be very long; when swimming may be steeply angled upwards

May droop primaries to reveal more grey

Eyecatching white wingtips separate these two species from Herring Gull group

Adult's pale eyes often look dark at distance

Immature
Older immatures difficult to age; become very pale overall before gaining grey back

Scarcer than the Glaucous Gull in Europe, the Iceland Gull breeds around Greenland and Arctic islands north of Canada. It visits Iceland in some numbers in winter, and variable numbers, some following fishing fleets, reach northwest Europe each winter. A few regularly move inland in Britain, roosting on reservoirs early in the year.

FEEDING It eats mainly fish, catching them in shallow dives; also eggs and young birds in summer, and refuse from beaches and tips in winter.

DISPLAY & VOICE The social behaviour is generally like that of the Herring Gull, but its calls are shriller.

BREEDING Most nests are on flat cliff ledges beside the sea. Two or three eggs are laid; they hatch after 28–30 days.

MIGRATION West Greenland breeders disperse locally in winter but some move farther; east Greenland breeders move to Iceland. Numbers reaching Britain and Ireland vary from a few score to a few hundred in exceptionally good years.

LENGTH 52–60cm (21–24in)

WHEN TO SEE Mostly November or December to April
WHERE FOUND Iceland, locally Ireland, Scotland, England, Norway in winter

Common Gull *Larus canus*

Resembling a small Herring Gull, the Common Gull is a less familiar bird and certainly not the most 'common' gull in many parts of Europe. Its distribution is curiously patchy: in Britain there are places where hundreds of Common Gulls march steadily across the fields looking for food in winter, while not far away they are rarely seen. In most wintering areas inland they are far outnumbered by Black-headed Gulls. Most of them withdraw to the north in spring, to nest in pairs, groups, or small colonies. In summer Common Gulls like boggy moors and sheltered coasts; they prefer little beaches and bays between rocky headlands and islands to open, windswept cliffs. In winter they are found on broad, sandy beaches and estuaries, and on farmland with long-established grassy meadows or freshly-ploughed fields. Like other gulls they fly to large reservoirs or lakes each evening to roost.

FEEDING Favoured food includes earthworms, insect larvae, and other invertebrates, pulled from the ground or stolen from other gulls or Lapwings. Common Gulls are chiefly ground-feeders, but they also pick scraps and occasional fish from water, take berries from shrubs, and catch insects in the air. It is only in recent years that Common Gulls have taken to urban feeding or visiting gardens.

DISPLAY & VOICE Most calls have a recognizable high, nasal, squealing quality, although with a pattern much like the calls of Herring Gulls. Their displays are also similar to those of Herring Gulls: the female begs and is fed by the male, both birds toss their heads and call with their bills stretched vertically upwards. There is also a good deal of posturing with heads stretched forwards or downwards and the wings pushed half-open at the carpal or 'wrist' joints.

BREEDING Nests are made of seaweed, grasses, and plant stems, and placed in shallow depressions in rocks, on stumps or earth banks, on fence posts or drystone walls, on piers, or even on the roof ridges of disused buildings. Typically three eggs are laid; they hatch after 22–28 days.

MIGRATION Most are migratory, moving south and west in autumn but not penetrating far into continental Europe: this is a species of coastal countries in the main.

LENGTH 40–43cm (16–17in)

WHEN TO SEE All year; September to April where it does not breed
WHERE FOUND Breeds on moors, islands, Britain and Ireland, Low Countries and Scandinavia, sparsely N Europe; widespread in North Sea countries in winter but not Iberia or Mediterranean

Juvenile
Chequered back and scapulars quickly replaced by plain grey (rarely some pattern remains in winter); tail usually plain white with broad black band; wingtips solid black-brown

Wings rather straight, quite broad to tip on adult (more pointed on juvenile); tail held closed, square

An elegant gull with basic pattern of a Herring Gull, but smaller, neater, more gentle-looking, never with pink legs, red bill spot, or yellow eyes. Long-winged, but rarely glides so masterfully as the larger gulls; typically seen foraging in flocks on fields or loafing on beaches

Adult, breeding
Extensive black wingtips with two large white spots near tip; broad white trailing edge to otherwise grey wing; dark eyes, yellow-green legs

Neatly patterned wing coverts of juvenile create rows of brown spots; secondaries make dark trailing edge to inner wing; outer greater coverts form a plainer grey central panel, much darker than on juvenile Mediterranean Gull

First summer has wings bleached to cream and brown, with darker grey saddle

Juvenile
Variable but typically with neat lines of brown spots on underwing coverts; white tail with clean black band

Adult underwing

Second winter (right)
Dark marks on coverts; dark outer primary coverts; extensive dark wingtip wedge with less white than adult

Second winter
Closed wingtip looks all black; bill often with broad black ring

Adult, winter
Large white crescent between grey back and black of wingtip; bill may have thin black ring; legs blue-green or grey

Adult, breeding
Green-yellow bill

First year
Bill clear-cut pink and black

First winter
Grey 'saddle'; neat covert pattern; pinkish legs and bill base

Ring-billed Gull *Larus delawarensis*

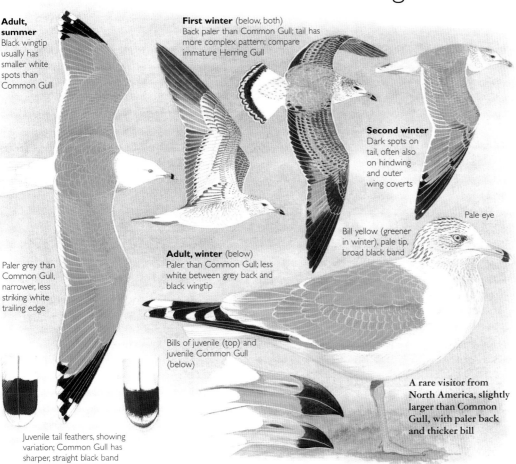

Adult, summer
Black wingtip usually has smaller white spots than Common Gull

First winter (below, both)
Back paler than Common Gull; tail has more complex pattern; compare immature Herring Gull

Second winter
Dark spots on tail, often also on hindwing and outer wing coverts

Pale eye

Bill yellow (greener in winter), pale tip, broad black band

Paler grey than Common Gull, narrower, less striking white trailing edge

Adult, winter (below)
Paler than Common Gull; less white between grey back and black wingtip

Bills of juvenile (top) and juvenile Common Gull (below)

A rare visitor from North America, slightly larger than Common Gull, with paler back and thicker bill

Juvenile tail feathers, showing variation; Common Gull has sharper, straight black band

Unknown in Europe until late in the 20th century, this common American gull is now a regular visitor, in small numbers, to northwest Europe. It mixes with Common and Herring Gulls in estuaries and around coastal lakes, roosting with them on beaches and feeding on fields, at sewage outflows, and along the tideline.

FEEDING Like other larger gulls it eats almost anything, from fish and molluscs to rubbish and waste food around quays and seaside resorts.

VOICE Calls resemble a Herring Gull's but tend to be higher in pitch and more nasal.

MIGRATION Adults appear on the coasts of northwest Europe in late autumn and remain through the winter. There is often an increase in records around March and April, when Common Gulls are moving north. Immatures tend to move later in spring and may be seen during the summer.

LENGTH 43–47cm (17–18½in)

WHEN TO SEE All year; most October to April
WHERE FOUND Annual in Ireland, Britain (mostly SW) and rare vagrant in many other countries from Iceland to Spain

Audouin's Gull *Larus audouinii*

A rare gull of the Mediterranean, dark-billed and dark-legged

Second year (right)
Narrow tail band, dark hindwing bar

Adult
Wedge of black on wingtip, small white spots; narrow wings, narrow tail

Juveniles
Very dark tail, U-shaped white rump, heavily marked underwing

Forehead slopes into long 'snout'; thick bill with black band has square-tipped look, looks black

Juvenile
Dark, blotched; very long wings

Adult has dark eye

Underwing white with Gannet-like wedge of black

Tiny white 'mirror' on outer feather of upperwing

Wingtip spots wear off by summer

Adult
White head; bill with variable yellow tip, looks very dark unless seen closely; body washed palest grey; legs dark grey-green

Adult

Juvenile

One of the most specialized of gulls, and until recently one of the rarest, Audouin's Gull is showing signs of a wider range of feeding methods and is increasing in numbers. In the 1960s only around 1000 pairs remained; by the end of the 20th century single colonies numbered several thousand pairs.

FEEDING Since they specialize in snatching fish from the surface of the sea Audouin's Gulls rarely feed on beaches, but some may now be seen inland. Typically, fish are caught in the bill without any other part of the bird touching the water.

DISPLAY & VOICE Displays are similar to those of the Yellow-legged Gull; calls are particularly hoarse and deep.

BREEDING Colonies occupy rocky islands; two or three eggs are laid in a scantily-lined nest on the ground.

MIGRATION Most disperse within the Mediterranean and along the west coast of Africa after breeding; a few reach the west coast of Iberia.

LENGTH 48–52cm (19–20½in)

WHEN TO SEE All year
WHERE FOUND Breeds locally E Spain, Balearics, Corsica, Sardinia, S Italy, Greece; widespread in W Mediterranean in autumn

Yellow-legged Gull *Larus michahellis*

Not long ago 'Herring Gulls' were Herring Gulls, and that was that as far as ordinary birdwatchers were concerned. It was, nevertheless, obvious that those in southern Europe looked different from the ones breeding in the northwest – but then, so did those in North America, others in the Middle East, and still more in northern or central Asia. It is still not entirely certain how many of these variations represent local races or different species, but the Yellow-legged Gull has clearly emerged as a separate species in its own right.

In Britain, the Netherlands, and France this is a regular, indeed increasing visitor. Most arrive after the breeding season, but a few remain all winter. Superficially they look like Herring Gulls, but with practice they are easily picked out. Summer adults are really handsome birds, their relatively dark backs and strong leg and bill colours most striking in a good view. In some towns they are tame, but in many Mediterranean areas they are rather sparse, not so easy to approach and difficult to see well in the prevailing heat shimmer over sandy beaches, estuaries, and salt pans.

FEEDING Like the Herring Gull this species takes fish, offal, and all manner of other material, feeding extensively on refuse tips.

DISPLAY & VOICE Their displays are like those of the Herring Gull, with some details more like those of the Lesser Black-backed Gull. Their calls resemble the Lesser Black-back's, with a deep, guttural, nasal quality. The long call is faster, longer, and more guttural than a Herring Gull's.

BREEDING They breed in colonies, usually on rocky islands and much less often on buildings or other man-made structures than Herring Gulls. The nest is a similar shallow dish or pad of grasses but may be much more scanty, or absent altogether. Two or three eggs are incubated for 27–31 days, and the chicks fly when 35–40 days old.

MIGRATION After breeding a proportion of the population evidently moves north, reaching North Sea coasts and penetrating central Europe along major rivers. This pattern seems to have developed since the 1970s, prior to which the species was more or less sedentary. Populations in Morocco are still resident all year round, and elsewhere in the Mediterranean many remain throughout the year.

LENGTH 59–67cm (23–26in)

WHEN TO SEE All year; in North Sea area mostly August to November
WHERE FOUND Breeds coasts of Spain, Portugal, S France, Italy, Balkans; also locally N Italy, Switzerland, Romania, Bulgaria

A large, handsome gull of the familiar white-headed, grey-backed, black-wingtipped type, adults having strikingly yellow legs and thick, bright bills; immatures not so easy but tend to be white-headed, dark-backed and dark-tailed

Adult male (left)
Head white, variably marked with soft streaks around and behind the eye in late summer and autumn but strikingly white in winter; legs rich yellow

Juvenile has whitish head, dark back; blackish bill; some darker-chested like Lesser Black-backed Gull

Wingtips of adult female shorter than male's, but still a long-winged bird

Juvenile (below)
Solid dark tertials with pale tips

Fourth year (right)
Like adult but often has black bill ring

Some juveniles obvious rusty-brown

Second year
Grey on back, still much dark brown on wings; legs pinkish

Juvenile (above)
Darker underwing than Herring Gull, neat tail band often edged white

First winter
Head pale, streaked; dark, neat tail band and pale rump; dark bill; much grey on back; dark tertials

Juvenile
White head; dark upperwing with weak paler patch behind bend of wing (more like Lesser Black-backed than Herring Gull)

Upperparts darker than British race of Herring Gull, obviously paler than Lesser Black-backed Gull

Third year
Legs yellowish

Striking white rump, dark band on tail

Wings long, narrower than Herring Gull, held flatter

Male (right) longer-tailed than female (left)

Adults in Portugal show grey primary coverts beneath wing

Second winter (right)
Still marked tail band; plain grey back same shade as adult

Third winter (above)
Blackish wingtips show little white; some dark on tail

Adult (right)
Typically large areas of white on outermost two primaries give big wingtip patch; white tips wear off in summer leaving extensive black

Black/grey wing contrast much stronger than Lesser Black-backed Gull

Herring Gull *Larus argentatus*

One of the most familiar gulls, white-headed in summer but streaked in autumn and winter, with a pale grey back and black and white wingtips; pale pink legs; northern birds are bigger and darker-backed but with less black in the wing

Juvenile *argenteus* (above)
British race: small, pale, lacy buff feather edges on back, pale base to bill, notched tertials

Juvenile *argentatus* (above)
Scandinavian race: big, bulky, broad white tertial tips

Adult *argentatus* (above)
Bigger, bulkier than *argenteus*; back darker; broader white tertial tips, more white, less black at wingtip (exceptionally much reduced); legs greyish-pink

First summer *argenteus*
Pale, but still marked over head and chest, little clear grey above; tertials markedly pale, unlike Yellow-legged Gull; bill pale at base

Scandinavian race *argentatus* (left) immaculate in summer, but head and chest dark in winter (above); big, thick bill largest on males

Adult *argenteus*
Smaller than *argentatus*, neat, pale silvery-grey, wingtips with much black, bold white spots (white tips wear off in summer)

Adult, winter *argenteus*
Some are much more heavily clouded and streaked grey-brown

Second summer
Race *argenteus*

Second summer
Race *argentatus*

Second summer / third winter
Race *argenteus*: rate of development towards adulthood varies

Third year
Retains traces of immaturity

Juvenile
Pale underwing, especially behind bend of wing

Adult *argentatus*
Big, broad-winged; some enormous compared with small *argenteus*

Adult *argenteus*
Small, pale, sharp wingtip contrast

Adult flight feathers much paler from below than Lesser Black-backed Gull

Juvenile
Mottled rump and tail base blend into tail band; pale patch behind angle of wing

Race *argentatus* has smaller band of grey-black under wingtip, sometimes reduced almost to nothing; large white tips to outer primaries

Brown on juvenile fades to creamy-buff in late spring to summer; pale patch on inner primaries often obvious

To most of us this bird is the quintessential 'seagull': yet it is a controversial and complex species with a range of variations that leave scientists (and birdwatchers) in disagreement and confusion. One way to treat the species complex in Europe is to separate the Yellow-legged Gull (chiefly of the Mediterranean) as *Larus michahellis*, and a more eastern form, the Caspian (or Steppe) Gull, as *Larus cachinnans*, leaving the pink-legged birds breeding in northern and western Europe as 'Herring Gulls'. The situation is more complicated than this, however, especially once the variety of forms breeding in Asia and wintering through the Middle East, into Africa, and eastwards to Southeast Asia are taken into account. In Europe the Scandinavian race *argentatus* is bigger than the race *argenteus* of Britain and Iceland; they mix in winter, the most extreme examples being quite strikingly different.

Herring Gulls as seen in summer beside the sea in Britain and most of northwestern Europe are big, bold, noisy birds. In seafront towns they wake people at an unearthly hour with their calls, frighten children by swooping down to steal their sandwiches, and make a mess over buildings, statues, and parked cars. Yet on sea cliffs these dramatic birds add immeasurably to the coastal atmosphere with their strident calls and mastery of flight. In winter hundreds roost on reservoirs far inland.
FEEDING Herring Gulls eat whatever they can get, on beaches, at fish quays, on the promenade, on refuse tips, from ploughed fields and pastures, and along built-up estuaries. Fish, earthworms, small mammals, eggs, grain, and waste human food are all eaten with relish.
DISPLAY & VOICE Gull displays are complex. The most familiar is the 'long call', given as the head is bowed deeply, then raised with bill wide open. Aggressive displays involve standing upright with the bill pointed down and wings pushed away from the body; birds also peck at the ground or tug at grass stems. The calls include the long call: a loud, clear, yelping *au-kyee-kau-kau-kau-kau-kau-kau-au-ow*, a barked *gagagag*, and an explosive, yelped *kyow!*
BREEDING Nests are grassy pads on rock ledges, islets, or roofs; three eggs hatch within 28–30 days and the young fly at about five weeks old.
MIGRATION Northern birds move south and west in winter.
LENGTH 55–64cm (22–25in)

WHEN TO SEE All year
WHERE FOUND Breeds Iceland, coasts of Norway, widely Sweden, Finland, Baltic states, locally Germany; North Sea coasts; Britain, Ireland, NW France; winters south to N Spain

Great Black-backed Gull *Larus marinus*

The largest of the world's gulls, the Great Black-back is a fearsome, yet handsome bird. The adult is one of the most contrasted of the gulls, really black-and-white in fresh plumage. Immatures are boldly chequered, but often best distinguished by their size and especially the weight of their bills.

The Great Black-backed Gull has a more restricted breeding habitat than the more widespread Herring Gull. Where nesting Herring Gulls are often numerous along the upper edges of sea cliffs on wide, grass-fringed ledges or steep crags, Great Black-backs are typically more scattered, with each pair occupying some prominence, such as the top of an offshore stack, or the end of a rocky promontory. Pairs may nest on ledges or even on flatter ground, but their first choice is a more obvious feature – as befits the biggest, most dominant of the gulls.

Outside the breeding season they move to all kinds of shores, including harbours and flat, sandy beaches. Many go inland: in England the numbers at winter roosts on reservoirs greatly increased in the late 20th century as more birds took advantage of the food available on refuse tips. In some areas Herring Gulls did this much earlier but then declined, so Great Black-backed Gulls now outnumber them.

FEEDING Great Black-backs kill many more birds and animals than most other gulls. Some specialize in taking Puffins, or various shearwaters and petrels, at their breeding colonies. They kill Manx Shearwaters on the ground, but grab Puffins by the neck in mid-air. In winter they may even attack wildfowl. They eat a lot of fish, and large flocks follow trawlers, seizing discarded fish and offal. They also scavenge for all kinds of dead animal matter and scraps on beaches and at rubbish tips.

DISPLAY & VOICE Their displays resemble those of the Herring Gull. Calls, however, are mostly distinctive, with a deep, barking, throaty quality. A deep, abrupt bark, *aouk*, is frequent, as is a throaty *uh-uh-uh*.

BREEDING The nest is a mound of seaweed, grass, and other vegetation, usually placed on top of a rock outcrop or offshore stack, or beside some prominent feature on the cliff edge. Two or three eggs are incubated for 27–28 days and the young are able to fly when seven or eight weeks old.

MIGRATION Northern breeders move southwest in winter.

LENGTH 64–78cm (25–31in)

Juvenile
Dark back (paler, more chequered in first winter); dark trailing edge to wing, slight pale 'window' beyond the bend of the wing; quite narrow tail band broken at basal edge

The biggest gull, always thick-set and heavy-billed; typically pale-headed and contrasty at all times. Previously mostly coastal, but increasing numbers winter inland in Britain

Second summer
White head and body; blackness of 'saddle' useful clue; some black wing coverts appear; dark band on yellow bill

Third summer
Wings become blacker with white spots at tip, tail whiter

Looks large and long-winged in flight, with protruding head, obvious heavy bill, and deep belly; wings often markedly arched

Adult, summer
Bright white head and body; much dark grey under flight feathers

Adult, summer
Large white wingtip spots

First winter
Massive bill blacker at first, paler by spring. Upperparts very chequered

Second summer
Black back; wings develop black at varying rate

Second summer bird has all-black wingtips and black saddle, but brown wing coverts, fading paler, and white tertial tips

Third winter

Birds with larger white tip to wing probably male

Adult female, summer
Very black (fades browner); legs pale pink to whitish

Adult, summer

Third/fourth summer
Near-adult has dark bill band, uneven wing colour

Adult, winter
Head much whiter than most Lesser Black-backs

Lesser Black-backed Gull *Larus fuscus*

A large gull, white-headed in summer, with a mid grey to dark grey or black back, black and white wingtips, red-spotted yellow bill and bright yellow legs when adult

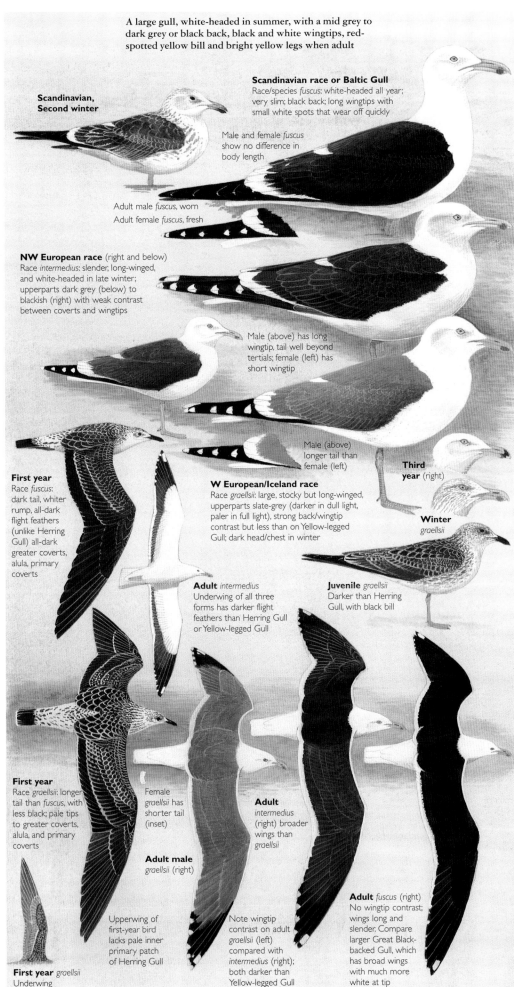

Scandinavian, Second winter

Scandinavian race or Baltic Gull
Race/species *fuscus*: white-headed all year; very slim; black back; long wingtips with small white spots that wear off quickly

Male and female *fuscus* show no difference in body length

Adult male *fuscus*, worn
Adult female *fuscus*, fresh

NW European race (right and below)
Race *intermedius*: slender, long-winged, and white-headed in late winter; upperparts dark grey (below) to blackish (right) with weak contrast between coverts and wingtips

Male (above) has long wingtip, tail well beyond tertials; female (left) has short wingtip

Male (above) longer tail than female (left)

Third year (right)

Winter *graellsii*

First year
Race *fuscus*: dark tail, whiter rump, all-dark flight feathers (unlike Herring Gull) all-dark greater coverts, alula, primary coverts

W European/Iceland race
Race *graellsii*: large, stocky but long-winged, upperparts slate-grey (darker in dull light, paler in full light), strong back/wingtip contrast but less than on Yellow-legged Gull; dark head/chest in winter

Adult *intermedius*
Underwing of all three forms has darker flight feathers than Herring Gull or Yellow-legged Gull

Juvenile *graellsii*
Darker than Herring Gull, with black bill

First year
Race *graellsii*: longer tail than *fuscus*, with less black; pale tips to greater coverts, alula, and primary coverts

Female *graellsii* has shorter tail (inset)

Adult *intermedius* (right) broader wings than *graellsii*

Adult male *graellsii* (right)

Upperwing of first-year bird lacks pale inner primary patch of Herring Gull

First year *graellsii* Underwing

Note wingtip contrast on adult *graellsii* (left) compared with *intermedius* (right); both darker than Yellow-legged Gull

Adult *fuscus* (right)
No wingtip contrast; wings long and slender. Compare larger Great Black-backed Gull, which has broad wings with much more white at tip

A Lesser Black-backed Gull in early summer is a beautiful bird by any standards, its slate-grey back contrasting with its immaculate white head and underparts, and set off by yellow legs and a really vivid waxy yellow bill. These gulls are less attractive in their feeding habits, however, since they kill a great many smaller seabirds including Puffins, Manx Shearwaters, and Storm Petrels.

Lesser Black-backs like to breed on flatter ground than Herring Gulls, on moors and on the tops of broad islands. In southwest Wales they nest on islands that are clothed in drifts of bluebells and red campion: surely some of the most beautiful seabird colonies anywhere in the world.

In the past nearly all the British breeders of the western European race *graellsii* migrated to Africa in winter, but since the mid 20th century more and more have been remaining in Britain all year. They are probably encouraged by the greater availability of food inland, especially at refuse tips, combined with the security of safe night roosts on reservoirs.

Scandinavian birds of the race *fuscus* – now proposed as a separate species, the Baltic Gull – move southeast in winter and are rare in western Europe at any time. A third group, *intermedius*, which breeds in Denmark and the Low Countries, is relatively frequent in Britain and France.

FEEDING Fish form a large proportion of their diet, but Lesser Black-backs take other seabirds in summer where they are available. At other times they forage widely for all kinds of animal and vegetable food, and often scavenge from refuse tips.

DISPLAY & VOICE Their displays are generally like those of the Herring Gull, but their calls have a throaty, sometimes strangled but typically deeper quality. These deep calls are easily identifiable in winter at a mixed roost. In spring the long call is often heard from birds migrating over land, or loafing about near feeding sites.

BREEDING Lesser Black-backs typically nest on the ground, often in vegetation, but increasingly they nest on roof tops. Three eggs hatch after 24–27 days and the chicks fly at 30–40 days old.

MIGRATION Most Lesser Black-backs are migratory, but in Britain many now remain inland all winter.

LENGTH 52–64cm (21–26in)

WHEN TO SEE All year; in N Europe, summer only
WHERE FOUND Breeds locally Iceland, widely throughout Scandinavia and Russia, locally N Germany, Low Countries, NW Ireland, and mostly N and W Britain

Common Tern *Sterna hirundo*

Terns are generally smaller, neater, more streamlined, longer-winged, and longer-tailed than gulls. The *Sterna* terns, which include the Common and Arctic Terns, are distinguished by pale grey wings, paler grey underparts, long, streamered white tails, and jet black caps in summer. Their bills are sharp and red, their legs very short.

Near the sea Common Terns like shallow lagoons in sandy or shingly places, or even quite small shingle beaches. Inland they have increased in recent years by colonizing flooded gravel pits with gravelly or sandy islands; in central Europe they nest on riverside shingle. In places they mix with Arctic Terns, but are typically not such northerly birds, less associated with rocky islands off wild coasts.

FEEDING Although they often eat crustaceans or insects Common Terns are essentially fish-eaters, catching them after a headlong plunge from the air and bringing them to the surface to swallow them. The plunge is often preceded by a Kestrel-like hover. Inland, Common Terns frequently feed on tiny fish fry or insects scooped from the surface, diving much less than they do at sea.

DISPLAY & VOICE Common Terns are colonial breeders. Pairs may be seen flying high over their territories in beautifully synchronized flight, swaying from side to side. Males often feed fish to females during the egg-laying period. Their calls are mostly harsh, with an irritating screechy or rasping quality, mostly slightly lower than the calls of an Arctic Tern. A grating *kee-yah* (the emphasis on the first syllable) is distinctive; also *kek-kek* and *karrr*. Yet whole colonies may suddenly fall silent and fly away in what is known as a 'dread'.

BREEDING Two to three eggs are laid in a bare, shallow scoop in sand or shingle, or often now on specially provided rafts. The eggs hatch after 21–22 days and the chicks fly when they are 25–26 days old.

MIGRATION Common Terns move south in autumn, becoming quite widespread inland and around many coasts where they do not breed. They spend the winter in Africa, chiefly off the west coast. A few fly round the Cape and head north along the east coast of Africa.

LENGTH 31–35cm (12–14in)

A typical grey sea tern with black cap in summer; greyer than Roseate and Sandwich Terns; fractionally broader-winged and shorter-tailed than Arctic Tern, with longer head and longer bill

Adult, summer
Outer primaries darker than inner ones; often a small dark wedge on fourth/fifth outermost (compare Arctic Tern)

Compared with Arctic Tern, head/bill projects more, tail less; longer inner wing ('arm') and shorter outer wing

Juvenile
Rump pale grey in centre, hindwing grey (midwing paler), forewing blackish; underwing like adult

Underwing shows broad, slightly diffuse, dusky tips to outer primaries; only inner few primaries look translucent

Cap rather flat; bill scarlet or orange-red with black tip

First summer
Forehead remains white; bill may be more extensively black; underparts whiter than adult

First winter
Bill becomes blackish

Adult, winter
Bill black; forehead white; legs brown-black

Adult, summer
Note blacker longest primaries against pale shorter ones (Arctic Tern has no such contrast); pale grey below; red legs longer than Arctic's; bill tipped black

Juvenile
Forehead and back initially tinged ginger; bill pale orange with black tip; back thinly barred brown; leg length as adult

WHEN TO SEE March to October
WHERE FOUND Widespread on all coasts except Iceland on migration. Breeds locally inland and around coasts of Ireland, Britain, Norway; most of Sweden and Finland east into Russia; also south locally to Mediterranean, but rare in Iberia

Arctic Tern *Sterna paradisaea*

The most delicate and lightweight sea tern, with very pale, clean wings and a very long tail; rounded head and short bill project much less than Common Tern's

Adult, summer
Outer wing all pale grey with no contrast between feathers; wingtip long, drawn into thin, tapered tip. Inner wing ('arm') shorter than Common Tern's

Long tail streamers, very white rump; back silvery; underside grey, leaving narrow white cheeks; round black cap; short, spiky, blood-red bill

Juvenile
Rump white; hindwing has triangle of very pale grey and white, paler than midwing; forehead pure white; bill black, at most only slight deep red at base

Underwing at all ages very white with a long, tapered, sharp dark grey line along primary tips. All flight feathers translucent

Body greyer than Common Tern, but beware variations of light and shade

Legs shorter than Common Tern; cap rounder; bill shorter, tapered, deeper red

Common   Arctic
First summer upperwings

First summer
Usually remains in wintering areas, rare in Europe; dark forewing, white forehead, dark bill, very short legs

Wingtips all grey, no contrast between inner and outer feathers

Juvenile
Small black cap with lobe onto ear coverts; black bill; variable dark scales on back

Juvenile
Buff wash on very fresh feathers wears off more quickly than on Common Tern

While the Common Tern is slim and elegant, the Arctic Tern is even more so: beautifully turned out at all times, shorter in the bill but longer in the tail and with long, slender, attenuated wingtips.

Arctic Terns are generally far less common inland, although a number visit reservoirs on migration (sometimes even large flocks for a few hours in spring). They like rocky islets and lonely, undisturbed shingle or sand beaches, especially on more remote coasts. In spring and autumn small numbers can be identified moving past headlands or pausing on low-lying coasts south of their breeding range. Since they spend the summer so close to the Arctic and the winter at sea in the Antarctic, these terns are said to experience more constant daylight than any other species.

FEEDING Small fish such as sandeels form the staple diet of Arctic Terns. In some years the fish supply is limited, probably because of overfishing by trawlers, and large numbers of Arctic Tern chicks starve in the nest. In these circumstances the adults turn to crustaceans; they survive but they rear fewer young. They catch fish in vertical dives, each tern usually just immersing itself and rarely going deeper.

DISPLAY & VOICE Displays are very much like those of the Common Tern. The voice may be useful, since most calls are higher in pitch; a sharp alarm note, *keearr*, with the emphasis on the second rather than the first syllable, is most characteristic. Other notes include a scolding *kit-it-it-aarr* and a squeaky *kee* and *peet*. Scolding notes should be taken seriously, as Arctic Terns at their colony are quite capable of striking an intruder's head and drawing blood.

BREEDING Up to three eggs are laid on the ground, in sand or shingle, or in a small depression on a rocky island. They are incubated for 20–24 days and the young fly at 21–24 days old.

MIGRATION In autumn small numbers visit lakes and reservoirs inland, often staying a little later than Common Terns. In spring scores or even hundreds appear at such sites in occasional 'rushes'. In winter Arctic Terns move south along the west African coast and then on to the Antarctic pack ice. In summer some breed on islands far to the north of the Arctic Circle.

LENGTH 33–35cm (13–14in)

WHEN TO SEE April to November
WHERE FOUND Breeds Iceland, Spitsbergen and other Arctic islands, Faeroes, Scotland, Ireland, very locally England; many more inland in N Scandinavia; also Baltic and North Sea coasts south to Low Countries

Roseate Tern *Sterna dougallii*

Unaccountably rare throughout its large world range, this is a superb tern: ghostly pale, especially in summer when the pink of spring has faded to leave its underside gleaming white. It is a marine species, and exceptionally scarce inland.

FEEDING Dives for fish after a rapid hover, almost 'flying into the water'.

DISPLAY & VOICE The extraordinarily long tail feathers look wonderfully elegant in the slow-winged, springy display flights; the tern also raises them in displays on the ground. By contrast the calls are harsh: a deep, grating *aahrk* and a sharper, bright *chu-vee*, often used around colonies.

BREEDING Nests are often hidden in long vegetation on rocky islets. At some colonies these rare terns are also provided with nest boxes as a conservation measure. One or two eggs are incubated for 21–26 days.

MIGRATION The western European population spends the winter off west African coasts.

LENGTH 33–38cm (13–15in)

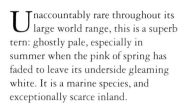

WHEN TO SEE In W Europe from April to October
WHERE FOUND Very few colonies in the Irish Sea, Brittany, NE Britain; rare elsewhere and very rare inland

Typically extremely pale, recalling Sandwich Tern, but with red on the bill for much of the year, relatively long red legs and very long white tail streamers in spring. Flight slightly stiff-winged and fast except during graceful display

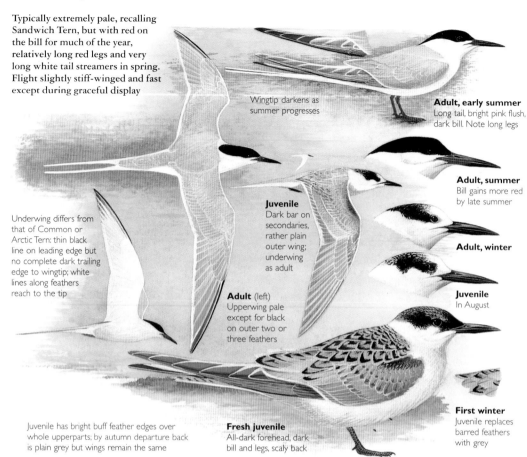

Wingtip darkens as summer progresses

Adult, early summer Long tail, bright pink flush, dark bill. Note long legs

Adult, summer Bill gains more red by late summer

Adult, winter

Juvenile Dark bar on secondaries, rather plain outer wing; underwing as adult

Juvenile In August

Underwing differs from that of Common or Arctic Tern: thin black line on leading edge but no complete dark trailing edge to wingtip; white lines along feathers reach to the tip

Adult (left) Upperwing pale except for black on outer two or three feathers

First winter Juvenile replaces barred feathers with grey

Juvenile has bright buff feather edges over whole upperparts; by autumn departure back is plain grey but wings remain the same

Fresh juvenile All-dark forehead, dark bill and legs, scaly back

Gull-billed Tern *Gelochelidon nilotica*

Unlike most terns Gull-billed Terns feed mainly over pastures and marshland, as well as on shallow lagoons near the coast, and are less likely to be seen fishing.

FEEDING They take insects, lizards, even voles and small chicks of other birds. In winter they migrate to the plains of east Africa, where they forage around the great herds of grazing wildebeest, gazelles, and zebras.

DISPLAY & VOICE Displays are much the same as those of other terns, but the calls are distinct: a nasal *chuvek* and a croaking *kway kway kway*.

BREEDING Small breeding colonies are widespread through the Mediterranean region. The nests are hollows on the ground on grassy banks and dunes near coastal lagoons or estuaries; less often on open beaches. Two or three eggs are incubated for 22–23 days.

MIGRATION European birds move south into Africa from August to October and return in March and April.

LENGTH 35–38cm (14–15in)

WHEN TO SEE March to October
WHERE FOUND Mostly freshwater and brackish marshes and wet meadows around the Mediterranean, also interior of Spain; only a vagrant in NW Europe, usually on the coast

A relatively stocky, long-winged, short-billed, long-legged tern. In summer its smooth, rounded black cap and all-black bill are distinctive; in winter it looks extremely pale despite its grey rump and variable grey or black eye patch

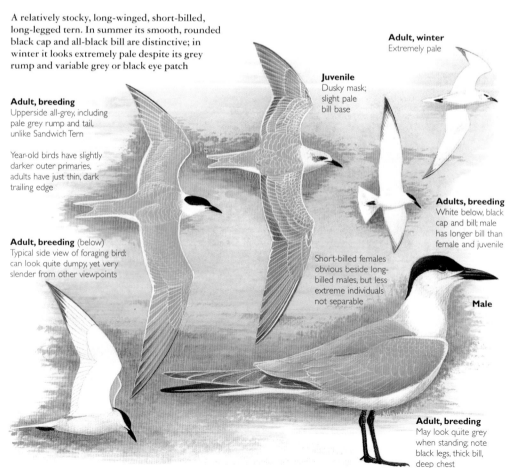

Adult, winter Extremely pale

Juvenile Dusky mask; slight pale bill base

Adult, breeding Upperside all-grey, including pale grey rump and tail, unlike Sandwich Tern

Year-old birds have slightly darker outer primaries, adults have just thin, dark trailing edge

Adults, breeding White below, black cap and bill; male has longer bill than female and juvenile

Adult, breeding (below) Typical side view of foraging bird; can look quite dumpy, yet very slender from other viewpoints

Short-billed females obvious beside long-billed males, but less extreme individuals not separable

Male

Adult, breeding May look quite grey when standing; note black legs, thick bill, deep chest

Sandwich Tern *Sterna sandvicensis*

A large, long-winged, dagger-billed tern: angular, lively, and expressive compared with smaller terns. Beside Common or Arctic Terns it looks extremely pale, with much brighter white underparts. Black legs and bill are useful clues

A **B**

Sandwich

Common

Sandwich Tern has much longer 'arm' (A) relative to outer wing (B) than Common Tern, even more so compared with Arctic Tern; gives different flight action and long-winged, rangy impression

On arrival in spring has complete black cap; white forehead appears from June or July

Adult, spring
Clean, pale grey above; increasingly black streaks along outer primaries during summer and autumn contrast with pale inner ones

Long head and bill balance short tail, giving rakish effect compared with Common Tern

Tail short, forked; tail and rump all white

Bill black with pale spot at tip: yellow at close range

Adult, spring
Very white below (Common much greyer)

Typical food-searching flight

Often detected at long range by harsh, rhythmic *kier-ink* calls

Adult, early summer
Black forehead; spiky crest

Juvenile, September
White head with dark mask effect; pale except for dark outer wing, darker hindwing and dark corners to tail

Adult, summer
Quickly loses black on forehead

Long wings give angular, 'big-shouldered' effect on ground; dark areas on wingtips wear much blacker by autumn

Juvenile, September
Dark Vs on upperpart feathers gradually lost during July and August, leaving dark marks on unmoulted wing coverts and tertials; all-black bill develops pale yellow tip

Juvenile, August/September
Shorter-billed individual; streaked crown, dark, streaky nape with hint of crest

Black legs at all ages and seasons

Juvenile Gull-billed Tern
Black restricted to eye-patch; bill slightly thicker, all-black

Adult, late summer
Bill long, angular; tip almost colourless to clear yellow

This is the largest tern in most of Europe (Gull-billed Terns are much more restricted and the huge Caspian Tern is mostly very rare). It is a rather lanky, angular, bony-looking tern – but its pale plumage, set off by a black crest and a long, spiky, black bill, give it a refined, clean, and handsome character. It is a lovely bird when seen close up, especially early in spring when it is at its best, with a full black cap. (It is also one of the first welcome signs of summer.) At long range over the sea it has a whiteness that marks it out from the greyer Common Tern, and because of its fishing technique – a faster dive from a greater height giving a bigger splash as it plunges headlong into the sea – it can often be discerned right out on the far horizon. Its extra whiteness is perhaps less obvious on a sunny day, when all gulls and terns tend to gleam in the bright light reflected from the sea, but on a dull day it can shine out from the gloom.

FEEDING It catches mainly small fish, especially sandeels, sprats, and herrings, after a vertical plunge into the sea.

DISPLAY & VOICE Its displays are much like those of other terns, involving pursuit flights over the nesting colony and posturing on the ground. It often crosses its angular wings over its raised tail, pushing their joints out from its body at the 'shoulders', while raising its head and expanding its pointed crown feathers into a spiky crest. During courtship males feed females with fish, both to cement the pair bond and to give her much-needed extra nutrition to build a clutch of large eggs. Calls are harsh, loud, far-carrying, and characteristically rhythmic, including *kier-ink* and *kirrik*.

BREEDING Sandwich Tern colonies are notoriously fickle, the birds deserting easily if disturbed and moving from place to place in different years. They usually nest on dunes, or sandy or shingly islands in coastal lagoons; some contain hundreds of pairs. The nest is a mere scrape; the one or two eggs hatch in 21–29 days and the chicks fledge in 28–30 days. Adults are aggressive but fall easy prey to foxes, hedgehogs, even badgers, and predatory birds.

MIGRATION In spring they arrive in Europe early, often in March, but most birds move south back to west Africa in August and September. Occasionally one or two are seen in winter in southwest Europe, or rarely Ireland, Britain, or the Netherlands.

LENGTH 36–41cm (14–16in)

WHEN TO SEE Mostly March to September, a few through the winter
WHERE FOUND Coasts of Britain, Ireland, Low Countries and Denmark, NW France; more widespread on W European coasts on migration; rare inland

Black Tern *Chlidonias niger*

The three small *Chlidonias* terns are often called 'marsh terns' because they are associated with shallow, reed-fringed freshwaters, overgrown lake shallows, riversides, and similar wetlands far more than with the open waters and coasts frequented by the *Sterna* terns. They have an easy, lazy flight over such places, quite distinct from Common Terns. On migration, however, Black Terns are just as frequent on large reservoirs, where groups of 10, 20, or sometimes a few hundred may appear in spring and autumn; they also pass by coastal headlands over the sea. In winter they form flocks, fly faster, and even hover more, resembling Common Terns in their behaviour. They are nevertheless delicate birds, usually dipping to the surface rather than diving for food (but migrating Common Terns, Arctic Terns, and Little Gulls do this too).

FEEDING In summer they eat mainly insects and small aquatic creatures, but on migration and in winter they turn to fish. They typically feed in groups, flying head-to-wind, rising and falling – but not hovering – between swoops to the surface to snatch food in their bills. Black Terns also catch insects in the air like overgrown swallows.

DISPLAY & VOICE In spring groups of pairs fly over the breeding colony in a high, jerky flight followed by a downward glide, in which the leading pair are followed at a distance by the rest. Males feed females with fish once they are paired. Calls are relatively quiet and simple, with a slight squeaky quality: *kik-kik*, *teek-teek* and *teeuw*.

BREEDING The birds breed in colonies of perhaps 20–30 nests together at the edge of a marsh, often close to (but not mixed with) other species of tern or Black-headed Gulls. The nests are built on floating vegetation or heaps of weed; they are little more than piles of damp waterweed. Two to four eggs are incubated for 21–22 days.

MIGRATION Black Terns winter in Africa. In autumn huge numbers gather in the Netherlands before moving south over the sea; adults move a month or so before juveniles. Many stop at inland reservoirs and lakes for a few days. In spring the northward movement tends to be more urgent and some cross the Sahara direct rather than going around to the west. Large groups that arrive at reservoirs may be gone within a few hours. Black Terns may migrate at night, at a considerable height, as well as by day.

LENGTH 22–24cm (9–9½in)

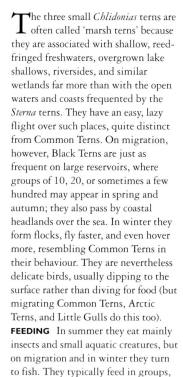

WHEN TO SEE April to October
WHERE FOUND Breeds very locally south from S Sweden and Finland, most in E Europe; commoner south of Baltic than in Mediterranean region. Widespread migrant

A small, delicate, short-legged tern, with a fine, spiky bill, round head, long wings. In spring sooty-black appearance obvious; in autumn dark shoulder smudge characteristic

Summer adult
Head, breast, belly, and bill all black; back smoky grey; white vent

Winter adult
Pale; mid-grey above; note three-lobed cap, dark shoulder/chest smudge, black legs

Closed wingtips extend well beyond tip of grey tail

Autumn juvenile
Three-lobed cap; large dark chest smudge; scaly brownish above, darker fore-edge of wing

Legs dull reddish

Black Tern, winter
Large cap, thin bill, shoulder patch

White-winged Black
Small cap, stubby bill, no shoulder patch

Autumn juvenile
Front edge of wing dark; washed brown above; rump pale grey, tail grey, only slight fork

Flight is buoyant, erratic, sometimes rising high over water before departure, returning in fast, sweeping dive

Summer adults
Smoky grey above includes tail, black on head and body, bright white undertail

Whiskered, immature, autumn
Scaly 'saddle', no white collar. Rump normally grey. Odd individual with white rump

Black, immature, autumn

White-winged Black, Breeding
White tail and forewing

Black, immature, autumn

White-winged Black Tern *Chlidonias leucopterus*

Adult, breeding
Bold black head and body, pale wings, white vent and tail; thick dark bill, bright red legs

Adult, moulting
Ragged dark central line on underwing

Sub-adult, summer
Less immaculate breeding plumage; some have darker outer flight feathers

Adult, breeding

Adult, winter
Pale head with small greyish cap, thick black bill; whole of neck, sides of chest, and underside unmarked white

Legs rather long, red

Juvenile, autumn
Narrow three-lobed cap; dark, barred brown saddle; white chest

Juvenile
Dark saddle, white rump, tail edged white

A small tern, slightly chunkier, dumpier, and less graceful than Black Tern to experienced eye; slightly stouter bill, steeper forehead, longer legs

Adult, winter
Clean white underside obvious

In summer the adult White-winged Black is a really stunning tern. In western Europe it is a rare visitor to shallow floods, swamps, and reed-fringed lakes, often among flocks of commoner Black Terns. These exciting finds are typically autumn juveniles; a spring adult is a real treat.

FEEDING The tern picks insects and tiny fish from the water surface.

DISPLAY & VOICE Courtship displays are similar to those of Black Terns; the calls are more slurred, less piercing; the *kerr*, *keek*, or *kek* alarm notes are rarely heard outside the breeding season.

BREEDING Like the Black Tern it breeds in waterside colonies, often close to those of other water birds. The nests are built on floating weed, less often on the solid shore. Two or three eggs are incubated for 18–22 days.

MIGRATION Most breeders move south through the Balkans in autumn, to winter in Africa (often in large flocks on east African lakes), and pass back through eastern Europe in spring.

LENGTH 20–23cm (8–9in)

WHEN TO SEE April to October
WHERE FOUND Breeds E Europe, rare west to Poland; regular in very small numbers west to Britain, mostly in autumn

Whiskered Tern *Chlidonias hybridus*

The largest of the marsh terns, but still remarkably light, buoyant, and elegant, broader wings and relatively shorter tail give it a distinctive appearance in flight

Whole upperside pale grey; lack of white collar diagnostic

Summer

Summer

Winter

Winter

Bill relatively long and thick

Breeding adult, summer
Black cap, white throat, grey underside almost black on belly

Large cap, rear crown broadly black, central crown slightly streaked

Autumn juvenile
Back ginger-brown with scaly black bars and white fringes; quickly becomes more uniform grey

Legs reddish, long

Compared with Arctic and Common Tern in winter (unlikely in Europe) grey (not white) short tail, shallow fork and no white collar

Of the marsh terns this is the largest; it is also the most like a Common or Arctic Tern in appearance and behaviour, especially in winter or juvenile plumage. It breeds in warmer regions than either of the black terns, in marshy areas with plenty of shallow, still water and the mats of floating vegetation that it needs for nesting.

FEEDING It picks insects and small fish from the water surface in a slow, swooping flight, head-to-wind.

VOICE Whiskered Terns are more vocal than Black Terns, with louder, more rasping calls at the colony: *kyick*, *cherk*, and a strident *kerch*.

BREEDING The nest is small heap of vegetation anchored to reeds or rushes. Two or three eggs hatch after 18–20 days' incubation.

MIGRATION Whiskered Terns spend the winter in west Africa. They are rarely seen inland once the central European breeders have migrated southwest along major rivers.

LENGTH 23–25cm (9–10in)

WHEN TO SEE April to October
WHERE FOUND Very local across Europe south of the Baltic, most occur in Iberia and E Europe; rare vagrant north of this range

153

Little Tern *Sterna albifrons*

The smallest, nimblest, fastest tern, the Little Tern looks too small and delicate for a seabird, yet it flies with a determination and energy that fit it well for its life over inshore waters, and for its long migrations at sea. When nesting it is particularly attracted to shingle beaches right at the edge of the waves, and prone to having its nest and eggs washed away by high tides, or buried in windblown sand. It also needs protecting from disturbance on popular holiday beaches.

FEEDING It catches small fish in quick dives that end with a sharp smack into the waves.

DISPLAY & VOICE Little Terns make noisy display flights and posture beside the nest; calls are typically quick, sharp, harsh: *kirree-ik kirree-ik*.

BREEDING Two to three eggs are laid on sand or shingle, rarely on old concrete buildings or rafts.

MIGRATION Many gather on estuaries in autumn before heading for Africa.

LENGTH 22–24cm (9–9½in)

WHEN TO SEE April to September
WHERE FOUND Mostly low-lying W European and Mediterranean coasts, also inland in S and E Europe; on migration off estuary mouths, sandy beaches, shingle banks, rare inland

A small, dynamic tern with fast, flickery wingbeats; white forehead at all seasons and a diagnostic yellow bill when adult

Juvenile
Black bill, mottled crown, dark forewing band and scaly upperpart pattern

Flickering hover, looking down for fish, before dive

Juvenile

Non-breeding

Tail fork varies: longer on breeding males

Outer primary feathers make black wedge on wingtip

Small, short body, but long wingtips stretch well beyond tail

Mainly silvery-grey above, always looks very pale

Flies with fast action; dives hurriedly with loud smack into waves

Diagnostic yellow legs and bill (usually with black bill tip)

Breeding

Some adults lose black bill tip in summer

Caspian Tern *Sterna caspia*

This very large tern approaches the size of a Lesser Black-backed Gull, although it stands lower and is less bulky. Its powerful bill and large size are usually very obvious, allowing immediate identification, but can be overlooked at long range if there are no smaller species nearby for comparison. Its long, angular wings with prominent black patches under the tips give an almost Gannet-like impression.

FEEDING These terns take fish in dramatic headlong dives; they fly from their offshore colonies to feed in fresh or brackish lagoons rather than the sea.

DISPLAY & VOICE Displays involve showing off the black cap and crest and large, red bill. Calls include several rasping notes, such as *kak-ra-racha*.

BREEDING Colonies occupy remote or secluded islands; the nest is a simple scrape in the sand. Two or three eggs hatch after 20–25 days' incubation.

MIGRATION Most spend the winter in Africa, migrating along the western European coast; rarely seen in Britain.

LENGTH 47–54cm (18½–21in)

WHEN TO SEE May to October
WHERE FOUND Scarce breeding bird on beaches and coastal marshes in the Baltic; rare migrant on most coasts

A dramatic, red-billed tern with black legs, identifiable by its large size, stout bill, and black under the wingtips

Juvenile has dusky tail bands and orange bill

Black underwing tip conspicuous

Juvenile

Breeding

First year
Dark wing covert band, dark secondaries

First year has thin tail band

Size of bill not always obvious in flight

Striking, heavy red bill with blackish marks near tip

First summer
Streaked cap, often dark bill tip

Adult, winter
Pale-streaked cap

Breeding
Adult has flat, bushy crest and black forehead until midsummer

Black legs

Little Auk *Alle alle*

Although remarkably abundant around some far northern islands, Little Auks are usually scarce in the southern North Sea and much rarer still in the eastern Atlantic. Sometimes northerly gales bring much bigger numbers farther south in late autumn. They are tiny, round-bodied, small-winged relatives of the larger Puffin.

FEEDING Little Auks dive easily and frequently to catch tiny crustaceans and occasional fish fry.

DISPLAY & VOICE Courtship displays involve much bowing and mutual head-wagging. Flocks form mass flights above breeding cliffs, and larger flocks call with prolonged, rippling trills; they also give these calls on the water and from cliff ledges.

BREEDING Nests are high on cliffs. The single egg hatches after 29 days and the chick flies at 27–28 days old.

MIGRATION Arctic breeding sites are occupied in April and May, and vacated in August; oceanic wintering areas are mostly occupied by November.

LENGTH 17–19cm (7–7½in)

| WHERE FOUND | Arctic Ocean, North Sea |
| WHEN TO SEE | Mostly October–March in Europe |

Round-bodied, narrow-winged, short-billed black and white seabird. Although tiny, rides out most winter storms; prolonged gales bring some inshore and even onto inland lakes

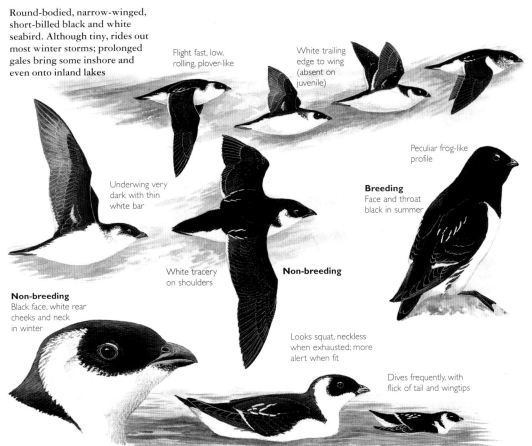

Flight fast, low, rolling, plover-like

White trailing edge to wing (absent on juvenile)

Underwing very dark with thin white bar

Breeding
Face and throat black in summer

White tracery on shoulders

Non-breeding

Peculiar frog-like profile

Non-breeding
Black face, white rear cheeks and neck in winter

Looks squat, neckless when exhausted; more alert when fit

Dives frequently, with flick of tail and wingtips

Puffin *Fratercula arctica*

Most seabird colonies have some Puffins, but they are common only in the far north and west of Europe. For most of the year they live far out at sea.

FEEDING They feed mainly on small fish but also take crustaceans and other small marine creatures. They dive frequently to search for food, using their wings vigorously underwater.

DISPLAY & VOICE Most Puffin displays involve their big, colourful bills. Courting pairs attract the attention of nearby birds which cannot resist joining in: they are the original nosy neighbours. Calls at the colony are deep growling and crooning notes.

BREEDING Puffins nest in burrows or crevices in clifftop earth or fallen boulders, in a colourful world of sea campion, thrift, lichens, and blue sea. The single egg hatches after 39 days and the chick flies when about 38 days old; it will breed after five years at sea.

MIGRATION The colonies are occupied from March to August or September; the birds then disperse to sea.

LENGTH 26–29cm (10–11in)

| WHEN TO SEE | Mostly October to March |
| WHERE FOUND | Islands and mainland cliffs, Iceland, Britain, Ireland, Scandinavia, NW France; scarce offshore elsewhere, very rare waif inland |

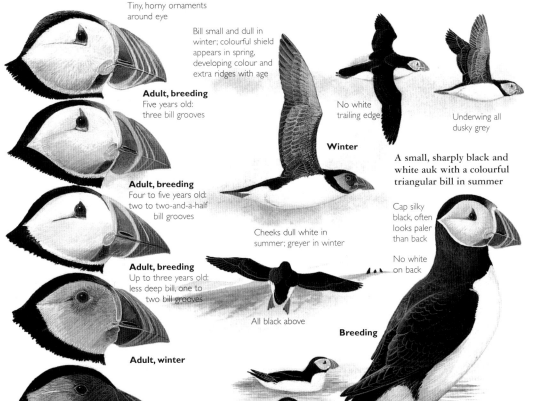

Tiny, horny ornaments around eye

Bill small and dull in winter; colourful shield appears in spring, developing colour and extra ridges with age

Adult, breeding
Five years old: three bill grooves

Adult, breeding
Four to five years old: two to two-and-a-half bill grooves

No white trailing edge

Underwing all dusky grey

Winter

A small, sharply black and white auk with a colourful triangular bill in summer

Cap silky black, often looks paler than back

No white on back

Cheeks dull white in summer; greyer in winter

Adult, breeding
Up to three years old: less deep bill, one to two bill grooves

All black above

Breeding

Adult, winter

Juvenile/first-winter
Grey-faced; small dark bill

Swims buoyantly; rarely driven ashore in gales

Vivid orange legs

Guillemot *Uria aalge*

Guillemots are individually fascinating, elegant creatures, but they are best seen *en masse* at the breeding colonies where they add life, noise, and spectacle to a seabird cliff.

FEEDING Guillemots catch fish in very deep dives, using their wings to 'fly' underwater.

DISPLAY & VOICE Displays are relatively simple bowing and bill-fencing bouts, which reinforce pair bonds and confirm ownership of a tiny territory on a ledge. The calls at the nest are loud, whirring, rising growls.

BREEDING Guillemots lay on open ledges on sheer cliffs, in the most precarious positions imaginable. A single egg is incubated for 28–37 days; the chick jumps from the ledge when barely half grown, encouraged and accompanied by a parent.

MIGRATION The colony is occupied from March to August, then most move well out to sea, wintering from the Arctic south to Iberia.

LENGTH 38–41cm (15–16in)

WHEN TO SEE All year
WHERE FOUND Breeds around coasts of Britain and Ireland, Iceland, Scandinavia, NW France, W Iberia. Widespread offshore in winter; extremely rare inland even in autumn storms

Non-breeding
White face with dark stripe through eye, dark crescent on side of chest

Northern birds have throat band and heavily mottled underwing

Northern birds blackish

A sleek, elegant auk; brown above with white front. Stands upright, resting on full length of leg; swims low with head raised, tail short and square; flies fast with whirring wing action

Most of underwing white; rear body longer than Razorbill's, feet project well beyond tail

Non-breeding

Juvenile
July/August: grey patch behind eye

Juvenile
Mid September: White patch

Minority in south have white eye-ring and 'bridle'; proportion increases northwards

Breeding
Whole of head and neck dark brown; flanks streaked brown

Juvenile calls to be fed with loud, musical whistle

Non-breeding

Brünnich's Guillemot *Uria lomvia*

This is a northerly counterpart of the Guillemot, slightly larger and thicker-billed but similar and with much the same lifestyle. It breeds in huge, dense colonies on cliffs and otherwise spends its life at sea.

FEEDING It catches fish and some marine invertebrates during deep dives from the surface, after searching for prey by swimming with its head held underwater.

DISPLAY & VOICE Its aggressive behaviour at nesting ledges is much the same as in Guillemots, but the pair-bonding activity is less obvious, with little bill-fencing and no upright stretched poses adopted by pairs.

BREEDING Brünnich's Guillemots nest on narrow ledges, but not the flat tops of sea stacks sometimes used by Guillemots. Some colonies total hundreds of thousands of pairs.

MIGRATION Colonies are occupied from April to August; otherwise the birds are at sea, mostly in the Arctic, in less saline water than Guillemots.

LENGTH 39–43cm (15–17in)

WHEN TO SEE All year; rare vagrant in NW Europe, mostly in winter
WHERE FOUND Breeds in Iceland, extreme N Norway and the Arctic; very rare elsewhere

A northern auk; heavier, thicker-billed, broader-winged than Guillemot but hard to distinguish at sea

Breeding
Thick white streak along gape in summer; white extends up throat as point (round on Guillemot)

Wingtip slightly broader, rounder than Guillemot's

Darker than the Guillemot beneath flight feathers and on greater coverts, otherwise white below

Non-breeding

Upperparts blacker than on Guillemot

Non-breeding

Non-breeding
In winter dark cap extends down to speckled cheeks, unlike Guillemot with its whiter face and dark eye stripe

Thick white tips to secondaries; long tail extends well beyond wingtips

Flanks unstreaked white all year (dark streaks on Guillemot); breastband often more complete. Note 'armpit' compared with Guillemot

Female (right) has slimmer bill than male (below)

Female

Male, breeding

Non-breeding

Guillemot

Razorbill *Alca torda*

A heavy-bodied, deep-billed auk; black above, with white front. Stands upright on full length of leg; swims low, head raised, tail pointed and often raised; flies fast on short, whirring wings

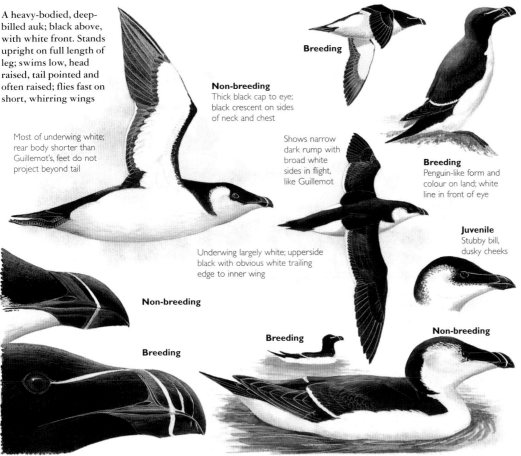

Breeding

Non-breeding
Thick black cap to eye; black crescent on sides of neck and chest

Most of underwing white; rear body shorter than Guillemot's, feet do not project beyond tail

Shows narrow dark rump with broad white sides in flight, like Guillemot

Breeding
Penguin-like form and colour on land; white line in front of eye

Juvenile
Stubby bill, dusky cheeks

Underwing largely white; upperside black with obvious white trailing edge to inner wing

Non-breeding

Non-breeding

Breeding

Breeding

Razorbills are quite extraordinary seabirds, being among the deepest-diving birds in the world. They are usually less numerous than Guillemots at seabird colonies, where several species cram together to nest on the sheer cliffs.

FEEDING Most of their food is fish, with a few other marine creatures. They usually catch several fish during each dive from the surface.

DISPLAY & VOICE Pairs indulge in bowing and preening, and also fly off the ledge in a beautiful downward flight with deep, slow beats of fully stretched wings. Their calls are gruff, rattling growls and short grunts.

BREEDING They prefer more sheltered nesting sites than Guillemots, laying their eggs in cavities or crevices rather than open ledges. The single egg hatches after 36 days and the young flutters down to the sea after 18 days.

MIGRATION Colonies are occupied from March to August or September.

LENGTH 37–39cm (14½–15½in)

WHEN TO SEE All year
WHERE FOUND Breeds around Iceland, Scandinavia, Britain, Ireland and NW France; in winter south to W Mediterranean, more often in mouths of estuaries and shallow bays than other auks

Black Guillemot *Cepphus grylle*

A stocky black and white seabird, usually seen bobbing on waves offshore or flying low over the sea

Breeding

White upperwing patches and larger white underwing eyecatching in flight

Non-breeding, winter
Recalls small grebe, but barred back and white wing coverts distinctive

Breeding, summer
Unmistakable: smoky black with oval white wing patch, red legs

Immature in summer has mottled white patch on browner wings

Juvenile

Juvenile dusky above, white below, wing patches barred; winter adult cleaner, wing patches white

Immature

Immature

Non-breeding, winter

While other guillemots breed on sheer cliff faces in large colonies and may be seen floating on the water beneath the cliffs in their hundreds, Black Guillemots are usually seen in ones and twos near low, rocky islands, or in sheltered bays along indented rocky shorelines.

FEEDING They eat mainly fish in the south of their range, with more marine crustaceans in the far north.

DISPLAY & VOICE The birds display using their red legs and mouths, and the white wing patches above and below their wings. Pairs also display on land by walking in an upright posture. They call with a thin, shrill piping.

BREEDING Nests are generally in crevices between boulders and in scree slopes under cliffs; also under debris such as driftwood and fish boxes.

MIGRATION There is little southward movement in winter and all the breeding areas remain occupied, although some birds move well out to sea, even in Arctic waters.

LENGTH 30–32cm (12–13in)

WHEN TO SEE All year
WHERE FOUND Breeds from Ireland and Scotland northwards, and in the Baltic; rare farther south

Black-bellied Sandgrouse *Pterocles orientalis*

Arid or semi-arid steppe – poor pasture with areas of almost bare, dry earth and stones, rocky plateaux and saltflats – is the preferred habitat of this localized bird. It is best seen in the morning when small flocks fly to lakes or even tiny pools to drink. Sandgrouse can tolerate extremely dry habitats, but they must have regular access to water which they visit in a daily rigid routine.

FEEDING They pick seeds from the ground, or less often from the stems of plants, with a precise, pigeon-like action of the head and small bill.

VOICE The flight call resembles that of a Turtle Dove or Black Grouse: a rolling or gurgling *ch-llll* or *churrr*.

BREEDING Two or three eggs are laid in a bare or scantily-lined hollow; they hatch after 23–28 days. The male brings water to the chicks by soaking his belly feathers in a pool; the chicks 'strip' water from the feathers by drawing them through their bills.

MIGRATION Resident.

LENGTH 33–35cm (13–14in)

WHEN TO SEE All year
WHERE FOUND Locally in Portugal and widespread but scattered through Spain; also Turkey, Russia, north Africa

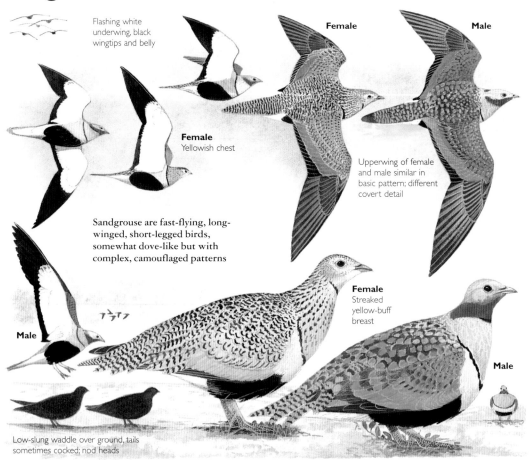

Flashing white underwing, black wingtips and belly

Female
Yellowish chest

Female

Male

Upperwing of female and male similar in basic pattern; different covert detail

Sandgrouse are fast-flying, long-winged, short-legged birds, somewhat dove-like but with complex, camouflaged patterns

Female
Streaked yellow-buff breast

Male

Male

Low-slung waddle over ground, tails sometimes cocked; nod heads

Pin-tailed Sandgrouse *Pterocles alchata*

Although it may live on dry steppe like the Black-bellied Sandgrouse, the Pin-tailed Sandgrouse is often found on the dried-out edges of low-lying grassy marshland, on hard-baked mudflats and dunes, among scattered bushes, and on dry, flat arable fields. Where it is still common it gathers in larger flocks than the Black-bellied, sometimes of hundreds. These typically fly to their drinking sites in the morning, less often at dusk.

FEEDING Virtually all its diet consists of seeds taken from the ground, supplemented by occasional green shoots and buds.

DISPLAY & VOICE Pairs may perform courtship flights at a great height. The flight call carries far, announcing the sudden arrival of a flock at a drinking pool: a slightly ringing *catarr-catarr*.

BREEDING Two or three eggs hatch after 19–20 days, in an unlined nest on the ground, sometimes in a tuft of grass. The chicks fly when about four weeks old. Several pairs may nest close together, while others are solitary.

MIGRATION Resident.

LENGTH 31–39cm (12–15in)

WHEN TO SEE All year
WHERE FOUND Rare S France; widely scattered but localized in Spain. Also north Africa and Middle East

Typically flies fast in irregular groups or lines, with deep, rapid wingbeats

Flight calls distinctive

Male

Female

White edges to primaries reduce contrast

Both sexes have tail point when adult

An exceptionally beautiful sandgrouse with a satin-white belly and long central tail point

Juvenile
No tail spike
Pale wingbar

Pearly-grey wingtips wear darker

Juvenile
Pale primary tips

Female
Double black throat band

Male
Unique pattern

Juvenile (A) moults to barred pattern (B) like female but without grey or head/breast pattern

Non-breeding adults may have some barred feathers (B) above

Laughing Dove *Streptopelia senegalensis*

Flight swift and energetic, wings usually bent back and blunt

Underwing very dark ;belly, vent and most of underside of tail pale grey to white

Compare plain red-brown back and blue-patched wings with paler (but chequered) Turtle Dove; tail less white at tip than Turtle Dove

Turtle Dove
Slimmer, with narrower wings

A rather dark, variable, pink-brown and slate-blue dove of extreme southeast Europe; long-tailed, round-winged; may be very tame in towns, where often darkened by urban grime

Flies on arched wings with jerky but rhythmic wingbeats

Feeds inconspicuously on ground but may enter streetside cafes to forage under tables; open country individuals brighter than this

Female
Male has more extensive black speckling on pink chest

Juvenile
No necklace or half collar

Doves and pigeons shown to same scale (main and flight images)

This is really a dove of the Middle East and Africa and eastwards through southern Asia, but it is a vagrant in the extreme southeast of Europe. In many places it is extremely tame, even feeding beneath occupied tables at streetside *tavernas*. It is associated with cultivation, towns and villages everywhere, but also lives in open woodland in quite wild regions.

FEEDING It feeds in typical dove fashion, picking seeds, a few insects, spiders, small snails, and other such small items from the ground.

DISPLAY & VOICE Males identify their territory and attract mates with gliding display flights. Their call has a rolling, bubbling, laughing quality: *ha-ha-hoo-hoo-hoohoo-hoo*.

BREEDING The nest is a frail, flat structure of twigs, typically in a tree or bush but often on a building. Two eggs are incubated for 12–14 days. The squabs fly when two weeks old.

MIGRATION Resident.

LENGTH 25–27cm (10–11in)

WHEN TO SEE All year
WHERE FOUND Istanbul; also north Africa and the Middle East

Rock Dove *Columba livia*

Pure northwest European Rock Doves are handsome birds with a white rump, white underwing, and two black bars across each wing. Domestic descendants (the basis of many feral populations) are varied, typically with a thicker bill and fatter white cere; racing pigeons have longer head and neck, and swept-back wings set farther back

Black wingbars, white rump

Slim head

Rock
Slim bill, tiny cere

White underwing patch (unlike Stock Dove but like most feral pigeons); dark beneath tail

Domestic
Thick bill, fat cere

Adult Rock Dove
Classically clean, pale grey with large white rump; black bar and trailing edge to inner wing; glossed neck with no white

The true Rock Dove is a handsome wild pigeon, but centuries of domestication, and the subsequent 'escapes' of pigeons of varied form and colour back into the wild, have created a confusion of hybrid forms. The pigeons found in most areas are pretty much a mixture of domestic breeds, although those on coastal cliffs tend to revert to the true type. Only on wilder coasts and mountain ranges are pure Rock Doves still found.

FEEDING They feed mainly on grain and smaller seeds, supplemented by a good deal of green matter such as shoots, buds, and soft leaves of herbs.

DISPLAY & VOICE Displays are the same as those of the familiar town pigeon, as is the call: a deep, moaning *ooorr* or *ooh-oo-oor*.

BREEDING Rock Doves nest on cliff ledges in sea caves and high crags. Two eggs are incubated for 16–19 days.

MIGRATION Resident.

LENGTH 31–34cm (12–13in)

WHEN TO SEE All year
WHERE FOUND Locally N Scotland, Ireland, Iceland, Scandinavia, mountain regions; domestic pigeons gone wild established almost everywhere except much of Scandinavia

159

Stock Dove *Columba oenas*

While Woodpigeons are large, long-winged, broad-tailed, slim-headed birds, and usually abundant, Stock Doves are generally much less common and distinguished in flight by their smaller size, shorter wings and tail, and rounder heads. They are more likely to be mistaken for feral pigeons, but their much greater partiality to trees (especially when roosting) is a helpful guide. Feral (and especially racing) pigeons tend to look longer-necked, and have more swept-back wings.

Stock Doves are not just woodland and farmland birds: they also like cliffs and crags, inland rather than at the coast, and they often occupy quarries. They fly out with a noisy clatter if disturbed. Lowland farms with plenty of trees and woodland edges are typical places for Stock Doves, especially where there are old trees with big holes for nesting in; the birds move out from the trees to feed on open fields. They often mix with Woodpigeons, Rooks, and Jackdaws, but sometimes form pure flocks of a few scores.

FEEDING Their main foods are seeds, leaves, shoots, and buds. Stock Doves feed in typical pigeon fashion on the ground, walking slowly or standing almost still as they forage. They prefer more or less bare ground and feed close to water, which they need for frequent drinking. They also take some food directly from trees.

DISPLAY & VOICE A displaying male will fly with slow, deep wingbeats, clapping its primary tips together over its back. It then glides with spread tail and raised wings, often from tree to tree or circling back to the same perch. Its song is characteristic: deeper than a Woodpigeon's, simpler in pattern and repeated several times: a rhythmic, almost booming *ooo-rooh* or *ooo-er*.

BREEDING The nest is built in a tree cavity, or on a shady ledge on a cliff or inside an old, derelict building. It is a scanty construction of a few twigs and stems, on which two eggs are laid. They are incubated for 16–18 days and the chicks fly when 20–30 days old.

MIGRATION Western birds are resident; northern and eastern populations (north of the Baltic and east from Denmark and eastern France) migrate south and west in winter.

LENGTH 32–34cm (12½–13½in)

WHEN TO SEE All year in west; March to October in N and E Europe
WHERE FOUND Breeds Ireland, Britain (except far N Scotland), S Finland, S and E Scandinavia, and most of mainland Europe, but scarce in Mediterranean region and absent from most Mediterranean islands

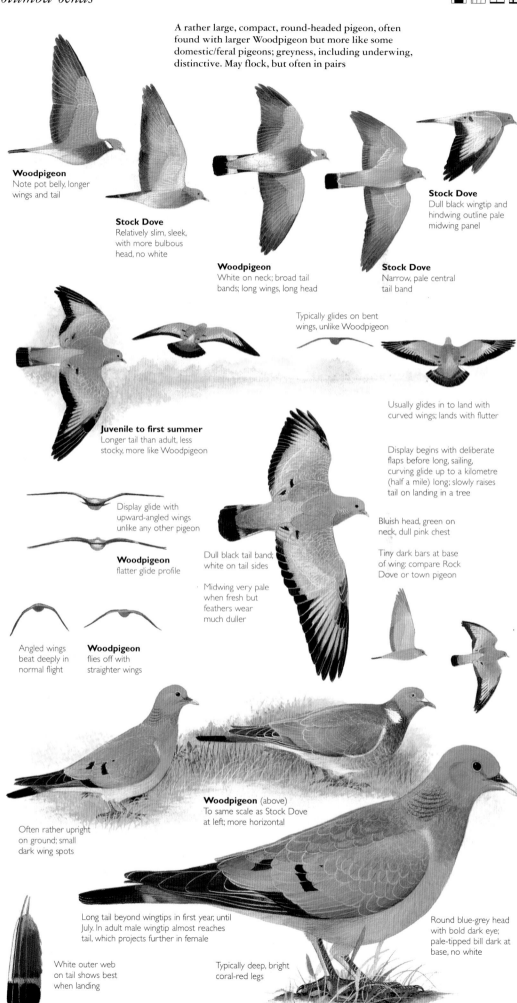

A rather large, compact, round-headed pigeon, often found with larger Woodpigeon but more like some domestic/feral pigeons; greyness, including underwing, distinctive. May flock, but often in pairs

Woodpigeon
Note pot belly, longer wings and tail

Stock Dove
Relatively slim, sleek, with more bulbous head, no white

Woodpigeon
White on neck; broad tail bands; long wings, long head

Stock Dove
Dull black wingtip and hindwing outline pale midwing panel

Stock Dove
Narrow, pale central tail band

Typically glides on bent wings, unlike Woodpigeon

Usually glides in to land with curved wings; lands with flutter

Display begins with deliberate flaps before long, sailing, curving glide up to a kilometre (half a mile) long; slowly raises tail on landing in a tree

Juvenile to first summer
Longer tail than adult, less stocky, more like Woodpigeon

Display glide with upward-angled wings unlike any other pigeon

Woodpigeon
flatter glide profile

Angled wings beat deeply in normal flight

Woodpigeon
flies off with straighter wings

Dull black tail band; white on tail sides

Midwing very pale when fresh but feathers wear much duller

Bluish head, green on neck, dull pink chest

Tiny dark bars at base of wing: compare Rock Dove or town pigeon

Woodpigeon (above)
To same scale as Stock Dove at left; more horizontal

Often rather upright on ground; small dark wing spots

Long tail beyond wingtips in first year, until July. In adult male wingtip almost reaches tail, which projects further in female

White outer web on tail shows best when landing

Typically deep, bright coral-red legs

Round blue-grey head with bold dark eye; pale-tipped bill dark at base, no white

Woodpigeon *Columba palumbus*

Striking flash of white across wing always obvious and instantly identifiable

Large, long-tailed; wings often slightly angled back to blunt, slightly indented tips. At full stretch, wings look long and quite straight, with slightly notched tips

Tail with broad, whitish central band, the black tail band always obvious as bird flies off

Stock Dove
Same scale as Woodpigeon above

A big, striking, heavyweight pigeon with boldly contrasted wings. In flight it appears heavy, deep-chested, small-headed, with long, rather broad wings and a broad tail. Flies up from ground or trees with a loud clatter; may sweep upwards, clap its wings and descend in a shallow glide

Display flight includes steep climb and 'stall' with sharp, snapped wing-clap

Typically flies up with loud clatter, twisting sideways, then dashing off with deep, fast wingbeats

When perched, small head and full chest obvious: quite long, broad, square tail

Broad body, narrow head

Juvenile
Duller, smokier grey than adult with pale scaly feather edges; white on wing but not on neck. Very young ones untidy, fluffy, weak-looking

Adult
Well-fed adults look immaculate, smooth, glossy, and colourful with bright bill and eye, rich pink breast. Back wears slightly browner

Woodpigeons evoke mixed reactions: most people probably ignore them or dismiss them as just 'pigeons'; sometimes, even in town parks where they are tame, they are regarded as pests. To farmers – and to many gardeners – they are undoubted pests: the enemies of greens and young shoots. To anyone with an eye to see, however, they really are splendid birds. Close up, even on bird tables in some areas, they are beautiful creatures: plump and shiny, their plumage patterns full of subtle variations on basic blue-greys, brownish-greys, and soft pinks. Distant flocks may number hundreds, even thousands, making a welcome sight in many open farming landscapes where there are relatively few birds, or against a winter sunset as they fly off to roost.

Where they are shot relentlessly, on farmland and in nearby woods where they roost, Woodpigeons are generally wild and understandably difficult to approach. In gardens and towns they may become quite tame, always wary but daring to let people get close unless they are given a fright, in which case their fragile relationship with people explodes in a clatter of alarmed wingbeats as they dash away.

FEEDING Woodpigeons eat seeds, grain, shoots, leaves, acorns, and many kinds of berries.

DISPLAY & VOICE Rival birds may fight quite dramatically, with feathers and white down spilling from the trees, but their most obvious displays are the special flights over treetops in their breeding areas. These involve a steady climb followed by a sharp wing clap and a shallow glide on spread wings. The Woodpigeon's song is a lovely, lazy, relaxing summer sound: a rhythmic coo, typically *cu-COO coo, coo-coo, cu-COO coo*.

BREEDING Nests are shallow and flimsy, see-through platforms of sticks in hedgerows and scrubby trees. Two pure white, shiny eggs are incubated for 17 days; their empty shells are often found later, dropped away from the nest by the parents. The young, or squabs, are fed on special 'milk' – a secretion from the parent's crop – and fly after 20–35 days.

MIGRATION Most British breeders are sedentary, moving around in winter to find the best sources of food; some winter visitors from the Continent swell their numbers. In Scandinavia and eastern Europe Woodpigeons are summer migrants. Large numbers migrate over southern Europe in September–October and April.

LENGTH 40–42cm (16–16½in)

WHEN TO SEE All year
WHERE FOUND In farmland and mixed woods, town parks, large gardens. Almost all Europe

Collared Dove *Streptopelia decaocto*

This ordinary-looking dove – although with an appeal and refinement of its own when seen at close range – is actually one of Europe's most remarkable birds. From the 1930s it spread north and west from the Middle East, crossing the whole of Europe within a few decades and reaching Britain in the 1950s. Its phenomenal expansion more or less stopped in the 1970s, but it is now one of the most widespread species in the UK. Much of Scandinavia and Spain are still 'Collared Dove free'.

FEEDING The dove's spread and subsequent increase in numbers throughout its new range was largely made possible by the availability of spilled grain around the places where grain is handled, from backyard chicken runs, farms, and stockyards to railway sidings and distilleries. Few such places now spill significant quantities of grain, and few people now keep hens in the suburbs, so Collared Doves tend to feed more in gardens, parks, and horse pastures. They eat a variety of small insects and vegetable matter, and in many areas they frequently feed at bird tables. In town parks and gardens they are particularly tame and approachable.

DISPLAY & VOICE The most obvious displays are steeply-climbing flights and long, flat, circling glides. These develop into rapid chases between pairs with more frenetic calling. The song is familiar: a loud, hollow, rather quick triple coo. The emphasis is on the second note, with the third more clipped: *coo-COO-cuk*. Excited males call with their necks inflated and an exaggerated bobbing of the whole body. Their frequently-heard flight call is a slurred, nasal, or sometimes more rasping *kwurrr*.

BREEDING The nest is a typical dove platform of thin sticks; flimsy and lightweight. It is usually in a dense conifer or shrub. Two pure white eggs are incubated for just 14–16 days and the young fly at just 17–18 days old.

MIGRATION A few are still seen in out-of-the-way places north and west of the main range, but most are resident. The reasons for the dove's initial spread are still not fully understood, since although suitable food made it possible, such food had been available for hundreds of years before the Collared Dove took advantage of it.

LENGTH 31–33cm (12–13in)

WHEN TO SEE All year
WHERE FOUND Suburbs, farmland, pinewoods throughout Britain and Ireland except for most remote coasts and islands, mountains and moors. From N Iberia to Norway, east throughout Europe and Middle East

Female

Male

Male

Male

Top three views to scale with those of Turtle Doves opposite

A large, long-tailed dove; small head and short legs typically dove-like and delicate, wings broad and curved back in flight. Generally pale and lacking in contrast, with greyer areas on wing, silky-grey underwings and wide, dull whitish band beneath tail tip

Wings broad, bent back towards tip, slightly rounded

Distinctive jerky, angle-winged flight action

Silver-grey underwing, often looking very dark; characteristic pattern beneath tail

Upperwing shows little contrast but blue-grey panel catches the eye in certain lights

Spread tail reveals pale grey corners: lacking the white of Turtle Dove

Looks slim and often erect when alert, but much more dumpy, small-headed when relaxed; frequently on wires, aerials, chimneys

Frequently rises at steep angle, then sails in wide arc on depressed wings (compare with raised wings of Turtle Dove in display flight). Loud flight call, unlike other doves and pigeons

Pale head and breast marked by thin, black, white-edged collar on adults; red eye often looks almost black

Female
Face more buff than male, but difficult to separate

Male

Wingtips of female (above) reach almost to tip of tail coverts; those of male (below) fall short

Juvenile is slightly scaly above with pale feather edges, and lacks dark collar

Turtle Dove *Streptopelia turtur*

Upperpart pattern more contrasted than Collared Dove's, with much richer colouring and brighter, bluer midwing panel

Normal flight speed 95 km/h (60 mph); seems to fly at this speed wherever it goes

Compare flight shapes and patterns with those of Collared Dove (to same scale opposite). Wings taper to narrower tip, usually swept back

Display flight ends with glide on raised wings, unlike Collared Dove's; silent in flight

Underside of tail largely white with narrow black base

Beautiful and delicate, this small, bright dove looks alert, quick, and lightweight. Flies with occasional sideways rolls and flicked, backward wingbeats, spreading its tail on landing to reveal a broad, pure white band across the tip

Turtle Dove

Alarmed adults fly off with spread tails revealing white band

Adult
Neck patch neatly striped

Collared Dove
Display flight: note paler underwing, different tail pattern

Adult
Crown grey, breast pink; much whiter belly than Collared Dove, upperparts chequered

Juvenile
Head grey, breast sandy, less pink than adult; upperside duller, less crisply marked; (compare with plainer Laughing Dove in SE Europe)

The Turtle Dove used to be a familiar and popular part of the 'English country scene', but for whatever reason – and probably there are several – the population has suffered a catastrophic decline. It has always been scarce or absent from most of Wales, Scotland, and Ireland. Indefensible spring shooting in southern Europe and France places excessive pressure on the diminished breeding population, but there may also be problems in Africa, where the Sahel droughts of the 1960s and 1970s affected Turtle Doves along with other species such as the Whitethroat and Sand Martin, and where pesticides might be doing damage now. There are also problems in England; these include the destruction of old hedges and especially the loss of farmland weeds: wild plants upon which many birds (not to mention insects) depend. As a result of all this the Turtle Dove is now rather scarce, but its populations fluctuate; in favoured spots there may still be small groups (often threes in summer, but larger flocks in late summer and autumn) to enjoy.

FEEDING It eats mainly green shoots and seeds. In late summer flocks of Turtle Doves may line overhead wires (sometimes mixed with Collared Doves) above the cereal fields, waiting to feed on the spilt grain after harvest.

DISPLAY & VOICE The display flight is similar to that of the Collared Dove but rather less obvious, and it ends in a glide on raised, rather than lowered, wings. The soporific summer song is a low, soft, purring coo: *toorrr toorrrr*. Like other pigeons, it has no alarm note or other call.

BREEDING Typical nesting habitat is the edge of a mixed wood with dense shrubbery, or an old, overgrown, dense hedgerow with tall, spreading hawthorns and odd trees overwhelmed by tangles of ivy. A thin dish of fine twigs holds two pure white eggs; these are incubated for 13–14 days and the young birds fly when they are only 19–21 days old.

MIGRATION Arrivals in spring reach northwest Europe in April and May; flocks or small parties may be seen heading north along coastlines. They leave again between August and September, although occasional individuals hang on into winter. Turtle Doves spend the winter in west Africa.

LENGTH 26–28cm (10–11in)

WHEN TO SEE Mostly April to September
WHERE FOUND Typically in wooded farmland and tall hedgerows, England and E Wales; widespread in Europe except for Scandinavia and higher mountains

Cuckoo *Cuculus canorus*

It is remarkable how many people say that they frequently hear Cuckoos but have never actually seen one. Yet they probably have seen one without knowing it, for Cuckoos are simply not recognized for what they are.

They are not especially difficult to see. Indeed, they perch freely on open wires and on the outer twigs of tall trees, as well as on fence posts overlooking rough grassland, pastures, or marshy places. In summer they need to find small birds' nests to parasitize, so they are often to be seen on bushy moorland looking for Meadow Pipits, beside marshes where they can find Reed Warblers, or near woods, hedges, and parks with breeding populations of small birds such as Wrens or Dunnocks.

FEEDING The Cuckoo is unusual in that it eats hairy caterpillars, which are strongly distasteful or very irritating to small birds. It even expels much of its stomach lining periodically to rid itself of caterpillar hairs. It also eats a variety of other insects; it catches them on the ground or picks them off bushes, often after a steep dive from a perch.

DISPLAY & VOICE Cuckoos often droop their wings and raise and spread their tails in aggression to other Cuckoos, or in courtship when close to potential mates. The male's song is the familiar double note: *cuc-coo*, or *u-oo* at close range, given with the bill almost closed. It often becomes *cu-cuc-coo* and may sound remarkably hoarse from some birds. They call to each other with a low, quick 'dirty laugh' sound, *kwak-ak-ak-ak*. Females have a quick, clear, throaty bubbling call with a remarkably liquid quality.

BREEDING A female may lay from one to 25 eggs. She watches small birds from a perch, or from overhead in open areas, until she locates a nest with fresh eggs. She then flies to the nest when it is left unguarded, removes an egg in her bill, and quickly lays one of her own directly into the nest (even into a 'difficult' nest with a side entrance such as a Wren's nest in a cavity). The Cuckoo egg, incubated by its foster parents, hatches in 11–12 days. The chick devotes much energy to evicting the 'rightful' occupants of the nest, hoisting both eggs and chicks to the nest rim and pushing them over the edge. The foster parents then feed it until it flies at 19 days old, by which time it is much bigger than they are.

MIGRATION Cuckoos spend the winter in Africa, mostly south of the equator. Adults go south before the juveniles.

LENGTH 32–34cm (12½–13½in)

WHEN TO SEE Mostly April to September
WHERE FOUND Breeds throughout Europe except for Iceland and the northern tundra

Male often raises and fans tail when it lands, and looks from side to side

Instantly identified by its unique call, yet unseen or unrecognized by many. Often perches on side of tree, fence post, or overhead wire; resembles a small bird of prey in flight, but flies with heavy, head-up, low-winged attitude

Flies with wings below horizontal; head looks thin, raised

Male, spring Clean grey chest

Juvenile, rufous type

Juveniles May be rufous type (above) or grey type (below)

Adult female Tinge of tawny-brown on chest

Juveniles are heavily barred; broad bars beneath unlike Kestrel, barred back unlike Sparrowhawk

Juvenile, grey type

Bold white spots on tail unlike hawks and falcons

Juvenile has pale nape spot

Pale band along midwing with dark patch each side in all plumages

Usually flies with shallow wingbeats below the horizontal, almost quivering as it lands in a tree

Female, first summer Retains brown-barred inner flight feathers of juvenile

Male, adult Broad-based, pointed wings unlike Sparrowhawk, grey unlike Kestrel; thin head and curved bill

Female has slightly shorter, blunter wing, but not distinguishable in field

Male makes angry growling noises when approached

Typical flight shapes: wings back, tail closed or fanned in diamond-shape, head raised

Juvenile

Adult

Adult female, red phase A rare form in Britain

164

Great Spotted Cuckoo *Clamator glandarius*

A large, rangy, long-tailed, southern European cuckoo, often difficult to watch

Often a flight view is puzzling: this is a 'peculiar' bird, unlike anything else

Adult
Pale spots in rows across wing; grey outer wing

First winter

Juveniles and first winter birds have unique rufous primaries

Adult
All-grey crown, larger tail spots than juvenile

Flight quick, rolling, slightly laboured, small head raised

Adults
Long tail characteristic; pale peachy flush on neck

Adult

Some first winter birds have grey crown and mostly dark primaries, but usually retain a few rufous feathers

Juvenile
Rufous on wing, black crown and cheeks

This wonderful large, long-winged, long-tailed cuckoo is a bird of warm Mediterranean regions with heath, scrub, and scattered trees in which Magpies nest. It also likes olive and almond groves and cork oak, pine, or mixed woodland with plenty of open, airy, sunny spaces.

FEEDING It favours hairy caterpillars but wipes off the hairs before eating them. It also catches and eats various other insects and spiders.

DISPLAY & VOICE A male has a dove-like display flight, rising quickly and gliding down. The pair then defend a territory that may contain up to 40 Magpie nests. The song is a chatter, becoming a gobbling sound: *kittera kittera kee-ow kee-ow -wow-wow-woh*.

BREEDING The female lays one egg, occasionally two or three, in the nest of a Magpie or other crow; each female lays up to 18. The chick hatches after 12–14 days, and does not evict other eggs or chicks; it flies after 24 days.

MIGRATION Most winter in Africa, south of the Sahara.

LENGTH 38–40cm (15–16in)

WHEN TO SEE February to September
WHERE FOUND Breeds Portugal, Spain, S France, W Italy, very locally Balkans; rare vagrant outside this range, mainly in spring

Hawk Owl *Surnia ulula*

Sparrowhawk-like flight profile

An exciting, long-tailed owl, often seen perching prominently on a high perch; has a unique combination of shape, pattern, and character; may attack people fiercely near its nest

Tail quite broad, but long, with obvious wedge-shaped tip

Pale 'braces' and dark stripes on sides of head

Underpart barring varies individually

Adult male
Female has shorter tail

Characteristic fierce expression with white cheeks, black lines, and striking yellow eyes

Ranging from the tundra in the north to the fringe of open steppe in the south, this is an owl of forests and forest edges. It likes clearings in birch and mixed woodland, but usually avoids solid conifer woods.

FEEDING In summer it eats mainly small voles; in winter it varies its diet with some small birds. It hunts by day, even in sunshine, but also at dusk when it is feeding young.

DISPLAY & VOICE Males advertise their territories for some weeks before they begin nesting. They call in a display flight or from a perch: a bubbling, rising trill lasting up to 14 seconds. They also give a wheezy *aaaa-ik*.

BREEDING Nests are unlined tree holes, old crow nests, or nest boxes. Up to 10 eggs hatch after 25–30 days, and the chicks scramble into nearby branches before flying at 25–35 days.

MIGRATION These owls are essentially nomadic, dispersing in winter. Large numbers sometimes move south when voles are unusually scarce.

LENGTH 36–39cm (14–15½in)

WHEN TO SEE All year
WHERE FOUND Breeds over most of Norway, Sweden (except south), Finland, and east through Russia. Very rare vagrant farther south

Tawny Owl *Strix aluco*

Tawny Owls really hoot in classic owl fashion, although their other calls are more common. They are responsible for the 'tu-whit-tu-woo' known to every child, actually a duet between the female's *ke-wick!* and the male's hoot. Seldom seen, the bird waits until dark before emerging to call and hunt. By day it sits motionless in dense ivy, a tall tree, or rarely low down in dense cover, given away only by a splash of white droppings below. It may, however, be betrayed by small birds mobbing it from a safe distance.

FEEDING It catches most of its prey on the ground, typically mice, voles, rats, earthworms, and beetles, but it also catches many birds at night.

VOICE The song is a breathy, wavering hoot: *hooh! hu, hu, ho-oooooo*. Its other calls are loud, wheezy, yelping notes: *ke-wick! yeick* or *ki-eeer*.

BREEDING The female lays two to five eggs in an unlined cavity in a tree or building, or an old Magpie nest, and incubates them for 28–30 days.

MIGRATION Resident.

LENGTH 37–39cm (14½–15in)

WHEN TO SEE All year
WHERE FOUND Absent from Iceland, Ireland, most of Scandinavia and Sardinia, but otherwise widespread in Europe

Bulky, heavy-headed, short-winged

Hunts from perch: listens for prey, then dives onto it

Black eyes; high brows above round face

A big, large-headed, black-eyed owl of woods and parks, strictly nocturnal and usually difficult to see unless discovered at its daytime roost in a tree

Usually rich brown above; line of white spots on wing coverts; grey and rufous forms occur, ranging from extremely rufous to light and dark grey

Barn Owl *Tyto alba*

Few birds match the extraordinary beauty of a Barn Owl. At a distance it looks bright yellow-buff and white, while a close view reveals an intricate peppering of grey. It is easier to see than many owls: in summer, when it has young to feed, it hunts quite early in the evening; in a hard winter, when it risks starvation, it may be forced to hunt by day. In arable farming areas Barn Owls are often restricted to hunting over roadside grass, where they are vulnerable to traffic.

FEEDING It eats mainly small rodents, especially voles, mice, and rats, which it locates by flying low and slowly over the ground, often hovering before diving headlong into the grass.

VOICE The adults make a strangled shriek; a hoarse snoring sound may betray young at the nest.

BREEDING Up to seven eggs are laid in barns, bell towers, or other roof spaces, in hollow trees, and among hay bales. They hatch after 30–32 days; the young fly at eight or nine weeks old.

MIGRATION Resident.

LENGTH 33–39cm (13–15in)

WHEN TO SEE All year
WHERE FOUND Widespread, but absent from Iceland, Scandinavia, E Europe, high altitude regions

Male has paler wings than female, less barred, but much variation

Pale-breasted race
W and S Europe: striking white underwing and white body

Large, big-headed owl with tapered wings, white, heart-shaped face with small black eyes; hunts at dusk and by day in cold weather

Light hunting flight with floating glides and quick wingbeats; dives onto prey

Dark-breasted race
N and E Europe: breast dark, upperparts much greyer (see also bottom left); underwing can be darker

Thin-legged, knock-kneed effect

Wingtip shape variable

Dark-breasted race

Short-eared Owl *Asio flammeus*

A large, long-winged, fierce-eyed owl with distinctive dark wrist patches in front of bold pale orange-buff areas on primaries; spends much time on the wing, often seen by day

Round head, long wings, very short tail

Flies high over moorland, calling and clapping wings under body

Perches on ground, rock, or fence post in angled pose; may roost in bushes or in ivy in trees

Yellow eyes set in black against white face; rich tawny body marbled with black and buff; may raise small ear tufts

Pale bars and trailing edge to upperwing and white tip to tail unlike Long-eared

Small ear tufts may be raised

Underwing pale with small, crisp dark marks

Bowed wings in glide

Unlike most owls this species hunts by daylight, flying low over open ground. In summer it is usually seen over moors, with or without small conifers, or over extensive marshes. In winter it visits a surprising range of habitats, from land cleared for building to rough, semi-urban heaths, as well as open farmland and reedbeds.

FEEDING Its main victims are field voles; when these are abundant, several owls may concentrate in a small area.

DISPLAY & VOICE During summer display flights it makes a deep, hollow *boo-boo-boo* and loud wing claps; in winter, rarely a nasal, yapping, whip-like bark.

BREEDING Four to eight eggs are laid on the ground in a simple shallow scoop, usually among tall heather or rushes. They hatch after 24–29 days; the young fly when 24–27 days old.

MIGRATION Many northern breeders move south and west in autumn. They also make erratic, nomadic movements, mostly connected with the varying abundance of small rodent prey.

LENGTH 34–42cm (13½–16½in)

WHEN TO SEE All year, but unpredictable
WHERE FOUND Widespread in Europe as a wanderer or winter visitor; breeds mainly in N Britain, Iceland, Scandinavia, and NE Europe

Long-eared Owl *Asio otus*

Occasionally discovered roosting in thorn or willow thicket in winter

Flattish wings in glide

A richly coloured, beautifully patterned, elusive owl of conifers and dense thickets near open moor or heath; long ear tufts characteristic if raised but less obvious when relaxed. Strictly nocturnal except in very cold weather

Deep orange eyes; V-shape on head continues up into raised ear tufts

Some individuals more creamy-buff, some more tawny

Tail all dark, barred, no white tip; longer than Short-eared Owl's

Underwing has more broken bars on tip than Short-eared

Grey area on wing

Where discovered by day, can be remarkably confiding, but vulnerable to repeated disturbance

Rear of wing barred with narrow bands, giving more uniform appearance than bold pattern of Short-eared Owl; pale trailing edge less distinct

Breeding Long-eared Owls are extremely elusive, since they are nocturnal and nest in forest edges, shelter belts, and copses with conifers where they are hard to see. The calls of young, demanding food, may give them away. In winter, however, groups of owls roost together in thickets and tree tops; it is sometimes possible to watch these over several weeks, so long as they are not scared off by anyone approaching too closely.

FEEDING Hunting mainly at night, Long-eared Owls catch small rodents, plus many small birds in winter.

VOICE In early spring the owl gives a deep, moaning or cooing hoot: *oo oo oo*. The young call like squeaky gate hinges: *peee-oo*. Silent in winter.

BREEDING Nesting owls take over old nests of crows, pigeons, magpies, sparrowhawks, or squirrels; the three to five eggs hatch within 25–30 days and the young fly when 30 days old.

MIGRATION Northern breeders move west and south in autumn, and some cross the North Sea.

LENGTH 35–37cm (14–14½in)

WHEN TO SEE All year
WHERE FOUND Absent from Iceland and N Scandinavia; breeds in Britain, Ireland, and N Europe; widespread in winter

Scops Owl *Otus scops*

Of the owls, only the Tawny forces itself upon our attention as often as the Scops, which calls so frequently in the wooded parks, gardens, and squares in and around Mediterranean towns and villages. It is extremely difficult to locate by day and often hard to see at night, but persistence is sometimes rewarded by an excellent view at dusk, or of a bird caught in the beam of a torch or a nearby street light.

FEEDING The Scops Owl eats insects and spiders, plus a few reptiles, frogs, and small birds. It seizes them in its feet after flying down from a perch, but sometimes catches moths in flight.

VOICE It repeats a slightly ringing, whistled, unvaried *peu* or *tyuu*, at a rate of about 22–26 notes per minute. It also has a shrill, squealed alarm call.

BREEDING Nests are in holes in trees or walls; the clutch of four or five eggs hatches after 24–25 days' incubation.

MIGRATION European Scops Owls winter in Africa, except for a few in southernmost Spain, Italy, and Greece.

LENGTH 19–20cm (7½–8in)

WHEN TO SEE Mostly March to September; all year in far south of Europe
WHERE FOUND Iberia, France, Italy, locally Austria, Balkans, E Europe north to W Russia; rare vagrant elsewhere

Often seen on rooftops at dusk; dives away if approached

Female will duet with male at different pitch

Can be called and seen by lights of street lamps

'Ears' raised or flat

Grey and rufous phases: some greyer than shown

A small nocturnal owl, easily located by its persistent whistling call but often seen merely as a rooftop silhouette; very elusive by day

Very rufous on forewing close to body

Long, narrow wings make it look much larger in flight

Very variable facial shapes and postures; yellow eyes show when fully open, alert

Strongly barred underwing

Pygmy Owl *Glaucidium passerinum*

Male Pygmy Owls sit in tree tops at dawn and dusk, at the edges of glades and boggy areas in mixed or coniferous woods, calling repeatedly for minutes on end. They often cock or wave their tails and generally have an active, fidgety character. Pygmy Owls are frequently active by day, and in winter they may come close to farms and villages in search of prey.

FEEDING They catch voles, mostly at dawn and dusk, and take small birds from perches or even on the wing. The owls store food in holes, including nest boxes, especially in winter when dead prey is preserved by frosts.

DISPLAY & VOICE Males defend their territories all year, using a flute-like call like that of a Bullfinch: *du*, *pyuh*, or *pyuk*. The note is given 30 to 60 times a minute for several minutes.

BREEDING The nests are in tree holes or nest boxes; four to seven eggs hatch after 28–30 days and the young fly at 27–34 days old.

MIGRATION Resident, dispersing in far north of Europe if food is short.

LENGTH 16–17cm (6–7in)

WHEN TO SEE All year
WHERE FOUND Scandinavia, east and south to Russia, Poland; S Germany and the Alps, locally in E Europe

A very small, round owl of thick forest, active at dusk, often bold and likely to approach if its call is imitated

Alert, often with tail raised. Pale 'face' marks on back of head

Great Tit prey shows small size

Pygmy   Scops   Little

Head has distinctive shape when feathers are raised

Small, rounded (same scale as Scops above)

Yellow eyes, white brows

Barred tail; some more marked on back and wings

Undulating flight, like woodpecker

Barred flight feathers beneath, but very clean coverts

Little Owl *Athene noctua*

A small, dumpy, rather flat- or square-headed owl with bright yellow eyes and white eyebrows; typically upright on short, slim legs. Often seen by day but hunts at dusk, from trees, poles, and fence posts; when curious, bobs whole body and twists head

Yellow eyes set in dark sockets; fierce look

Female has longer tail than male

Female

Males

Barred underwing

Quick, bounding flight with frequent wing closures; sweeps up to perch

Upperparts brown, white-spotted

Male

The only small, white-spotted owl in Britain; Tengmalm's occupies different habitat in mainland Europe

Female

The Little Owl's alert expression became familiar in southern Britain after it was introduced from Europe in the late 19th century. It took well to the mixed farmland of England and even spread to remote, bleak islands and coastal cliffs. Yet it remains a bird of warmer habitats in much of southern Europe and north Africa: anywhere from Egyptian temples to the terracotta tiles of barn roofs and stony yards of old Spanish farmsteads.

FEEDING Although often obvious by day, the Little Owl hunts chiefly after dark, catching beetles, moths, worms, small voles, and small birds.

VOICE Most of its calls are far-carrying whistles, including a clear, mellow *gooeek* and a sharper *k-weeew*.

BREEDING Nests are typically in rather long, deep holes, in hollow branches, among rocks, or in earth banks. Two to five eggs hatch after 27–28 days; the chicks fly five weeks later.

MIGRATION Resident.

LENGTH 21–23cm (8–9in)

WHEN TO SEE All year
WHERE FOUND England and Wales, widespread over most of mainland Europe north to Denmark, Latvia, and Russia

Tengmalm's Owl *Aegolius funereus*

A highly nocturnal forest owl, rarely seen except in high latitudes in summer. Warmer brown than Little Owl, more rufous-buff below; raised eyebrows give questioning or surprised look, less frowning

Degree of spotting variable

Underside varies, may be more or less barred or paler on belly; smaller white upperwing spots than Little Owl

Juvenile leaves nest in all-dark down, gradually develops adult pattern

Spotted crown, white V-shape between eyes, high points to white cheeks, line of white spots on coverts

Flight quite direct with short glides. Prefers to keep within canopy, using well-concealed perches (Pygmy Owl often uses tree top perch, Little Owl perches in the open)

This is a curiously large-headed, high-browed owl with a look of constant surprise or inquiry. It is difficult to see, being strictly nocturnal in its behaviour. It has some preference for spruce forest, but is also widespread in mixed stands of pine, birch, and poplar in mountain forest and in the northern taiga.

FEEDING Its staple prey are small voles, although it also catches some mice, shrews, and small birds. It hunts from a perch within woodland.

VOICE The usual call is a soft, repetitive *po-po-po-po-po*, with up to 25 notes in succession, which carries for 2 kilometres (1¼ miles). The rhythm of the hollow, barking hoots varies individually from male to male.

BREEDING Tengmalm's Owls nest in holes in trees, but also use nest boxes; three to seven eggs hatch after 25–32 days' incubation. The chicks fly when about four to five weeks old.

MIGRATION Mostly resident; some dispersal when food is short.

LENGTH 24–26cm (9½–10in)

WHEN TO SEE All year
WHERE FOUND Most of Norway, Sweden, Finland, Baltic states, and Russia; scattered through central Europe, rare and local in Pyrenees, Balkans, E Europe

Ural Owl *Strix uralensis*

This is an aggressive owl that chases other owls and birds of prey from its territory – and is liable to strike human intruders in the face. It needs mature, undisturbed forest, and pressure on its habitat has reduced numbers over most of its range.

FEEDING It captures rodents in forest clearings and bogs, but it also eats medium-sized or large birds such as Jays and Willow Grouse, especially in years when small rodents are scarce.

DISPLAY & VOICE The owl's territorial call carries up to two kilometres (1¼ miles): a soft, deep *VOOhoo – voohoo-oVOOho*. Various other gruff hoots and barks are heard near the nest.

BREEDING Ural Owls nest in big holes in tree stumps, rarely in old stick nests and increasingly in nest boxes. Two to four eggs are usual; they hatch after 27–34 days. The young leave the nest after about four weeks, but do not fly until they are 40 days old.

MIGRATION Resident; requires an all-year round territory to ensure survival.

LENGTH 60–62cm (24–24½in)

WHEN TO SEE All year
WHERE FOUND Sweden, Finland,Russia, Belarus and locally south to N Germany; Romania; rare and local Carpathians and Balkans

A unique round-headed, grey owl with a barred and streaked look; mild facial expression with small, beady eyes

Long wedge-shaped tail distinctive

Tawny Owl (left) at same scale and showing shorter tail

Large head distinctive

Adult
Pale patch near wingtip, juveniles have narrower bars

Adult

Round head; small, round, dark eyes

Adult

Adult

Tail of some juveniles less heavily barred

Adult (left)
Pale underwing, darker breast

Note long tail beyond wingtips

Great Grey Owl *Strix nebulosa*

A truly extraordinary giant owl of northern forests, the Great Grey is one of Europe's most dramatic birds. It may be seen by day in mixed or coniferous forests, as well as adjacent clearings and boggy areas. It is famous for its dangerous aggression towards humans at the nest, and for its ability to detect (by sound) and catch small rodents hidden under deep snow. Yet it is often extremely hard to find: in years when food is scarce, especially, it can be most unobtrusive for such a huge bird.

FEEDING Small voles make up the bulk of its prey, supplemented by shrews and small to medium-sized birds.

VOICE The territorial call is a deep, muffled, pumping boom of 10 to 12 hoots. Given only in the darkest hours of the night, it carries barely 400 metres (¼ mile). Other feeble notes are given by the female.

BREEDING Great Grey Owls nest on broken stumps or in the stick nests of hawks and Buzzards. Up to six eggs are usual; they hatch in 28–30 days.

MIGRATION Resident, but may roam in search of food if vole numbers crash.

LENGTH 64–70cm (25–27½in)

WHEN TO SEE All year
WHERE FOUND NE Sweden, sporadic N Norway, more commonly Finland, rare Belarus, Russia, Ukraine

A massive, rare, elusive owl, with an enormous head and facial disc but small, piercing yellow eyes; very variable plumage

Will perch on treetop looking slim, tapered

Black eye-rings inside white crescents; black around small, pale bill

Adult

Adult
Bold bars on wing (juvenile has narrower, weaker bars)

Adult
Pale wingtip patch rich buff (compare Ural Owl), juvenile paler overall on wingtip, with more uniform bars

Diving to catch prey in snow

Juvenile
Less strongly barred than adult

Note shoulder straps

Eagle Owl *Bubo bubo*

A huge 'eared' owl; heavily built, broad-winged, but usually elusive; inactive and well-hidden by day

Adult
Note ample wings, buff below, well marked at tip

Ear tufts tend to be flattened outwards or raised in wide V; deep orange eyes

Juvenile
Much like adult except for weaker wingtip barring

Adult
Variable but typically very dark on forewing, some almost solidly blackish

Short, square tail; long, broad wings, easy flight

Glides on flat wings

Adult
Ear tufts raised

The size and intensity of colour of Eagle Owls varies from region to region; pale Siberian birds are truly giant owls, while darker, more richly coloured western ones are somewhat smaller. Eagle Owls are ten times the weight of Long-eared Owls, giving an idea of their real bulk and great power.

FEEDING They take a great range of prey, regularly killing gulls, ducks, grouse, crows, other owls, and birds of prey, as well as rabbits, hares, and even young deer. They take most of their prey at night, except in the far north in summer when Eagle Owls hunt over the tundra in daylight.

VOICE Just after sunset in late winter males call with deep, short, booming hoots which carry up to five kilometres (3 miles): *HOO-o*. Hoarse notes and a sharp *ke-ke-kekayu* in alarm can also be heard near the nest.

BREEDING They nest on cliff ledges, in caves or in large holes in old trees. Two to four eggs hatch after 32–34 days.

MIGRATION Resident.

LENGTH 60–75cm (24–30in)

WHEN TO SEE All year
WHERE FOUND S and W Norway, S and central Sweden, Finland and east into Siberia; Denmark, very locally central Europe to Balkans, Italy, S France, Iberia

Snowy Owl *Nyctea scandiaca*

A unique, massive, rounded, white or heavily barred owl of wild, open regions

Yellow eyes look dark at distance

Adult males
Whitest plumage

Adult male
Smaller than female

Juveniles (above and left)
Great variation; males (above) less barred than females (left) but some overlap; some look dark with bold white face

Adult female
Variable but evenly barred over body and upperwings, barred tail

Adult female
Piercing yellow eyes at close range

Barn Owl

Juvenile male
Much bigger than Barn Owls, which are very white below in UK. European Barn Owls have all or partly buff underwings

Big, round, with pure white males, Snowies are tremendous birds. Females are bigger still, but not quite so pristine. These are owls of open, cold, windswept moors, high mountain plateaux and stony, snow-covered ridges on remote tundra: highly nomadic and settling wherever there is a good supply of food.

FEEDING Lemmings and small rodents make up the bulk of their diet; if these are not available the owls catch rabbits, arctic hares, and a variety of birds, ranging from Oystercatchers to skuas.

VOICE The territorial 'hoot' is a rather weak, soft *gawh* or a rougher, more drawn-out *hoo*. The alarm is a harsh, quacking *kraik-kraik-kraik*.

BREEDING Snowy Owls lay their eggs on a raised hummock or rock, often protruding from surrounding snow. The clutch of three to nine eggs is incubated for 30–33 days, and the chicks fly when 45–50 days old.

MIGRATION Nomadic; rare far to the south of the usual breeding range.

LENGTH 55–65cm (22–26in)

WHEN TO SEE All year
WHERE FOUND Locally N and W Norway, N Sweden, N Finland, N Russia; very few breed Iceland. Has bred Shetland, but now rare vagrant in Britain

Alpine Swift *Apus melba*

Although every inch a swift in its shape and actions, the Alpine Swift is a big, powerful species that flies with strong, deep wingbeats and purposeful glides. It is characteristic of southern European mountain ranges and gorges, especially with limestone cliffs full of cavities in which it can nest, but it also mixes with Swifts and Pallid Swifts over southern towns.

FEEDING Insects caught in the air are the standard prey of all swifts. Alpine Swifts eat large insects, including moths attracted to lights at night.

DISPLAY & VOICE Small groups dash around cliff faces and fly up to nesting cavities with noisy, chattering or trilling calls, sometimes fighting.

BREEDING Each pair rears three chicks that fly when 45–55 days old; they will not breed until two or three years old. As with other swifts, they spend their immaturity entirely on the wing.

MIGRATION They all move to Africa in the autumn; a few 'overshoot' in spring and turn up unusually far north.

LENGTH 20–22cm (8–9in)

WHEN TO SEE March to October
WHERE FOUND Mostly in mountains in S Europe north to Alps; often in high altitude towns and villages

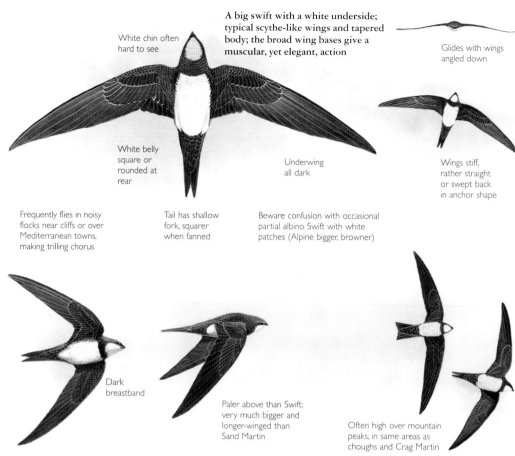

A big swift with a white underside; typical scythe-like wings and tapered body; the broad wing bases give a muscular, yet elegant, action

White chin often hard to see

White belly square or rounded at rear

Underwing all dark

Glides with wings angled down

Wings stiff, rather straight or swept back in anchor shape

Frequently flies in noisy flocks near cliffs or over Mediterranean towns, making trilling chorus

Tail has shallow fork, squarer when fanned

Beware confusion with occasional partial albino Swift with white patches (Alpine bigger, browner)

Dark breastband

Paler above than Swift; very much bigger and longer-winged than Sand Martin

Often high over mountain peaks, in same areas as choughs and Crag Martin

White-rumped Swift *Apus caffer* Little Swift *Apus affinis*

These two small, white-rumped swifts are essentially African species, rare in Europe. Both are fast fliers, the Little Swift typically of town and city skies, twinkling on stiff, straight wings. The White-rumped Swift is a bird of more remote areas and villages, and rather more elegant.

FEEDING Both catch small insects on the wing, usually high up.

DISPLAY & VOICE Parties fly over their nesting areas, White-rumped Swifts calling with low twittering notes, Little Swifts with high, screeching, rippling calls.

BREEDING Pairs of Little Swifts make globular nests of straw, feathers, and saliva, on buildings. White-rumped Swifts use old Red-rumped Swallow nests under eaves, and also beneath bridges and even roadside culverts.

MIGRATION White-rumped Swifts migrate to central Africa from Spain and Morocco; Little Swifts are resident in north Africa and a few places in the Middle East, and sporadic elsewhere.

LENGTH White-rumped Swift 14cm (5½in); Little Swift 12cm (5in)

WHEN TO SEE May to October
WHERE FOUND White-rumped breeds S Spain near coast; Little is rare vagrant in Europe, rare UK, mostly on coasts, islands

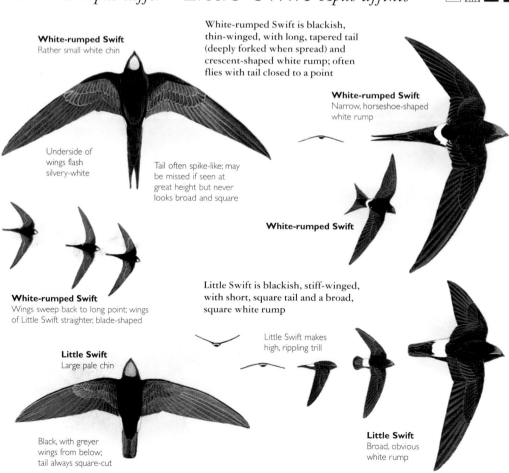

White-rumped Swift
Rather small white chin

White-rumped Swift is blackish, thin-winged, with long, tapered tail (deeply forked when spread) and crescent-shaped white rump; often flies with tail closed to a point

White-rumped Swift
Narrow, horseshoe-shaped white rump

Underside of wings flash silvery-white

Tail often spike-like; may be missed if seen at great height but never looks broad and square

White-rumped Swift

White-rumped Swift
Wings sweep back to long point; wings of Little Swift straighter, blade-shaped

Little Swift is blackish, stiff-winged, with short, square tail and a broad, square white rump

Little Swift
Large pale chin

Little Swift makes high, rippling trill

Black, with greyer wings from below; tail always square-cut

Little Swift
Broad, obvious white rump

Swift *Apus apus*

A slim, dark, scythe-winged bird of the air, never seen perched; often in noisy groups, flying between buildings

Whitish chin at close range

UK breeders all depart in August; birds seen in late September/October have come in from eastern Europe on weather systems

Very short inner wing; long, tapered outer wing: compare shape with swallows and martins

Wingtip pointed, swept back

All dark at distance

Birds can mate in the air, using slow, synchronized wingbeats, with little loss of height

Sharp-cornered forked tail

Looks all sooty-black but actually glossed green; may fade browner by autumn; underwing may shine paler in sun

Wingbeats quick, flickering, stiff

Cannot perch on wires or twigs

Often low over water in bad weather; often seen feeding in front of thunderstorms which push insects along

Loud, strident, screaming calls

Juvenile
White feather fringes

Spending most of its life on the wing, the Swift circles high in the air to feed and even sleep, but swoops low around the rooftops in noisy displays, especially towards dusk.
FEEDING It feeds entirely on flying insects and small airborne spiders, which it catches in its gaping mouth.
DISPLAY & VOICE Parties career over breeding sites, females screaming a high *swee*, males a loud, slightly lower *sree*, in a prolonged duet of *swee-ree* sounds. They fight and display in the dark of the nest cavity, recognizing each other by sexual and individual variations in voice.
BREEDING The Swift collects feathers, bits of grass, and other material in the air and builds a nest in a roof or church tower; some use natural holes in cliffs. The two chicks fly after 37–56 days, depending on the availability of food; they do not breed until four years old.
MIGRATION Immatures may spend three years aloft in Africa. Adults arrive in Europe late in spring and leave early, heading for southern Africa.
LENGTH 16–17cm (6–7in)

WHEN TO SEE Late April to September (most leave Britain in August)
WHERE FOUND Over almost any open landscapes and freshwater, in all but extreme N Europe

---

Pallid Swift *Apus pallidus*

Flight fractionally less rapid and agile than Swift; more slow turns and flat glides

A dull, muddy-brown swift, with slightly blunter wings and shorter tail than Swift

Adults very dark when freshly moulted

Note dark saddle

Underside has pale, scaly feather edges

Pale area on wing; short rear body

Paler inner and rear upperwing

Adult, underside

Tail shorter, blunter than Swift's; the two outer feathers more equal

Adult, mantle above

Pallid Swift   **Swift**

Pallid Swift   **Swift**

Dark sandy- or earthy-brown

Juvenile underside

Middle primaries longer than on Swift, giving slight bulge towards wingtip

Swift

Whiter face than Swift; Black eye stands out against pale forehead

Pallid Swift

Alpine Swift   **Pallid Swift**   **Little Swift**   **Swift**

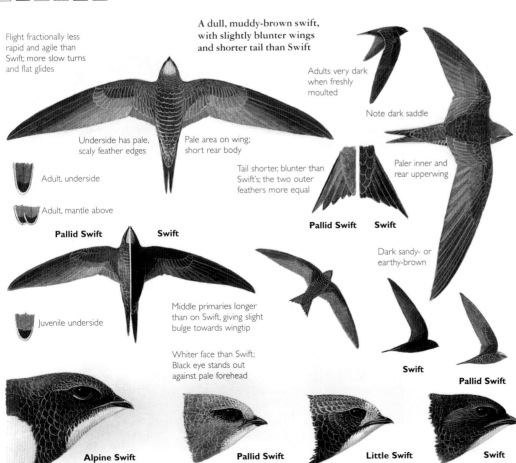

This is the Mediterranean swift, a bird of ancient towns and villages with plentiful cavities beneath roof tiles or wooden eaves. It is just as gregarious as the Swift, and the two species are often seen together. When seen apart they are harder to identify: Pallid Swifts can look dark in poor light while Swifts may look browner in strong sun, but a good view of a Pallid in clear conditions usually reveals its distinctive muddy-brown appearance.
FEEDING It eats airborne insects, caught in high, swooping flight.
DISPLAY & VOICE Its screaming calls are not quite so shrill as those of the Swift, but it chases around the houses and rooftops in similar fast-flying, noisy parties.
BREEDING It nests in dark spaces, like the Swift, under eaves or in ancient towers and walls; each pair rears two chicks which fly after about 46 days.
MIGRATION It arrives in southern Europe earlier than the Swift and is occasionally seen in winter, but it is extremely rare north of its usual range.
LENGTH 16–17cm (6–7in)

WHEN TO SEE March to October
WHERE FOUND Towns, villages, cliffs near Mediterranean coastal strip

Nightjar *Caprimulgus europaeus*

Few birds exercise the imagination in quite the same way as the Nightjar: a strange voice of the short summer nights, a shadowy shape at twilight. It becomes active around sunset and is not easy to see, although at times it seems to be remarkably inquisitive. By day it hides, either on the ground among dead leaves and bracken stems, or by sitting still and invisible along a horizontal branch.

FEEDING It catches moths and large beetles in the air, snapping them up in its wide, bristle-fringed gape as it hawks over heaths, around bushes, and in woodland clearings.

DISPLAY & VOICE The male sings from a perch at dusk, with a prolonged, even, mechanical churr or rattle, with occasional changes in pitch, like a distant motorbike. He flies from the perch with two or three loud wing-claps. The flight call is a nasal *goo-ik*.

BREEDING Two eggs are laid on bare ground; they hatch after 17–18 days.

MIGRATION Nightjars fly to Africa in August–September, returning in May.

LENGTH 26–28cm (10–11in)

WHEN TO SEE May to September
WHERE FOUND Locally through Europe except Iceland, N and W Scandinavia, high mountain regions

Flight extremely agile, light, manoeuvrable with skipping twists and turns, hovers, glides

Wings long, tapered, broadest in middle; tail full, long, often fanned

A strange, mysterious bird, active at dusk and dawn, revealed by distinctive calls and a unique, mechanical song

Sits along open, dead branches; sometimes silhouetted at dusk

Female has all-brown tail

First summer male has buff tail corners

First summer male   Adult male

Female Buff wing spots

Adult males Striking white wing spots and tail corners, visible late into dusk

Males can be lured by giving the *goo-ik* call

Red-necked Nightjar *Caprimulgus ruficollis*

A speciality of Iberia and north Africa, the Red-necked Nightjar is a fraction bigger and brighter than a Nightjar, but nine times out of ten it is identified by its distinctive voice. Like the Nightjar it has a superb light, airy, acrobatic flight, with springy wingbeats, long glides on raised wings and rapid spins and turns in pursuit of flying insects. It prefers open, flat areas with dry sandy soil and scattered bushes or trees, thickets, or groves of olive, cork oak, and eucalyptus.

FEEDING It captures moths and beetles in the air; more rarely it picks insects from the ground.

VOICE The song is a hollow sounding, monotonous, rhythmically repeated double note, like a blow on a piece of wood: *ku-TOK, ku-TOK, ku-TOK*, with a slightly squeaky effect at close range.

BREEDING Two eggs are laid on the ground among low bushes.

MIGRATION The whole population winters in West Africa, mostly in Mali.

LENGTH 30–32cm (12–12½in)

WHEN TO SEE March to October
WHERE FOUND S Portugal, central, E, and S Spain; very rare vagrant elsewhere

A typical nightjar, active very late or after dark; distinctive repetitive song; in Europe restricted to Iberia

Both sexes have clear white wing spots

Agile, gliding flight, often with wings raised in V

Rufous collar and white throat marks rarely seen

Both nightjar species have the smallest ratio of body weight to wing area of any European bird, which accounts for their floating, bouncing flight

Female has no white on outer tail feathers

Like all nightjars, superbly camouflaged when roosting, either on the ground or on a branch

Kingfisher *Alcedo atthis*

A uniquely large-headed, long-billed, short-tailed bird of watersides, smaller than most people imagine. Typically seen flying low and fast over water, giving sharp call, when electric-blue rump most obvious; far less conspicuous when perched, despite colours

Unique green-blue and orange pattern. White on cheeks often conspicuous from side or rear

Flight very fast, direct, swerving to avoid obstructions or follow course of stream; flies under very low bridges. Occasionally flies more slowly and slightly jerkily across a pond

Frequently hovers over water, especially in open sites with few perches; visits small garden ponds; dives with audible splash

Vivid blue rump; wings and crown greener in some lights

Male
Lower mandible black

Female
Lower mandible mostly orange-red

Juvenile is duller, with blackish feet

Nests in bank over water; occupied tunnel revealed by trickle of oily white droppings from entrance

Despite its genuinely vivid and beautiful colouring, the Kingfisher can be surprisingly easy to miss. It likes to perch in the dappled shade of low, overhanging vegetation, where it can be virtually invisible against a background of yellowing leaves or reeds, and sparkling or dark, rippled water. It is shy, but occasionally lets itself be watched at very close range: a breathtaking experience.

FEEDING It dives for fish and small aquatic insects, either from a perch or a hover, and eats them at the perch.

DISPLAY & VOICE Pairs chase through and over waterside trees in spring. The typical call is a sharp, slightly ringing *keeee* or *ch'keee*, with more of a trill in courtship or territorial displays.

BREEDING It digs a narrow, round tunnel into an earth bank, laying six or seven eggs which hatch in 19–21 days.

MIGRATION Some move to the coast in cold weather; those from eastern Europe move south and west in winter.

LENGTH 16–17cm (6½in)

WHEN TO SEE In W Europe, all year; in extreme north of range and east from Germany, mostly March to October
WHERE FOUND Breeds widely through Europe except in mountains, Iceland, Norway, most of Sweden and Finland

Bee-eater *Merops apiaster*

An elegant, long-tailed, slim-headed bird with stiff, straight, tapered wings rather like a very elongated Starling; perches on dead branches and wires, often in groups, and flies in sweeping arcs, wheeling on flat wings with bursts of quick, stiff beats

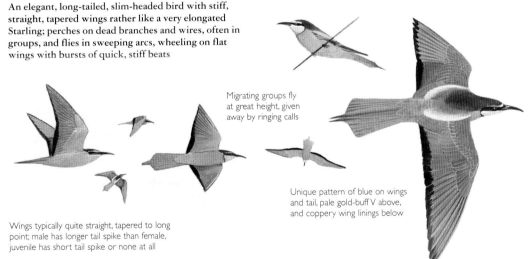

Migrating groups fly at great height, given away by ringing calls

Unique pattern of blue on wings and tail, pale gold-buff V above, and coppery wing linings below

Wings typically quite straight, tapered to long point; male has longer tail spike than female, juvenile has short tail spike or none at all

Breeding groups around sand cliffs call noisily as they fly or perch nearby

Adult

Juvenile

Adult is bright with rich chestnut, yellow, green, and pale blue; juvenile duller, more green on upperside; yellow throat always distinctive

Of the few really exotic-looking European birds, the Bee-eater is perhaps the most glorious-looking of all, both on the page and in real life. Its colours may be muted in early spring and autumn but its shape and actions are always superb; at its best, its dazzling pattern is rich beyond compare. Bee-eaters are not shy, and with a little patience it is possible to get some wonderful views.

FEEDING True to its name, it catches insects such as bees and wasps on the wing, in swooping, gliding flights. It takes large ones to a perch to deal with, although it usually eats their stings.

DISPLAY & VOICE Males and females behave similarly around the nest, except when males feed females in courtship. The voice is rather liquid, with far-carrying, quite deep, abrupt notes: *quilp*, *prrup* or *pruuk-pruuk*.

BREEDING They nest in holes dug in banks or almost flat sandy ground; six or seven eggs hatch after 20 days.

MIGRATION Bee-eaters winter in the African tropics; a few overshoot north of the breeding range in late spring.

LENGTH 25–27cm (10–10½in)

WHEN TO SEE April to September
WHERE FOUND Breeds S and E Europe, locally north to NE France, E Europe, Russia

Roller *Coracias garrulus*

The glorious azure plumage of the Roller is a frequent sight in Africa, where it spends much of the year in the company of other species of rollers, but it comes north to Europe to breed. At times it can be watched closely as it concentrates on finding food, almost oblivious to people in vehicles close by.

FEEDING Rollers eat large insects and small frogs, caught on the ground after a quick pounce or a short flight from a post, overhead wire, or bush, with an eyecatching flash of blue.

DISPLAY & VOICE A displaying male flies over his nesting area with jerky wingbeats, gaining height and calling all the time with a harsh *rak rak* note, then drops suddenly with a twisting, tumbling action, a wonder to behold.

BREEDING Rollers nest in tree holes in parkland or at woodland edges near sunny clearings; three to five eggs hatch in 17–20 days.

MIGRATION Rollers move to Africa south of the Sahara in autumn; in spring some fly too far north, but they are very rare in northwest Europe.

LENGTH 30–32cm (12–12½in)

> **WHEN TO SEE** April to September
> **WHERE FOUND** Iberia, S France, rare UK, more widespread E Europe north to Baltic States

Flight strong, direct, with slight 'rowing' action of wings

A Jackdaw-sized, stout-billed, broad-winged bird fond of using exposed perches; nothing else so large has a pale blue head and breast, or such vivid wing colours

Juvenile
Rather dull, especially on head and breast which are browner than adult's

Upperwing flashes brilliant blue and turquoise

Adults, summer
Vivid blue, greenish, and rich brown: brightest colour shows on wings in flight

Typical upright pose on perch, settled on short legs. Drops to ground in sudden outburst of blues

Autumn adults much duller, as fresh feathers have pale buffish fringes

Hoopoe *Upupa epops*

Surprisingly elusive despite its contrasted plumage, the Hoopoe is easily overlooked as it feeds in the shade of hedges and trees at the woodland edge. It catches the eye only when disturbed, often at close range, and flies off, low and quite quickly.

FEEDING The Hoopoe feeds mainly on insects such as beetles, various grubs, and caterpillars, as well as frogs and lizards, which it takes from the ground or extracts from bark with its long bill.

DISPLAY & VOICE The male calls with his crest raised, from a rooftop or bare tree, but displays are not particularly obvious. The call is a far-carrying, soft, quite quick, hollow *poo-poo-poo*.

BREEDING Nests are found in May and June, in large holes in trees or walls. The sites quickly become fouled by droppings and food remains. Seven to eight eggs hatch in 15–16 days.

MIGRATION A few remain in southern Europe all year, but most fly south each autumn and return early in spring; some overshoot to Britain in April and May, and a few appear in autumn.

LENGTH 26–28cm (10–11in)

> **WHEN TO SEE** Mostly March to October
> **WHERE FOUND** Europe north to the Baltic, more sporadic in central Europe; rare in UK and Ireland

Head and bill held up, tail closed in flight

The Hoopoe in flight combines the black and white of a spotted woodpecker with unique broad, floppy wings and a thin bill

Duller, more grey-brown, less pink-buff, in autumn and winter

Erratic flight has jerky, springy effect, almost like a butterfly

Crest fans upwards and forwards when excited, and often immediately after bird settles

On ground, has shuffling, rolling action on short legs; remarkably easy to overlook

Bill long, slightly curved

Crest may be raised in flight

Wryneck *Jynx torquilla*

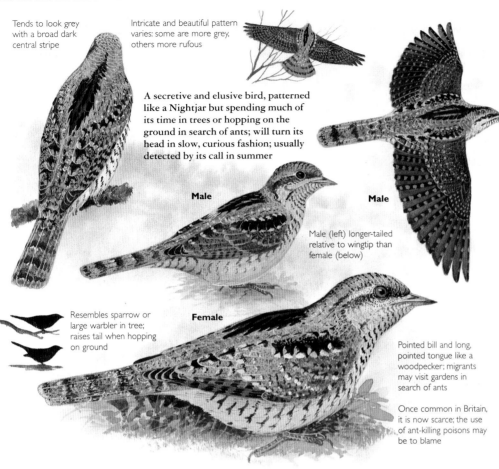

Tends to look grey with a broad dark central stripe

Intricate and beautiful pattern varies: some are more grey, others more rufous

A secretive and elusive bird, patterned like a Nightjar but spending much of its time in trees or hopping on the ground in search of ants; will turn its head in slow, curious fashion; usually detected by its call in summer

Male

Male

Male (left) longer-tailed relative to wingtip than female (below)

Female

Resembles sparrow or large warbler in tree; raises tail when hopping on ground

Pointed bill and long, pointed tongue like a woodpecker; migrants may visit gardens in search of ants

Once common in Britain, it is now scarce; the use of ant-killing poisons may be to blame

Its sharp bill, two-forward and two-back toe arrangement, and habit of nesting in holes are clues that the Wryneck is a close relative of the woodpeckers, although it looks quite different. It is difficult to track down but persistence is worthwhile, since it often allows a close view of its intricate, beautifully coloured feather patterns.

FEEDING It eats ants, and very little else, digging them from their nests with its bill or extracting them from holes with its long, sticky tongue.

VOICE The song is a nasal, quite low, 'complaining' *quee-quee-quee-quee-quee*.

BREEDING The wryneck nests in holes in trees and walls (but does not excavate them itself), even if they are already being used by sparrows or tits. Up to 10 eggs hatch after 12–14 days. The young fly when 18–22 days old.

MIGRATION Wrynecks are scarce but annual migrants in early autumn in much of northwest Europe, including Britain, especially in coastal scrub and dunes, occasionally well inland.

LENGTH 16–17cm (6½in)

WHEN TO SEE Late March to October
WHERE FOUND Breeds over most of Europe but local in west and southeast; migrant in Britain, including northern isles

Black Woodpecker *Dryocopus martius*

Male
Red crown, whitish eye

Typical of forest with big pine or beech trees, also suburban parks, gardens where common

A giant woodpecker, all black except for red on head, pale bill and pale eye. Hard to see despite size, but distinctive calls echo far through forests; has distinctive nest holes

Female
Red only on nape

Red cap shows prominently in rear view

Flight erratic, with Jay-like flaps

Typical slim, gaunt look gives way to puffed-out shape in cold weather

Broad bill

In winter this dramatic bird forages through well-wooded town parks and even gardens, but for nesting it is confined to mature woods with big beech, pine, or larch trees. It is easiest to find in spring and early in the day, when it is most vocal; at other times it can be elusive, despite its size and bright red nape or crown.

FEEDING It eats mainly ants and both the adult and larval stages of beetles, especially wood-boring grubs. Its sticky tongue is armed with backward-pointing barbs for impaling and extracting grubs.

DISPLAY & VOICE It employs a loud, dramatic drumming and an equally loud, melodious *kwih kwih kwih kwih* territorial call repeated 10–20 times. A plaintive, far-carrying *peee-a* or *ki-ya* is often heard, while in flight it gives a rolled *krrrri-krrrri-krrrri*.

BREEDING Holes are distinctively oval, 11–12 cm high by 8–11 cm wide; the clutch is usually of 4–6 white eggs.

MIGRATION A few move quite long distances in winter; most are resident.

LENGTH 45–57cm (18–22½in)

WHEN TO SEE All year
WHERE FOUND W Norway, most of Sweden, Finland, Russia; mainland Europe south to Balkans, central France; local N Spain, S Italy; rare outside breeding range

Green Woodpecker *Picus viridis*

As common in open heathy places or on rough, grassy pastures as it is in woods, the Green Woodpecker makes itself known by frequent loud calls. If disturbed it flies off low and fast, then sweeps up into a tree, often perching around the back of a thick branch and peering out at the intruder.

FEEDING Its principal food is ants, both adults and larvae. The bird digs them out of the ground and soft anthills with its relatively weak bill, and licks them up with its extremely long, wide, sticky tongue, which has a flexible, mobile tip.

DISPLAY & VOICE It rarely drums against branches, but has loud, ringing calls, evenly pitched but variable in speed: *plue plue plue, klee klee klee* and variants; Iberian race has a sharper call.

BREEDING The nest is a 6cm (2½in) wide hole in a branch, often quite low. Five to seven white eggs hatch after 17–19 days; chicks fly at 23–27 days.

MIGRATION Resident.

LENGTH 31–33cm (12–13in)

WHEN TO SEE All year
WHERE FOUND Britain (not Ireland or Iceland), S Norway and Sweden, Baltic states and south throughout central and S Europe, except for entirely treeless areas and highest mountains

Spanish race Female above, male below

A large, green and yellow, long-bodied bird, often seen on ground; flies up into trees with loud laughing call

Spanish race Juvenile with orange-red cap

Juvenile Spotted and barred below, cheeks and throat streaked; duller than adult

Adult female All-black moustache

Adult male Red centre to black moustache; bright green when fresh, wears duller; wings wear to dark brown

Striking, bright greenish-yellow rump

Undulating flight with 4–5 flaps between swoops

Dull, worn feathers

Grey-headed Woodpecker *Picus canus*

This species is often betrayed by its distinctive call: sufficiently similar to that of the Green Woodpecker to give a good clue, but different enough to sound 'odd' and suggest something else. If the bird can be tracked down, a good view will reveal subtle differences in plumage. It likes small, moist woods, riverside trees, and often small or young trees.

FEEDING Less specialized than the Green Woodpecker, it eats many ants but varies its diet with more insects and spiders. It also forages more on trees, walls, and rocks.

DISPLAY & VOICE Drumming is occasionally heard but the call is most useful: slightly sharper, more fluting than a Green Woodpecker's, with the sequence of *ku* or *kee* notes distinctly more melancholy and becoming slower, quieter, and lower in pitch, and fading away.

BREEDING Seven to nine eggs are laid in a hole excavated in a tree – usually an aspen, beech, oak, or lime.

MIGRATION Resident, but with some local dispersal.

LENGTH 25–26cm (10–10¼in)

WHEN TO SEE All year
WHERE FOUND S Norway, central Sweden, S Finland, central Europe from middle of France eastwards, S to Balkans

Juvenile No red; dull moustache; yellowish on bill; slightly marked below

Green Note long head

Grey-headed 'Neckless' shape

Adult male Red crown, grey nape

Note plain tail without Green's spots

Adult female No red; black moustache

Plain tail; greenish-yellow on rump

Adult male

Like Green Woodpecker, but short-necked, compact, slim-billed, with a slightly rounder head

Three-toed Woodpecker *Picoides tridactylus*

A small, rare, elusive woodpecker characterized by dark plumage with broken, mottled white markings; never shows any red

Adult male (left)
Race *tridactylus*:
yellow often
inconspicuous

Adult female
Southern race *alpinus*:
darker beneath than
northern birds;
darker tail

Adult female
Northern race
tridactylus: blackish
above with white
back

Only one hind
toe; most
woodpeckers
have two

Adult female
Race *alpinus*: central
Europe, Alps, SE Europe;
more barred above and
below than *tridactylus*

Adult female
Race *tridactylus*: some
more strongly barred
than this; pale tail

Some birds
of both sexes
have this clear
white back
without bars

Both sexes, both races, have striped
face unlike any other European
woodpecker; barred back recalls
Lesser Spotted (below) but it is a
blacker bird with smaller white spots

This is a medium-sized, tame, rather sluggish woodpecker that tends to remain for long periods in one tree. This makes it rather hard to find, but good to watch once located. It lives in northern lowland conifer forests with many damp hollows and dead trees, and in higher Alpine woods of mature spruce.

FEEDING It digs adult and larval wood-boring beetles from under bark, and takes other insects from the surface. It also eats sap that oozes from holes bored in trees.

DISPLAY & VOICE It drums on trees in a long, loud, rapid salvo. Its calls are low and soft compared with a Great Spotted Woodpecker's: *ptuk* or *ptik*.

BREEDING The nest is a hole excavated in a dead or dying tree, its entrance diameter 4.7cm (1¾in). Three to five eggs are usual, incubated for just 11 days; the chicks fly after 22–25 days.

MIGRATION Resident, except for local dispersal; sometimes moves out from breeding areas, rarely to unlikely places, in small irruptions.

LENGTH 21–22cm (8¼–8½in)

WHEN TO SEE All year
WHERE FOUND Scandinavia, Baltic states, E Germany and Poland eastwards; locally in Alps, N Balkans, Carpathians

Lesser Spotted Woodpecker *Dendrocopos minor*

Often up in
treetops in
slender twigs

Adult male
Red cap (compare
juvenile Great
Spotted)

Female

Male
Bars above may
wear into
square white
patch on back

Chaffinch (top left),
Lesser Woodpecker
(top right) and Great
Spotted (right) to
same scale

Barred underwing
often hard to see
well against sky in
quick, jerky flight

A very small, elusive woodpecker, often
in high twigs (or twiggy undergrowth),
revealed by call; blurry black and white
above, no red beneath

Female
No red
on head

Females
Juvenile male has
rear of crown red;
juvenile female has
some red spots

Barely bigger than a sparrow, this miniature woodpecker tends to stay in the tops of trees or tall, spindly hedges, where it is inconspicuous and hard to find unless it is calling. It occasionally visits gardens, but does not feed at peanut baskets (unlike Great Spotted), generally feeding in fruit trees or ornamental cherries.

FEEDING Its diet is almost entirely insectivorous: it hacks out some grubs and beetles from under loose bark, but takes most of its food from the bark surface, often from quite small twigs.

DISPLAY & VOICE Its drumming is slightly longer, higher, more 'brittle' than that of the Great Spotted. The typical call in spring is a peevish, nasal *pee-pee-pee*, with up to 20 notes. It has a rather weak *chik* contact call.

BREEDING Excavated in a small side branch, the nest hole has a diameter of 3–3.5cm (1¼–1½in); the four to six eggs hatch after 11–12 days.

MIGRATION Resident, with some random dispersal and more extensive movements in the far north of its range.

LENGTH 14–15cm (5½–6in)

WHEN TO SEE All year
WHERE FOUND S Britain, almost all mainland Europe except most of Spain and Portugal and highest, most treeless regions

Great Spotted Woodpecker *Dendrocopos major*

By far the most common and familiar of the 'spotted' woodpeckers in Europe, this is the yardstick by which to compare others. It is a splendid bird: a wonderful splash of colour in a dreary winter wood, or on a bird table, or in the leafy green of a summer forest. It is equally at home in coniferous or broadleaved woodland, or even in low willow carr.

FEEDING It eats insects all year and many seeds in winter; it also takes eggs and nestlings. It probes into crevices, digs under bark, and hacks into hard wood, using its strong, stout bill as a chisel, and scoops out food with its long, flexible, sticky, bristled tongue.

DISPLAY & VOICE It drums against a branch to produce a sudden, short, fast *brrrrp*. The main call is a loud, sharp *tchik!* A fast rattle is less often heard.

BREEDING It excavates a nest hole with a diameter of 5–6cm (2in); four to seven eggs hatch after 10–13 days.

MIGRATION Resident, but northern populations, especially, sometimes irrupt when food is short.

LENGTH 22–23cm (8½–9in)

WHEN TO SEE All year
WHERE FOUND All of Europe except Iceland, Ireland, Scottish islands, extreme N Scandinavia, parts of E Spain

Male
Red nape patch obvious

Juvenile
Red cap of variable extent, edged black

A handsome, medium-sized woodpecker: black, white, and buff, with splashes of red. Easily located by its loud drumming from late winter onwards, and by its frequent sharp call at all times

Black bar across cheek reaches both nape and shoulder

Typical bounding, undulating flight with steep rise to perch

Female
No red on head

Female
Plumage combines large white 'shoulder' patch and extensive red undertail

Male

Juvenile
Underside dusky yellow-buff

Syrian Woodpecker *Dendrocopos syriacus*

In its restricted range in eastern Europe this is often a quite obvious bird, but you need a good view to be sure that it is a Syrian Woodpecker and not a Great Spotted. These are the most similar of all the black and white woodpeckers. It is mostly a bird of lowland woods, orchards, even lines of trees along roads or beside rivers.

FEEDING It eats mainly insects, but it also eats more seeds, fruit, and nuts all year round than most woodpeckers; it even feeds fruit to its young.

DISPLAY & VOICE Bursts of drumming are longer than a Great Spotted's and die away at the end. The typical call is softer than the Great Spotted's familiar *tchik* note: more *chuk*, sometimes running into a chatter or rattle.

BREEDING A hole, 3.5cm (1½ in) wide, is dug into a tree branch; up to seven eggs are incubated for just 9–14 days.

MIGRATION Resident, but there is some dispersal as it is expanding its breeding range quite quickly in southeast Europe.

LENGTH 22–23cm (8½–9in)

WHEN TO SEE All year
WHERE FOUND Mostly SE Europe, but has spread north. Still increasing in Poland, Czech Republic, Romania, Ukraine; stable Hungary, Austria, Bulgaria, even declining slightly in Greece, Albania

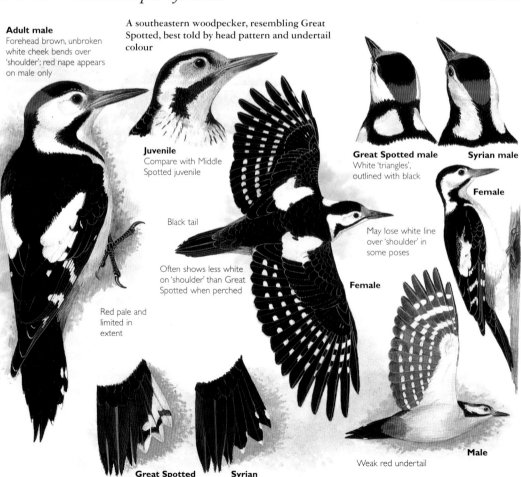

Adult male
Forehead brown, unbroken white cheek bends over 'shoulder'; red nape appears on male only

A southeastern woodpecker, resembling Great Spotted, best told by head pattern and undertail colour

Juvenile
Compare with Middle Spotted juvenile

Black tail

Great Spotted male
White 'triangles', outlined with black

Syrian male

Female

Often shows less white on 'shoulder' than Great Spotted when perched

May lose white line over 'shoulder' in some poses

Female

Red pale and limited in extent

Great Spotted   **Syrian**

Weak red undertail

Male

Middle Spotted Woodpecker *Dendrocopos medius*

Obviously a 'spotted' woodpecker, but rather small, quite dumpy, with a slim bill and a gentle facial expression; often shuffles and flits around on outer branches

White-backed

Middle Spotted
Bill short, slender

Large white patch under wing; red crown above white cheek

Underside pink-buff, intensifying into diffuse pink-red patch under tail

Adult male
White 'shoulders', red crown (compare juvenile Great Spotted)

Streaked flanks; underside of tail blends into buff belly

Adult female
Like male; wing patch differences are individual variations

Adult male
Flame-red crown often raised; white cheek with no dark line joining nape and black side of neck

Juvenile
Little red on cap; dull face; round head, weak bill

While its basic pattern is much like that of other spotted woodpeckers, the Middle Spotted's plumage is particularly attractive: flushed buff and pink below, and with a particularly bright, almost glowing red cap. It tends to keep high in trees, moving around a lot, making a good, long, close view difficult.

FEEDING It eats insects all year; mostly picking them from branches and twigs rather than hacking them out of wood or from beneath bark. The bill is a tweezer more than a chisel.

DISPLAY & VOICE Drumming is rare; calls include a 'throttled' *quah quah* or *ahk-ahk-ahk* at varying speed and a rattling *kik kekekekek*.

BREEDING It excavates a nest hole just 5cm (2in) wide in a decaying tree. It lays four to seven eggs and incubates them for 11–14 days.

MIGRATION Resident, except for a few wanderers in the northeast of its range in winter.

LENGTH 20–22cm (8–9in)

WHEN TO SEE All year
WHERE FOUND W Russia; Latvia south to Ukraine, Balkans; locally through central Europe north of Alps west to France; rare N Spain, central Italy

White-backed Woodpecker *Dendrocopos leucotos*

A large 'spotted' woodpecker with bars across the wings and a white lower back, declining and rare in most of its range

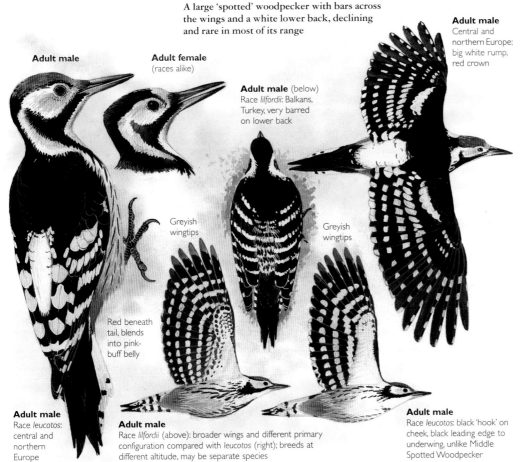

Adult male

Adult female
(races alike)

Adult male (below)
Race *lilfordii*: Balkans, Turkey, very barred on lower back

Adult male
Central and northern Europe: big white rump, red crown

Greyish wingtips

Greyish wingtips

Red beneath tail, blends into pink-buff belly

Adult male
Race *leucotos*: central and northern Europe

Adult male
Race *lilfordii* (above): broader wings and different primary configuration compared with *leucotos* (right); breeds at different altitude, may be separate species

Adult male
Race *leucotos*: black 'hook' on cheek, black leading edge to underwing, unlike Middle Spotted Woodpecker

The biggest spotted woodpecker, and sometimes more approachable than most, this is generally a rare bird. It must have big, mature woods with a lot of standing and fallen dead wood, and cannot thrive in over-managed woodland or plantations. It has decreased in Scandinavia, and even where conditions are good, pairs are few and far between.

FEEDING Like other pied woodpeckers, it eats mostly wood-boring beetles, their larvae, and various other insects, but also nuts, seeds, and berries.

DISPLAY & VOICE Drumming by males (less often by females) is very loud and accelerates. Calls include a soft *kiuk* and a longer *kweek*, sometimes repeated.

BREEDING The birds usually dig holes in rotten wood, 25–37cm (10–14½in) deep and 6–7cm (2½–3in) wide at the entrance. Three to five white eggs hatch after just 10–11 days.

MIGRATION Resident; a few move quite widely, occasionally beyond the breeding range, in the east of Europe.

LENGTH 24–26cm (9½–10in)

WHEN TO SEE All year
WHERE FOUND Locally S Norway and Sweden; S Finland, Baltic states eastwards and south to Balkans; local Italy, central Pyrenees

Skylark *Alauda arvensis*

Despite widespread and even quite catastrophic declines in many areas, largely connected with changes in agricultural practices, the Skylark remains a familiar and generally quite common bird. In spring and summer the song of the Skylark is still to be heard over large areas of farmland and moorland: one of the most evocative countryside sounds. In winter Skylarks abandon the upland moors and bleaker heathlands, moving downhill to forage on softer ground, especially on ploughed fields and old pastures. At this time resident birds are often found in small groups, while migrants to western Europe from farther east tend to be in much bigger flocks.

FEEDING Skylarks locate food by sight and pick it up with deft, quick movements of their heads and bills. In winter they eat various seeds, including cereal grains, which they gather from the ground in a low, shuffling walk; they also pick some seeds directly from low stems, and uproot tiny shoots to reach the attached grain in the soil beneath. In spring and summer they also eat a variety of insects and other invertebrates. Dense, autumn-sown cereal crops tend to make feeding more difficult, and this may partly explain Skylarks' absence from what, at first sight, looks like suitable habitat.

DISPLAY & VOICE If both members of a pair survive the winter they are likely to pair again the following spring, so Skylarks are both monogamous and frequently pair for life. The male's song flight lasts from one to five minutes, and rarely for 10 or even 20 minutes without a break. He flies up silently, at an angle, into the wind, then spirals upwards singing. He may reach around 100 metres (330 feet), fluttering on flexed wings, hovering and singing all the time, before a slow descent and a final steep, fast plunge. The song is a wonderful outpouring of fast and varied warbling with a lot of repetition of short phrases; at close range many throaty notes are heard, but at a distance the song has a higher, silvery, whistling quality. Calls include a rippling *chirrrup* and thinner whistles.

BREEDING Nests are on the ground, neatly lined with leaves and fine stems. Three to five eggs hatch after just 11 days; the chicks fly at 18–20 days old.

MIGRATION Many are seen on the move in autumn or after snowfall, usually in loose, straggly flocks, quite low down. Migration occurs in most areas almost any time between September and March.

LENGTH 18–19cm (7–7½in)

WHEN TO SEE All year
WHERE FOUND Almost all Europe except Iceland, upland Scandinavia; migrates south and west from Scandinavia and E Europe, resident in west

Male

Female
Eastern birds wintering in Britain tend to flock more, fractionally larger, paler

Male, first winter
In December

Plump but long-winged; dusky underwing; sharp breast/belly contrast

Female, first winter
Female's wingtips fall close to tail tip

Adult male, autumn
Male's wingtips fall well short of long tail

First-winter tail | Adult tail

Needs wide open ground, avoiding proximity of hedges or trees, but will sing from a fencepost

Female
Shorter tail

Male
Longer tail

Variable action and shape; typically bursts of quick wingbeats, short swoops; wings angled at front, straight at back, slightly square tips. Compare overhead flocks with Redwing

In song-flight looks as if suspended on string

Distinctive white outer tail and pale trailing edge to wing above and below

Descends with fluttering glide, then drops like a stone before levelling out to hover briefly before landing

The classic aerial singer of wide open spaces: a streaky brown bird, bigger than a sparrow but smaller than a thrush, with a short, stubby crest and angular wings that are almost white on the trailing edge

Always calls when flushed; squats low then dashes away

Hangs in wind, looking back at intruder

Head rounded with crest depressed; stout pointed bill

Adult (right)
Darker than bright first-winter, as pale feather tips wear off to create 'colourless' grey-buff

Very long hind claw

Juvenile
Dark, with dark and whitish loops on upperparts giving scaly effect

182

Woodlark *Lullula arborea*

A neat, streaked lark with prominent head stripes, black and white wing markings, and a short tail. Slow, bounding flight; high circling song flight ending in plunge to ground

Looks broad-winged, short-tailed in flight: an almost bat-like outline

Perches in trees like more slender Tree Pipit, unlike terrestrial Skylark. Where common, forms small, quiet, inconspicuous winter flocks

Short, streaked crest; broad cream line over eye almost to back of head, encircling crest

Upperwing plain brown except for leading edge; no pale trailing edge as on Skylark

Well-marked face with rusty- or ochre-brown cheeks; breast striped, belly clean white

Sides of tail duller than Skylark's tail, whiter on corners

Black-white-black mark on edge of folded wing is very distinctive

A rather small but broad-winged, streaky lark, the Woodlark is best known for its beautiful song. It is quite elusive, often staying well-hidden in short grass or crouching on sandy ground until approached, when it flies off with a peculiarly bounding, almost floppy action.

FEEDING Woodlarks pick small seeds and insects from the ground in dry places with plenty of bare earth, on heaths or, in winter, on stubble fields.

DISPLAY & VOICE During the high, undulating song flight the male covers wide circles over the nesting area. Songs are fluty, liquid, and melodious, in short, usually descending, repetitive phrases without the free-flowing, sparkling sound of the Skylark: *tlu tlu tlu tlu, luee luee luee, teeeoo teeoo tioo tioo tioo*. Ordinary calls include *tit-lee-o*.

BREEDING The nest is tucked away in long grass near a stump or bush; three to five eggs hatch after 12–15 days.

MIGRATION Most move south and west in winter.

LENGTH 15cm (6in)

WHEN TO SEE All year
WHERE FOUND Central Europe, scattered north and west to England, Denmark, S Sweden

Shore Lark *Eremophila alpestris*

A neat, ground-loving, shuffling lark with prominent head markings, likely to get up and fly fast, swerving over a beach or marsh in small groups, before returning to settle again nearby

Male, Balkans
Broad black band from cheek to chest

Female, spring
Strongest yellow on forehead and throat

Female, Balkans
Balkan birds have grey backs to match rocky terrain

Upperwing plain pale brown; tail has narrow white sides, darker outer section and pale centre

Male, non-breeding (right)
Tiny black 'horns'; faded yellow, breastband browner, often with brown smudges beneath

Female
No 'horns'

Very thin white outer edge to tail

This is a long-bodied, slim-winged lark, most familiar in winter when it frequents flat, damp areas of saltmarsh and wave-washed sand with strandlines and beach debris. In summer it is a mountain bird of the far north, also very rarely in Scotland.

FEEDING Shore larks eat mostly seeds, supplemented by insects in summer.

DISPLAY & VOICE Males display on the ground with bowing actions, showing the colourful head and breastband. The song, sometimes given from the ground but mostly during short, fluttery flights, has short, twittering phrases; calls include a soft *zeeih* and pure-sounding *tseeep* notes.

BREEDING Two to four eggs are laid in a neat nest of twigs, leaves, and grass in a depression on the ground; they hatch after an incubation of 10–11 days.

MIGRATION Northerly breeders move southwest to North Sea coasts in winter. In north Africa and southeast Europe the birds are resident in mountain areas.

LENGTH 14–17cm (5½–7in)

WHEN TO SEE All year
WHERE FOUND Central spine of Scandinavia; Balkans; in winter on North Sea coasts, on saltmarsh and beaches

Lesser Short-toed Lark *Calandrella rufescens*

A bird of steppe and semi-desert areas, the Lesser Short-toed Lark is most easily seen in Spain along hot, dry river valleys, in bare coastal dunes and on extensive sun-dried mud, gravel, and rushy places around coastal marshes. It is not very obvious and easy to confuse with other larks, especially young ones.

FEEDING In summer it eats mainly insects, but from autumn to spring its basic food is a variety of small seeds taken from the ground.

DISPLAY & VOICE Males have a low, circling song flight, keeping level but sometimes faster, sometimes slower. The song is a continuous flow of metallic, thin, jangly phrases. The call, a useful clue to identity, is a rattled or buzzy *chirr-rit, prrt,* or *prrirrik*.

BREEDING Nests are well-hidden on the ground, typical of the larks; the clutch is of three to five eggs.

MIGRATION There is little coherent migration but a rather nomadic wandering in winter in Spain.

LENGTH 13–14cm (5–5½in)

WHEN TO SEE All year
WHERE FOUND Locally in N Spain (Ebro valley), around SE coast, and in SW Spain; rare in extreme S Portugal

A small lark, like a diminutive Skylark with its streaked breast and slightly crested cap

Longer exposed wingtip than Short-toed, clearly visible at distance; even longer on male

Streaked cap; pale around eye; pale throat but whole of breast evenly streaked, unlike Short-toed

Adult female

Female Narrower wingtip than male

Adult male Longer wingtip; more attenuated, more Linnet-like shape than female

Spanish race Thin bill

Turkish race Asia Minor, north Africa: short, thick bill

Crest raised in display

Turkish race (left) Thick-billed, fine-streaked; rare vagrant in west

Wings quite plain, no white trailing edge

Male Broader wingtip than male Short-toed Lark

Even width of white on tail sides

Short-toed Lark *Calandrella brachydactyla*

In many areas of the Mediterranean region this is a common and easily-seen little lark. It has its own character, as do many apparently dull, small brown birds. It is lively, frequently in parties or small flocks, and often stays together in tight groups in flight.

FEEDING It shuffles along the ground picking up seeds, as well as insects in summer; sometimes it digs for grubs or seeds, or stretches up to pull seeds from dry stems.

DISPLAY & VOICE Displaying males flutter upwards, circle in undulating flight as they sing, then plummet to earth. The song is quite light, almost spitting in effect, mixed with mimicry of other species, with each phrase descending towards the end. The call is a full, sparrowy *chup* or *chirrup*.

BREEDING Three to five eggs hatch after 13 days; the young fly when 12 days old, but leave the nest earlier.

MIGRATION Migrating birds cross the Mediterranean throughout its length, to winter in northern Africa.

LENGTH 14–16cm (5½–6½in)

WHEN TO SEE March to October
WHERE FOUND Local France, Romania; widespread Iberia, Italy, Balkans; rare but annual vagrant in NW Europe

Male Narrower wings, longer tail than Lesser Short-toed Lark

Male

Female

May show dark lower cheek and at side of neck, but no breast streaks

A small lark with a pale underside, dark cap and dark spots at side of chest; common in southern Europe

Eastern race East European, north African race is pale, rufous-capped, with stocky bill and breast patch; may appear in western Europe, some seen in UK

Dark band across lesser coverts, pale midwing band

Female (above) Broader wingtip than male

Fresh

Worn

Female

Long tertials cloak wingtip when fresh; they wear off to reveal more wingtip, but never so much as on Lesser

Wingtip detail difficult to see at distance; longer exposed wingtip of Lesser Short-toed Lark easier

Male Longer tertials than female, attenuated look

SW European race Longer bill, chest may be finely marked like Lesser: check wingtip projection to confirm

Crested Lark *Galerida cristata*

Common farmland and wasteland lark in south Europe; flies up with broad, floppy wings; can raise pointed crest

Pale sandy outer tail

Puffed out in cold – taut and sleek in heat

Underwing much more rufous than Thekla Lark: compare coverts

Adult
Typical lark pattern with drooping pale feather fringes

Crest is a spike when flattened

Wings are narrower than Thekla Lark

Pale, blurred, or clearer streaks on chest; belly whitish

Fresh plumage (above) pale, bright; worn plumage (below) duller, darker

Crest sharp when raised

Bills vary, but typically longer, stronger than Thekla Lark

Adult
Worn plumage; basic colour can vary with local soil conditions

First year, late summer

In much of southern Europe Crested Larks are remarkably common, and often seen on roadsides and in cereal fields. They can be recognized at a glance by their pale colour, short-tailed, round-winged shape, and floppy flight. They are mostly birds of open, flat, warm lowlands, but often occupy small, sandy patches by railways, docks, airfields, and industrial sites.
FEEDING They pick seeds, leaves, shoots, beetles, and other insects from the ground, using their strong bills to turn over leaves and stones, and dig or probe into loose earth.
DISPLAY & VOICE The song flight is high, fluttering, with some hovering, between spells of level 'cruising'. The birds also sing on the ground. The song is loud and fluty, with short whistles, more complicated notes, and twitters. The call is a pure, liquid, evenly-pitched *pee-lee-veee* or *twee-tee-tooo*.
BREEDING Three to five eggs hatch after 11–13 days; chicks move off at nine days and fly when 15–16 days old.
MIGRATION Mostly resident.
LENGTH 17cm (7in)

WHEN TO SEE All year
WHERE FOUND Mainland Europe north to Baltic, absent from large areas in central Europe; very rare vagrant in Britain

Thekla Lark *Galerida theklae*

A dumpy, shortish-billed lark, rather scarce on bushy or bare, stony slopes and rocky plains

Outer tail contrasty with rich sandy-orange

Broad, plain wings, orange-sided tail, more contrasted rump than Crested Lark

Chest generally firmly, sharply-streaked blackish (less on juvenile)

Orange on underside of wing can 'flash' to grey at some angles

Well-marked with dark back when fresh (above); pale when worn (below)

Crest fan-shaped when raised (not a sharp spike)

Often dives from a height

Underwing greyer than Crested Lark, especially on coverts

Adults, late summer
Upperparts worn pale

Floats high up in sky, with occasional light wingbeat; may momentarily close wings in high flight

Underside of tail dark, obvious in flight; underwing colour hard to see clearly

While Crested Larks like a range of places that are mostly flat and open – often vast cereal fields – Theklas prefer bushy hillsides with scattered trees, rocks, areas of bare earth, heaths, and woodland edges. They are generally much less easy to find than Crested Larks and less well-known to the average birdwatcher.
FEEDING They pick insects and seeds from the ground, often discovering them under stones which they flick over – although they do not dig for food like Crested Larks.
DISPLAY & VOICE Song flights are wide circles on weak, fluttery wingbeats, but the Thekla often sings from a barn roof, a bush top, or the ground. The song is loud and fluty, with fewer variations than a Crested Lark's. The call is lower, but ends with a long, rising and falling note: *doo-dee-doo-deeeee*.
BREEDING The nest is a typical lark cup-shape on the ground, lined with grass; three or four eggs are usual.
MIGRATION Strictly resident.
LENGTH 17cm (7in)

WHEN TO SEE All year
WHERE FOUND Portugal, Spain including Balearics, extreme S France

Calandra Lark *Melanocorypha calandra*

This big, muscular lark is found in a restricted area of southern Europe in a relatively narrow range of habitats: lowland grasslands and crops, sometimes bushy or with thick, low shrubs, but usually wide open and hot in summer. It is usually easy to see, although even big flocks can disappear from sight when feeding in tall grass.

FEEDING It eats insects in summer, but seeds and shoots are more important in winter. It digs for food with its large bill, but also picks items from the ground as it runs or walks.

DISPLAY & VOICE The male sings from bushes or stones, but mostly in display flight. He circles low before rising to a great height, singing all the time and flying with slow beats of his fully-extended wings, quite unlike a Skylark. The song is like a Skylark's in quality, but louder and richer.

BREEDING Four or five eggs, laid in a well-lined hollow on the ground, hatch after 16 days. The chicks leave the nest after 10 days and fly a week or so later.

MIGRATION Resident in Europe.

LENGTH 18–19cm (7–7½in)

> **WHEN TO SEE** All year
> **WHERE FOUND** S Portugal, much of Spain except far north; extreme S France, Sardinia, S Italy, locally in Balkans, rare Britain

A big, heavy, southern lark with a striking wing pattern, heavy bill, and dark chest patches; high song flight has slow wingbeats

Distinctive dark underwing; broad white trailing edge

Upperwing has white trailing edge and two pale bars; wings angled down

Big dark neck patch characteristic, but varies individually and with pose (hunched head hides patch, stretched neck reveals it)

Broad, long wings with white rear edge; white sides to tail

Female
Smaller than male, shorter wingtip projection

Male sings with tail cocked

Male
Long wingtips extend well down tail

Big bill compared with Skylark; chest streaked at sides, pale in centre

Dupont's Lark *Chersophilus duponti*

This is a strange and elusive lark, found in quite isolated areas of Spain and north Africa, mostly in dry places that are often searingly hot in summer and very cold in winter. Most of these regions have short, often sparse vegetation with areas of bare stony ground, over which the birds run when approached. They are difficult to locate and see well except when singing.

FEEDING Dupont's Lark takes insects and small seeds from the ground, using its long bill to dig into friable earth, probe tussocks of grass, and split open balls of dung with insects inside.

DISPLAY & VOICE Males sing in flight or from the ground, often rising higher in song flight than a Skylark until the bird is almost out of sight. The song is a twittering, Linnet-like affair; the usual call is a nasal *hoo hee*.

BREEDING Nests on the ground under a bush, beside a tuft of grass, or against a large stone. Three or four eggs are laid, but other details are unknown.

MIGRATION Usually resident, with only sporadic dispersal.

LENGTH 18cm (7in)

> **WHEN TO SEE** All year
> **WHERE FOUND** Locally in inland NE Spain and small parts of SE Spain, range has contracted slightly recently

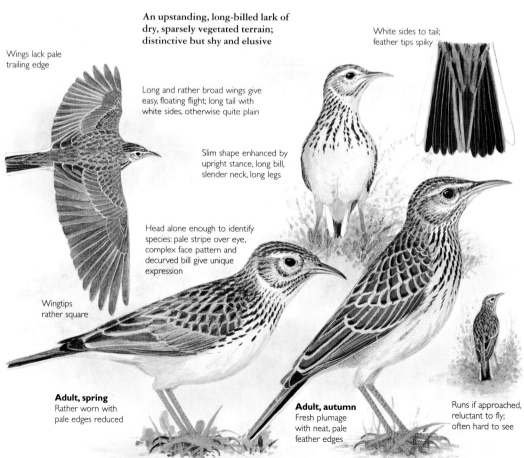

An upstanding, long-billed lark of dry, sparsely vegetated terrain; distinctive but shy and elusive

Wings lack pale trailing edge

White sides to tail; feather tips spiky

Long and rather broad wings give easy, floating flight; long tail with white sides, otherwise quite plain

Slim shape enhanced by upright stance, long bill, slender neck, long legs

Head alone enough to identify species: pale stripe over eye, complex face pattern and decurved bill give unique expression

Wingtips rather square

Adult, spring
Rather worn with pale edges reduced

Adult, autumn
Fresh plumage with neat, pale feather edges

Runs if approached, reluctant to fly; often hard to see

Crag Martin *Ptyonoprogne rupestris*

A stocky, broad-winged martin with a shallow tail fork and characteristic white tail spots; dull clay-brown in late summer, greyer in fresh plumage; pale underside

Fresh plumage has grey bloom, which wears off to become browner on upperparts

Looks quite dull, without clean white of Sand Martin; less dashing, less scythe-winged than Alpine Swift

Underwing has distinct dark wedge

Rounded head, short stout bill

Tail square when fanned

Elegant, confident flight even in strong wind, swinging pendulum-like to and fro across cliff face, soaring over peaks or dashing through gorges

White tail spots show from below or when tail is fanned in turns

Tiny legs, like other martins

The Crag Martin makes up for a lack of colour by its superb flight. Most elegant of all the swallows and martins, it has a swooping, free-flowing action across the faces of cliffs, or deep into narrow river gorges.

FEEDING Like other martins, a Crag Martin captures insects in its mouth in the air; in dull, cold weather it feeds lower over rivers and lakes.

VOICE The call is an occasional short, feeble chirp, easily lost in the dramatic gorges that the birds prefer.

BREEDING The nest is a mud cup, almost invisible on a similarly coloured cliff face, often just inside a road or rail tunnel. The adults allow a close approach as they sit at the lip of the nest. They rear two broods of three to five young between May and July.

MIGRATION Crag Martins from southern France and the Alps move south each autumn, as far as northern Africa, but in Spain, Italy, and Greece some remain all year.

LENGTH 14.5cm (5¾in)

WHEN TO SEE Mostly March to September, some all year in the south
WHERE FOUND High gorges, cliffs, over rivers; in the Alps, S France, Spain, Italy, Mediterranean islands, Balkans, rare UK

Sand Martin *Riparia riparia*

A small, fluttery martin with a sharply-forked tail and broad-based wings, with narrower tips angled back. White underside with brown breastband distinctive

All sandy-brown or mud-brown above

Typical wingbeat is quick, backwards flick

Underwing and underside of tail contrastingly dark

Underside dull white except for breastband

Flocks roost in reedbeds in autumn

No tail spots

Likes river valleys, flooded gravel pits, sand pits

Often perches on wires, dead trees, or reed stems, sometimes on flat ground or shingle banks

Of all the swallows and martins this is the smallest and weakest in flight, typically feeding low over water with frequent tight twists and turns. Flocks often rise higher, especially if a predator such as a Hobby is nearby.

FEEDING It hunts small flying insects, often over expanses of freshwater.

DISPLAY & VOICE Small groups fly around over the colony, giving short, dry, twittering flight calls.

BREEDING Sand Martins tunnel into the faces of vertical earth banks, disused or active quarries, and sand pits, where they can occupy scores of holes. Each pair rears two broods of four or five chicks each summer.

MIGRATION Sand Martins are among the earliest of the summer migrants to return in spring. The first may arrive very early in March, often in sleet or snow; they concentrate over lakes and reservoirs seeking insects, but some perish in poor weather. They return in September to Africa, south of the Sahara and almost to the Cape.

LENGTH 12cm (4¾in)

WHEN TO SEE March to October
WHERE FOUND In quarries, gravel and sand pits, over lakes; most of Europe except interior of Italy, Alps, Balkans

Swallow *Hirundo rustica*

Swallows are among the favourite birds of birdwatchers, although they might be outvoted by fans of the Robin in a public poll. They are symbolic of summer, yet they are in serious decline in many areas where modern buildings offer few nesting opportunities. A nesting pair needs an old barn, or a shed with a broken window – even an open car port will do in a rural village. Unlike House Martins and Swifts they are not at home in towns: Swallows require open spaces, where they can fly much lower down and swoop close to the ground as they hunt flies. Insecticides are also denying them food; even the drugs used to 'worm' cattle have had a lasting effect on the populations of insect-eating birds such as Swallows, since they make cow-pats sterile and devoid of flies, beetles, and other insects.

FEEDING Swallows prefer large flies, such as bluebottles and dung flies, catching them in the air in their open bills. They take fewer aphids and tiny flies than is usual for House Martins and Sand Martins, their average prey size being noticeably bigger.

DISPLAY & VOICE Swallows frequently sit on television aerials, dead branches, overhead wires, or other perches close to a nest site, singing with a soft, fast, twittering warble interspersed with a short, wooden trill: a much more sophisticated performance than the martins manage. Other calls tend to be rather liquid and slurred, with a slightly nasal quality.

BREEDING They build their nests on beams or other small supports against walls inside buildings; the nest is made of mud and straw, and lined with feathers. They lay four or five eggs, which hatch after 15 days. In southern Europe Swallows lay more eggs and rear more broods than in the north. The young fly after 19 days in the nest.

MIGRATION All Swallows migrate to Africa in the autumn. They gather in flocks first, then move south in about September and October; a very few remain in Europe until December. While many birds skirt around the western or eastern edges of the Sahara, Swallows enter Africa all along the north coast and head off across the desert: a severe test of fitness and stamina. They reach the southernmost parts of Africa and return in spring, reaching Spain in March and Britain by early April.

LENGTH 17–19cm (7–7½in)

WHEN TO SEE March to October
WHERE FOUND Wide variety of farmland, with open spaces such as pastures with horses, sheep, or cattle, marshes, and over freshwater; almost all Europe except extreme N Scandinavia

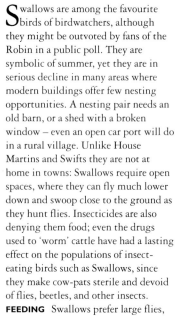

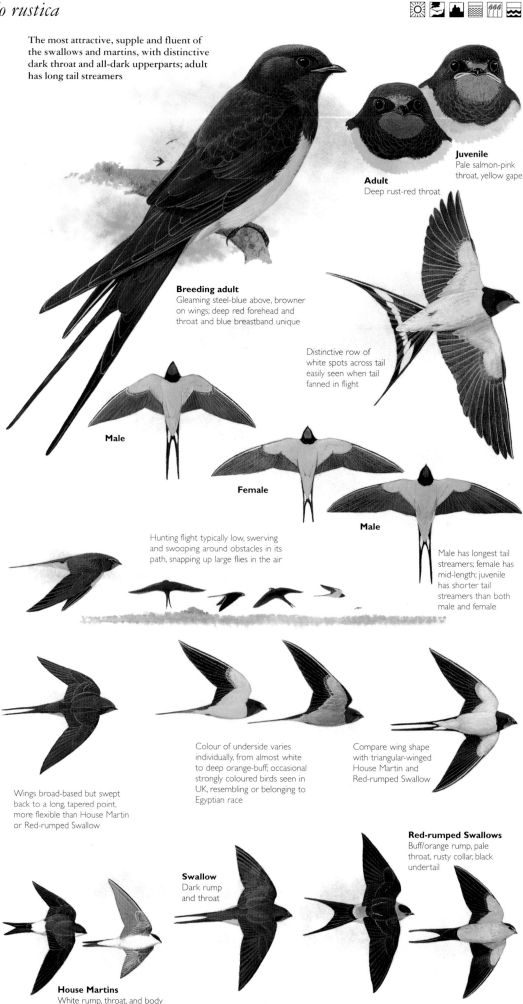

The most attractive, supple and fluent of the swallows and martins, with distinctive dark throat and all-dark upperparts; adult has long tail streamers

Adult
Deep rust-red throat

Juvenile
Pale salmon-pink throat, yellow gape

Breeding adult
Gleaming steel-blue above, browner on wings; deep red forehead and throat and blue breastband unique

Distinctive row of white spots across tail easily seen when tail fanned in flight

Male

Female

Male

Male has longest tail streamers; female has mid-length; juvenile has shorter tail streamers than both male and female

Hunting flight typically low, swerving and swooping around obstacles in its path, snapping up large flies in the air

Wings broad-based but swept back to a long, tapered point, more flexible than House Martin or Red-rumped Swallow

Colour of underside varies individually, from almost white to deep orange-buff; occasional strongly coloured birds seen in UK, resembling or belonging to Egyptian race

Compare wing shape with triangular-winged House Martin and Red-rumped Swallow

Red-rumped Swallows
Buff/orange rump, pale throat, rusty collar, black undertail

Swallow
Dark rump and throat

House Martins
White rump, throat, and body

Red-rumped Swallow *Hirundo daurica*

A swallow with a blue-black back and cap, rusty collar, pale buff-pink rump and no dark throat. Looks sturdy, straight-winged, and less fluent than Swallow, flying slower on straighter course or circling to a height on flat wings

Stiff-winged, almost falcon-like soaring

Black beneath 'stuck-on' tail on adult

Rump two-tone pink or rusty-buff

Underside pale from chin to vent

Rusty collar often hard to see in flight but rules out rare hybrid between Swallow and House Martin

Juvenile
Lacks tail streamers

Adult

This distinctive swallow of Iberia and the Balkans combines the blue-black and buff colouring of a Swallow with the pale rump and stiff-winged flight of a House Martin, yet with familiarity it reveals a distinctive character all of its own.

FEEDING Like the Swallow it feeds in the air, taking insects on the wing – yet with fewer wingbeats, more glides, and higher foraging flights, sometimes in small groups like House Martins.

DISPLAY & VOICE A female may perch with her tail raised while a male sidles up to her on the same perch, singing loudly with short, twittering phrases. The typical flight call is a low-pitched, sparrow-like chirp: *tchreet* or *djuit*.

BREEDING The nest is a cup-like structure of mud under overhanging rocks or eaves, with a characteristic entrance 'spout'. Two or three broods of four or five young are reared.

MIGRATION European Red-rumped Swallows winter in Africa, joining others that breed in southern Asia, Japan, and tropical Africa.

LENGTH 16–17cm (6½in)

WHEN TO SEE April to October
WHERE FOUND In villages and adjacent open, warm countryside in Spain, Portugal, Yugoslavia, Greece

House Martin *Delichon urbica*

A small black and white aerial bird, with triangular wings and a forked tail; blackish upperparts marked by broad white rump distinctive. Flies high, with fluttery or flickering wings between short glides

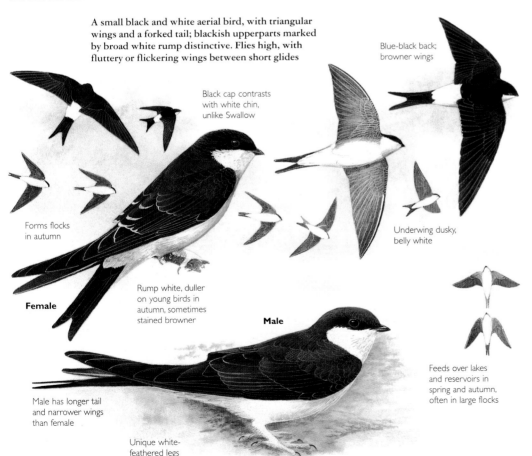

Blue-black back; browner wings

Black cap contrasts with white chin, unlike Swallow

Forms flocks in autumn

Underwing dusky, belly white

Female

Rump white, duller on young birds in autumn, sometimes stained browner

Male

Male has longer tail and narrower wings than female

Unique white-feathered legs

Feeds over lakes and reservoirs in spring and autumn, often in large flocks

Abundant in the clean air over unpolluted towns and villages, House Martins breed throughout Europe. They are especially numerous above old Mediterranean towns.

FEEDING They tend to feed higher than Swallows, above roof height, often high up with Swifts and frequently in small groups. Swallows tend to be more solitary.

DISPLAY & VOICE A pleasant twitter passes for song, in flight near the nest; the call is a dry, simple *chirrup*.

BREEDING They mostly nest under the eaves of buildings, but in remote parts they still use natural sites on inland or sea cliffs. The nest is the familiar cup of mud, with a mess of droppings below; it may be taken over by House Sparrows in spring.

MIGRATION On warm autumn days they gather on roofs to bask in the sunshine or join Swallows on wires before migrating south to Africa, where they live mysterious lives high in the sky, almost out of sight.

LENGTH 12.5cm (5in)

WHEN TO SEE Late March to October
WHERE FOUND In rural and suburban areas throughout Europe except extreme north and mountain peaks

Rock Pipit *Anthus petrosus* Water Pipit *Anthus spinoletta*

The Rock Pipit and Scandinavian Rock Pipit are usually treated as one species, with the Water Pipit given separate species status. Research for the illustrations on this page shows that the Scandinavian Rock Pipit and Water Pipit are identical in structure, and that the Rock Pipit is the odd one of the trio. Provisionally, therefore, we propose to treat them as three species.

The Rock Pipit is a bird of rocky coasts; it is resident, except for some short-distance movements in winter. Any 'Rock' Pipits seen in saltmarsh creeks, on groynes, and around piers in winter, and certainly any inland in spring and autumn, are more likely to be migrant Scandinavian Rock Pipits. This species breeds on coasts, but the whole population migrates in autumn and returns in spring. In Britain migrants appear at inland waters in March–April and September–October. Water Pipits breed on mountains, including high-altitude pastures in the Alps and Pyrenees. They move lower for the winter, often to the north, to muddy freshwater shores, marshes, and brackish pools near the coast.

Rock Pipits hold small feeding territories in winter, and breeding ones (often in a different area) in summer, so songs and aggressive calls towards intruders usually make them easy to locate all year round. Water Pipits are often shy and likely to fly off when approached: a Scandinavian Rock Pipit might go a short distance and double back, while a winter Water Pipit often flies straight to the far side of the lake.
FEEDING They pick invertebrates from the debris of the strandline and rocks in winter, and insects from grassy areas above the beach in summer. Water Pipits catch insects on the ground, sometimes in flight, or in short leaps or flycatching sallies.
DISPLAY & VOICE Males sing in flight, rising steeply and then parachuting down; the song is a louder version of a Meadow Pipit song, with a stronger trill at the end. Both Rock Pipits call a loud, full *phist* or *feest*. Water Pipit calls are less squeaky than a Meadow Pipit's, less full than those of a Rock Pipit.
BREEDING Nests are hidden in rocky crevices close to the shore or on grassy slopes. Four to six eggs hatch in 14–15 days; chicks fly at 14–15 days.
MIGRATION Scandinavian Rock and Water Pipits migrate; Rock is resident.
LENGTH 16.5–17cm (6½–7in)

A complex group of medium-sized pipits, with distinctively dark legs. Rock Pipit and most Scandinavian Rock Pipits remain dull all year, while the Water Pipit has a brighter, striking breeding plumage

Richard's Pipit *Anthus novaeseelandiae*

Outer feather all white except shaft

A large, bold pipit, striding easily through tall grass, or flying up and away over a long distance, briefly hovering before settling again

Some begin moult in autumn, back is patchy

Juvenile has shorter tail than adult

Juvenile
Note thin white edges to median wing coverts

Adult
Large, broad-based wings, long tail

Adult, autumn
Well-streaked chest sides

Meadow Pipit and Richard's Pipit to same scale; Richard's long-winged, pot-bellied

Grey-brown to buffy above, white to bright buff below, streaked chest, plain flanks

Adult
Note thick buff edges to median wing coverts

Adult
Typical upright, alert, ready-to-go pose, reveals big pale underbody

Hind claw: long variant and average

Heavy wagtail shape, with long tail (length varies) and long, thick, pale legs with very long hind claw

In fresh autumn plumage, buff back with fine streaks contrasts with pale-edged dark tertials (pale edges show as Vs from rear)

Hind claw of Tawny Pipit

A handful of Richard's Pipits, rarely a few hundred, move west instead of south in autumn and reach western Europe, where they are annual vagrants in favoured places near the coast. Compared with most European pipits they are big, long-tailed, eyecatching birds.

FEEDING They take insects from the ground, often in lengthy grass as the birds walk boldly along; they also catch some in short, leaping flights.

VOICE Their calls are mostly loud, strident, even explosive, or more sparrowy and sometimes quite subdued: *shrriw*, *shreep*, *chup*, or *chirp*.

MIGRATION Their breeding areas are in the steppes of central and eastern Asia; most move to India and Southeast Asia, but a few head west. They cross western Siberia to reach Europe, where most are identified on Baltic and North Sea coasts; in some years they are rare, in others a few score or even a hundred or more may reach Britain from late September to November.

LENGTH 18–20cm (7–8in)

WHEN TO SEE Late autumn, most end of September to November
WHERE FOUND Annual Britain, Belgium, Netherlands, Germany, Sweden, rare or sporadic many other countries

Tawny Pipit *Anthus campestris*

Juvenile (below)
Onset of moult gives uneven pattern on back, new feathers edged yellow

A big, wagtail-like pipit, obviously pale except in short-lived autumn juvenile plumage

Compare streaked chest, back, with Richard's Pipit

Juvenile has shorter tail than adult; mottled rump

Adult, spring
A large pipit, but quite delicately proportioned

Adult, spring
Back softly marked or plain; bold line of dark coverts across wing

Adult, spring
Plain back and rump; bright buff to sandy, wears to greyer-brown

Wagtail-like shape; slim, pale legs with short hind claw

Adult, winter
Greyer, slightly more contrasty than in spring

Outer tail fades to white

This is a 'big' pipit, although only the size of a Yellow Wagtail. It is typical of sunny slopes and dry heaths, sandy fields and along riversides, but is generally scarce. It tends to be quite shy, flying up at some distance and going far away if approached.

FEEDING It picks insects from the ground or short plants in wagtail-like fashion, with short runs, deft lunges, and occasional flutters into the air.

DISPLAY & VOICE Males sing from the ground but mostly in a high, long, deeply undulating song flight, with a simple repetition of a ringing *chiree* or *chy-vee*. The call is *tzeep* or *trreep*, a little harsher than the similar call of western Yellow Wagtails; also a sparrowy *chup*.

BREEDING The nest is of grass stems, on the ground beside a tuft of grass or leaves. Four or five eggs hatch after 12–13 days; chicks fly at 13–14 days.

MIGRATION This is a scarce but regular spring and autumn migrant north of its breeding range, including Britain, usually found on the coast.

LENGTH 16.5cm (6½in)

WHEN TO SEE April to October
WHERE FOUND Iberia, locally central and S France; Italy, Balkans, sporadically north to Denmark, extreme S Sweden; rare migrant in Britain

Tree Pipit *Anthus trivialis*

A small pipit, but subtly stronger, more confident than the Meadow Pipit, the Tree Pipit is blessed with a fine song. It is an elegant bird of woodland edges and clearings, felled or newly-planted conifers, or scattered trees and bushes both on heaths and high on mountain slopes.

FEEDING It eats mainly small insects with a few seeds, picking most of its food off the ground but taking some from leaves or twigs. Now and then it snatches a passing insect from the air.

DISPLAY & VOICE Males sing from fence posts, wires, trees, and also in a song flight, typically from a treetop. The Canary-like song rises and falls, stutters, then develops into a series of loud, full double-notes: *chia-chia-wich-wich tsee-a tseee-a tseee-a*. In flight the call is a flat, buzzing *teees* or *tease*.

BREEDING It nests on the ground; two to six eggs take 12–14 days to hatch.

MIGRATION Tree Pipits often appear on migration near reservoirs and on the coast; they are detected by their calls.

LENGTH 15cm (6in)

WHEN TO SEE April to October
WHERE FOUND Breeds in most of Europe except Iceland, Ireland, most of Spain and Mediterranean coasts

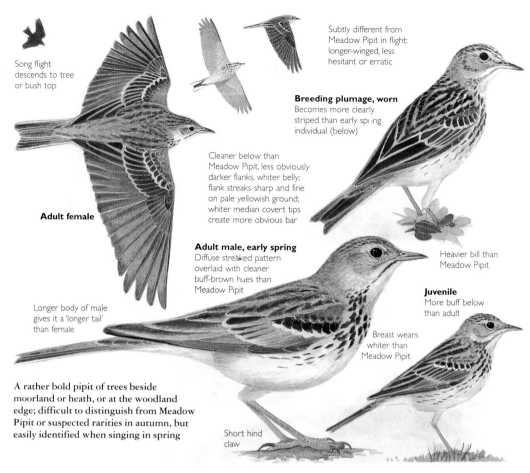

Song flight descends to tree or bush top

Subtly different from Meadow Pipit in flight: longer-winged, less hesitant or erratic

Breeding plumage, worn
Becomes more clearly striped than early spring individual (below)

Cleaner below than Meadow Pipit, less obviously darker flanks, whiter belly; flank streaks sharp and fine on pale yellowish ground; whiter median covert tips create more obvious bar

Adult female

Adult male, early spring
Diffuse streaked pattern overlaid with cleaner buff-brown hues than Meadow Pipit

Heavier bill than Meadow Pipit

Juvenile
More buff below than adult

Breast wears whiter than Meadow Pipit

Longer body of male gives it a 'longer tail' than female

A rather bold pipit of trees beside moorland or heath, or at the woodland edge; difficult to distinguish from Meadow Pipit or suspected rarities in autumn, but easily identified when singing in spring

Short hind claw

Most Red-throated Pipits seen on migration in western Europe are in non-breeding or juvenile plumage, but in spring a few – and many in southeastern Europe – are really colourful. They like clear areas in grassy marshes, damp patches in dunes, and muddy places where livestock comes to water to drink. In summer they are birds of the Arctic, breeding on the tundra and adjacent fields.

FEEDING They pick insects, snails, and seeds from the ground and water's edge, or even from seaweed strandlines when on beaches on migration.

DISPLAY & VOICE The song flight is high, gliding in wide arcs, with a richer song than a Meadow Pipit. Calls are an abrupt *chup* and more often a high, penetrating note that fades and falls away: *p-seeeee* or *pee-eeez*.

BREEDING The nest is on the ground, sometimes a 'tunnel' into a soft mound; 5–6 eggs hatch after 11–14 days.

MIGRATION These Arctic breeders winter in Africa; migrants are frequent in southeast Europe, rare on coasts of northwest Europe and UK in autumn.

LENGTH 15cm (6in)

WHEN TO SEE March to October
WHERE FOUND Breeds N Scandinavia; widespread migrant (most in autumn in Britain, Ireland); some winter Italy, Greece

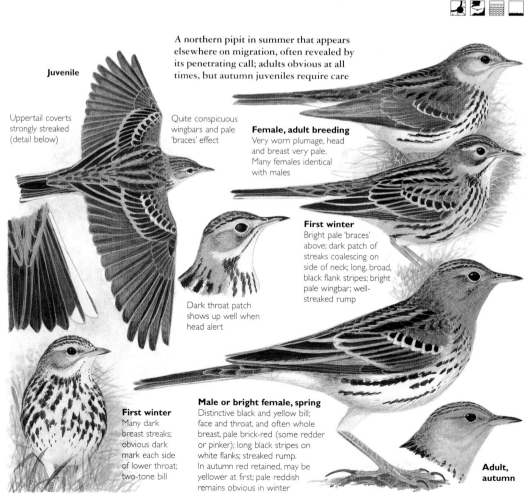

A northern pipit in summer that appears elsewhere on migration, often revealed by its penetrating call; adults obvious at all times, but autumn juveniles require care

Juvenile

Uppertail coverts strongly streaked (detail below)

Quite conspicuous wingbars and pale 'braces' effect

Female, adult breeding
Very worn plumage, head and breast very pale. Many females identical with males

First winter
Bright pale 'braces' above; dark patch of streaks coalescing on side of neck; long, broad, black flank stripes; bright pale wingbar; well-streaked rump

Dark throat patch shows up well when head alert

First winter
Many dark breast streaks; obvious dark mark each side of lower throat; two-tone bill

Male or bright female, spring
Distinctive black and yellow bill; face and throat, and often whole breast, pale brick-red (some redder or pinker); long black stripes on white flanks; streaked rump. In autumn red retained, may be yellower at first; pale reddish remains obvious in winter

Adult, autumn

Meadow Pipit *Anthus pratensis*

A slight, streaked, ground-loving, frenetic bird with a thin bill and spindly legs, white tail sides and thin, peevish calls. Typically a moorland bird in summer, widespread in lowlands in winter

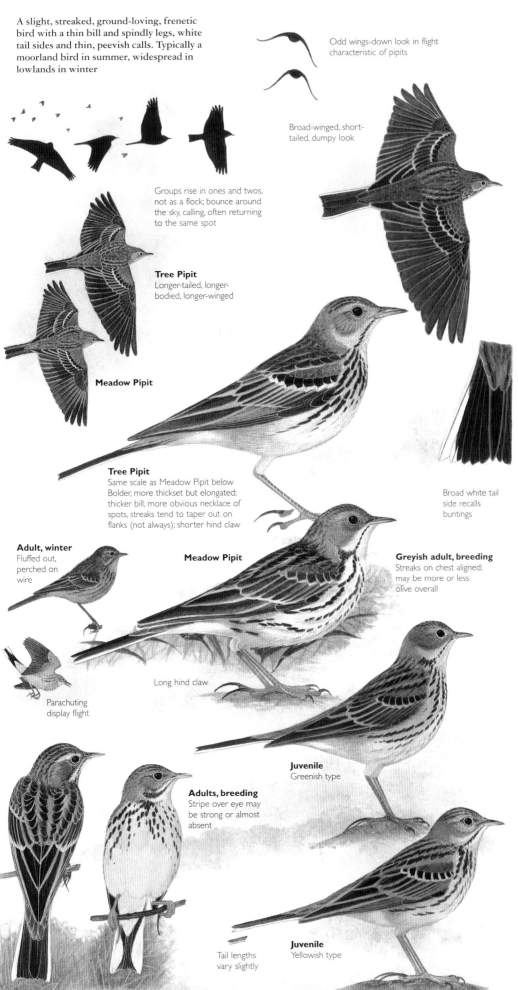

Odd wings-down look in flight characteristic of pipits

Broad-winged, short-tailed, dumpy look

Groups rise in ones and twos, not as a flock; bounce around the sky, calling, often returning to the same spot

Tree Pipit
Longer-tailed, longer-bodied, longer-winged

Meadow Pipit

Tree Pipit
Same scale as Meadow Pipit below
Bolder, more thickset but elongated; thicker bill, more obvious necklace of spots, streaks tend to taper out on flanks (not always); shorter hind claw

Adult, winter
Fluffed out, perched on wire

Meadow Pipit

Greyish adult, breeding
Streaks on chest aligned; may be more or less olive overall

Broad white tail side recalls buntings

Parachuting display flight

Long hind claw

Juvenile
Greenish type

Adults, breeding
Stripe over eye may be strong or almost absent

Juvenile
Yellowish type

Tail lengths vary slightly

Almost everywhere this is the most common pipit, the typical little streaky, frenetic bird, always nervous and ready to fly away at the least provocation. On migration in spring it often appears in little groups by reservoirs, mixed with Pied and Yellow Wagtails, and Reed Buntings, searching the water's edge and nearby grassy areas for early insects. In the hills it is a summer visitor; on lowland farmland a winter bird. On lowland heaths and some other rough, grassy places like those surrounding old gravel pits it can be found all year round. Meadow Pipits are usually approachable and easy to see, but like other pipits and wagtails they may suddenly decide to fly up and away out of sight if disturbed. Pity the poor little pipit: on the moors it is the chief prey of Merlins and Hen Harriers, and its nests are frequently found and parasitized by Cuckoos. But it remains a common and distinctive bird over vast tracts of open countryside.

FEEDING It picks insects from the ground and low vegetation in a steady, even walk, with few runs or lunges. It also snatches them from the air as they fly up, but does not follow them in proper aerial flycatching chases.

DISPLAY & VOICE Territorial songs are given in a song flight, a sight-and-sound combination typical of heaths and hillsides in summer. The male flies up from the ground, climbing in a steep, fluttery flight, then sails back down with wings half open and raised and its tail spread, like a miniature parachute or shuttlecock. The song is a long series of thin trills and rattles, accelerating at first, at its best with a more musical trill to finish but without the rich, Canary-like notes of a Tree Pipit. Calls are often given in twos or threes: a short, high, thin *seep seep* or *swip swip swip*, or sometimes more frantic repetitions. Alarm notes at the nest include a shorter *chip*.

BREEDING The nests are well hidden on the ground: neat little cups lined with grass and hair. The three to five eggs are incubated for 11–15 days, and the chicks fly after 10–14 days.

MIGRATION In Iceland, Scandinavia and northeast Europe it is a summer visitor; in Britain and Ireland and much of mainland northwest Europe it is found all year, but migrates to lower altitudes in winter. In parts of central and southern Europe it is a winter visitor only.

LENGTH 14.5cm (5¾in)

WHEN TO SEE All year in Britain and Ireland, N France to Denmark; April to September farther north; September to April farther south
WHERE FOUND Breeds Iceland, Ireland, Britain and mainland Europe south to central France; migrant elsewhere

Grey Wagtail *Motacilla cinerea*

In summer a bird of rushing rivers, mill races, and upland streams, the Grey Wagtail moves downhill in winter to softer landscapes with calmer, more open waters, as well as visiting the smallest of puddles or the most insignificant garden ponds. It is the most 'extreme' wagtail in shape and actions, but the main clue to its presence is its distinctive flight call.

FEEDING It flits from rock to rock, walks along gravelly shores, or potters slowly beside pools, picking insects from the ground and the water's edge.

DISPLAY & VOICE Males sing and quiver their wings from trees or rocks, or in a pipit-like song flight. The song is a penetrating trill based on the call: a sharp, explosive *tzi* or *tzitzi*, more penetrating than a Pied Wagtail's.

BREEDING Nests are cups of moss and grass built in crevices in banks, among tree roots or rocks above water. Four to six eggs hatch after 11–14 days.

MIGRATION Moves to lowland areas in winter; breeders from N and E Europe move south and west as far as Africa.

LENGTH 18–19cm (7–7½in)

WHEN TO SEE All year
WHERE FOUND Breeds Ireland, Britain, S Scandinavia south to Mediterranean; in northeast only in summer, central Spain only in winter

Europe's slimmest wagtail, with the longest tail and most exaggerated tail-swinging action; bounding flight with sharp calls; often seen on town roofs in winter

White wingbar

Green-yellow rump

Juvenile

Juvenile

Slaty-grey above; yellow rump obvious

Female, breeding
Variable black on throat

White wingbar shows well from below

Male, breeding
Some are whiter on flanks/belly; much individual variation in summer adults of both sexes

Male, winter

First winter
Whitish or buff on breast and belly

Very long white-sided tail, always yellow beneath

Female, breeding
Some have whiter belly and/or blacker throat

Citrine Wagtail *Motacilla citreola*

Citrine Wagtails breed in the Arctic tundra, and in mountains and damp clearings farther south. In western Europe they are vagrants, rare even in the east, although they appear every year and sporadic breeding has been recorded far from the usual range. They are usually found close to water.

FEEDING They pick insects from the ground and from water, often when wading in the shallows. They also catch flies disturbed by grazing cattle.

VOICE The typical migrant's call is a slightly harsh or buzzed short note: a little more grating but higher, less upswept, than western races of the Yellow Wagtail: *sreep*, *drreep*, or *deesp*.

BREEDING The cup nest is well hidden in vegetation, in a hollow in a bank, or beside a stone, with four to six eggs.

MIGRATION The great majority move south and southeast to the Middle East and India, but a few head west in autumn to reach far-flung coasts and islands of northwest Europe.

LENGTH 17cm (6½in)

WHEN TO SEE September to November in W Europe; increasingly in spring
WHERE FOUND Breeds locally Belarus, Ukraine, commonly in Russia, rarely and erratically elsewhere; rare migrant/vagrant in most of Europe

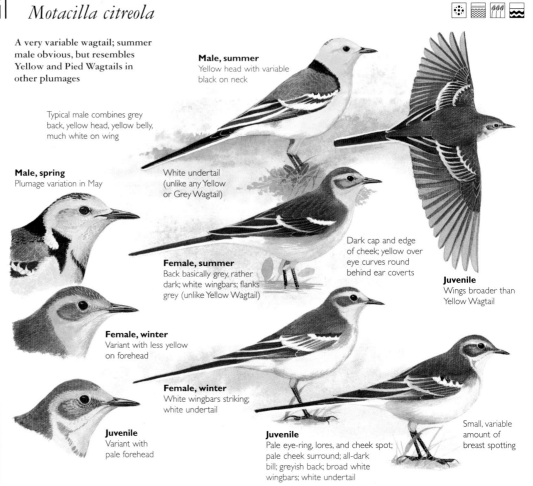

A very variable wagtail; summer male obvious, but resembles Yellow and Pied Wagtails in other plumages

Male, summer
Yellow head with variable black on neck

Typical male combines grey back, yellow head, yellow belly, much white on wing

Male, spring
Plumage variation in May

White undertail (unlike any Yellow or Grey Wagtail)

Dark cap and edge of cheek; yellow over eye curves round behind ear coverts

Female, summer
Back basically grey, rather dark; white wingbars; flanks grey (unlike Yellow Wagtail)

Juvenile
Wings broader than Yellow Wagtail

Female, winter
Variant with less yellow on forehead

Female, winter
White wingbars striking; white undertail

Juvenile
Variant with pale forehead

Juvenile
Pale eye-ring, lores, and cheek spot; pale cheek surround; all-dark bill; greyish back; broad white wingbars; white undertail

Small, variable amount of breast spotting

Yellow Wagtail *Motacilla flava*

Juvenile
Race *flavissima*; compare Pied

First winter
Race *flavissima*; often seen in autumn

Female
Race *flavissima*; some greyer, paler, less yellow

Male, spring
Race *flavissima*; uniquely green and vivid yellow ground bird

Top four birds all UK 'Yellow' race *flavissima*

A spindly-legged, slim-tailed bird of open, grassy places, often near water or livestock; complex races or closely-related species

Male, spring
Central Europe, 'Blue-headed' race *flava*

Male

Beware confusion with Grey Wagtail, especially non-breeding; Yellow Wagtail not present in winter in N Europe, unlike Grey

Male
Iberian 'Spanish' race *iberiae*

Male
France, 'Blue-headed' race *flava*, scarce UK

Female

Whitish wingbars and tertial edges; slim black tail with white sides. Flight deeply undulating over long distance

Female (left)
Italy, race *cinereocapilla*

Male Italy, race *cinereocapilla*

Races may be hard to identify: study crown, cheeks, 'eyebrow', chin, and throat – and note call

Male
Kirghiz steppe, race *beema*

Female
N Scandinavia, 'Grey-headed' race *thunbergi*, rare UK

Male
Romania, SE Russia, races *superciliaris* and *dombrowskii*

Male
Race *thunbergi*; darkest may look like Black-headed race, but nape duller, back less deep green

Male
Balkans, 'Black-headed' race/species *feldegg*, very rare in W Europe

Female
'Black-headed' race/species *feldegg*

Recent developments in classifying wagtails suggest that we may eventually separate 'yellow' wagtails into several species. The black-headed form of southeast Europe and the mainly yellow type of Britain and northern France are particularly well-marked, and seem to breed alongside other types without hybridizing; other races are more variable, and the boundaries between them are complex. The variety of racial types has always fascinated birdwatchers, especially in spring when two or three kinds may be seen side by side tripping about in a field of sheep or cattle. Yellow Wagtails like short grass with grazing animals; they favour wet places, especially seasonally-flooded meadows, but also breed in fields of cereals close to water. They appear in all kinds of open spaces on migration, from ploughed fields to sand dunes and golf courses. In spring they often pause in grassy pastures high on mountainsides in southern Europe, waiting for improved conditions before making the final crossing.

FEEDING Yellow wagtails eat small insects, picking them from the ground or shallow water while walking steadily, or snatching them in fast runs or lunges (especially insects disturbed by animals). They may chase them into the air, snatching them in their bills or simply knocking them to the ground. They also pick insects and ticks from the backs of animals, especially sheep.

DISPLAY & VOICE They pair up from late winter, and form spring flocks soon after migration. Small groups of breeding pairs often gather in suitable areas, with more or less overlapping territories. Males sing from the ground and low perches, or in rather ill-defined undulating song flights. The song is a long, fast, twittering performance of little musical merit. Flight calls vary individually and by race: western birds have a musical, upswept, full *tsweep* or *tsree-ee*; eastern races tend to produce more grating versions of these calls.

BREEDING Nests are neat cups, built on the ground in grass, lined with fine stems, hair, and wool. Four to six eggs hatch after 11–13 days. The chicks leave the nest a few days before they can fly, and fledge at about 16 days old.

MIGRATION All European Yellow Wagtails move south in autumn, to spend the winter in Africa. A few spend the winter in southern Spain but most go south of the Sahara. They leave Europe from July and August through to early November, and return in March, April (the majority), and May.

LENGTH 17cm (6½in)

WHEN TO SEE March to November
WHERE FOUND Breeds England and Wales, widely over mainland Europe; local in much of S Europe; widespread migrant

White & Pied Wagtails *Motacilla alba*

The White and Pied Wagtails are usually treated as races of the same species, *Motacilla alba*, but increasingly the Pied is being regarded as separate species, *Motacilla yarrelli*. Yet whether they are technically races or species, the two are clearly very closely related. The neat, dapper little Pied Wagtail is a British resident: a familiar bird of the suburbs, where it happily feeds on tarmac and concrete, on roofs and beside garden ponds, as well as in many places that are more or less associated with water. It is equally likely to be seen in gravel pits, old quarries, stony rivers, woodyards, railway sidings, and village streets. Over most of the rest of Europe the breeding birds are White Wagtails: common and easy to see in towns and village streets (even deep down in narrow, concrete streets between high walls), along stony riverbeds, and in more open fields and high, rocky meadows. Both Pied and White Wagtails spend most of their time on the ground, usually away from tall or dense vegetation except when roosting.

FEEDING Both eat insects washed up at the water's edge throughout the year, and pick others from the ground after short, fast dashes and lunges. They also snatch insects from the air, chasing them in lively, bouncy, tail-flirting runs or in brief, fluttering, fly-catching flights.

VOICE Male Pied Wagtails do not sing much, but call from rooftops and other raised perches near the nest. Their calls include a cheery, liquid *cheweeoo* or *chiwoo* and a distinctive harder *chiss-ick*. White Wagtail calls are like those of Pied's, but softer, more like *pee-vit*.

BREEDING They nest in holes in banks, rocks, piles of wood, in old walls, or inside derelict buildings. Five or six eggs take 11–16 days to hatch, and the chicks fledge in 13–14 days.

MIGRATION The Pied Wagtail is more or less resident, with movements to lower ground, urban areas, and the coast in winter; some birds that breed in northern Scotland move well south within Britain. White Wagtails that breed in Iceland, northern Europe, eastern Europe, and the Alps move south in autumn. They are regular passage migrants in Britain in spring, but less often identified in autumn.

LENGTH 18cm (7in)

A small, long-tailed, fearless, strikingly patterned bird of watersides, housing and industrial estates, car parks, and grassland, drawing attention by frequent, characteristic calls

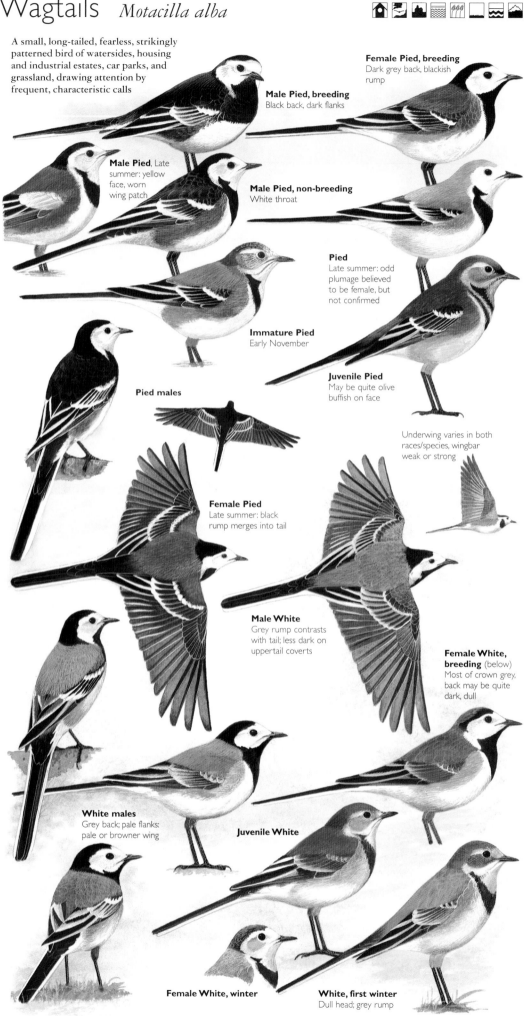

Female Pied, breeding Dark grey back, blackish rump

Male Pied, breeding Black back, dark flanks

Male Pied, Late summer: yellow face, worn wing patch

Male Pied, non-breeding White throat

Pied Late summer: odd plumage believed to be female, but not confirmed

Immature Pied Early November

Juvenile Pied May be quite olive buffish on face

Pied males

Underwing varies in both races/species, wingbar weak or strong

Female Pied Late summer: black rump merges into tail

Male White Grey rump contrasts with tail; less dark on uppertail coverts

Female White, breeding (below) Most of crown grey, back may be quite dark, dull

White males Grey back; pale flanks; pale or browner wing

Juvenile White

Female White, winter

White, first winter Dull head; grey rump

WHEN TO SEE Pied all year in Britain; White all year in central and SW Europe; April–October in north and east; most April–May, September–October in Britain
WHERE FOUND Pied throughout Britain and Ireland, rare breeder N France and also irregularly to NW Germany; White throughout Europe

Waxwing *Bombycilla garrulus*

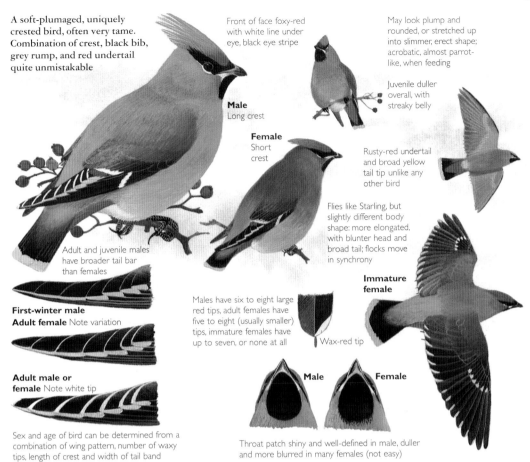

A soft-plumaged, uniquely crested bird, often very tame. Combination of crest, black bib, grey rump, and red undertail quite unmistakable

Front of face foxy-red with white line under eye, black eye stripe

May look plump and rounded, or stretched up into slimmer, erect shape; acrobatic, almost parrot-like, when feeding

Juvenile duller overall, with streaky belly

Male Long crest

Female Short crest

Rusty-red undertail and broad yellow tail tip unlike any other bird

Flies like Starling, but slightly different body shape: more elongated, with blunter head and broad tail; flocks move in synchrony

Adult and juvenile males have broader tail bar than females

Immature female

First-winter male
Adult female Note variation

Males have six to eight large red tips, adult females have five to eight (usually smaller) tips, immature females have up to seven, or none at all

Wax-red tip

Adult male or female Note white tip

Male **Female**

Sex and age of bird can be determined from a combination of wing pattern, number of waxy tips, length of crest and width of tail band

Throat patch shiny and well-defined in male, duller and more blurred in many females (not easy)

When Waxwing numbers build up after a good breeding season, but the berry crop happens to be poor, large flocks leave northern Europe in search of food elsewhere: these 'irruptions' into countries where Waxwings are usually scarce are among the most exciting events of winter birdwatching.

FEEDING Groups, rarely large flocks, gather in places with hawthorn or cotoneaster berries, eating greedily and regularly flying off to drink before the next feast. In summer, they eat insects.

DISPLAY & VOICE A displaying male shows off his crest and ruffles up his grey rump feathers; he will also pass a berry to a suitably willing female. The song is poorly developed: a version of the typical call which is a rather shrill, silvery trill, with a slight rattling quality at close range.

BREEDING Pairs build cup nests in belts of tall spruce and pine trees close to open tundra. Five to six eggs hatch after an incubation of 14–15 days.

MIGRATION Erratic movements west and south in winter.

LENGTH 18cm (7in)

WHEN TO SEE All year; November to April in central and W Europe
WHERE FOUND N Sweden, N Finland; winters farther south, sometimes to UK

Dipper *Cinclus cinclus*

A waterside bird of Wren-like shape but closer to size of small thrush; bobs up and down as if on springs. Unique white bib and aquatic behaviour

Most of body dark grey-black with steely gloss; head browner, white eyelid often seen

Northern race

Flight low, fast, body looking rather too heavy; follows course of stream

North European race has black belly; British race has broad ginger-brown breastband; Irish and Scottish Dippers have darkest heads; central European Dippers are brightest of all below

Northern race

British race

British race

Typical action is a quick, springy, rhythmic down-up bob of the whole body

Large, strong legs and toes give excellent grip on stones even in fast-flowing water

Juvenile Paler and greyer, dull whitish below with barred, less crisp bib

Underwater, Dippers open their wings and lower their heads, using the flow of water over their backs to push them down while they forage for food under stones and weeds

Few birds are quite so restricted to one habitat as the Dipper, which is rarely found away from a stream and then only by water of some sort: in winter some move to the shore of a large lake or even the sea for a time.

FEEDING Uniquely among songbirds the Dipper feeds in and under water, wading, swimming, and diving, to find insects and crustaceans on the water's edge or stream bed. The flow of water against its opened wings helps keep the Dipper submerged.

DISPLAY & VOICE Dippers fly along their river territories, calling loudly, and sing from low branches and boulders with loud, rich, warbling notes. The usual call is a short, hard, slightly grating, low-pitched *dzit*.

BREEDING The nest is always over water, under a bridge or overhanging rock or tree root, sometimes even under the cascade of a waterfall. Four or five eggs hatch after 16 days.

MIGRATION Most are resident, but there is some movement in cold winter weather to lower areas or the coast.

LENGTH 18cm (7in)

WHEN TO SEE All year
WHERE FOUND On clean rivers, less often lake shores, in most of the higher parts of Europe, lowlands in winter

197

Dunnock *Prunella modularis*

Best known as little garden birds that sing from the hedge and scuttle into thick cover at the least sign of disturbance, Dunnocks are as likely to be found among the brambles and bracken of coastal clifftops. They are full of surprises when breeding, with extra-pair matings and trios being quite normal.

FEEDING In summer they pick insects from the ground and low vegetation; in winter they eat seeds.

DISPLAY & VOICE Dunnocks display in twos and threes by singing and waving their wings, often one at a time, from low perches. The song is a slightly flat, fast warble with less emphasis or melody than a Robin's. Calls are loud, sharp, simple notes, *tseee* or *tsip*.

BREEDING A neat nest, lined with hair and feathers, is hidden in a bush or hedge; four or five eggs hatch in 12 days; the chicks fly when 12 days old.

MIGRATION Birds breeding in northern and eastern Europe move south and west in winter.

LENGTH 13–14cm (5–5½in)

WHEN TO SEE All year in W and central Europe; winter visitor in south, summer visitor in east and north
WHERE FOUND Breeds most of Europe except Iceland and Mediterranean

A small, streaky, dark brown and grey bird, shuffling under shrubberies and through flowerbeds but also found widely in many habitats from forest to coastal heath

Pairs and trios wave wings in display

Flies with flicking action and gentle undulations, dives into cover

Adult, autumn Brown cap and ear coverts within blue-grey; pale brown eye; brown wash on flanks

Rapidly flicks tail open and shut; no white

Stands more upright when alarmed

Adult, spring Tiny white spots on wing soon wear off

Reddish/orange legs

Short, thin bill

Female's tail shorter than male's

Typically feeds in horizontal pose

Juvenile Streaked beneath

Adult Pale belly

Alpine Accentor *Prunella collaris*

In summer this is a bird of wild, open, windswept mountain regions, usually 1800–3000m (6000–10,000ft) above sea level, with plenty of rocky ground or bare crags. In winter it may move much lower. It can be located by its song, although distant snatches of song and calls from Black Redstarts or Water Pipits carried on the breeze often confuse the issue.

FEEDING It eats small insects, spiders, and seeds, picking them from the ground or extricating them from crevices in the rock.

VOICE The song is a creaky trill of uncertain pattern, sometimes more rippling, usually slower than a Dunnock's but more musical. Its calls are rolling *tschirr* or *drru* notes.

BREEDING Nests are loose grassy cups lined neatly with moss, feathers, and hair, in cavities among rocks. Three or four eggs hatch after 14–15 days.

MIGRATION Mostly resident; some move lower in winter, but rarely make long-distance movements.

LENGTH 15–17.5cm (6–7in)

WHEN TO SEE All year
WHERE FOUND Breeds in highest ranges of central and N Spain, Pyrenees, central France, Alps, Italy, Balkans, and E Europe; rare outside breeding range in winter and only a vagrant farther north

Adult, spring Dark streaks above and dark orange on flanks not easy to see at long range; bold streaks under tail

Adult, winter Back wears greyer

Flies low and fast like small thrush

Yellow bill base obvious, but spotted throat harder to see, often like a pale bar

Blackish bar across wing shows well

Adult, autumn Buff-brown back

Often elusive but sometimes confiding bird of high-altitude rocks and grassland, larger and brighter than Dunnock, but with much the same character

Male (main bird) has longer tail projection than female (inset)

Adult, October Bright, fresh colours in autumn; dull and worn in summer

Dull, dark in flight with plain tail but double blackish and thin white wingbars

Same scale as Dunnock, above

Big white tips under tail

Juvenile Body like October adult

Wren *Troglodytes troglodytes*

Loud, very rapid, full-throated song includes distinctive low trill

Pale stripe over eye

Bill slightly curved, tapered

Warm brown; darker bars across wing and flanks

Tail often cocked

Slips through cover or flies to next bush; flight low, fast, and whirring, on tiny round wings

A tiny but rounded, deep-bellied bird of dense undergrowth and shady places; irascible and inquisitive, with noisy calls and remarkably loud, very fast song

Widespread and often very abundant, the Wren can be found anywhere from parks and gardens to rocky islands far offshore. Some isolated island groups have their own races. It is rarely seen in the tree tops, preferring low undergrowth, hedgerows, and shrubs.

FEEDING It hunts insects and spiders in nooks and crannies in and beneath dense tangles of vegetation.

VOICE Males sing from low perches with a remarkably loud, vibrant, fast warble, more emphatic than the song of a Dunnock and incorporating a distinctive low, rapid trill. Other calls include a harsh *tchurr* and dry *chit-it*.

BREEDING The male builds several nests, each a ball of grass and leaves with a side entrance, and lines the one chosen by the female. Five or six eggs hatch after 14–15 days; chicks fly at 16–17 days.

MIGRATION Northern birds move south and west in winter.

LENGTH 9–10cm (3½–4in)

WHEN TO SEE All year except much of S Scandinavia and NE Europe, where summer only
WHERE FOUND Absent from high mountains, open moors, and N Scandinavia, otherwise almost everywhere

Robin *Erithacus rubecula*

An unmistakable bird in adult plumage, bright when fresh but fading during the summer; juveniles without red are less distinctive but have same alert, intelligent character

Both sexes aggressive and territorial; breast patch used in display

Face and breast clear, unmarked reddish-orange, fading paler

Bluish-grey sides of face, neck and chest

Thin blackish bill, big dark eyes; stands well clear of ground on spindly legs

Warm brown back, thin pale wingbar

Juvenile
Pale spots above, dark mottles on gingery chest; tail dull; develops red in irregular spots from centre of chest

Robins are bold and confiding in Britain, but much less so elsewhere in Europe where they tend to be quite shy. They like deciduous or mixed woods, spruce, parkland with plentiful trees and, in Britain, gardens, avoiding wide open spaces.

FEEDING They eat a variety of insects and spiders, taking them mostly from the ground; they also eat small berries in autumn and winter.

DISPLAY & VOICE Both males and females are notoriously aggressive, posturing to show off their orange-red breasts in threat displays. The song is a flowing, rich, even warble, clear and rippling; in autumn it has a rather melancholy quality as each phrase fades away. Calls include a sharp, clicking *tic* or *tic-ikik* and a thin *seei*.

BREEDING Robins nest in banks, under roots or in nest boxes with open fronts; the nest is usually a hair-lined cup of grass and leaves. Four to six eggs hatch in 13–14 days.

MIGRATION Many birds from northern and eastern Europe move south and west in winter.

LENGTH 14cm (5½in)

WHEN TO SEE All year in south and west, summer visitor in N and E Europe
WHERE FOUND Widespread except for Iceland, Norway

Nightingale *Luscinia megarhynchos*

Famous as it is, the Nightingale is not widely known to people in England, where Robins singing at night are likely to be confused with the real thing. Nightingales require dense bushes down to ground level, best provided by coppiced shrubs such as sweet chestnut and hazel, and thickets of blackthorn, bramble, and wild rose. In such places they are a challenge to see, yet sometimes sing in full view.

FEEDING They pick beetles, ants, worms, and berries from the ground, taking them from deep leaf litter and from bare patches in deep shade.

VOICE The song is superb, but rather poorly-structured. It is best recognized by its unique mixture of slow, piping notes, high warbles, and sudden, deep, throbbing and full-throated phrases at great speed, separated by long pauses. Calls include a sweet *hweee* and a peculiar low, croaking, mechanical *kerrrr*.

BREEDING Nests are cups of leaves and grass built on or near the ground; four or five eggs hatch after 13 days.

MIGRATION Winters in Africa.

LENGTH 16.5cm (6½in)

WHEN TO SEE April to September
WHERE FOUND Breeds S and E England, Europe north to S Denmark and Germany, east to Poland, Romania

A skulking bird with a glorious voice but undistinguished appearance; plain face with dark eye and rufous tail are distinctive if seen

Rufous tail contrasts with warm olive-brown body

Juvenile (right)
Very dark, wings much darker than adult at first, fade paler by autumn. Spotted like young Robin or Redstart

Very faint malar stripe (dark line from base of bill) at some angles, less marked than on Thrush Nightingale

Faint breastband on some

Only slight pale base to large bill

Sturdier than Robin, hops on ground or through dense vegetation; plain head but pale eye-ring, slight capped effect, greyer side of neck

Undertail and wings rich buff, unlike Thrush Nightingale

Bright upperparts and rufous tail separates Nightingale from most Thrush Nightingales (some Russian Thrush Nightingales can be as rich). Lower belly whiter

Small first primary (dark) shown drooped, equal to or longer than primary coverts

Thrush Nightingale *Luscinia luscinia*

A real rarity in Britain, this is the eastern counterpart of the Nightingale. It is slightly duller than its relative in appearance, but its equal as a songster. It occupies much the same types of terrain, favouring tall, dense bushes and shrubs in extensive, shady woodland, with soft soil thickly covered in dead and rotting leaves.

FEEDING It eats mainly insects, varied with a few berries and fruits, obtaining them mostly from the ground. It searches leaf litter and herbs like a small thrush.

VOICE Males sing from several low perches within their territory. The song is louder, more repetitive and more staccato than a Nightingale's, with a 'solemn' character. It usually lacks the thin, rising notes but has many pure, bell-like phrases.

BREEDING Nests are bulky, made of grass and stems with a fine lining, on the ground in deep shade. Four or five eggs hatch after 13 days' incubation.

MIGRATION Migrates to east Africa in autumn; rare in western Europe.

LENGTH 16.5cm (6½in)

WHEN TO SEE April to September
WHERE FOUND Breeds extreme S Norway, S Sweden, from Denmark and east side of Baltic eastwards, south to Romania

Very like Nightingale but more easterly in range; duller, with faint or stronger mottling on breast, duller tail, more definite dark stripe beside throat

Head rounder than Nightingale, eye-ring less prominent, malar stripe stronger, yellow gape line more marked

Tail dull rufous; undertail whitish; underparts whitish with faint, fine streaks, fine shaft-streaks on chest

Stronger pale gape than Nightingale, darker malar stripe, more mottled breast; plumage variable: some greyer, some more rufous

First primary very short, hidden beneath primary coverts; usually eight primary tips visible (not seven, like Nightingale); mottled breast may help

Sides of tail, but not uppertail coverts, can be redder in flight; underparts whiter than Nightingale, but difficult to distinguish

Bluethroat *Luscinia svecica*

A real gem, beautiful and tuneful, but secretive in wetlands. Spring males vary and are different from females and young, but all have red tail-sides and bold face patterns

White line over eye; dark bill with yellow gape patch

Male, breeding
Spain: blue and red bib, no black band

Rufous tail sides obvious in flight

Male, breeding
Netherlands: blue and red separated by black

Female, breeding
Some have blue

Male, breeding
'White-spotted', central and S Europe: central white patch in blue

Female, breeding
Bold white and dark stripes, dark breastband

Male, first winter

Female, winter
Black and tawny on chest, dark stripe from bill, white over eye and under cheek

Male, breeding
'Red-spotted', N Europe: central red patch in blue

In Britain the Bluethroat is a scarce migrant, usually in non-breeding plumage and difficult to see, but in spring and summer it is a real joy, combining richness of colour with a fine song. It likes a mixture of open and wooded ground, often frequenting the edges of reedy fens and marshes with willow thickets. It breeds from low plains to high hills.

FEEDING Bluethroats feed on the ground, scuffling and hopping about in search of insects and seeds.

DISPLAY & VOICE Males puff out their throat and breast feathers to exaggerate the central spot as they sing. The song is loud, sweet, and prolonged, varied by a great deal of imitation. It recalls a Nightingale's, but is less richly toned.

BREEDING It nests on the ground in thick vegetation. Five or six eggs take 13–14 days to hatch.

MIGRATION Winters in Africa (a few in Spain). Migrants appear in varying numbers on western European coasts and islands in late spring and autumn.

LENGTH 14cm (5½in)

WHEN TO SEE April to October
WHERE FOUND Breeds locally W and E France, Low Countries; N Scandinavia; erratically across central Europe and east from N Germany into Russia

Rufous Bush-robin *Cercotrichas galactotes*

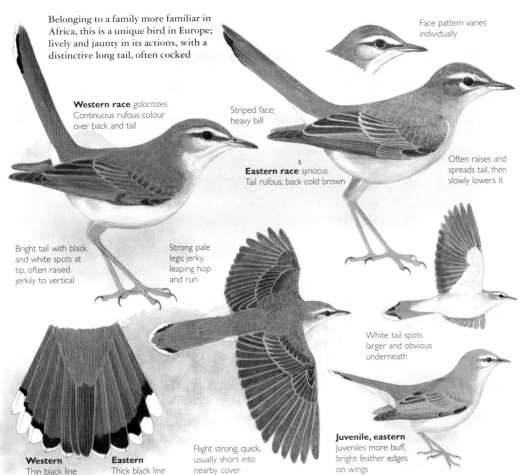

Belonging to a family more familiar in Africa, this is a unique bird in Europe; lively and jaunty in its actions, with a distinctive long tail, often cocked

Face pattern varies individually

Western race *galactotes*
Continuous rufous colour over back and tail

Striped face; heavy bill

Eastern race *syriacus*
Tail rufous, back cold brown

Often raises and spreads tail, then slowly lowers it

Bright tail with black and white spots at tip, often raised jerkily to vertical

Strong pale legs; jerky, leaping hop and run

White tail spots larger and obvious underneath

Western
Thin black line

Eastern
Thick black line

Flight strong, quick, usually short into nearby cover

Juvenile, eastern
Juveniles more buff, bright feather edges on wings

The bush-robins are mostly African birds; this is the only species that breeds in Europe, where it likes dry, sunny places such as orange groves, prickly pear thickets, and sandy gorges with bushes. It is lively and almost extravagant in its actions, but can be extremely elusive. It often flies off into a deep bush if disturbed, but patience may be rewarded when it returns to show itself off on the ground.

FEEDING It digs large insects and worms from loose soil, catches moths in flight, and snatches flies and wasps while hovering over flowers.

DISPLAY & VOICE Males stand upright with drooped wings and fanned tail as a threat to intruders. They sing from high perches with a disjointed but exceedingly rich, varied song, with clear, lark-like notes and throaty phrases like those of a Nightingale.

BREEDING They build untidy nests of twigs, grass, and roots in bushes, and incubate four or five eggs for 13 days.

MIGRATION It winters in Africa; very rare north of breeding range.

LENGTH 15cm (6in)

WHEN TO SEE April to October
WHERE FOUND Breeds sparsely in S Spain and Portugal; small numbers in Albania and Greece, very rare UK

Redstart *Phoenicurus phoenicurus*

The breeding range of this delightful little chat is curiously erratic: in Britain it is largely a bird of western woods, but can be found locally over much of southern and eastern England too. In the west it likes old oak woods and scattered oaks on the slopes of rocky hillsides. In other areas it likes mature oaks with a lot of dead wood in parkland or near lowland heaths.

FEEDING It picks insects from the surface of leaf litter, or from leaves high in trees; it also snatches them from the air in short 'flycatching' flights.

VOICE Males have a rich, full song on arrival at their territories, but soon change to a shorter song close to the nest site as they advertise it to potential mates. This song is sweet, short, and rather unfinished, beginning with several rolled *srree* notes. Calls include a high *hweet* and a harder *tuik*.

BREEDING It nests in holes in trees, rocks, walls, or sometimes nest boxes. Up to seven eggs hatch in 12–14 days.

MIGRATION Winters in Africa; regular migrant on western European coasts.

LENGTH 14cm (5½in)

WHEN TO SEE April to October
WHERE FOUND Rare Ireland, local in Iberia; absent Iceland; otherwise breeds in most of Europe and is a widespread migrant

A small, elegant, colourful chat distinguished by its light rusty red tail and rump and woodland habitat

Male, spring
Slaty-grey above, white forehead, inky black face and bib

Female

Female and juvenile pale; rump and tail like male but body mostly buffish; black eye in plain face

Juvenile

Male, autumn/winter
Pale feather tips obscure black and white areas

In SE Europe may show whitish wing panel

Both sexes have more red on rump than Black Redstart

Male underwing brighter than that of paler female

Female

Male

Black Redstart *Phoenicurus ochruros*

Although clearly a close relative of the Redstart, this species breeds in very different habitats. Common in old towns and villages, it is also found on derelict sites and in industrial areas which simulate rocks and cliffs. Many breed on remote cliffs and in mountain gorges far from urban influence.

FEEDING Hopping and running on the ground, or dropping briefly from a perch before flying back up, the Black Redstart snatches small insects and sometimes picks up small berries.

VOICE Males sing from rooftops, chimneys, and wires, often on very high buildings, as well as from rocks high above screes and boulder-strewn quarries. The song has short, quick, sweet trills mixed with rattles and a grating, slurred *tch-r-r-rrrrt*.

BREEDING The nest is on a ledge or in a crevice, in a building, a cave, or on a cliff. Four to six eggs take 13–17 days to hatch; the chicks fly in 12–19 days.

MIGRATION Disperses widely in the autumn to the south and west.

LENGTH 14.5cm (5¾in)

WHEN TO SEE All year
WHERE FOUND Breeds very locally in Britain; Europe south from S Sweden and Denmark; from N and E Europe moves west and south in winter as far as S Ireland, SW England

Male, Iberia
Steely-black with paler cap, bold white wing panel

Typically a bird of old towns and villages, industrial sites, cliffs, and mountain crags; also coasts and quarries in winter

Adult male, summer
Black and slaty-grey with dark reddish tail and vent. Immature males much greyer

Male's tail longer than female's

Adult female
Sooty brown-grey, darker than Redstart; red more restricted on uppertail

Note Robin-like shape, dark eye in grey face, dark legs

Male

Female

Male, first winter
Some first-winter males have a little white on inner wing

Female, first winter

Whinchat *Saxicola rubetra*

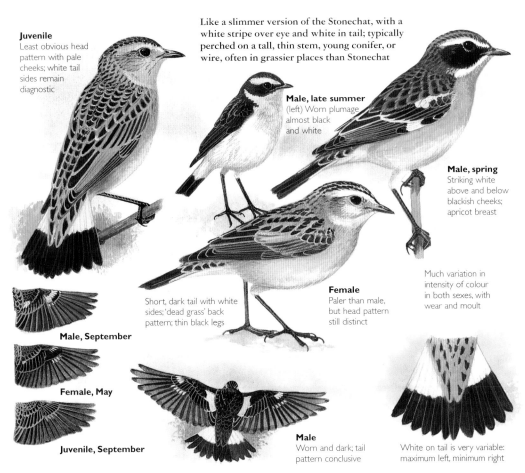

Juvenile
Least obvious head pattern with pale cheeks; white tail sides remain diagnostic

Like a slimmer version of the Stonechat, with a white stripe over eye and white in tail; typically perched on a tall, thin stem, young conifer, or wire, often in grassier places than Stonechat

Male, late summer
(left) Worn plumage, almost black and white

Male, spring
Striking white above and below blackish cheeks; apricot breast

Much variation in intensity of colour in both sexes, with wear and moult

Female
Paler than male, but head pattern still distinct

Short, dark tail with white sides; 'dead grass' back pattern; thin black legs

Male, September

Female, May

Juvenile, September

Male
Worn and dark; tail pattern conclusive

White on tail is very variable: maximum left, minimum right

Sadly declining in many areas where intensive farming has swept away great tracts of ancient, species-rich pasture, the Whinchat needs slender stems rising from rough grassland, heathery slopes, or young, open conifer plantations. Like other chats, it often pauses on open ground near the coast while on migration.

FEEDING The Whinchat drops from a perch to take insects from the ground, less often taking them in the air.

VOICE Isolated pairs are often rather quiet, but where several pairs are close together the males sing much more. Their song is Robin-like but with throaty churrs and rattles and much mimicry. Calls are a scolding *tik-tik* and a rising *huee*, often combined as *huee-tik-tik*, less hard than a Stonechat.

BREEDING The neat cup nest is extremely well hidden on the ground among thick grass. Four to seven eggs hatch within 12–13 days.

MIGRATION All Whinchats leave Europe to spend the winter in Africa.

LENGTH 12.5cm (5in)

WHEN TO SEE April to October
WHERE FOUND Breeds from N Spain and C Italy north and east through Europe, except for extreme N Scandinavia, Iceland, most of Low Countries, and S Greece

Stonechat *Saxicola torquata*

A stocky little bird, typically on exposed perches on bushes or overhead wires, scolding intruders with insistent, tetchy notes

Male
Typical posture: black face and throat, white neck patch obvious

Female
Small white wing marks, all-dark tail

Male, spring
Short, rounded wings, large white shoulder patches

Female
Dark extreme

Male, late summer
Worn to most contrasted effect

Female, first winter (above)
Streaky chin edged pale; least distinctive plumage

Male, first winter
(above) Dark face and throat, with paler lower edge; all-black tail

Female
Fades paler below in late summer

Male, spring
White shoulder patches more exposed in display

Male, September
Spanish race

Should you walk close to its nest, the Stonechat will scold you from a bush or wire with endlessly repeated, agitated calls. This is a bird of rough heaths and slopes, moors and hillsides with plenty of gorse, tall bushy heather, and small shrubs. It is fond of the narrow strip between enclosed fields and rocky cliffs on the coast.

FEEDING Gliding to the ground from an open perch, the Stonechat picks up an insect, sometimes after a short chase, then flies up again – often to a fresh perch nearby.

DISPLAY & VOICE Males sing from exposed perches, including wires, and also in bouncy, hovering song flights. They often spread their wing covert feathers to expose large areas of white. The song is a scrappy warble, more uniform than a Whinchat's; calls are hard, chacking notes and a plaintive *hweet*, often together as *hweet-tsak-tsak*.

BREEDING The nest is in grass, often with a short entrance tunnel, holding 4–6 eggs which hatch in 13–14 days.

MIGRATION They disperse in autumn, often moving to coasts in cold weather.

LENGTH 12.5cm (5in)

WHEN TO SEE All year
WHERE FOUND Ireland, local Britain, Europe south of Denmark, Germany, Ukraine

Black-eared & Pied Wheatear *Oenanthe hispanica, O. pleschanka*

Black-eared and Pied Wheatears form a closely-related species pair, not always easy to distinguish. While they are clearly wheatears, both have some characteristics typical of the smaller chats, especially a tendency to perch on bushes. Compared with other wheatears they are small and slim, and their light weight allows them to perch on quite slender stems.

The Black-eared is much the more familiar of the two. It is one of the few birds in Europe with two different plumages: the 'pale-throated' and 'black-throated' forms. There are also two races, both of which occur in the two plumage forms. Males of the race *melanoleuca*, found east of Italy and Yugoslavia, have more black above the bill than the western race *hispanica*. The eastern black-throated form has more black than the western black-throated form, and in spring eastern birds are greyer, less richly cinnamon-buff, than western ones.

The Black-eared Wheatear lives chiefly in the Mediterranean area. It prefers low-lying landscapes with scattered shrubs, rocks, and exposed earth. Stony fields, gullies, heaths, vineyards with rocky walls, and open Mediterranean scrub suit it well.

The Pied Wheatear breeds in similar terrain from the western side of the Black Sea eastwards, and is a rare vagrant in the UK, typically very late in the autumn.

FEEDING Both species eat mainly insects, taking them from bare earth and short herbs – typically in short, accurate flights from perches, to which they usually return quite quickly.

DISPLAY & VOICE Males sing for long periods from rocks, walls, bush tops, and wires. They also have a song flight, expanding their tails to show the large areas of white and then diving in a steep plunge to the ground. The song is a series of short, loud, warbling phrases, with a scratchy effect. Calls are dry clicking notes and short rattles.

BREEDING Both build a cup nest of grass and moss with a finer lining, on the ground, either in a hollow or beneath a stone or bush, with a heap of fine twigs at the entrance forming a small platform. Four or five eggs are incubated for 13–14 days. The chicks fledge after 11–12 days.

MIGRATION They winter in semi-desert regions in Africa just south of the Sahara. They are rare north of the breeding range, either as 'overshoots' in spring or strays in the autumn.

LENGTH Both species 14.5cm (5¾in)

WHEN TO SEE March to October
WHERE FOUND Black-eared Wheatear: Iberia, S France, S Italy, Balkans; rare migrant elsewhere; Pied Wheatear: extreme E Europe, S Asia, very rare vagrant in W Europe, often very late in the autumn

Black-eared is a neat, bright, handsome wheatear that often perches on bush tops and posts; tail pattern is distinctive

Spring males
Race *hispanica*

Variation in tail pattern, all forms: left most like Wheatear but width of black uneven; right most typical and distinctive, with uneven black tip and thin black line on side

Male

Female

Male
Both black-throated and pale-throated forms have black underwing, or dark grey with pale tertial edges

Spring males
Race *melanoleuca*: black throat deeper, black mask wider than *hispanica*

Female, spring
Race *hispanica*

Male, spring
Race *hispanica*

Compare yellow-brown back, tail pattern, dark wing, and black underwing with Wheatear

Often perches on slender bushes, unlike Wheatear

Male, autumn
Race *hispanica*: broader pale tertial, secondary, and covert fringes

Male, first winter
Race *melanoleuca*: black-throated form

Female (below)
Race *melanoleuca*

Male, first winter
Race *melanoleuca*
Probably pale-throated form

Male, spring
Race *melanoleuca*:
orange wears to white

Pied Wheatear has same tail pattern, shape, and behaviour as Black-eared, making it hard to distinguish in some plumages

All below are Pied Wheatear

Male

Male, spring
Rare white throat

Male, spring
Typical black throat; often grey on crown

Female, summer
Tail like Black-eared; white rump extends higher onto back in all plumages

Shorter tail projection than Black-eared; more rusty- or grey-brown on chest; some are faintly mottled with firmer border against pale belly

Female, first winter
Typical pale throat; very like eastern Black-eared, but colder back colour, less yellowish below; note scaly back feathers

Female, first winter Rare black throat

Wheatear *Oenanthe oenanthe*

A small, smart, upright, terrestrial chat with a bold splash of white over a T-shaped black tail; spring males are beautifully grey above, other plumages much more brown and buff

Grey underwing unlike Isabelline or Black-eared Wheatear

Simple tail band below

Juvenile

Immature or adult, autumn to winter (left)

Male, spring
Greenland race: fractionally longer primaries than European race

Male, first spring
Wings brown; just a thin dark smudge on ear coverts

Adult male, spring
Black wings, ear coverts have wide black band; back much greyer than Black-eared Wheatear

Male, spring
Spanish race: strikingly pale grey and black

Adult female, spring
Grey bloom wears off to give brown back by June; breast becomes whiter

Male, first year (below)
Greenland race: crown and ear coverts differ from those of adult

Juvenile female
Primaries browner than young male

Male, autumn (below)
Female's wings browner

Female, autumn

Wide, pale primary tips distinguish juvenile from adult

Autumn birds have boldly contrasted wings, unlike Isabelline Wheatear; more obvious T-shape on tail, wider white rump, grey underwing

Juvenile
Greenland race: longer wingtip than European, with six visible tips

Some Greenland birds have shorter tail than European, but not all

Adult male, spring
Greenland race: biggest, brightest Greenland birds with longest wings are distinctive, but many are not distinguishable

The first Cuckoo or Swallow may be a more popular symbol of spring, but to many birdwatchers it is the arrival of the Wheatear that lifts the spirits early in March. Usually it will be a male first, a few days ahead of the females, and he looks unbelievably smart. He may be on a grassy strip near the coast, or on a high chalk down inland, but wherever he is seen he will probably fly ahead a few dozen yards and then settle again, his vivid white rump catching the eye for a moment before disappearing as quickly. Wheatears behave in the same way in autumn, when migrant birds appear in open spaces with grass, sandy areas, golf courses, ploughed fields, and the shores of lowland reservoirs. In the summer breeding season, by contrast, Wheatears need a combination of short grass on which to forage, and tumbled rocks or stone walls in which to nest.

FEEDING The birds feed mainly on insects and spiders. They usually take them from the ground, either in short runs with frequent stops to stand upright and look around, or in quick, deft flights from a low perch. A Wheatear tends to fly from a perch to the closest areas of open ground first, then fly farther afield but still return to the same bush or post. Once that area has been exhausted, the bird flies on to a new perch: in this way it often covers a large area along a linear habitat such as a strip of dunes or shingle behind a beach, or a band of grass along a rough track bulldozed across a moor.

DISPLAY & VOICE Wheatear song flights are frequent, quite long and high, with a fast, fluttering action. At the peak of the climb the bird 'dances' in the air before slanting back to the ground. The song is musical and quick, but with many hard notes, creaky calls, and rattles. Calls are typically hard and double or treble: *chak-chak* or *hweet-chak-chak*.

BREEDING The female builds a rough nest of grass, heather, feathers, and moss in a hole in a wall, a collapsed rabbit hole, a space beneath fallen rocks, or a tunnel into a scree slope, and incubates her four to seven eggs for 13 days. The chicks move from the nest when about 10 days old and fly after two to three weeks.

MIGRATION Frequently seen on migration outside their breeding areas, Wheatears move south to Africa for the winter. Even breeders from Greenland winter in tropical Africa, passing through Britain in spring.

LENGTH 14.5–15.5cm (5¾–6½in)

WHEN TO SEE March to October
WHERE FOUND Breeds over most of Europe, including Iceland, but sparse and local in France and much of S Spain. A widespread migrant both on coasts and well inland

205

Black Wheatear *Oenanthe leucura*

This large wheatear is never very common, often occurring just a pair or two at a time in suitable spots with broken rocky slopes, screes, cliffs, and scattered bushes. It is an Iberian speciality, reaching the southern foothills of the Pyrenees, but it also breeds in Morocco and Tunisia where it must be distinguished from the similar White-crowned Black Wheatear.

FEEDING It catches most of its insect prey as it hops about like a thrush or explores cavities under rocks, but it takes some in dives from a perch or in flight. It also eats berries in autumn.

VOICE The song has a curiously distant, subdued quality even at close range. The call is a thin *pee-pee-pee*; also a hard *chak* in alarm.

BREEDING The birds nest in cavities in cliffs or walls, laying three to five eggs; they hatch after 14–18 days, and the chicks fly within two weeks.

MIGRATION Higher breeding areas such as the Sierra Nevada are vacated in winter, but little other movement occurs; very rare outside usual range.

LENGTH 18cm (7in)

WHEN TO SEE All year
WHERE FOUND Spain, extreme eastern edge of Portugal; almost extinct in extreme S France; perhaps breeds Italy

Typically stocky but can look very slim in extreme heat

A large, dark wheatear with a striking white rear end, the only all-dark wheatear likely in Europe

Male
Black-brown; wings black, but wear browner

Looks big, heavy, broad-winged in flight

Female/juvenile
Dark sooty-brown; wings black when fresh but wear to dull brown

Paler webs of flight feathers inconspicuous from above

Very striking white tail, rump, and vent

Isabelline Wheatear *Oenanthe isabellina*

Within its usual range this stocky, pale wheatear can look so striking that its identity is never in doubt. If it turns up as a rare vagrant elsewhere in Europe, however, it is likely to be confused with the northern Wheatear; this makes careful observation essential for a correct identification. It is a lowland bird, found in dry areas from semi-deserts to open fields and scrubland.

FEEDING It favours ants and beetles, usually catching them on the ground in short, quick dashes. It may also dig them from loose soil, or snatch them in dives from a perch rather like a shrike.

DISPLAY & VOICE The song, often given in a low, whirring flight, is rich and musical with much mimicry. Typical calls include a loud *weep* and quieter *cheep* and *wheet-wit* notes.

BREEDING It usually nests in a burrow made by a bee-eater or a souslik. Five or six eggs are incubated for 12 days, and the chicks fledge after 15 days.

MIGRATION European breeders move to sub-Saharan Africa in winter.

LENGTH 16.5cm (6½in)

WHEN TO SEE March to October
WHERE FOUND Breeds from Greece very locally to Black Sea; very rare elsewhere in Europe

A big, pale wheatear, easily confused with some forms of the northern Wheatear: check the structure, face, wing pattern, and tail; often wags tail more and runs more than Wheatear

Upright, big-headed, thick bill

Stripe over eye usually short, well-defined; male has dark line to bill

Rather uniform upperwing except for dark alula spot

Broad dark tail band with short 'stem', small dull white/buffish rump

Male, breeding
Note longer tail than female but shorter than northern Wheatear; often more exposed 'thigh' above leg joint than on Wheatear

Juvenile female, autumn
May be sandy or a colder clay colour

Adult, autumn
The darkest extreme: note wing pattern, sharp stripe over eye

White underwing with darker rim distinctive

Rock Thrush *Monticola saxatilis*

A small, sturdy, short-tailed thrush of mountain pastures and rocky slopes; spring males have bold colouring, other plumages mostly rusty and barred

Unique tail colour

Females, spring

Back feathers have white tips in spring

Rich tail and underwing colour diagnostic

Female, spring
Less white on back than male; grows darker in summer as feather tips wear off

Younger females more spotted above, paler below

Juvenile, autumn
Pale, scaly upperparts, white wingbar; pale orange underside

Male, spring
May have more white on back

Male, spring
Unique, beautiful pattern

Male, autumn
Pale spots wear away in spring

Very shy in summer; tame on migration

Although its subtlety of colour and pattern make the male Rock Thrush less obvious than might be expected, a close view reveals its true beauty. It is found in grassy Alpine meadows and on high, open slopes with plenty of rocks, dry stone walls, and scattered bushes, often higher up than the Blue Rock Thrush.

FEEDING It catches beetles and other large insects on the ground, often after a dive from a rock or wire. Sometimes it catches several insects in a shuffling run before returning to the perch.

DISPLAY & VOICE The male sings from a perch or in high, fast, fluttering song flights. The song is a soft, flowing warble with much mimicry, especially of the Chaffinch. Calls are a short, hard *tak*, *schak-schak* and a fluty whistle.

BREEDING The nest is placed in a crevice in a crag or wall; four or five eggs hatch within 14–15 days.

MIGRATION A few birds winter in north Africa, but most go south of the Sahara as far as Tanzania.

LENGTH 18.5cm (7¼in)

WHEN TO SEE March to September
WHERE FOUND Iberia, SE France, Alps, Italy, Balkans, E Europe

Blue Rock Thrush *Monticola solitarius*

Long-bodied, square-tailed, and noticeably long-billed, a thrush of rocky crags and gorges, where it can be elusive and hard to approach over difficult terrain, but not wary around human habitation

Long wings and tail, strong flight with easy, floating action

Spends long periods standing still on cliff ledges or boulders

Male

Juvenile

Long bill distinctive

Female

Female, spring
Combination of blue and barred brown; wings fade browner until moult from July to October

Wings fade to brown before autumn moult; much duller overall by late summer

Male
Dark at distance; close up in good light shows intense blue

Male, first year

While the Rock Thrush is a bird of high meadows, the Blue Rock Thrush is more likely to be found in warm, rocky places, including deep, wild gorges and coastal sites with cliffs and buildings. It also lives on large stone buildings that reproduce its natural cliff habitat, such as castles and even the Coliseum in Rome.

FEEDING Its main foods are insects and small lizards, with a few berries.

DISPLAY & VOICE Its song flights are more swooping, less powerful, than those of the Rock Thrush. It often sings from a high perch above a gorge with a far-carrying, rich, throaty warble, recalling a Blackbird or Mistle Thrush but with shorter, simpler phrases. The calls are a hard *tchuk tchuk* and a high *peep*.

BREEDING It nests in holes in rocks, walls, buildings, or pipes. Four or five eggs hatch in 12–15 days.

MIGRATION The Blue Rock Thrush is a resident or partial migrant, with some winter dispersal to milder areas in the Mediterranean region.

LENGTH 20cm (8in)

WHEN TO SEE All year
WHERE FOUND Widespread in Iberia and Mediterranean region, including major islands

Blackbird *Turdus merula*

Few birds have such a presence in and around places where people live and spend much of their time: gardens, town parks, woodland edges, tall trees, and farmland with hedges. In all of these habitats, and others, the Blackbird is a familiar neighbour. It draws attention to itself by its loud, persistent, and sometimes irritating alarm notes, especially if there is a cat or a Magpie about, its sudden outburst when scared into flight, and – much more welcome – its beautiful song. Of all the fine songsters of Europe, the Blackbird has the most 'musical' song in our terms, with beautifully modulated notes and phrases that seem almost capable of developing into human musical forms.

FEEDING The Blackbird eats a great many earthworms, and it is most characteristically seen hopping and shuffling across a lawn, stopping periodically to look and listen, lean forward and then suddenly seize a worm, pulling it from the ground only after a long struggle. It is also a noisy feeder in dry leaf litter, throwing aside piles of leaves as it searches for grubs. It eats various insects, their larvae, berries, and fruits – the berries especially in autumn – as well as occasional newts, fish and lizards.

DISPLAY & VOICE Blackbird displays are overlooked by most people, but they include a variety of postures in which the bird raises, depresses, or fans its tail, and puffs out its rump feathers. Its song, however, is obvious everywhere: a long, flowing sequence of varied phrases, most of which include fluty, throaty, musical notes which peter out into thin, scratchy, hesitant endings. The song has far less repetition than that of the Song Thrush, and is less wild, more varied, and mellower than a Mistle Thrush song. Typical calls include a staccato *pink pink pink*, especially at dusk; *clink clink* in alarm; a soft, 'comfortable' *chook*; a slightly vibrant *seee* in flight and a loud rattling outburst if suddenly frightened.

BREEDING The nest is a deep, thick cup of grasses and stems, with a mud inner layer covered by a fine lining. Three to five eggs hatch after 12–14 days and the chicks fly after 13 days, leaving the nest a few days earlier.

MIGRATION A frequent migrant, the Blackbird is often seen at coasts in autumn. Eastern birds move south and west in autumn.

LENGTH 24cm (9½in)

WHEN TO SEE All year in most of range; summer only in far north and east
WHERE FOUND Breeds Iceland, all but extreme N Scandinavia, and throughout rest of Europe; birds from east of Germany migrate in autumn to W Europe and N Africa

A common garden, woodland, and farmland thrush; all-black male unique, the female darker than any other brown thrush. Raises tail on landing, gives loud, hysterical rattle of alarm; not found in flocks

Adult male
Diagnostic yellow bill and eye-ring against black plumage

Female adult
Dark brown; bill yellow in summer

Male, first winter
Young male has dark bill, browner wings than adult

Female, first winter

Juvenile
Rufous brown with mottled breast, pale spots on wing coverts

Adult female
More rufous individual, with whiter throat; obvious dark mottles below but much darker than Song Thrush

Flight direct and strong, wings broad and round, tail long and full

Male

Female
Rounder wings than male

Ring Ouzel
Pale coverts

Blackbird

Pale greyish outer wing of adult male contrasts with black body in flight

Feeds with series of short, two-footed, bounding hops, runs, and pauses, bending forwards to pick up food

Typically raises tail and then lowers it slowly on landing

Fieldfare *Turdus pilaris*

A bold, handsome, gregarious thrush with a distinctively contrasting grey head and rump, a dark back, and flashing white underwings

Female (left) longer tailed than male (right). Flight strong, quick, often high; flocks have low, throaty, chuckling calls

White belly striking when perched

Grey rump, black tail

Bright white underwing coverts obvious (but compare Mistle Thrush); sharp contrast with dark chest

Yellow bill with dark tip often conspicuous

Female (above) has longer tail than male (below)

Handsome grey head, blacker mask, and orange-buff chest with bold black spots; flanks more solidly black in spring

This is a social bird all year round, but particularly familiar in its roaming, chattering winter flocks, when it often mixes with Redwings. It likes farmland with tall, old hedges and trees, as well as bushy heaths.
FEEDING It eats mostly insects and worms taken from the ground, with many berries in autumn and winter.
DISPLAY & VOICE Pairs defend their loose nesting colonies against predators, and males sing from a perch or in a song flight. The song is a mixture of weak chuckles, rattles, and squeaks. Calls include a nasal, slightly Lapwing-like *weep* and a chuckling, guttural chatter: *chak-chak-chak*.
BREEDING The female builds a heavy nest of roots, grasses, and mud in a tree; five or six eggs hatch in 10–13 days.
MIGRATION Fieldfares migrate south and west in autumn in flocks of 10–100 or more, often moving by day, and return to breed in spring.
LENGTH 25.5cm (10in)

WHEN TO SEE In N Europe, mostly April or May to September; in central Europe, all year; in W and S Europe, September to May
WHERE FOUND Breeds from E France and Alps region eastwards; in winter, widespread except in Scandinavia and N Russia where breeding areas are vacated

Ring Ouzel *Turdus torquatus*

A shy, wild, dark thrush of uplands, rocks, and coastal scrub. Small head, long square tail, long wings combine shape of Blackbird and Mistle Thrush, but typically slender

Male, spring

Long-winged shape recalls Mistle Thrush; longer, narrower wings than Blackbird

Pale feather edges make a light greyish 'flash' on upperwing (on Blackbird, tips of wings look pale, inner wings dark)

Female, first winter Dark, pale scaling and chestband often obscure

Male, spring

Male, winter Dull breastband, broader pale scales on body

Female Alps/Pyrenees

Female, spring Brown with pale breast crescent, pale wing panel

Juvenile Pale wing panel; black bars on rufous flanks

Male (below) Alps/Pyrenees broad pale scales

In spring and autumn many people see migrating Ring Ouzels on the coast, or along ranges of quite low hills, but as breeding birds they are restricted to higher ground with rocky tors, cliffs, and crags. The popularity of such places among walkers and climbers puts great pressure on Ring Ouzels in many hilly areas.
FEEDING They eat grubs, adult insects, and earthworms, supplemented in autumn by the berries of hawthorn, rowan, juniper, and other small trees.
DISPLAY & VOICE Males sing from high rocks in early spring, with loud, fluty, melancholy phrases of two to four notes, each clearly separated from the next. Calls include a rattle and a loud *tac-tac-tac* in alarm.
BREEDING Ring Ouzels build their cup nests in vegetation, on steep banks, or in rock crevices; the four eggs hatch after 12–14 days.
MIGRATION A scarce but regular migrant on coasts and hills away from breeding areas, often early in spring.
LENGTH 23–24cm (9–9½in)

WHEN TO SEE Late February to October or November
WHERE FOUND Breeds in N and W Britain, very locally Ireland; N and W Scandinavia, Pyrenees, E France, Alps, Balkans, Carpathians

Song Thrush *Turdus philomelos*

While Song Thrushes that breed in the shrubberies and hedges of parks and gardens do well, those that live on intensively farmed land find too little food and too few nest sites, and have been in steep decline for some time. They are justifiably garden favourites, with a most vigorous, energetic song that can include notes of unmatched clarity and purity.

FEEDING Earthworms and grubs are staple fare, but snails are important – especially in dry periods when worms are hard to find. In autumn and winter Song Thrushes eat many berries.

DISPLAY & VOICE Their displays are rather inconspicuous, but the song is loud and highly distinctive. It includes short phrases, some rich and fluty, others scratchy or strained, each repeated. The typical call is a thin *sit*; also a hard rattle of alarm.

BREEDING The nest, lined with hard mud or dung, is built in a tree, shrub, or creeper. Three to five eggs hatch after 10–17 days, typically 13.

MIGRATION Birds from northern and eastern Europe move west and south in autumn, returning in spring.

LENGTH 23cm (9in)

> **WHEN TO SEE** All year; in north and east mostly April to October
> **WHERE FOUND** Throughout Europe

Neat olive brown; lines of V-shaped spots beneath, on yellow-cream breast

Sexes alike

Often feeds with wings drooped

Juvenile
Streaks above less obvious than on Mistle Thrush

A small, neat, spotted thrush, with a rather plain head pattern and neat, V-shaped spots underneath. Loud, bright, repetitive, challenging song

Some races look dark

If flushed, typically flies low into nearest cover (Mistle Thrush flies off far and high)

Underwing soft orange-buff (white on Mistle Thrush, rusty on Redwing)

Longer tail than Redwing

Redwing *Turdus iliacus*

Redwings often mix with Song Thrushes and Fieldfares, when they look smaller and darker. In Britain they are mostly winter visitors, and flocks of autumn migrants can be heard calling at night as they fly west.

FEEDING They eat insects in summer and many berries in autumn and winter, but earthworms are an important part of their diet throughout the year. They typically forage on the ground, moving a few hops at a time between pauses.

DISPLAY & VOICE Males sing from high perches; most phrases are simple, short, and fluty, with a final light 'chuckle'. Calls include a rattle of alarm and the distinctive high, thin flight call, *seeee*, penetrating and far-carrying.

BREEDING Pairs may breed in small, loose colonies, each nesting in a bush or shrub and laying four to six eggs in a nest lined thinly with mud.

MIGRATION Icelandic breeders move to north and west Britain, Ireland, France and Iberia; others move south and west.

LENGTH 21cm (8½in)

> **WHEN TO SEE** In north and east mostly April–October; reverse in south and west
> **WHERE FOUND** Breeds Iceland, Faeroes, N Scotland, Scandinavia, and N Europe east from N Germany; central, S and W Europe in winter

Narrow wings; flight quick, flicking, more impetuous than other thrushes

Small, broad-winged, short-tailed in flight; flocks may recall Skylark but flight more fluent

Female

Male
Shorter tail than female

Underwing rusty-reddish, not usually very striking

This small, sociable thrush is dark above, silvery-white below, with neat lines of dark streaks; head pattern distinctive

Bright pale stripes above and below dark cheek patch

Feathers often fluffed up for warmth in cold winter weather

Yellow bill base

Adult female
Neat lines of streaks bolder in spring, rusty flanks and white vent

Juvenile/first winter male
Pale tips to coverts; less organized streaks on underside

Mistle Thrush *Turdus viscivorus*

This is a big, bold, vigorous thrush, quite capable of attacking an intruding cat near its nest – or, for that matter, anyone who walks too close beneath the nesting tree. In winter the males defend berry-bearing trees from all comers. In autumn, however, Mistle Thrushes form flocks, based around family groups, which gather wherever there are abundant berries or a feast of crab apples. These straggling groups, sometimes 30 or 40 strong, fly from treetop to treetop, staying in contact with their distinctive dry, rattling calls. They are seen far less often in small gardens than Song Thrushes, for they tend to prefer more open places that offer a good view, and plenty of room to escape with a high flight into the distance if disturbed. By contrast the Song Thrush is content to slip into the nearest shrubbery, or over the garden fence.

FEEDING The Mistle Thrush finds food on open ground, or in trees and bushes: mostly worms, insects, and various berries. It is less likely to join mixed flocks of other thrushes than the Song Thrush or Blackbird, and more vigorous in defence of a fruitful winter feeding territory.

DISPLAY & VOICE Mistle Thrushes sing from late autumn through the winter into the breeding season, even on the gloomiest of days. The song is loud and fluty with a strikingly wild and challenging quality. It is far-carrying and probably the loudest song of any European songbird. Each phrase is quite short and simple: it is less varied and developed than a Blackbird's song, but not so high-pitched nor so repetitive as that of a Song Thrush. The usual call is a dry, rasping, almost hissing chatter, with no equivalent from other common thrushes.

BREEDING These thrushes build their nests early in spring, often on quite exposed branches in tall trees. They line the outer layer of grass and stalks with mud, then add an inner lining of fine grasses. The three to five eggs hatch after 12–15 days, and the chicks fledge after a similar period in the nest.

MIGRATION Birds breeding in the north and east of Europe move south and west in winter, joining the local resident populations. Some from the west of Europe, including Britain, also move south, but most stay in their natal area all year. Migrating birds are generally much less obvious than the more social thrushes.

LENGTH 27cm (10½in)

WHEN TO SEE All year in S and W Europe; in N and E mostly in summer
WHERE FOUND Breeds in most of Europe except Iceland, N Scandinavia; a summer visitor to the north and east of Denmark and Germany

A large, bold, long-tailed and long-winged thrush, rather wild and aggressive

Surprisingly large and powerful in flight; almost dove-like shape

Underwing flashes even more brilliant white than Fieldfare

Long wings with row of inconspicuous pale spots; dull white outer tail feathers

Long, quite pointed wings momentarily close in bounding flight with long undulations, often above treetop height

Paler than other thrushes, with pale edges to wing coverts; greyer when plumage is worn

Breast spots black, round or broad crescent shaped, less aligned or V-shaped than on Song Thrush

Sexes alike

Variable white in tail

Typical stance upright, with small, round head held up, tail angled down

No sexual differences detected

Powerful on the ground, with long, leaping hops

Greyer, smaller in Corsica and Sardinia (above) compared with N Europe (left)

Juvenile (below)
Bold pale spots and dark flecks on back, pale wingbars and mealy head can be perplexing; dark marks on uppertail coverts; small spots below

211

Savi's Warbler · *Locustella luscinioides*

Being a small, brown warbler of extensive reedbeds, this species could be confused with the Reed Warbler, but its relationship with the Grasshopper Warbler becomes apparent with close observation. Its shape and song are both typical of the *Locustella* group of warblers.

FEEDING It feeds on insects, spiders, and snails which it finds in low growth; it may walk or hop on the ground within deep cover.

DISPLAY & VOICE Males sing from reed tops and chase each other across reedbeds, more visibly than Grasshopper Warblers. The song accelerates into a prolonged trilling buzz lasting half a minute or more: faster, duller, and less ticking than Grasshopper Warbler's; calls include a sharp *pit* or *zick*.

BREEDING A nest of grass stems and leaves is built in tall plants over water; three to six eggs hatch in 10–12 days.

MIGRATION These warblers move to Africa, probably south of the Sahara, for the winter, but they are rarely seen away from their breeding areas.

LENGTH 14cm (5½in)

WHEN TO SEE Late April to September
WHERE FOUND Very rare SE England; locally scattered through Europe south of Baltic where extensive reedbeds are found

A long-tailed, slim, small-headed, narrow-necked warbler found in reedbeds, often hard to see; similar to Reed and Grasshopper Warblers

Sings with head raised, throat fluffed out

Male

Male
Pale-breasted

Dark-breasted individual

Pale type, extreme | Pale type | Dark type

Undertail coverts are variable

Male

Female has shorter tail than male

Compare short wing coverts and tertials of Savi's Warbler (top) with River Warbler

Savi's

River

River Warbler · *Locustella fluviatilis*

While clearly a *Locustella* warbler, resembling the more familiar Grasshopper Warbler in its shape, actions, and song, this is a bird of dense, low thickets, from riverside vegetation to boggy willow, bramble, and birch scrub; it even lives in overgrown orchards and town parks. In recent decades it has spread westwards across north-central Europe.

FEEDING It finds beetles, spiders, and other small prey items in grass, bushes, nettles, and other low cover.

DISPLAY & VOICE Males sing mostly at night from quite high perches. The song has a rhythmic 'chuffing' or fast, pulsing 'sewing machine' pattern, with a sharp, metallic, insect-like quality.

BREEDING Pairs build their nest close to the ground in thick grass or a bush, laying five or six eggs that hatch after 14–15 days.

MIGRATION A few appear west of the usual range in late spring or summer; they all migrate to Africa in winter.

LENGTH 13cm (5in)

WHEN TO SEE Mostly mid May to August
WHERE FOUND Local in E Europe from S Finland and N Germany eastwards, south to Danube; a rare but increasing summer vagrant in west

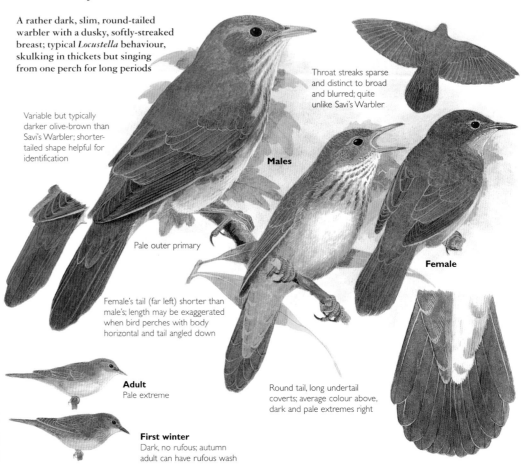

A rather dark, slim, round-tailed warbler with a dusky, softly-streaked breast; typical *Locustella* behaviour, skulking in thickets but singing from one perch for long periods

Variable but typically darker olive-brown than Savi's Warbler; shorter-tailed shape helpful for identification

Throat streaks sparse and distinct to broad and blurred; quite unlike Savi's Warbler

Males

Pale outer primary

Female's tail (far left) shorter than male's; length may be exaggerated when bird perches with body horizontal and tail angled down

Female

Adult
Pale extreme

First winter
Dark, no rufous; autumn adult can have rufous wash

Round tail, long undertail coverts; average colour above, dark and pale extremes right

Grasshopper Warbler *Locustella naevia*

Usually olive, some greyer or much yellower; breast unstreaked or with very fine marks, but shows slightly darker breastband

Males, singing
Head turns from side to side; yellow inside mouth often visible

At long range shows little contrast between upperside and underside, but throat paler

Female has shorter tail than male

Long, diffuse streaks beneath tail

Creeps mouse-like through grass; once located, may allow very close views

Juvenile female
Very neat with immaculate pale feather edgings and dark streaks; pale eye-ring moderately prominent; typically few flank streaks, but variable

Often fans tail in flight as it swerves and dives into cover

A slim, round-tailed, fine-billed, secretive warbler found where grass grows up through low bushes; usually located by its diagnostic song at dusk or in still, warm, cloudy weather, it may be seen when singing from a more exposed perch

Flight brief and low, diving down or sideways into thick cover

Pale edges to tertials widest on outer webs, slightly diffuse

Adult, autumn
Dull, yellowish individual

The Grasshopper Warbler is easier to locate and more familiar than its relatives in the *Locustella* group, and it acts as a yardstick with which the others can be usefully compared. It is a slim bird, with a narrow head and slender bill, a tapered or rounded tail, and long undertail coverts. Most distinctively, the male has a high, fast, ticking or reeling song that may continue without alteration for a minute or more. The vast majority of Grasshopper Warblers seen by birdwatchers are located by this song, but it is so high-pitched that those suffering from high-frequency deafness – common from middle age – cannot hear it at all. Grasshopper Warblers like grassy places with low bushes and small, clumpy thickets; they skulk in these, demonstrating a frustrating ability to avoid being seen. If a Grasshopper Warbler is flushed from cover it will usually fly off fast and low to the next clump and dive out of sight, often not to be seen again. But if it can be located without alarming it, a quiet and careful watcher may be rewarded with excellent views.

FEEDING Grasshopper Warblers eat mainly insects, taking them from low vegetation, from the ground beneath clumps of grass or dense brambles, or from the stems of reeds which they carefully search from top to bottom.

DISPLAY & VOICE Little of the display can be seen except for the male singing on his song perch. Typically this is within a small hawthorn or bramble bush, but he may gradually climb to a clearer perch at the top, or to one side. His song is a remarkable, prolonged performance. At long range it is a light, fast, metallic reel, like a fast freewheeling bicycle, but at close range the individual notes sound harder and more rattling. For a few moments at the beginning of the song the trill is slower and lower, working up to 'full speed', and it may seem to rise and fall as the bird turns his head. Calls include a quite loud, sharp *tik*.

BREEDING The nests are thick cups of grass stems and leaves, built on or near the ground in tussocks of grass, sedge, or rushes. Typically five or six eggs are laid and incubated for 12–15 days. The chicks fly after just 10–12 days.

MIGRATION A few are seen away from their breeding areas in spring and autumn, but this is not a commonly-seen migrant. All Grasshopper Warblers migrate south in autumn to spend the winter in west Africa.

LENGTH 12–13.5cm (4¾–5¼in)

WHEN TO SEE April to September
WHERE FOUND Widespread in Europe but absent from most of Norway and Finland, most of Sweden except for the Baltic fringe, and most of Iberia, Italy, and the Balkans

Aquatic Warbler *Acrocephalus paludicola*

Never common nor widespread, the Aquatic Warbler has in recent years become the object of real concern to conservationists, being one of the rarer and more endangered breeding birds of Europe. It nests in wet marshes with clumps of sedge and iris, and not in the reedbed habitats used by Reed Warblers; on migration, however, reedbeds with plentiful insect food are essential to its survival.

FEEDING It takes insects from leaves and stems in low vegetation.

DISPLAY & VOICE Males move around while singing from perches, or rise in song flights, descending with head raised and tail cocked. The song is a series of short, simple phrases quite unlike that of a Sedge Warbler. Calls include a hard *tak* and a soft *tucc tucc*.

BREEDING Nests in sedges, laying four to six eggs which hatch in 12–15 days.

MIGRATION A few reach extreme western parts of Europe, such as southwest England, each autumn. All migrate to west Africa for the winter.

LENGTH 13cm (5in)

WHEN TO SEE April to September; mostly in August in W Europe
WHERE FOUND Breeds in extreme NE Germany, Poland, very locally farther east

Central crown stripe, black and cream back stripes, streaked breast, spiky tail feathers

Breast and flank streaks stronger than on juvenile Sedge Warbler

Juvenile **Adult**

Black crown-sides of juvenile (above) reach bill, unlike adult (right)

Both tail coverts and tail show pointed tips, unlike Sedge Warbler

Note pale 'braces' and broad pale area on secondaries

Adult

Juvenile

Bright orange panels on coverts, unlike Sedge

Streaks on back, rump, tail coverts, unlike Sedge Warbler

Juvenile Sedge Warbler
Duller pale crown stripe

A striking, small warbler of reedbeds and wet scrub, often rounder-bodied, less crouched than Sedge Warbler, and showing more obvious leg

Sedge Warbler *Acrocephalus schoenobaenus*

In spring and summer, waterside sedge and nettle beds, banks of rosebay willowherb, hawthorn clumps, and reedbed edges are enlivened by Sedge Warblers in full song. They are less restricted to reedbeds than Reed Warblers, for while they often breed alongside them they are frequently found by quite small ditches or even thickets away from open water.

FEEDING They take insects from low down in reeds and sedges, from cereals, and from nettles or similar vegetation.

DISPLAY & VOICE Males perform a short, rising song flight (unlike Reed Warblers) but also sing from perches. The song is varied and fast; it has a scolding, irritated quality, with buzzing or chattering notes between more musical, rhythmic sequences. It often begins with a few rich, sweet notes. The call is a grating *tucc* or *churr*.

BREEDING Five or six eggs are laid in a deep cup of leaves, stems, moss, and cobwebs, near the ground or over water.

MIGRATION It winters in tropical Africa, and often stops off in bushy or wet places away from breeding areas.

LENGTH 13cm (5in)

WHEN TO SEE April to September
WHERE FOUND Breeds in most of Europe except Iceland, upland Scandinavia, Iberia, S France, and Italy; local in SE Europe

A small, dark, rusty warbler of waterside scrub and thickets; noisy spring song; striking pale stripe over eye

Juvenile
More buff than adult, faint chest streaks sharper

Juvenile
Wings broader than Aquatic Warbler

Song flight

Note rusty, unmarked rump; black, pale-edged tertials

Wing coverts darker than Aquatic Warbler

Adult
By late summer plumage wears to more uniform, browner appearance

Adult
Broad white stripe over eye, faint, soft chest streaks

Can look silky white against dark bush

Rump plain, with blunt tail feathers (slightly pointed on juvenile)

Moustached Warbler *Acrocephalus melanopogon*

A secretive and skulking bird, usually low down in dense waterside vegetation, with rich colours and a striking head pattern

May sing on exposed perches

Cocks tail, unlike Sedge Warbler

Dark crown, bright stripe over eye and rufous back distinctive; dark, rounded tail, contrast between white throat and rusty flanks are helpful features

Wingtips do not project as far as Sedge Warbler's

Black streaks on back in fresh plumage wear duller over time; clear, bright rump

Wingtip projection shorter than Sedge Warbler

Moustached

Sedge

Short tail and broad wings

Male
Bold dark cheek patch below white stripe, white throat

Juvenile
Duller throat

While the Sedge Warbler is a widespread, successful, and adaptable bird the similar Moustached Warbler is rather rare, occurring in restricted habitats in south and east Europe. It favours reed and sedge beds with scattered bushes.

FEEDING It prefers small beetles, but also eats water snails, both taken from dense vegetation over water.

DISPLAY & VOICE The song is long and rich: less scolding than that of the Sedge Warbler, thinner and softer with fewer jarring notes. It starts with distinctive low, pure notes recalling both the Nightingale and Woodlark. Calls include a low *trk* and a hard *tac*.

BREEDING Three to five eggs are laid in an untidy nest of leaves and stems lined with reed flowers and feathers, attached to plant stems over water.

MIGRATION Birds from the north of the breeding range migrate to the south of the range in winter; otherwise sedentary, unlike the Sedge Warbler. Very rare north of usual range.

LENGTH 12–13cm (4¾–5in)

WHEN TO SEE All year
WHERE FOUND Very scattered and localized in Spain, S France, Balearics, Italy, and Balkans; also Neusiedler See in Austria, locally Hungary; commoner S Russia

Cetti's Warbler *Cettia cetti*

An extremely skulking warbler, hard to see except in short flight across open space, but obvious loud, explosive song

Lurks in dense vegetation

Dark rufous brown with greyish underside, dull pale stripe of variable strength over eye

Cocks tail

Tail broad, rounded; may spread and 'wobble' in flight

Short, rounded wings

Pale throat and breast against darker flanks

Occasionally appears on open perch to give clear view, when quite tame

Broad tail of just 10 feathers; may be more rounded; dark rufous undertail coverts

One of the Asian bush-warblers with a range that extends into Europe, Cetti's Warbler is one of the few warblers resident in Europe all year. It can be approached very closely, but is usually so skulking that it gives scarcely a glimpse as it moves through low, dense, waterside vegetation. It is usually its joyous explosion of song that gives it away – but you may stare in vain at the place from which the song came, until you hear it again from a quite different location.

FEEDING It finds insects, spiders, and aquatic creatures deep within thick vegetation over or around fresh water.

DISPLAY & VOICE Males (and less frequently females) sing from low, hidden perches with sudden, loud outbursts. Two or three separate notes precede a short, fast, rich phrase: *chi-chuwee, chuweewewewewewe!* Characteristic loud, staccato *chip* call.

BREEDING Four or five eggs hatch after 16–17 days; the nest is hidden in reeds or in a bush interlaced with stems.

MIGRATION Resident; some wander in winter and colonize new sites.

LENGTH 13.5cm (5¼in)

WHEN TO SEE All year
WHERE FOUND S Britain, France, and Iberia east through Italy to Balkans

Reed Warbler *Acrocephalus scirpaceus*

Few species are quite so tied to a habitat as the Reed Warbler. It is not, perhaps, as specialized as the Dipper or the Treecreeper, or even the Bearded Tit, but nine times out of ten a Reed Warbler seen in summer will be in a reedbed. They do, however, feed in adjacent willows, even singing and sometimes nesting in bushy thickets, and migrants are often found away from water in unexpected places. These are the ones that can throw even experienced birdwatchers into temporary confusion. In summer a visit to a reedbed at dawn is well worth the effort, as the chorus of singing Reed Warblers can be unforgettable.

Because reedbeds themselves are so limited and widely scattered, Reed Warblers may be absent from wide areas but abundant in local pockets of suitable habitat. Reedbeds tend to dry out if not managed properly, causing a decline in Reed Warbler numbers; on the other hand reed growth on the margins of flooded gravel pits can draw them into new areas quite quickly.

FEEDING They pick insects, spiders, and a few small snails from the leaves and stems of reeds or waterside bushes, the preferred prey depending on its abundance at the time.

DISPLAY & VOICE Males sing from a few regular perches; unpaired males sing with the greatest persistence. A singing bird perches on a vertical reed stem in a dense or tall clump, often out of sight but in calm weather gradually creeping up into full view. Often heard where there are Sedge Warblers, the song of the Reed Warbler is usually quite distinct. It is less angry and scolding; more even, rhythmic and repetitive, with fewer abrupt changes in pitch and speed: typically a low, churring *kerr-kerr-kerr chirruc chirruc chrip chrip chrip chirr chirr chirr* and so on. Calls are mostly soft, low churrs and a harder, grating *churrr* of alarm.

BREEDING Nests are mostly in upright reed stems over water: deep, woven around several stems, and lined with fine grass and hair. Three to five eggs are incubated for 9–12 days and the young fly after 10–12 days. Many nests are parasitized by Cuckoos.

MIGRATION The European population moves to Africa in the autumn. Migrants stop off in thickets near or away from water, inland or at the coast, as well as in reedbeds. A few turn up in quite unsuitable habitats on offshore islands, especially in autumn.

LENGTH 13cm (5in)

One of the more common *Acrocephalus* warblers, mostly restricted to reeds, but some breed (and many feed) in willows and other dense vegetation. The most rufous of the plain brown 'reed' warblers, but individuals with slight variations can be mistaken for rarities

Unstreaked back and plainer face distinguish Reed from Sedge Warbler

Wingtips tend to be plainer than Marsh Warbler

Sings from reed stem, near top or more often well-hidden; dives out of sight among stems

Shorter wingtip projection than Marsh Warbler

Mouth of both Reed and Marsh Warbler bright orange-yellow, but Marsh sings with bill open wide, Reed less so

Can adopt dumpy shape when singing

Very slight pale line over eye, brighter eye-ring; no broad pale line like Sedge Warbler

Juvenile, first winter
A little more rufous than adult; plumage wears paler, sandier by autumn

Obvious white throat

Adult, late summer
Worn plumage sandier brown than spring, rump brighter

Compared to Marsh Warbler, tips of greater coverts project farther beyond primary coverts

Adult, spring
Typically slightly greyer on back than rump, which is more rusty; legs darker, greyer than Marsh Warbler

Facial expression differs slightly from Marsh Warbler: more robust and masculine, bill slightly longer, more pointed

Sometimes shows whitish over bill, creating effect of pale face stripe like Blyth's Reed Warbler

Marsh

Reed

Flies off low and fast over reeds

Reed

Marsh

Reed Warbler has seven obvious tips in shorter wingtip projection, Marsh Warbler has eight; paler edges wear away in summer

Marsh

Reed

Tail shapes vary, but Reed Warbler generally squarer than Marsh Warbler

Wings rounder than Marsh Warbler

Marsh Warbler *Acrocephalus palustris*

It takes more than a casual glance to be certain this bird is not a Reed Warbler, let alone the rarer Blyth's Reed Warbler: the *Acrocephalus* genus is notoriously difficult. Add to that its similarities with some *Hippolais* warblers and the rare possibility of hybridization, and this is clearly not an 'easy bird'. Song helps, but assessing the small differences in shape and pattern takes experience. The habitat can give some useful clues: it is less of a reedbed bird than the Reed Warbler, with a liking for rank wetland vegetation including nettle beds, thick growths of tall umbellifers, hawthorns, and many other plants from wild rose to meadowsweet. It does not often occupy vegetation growing from water, preferring the edge of a marsh.

FEEDING It takes insects, spiders, a few small snails, and similar prey from grass and other stems, or from bushes. Migrants may eat berries in autumn.

DISPLAY & VOICE Males sing either openly or from hidden perches in bushes or tall, thick vegetation, often by night (unpaired males sing most persistently, while paired males soon cease). Their song is greatly influenced by the songs and calls of birds heard in winter in Africa: the Marsh Warbler is a superb mimic of both these and European birds. The basic pattern of the song is fluent, flowing, and energetic. It is sometimes gurgling and undistinguished, much like that of a Sedge Warbler, but at its best it is rich and beautiful with Canary-like trills and throbbing, Nightingale-like phrases. At least 99 European and 113 African species have been recognized in its repertoire. Its calls are rather hard and loud, *tacc* or *tchuk*.

BREEDING The nest is built in tall bushy vegetation, but often close to the ground. It is shallower than a Reed Warbler's nest, and distinguished by more obvious 'basket handles' suspending it from upright stems (the Reed Warbler's nest is rounder, with stems growing up through the sides). The female lays three to five eggs; they hatch after 12–14 days and the chicks fly within 10–11 days.

MIGRATION This is a very late arrival in summer in western Europe, in itself a useful clue to identification. A few migrants appear on the coast in early summer and late autumn. The whole European population moves to south and east Africa in winter.

LENGTH 13cm (5in)

Primary projection (wingtip length) greater than on Reed Warbler

Compare also with Olivaceous Warbler

Tail usually more rounded than Reed Warbler's

A dull, pale, brownish warbler of dense vegetation near water; closely resembling other plain *Acrocephalus* warblers. Looks slim, usually holds itself very horizontally; movements more fluent and graceful than clumsier Reed Warbler

Juvenile, first autumn
This is the most rufous plumage, very like Reed Warbler, but legs paler, claws pale (Reed Warbler dark)

Acrobatic feeder in dense vegetation; climbs up to pick off insects, drops swiftly out of sight with vertical fall

Breeding adults
Variable colour recalls either wet or dry earth, sometimes faintly tinged greenish above, yellowish below, without rufous flanks of Reed Warbler; duller rump; cold whitish on chin, throat, and belly

Marsh

Reed

Bill fractionally wider than that of Reed Warbler

Tertials and primary tips very dark, often with sharper pale edges than on Reed Warbler; alula usually darker on Marsh

Greater covert and primary covert tips more equal than those of Reed Warbler

Juvenile, October
Relaxed, fluffed out in cool weather, as often seen on migration; head often rounder than Reed Warbler

Tends to sing more openly than Reed Warbler, from bush or rank herbage, not reeds

Adult
Taut, tightly-feathered shape in summer; flatter head with more delicate forehead/bill profile than Reed Warbler; angular nape

Legs paler, browner than Reed Warbler, but not always conclusive

Wing profiles of Marsh Warbler (red) and Reed Warbler (black)

Adult
Subtly narrower wings than Reed Warbler; tail has hint of paler edge but, as on Reed, may look translucent against the light

WHEN TO SEE From late April in E Europe, May or June in W, until September
WHERE FOUND Breeds from extreme SE England locally from France eastwards through central Europe, S Sweden, and Finland to most of E Europe and Russia

Great Reed Warbler *Acrocephalus arundinaceus*

This is essentially a 'giant' Reed Warbler that inhabits dense marshes with tall stands of stout reed, as well as small wet spots with reeds beside rivers or even along deep ditches. It is sometimes very hard to see, but often easy to hear when it sings boldly from an exposed reed top.
FEEDING It finds a variety of insects in and around the reeds and other marsh vegetation.
DISPLAY & VOICE Males sing from reeds, often sporadically by day as if they can't quite 'get going'. The full song is loud, and characterized by a rhythmic repetition of frog-like, croaking, grating, and strident notes: *krik krik krik, gurk gurk, eeek-eeek-eeek, kara karra chrruk chrruk* and so on. Also a hard *chack* and a *churr*.
BREEDING Three to six eggs are laid in a cylindrical nest attached to thick reed stems, and hatch within 14 days.
MIGRATION Winters in Africa; a few overshoot their normal breeding range on returning in spring.
LENGTH 19–20cm (7½–8in)

WHEN TO SEE March to September
WHERE FOUND Breeds much of mainland Europe south of Baltic but localized; also S Sweden; rare non-breeder in spring in Britain

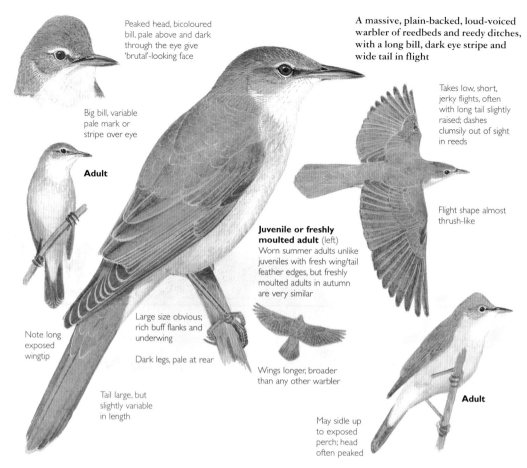

A massive, plain-backed, loud-voiced warbler of reedbeds and reedy ditches, with a long bill, dark eye stripe and wide tail in flight

Blyth's Reed Warbler *Acrocephalus dumetorum*

A westward spread has made this a more familiar bird in parts of eastern Europe than it used to be. It is a fine songster of willow and alder thickets beside rivers, overgrown ditches, and wet, bushy forests. Unless it sings it is a serious identification challenge for any birdwatcher.
FEEDING It finds insects, spiders, and snails both high in trees and in dense bushes, or on the ground beneath.
VOICE The song is energetic, rich, and full of mimicry, containing many pure, whistling sounds interspersed with harsh or chirping phrases. Its slow pace recalls that of a Song Thrush. Calls are a soft *thik* and *trrk*.
BREEDING Three to six eggs are laid in a compact cup-shaped nest in reeds, nettles or a thick bush, and hatch in 12–14 days.
MIGRATION The entire population moves southeast in autumn, to winter in south Asia. In spring a very few move farther west than the usual breeding range.
LENGTH 13cm (5in)

WHEN TO SEE May to September, a late spring arrival in N Europe
WHERE FOUND Breeds S Finland, Baltic states and eastwards through Russia

Icterine Warbler *Hippolais icterina*

A rather large, long-headed, spike-billed warbler with a square tail and short, abrupt undertail coverts; moves quite heavily through foliage

Bold dark eye in quite plain head

Long wings

Cutting edge and base of bill pale orange

Wingtips rather long compared with Melodious Warbler; also compare Olive-tree Warbler

Legs can be brown or bluish

Adult, spring
Dull, brownish type, white below

Juvenile

Typically pale between eye and bill; dark mark from some angles in some lights

Adult, spring
Green and yellow; long, bright bill; legs typically bluish

Yellow underwing, unlike Olive-tree Warbler

Some juveniles have this stronger head pattern

Pale feather edges create pale wing panel

Juvenile
Pale edge to tail; strong pale wing panel; no yellow on some individuals. Note long wing projection, long tail

Dagger bill, broad from above or below

Warblers are divided into several groups, each defined by its genus: the first word of the scientific name. *Hippolais* warblers are typified by this one: a medium-large warbler with a rather long, pale, spiky bill. It is stouter, squarer-tailed, longer-winged and bigger-billed than a Willow Warbler. It is a bird of open woodland and woodland edge – especially with mixed trees – and copses, spinneys, lines of bushes, and overgrown gardens.

FEEDING Insects are its chief food, with some fruit in late summer.

VOICE The song is far-carrying and energetic: a striking mix of harsh, strident and musical sounds, more rapid and powerful than a Marsh Warbler. Calls include short *tuk* notes.

BREEDING Nests are in fruit trees or bushes. Four or five eggs hatch within 13–15 days; chicks fly in two weeks.

MIGRATION It winters in Africa; a few regularly turn up on the east coasts of Britain in autumn.

LENGTH 13.5cm (5¼in)

WHEN TO SEE April to October
WHERE FOUND Most of Europe east of NE France from central Scandinavia, south to the Alps and Danube region

Olive-tree Warbler *Hippolais olivetorum*

A B C

Short flights between trees reveal long wings and square tail

Female
'C' dimension shorter on female than male

Proportion of A (tail projection) to B (wingtip projection) to C (tertial length) important in identifying *Hippolais* warblers

Female

Male
(drawn to same scale as female above)
'C' dimension long on male

A really big, long, heavy, spike-billed warbler of olive groves and fruit orchards, rather plain and greyish

Bill pale beneath; plain face except pale eye-ring

Male, spring
'A' dimension long on male: this is a particularly long-tailed warbler

Very large; very long bill; pale, olive-grey to brownish, with distinct pale wing panel

Very pale below, white on belly and underwing; white edge and tip to tail

Of the *Hippolais* warblers this is the biggest and most extreme in its long- and broad-billed, stout-bodied, wide-tailed form. It is genuinely a bird of dense olive groves, but it also lives in oakwoods, orchards, and almond plantations. It is typically skulking in its habits and hard to observe, but repays patience and careful watching from a little distance.

FEEDING It eats insects and other small creatures, as well as figs in late summer, finding them mostly within the canopy of thick, leafy trees but also on the ground.

VOICE A distinctively deep, throaty song is lower, slower, and more uniform than an Icterine Warbler's, combining deep notes with squeaks. Calls are mostly variants on *tuk* or *chuk*.

BREEDING Nests are made low down in olives, oaks, or smaller bushes. Three or four eggs are laid; other details are not accurately recorded.

MIGRATION Its wintering areas are in east and south Africa. In summer it is almost unknown outside its breeding range in Europe.

LENGTH 15cm (6in)

WHEN TO SEE May to September
WHERE FOUND Breeds in SE Europe, mostly Greece and Albania

Wood Warbler *Phylloscopus sibilatrix*

Of the more widespread leaf warblers this is the largest, most colourful, and also the most exacting in its requirements. It is restricted to tall, leafy woods with open spaces and dead leaf litter beneath the trees: hillside oaks and tall beech woods meet its needs.

FEEDING It picks insects and spiders from foliage and twigs in trees, usually in less active searching than a Willow Warbler. It also catches flies in the air in fluttering sallies.

VOICE The song mixes two distinct phrases. Most frequent is a sharp, metallic ticking that accelerates into a short, silvery trill: *ti ti ti tik-tik-tititrrrrrrrrrr*. Interspersed are sweet, sad piping notes: *peuw peuw peuw*.

BREEDING Nests are in leaf litter on the ground, domed, of grass and leaves. Up to seven eggs hatch in 12–14 days.

MIGRATION Moves to middle Africa in autumn. Few seen away from their breeding sites in spring or autumn.

LENGTH 12cm (4¾in)

WHEN TO SEE April to September
WHERE FOUND Widespread Britain, mostly in uplands, rare Ireland; across Europe north to Norway and Sweden and south to Pyrenees, S Italy and N Greece

Juvenile Tiny sharp white primary tips; broad whitish tertial edges

Female

Male Sings from leafy canopy or open branch beneath

Strongly yellow underwing

Adult female, spring Long tail is equal to length of wingtip projection; unusually female has the longer body

Bright yellow stripe over eye and dark green band through eye; variable amount of yellow on cheeks and throat contrasts with silky white belly

Male, spring Short body of male reduces length of tail beyond wingtip

Male Long wings unlike Willow

A long-winged, yellow-faced, white-bellied woodland warbler, easily found by following up its distinctive song in its breeding woods, but rarely seen elsewhere on migration

Bonelli's Warblers *Phylloscopus bonelli, Phylloscopus orientalis*

Eastern Bonelli's Warblers, breeding in the Balkans, are now regarded as a separate species from the Western Bonelli's Warblers of the rest of Europe. In the west they prefer oak woods, birch, beech, or mixed woods with plenty of clearings and bushy undergrowth. Eastern birds occupy similar areas, often in small trees on bushy slopes.

FEEDING They find insects in the foliage of trees, usually well up in the canopy or out at the edge.

VOICE Both sing with a loose, bubbly, fast trill, softer than a Cirl Bunting, quicker than Lesser Whitethroat. The Western Bonelli's call is a sharp, finch-like *chweet* or *hoo-eet*; the Eastern's is a hard, dry *tup*, *djip-djip* or *chip*, but also a wagtail-like *tsioup*.

BREEDING Five or six eggs hatch in 12 days in a ground nest under vegetation.

MIGRATION Western Bonelli's winter in Africa west of Chad; Easterns in northeast Africa. Otherwise both are rare outside their breeding areas.

LENGTH 11.5cm (4½in)

WHEN TO SEE April to September
WHERE FOUND Western breeds in Iberia, France, Italy, Alps east to Slovenia. Eastern breeds S Balkans and Turkey

Rather like duller Wood Warblers, with no yellow beneath, singing softer, bubbling, trilled songs in southern and eastern Europe, these are both real rarities on migration in northwest Europe

Western, male

Western, male (left) Greyish about head, greener on wings and rump, but brighter rump not easy to see

Pale over eye but little or no dark mark through it

Western, female Tertial edges whitish; secondary edges brighter green; greater covert edges and tips bright green; back duller; underparts silky white

Pale face, greyish cheeks, faint or diffuse pale stripe over eye, complete pale eye-ring

Eastern (right) Tends to be slightly greyer, rump contrastingly brighter, tertial tips whiter, whitish bar across coverts

Eastern, juvenile

Note on all Bonelli's 'double step' created by curved shape of feather edges, unlike other species

Eastern has more obvious pale line over eye and dark spot between eye and bill

Yellow underwing contrasts with white belly

Arctic Warbler *Phylloscopus borealis*

An obvious *Phylloscopus* warbler but stocky, thick-billed, and marked by a thin wingbar (sometimes two) and long, striking stripe over eye; hard call is valuable clue

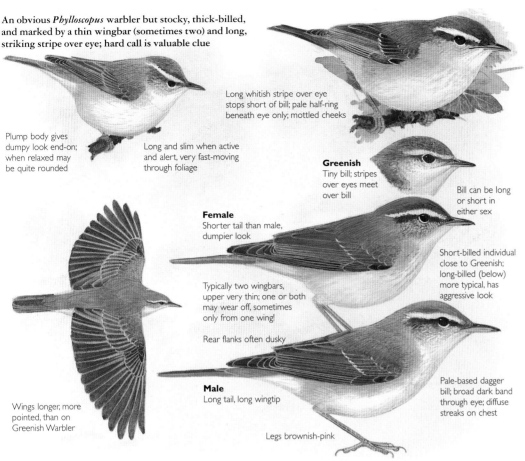

Plump body gives dumpy look end-on; when relaxed may be quite rounded

Long and slim when active and alert, very fast-moving through foliage

Long whitish stripe over eye stops short of bill; pale half-ring beneath eye only; mottled cheeks

Greenish
Tiny bill; stripes over eyes meet over bill

Bill can be long or short in either sex

Female
Shorter tail than male, dumpier look

Short-billed individual close to Greenish; long-billed (below) more typical, has aggressive look

Typically two wingbars, upper very thin; one or both may wear off, sometimes only from one wing!

Rear flanks often dusky

Male
Long tail, long wingtip

Pale-based dagger bill; broad dark band through eye; diffuse streaks on chest

Wings longer, more pointed, than on Greenish Warbler

Legs brownish-pink

Often easy to confuse with Greenish Warblers, Arctics are more northerly breeders but turn up as rare migrants on coasts in western Europe in much the same places. They nest in birch, poplar, or willow stands within conifer forest, usually near water, north to the tree line bordering open tundra.

FEEDING This is an active warbler, foraging with quick flits and hops through foliage for insects. It flies from bush to bush with a more confident, faster action than most warblers.

VOICE The song is loud, musical but repetitive, with a few short notes followed by a trill, lower but faster than a Wood Warbler's. The call is distinctive: a hard, Dipper-like *tzik* or *zrik*, or a quieter *zit*.

BREEDING The domed nest is built on the ground; six or seven eggs hatch in 11–13 days.

MIGRATION All Arctic Warblers winter in Southeast Asia, but a handful move southwest in autumn and appear in coastal woods and thickets.

LENGTH 10.5–11.5cm (4¼–4½in)

WHEN TO SEE June to September
WHERE FOUND Breeds extreme N Norway and Sweden, NE Finland, N Russia

Greenish Warbler *Phylloscopus trochiloides*

Wings shorter, more rounded, than on Arctic Warbler

Juvenile, September
Faintly yellow beneath

Short wingtip compared with Arctic Warbler

Single thin wingbar (compare with Chiffchaff); rarely faint pale tips form hint of second one; some have dark band across tips of primary coverts

Grey-brown legs

Striking stripe over eye, shorter than on Arctic but narrows over top of bill

Typically active feeder; often raises crown feathers

Stripe over eye flares at rear, unlike Chiffchaff

Rear flanks usually cleaner, whiter than on Arctic Warbler

Adult male

A small, rather bright grey-green and whitish warbler with a thin pale wingbar; has a rather large, rounded head, but small bill

Adult female, August
Typically rounded, but can look long and slim

Bill small, pale right to tip of lower mandible (Arctic has dark spot)

Greenish Warblers like woodland edges and clearings, with birch, aspen and scattered spruce trees. A slow westward spread has been noted for decades, but although singing birds have been recorded in summer west as far as Britain they have not bred there.

FEEDING They take small insects and spiders anywhere from the ground to the high canopy of trees, with agile, quick hops and leaps, fluttering from twig to twig. Wing flicking may help disturb insects which are then caught.

VOICE The song is fast, loud and lively, with a Wren-like pattern of chattering and changes in pitch. Calls include a cheery, chirrupy, squeaky note like a call of the Pied Wagtail or House Sparrow: *chi-vee* or *tsi-yip*.

BREEDING Nests are on the ground; up to seven eggs hatch in 12–13 days.

MIGRATION In autumn Greenish Warblers move to Nepal and India; a few always head west and turn up on northwest European coasts in August and September.

LENGTH 10cm (4in)

WHEN TO SEE April to October; a very few in May or June, more in autumn in W Europe
WHERE FOUND Breeds west to S Finland, Baltic States, Gotland, very locally along S Baltic

Chiffchaff *Phylloscopus collybita*

Warblers of the genus *Phylloscopus* are mostly small, slender, slim-billed, greenish birds, smaller and narrower-billed than *Hippolais,* shorter-billed and less brown than *Acrocephalus* and many *Sylvia* species. While these others mostly have simple, hard calls such as *tak* or *churr,* the *Phylloscopus* warblers have variations on a theme of *hoo-eet.* These differences are very useful in identifying and understanding these warblers, and the Chiffchaff and Willow Warbler, being so common and widespread, are the classic *Phylloscopus* benchmark species. They are also a considerable identification challenge in themselves.

Chiffchaffs like mature woodland, with a variety of mainly broadleaved trees. The canopy need not be dense and the undergrowth is typically much richer than in woods occupied by Wood Warblers. Migrating Chiffchaffs are often found in much bushier places, including insect-rich willow thickets, especially early in spring.

FEEDING Insects form almost the whole of their diet, mostly taken from high in trees; they also eat just a few berries in autumn.

DISPLAY & VOICE Male Chiffchaffs sing persistently in spring and also on migration, both in spring and autumn. They sing as they wander through the treetops. The song is an instantly identifiable repetition of simple, short, musical chirps on two or three notes. The sequence varies: *chip chap chip chep chep chap chap chip chap,* and may be interspersed with a quiet *churr churr.* The call is more nearly monosyllabic than the notes of the Willow Warbler or Wood Warbler, a simple *hweet.* In autumn shrill, descending *shlip* or *cheep* notes are heard.

BREEDING The nest is a spherical ball of grass stems and leaves with a side entrance, on or just above the ground in a bush, thick herbs, or creepers. Four to seven eggs are laid; smaller clutches replace those that are lost, and second broods are also smaller than the first. The eggs are incubated for 13–15 days and the chicks fly at two weeks.

MIGRATION This is one of the earliest migrants to move north in spring. Wintering areas include the southern fringe of Europe, and north Africa. In spring migrants often appear first near water where there are insects. In autumn they are frequent in similar places, such as willow thickets, and also turn up in gardens, often singing briefly. Northeastern races are scarce migrants in northwest Europe.

LENGTH 10–11cm (4–4¼in)

WHEN TO SEE March to October; all year S Europe; a few winter north to Britain
WHERE FOUND All Europe except for Iceland, upland Scandinavia, S Sweden

A generally common, widespread, small, slim warbler, characterized by rather dull olive-green colours, lack of strong pattern, dark legs, white crescent under the eye and frequent downward dip of the tail, as well as a diagnostic song

Adult, spring
Rounder head than Willow Warbler

Shorter wingtip than Willow Warbler

Adult, spring
Western/southern European race *collybita*: quite bright; dark legs

May show yellow feathers from underwing poking through

Adult

Juvenile (right)
Weak pale line over eye, sometimes stronger, yellower; pale crescent under eye

Sometimes hovers while picking flies from foliage

Adult, winter
Dull, brownish; legs spindly, very dark (only rarely paler)

Frequent downward bob of tail, unlike Willow Warbler

Spanish race *brehmii/ibericus* (top left) has longer wing than European *collybita* (below left)

Spanish race *brehmii/ibericus* can occur in a duller form (below)

Adult, spring (above)
Spanish race *brehmii/ibericus*: bright in spring, wings striped green and 'oily' brown, breast yellow; wingtip longer than most European birds, legs may be paler

Some birds are intermediate between northern and southern European forms, and not safely identifiable; *tristis* type (right), migrant or wintering in western Europe, merges into *abietinus*

Adult

Adult
North European race *abietinus*: colder, greyer than western birds

Western/southern European race *collybita*

Adult
Siberian race *tristis*: cold brownish, buff and white; may show curved, thin wingbar (compare Greenish Warbler); rare in western Europe. A few winter in England.

Siberian race *tristis* has very yellow or pale yellow underwing

222

Willow Warbler *Phylloscopus trochilus*

A slender warbler, widespread and common in bushes and open woods; song instantly identifies it in spring, call and leg colour help at other times. Slips easily through foliage with occasional forays after flies; very rarely winters in Europe, unlike Chiffchaff

Male, spring
May be rather dark olive above, whitish below with clean lemon-yellow wash; pale brown legs (rarely darker); unique song

Male, summer
Becomes duller with wear

Female's tail shorter (compare with primary projection) than male's

Juvenile female
Juveniles commonly seen in autumn; very yellow below and on long stripe over eye but some much paler; dark-centred tertials

Juvenile

Adult

Adult male
Northern Scandinavia: greyer above, paler below with a hint of yellow, but many indistinguishable from southern birds. Pale birds like this occur on migration in Britain

Juvenile
Yellow beneath wing

Compare structure of head (flatter in Willow), also tertial length (pale green) against primary projection (yellow, longer in Willow) and against tail length

Willow

Chiffchaff
Rounder head, thinner bill, spindly legs always blackish (rarely dark brown on Willow Warbler)

Male
Flight quick, low, jerky, into nearest thick cover: too small and quick to see detail

Female **Male**
Female has narrower, rounder wing, and shorter tail

Willow Warblers are, on average, a little longer, a little slimmer, a little 'cleaner-looking' and fresher than Chiffchaffs, but the differences are subtle at best. Fortunately, their song allows instant identification.

While Chiffchaffs arrive very early in northwest Europe – early March onwards in Britain, for example – Willow Warblers appear a month or so later. A few Chiffchaffs also remain in winter, while Willow Warblers do not. Habitat differences, however, are not clear cut. Willow Warblers are less likely to be seen within tall, mature, broadleaved woods. They like a variety of bushier places: low willows, mixed thickets of hawthorn, elder, young oak, and various other species growing in abandoned railway cuttings, hedgerows with standard trees, forest clearings, and woodland edges; all these are typical sites. Birch trees are especially favoured as they support thriving populations of insects.

FEEDING A light, agile, quick feeder, the Willow Warbler slips through foliage while picking insects and spiders from leaves and twigs. It also catches some in the air. A few berries are eaten in autumn.

DISPLAY & VOICE In areas where Willow Warblers return in good numbers each year their sudden chorus of song is one of the great joys of spring. Given from a perch, or while the bird feeds, the song is a particularly pleasing, silvery, lyrical phrase, starting quietly and high in pitch, strengthening in the middle and dying away to a slower, quieter finish. The pattern is Chaffinch-like, but the quality far less rattling. A Treecreeper's song has a similar pattern but is weaker and much less musical, and a Robin's song is stronger and more varied: Willow Warblers repeat their phrase over and over. The call is a more disyllabic *hoo-eet* than a Chiffchaff's.

BREEDING The domed nest is built on the ground, well concealed in vegetation. Four to eight eggs are incubated for 12–14 days. The chicks fly when 11–15 days old.

MIGRATION Willow Warblers winter in Africa, from Senegal and Ethiopia south right down to South Africa; the silvery song of a Willow Warbler is often heard from a tall African acacia tree. Migrants arrive in mid or late March in the Mediterranean, and in mid April in Britain.

LENGTH 10.5–11.5 cm (4–4½in)

WHEN TO SEE April to September
WHERE FOUND Breeds widely in Europe north from central France and Alps; also locally in Pyrenees and N Spain. Absent from Hungary, Bulgaria, Balkans, Italy, most of Iberia

Melodious Warbler *Hippolais polyglotta*

This species forms a natural pair with the Icterine Warbler: both are 'green' *Hippolais* warblers, they look very alike, and they replace each other geographically. The Melodious Warbler likes bushy places, tall scruffy hedges, narrow strips of roadside trees, bushy gullies, and waterside woods.

FEEDING It uses its large bill to seize insects from foliage and in flight, and pulls berries from stalks with a backward jerk. It is clumsy compared with a Willow Warbler.

DISPLAY & VOICE Males sing from both deeply hidden and exposed perches. The song begins with quiet, simple notes, followed by a long, fast, chattering of even pitch . Calls include a sparrow-like *tert* and hard chattering.

BREEDING The nest is a deep, tapered cup of stems and leaves; four or five eggs are incubated for 12–13 days.

MIGRATION All winter in west Africa. A few appear in spring and autumn on British coasts, mainly in southern and western England; Icterine Warblers are generally east coast birds.

LENGTH 13cm (5in)

WHEN TO SEE April to October
WHERE FOUND Breeds Iberia, France, Italy, Slovenia; absent from Mediterranean islands

A typical pale green-and-yellow *Hippolais* warbler, very like Icterine; rather heavy and thickset, spike-billed, strong-legged and square-tailed, with a pale facial pattern

Adult, breeding
Can be very yellow; pale wing patch usually weak

Wingtip quite short: it equals tertials on Icterine, but is shorter on Melodious

Pale eye-ring; pale yellow over and in front of eye, no obvious dark stripe

Bill quite long, broad, less dagger-like than Icterine

Legs dull brown or greyish

Broader-winged than Icterine Warbler

Quite heavy flight; shows subtle whitish edge to tail

Flatter-headed if alarmed, stretching

Typically round-headed, crown feathers sometimes peaked

Juvenile, autumn (left)
Dull, sometimes whitish below with very little yellow, but flushed yellow around throat, neck sides, and on pale wing panel; compare Marsh Warbler

Adult, autumn
Worn, dull, can be whiter below; primaries uniform, no pale tips (which show on Icterine)

Postures vary, but typically pot-bellied

Paddyfield Warbler *Acrocephalus agricola*

Warblers are best considered in generic groups, identified by their scientific names: the Paddyfield is an *Acrocephalus*, and so has similarities to Reed and Sedge Warblers. It breeds in reeds beside pools and lakes, sometimes far from a solid shore. It finds such spots in river valleys, or even surrounded by semi-arid steppe.

FEEDING It picks insects from stems of reeds and other aquatic plants.

DISPLAY & VOICE Males tend to sing in full view at the top of a reed stem. The song is quick and varied, more continuous than a Reed Warbler's and more even than a Marsh Warbler's. Calls are a short *chuk* and a soft, ticking note while feeding: *chek* or *chik-chik*.

BREEDING Three to six eggs are incubated for 12 days in a cylindrical nest suspended from reed stems or in the base of a bush.

MIGRATION Paddyfield Warblers go east to winter in India. A very few overshoot in spring to turn up north and west of their usual range.

LENGTH 13cm (5in)

WHEN TO SEE April to September
WHERE FOUND Breeds on western shore of Black Sea and eastwards through Asia; rare autumn vagrant in NW Europe

Adult male
Yellowish-rufous rump against dark tail; strong pale stripe over eye

Male
Both adult and juvenile males have much longer tails than females

Quite rusty above, buffy below, throat white, pale base to bill; rump can wear duller

A brownish warbler resembling a Reed Warbler, but paler, rustier, more well-marked on the head, shorter-billed and longer-tailed

Adult tail from above (far left) juvenile from below; undertail very dark; juvenile's has narrow, pointed feathers

Bristles beside bill sometimes visible in the field, unlike Booted Warbler

Striking head pattern, unlike Reed, Blyth's Reed, Booted or other difficult warblers; dark line above wide, whitish stripe over eye, broad dark eye stripe

Juvenile female
Shorter tail than male, very short wingtip; quite dumpy compared to elongated male

Bill distinctively two-toned

Male
Long shape when singing; yellow gape

Olivaceous Warblers *Hippolais elaeica, Hippolais opaca*

A small, neat, long-billed, flat-crowned warbler, with short undertail coverts, a deep belly and a long tail that is often dipped downwards as it moves through foliage, unlike similar Reed Warbler. Two forms, best treated as two species

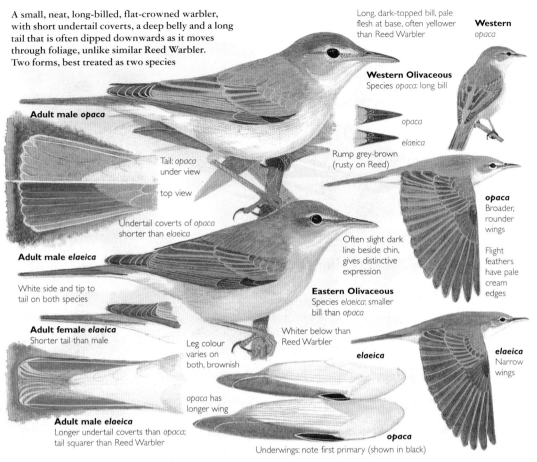

Adult male opaca

Tail: *opaca* under view

top view

Undertail coverts of *opaca* shorter than *elaeica*

Adult male elaeica

White side and tip to tail on both species

Adult female elaeica
Shorter tail than male

Leg colour varies on both, brownish

opaca has longer wing

Adult male elaeica
Longer undertail coverts than *opaca*; tail squarer than Reed Warbler

Long, dark-topped bill, pale flesh at base, often yellower than Reed Warbler

Western
opaca

Western Olivaceous
Species *opaca*: long bill

opaca

elaeica

Rump grey-brown (rusty on Reed)

Often slight dark line beside chin, gives distinctive expression

Eastern Olivaceous
Species *elaeica*: smaller bill than *opaca*

Whiter below than Reed Warbler

elaeica

opaca
Broader, rounder wings

Flight feathers have pale cream edges

elaeica
Narrow wings

Underwings: note first primary (shown in black)

A 'dull' *Hippolais* warbler, lacking green or yellow, the Olivaceous is a slender, long-billed bird. It prefers shrubby growth with tamarisk, figs, palms, and various broadleaved trees and bushes, in warm, dry places including dunes. Two closely similar forms are treated here as two species.

FEEDING It forages for insects in foliage with heavy hops and flits, and takes fruit in summer and autumn.

DISPLAY & VOICE The male sings from a hidden perch, but also while moving within a tree and sometimes in flight. The song has a characteristic cyclical pattern, a fast, rising and falling, chattering phrase repeated several times without pause. Calls include a sharp, hard *tack* and *tset-tset*.

BREEDING Nests are twig cups built in low bushes; two to five eggs hatch in 11–13 days.

MIGRATION Wintering areas are in Africa from Senegal east to Somalia, just south of the Sahara; very rare outside breeding range.

LENGTH 12–13.5cm (4¾–5¼in)

WHEN TO SEE Late April to September
WHERE FOUND Western breeds locally in Spain; Eastern in Balkans and E Europe, north to Hungary; rare vagrants elsewhere

Booted Warbler *Hippolais caligata* Sykes's Warbler *Hippolais rama*

Rather Chiffchaff-like *Hippolais* warblers, also much like Eastern Olivaceous Warbler but with short, usually distinct stripe over eye and darker lores. Two similar forms distinguished by structure and song

Male Booted (below) has longer tail than female (above)

Pale-edged tail, pale-based bill with broad base and paler legs separate both from Chiffchaff; longer tail, short wingtip, pinker legs, upward tail flick separate them from Eastern Olivaceous Warbler

Booted warbler, female
Small, spiky bill; pale-edged tail; pale-edged tertials; pinkish or greyish legs with darker feet

Male Sykes's (below) has longer tail than female (above)

Booted
Longer under-tail coverts

Sykes's
Shorter under-tail coverts

Booted
Short, round wings

Pale, 'milky-tea' colour, whiter throat, pale line over eye subtly edged darker above

Booted

Sykes's

Sykes's, female
Larger bill than Booted; tertials/secondaries often plainer

Greyish legs with darker feet

Underwings: note length of first primary (shown in black); underside of flight feathers darker than both Olivaceous Warblers

Sykes's
Longer, broader wings

Booted

Sykes's

The smallest of the *Hippolais* genus, and in some ways the most like a Chiffchaff, the Booted Warbler is also much like a small Olivaceous Warbler. It breeds in varied habitats from dry grassy places and bushes beside fields to green shrubs and riverside thickets. The central Asian form, Sykes's Warbler, is treated here as a separate species rather than a local race.

FEEDING Perhaps the most restless, quickest feeders of the *Hippolais* group, they find insects anywhere from the ground to treetops, and catch them in flight. They pluck berries acrobatically.

DISPLAY & VOICE Males sing a lot in spring, even at night, but their songs cease when the eggs are laid. The song is a fast, energetic, even phrase, that of Sykes's being harder in quality. Calls are simple *tsik, zet* or *chik* notes.

BREEDING Up to six eggs, laid in a strong cup of twigs and roots in a bush or herb, hatch after 12–14 days.

MIGRATION Most winter in India; a very few stray westwards in spring and autumn, rarely to western Europe.

LENGTH 11.5–12cm (4½–4¾in)

WHEN TO SEE May to September
WHERE FOUND Breeds in Asia, west to Lake Ladoga, south to Caspian Sea, rare vagrant in western Europe; *rama* east of Caspian, even rarer in Europe

Whitethroat *Sylvia communis*

Many of the *Sylvia* warblers are more or less restricted to southern and eastern Europe. The two whitethroats are exceptions, and they in particular (rather than the Blackcap and Garden Warbler) offer a taste of the *Sylvia* character to people living in more northern parts. Both species winter in Africa south of the Sahara, and they suffered enormous declines when the region suffered several successive years of drought. Their consequent rarity in northern areas like Britain helped to draw attention to the fact that protecting migrant birds on their breeding grounds is not enough to ensure their survival if they are at risk elsewhere, at other times of the year. In its breeding range, the Whitethroat likes dry heaths, the edges of woods and the fringes of fields where there are patches of rough ground. Poorly maintained hedgerows with gaps, and overgrown ditches with nettles and willowherb are ideal. They occupy what is too often described as 'waste' or derelict ground: the kind of habitat that develops around an old gravel pit or along a railway cutting, with a few tall trees but mostly low, bushy thickets scattered over open ground. And most of all, they enjoy a dense, thorny, food-rich bramble patch.

FEEDING The Whitethroat eats insects, in particular various species of beetles, which it finds by thoroughly searching low bushes and herbs. As the summer progresses it eats more berries, and by autumn berries make up most of its diet.

DISPLAY & VOICE Male Whitethroats define their territories by singing from perches such as bush tops and overhead wires. They frequently sing in short, fluttery song flights (which Lesser Whitethroats do not). The song is a short, fast medley of notes, both harsh and sweet, and of variable quality: *cheechiwee-cheechiweechooo-chiwichoo*. The calls are varied, including a churry *wichity wichity wichity*, a croaking *churr*, *wheet* and a hard *tak tak*.

BREEDING Whitethroats nest low down in shrubs or in tall herbaceous growth. Four or five eggs are incubated for 11–12 days and the chicks fly at 10–12 days old.

MIGRATION The Whitethroat spends the winter in Africa along the southern edge of the Sahara, in the semi-arid Sahel zone. Migrant Whitethroats turn up at many places in the autumn, including gardens where they eagerly eat honeysuckle berries.

LENGTH 14cm (5½in)

WHEN TO SEE April to September
WHERE FOUND Absent from Iceland, N Scotland, interior of Norway and Sweden, also S Spain, otherwise appears widely across Europe

Adult (right) has white tail edges and whiter underparts than juvenile (left)

Song flight from bush, hedge, or wire reveals thin tail

A quite large, long-tailed warbler of low bushy vegetation, with a puffy throat and large head; white tail sides, greyer head, white throat, rusty wings, and pale legs are distinctive

Male
Tail of female and juvenile shorter; note ample wings compared with Lesser Whitethroat

Male, spring
Head evenly grey, contrasting with white throat

Bright wing feathers fade to buff during summer

Jerky, erratic, excitable actions; steep climb at beginning of display flight

Male, first summer
Adult male fades to similarly dull colours in late summer

Female, autumn
Fresh pale tips to primaries

Bill thick, pale at base; legs pale (see Lesser Whitethroat); face pale (see Spectacled Warbler)

Juvenile
Bright, buffy, with striking rusty wings, dull tail edges, bright pale tips to primaries; white crescents around eye obvious

Female
Typical pose, diving into low vegetation

Female, breeding

Lesser Whitethroat *Sylvia curruca*

Male, spring

A neat, grey-brown, dark-legged, grey-capped warbler with a bright white throat, usually in dense shrubbery, betrayed in spring by its rattling song

Female, summer

Easily overlooked when feeding quietly in thick hedge

Rounder wings, shorter tail than Whitethroat

Juvenile
Extremely neat; dark edge to cheek and between eye and bill; bright white throat

Juvenile   **Adult**

Tail of juvenile duller than adult

Male, singing
Always moves to a new perch before next song

Male, spring
May be pinker beneath; angle of view and light varies strength of dark patch on ear coverts

Female, spring
Head paler than that of male, but pattern the same

Adult, September
Browner; ear coverts slightly darker than cap; note pale primary tips, plain wings, grey legs

Eastern race
Paler head and back, but grades into western form so not reliably identifiable in the field

Juvenile, September
Grey cap, dark ear coverts, white eye-ring; wing feathers edged paler (unlike adult); primaries have neat pale tips

While Whitethroats tend to live in low, bushy vegetation, Lesser Whitethroats go for taller, denser growth. So rather than selecting a straggly hawthorn hedge, for example, a Lesser Whitethroat pair may prefer a tall, dense, widely-spreading hedge of hawthorn and blackthorn, punctuated with large trees such as oak or ash. They are also often found in the denser thickets that grow along the edges of broadleaved woodlands. Partly because of this preference for taller, thicker growth, Lesser Whitethroats are less easy to see than Whitethroats – although the frequent singing of a territory-holding male may give away his position. In autumn they become more conspicuous, visiting elders and honeysuckle to feed on berries along with Blackcaps and Garden Warblers. They sometimes visit gardens, and quietly watching a heavily-fruited bush can be rewarding.

FEEDING Most of their diet consists of insects that they glean from foliage and twigs. They eat a lot of berries in late summer and autumn, and take nectar and pollen from flowers in spring.

DISPLAY & VOICE The male sings as it moves around a territory, often from perches hidden in the depths of a bush. Each song is typically given from a different spot within the thicket as it moves, rather than from a single perch. It never sings in flight. The song has a quiet, warbling introduction, often too quiet to be heard at longer ranges, followed by a hollow, wooden rattle, not nearly so metallic as a Cirl Bunting or Yellowhammer and harder, less bubbling, than a Bonelli's Warbler: a quick *chika-chika-chika-chika-chika*. Calls include a high, thin *seep* and a hard, low *tuk*, not so 'thick' as a Blackcap's *tak* note.

BREEDING The pair build a nest of grasses and stems in a bush or tree, fixed to creepers close to the trunk or among clusters of suckers, and line it with finer material such as rootlets, moss, some hair, and plant down. The four to six eggs are incubated for 11–14 days and the chicks fly when just 10–13 days old.

MIGRATION This is an unusual species in that even western populations migrate around the eastern end of the Mediterranean, rather than south through Spain. This means that in Britain migrants arrive and depart via the east coast rather than the south. They winter in Africa south of the Sahara, as far west as Niger.

LENGTH 13cm (5in)

WHEN TO SEE April to September
WHERE FOUND Breeds S Britain, N and E France and east through Europe, north to Norway, Sweden, and Finland; absent from Italy, S Greece, and Mediterranean islands

Subalpine Warbler *Sylvia cantillans*

One of the 'Mediterranean' warblers, but well distributed through Spain and Portugal as well as on the Mediterranean coastal strip, the Subalpine Warbler is found in bushy, thorny scrub with scattered oaks, as well as open slopes with low heath. It is small, long-tailed, lively, and attractive, but except in spring plumages it can be confusingly difficult to identify.

FEEDING Insects are its main food, but in autumn it also eats many small fruits and berries. It feeds both low in bushes and higher in oak and olive trees.

DISPLAY & VOICE Males sing from perches and in short, fluttery song flights. The song is musical, prolonged, and varied, but rather even-toned. Its calls are a loud *tec*, *tec-ec-ec-ec* and *krrrr*.

BREEDING The pair build a deep cup of grass stems and cobwebs in a bush or tree, and incubate three or four eggs for 11–12 days.

MIGRATION Subalpine Warblers winter along the southern edge of the Sahara; a few turn up north of the breeding range in spring.

LENGTH 12cm (4¾in)

WHEN TO SEE March to September
WHERE FOUND Iberia, S France, Italy, and Mediterranean islands, Balkans

A tiny, bright, lively, slim-tailed warbler of Mediterranean scrub

Juvenile Rather oval wings, longish tail

Tail of male

Southeast European race has darker breast, more abrupt white vent and belly

Male, spring Blue-grey and pink; white moustache, red eye

Long tail edged white; wings rather plain

Female, spring Pale ring around brick red eye-ring; more or less marked white moustache; first year has paler throat

Female, winter

Male, first winter (right) Grey-brown nape, browner cheeks; dull eye, pale eye-ring; ochre-brown edges on wings

Tail of juvenile

Juvenile Brown head; pale eye-ring

Tail of female

Spectacled Warbler *Sylvia conspicillata*

Of the various *Sylvia* warblers in southern Europe, this is one of the most restricted in range and habitat. It prefers very low heathy growth on dry, stony slopes, or short vegetation in saline depressions, and it avoids taller bushy growth or trees. Consequently it is both harder to find and generally less well known than most of its relatives.

FEEDING Although it eats some fruit in season, insects are by far its most important food. It creeps and hops among low growth, searching for food on the ground and among foliage.

DISPLAY & VOICE Males have a typical quick, fluttery song flight; they also sing from a perch. The song is a short, sweet warble. Calls are a high *tseet* and a variety of churring and rasping notes.

BREEDING The nest is built in very low vegetation; three to five eggs are incubated for 12–13 days and the chicks fly within 12 days.

MIGRATION A few are resident in the south of France and eastern Spain, but elsewhere it is mostly a summer visitor. It probably winters in north Africa.

LENGTH 12.5cm (5in)

WHEN TO SEE All year
WHERE FOUND Breeds locally Spain, Balearics, S France, Sardinia, S Italy including Sicily

A dark-headed, rusty-winged warbler that lives in very short Mediterranean scrub

White crescent above and below eye; white throat with blurred grey lower edge

Adult male has a long, slim, white-edged tail

Male Dark head with blackish face; wings show bright rusty panel

Female Male's tail is longer

Compared with Whitethroat wingtip projection is short, body small, head large, bill spiky, legs yellower

Female White above and below eye; pale line from eye to bill

Wings short and rounded; note rusty patch compared to Subalpine

Female, first winter Bill thin, pointed

Male, first winter

Male Dark cheeks frame white throat; pink chest; white underside of tail

Sardinian Warbler *Sylvia melanocephala*

Always lively but often skulking, drawing attention to itself by its calls, this is a slim, long-tailed, dark-capped warbler of Mediterranean regions

Male, breeding
White throat shines brightly against grey chest and black cap

Juvenile
Long thin tail and narrow-based, broad wings

Male, breeding
Always looks grey

Often cocks and flicks tail

White spots on tail

Male, breeding

Leg colour varies, often pinkish-orange

Male, breeding
Browner-backed individual

Female
Duller than male but pattern similar; dark head with red eye and white throat

Juvenile
Duller and browner; wing feathers edged paler; flanks dark

Female, first winter

Broad white band across underside of tail

Tail of juvenile

Tail of adult

Often crouches with head low, flitting through low vegetation or on ground beneath, with tail raised; also in taller trees

Warm, bushy slopes and rocky clifftops along Mediterranean shores have many characteristic scents and sounds. They include the machine-gun rattle of this little warbler, which calls over and over again as it skulks and scuttles about in the bushes, or flits across a footpath with its long tail waving, only to disappear from sight. But wait a while and it is bound to poke its head out of the top of a bush to check where you are, since Sardinian Warblers seem to be inquisitive and unable to keep still or entirely out of sight for long. Even so, it might be quite some time before you get a really good, clear view. Sardinian Warblers also move easily through the tops of oaks and pines, as well as varied landscapes of shrubs, herbs, rocks, and very often the shrubberies of gardens and hotel grounds. They are happy to occupy relatively built-up areas so long as some scrubby habitat remains. Their slim shape and long, slender tails make them distinctive even in a silhouette view or a brief glimpse.

FEEDING Sardinian Warblers find insects by active foraging, both through low scrub and on the ground. In autumn they also eat a variety of small berries.

DISPLAY & VOICE These birds occupy territories throughout the year, but their song is basically restricted to spring and summer. The male sings from an exposed perch on a tree or bush, and also in a short, fluttery song flight. The song is a musical warble with a mixture of harder, rattling notes. The typical call is like a fast, wooden rattle, repeated several times: *tratratratratratra* or *kre-kre-kre-kre-kre*. Males use the call all year; it probably helps them to identify themselves and defend their territories.

BREEDING The pair build a cup nest in a bush, using grass and plant stalks mixed with cobwebs, roots, and plant down, and lined with finer material. The female lays three to five eggs; they are incubated by both parents for 13 days, and the chicks fly when 12–13 days old.

MIGRATION Mostly resident; in eastern Europe, northerly birds move south in winter, while in western Europe a few move short distances, some to north Africa.

LENGTH 13.5cm (5¼in)

WHEN TO SEE All year
WHERE FOUND Widely in Iberia, locally S France, Italy, Balkans, and Mediterranean islands; occasional vagrant outside breeding range

Dartford Warbler *Sylvia undata*

I n southern Europe the Dartford Warbler is found on warm slopes with short, aromatic herbs and dense thorny scrub. In southern Britain it is confined to heaths with gorse and heather, mixed with a few pines. Being resident in Britain it suffers severely in hard winters, and this causes marked fluctuations in numbers.

FEEDING It takes various small caterpillars and other invertebrates from foliage and vegetation close to the ground.

VOICE Males in spring briefly abandon their skulking habits to sing from bush tops; the song is an even, rapid, churring warble. Calls are distinctively slurred, buzzy *jrrrr* notes.

BREEDING The birds build their nests of moss, wool, and grass, deep within gorse or heather. Up to five eggs are incubated for 12–13 days.

MIGRATION Although basically resident, Dartford Warblers make sporadic movements when high numbers put too much pressure on their food supply.

LENGTH 12.5–14cm (5–5½in)

WHEN TO SEE All year
WHERE FOUND On Mediterranean scrub and heaths, S Britain, NW France, Iberia, Italy, Mediterranean islands

Adult male, spring
Britain, May. Blue-grey head, browner-grey back, looks dark and slaty; equally dark brown-red underparts

A tiny, long-tailed warbler, small-billed but peaky-headed. Usually elusive and skulking, it may perch on bush tops or fly low with its long, slightly flicking tail trailed behind; its short, soft, buzzing churr is distinctive

Adult male
Long, slim tail; broad wings

Pale throat spots may align in slight moustache

Adult male
Northwest Spain, May

Pale outer tail feather

Female, first winter
Eastern Spain, January. Dull brown, dark eye

Tiny spiky bill

Juvenile male
Northern France, August

Adult female
Slightly browner than male; may look dull and greyer

Bright orange legs

Male, first winter
Wears duller in summer, often lacks white throat spots. Female paler below

Marmora's Warbler *Sylvia sarda* Balearic Warbler *S. balearica*

T hese two warblers are even more restricted in numbers and range than the very local Dartford Warbler, which has now replaced the Balearic in Menorca. They are birds of exposed coastal scrub and higher heathy places, often found among rocks with sparse herbaceous growth.

FEEDING They pick small insects, spiders, cocoons, and similar minute creatures and their young from foliage near the ground.

VOICE The song of the Marmora's is a short, sweet, twittering warble; that of the Balearic is more grating. The call of the Marmora's is a hard, throaty *tak* while that of the Balearic is a nasal *tsrek* or *trt*.

BREEDING The nest is a neat, deep structure of moss and grass, sited deep inside a small bush. Up to five eggs are incubated for about 12 days.

MIGRATION Balearic Warblers are resident, but some Marmora's Warblers move to the coastal areas of northwest Africa; rare vagrants in Britain.

LENGTH 13–14cm (5–5½in)

WHEN TO SEE All year
WHERE FOUND Marmora's: Sardinia, Corsica, small islands in area, and Pantelleria; Balearic: Balearic islands, but not Menorca

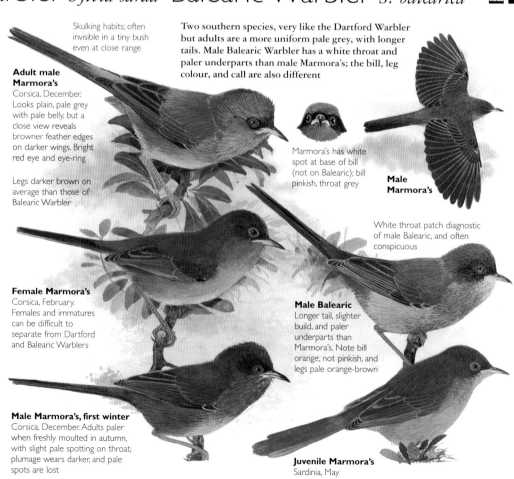

Skulking habits; often invisible in a tiny bush even at close range

Adult male Marmora's
Corsica, December. Looks plain, pale grey with pale belly, but a close view reveals browner feather edges on darker wings. Bright red eye and eye-ring

Legs darker brown on average than those of Balearic Warbler

Two southern species, very like the Dartford Warbler but adults are a more uniform pale grey, with longer tails. Male Balearic Warbler has a white throat and paler underparts than male Marmora's; the bill, leg colour, and call are also different

Marmora's has white spot at base of bill (not on Balearic); bill pinkish, throat grey

Male Marmora's

Female Marmora's
Corsica, February. Females and immatures can be difficult to separate from Dartford and Balearic Warblers

White throat patch diagnostic of male Balearic, and often conspicuous

Male Balearic
Longer tail, slighter build, and paler underparts than Marmora's. Note bill orange, not pinkish, and legs pale orange-brown

Male Marmora's, first winter
Corsica, December. Adults paler when freshly moulted in autumn, with slight pale spotting on throat; plumage wears darker, and pale spots are lost

Juvenile Marmora's
Sardinia, May

Rüppell's Warbler *Sylvia rueppelli*

A quite large, thick-necked, grey warbler, recalling Sardinian Warbler but much more restricted in range; pale edges on wing feathers always distinctive

Juvenile male

Juvenile female
Pale reddish eye; grey above, wings edged buff; legs yellowish

Pale primary tips wear off by August/September (above)

Female, first summer

Adult female, spring

Adult female, autumn (left)
Fresh primaries pale-tipped

Female's throat may be white (as above) or spotted dark (as left)

Tail of juvenile

Tail of adult female

Male, spring
Bold head pattern unmistakable

Bright wing feather edges; blackish alula

Restricted to extreme southeast Europe and Turkey, this warbler is normally found only on dry, sunny slopes with thorny bushes, aromatic herbs and scattered trees. It is less active than most smaller warblers, skulking but not especially shy, so it is usually quite easy to watch once located. It is often attracted to rocky places, especially where scrub grows up from deep clefts.

FEEDING It forages for insects within the cover of trees and bushes; it also eats berries in autumn.

DISPLAY & VOICE Males sing from a perch or in a 'parachuting' song flight. The song is a mixture of short, dry chattering phrases and clear whistles. Calls are a hard *tak* and a ticking, 'clock-winding' *tictictictictic*.

BREEDING The nests are solid structures of grass and stems, sited in thick, thorny bushes. Four or five eggs are incubated for 13 days.

MIGRATION The wintering area is in Chad and Sudan; in Europe very few turn up outside the breeding range.

LENGTH 14cm (5½in)

WHEN TO SEE March to September
WHERE FOUND Breeds S Greece, Crete, a few Greek islands, Turkey

---

Fan-tailed Warbler *Cisticola juncidis*

A tiny warbler: sandy, round-bodied and thin-tailed in side view, but broad- and short-tailed from rear, most easily seen in frequent song flights over grassland

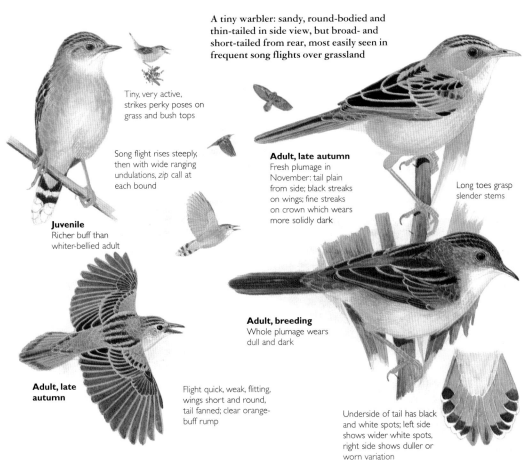

Tiny, very active, strikes perky poses on grass and bush tops

Song flight rises steeply, then with wide ranging undulations, *zip* call at each bound

Juvenile
Richer buff than whiter-bellied adult

Adult, late autumn

Flight quick, weak, flitting, wings short and round, tail fanned; clear orange-buff rump

Adult, late autumn
Fresh plumage in November: tail plain from side; black streaks on wings; fine streaks on crown which wears more solidly dark

Long toes grasp slender stems

Adult, breeding
Whole plumage wears dull and dark

Underside of tail has black and white spots; left side shows wider white spots, right side shows duller or worn variation

In Africa there are many species of *Cisticola* warblers, but this is the only one found in Europe. It requires large areas of grassland, damp or dry, with sparse bushy growth at most, and more or less bare earth beneath. Cereal fields make a fair substitute in places. It is typically seen beside coastal marshes or around the fringes of salt pans or shallow lagoons.

FEEDING It picks small insects from soft, level ground beneath grass or cereal stems.

DISPLAY & VOICE The best way to detect Fan-tailed Warblers is to listen for their distinctive song. Males have a high, undulating song flight, calling at each bound with a sharp, metallic, vibrant *tzip, tzip, tzip*. They also sing from a perch.

BREEDING The nest is a pear-shaped, bottle-like mass of grass and cobwebs with a high side entrance, fixed to tall stems. Four to six eggs are incubated for 13 days; the chicks fly at 14 days.

MIGRATION Resident; hard winters cause severe declines but periodic dispersals help populations recover.

LENGTH 10cm (4in)

WHEN TO SEE All year
WHERE FOUND Iberia, local W and S France, Italy and Mediterranean islands, S Balkans

Barred Warbler *Sylvia nisoria*

Big, heavy, almost clumsy for a warbler, and in summer almost resembling a Wryneck in some ways, the Barred Warbler is usually easy to identify but not to see. It skulks in low bushes and undergrowth, particularly in banks of brambles, thorn bushes, and overgrown woodland edges.

FEEDING It eats insects in summer and takes berries in autumn, using its large bill to pluck them from twigs with a firm grip.

DISPLAY & VOICE Males skulk even in spring, but they sing from trees (not while moving around as other *Sylvia* warblers do) or in a song flight. The song is a vigorous warble with much mimicry, especially of Red-backed Shrikes. The typical call is a hard or rattling *trrrt* or *tsak* like a Blackcap.

BREEDING The nest is often close to that of a Red-backed Shrike. Four or five eggs hatch within 12–13 days.

MIGRATION Barred Warblers winter in east Africa, but a few move west in autumn to reach northwest Europe, including the east coast of Britain.

LENGTH 15.5cm (6in)

WHEN TO SEE May to August; migrants in west August to September
WHERE FOUND Breeds very locally S Sweden and Finland, widely south of Baltic east from E Germany and N Italy

Male, first autumn
Dark eye, bill tip

Male (above) larger-bodied than female (below), giving longer tail projection

Female, breeding
Yellow eye; weak barring

Wing long, pointed

Grey arrows beneath tail diagnostic

A bulky, broad-tailed, pale-eyed warbler with stout legs and bill, that often moves heavily through low bushes. Thin, pale wingbars, dark bars under tail, and pale tail sides/corners are distinctive

Male, spring
Weak barring in first year, more in second, strongest in third

Grey legs

Male, first spring
Retains dark eye

Upperside of adult tail | Below

Orphean Warbler *Sylvia hortensis*

This large warbler is a bird of the Mediterranean and Iberia, found in open woodland and tall bushes on shrubby slopes, in olive groves, and in orchards. It is easy to overlook, but often attracts attention with its song.

FEEDING The Orphean Warbler eats mainly insects in summer and berries in autumn. It feeds in larger bushes or trees rather than scrubby undergrowth, picking food from the foliage.

DISPLAY & VOICE Males sing loudly, but usually from a hidden perch inside the canopy of a tree or bush. In western Europe the song is a loud, repetitive warble in short, distinct phrases; in the east it is flowing and varied, almost Nightingale-like at its best. Calls are simple hard *tak* or *tek-tek* notes.

BREEDING The nest is a well-built cup of grasses and stems lined with cobwebs and moss; three to five eggs hatch after 12–13 days.

MIGRATION Orphean Warblers winter in Africa; they are rare vagrants outside their breeding range.

LENGTH 15cm (6in)

WHEN TO SEE April to September
WHERE FOUND Breeds patchily Iberia, S France, Italy, Balkans, including Crete, but absent from other Mediterranean islands

Male, first winter
Dark, dull on head but dark cheeks contrast with throat; bright flanks

Male (above) has longer body, giving longer tail projection, than female (below)

Female, breeding
Pale eye

Broad, round wing, wide tail

Bill long and heavy

A big Mediterranean warbler with a dark head and obvious white throat; heavy bill and thick legs

First summer
Both male (left) and female (right) first-summer have dark eyes

Male, breeding
Blackish crown and cheeks blend into dark nape

Upperside of adult tail | Below

Blackcap *Sylvia atricapilla*

From a woodland thicket in early spring comes a rich warbling song: a rapid, throaty performance, initially subdued but quickly becoming a faster, louder outburst. The Blackcap is back. Yet while traditionally a summer visitor in Britain, the Blackcap has changed its habits and is now often seen in winter as birds from central Europe move west to replace UK breeders that fly south in autumn. These winter birds frequently appear in gardens, dominating smaller birds at the bird table.

FEEDING It eats insects and berries, plus food from bird tables in winter.

DISPLAY & VOICE Few displays are seen but the song is frequently heard: it has shorter phrases than the prolonged song of a Nightingale or thrush, and is more rushed. Calls are the hard, short *tak* notes typical of *Sylvia* warblers.

BREEDING The small, rounded cup of thin stems in a low bush holds four to five eggs that hatch after 10–12 days.

MIGRATION Most winter in the Mediterranean area and north Africa.

LENGTH 13cm (5in)

WHEN TO SEE All year, but most April to September; increasingly winter in W Europe
WHERE FOUND Open woodland, parks with plentiful undergrowth and shrubberies; all but extreme N Europe

Spring male
Fresh grey, becoming browner later in the season; striking black cap; grey above bill base unlike Marsh Tit or Willow Tit

Rear body looks silky white from below

Juvenile male
Duller and darker above and below than adult female, with darker cap

A large, thickset but sprightly warbler; can be sluggish in movements, especially if feeding on berry clusters on honeysuckle or elder; sometimes aggressive, noisy, with hard, abrupt calls and a brilliant song

Pointed outer tail feathers show this is a male

Wingtips of female equal tail coverts: male has longer body, tail extends farther beyond wings

Spring female
Bright red-brown cap, grey collar, olive-brown back

Male   **Female**

Garden Warbler *Sylvia borin*

An inhabitant of mixed woods and shrubberies with dense undergrowth, the Garden Warbler shows little in the way of colour but has a beautiful song. Even experienced birdwatchers have to see the singers to be certain some Garden Warblers are not Blackcaps, despite the slight differences 'on average' in their songs. Despite its name it is not common in gardens, although it will come to feed on honeysuckle and other berries.

FEEDING It eats mostly insects, with a variety of berries in autumn.

DISPLAY & VOICE The song is typically long, fluent, and rather less exuberant than a Blackcap's, without the slightly higher, fluty acceleration in the middle, but many are practically indistinguishable. Calls are a slightly softer *tsak* and a 'chuffing' *ch ch ch*.

BREEDING Four or five eggs hatch after 10–12 days; the chicks fly just 9–12 days later.

MIGRATION They leave for Africa in August–October and return in April.

LENGTH 14cm (5½in)

WHEN TO SEE April to September, a few in October
WHERE FOUND Open woodland, most of Europe except S Spain, N Scandinavia, most of Ireland

A relatively large warbler with a round head and stubby bill, otherwise few distinctive characters; soft and subtle in colouring, with a rich, flowing song

Male
Round head, thickish bill; notice the plain face with pale eye-ring and subtle grey patch on side of neck

Tail coverts of male extend beyond wingtips

Fresh plumage neatly edged paler buff on wing feathers; generally unmarked, soft olive-brown, paler beneath, with just a hint of a paler line over the eye and paler throat

Fast, flitting, rather Robin-like flight

Wingtips of female equal in length to uppertail coverts: male has longer tail/body extension beyond wings

Female
Gentle face with large eye a distinctive feature of the species

Fresh juveniles can look warm yellow-buff below, but become paler in time

Juvenile female

233

Goldcrest *Regulus regulus*

Tiny, fearless, often indeed simply ignoring people, the Goldcrest is a familiar bird of coniferous trees and thickets. It likes parks and gardens with yews and ornamental firs, and woods with spruce and silver fir (it is less attracted to Scots pine and larch). In winter it roams widely through low thickets of willow and alder.

FEEDING It picks tiny insects and spiders from twigs high in dense trees.

DISPLAY & VOICE The 'crest' is fanned in display. The song is thin, rhythmic, fast, with a flourish at the end: *tidl-de-ee tidl-de-ee tidl-de-ee tidl-de-ee-didl*, or *cedar cedar cedar* at a distance. Calls are needle-sharp, both less shapeless and more emphasized than those of a Long-tailed Tit: *seee seee*. Both song and calls are a test for high-frequency hearing loss: many people cannot hear them.

BREEDING A tiny nest of moss and lichen suspended from a twig holds up to 11 eggs; they hatch in 15–17 days.

MIGRATION Many northern breeders move south in winter; others are resident or wander short distances.

LENGTH 9cm (3½in)

WHEN TO SEE All year
WHERE FOUND Widespread breeder; absent from Iceland, N Scandinavia, S Spain and Portugal; winter visitor to much of S Europe

Yellow crown stripe often very thin in narrow black cap

Adult female
Yellow crown stripe

Tiny, dumpy, or quite slim; pale area around eye, faint dark moustache, two pale bars on blackish wing

Juvenile
Plain crown, pale around eye

Thin dark legs with paler feet

Forages high in trees; often hovers, catching insects in foliage

Male
Bright orange centre to crest, fanned broad and flat in aggression or display

Broad pale wingbar often has V-shape

Constant wing flicking reveals white underwing

A minute woodland bird combining some features of warblers and tits; oblivious to human presence, especially in autumn and winter when foraging low down in bushes and undergrowth

Firecrest *Regulus ignicapillus*

Through much of Europe the Firecrest is quite common, but in Britain it is much rarer: a treat in winter or at the coast on migration, and a rare find in summer. It likes mixed woodland with holly and oak, maples within conifer forest, and pure conifer stands, especially spruce.

FEEDING It eats similar food to the Goldcrest but often feeds in more open places. It is less restricted to conifers.

DISPLAY & VOICE Males display with their crown feathers widely spread. The distinctive song lacks the rhythmic repetition and flourish of a Goldcrest: an accelerating *zi zi ziziziziziii*. Calls are slightly lower and firmer, *zit* or *zizi*.

BREEDING The nest is an elastic cup of moss, lichens, and cobwebs similar to the Goldcrest's; up to 12 eggs are incubated for 15 days and the chicks fly when they are about 22 days old.

MIGRATION Mostly resident, but some move south and west; a few winter in southern Britain.

LENGTH 9cm (3½in)

WHEN TO SEE All year
WHERE FOUND Breeds very locally S Britain, widespread in Europe north to the Baltic and east to Baltic States, Bulgaria, and Greece

Adult female
Crown stripe rich orange-yellow; broad black band each side of crown; yellowish forehead, broad white stripe over eye may look wedge-shaped; grey cheek

Juvenile
Lacks crown pattern; dull pale stripe over eye

Female, winter

Male fans crown in display

Adult male
Centre of crown stripe orange-red; sides of neck more strongly bronzy-orange; whiter below than Goldcrest

Striped face pattern eyecatching head-on

A tiny woodland gem, revealing bright colours in close views but often a dull silhouette high in trees; song typically unlike Goldcrest's, calls subtly different

Spotted Flycatcher *Muscicapa striata*

A Spotted Flycatcher perches on open twigs or fences, high or low, and snatches insects on the wing with sudden, fluttering sallies. Tiny legs, upright stance, long wings, and a longish tail combined with a relatively flat head and thicker bill prevent confusion with brownish warblers

Sits upright with alert, intelligent air, often flirting its long wingtips, watching intently for flying insects

May drop to the ground to snatch an insect, but most prey caught in the air from a perch

Adult male

Juvenile

Long-winged and narrow-tailed in flight, with angular, straight-winged shape

Juvenile male
Silver-grey and buff feather centres on crown, ear coverts, back and scapulars produce pale-spotted effect above; wing feathers broadly edged yellow-buff

Pied Flycatcher
Note pale wingbar, white edges to tertials and short, white-edged tail

Adult female
Soft, fine streaks on crown; broader, gentle streaking on chest. Upperparts mostly plain, pale olive-brown to grey-brown, but wing feathers have obvious pale edges

Underside pale, silvery-white on belly: typically gives very pale-fronted look to upright bird

Males are longer-tailed then females

Short legs set well back, long tail and long head profile create upright, alert look on perched bird

Bill looks slim from side, but more substantial than most warblers'; viewed from above, has typically broad flycatcher form, with fine bristles at base

Not every bird with 'character' has obvious plumage patterns or bright colours. The Spotted Flycatcher is a clear case of a species with basically dull, brown plumage yet a really distinctive and individual appeal. It is bright-eyed, ever on the lookout for insects, lively, and active: always a joy to watch and welcome back in spring. It often draws attention to itself by its acrobatic flycatching behaviour despite its lack of conspicuous colours. Spotted Flycatchers are among the last of the summer visitors to Europe to arrive in spring: indeed, some of their traditional territories may not be occupied until the very end of May, or even early June – to the relief of those people who wait for 'their' flycatcher to return to a familiar garden or park perch. This is a bird of tennis courts, churchyards, and park benches; also of creepers on walls, the ivy around an old apple tree or an open-fronted nestbox fixed on a stump among the climbing roses and clematis flowers.

FEEDING A Spotted Flycatcher catches flies and other insects on the wing with a quick sally from its perch and a loud snap of its bill; it needs clear air and open space to see and hunt its prey. It may use perches as low as gravestones or as high as bare branches at the tops of trees. Unlike a Pied Flycatcher it often flies out from a perch, catches its fly, and returns to the same place.

DISPLAY & VOICE An undemonstrative bird, the Spotted Flycatcher has an insignificant song that most people would not recognize: a brief, thin, squeaky repetition of a few short notes. The calls are similarly short, scratchy, slightly creaky or squeaky in character: *tseet*, *sirr*, or *tsee-chup-chup*.

BREEDING The nests are often built among creepers, sometimes on old thrushes' or wagtails' nests; some sites are used year after year. They may use nestboxes or even half coconut shells placed out for them, but they need a shallow dish or open-fronted box, with a clear view for the incubating bird. Three to five eggs are laid, and hatch after 12–14 days; the pale-spotted chicks fly when 12–16 days old.

MIGRATION European breeding birds move into central and southern Africa, where Spotted Flycatchers are common in parkland and savannah regions. Most migrate in September, but a few stragglers remain into October, mainly at coastal sites; they return in May.

LENGTH 14cm (5½in)

Pied Flycatcher *Ficedula hypoleuca*

Male Pied Flycatchers are splendid little birds with a beautifully contrasted pattern. In autumn the males have a duller brown-and-white version of the same pattern, like summer females and juveniles, yet they remain striking, if unobtrusive in behaviour. They can be surprisingly elusive in the woods where they breed, and once the nesting season is over it is a virtual mystery where they spend the few weeks before they migrate: they simply melt away into the woods. Like Redstarts and Wood Warblers, which are often linked in the minds of birdwatchers – in Britain at least – as 'birds of the western oakwoods', they like leafy canopies above open, tree-shaded spaces. Overgrazed slopes under oak, with no undergrowth, are ideal. The clear space allows them room to manoeuvre when feeding.

FEEDING The Pied Flycatcher catches small insects, both in the air and on the ground after fluttering dives from a perch. It is more of a ground feeder than the Spotted Flycatcher. Protein-rich caterpillars are vital food for chicks in early summer.

DISPLAY & VOICE Males find territories around suitable nest holes or (especially in Britain) nest boxes. They sing frequently at first, with a simple, hesitant phrase, changing in pitch: *tri tri tri, trip trip, chichi-chwee*. Calls include a loud *hweet* or *whit* and a sharp *tic*, often combined as *whee-tic*.

BREEDING The nest is in a hole in a tree such as might be used by a Blue or Great Tit. Such holes are often in short supply, and many woods with thriving Pied Flycatcher populations had few or none at all until nest boxes were put up for them. This bird responds to their provision more positively than any other, occupying suitable woods in high densities once the shortage of nesting holes is no longer a problem. The nest is made of leaves, roots, and bark, lined with feathers, fine roots, and strips of soft bark. Six or seven eggs are incubated for 13–15 days. The chicks fly when 14–17 days old.

MIGRATION Pied Flycatchers spend the winter in west Africa, between the Sahara and the Gulf of Guinea. In spring they return quite swiftly, and relatively few stop off on coasts or at other places where they do not breed. In autumn, however, they are more widespread and northern birds are regularly seen on coasts in August and September. They are also seen in smaller numbers inland.

LENGTH 13cm (5in)

WHEN TO SEE April to October
WHERE FOUND Breeds N and W Britain; locally Iberia and France; more widely across N and central Europe but absent from Italy, SE Europe, and Mediterranean islands except Mallorca

A neat, quiet, round-headed bird with a bold eye in a plain face and some white in the wing; breeds in open woodland, but migrants often appear in low scrub or more unexpected places

Juvenile, August
Typically smaller white wingbar than adult female

Adult male typically has two white spots on forehead, but sometimes just one

Male, breeding

Female, breeding
First winter may have similar white pattern but slight individual variation

Male, breeding, Spanish race
Large single forehead patch, extensive white in wing, pale grey patch on back, no white in tail

Male, breeding
Tiny white spot at base of primaries beyond primary coverts varies

Male, first summer
Browner wings than full adult

Flycatches from a perch, but doesn't return to it; often forages on ground

Female resembles a small female Chaffinch with only one wingbar and white edges to tertials; not streaked like Spotted Flycatcher

Adult female
Small, narrow white primary patch may show or be hidden

First-winter female shows more or less marked dark malar stripe below bill

Female, first winter
Thin white streaks in wing, pale brown wings, white side to tail. Some (lower figure) have more white in wing including white primary bar

Short black legs

Adult female
Whiter below than immature bird

Male, first winter
Blacker wings than young female; some show pale edges to smaller coverts

Collared & Semi-collared Flycatchers *F. albicollis, F. semitorquata*

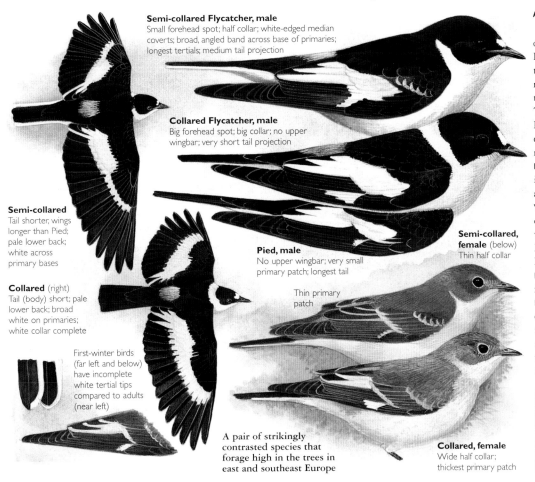

Semi-collared Flycatcher, male
Small forehead spot; half collar; white-edged median coverts; broad, angled band across base of primaries; longest tertials; medium tail projection

Collared Flycatcher, male
Big forehead spot; big collar; no upper wingbar; very short tail projection

Semi-collared
Tail shorter, wings longer than Pied; pale lower back; white across primary bases

Collared (right)
Tail (body) short; pale lower back; broad white on primaries; white collar complete

First-winter birds (far left and below) have incomplete white tertial tips compared to adults (near left)

Pied, male
No upper wingbar; very small primary patch; longest tail

Thin primary patch

Semi-collared, female (below)
Thin half collar

Collared, female
Wide half collar; thickest primary patch

A pair of strikingly contrasted species that forage high in the trees in east and southeast Europe

The eastern counterpart of the Pied Flycatcher, with even more contrasted plumage, the Collared Flycatcher lives in warmer regions with tall broadleaved woodland. It hunts more in the treetops, and less often on the ground than the Pied Flycatcher. The closely related Semi-collared Flycatcher, once considered a local race of the Collared, is mostly found in mountain woods of oak and hornbeam.

FEEDING They catch airborne insects in flycatching sallies, and take insects and larvae directly from foliage.

VOICE The song has a Robin-like quality, but is slower, more broken, with a mixture of harsh whistles. It is longer, but less loud, than a Pied Flycatcher's. Calls include a thin *eeep*.

BREEDING They nest in tree holes; four to seven eggs hatch in 12–14 days.

MIGRATION Wintering in Africa south of the Sahara, they move south through the Mediterranean in autumn, only rarely west of their breeding ranges; a very few 'overshoot' in spring.

LENGTH 13cm (5in)

WHEN TO SEE April to September
WHERE FOUND Collared east from W Germany and Italy through central Europe, north to Baltic islands; Semi-collared much more local, breeds Greece, Bulgaria, Turkey, Azerbaijan

Red-breasted Flycatcher *Ficedula parva*

One of Europe's most delightful small birds: tame and confiding, it flits about in the treetops, occasionally flying out to snap up a tiny insect in the air, when it reveals its distinctive white tail patches

Male, summer
Dark brown, greyish on the cheeks and neck, white beneath; orange-red gorget

Male, first summer
Reduced red

Bold white side patches on black tail distinctive in all plumages

Adult female
No grey or red on head; whitish throat above soft brown breastband

Autumn juvenile
Peachy-yellow or dull orange-buff below; pale wingbar; pale eye-ring

Often cocks tail

All the flycatchers are delicate, engaging birds, but in many ways this is the most charming of all. It is tiny, tame, active, and characterized by a boldly-marked tail. It prefers tall trees with thick undergrowth, near water, orchards, and vineyards.

FEEDING It hovers to glean insects and spiders from tree foliage, mostly within the middle canopy; it also catches a few in the air or on the ground.

DISPLAY & VOICE Its song is loud and far more attractive than that of other flycatchers; it has a silvery, melodious character as if combining Wood and Willow Warbler songs. Calls include a Robin-like but distinctive *zit* or *zirrt*.

BREEDING The nest is in a hole in a tree or wall. Five or six eggs are incubated for 12–13 days.

MIGRATION In winter Red-breasted Flycatchers move to southern Asia rather than Africa; they take an easterly route in autumn, but a handful go west instead and turn up as rare but regular migrants in western Europe.

LENGTH 11.5cm (4½in)

WHEN TO SEE April to October
WHERE FOUND Breeds S Sweden, Germany and east across NE Europe, also locally south to Balkans

Bearded Tit *Panurus biarmicus*

Unless forced to leave its native reedbed and roam more widely by lack of food, or too many individuals in one small marsh after a good breeding season, the Bearded Tit is a strict resident in freshwater (or slightly brackish) marshes with dense reeds. Consequently it has a very localized distribution, and it is easily wiped out from large areas if its fragile wetland habitat is destroyed.

FEEDING It eats small insects and seeds, taken from reed heads and the leaf litter at the base of the reedbed.

DISPLAY & VOICE Their displays are relatively inconspicuous in the dense reeds but Bearded Tits are easily heard, giving a variety of abrupt, ringing, or twangy notes, especially *tying* and *ping*.

BREEDING Nests are well hidden in reeds, over water, or in dense leaf litter, lined with reed heads. Five to seven or more eggs hatch after 12–13 days.

MIGRATION Usually resident, it sometimes makes wide-ranging winter movements over Europe.

LENGTH 16cm (6¼in)

WHEN TO SEE All year
WHERE FOUND In reedbeds (in winter, less often in reedmace and sedge); breeding range very erratic over Europe from Sweden, Britain, and Spain eastwards

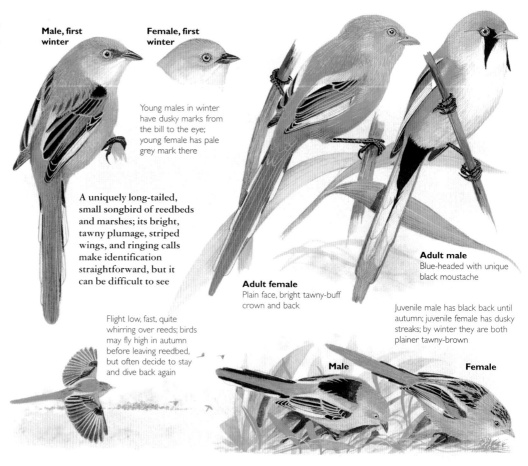

Male, first winter

Female, first winter

Young males in winter have dusky marks from the bill to the eye; young female has pale grey mark there

A uniquely long-tailed, small songbird of reedbeds and marshes; its bright, tawny plumage, striped wings, and ringing calls make identification straightforward, but it can be difficult to see

Flight low, fast, quite whirring over reeds; birds may fly high in autumn before leaving reedbed, but often decide to stay and dive back again

Adult female
Plain face, bright tawny-buff crown and back

Adult male
Blue-headed with unique black moustache

Juvenile male has black back until autumn; juvenile female has dusky streaks; by winter they are both plainer tawny-brown

Male   **Female**

Penduline Tit *Remiz pendulinus*

Unrelated to the typical tits, the Penduline Tit is a marsh bird that likes a mixture of reeds and reedmace, tall poplars, and willows. It is easily overlooked, but its characteristic call draws attention to it once learned.

FEEDING It forages for insects and a few small seeds, usually in reedbeds in winter but more widely in summer.

VOICE Its song is a rather quiet development of its high, thin call – a quite long, simple *tseeeh* or *tseeuh*, rather stronger and longer than the similar call sometimes heard from a Reed Bunting.

BREEDING The nest is extremely distinctive, made of reedmace down and poplar or willow catkins, fashioned into a deep pouch with a short entrance 'spout' near the top and hanging from the end of a thin twig. The six to eight eggs hatch in 13–14 days.

MIGRATION Birds from eastern Europe move south in winter; but southern birds are resident.

LENGTH 11cm (4¼in)

WHEN TO SEE All year
WHERE FOUND Mostly in poplars and willows, in damp farmland mixed with reed-fringed streams and ditches, in Europe and the Mediterranean fringe; spreading west; in reedbeds in winter

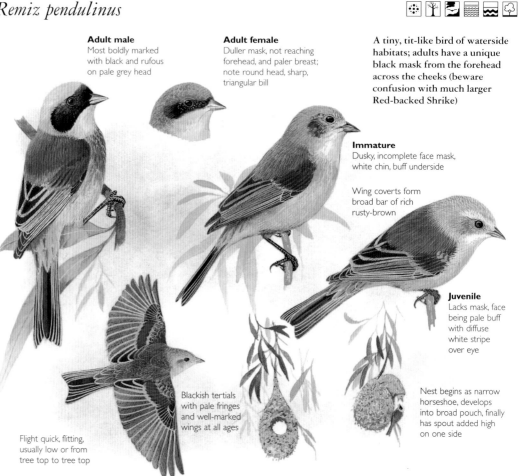

Adult male
Most boldly marked with black and rufous on pale grey head

Adult female
Duller mask, not reaching forehead, and paler breast; note round head, sharp, triangular bill

A tiny, tit-like bird of waterside habitats; adults have a unique black mask from the forehead across the cheeks (beware confusion with much larger Red-backed Shrike)

Immature
Dusky, incomplete face mask, white chin, buff underside

Wing coverts form broad bar of rich rusty-brown

Juvenile
Lacks mask, face being pale buff with diffuse white stripe over eye

Blackish tertials with pale fringes and well-marked wings at all ages

Flight quick, flitting, usually low or from tree top to tree top

Nest begins as narrow horseshoe, develops into broad pouch, finally has spout added high on one side

Long-tailed Tit *Aegithalos caudatus*

No other bird of bushes, trees, and woodland edge has such a combination of tiny bill, round body, and long, stick-like tail. The black, pink, and dusky white colouring is equally distinctive. Small parties usually move from bush to bush in a thin stream, calling as they go

Adult, British Isles
Dark race *rosaceus*,
with black head bands

Adult, northern Europe
Pale race *caudatus*, with
all-white head

Adult
Intergrades between
dark and pale
races occur

Juvenile
Typically white crown
but blackish upperside
lacks pink on scapulars

Adult
White-headed

Juvenile

Typical party flying in line
astern from tree to tree,
at roughly 30-second
intervals

Adult
Dark-headed

Adult, breeding
Black/pink/white plumage;
bright white edges to wing
feathers, white-sided tail

Adults, breeding
British type (left) grades
into grey-backed type
found in Italy (right)

Increasingly visits garden
peanut baskets; may feed
on ground, holding tail
slightly above horizontal

Nests in bush (left) or fork of tree
(above); nest is faced with lichen,
hair, and feathers; note yellow
gapes of young calling to be fed

Adults, breeding
Central Iberian/Corsican form
(left); Sicilian form (right)

Adult has long central tail
feathers, while juvenile
has short ones

Adult   **Juvenile**

Despite marked variation from place to place across Europe, all Long-tailed Tits are immediately identifiable: tiny, round-bodied birds with minute bills and long, slim, straight tails giving a distinctive 'ball and stick' shape. They are sociable birds, showing more of an affinity with the babblers than with the true tits. Whole families may roost together in their elastic nest to keep warm: not many European species exhibit such regular close body contact. In winter they huddle together in parties to conserve energy, for they suffer badly in hard weather, especially when heavy snow or spells of hoar frost and glazed ice lock away their food. Fortunately they have the ability to rear large broods of young, so they are able to 'bounce back' given a few years when the winters are milder.

FEEDING Most of their food is animal matter: tiny insects, including larvae of all kinds, and spiders and their eggs. They usually forage high in the tree canopy or in the top of the shrub layer, and rarely on the ground.

DISPLAY & VOICE Winter flocks are based around family parties; these break up in spring, so avoiding inbreeding, although previous adult pairs may remain together. Pair formation is a subdued affair: the two birds perch side by side and shiver their wings, the female slightly opening her wings a little away from her body. Voice plays little part: both sexes have a quiet, twittering song of no fixed pattern. They call all the time, however, to keep contact as they move through the trees: high, colourless, single or repeated *seee* notes, a soft but slightly metallic *pit* and a trilled *purrrp*.

BREEDING Despite their social nature Long-tailed Tits nest in solitary pairs, but additional 'helpers' may assist a pair to feed their large brood of hungry young. The nest is an extraordinary flask-shaped construction of moss, lichen, and spider silk, with a side entrance and a thick feather lining, usually in a low, thorny bush. Up to 12 eggs (highest numbers in the north) are laid and incubated for 13–17 days; the chicks fly at 14–18 days old.

MIGRATION Long-tailed Tits are mainly resident and do not usually travel far. In some years, however, the populations in north and central Europe build up to high levels; if there is then a shortage of food they are sometimes forced to move to other regions in spectacular irruptions.

LENGTH 14cm (5½in)

WHEN TO SEE All year
WHERE FOUND In mixed woods, farmland with tall hedges and bramble brakes, thickets, gardens, and parks. Almost all Europe except Iceland

Sombre Tit *Parus lugubris*

Even compared with a Great Tit this is a bulky little bird, and much bigger than the similarly-patterned Marsh and Willow Tits. It is also less acrobatic in its behaviour. It occupies warm forests of oak, willow, poplar, or conifers, as well as orchards, and favours slopes with a mixture of trees and big rocks.

FEEDING It picks caterpillars, grubs, and adult insects from trees and shrubs, or takes them from the ground beneath to be eaten on a nearby perch. It rips seedheads to pieces with its bill, acting more like a finch than other tits.

VOICE The song is a loud, repeated phrase, variable but with a buzzy effect: *chriv-chriv-chriv*. Calls include a deep, chattering, un-tit-like *chrrrt* or *chaerrrrr*, and a high *si-si-si*.

BREEDING A hole in a tree or among rocks is lined with feathers and wool. Five to seven eggs are incubated for 13 days; the chicks fly when 22 days old.

MIGRATION Resident, except for short-distance wandering in winter.

LENGTH 14cm (5½in)

WHEN TO SEE All year
WHERE FOUND Breeds south from Slovenia to Greece, and east to Romania and Turkey

Large black cap and broad black bib outline white cheeks

Its Great Tit proportions and black-white-brown-buff pattern with no bright colours make this bulky, bold bird unique within its range

Underside plain, pale buff

Very wide bib and cap striking in most views, especially from front, white cheeks create narrow wedge

Tail plain, greyish, with only faintest pale edge

Sometimes works its way up tree trunks in search of food like a Nuthatch

Wing feathers edged pale

Siberian Tit *Parus cinctus*   Azure Tit *P. cyanus*

The Siberian Tit is a bird of old, undamaged and undisturbed northern conifer forests with plentiful, streaming lichens, although it also breeds in birch forest. The largely central Asian Azure Tit prefers riverside willows and damp scrub.

FEEDING Both birds eat small insects, spiders, and seeds. In winter the Siberian Tit visits rubbish tips and sometimes bird tables to find food. It hides food among twigs and pine needles, to be rediscovered later during normal foraging.

VOICE The calls of the Siberian Tit are like a Willow Tit's, but less emphatic and not so drawn out at the end: *zi-zi tah tah tah* or *tchay*. The song is rasping and unmusical: *cheeurr cheeurr cheeurr* or *prrree prrree prrree*. The Azure Tit's call is more like that of a Blue Tit.

BREEDING Nests are in tree holes or rotten stumps lined with soft wood chips, moss, and hair; up to 10 eggs hatch in 15–18 days.

MIGRATION Both are resident.

LENGTH Siberian 13.5cm (5¼in); Azure 13cm (5in)

WHEN TO SEE All year
WHERE FOUND Siberian breeds mid Norway, N Norway, and Sweden, N Finland, N Russia; Azure breeds in Russia, only a very rare vagrant farther west

Siberian Tit is a big brown, grey, and white tit, with a large bib and cap outlining broad white cheeks

Siberian Tit
Back has grey bloom when fresh, wears off to brown

Wings and tail edged pale grey, wearing to dull brown (below)

Bib is rough, fluffy, and loose-looking

Siberian

Siberian Tit
Cap is dark brown, back warm ochre-brown

Azure Tits
Long slim tail; broad white band across blue wing; head pattern recalls Blue Tit, but crown white

Pure Azure Tits have white uppertail covert spots and pure white on tail

Azure Tit is uniquely blue and white, with no yellow; a faint yellow flush indicates a hybrid with the Blue Tit; most such hybrids lack yellow, but have a short tail and blue cap

Marsh Tit *Parus palustris*

No white nape or wingbars as on Coal Tit; black chin and more black in front of eye than Blackcap

Male
Long tail

Neat shape, with head in proportion (compare with Willow Tit below)

Flanks may look whiter in spring and summer, and on juvenile

Female
Shorter tail projection than male

Black cap and small black chin; plain brown upperparts, but variable pale wing panel can be quite marked; flanks typically less rich than on Willow Tit

Marsh

Adult

Willow

Juvenile

Difficult to distinguish from Willow Tit on sight, but loud, bright *pi-chew* call diagnostic. Looks grey, neat, smooth, glossy-capped

Hammers food and feeds on ground more than Willow Tit

Adult, Scandinavia, central Europe
Larger, greyer, with pinkish wash on flanks

Bright, lively and acrobatic in its behaviour, the Marsh Tit lacks bright colours but its subtlety is itself attractive. It poses a real identification problem, since it so closely resembles the Willow Tit: even experienced observers may confuse them unless they call. The Marsh Tit likes woods – often drier, with more mature trees, than the places favoured by Willow Tits. A beechwood is ideal, but it also lives in wooded parks or mixed woods.

FEEDING It eats insects and spiders in summer, and seeds, berries, and nuts in winter, including beechmast.

VOICE The song is rather infrequent: a rattling or bubbling *schip-schip-schip-schip*. The most distinctive call is a loud, explosive, bright *pi-chew* quite unlike the Willow Tit; also a buzzy *chicka-dee-dee-dee*.

BREEDING A hole in a stump or branch is used for nesting; six to nine eggs hatch after 13–15 days and the chicks fly when 17–20 days old.

MIGRATION Resident.

LENGTH 11.5cm (4½in)

WHEN TO SEE All year
WHERE FOUND S Britain, N Spain, and France eastwards, north to S Sweden and Norway; absent from most of Spain, Mediterranean coastal areas and islands

Willow Tit *Parus montanus*

Longer black cap and broader head than Marsh Tit; long head, short back

Large cap of Willow Tit duller black than that of Marsh Tit, but often not easy to judge; bib frequently more diffuse

A chunky, thick-necked, bull-headed bird with a big, dull black cap, large black chin, and typically warm-coloured flanks and pale wing panel. Deep buzzing call is a helpful clue

Willow Tit

Marsh Tit

Marsh Tit
Shorter head, longer back, usually less obvious wing panel

Central Europe
Intermediate form, less buff than British birds

Wide head, broad white cheeks unique to Willow Tit

Willow Tit
Pale edges to flight feathers most distinct in rear view

Flanks more strongly washed rusty-buff than Marsh Tit

Scandinavian race
Larger, paler, greyer, with whiter cheeks, whiter beneath

Looking like a stocky, slightly more richly coloured, less neat and tidy version of the Marsh Tit, the Willow Tit can be hard to distinguish. It is more often seen in willow and alder thickets and marshy places, in dense, tall hedgerows or bushy places beside heaths, and in upland birchwoods. Both visit gardens and peanut baskets.

FEEDING It seeks out insects, spiders, seeds, and berries, mostly rather low down in bushes.

VOICE Males sing a simple, repeated, liquid and sad *tsew tsew tsew tsew* and more rarely a short warble. Calls include a harsh, buzzing, thickly nasal *zi taah taah taah taah* or *eez eez eez*, which is rougher and deeper than Marsh Tit calls, and thin *zi zi* sounds. It never gives the *pi-chew* characteristic of the Marsh Tit.

BREEDING Holes are chipped out of rotten stumps; six to nine eggs are incubated for 17–20 days.

MIGRATION Mostly resident, but some wander short distances in winter.

LENGTH 12–13cm (4¾–5in)

WHEN TO SEE All year
WHERE FOUND From Britain and NE France east through central Europe, north through Scandinavia, locally south to Italy and Balkans; absent from Iberia and Iceland

Crested Tit *Parus cristatus*

In Britain, where Crested Tits are confined to Scotland, they are strictly pine forest birds. Elsewhere in Europe they like mixed woods, even beech forest or cork oak in places. They are not quite so easy to watch as other tits; they seem a little shyer and are less likely to make a close approach.

FEEDING Their chief foods are insects, spiders, and conifer seeds. In a few places they come to peanut baskets in winter. They store food, rediscovering it later during normal foraging in the winter and spring.

VOICE Crested Tits' songs differ little from their calls, which are distinctive and very useful in locating them. They have a quick, purring, stuttering character: *chr-r-r-r-rrrup* or *pt-rrr-r-p.*

BREEDING The female excavates a hole or enlarges a smaller one, and lines it with moss, hair, and wool. Six or seven eggs are incubated for 13–16 days; chicks fledge after 18–22 days.

MIGRATION Resident.

LENGTH 11.5cm (4½in)

WHEN TO SEE All year
WHERE FOUND Local in N Scotland; widespread Europe except extreme north and Italy; local in Hungary, Romania, Bulgaria

A tiny, lively, acrobatic tit of coniferous woods, located by its trilled, purring call and identified by its unique crest

Crest varies in length; black feathers edged white in streaky pattern

Adult
Black cheek crescent, black bib

Juvenile
Crest short, dull; face pattern weaker

At nest site: a hole excavated in a pine trunk

Often difficult to see as it forages in tall trees

Basically warm brown above, buffy below, with black and white head

Very active as it climbs trunks and branches looking for food

Coal Tit *Parus ater*

Tiny, almost Goldcrest-like, lacking bright colours but with boldly patterned plumage, the Coal Tit is a charming little bird. It prefers conifer trees, principally spruce, and is far less common in deciduous woods.

FEEDING Its feet and slim bill are adapted to searching the tightly-bunched, long needles of conifers for insects and spiders, their eggs and young. They also hide a lot of food in such places; they probably forget where, but find it again in the course of normal foraging.

VOICE Their songs recall a Great Tit's but are less strident: a rhythmic *teechu teechu teechu* or *tchuwee tchuwee.* Their calls also have a sweet, full quality: *chiwee* and *syew;* also a high, thin *seeee.*

BREEDING They nest in holes in trees and in the ground; eight or nine (rarely more) eggs are incubated for 14–16 days. The chicks fly when 19 days old.

MIGRATION Parts of northern populations move south in autumn, sometimes in very large numbers.

LENGTH 11.5cm (4½in)

WHEN TO SEE All year
WHERE FOUND Absent Iceland, N Scandinavia, otherwise widespread in Europe; largely a winter visitor in Mediterranean areas

Miniature, acrobatic bird of conifers, often visiting garden feeders; bold white patch on back of head diagnostic

Glossy black head with oblong nape patch, bold white cheeks, large triangular bib

Coal Tit (above) barely bigger than Goldcrest (below)

Adult, Europe
Continental birds are greyest on back

White wingbars prominent

Adult, Britain, Iberia
Back plumage more olive

Irish

British
Irish birds (far left) yellowish on cheeks and nape

Lacks blue, green, and yellow of Blue Tit; no central stripe on underparts

Fast, bounding in flight, with large head, short tail

Blue Tit *Parus caeruleus*

A bright, tiny garden favourite, looking blue, pale green, or light yellow according to the angle of view and light; usually looks plainer at a distance, brighter and more contrasted at close range

Blue cap, white ring around top of head, white cheeks and blue-black chin unique

Juvenile
The pattern is familiar but the colours are dull: yellow face and greenish cap most obvious differences from adult

Highly acrobatic when feeding

Spring male
At his brightest the male looks vivid blue on cap, wings, and tail; these areas become dull with wear

In winter roams woods, gardens, and hedges in mixed flocks with other tits and finches

Flight is quick, direct; lands on perch with sudden 'stop dead' effect

Short display flights are fluttering 'butterfly' glides from tree to tree

Deciduous woods with abundant caterpillars in spring provide the best breeding habitats for the Blue Tit. It also nests in gardens, often in nest boxes, but most suburban plots do not provide enough insect food for really successful breeding and brood sizes are consequently rather small.

FEEDING It eats insects, especially caterpillars, spiders, buds, and seeds; peanuts are garden feeder favourites. It takes food from the tips of thin twigs that cannot support heavier Great Tits.

DISPLAY & VOICE In spring the male's fluttering display flight involves frequent inspection of suitable nest holes. The song is a quick, stuttering trill, *tsee tsee tsee trrrr*, and most calls have a similar quality: *tseee-tseee-tseee tsit* and *churr-rr-rr*.

BREEDING Nests are made in tree holes and other cavities; 7–16 eggs take 12–15 days to hatch; the chicks leave the nest quietly after 16–22 days.

MIGRATION Resident, but some Continental birds winter in Britain.

LENGTH 11.5cm (4½in)

WHEN TO SEE All year
WHERE FOUND Mixed and deciduous woods, hedges, parks, and gardens; in winter also reedbeds. All Europe except Iceland, N Scandinavia

---

Great Tit *Parus major*

Compared with the Blue Tit, a bigger, heavier, bolder bird, marked by vivid white cheeks on a blue-black head and a long, dark stripe down the centre of the yellow chest; spring song is a strident, simple repetition of two notes

Male
Bold, aggressive at feeders, less agile than Blue Tit

Female has matt black on head, male deep blue

Some variation in the strength of green and yellow in Europe; Majorcan birds particularly pale

Female
Striking white cheeks and yellow underparts with black central stripe; white-sided tail

Female
Belly stripe narrows between legs

Male
Belly stripe broadens between legs

Typical pale V-shapes (tertials) on back

Juvenile
Dull cap, yellow cheeks, short central stripe underneath

Male
Longer body extends farther beyond wingtips than on female

Some English birds now pale yellow below, perhaps caused by a break in the food chain

The largest and boldest of the tits, the Great Tit is not so common as the Blue Tit in most gardens, nor in the mixed bands of birds that wander in search of food in winter.

FEEDING Its greater weight makes the Great Tit less acrobatic than the Blue and Coal Tits, and less able to gather food from fine twigs, so it tends to feed more on larger tree trunks. It also feeds on the ground, often under beech trees where it eats fallen beechmast.

VOICE The spring song is a loud, strident, but joyful repetition of simple notes, with many variations: *tee-cher tee-cher*, or *suee-suee-suee*. Calls include a loud *chink!* and many churrs and thin *seee* notes.

BREEDING It nests in holes in trees, walls, or preferably nest boxes; the 5–11 eggs hatch after 12–15 days. Like the Blue Tit, it rears just one brood each year.

MIGRATION Some Continental birds move south and west; British Great Tits are resident.

LENGTH 14cm (5½in)

WHEN TO SEE All year
WHERE FOUND Mixed woods, parks, and gardens. All of Europe except Iceland and highest mountains

Treecreeper *Certhia familiaris*

Now and then a Treecreeper is seen on a wall or even a cliff, but these are exceptions to the rule: it is a bird that normally spends its life wholly on the trunks and branches of trees. It likes parkland, mixed and deciduous woods, hedges with tall trees, and pine forest, especially where its range overlaps with Short-toed Treecreepers.

FEEDING It finds insects, spiders, and some seeds by diligently searching the rough bark of trees, typically climbing spirally up one trunk before flying down to the base of the next.

VOICE Its song is frequent, a little like a Goldcrest or Willow Warbler: thin, musical, and quick, with a terminal flourish. Confusingly, it often mimics the Short-toed Treecreeper. The call is a high, thin *tsreee*.

BREEDING Nests are in cavities under loose bark; five or six eggs hatch in 13–15 days; chicks fly in 13–18 days.

MIGRATION Resident, but some northern birds wander in winter, sometimes in large numbers.

LENGTH 12.5cm (5in)

WHEN TO SEE All year
WHERE FOUND Breeds Ireland, Britain, very local central and N Spain, N and E France, Italy; more widely through E Europe, Norway, Sweden, Finland, south to Balkans

Sometimes with mixed winter flocks of tits in hedgerows

A mouse-like, shuffling bird that creeps up trees, often spiralling around trunks and out onto smaller branches, hanging underneath, and probing with fine, curved bill

British race

Scandinavian race

Strikingly long pale wingbar in flight

Flies with weak, flitting action

Distinct pale shafts to central tail feathers

Note short, open V-shape of pale band across primaries (longer, more acute shape on Short-toed Treecreeper)

Each bird excavates a body-shaped recess in soft bark and sinks into this to roost with fluffed-out feathers

Pale primary tips of Treecreeper (below left) more even than V-shaped tips of Short-toed Treecreeper (below right)

Long, often forked, brown tail pressed against tree

Mottled brown upperparts, but some more spotted, looking like mottled lichen; more orange on rump; white underside

Scandinavian birds have brighter stripe over eye and whitest underparts; faintly washed buff and palest grey on British race

Short-toed Treecreeper *Certhia brachydactyla*

The treecreeper pair present as great an identification challenge as any in Europe: the best bet is to listen for the song or to go by distribution and habitat. Short-toed Treecreepers are more lowland birds than Treecreepers, occupying a variety of broadleaved and conifer woods, often with dense undergrowth.

FEEDING Like the Treecreeper it creeps about like a mouse on trees, searching for insects and spiders, insect eggs and pupae. It is perhaps slower in its movements, with more hops and tight spirals.

VOICE The song is distinctively different from the Treecreeper's: less flowing, less thin, a series of distinctly separate notes, *teet, teet, teet-er-oi-tit*. The call is more piping, less drawn out or thin, sometimes almost explosive, sounding like *sreeet* or *zeet*.

BREEDING It nests in bark cavities; six or seven eggs hatch in 13–14 days and the chicks fly in 16–18 days.

MIGRATION Resident in Europe; a rare vagrant in southeast England.

LENGTH 12cm (4¾in)

WHEN TO SEE All year
WHERE FOUND Iberia, France, north and east through Europe to S Denmark, Poland, Hungary; south as far as Italy, Balkans, Crete

Almost identical to Treecreeper; safest way to identify is by the song, since checking plumage features requires exceptional views and close attention to finest detail

Typically duller beneath than Treecreeper, greyish or browner on flanks, with contrasted white throat

Some birds have darker, more rufous-cinnamon rump than Treecreeper

Plain tail without pale shafts

Compared with Treecreeper has longer, more acute pale V across primaries

Typically pale edge of longest alula feather is complete and of even width

Sometimes looks rounder-bodied than Treecreeper, with tail more sharply angled into tree

Treecreeper

Black forms sharp, angled notch against upper edge of pale band

Smaller, smoother primary tips farther apart, irregularly spaced

Short-toed Treecreeper

Black forms blunt, saw-tooth shape against upper edge of pale wingbar

Larger, 'notched', pale primary tips close together and evenly spaced

Nuthatch *Sitta europaea*

British race (right)
Soft blue-grey and
pale orange-buff
with richer flanks

Much whiter
underparts in far
north and eastern
Europe (below)

A dumpy, large-headed bird
with a square tail, grey above
with black mask, unique in
most of Europe; noisy calls
echo around woodlands

Exceptionally
agile, does not
use tail as prop

Weak flight
with looping
undulations

Sweden

Spain

Black and white tail,
unlike Rock Nuthatch

Italy and Balkans
Bill narrow, pointed

As the Dipper is forever tied to the river, so the Nuthatch must live on the larger branches and boles of big trees, with only an occasional excursion to feed on open ground, old walls, or rocks, or even from a basket of peanuts.

FEEDING It eats a wide variety of insects, nuts, and berries, and often stores them in autumn. It wedges large insects and tough seeds in crevices in bark or walls so it can break into them more easily with its sharp, stout bill.

DISPLAY & VOICE It displays with strange head-waving movements in spring. Songs are loud, ringing, and far-carrying: a fast trill or a slower series of rounded, almost human whistles. The calls include a sharp *twit* like a pebble striking ice, and a loud, tit-like *sit*.

BREEDING The nests are in holes, usually in trees, with mud plastered at the entrance; up to 11 eggs are laid on a layer of bark and chippings.

MIGRATION Resident, but in northern Europe many may move south in autumn when numbers are high.

LENGTH 14cm (5½in)

WHEN TO SEE All year
WHERE FOUND Breeds from Wales and England east through S Norway and Sweden, sporadically Finland, east through Russia and south to Mediterranean

Rock Nuthatch *Sitta neumayer*   Corsican Nuthatch *S. whiteheadi*

Corsican is a small, neat nuthatch of
mountain pine forests; adult male
has black and white head stripes

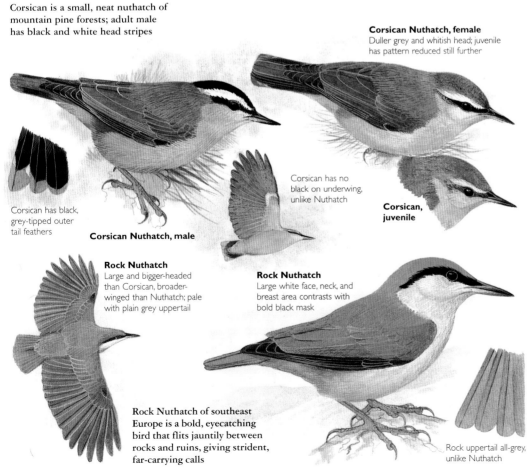

Corsican Nuthatch, female
Duller grey and whitish head; juvenile
has pattern reduced still further

Corsican has black,
grey-tipped outer
tail feathers

Corsican Nuthatch, male

Corsican has no
black on underwing,
unlike Nuthatch

**Corsican,
juvenile**

Rock Nuthatch
Large and bigger-headed
than Corsican, broader-
winged than Nuthatch; pale
with plain grey uppertail

Rock Nuthatch
Large white face, neck, and
breast area contrasts with
bold black mask

Rock Nuthatch of southeast
Europe is a bold, eyecatching
bird that flits jauntily between
rocks and ruins, giving strident,
far-carrying calls

Rock uppertail all-grey,
unlike Nuthatch

The Rock Nuthatch is a Balkan equivalent of the Nuthatch that lives on limestone crags and scattered hillside rocks; it is often conspicuous at Ancient Greek sites. The Corsican Nuthatch lives in mountain forests of Corsican pine, with 2000–3000 pairs confined entirely to Corsica.

FEEDING Rock Nuthatches eat mainly insects, with seeds and snails in winter. Corsican Nuthatches feed on pine seeds, except from May to August when they eat insects and spiders.

VOICE Rock Nuthatches are noisy birds: their loud trills, repeated at varying speeds, echo among the rocks and ancient columns and are audible at great range. Corsican Nuthatches have quieter trilling songs and a variety of short, whistled calls.

BREEDING Rock Nuthatches make flask-shaped nests of mud against rocks or on buildings. Corsicans nest in holes in pines; the holes are left unplastered.

MIGRATION Both species are resident.

LENGTH Rock Nuthatch 15cm (6in); Corsican Nuthatch 12cm (4¾in)

WHEN TO SEE All year
WHERE FOUND Rock Nuthatch along Balkan coasts, widespread in Greece, Turkey; Corsican Nuthatch confined to forests of central Corsica above 1000m

Wallcreeper *Tichodroma muraria*

No European bird is more beautiful than this unreal-looking creature. It may require a long search in difficult terrain, but when it appears the Wallcreeper is stunning, making all the trouble worthwhile. It may fly high onto a barren cliff or drop into a gorge, but if you can reach the spot you may get very close views. In winter Wallcreepers often move lower in gorges or appear on large buildings in the mountains. The bird bobs like a Dipper and constantly flicks its wings; it may remain in one spot for a long time, restlessly leap from rock to rock, or spiral away out of sight on rising currents of air.

FEEDING It captures insects and spiders under overhangs, beside rivulets or from the walls of buildings. Shady, moist spots are often preferred.

VOICE The elusive song is a repetitive, high whistle: *ti-tiu-treee*. The call note is a piping *tuee*.

BREEDING It nests in a hole in a cliff face, usually above the tree line but lower in eastern Europe.

MIGRATION Moves lower in winter.

LENGTH 16cm (6¼in)

WHEN TO SEE All year
WHERE FOUND Breeds in N Spain, S France, Alps, N Italy, Balkans; rare vagrant outside breeding range

Male, summer Variable black throat against grey

Female, summer Variable black throat with white surround

Male, winter Flicks wingtips as it feeds

An extraordinary, elusive, beautiful bird of gorges, mountains and crags, quite unmistakable. Flies with jerky, skipping action; short flights while feeding include spins, dives, and flutters

Outer tail of adult male

Female, winter Bill slimmer than male's

Juvenile Outer tail has smaller white tips

Spots on midwing more orange-red; from distance, white spots more obvious than red

Lesser Grey Shrike *Lanius minor*

The Lesser Grey Shrike is an open country bird of dry southern grasslands with scattered shrubs and trees. More contrasted and pinker beneath than the more northerly Great Grey Shrike, it looks more compact and less rangy.

FEEDING Like other shrikes it takes large insects, small reptiles, and small birds, but grasshoppers and beetles form the bulk of its diet. It requires drier, sunnier habitats than other shrikes mainly for this reason.

VOICE It is generally quiet, but in spring a varied, chattering, thrush-like song includes mimicry of other species. Unmated males sing loudly, while paired birds have a quieter song.

BREEDING The nests are neatly-made cups of twigs and rootlets; five or six eggs hatch after 15–16 days.

MIGRATION Most arrive from Africa in May and leave again in August to September, when many are seen in the eastern Mediterranean region.

LENGTH 20cm (8in)

WHEN TO SEE Mostly May to September
WHERE FOUND Breeds in extreme S France/N E Spain, but mostly Italy and SE Europe; rare vagrant north and west of this range, mostly in late spring

An eastern shrike with long wings, a relatively short tail and a stout bill. Large white patches on narrow, pointed wings are obvious, especially in flight.

Female, summer Forehead often slightly flecked; duller than male

Male, summer Broad forehead band and thick bill distinctive

Male

Juvenile Pale forehead but no white over eye

Broad white band on underwing, unlike Great Grey Shrike

Note long wings reach beyond upper tail coverts

First winter (September–October) Head pattern more like Great Grey; best identified by structure

Lesser Grey

Lesser Grey has diagnostic long wingtip; short on Great Grey Shrike

Great Grey

Great Grey Shrike *Lanius excubitor*

A large, long-tailed, short-winged shrike, often perched boldly on top of a bush or tree, or on a wire, flirting its tail or balancing by twisting it to one side

Some populations have paler bill base

May fly low, flat, and swoop up to bush, fly in bounds, occasionally rising very high; or in regular, thrush-like undulations

Adult
Single wing patch on some (right)

Adult
'Double' wing patch, often on female

Adult
Female may have faint chest bars

Juvenile
Faint pale bars above, browner bars below; pale base to bill; wingbar wears off, primary patch small

Adults
Single (top) or 'double' wing patch variations

Unmistakable grey/black/white, with black mask, grey back, black and white wings

Wingtip shows seven primary tips, four in a close group (compare with Steppe)

Race *homeyeri* (left) in Ukraine has structure of Great Grey but paler, more white on wing, tail and rump

Steppe Grey Shrike
Paler, with shorter body than Great Grey, longer wingtip, narrower wings with big white primary patch

Eight primary tips show on drooped wingtip: long tip is critical identification point

Wingtip partly hidden under tertials when tightly tucked up

First winter
Pale in front of eye; pale bill

Steppe Grey Shrike
Long narrow wings with huge white primary patch

**Southern Grey,
first winter**
Restricted pale bill base, pale grey bars below

Southern Grey Shrike
Underwing

Southern Grey Shrike
Body longer than Great Grey, wings shorter and broader, tail longer and slim; much darker above, deep pink below (fades whiter)

Southern Grey
Contrasting white throat and pink breast; bold white patch on outer wing only

Shrikes are exciting and charismatic birds, yet although they often perch on the exposed tops of bushes or even on overhead wires, they can be notoriously hard to find.

Great Grey Shrikes like heathland with scattered trees and bushes, forest clearings, and rough ground with scrub, from marshes to farmland. The similar Southern Grey Shrike *Lanius meridionalis* is a recent 'split' from the Great Grey Shrike, having previously been considered the same species. It occupies dry, warm, bushy places with scattered trees, olive groves, and orchards. The eastern forms of these shrikes are rather complex, and the inclusion of some within the Great Grey or Southern Grey remains contentious; one of these forms, the Steppe Grey Shrike, is best considered as a full species: *Lanius pallidirostris*. This is a rare migrant to the UK and Western Europe and has been confused with the Great Grey.

FEEDING The Great Grey Shrike takes large insects from the ground after gliding down from a perch; it also kills various mice, voles, and small birds. These shrikes often impale large prey on thorns or wedge it in twigs to make it easier to tear apart. The Southern Grey eats more lizards because of its southerly distribution, but otherwise the variety of food and feeding techniques are the same.

DISPLAY & VOICE Pairs may remain together all year, but in some areas males stay in the territory in winter, vigorously defending it against intruders, while females move away. Both sexes sing, the males to attract mates. The song of both species is a rough mixture of warbles and coarse, chattering notes. Surprisingly, very few calls are heard in winter.

BREEDING The nest of the Great Grey Shrike is a mixture of stems, roots, and moss, woven around twigs in a tree. Four to seven eggs hatch after 15–17 days. Southern Greys select the fork of a tree, or twigs in the canopy well out from the trunk, as the base for a bulky nest of twigs, and incubate five to seven eggs for 18–19 days.

MIGRATION Northern populations move south and west in winter; other populations include both resident and migrant groups. A few Southern Greys cross the Strait of Gibraltar in spring and autumn, but most remain in or close to their breeding areas in winter.

LENGTH 24–25cm (9½–10in)

WHEN TO SEE All year; migrant Great Greys in NW Europe September to April
WHERE FOUND Great Grey breeds through N and central Europe; migrates west to Britain and south to Mediterranean countries. Southern Grey breeds S France, widespread through Iberia; also Middle East. Rare vagrant outside this range

Woodchat Shrike *Lanius senator*

Shrikes have a distinctive habit of dashing across open spaces and swooping to new vantage points. The Woodchat Shrike is typical, but its flight is less undulating than others and it tends to choose higher perches. It prefers farmland with scattered trees, tall hedges, bushy slopes, or the aromatic heath, spiny bushes, and trees found in Mediterranean areas.

FEEDING It eats insects, especially big beetles, catching them on the ground after dropping from a perch. It also occasionally catches small birds.

DISPLAY & VOICE Pairs stand face to face, very upright, bobbing their heads and calling. The song is a prolonged mixture of warbles and harsh chatters. Calls are infrequent but varied, with a creaky *kiwik* and a hard *grack kjak kak*.

BREEDING The nest is lined with hair and wool. Five or six eggs hatch in 14–15 days; chicks fly in 15–18 days.

MIGRATION Woodchat Shrikes winter in Africa south of the Sahara.

LENGTH 18cm (7in)

WHEN TO SEE March to October; most vagrants May–June, August–September
WHERE FOUND Widespread in Iberia, S and E France; locally S Germany and south through Italy, Balkans, Greece, Turkey

Often perches on wire or high twig

A typical shrike, at times obvious, at times elusive, patterned with rusty cap and white shoulders

Adult male
Pale edges worn off; bold primary patch

Mark in front of eye looks whiter in some lights; buff/peach wash wears away

Female's head paler than male's, black reduced

Adult female
Fresh, pale edges, peachy wash

Adult female

Adult female
Worn plumage; white rump

Juvenile
Pale scapulars, buff greater coverts

Juvenile
Mainland birds have pale primary patch

W Mediterranean islands: no white wing patch

Underside of adult tail

Juvenile has pale rump/uppertail coverts; black tertials with rufous-buff edges (compare Masked Shrike)

Distinct bars on flanks

First winter

Underside of juvenile tail (compare with Masked Shrike)

Masked Shrike *Lanius nubicus*

This species is restricted to hot, sunny parts of southeast Europe in summer. It breeds in areas of cultivation with olives, almonds or other orchards mixed with stone pines and thorn bushes. It is frequently hard to see, perching inside or low down on the edges of bushes. A small, slender shrike, it is easily identified when adult, but in juvenile plumage it looks similar to a Woodchat Shrike .

FEEDING Like other shrikes it takes mostly large insects, with the occasional small lizard, often flying out from hidden, shady perches.

DISPLAY & VOICE The song is a fairly long, repetitive performance with a rhythmic, cyclical effect. Its calls include a short, dry rattle and a short, hoarse *chair*.

BREEDING The nests are well hidden in small trees or bushes, built of leaves and twigs and lined with a variety of softer material such as feathers or hair. Five or six eggs are incubated for about two weeks, and the chicks fly at 18–20 days.

MIGRATION A scarce migrant through the Middle East, to and from Africa.

LENGTH 17–18cm (6¾–7in)

WHEN TO SEE March to October
WHERE FOUND NE Greece, Turkey

Female
Pied effect; very long, dark tail

An unusual shrike, the only European one with a white forehead; white shoulders and buff flanks distinctive

Male
Fresh spring plumage: chest wears white by September

Male
Strikingly pied in flight

Dark parts of both sexes wear solidly brown-black by autumn

Female
Duller, greyer than male, but white forehead, neck sides, shoulders equally distinct

Juvenile
Dull, but broad white wing patch

Juvenile (below)
Centres of back feathers, scapulars, greater coverts all greyer, paler than Woodchat Shrike; tertials pale-centred, rump darker, tail blacker

Juvenile male
Bolder underwing than the Woodchat Shrike; female has smaller white outer panel

Juvenile undertail more pied than Woodchat Shrike

Red-backed Shrike *Lanius collurio*

A small, upright, colourful shrike, the male distinguished by a bold combination of black, grey, pink, and chestnut. Females and young are more puzzling but share the same hook-billed, strong-clawed, square-tailed character

Female
Grey-headed type

Thin white edge to tail

Males
Blue-grey cap and broad black mask, contrasting with bright, pale, pink-washed underside

Black tail broadly edged white

Juvenile

Juvenile
Rufous but barred on back, uppertail coverts, flanks

Female variably bright, plain rusty-brown above, tail narrowly edged white

Female
Brown-headed type

Male
A few (especially in eastern Europe) have thin white line at base of primaries

Despite substantial declines and reductions in range this remains the most 'typical' shrike throughout much of western and central Europe. In Britain its status has declined from that of a common breeding bird to complete absence, other than as a scarce spring and autumn migrant, mostly on the coasts. It is hard to say why, but the reduction in large insect prey must be to blame, more so than habitat change. Although it often occurs in warm, sunny areas with a good deal of bare ground, and is capable of breeding in quite dry, hot areas, the Red-backed Shrike can also survive in lush, green, damp places such as the small meadows and bushy hedgerows on the slopes of the Pyrenees and Alps.

FEEDING Beetles form the bulk of its prey, together with other insects. It also captures small birds and lizards. It chases insects in the air in rapid, twisting pursuits, but spots most of its victims on the ground and catches them after a long, descending swoop from a perch. It carries even small insects back to a perch to be swallowed, and impales large prey items on thorns or barbed wire. This has two functions: it creates a 'larder' of food for future use, but it also helps the shrike dismember large or tough meals.

DISPLAY & VOICE The male establishes a territory by moving around from perch to perch and singing; any neighbouring males call and sing in retaliation. The songs, often given from treetop perches or high wires, are prolonged but subdued warbles intermixed with a variety of harsh notes and much mimicry. If a female is nearby the song becomes a more excited, rapid twittering. Calls include loud, hard chirps: *cha* or *chee-uk*, and a short, hard alarm note: *tak* or *tek*.

BREEDING The nests are usually built in thick thorny bushes, sometimes in taller trees or even woodpiles. Various kinds of rubbish, from paper or cloth to string, are included in the structure, which is neatly lined with grass, hair, moss, or reedmace down. Three to seven eggs are incubated for 14 days; the chicks fly after a further two weeks.

MIGRATION European Red-backed Shrikes spend the winter in Africa, some in Kenya but mostly farther south. In Europe small numbers appear on coastal strips outside the breeding areas, especially in autumn.

LENGTH 17cm (6¾in)

WHEN TO SEE Mostly April to October; most breeding areas vacated by August or September
WHERE FOUND Breeds in S Norway, S and E Sweden, Finland and most of Europe south to N Spain, Italy, Balkans, but absent from Iceland, Britain and Ireland and most of the Low Countries

Rose-coloured Starling *Sturnus roseus*

Essentially Asiatic, with variable numbers reaching Europe from year to year, Rose-coloured Starlings live in semi-desert and dry grassland areas – although they must have access to water. They roost socially, often in reedbeds and bushes far from their favoured feeding areas.

FEEDING They feed on the ground, where they eagerly capture swarming grasshoppers and locusts. They also eat grapes, other fruit, and seeds in autumn and winter.

VOICE Their song is like a Starling's but even less musical; their calls are harsh, rasping notes.

BREEDING Colonies, often large, nest in holes in rocks and buildings. Three to six eggs hatch after 15 days.

MIGRATION In autumn most Rose-coloured Starlings move southeast, to India. Small numbers move northwest in spring and autumn. Occasionally large flocks invade southeast Europe in spring (but fewer and smaller flocks recently owing to declining numbers).

LENGTH 21.5cm (8½in)

WHEN TO SEE May to October
WHERE FOUND Sporadic breeder in Balkans, especially N Greece, Turkey; rare but regular in Italy and west as far as Britain and Ireland, rarely Iceland

A blunt-billed, dumpy starling of open ground; social, but as a vagrant usually solitary. Often seen in dull immature or non-breeding plumages

Female
Newly moulted: buff tips wear off to reveal pink

Juvenile
Contrasting pale rump

Some very pale juvenile Starlings mistaken for this species; check shape and colours of bill

Flight like Starling but wings more tapered at base, less triangular

Juvenile
Dark eye in plain face; round head; blunt, thick yellow bill

Remains pale brown into winter, unlike Starling; note darker wings, pale rump

Breeding adult
Unmistakable pink and glossy black

Spotless Starling *Sturnus unicolor*

Usually seen in towns and villages and on nearby farmland and pasture, this is a bird of Iberia, the extreme south of France, Corsica, Sardinia, and Sicily, as well as adjacent parts of north Africa. Common Starlings move into its range in winter and the two species may then flock together, but mostly they separate for the breeding season.

FEEDING Like Starlings they forage on the ground: walking and running, often in small groups, to find insects in summer and seeds in winter.

DISPLAY & VOICE Males sing from roofs, aerials, and overhead wires, with a prolonged, Starling-like song that includes longer, louder whistles and purer fluty notes. Alarm notes are similar to a Starling's: *fit* or *chip*.

BREEDING Four to five eggs are laid in a hole in rocks or under a roof tile. They hatch after 11 days' incubation.

MIGRATION Resident.

LENGTH 21–23cm (8¼–9in)

WHEN TO SEE All year
WHERE FOUND Extreme S France, Spain, Portugal, Corsica, Sardinia, Sicily

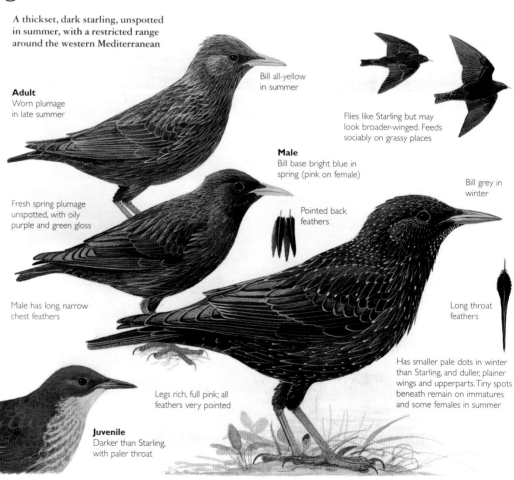

A thickset, dark starling, unspotted in summer, with a restricted range around the western Mediterranean

Adult
Worn plumage in late summer

Bill all-yellow in summer

Flies like Starling but may look broader-winged. Feeds sociably on grassy places

Male
Bill base bright blue in spring (pink on female)

Bill grey in winter

Fresh spring plumage unspotted, with oily purple and green gloss

Pointed back feathers

Male has long, narrow chest feathers

Long throat feathers

Legs rich, full pink; all feathers very pointed

Has smaller pale dots in winter than Starling, and duller, plainer wings and upperparts. Tiny spots beneath remain on immatures and some females in summer

Juvenile
Darker than Starling, with paler throat

Starling *Sturnus vulgaris*

Flocks often develop swooping, undulating track; synchronized aerobatics above roost; will rise and encircle a Sparrowhawk

Flight typically fast and direct; singly, often making long, straight bee-line to nest or feeding place

Fan-shaped tail

Pale underwing contrasts with blacker body

A sharp-faced, square-tailed, fast-walking, boisterous bird: common, familiar, sociable, and quarrelsome. Pointed head and triangular wings distinctive in flight

Shows a multitude of flight profiles

Juvenile
Looks pale mouse- or donkey-brown in flight; rarely creamy or biscuit coloured

Juvenile
Brown with blacker mask and black, pointed bill

Males sing with drooped, waved wings

Male, summer
Blacker than winter, with green and purple gloss; spots almost worn off

Female, winter
Bold spots of buff and creamy-white, merging into silvery face and throat; bright orange-buff feather edges on wings

Dark bill turns yellow in summer; male has blue bill base, female has pink bill base

Male, winter (right)
Smaller spots than female; bill dark in winter

Male

Female

Female, summer
Bright wing feather edges and orange-pink legs, unlike Blackbird

Before their recent widespread decline Starlings could often be seen in winter in huge flocks, drifting like smoke across the sky, sometimes numbering tens or hundreds of thousands. The flocks gathered to roost in reedbeds and woods, sometimes millions together. Such concentrations are rarer now because changes in agricultural practice have reduced Starling numbers in most areas. Yet in some town centres tens of thousands can still be seen gathering in the winter dusk to roost on giant bridges and other man-made structures. They attract Sparrowhawks, and sometimes Peregrines, which swoop through the flocks trying to catch a late meal. Starlings remain familiar in gardens all year, squabbling over food in winter, singing from roofs and aerials in spring, and nesting in roof spaces and eaves where cavities still exist. Most, however, nest in woodland or in old trees on farmland. They feed on more open ground, especially grassland.

FEEDING A foraging Starling typically probes in the grass, opening its bill to make a small but distinct hole, hoping to grasp some large grub such as a leatherjacket. It will eat insects of many kinds, seeds, grain, and food put out on bird tables. In winter, especially, flocks gather around animal feed troughs, on refuse tips, and in other places where food is unnaturally concentrated. They also search seaweed on beaches for small invertebrates.

DISPLAY & VOICE Males sing with their bills open and held upwards, and their wings loosely flicked open at each side. The song is a mixture of wheezy notes, rattling trills, and clicks, with more musical whistles and a variety of mimicry. Calls include a buzzy *churrr* on take-off, a loud, whistled *teeuw*, a grating *tschee-eer*, squawking notes and a sharp *klik* in alarm – a cue to look for a Sparrowhawk overhead.

BREEDING Starlings build their nests in holes, such as woodpecker holes in trees, large nest boxes, and under the eaves of a variety of buildings. The nest is made of straw, grasses, roots, and other material, lined with feathers and moss. Four to seven eggs are incubated for 12–13 days, and the chicks fly when they are 20–22 days old.

MIGRATION Northern and eastern breeding birds move west and south in autumn. Many of these migrants reach Britain in late autumn, to join the resident Starlings.

LENGTH 21.5cm (8½in)

WHEN TO SEE All year
WHERE FOUND Breeds widely south to Pyrenees; absent S Italy, S Balkans. In winter, range extends south to Mediterranean area

Golden Oriole *Oriolus oriolus*

I n a picture a male Golden Oriole looks stunning: in reality it is sensational. Few birds are quite so vivid, yet few are so difficult to see well. An oriole's presence is usually betrayed by its song, from the depths of a poplar plantation or a streamside copse, but it may take hours of patient watching to get more than a glimpse. Now and then, though, it allows a clear, close, and truly memorable view.

FEEDING It takes caterpillars, beetles, and berries in leafy tree canopies, more rarely from lower vegetation.

DISPLAY & VOICE Males advertise their territories with frequent songs, especially at dawn and dusk; females sing less often. The song is full-throated and fluty but short: a yodelled *eee-oo*, or *weedle-eeoo*, *doo-dl-iu* or similar. Both sexes make a cat-like squawl.

BREEDING The nest is slung within a horizontal fork high in a tree; three or four eggs hatch after 16–17 days.

MIGRATION Iberian birds move south, probably into west Africa; birds from farther east take a more southeasterly course to east Africa.

LENGTH 24cm (9½in)

WHEN TO SEE April to September
WHERE FOUND Europe south of Baltic; rare breeder in E England, S Sweden

Male
Bright yellow and black; black from eye to bill

Some old females almost as yellow as male

A thrush-sized, long-winged, secretive bird of leafy treetops; despite vivid plumage of male, extremely hard to see unless it flies to another clump of trees; buttercup-yellow and black of male unique in Europe, but female resembles Green Woodpecker

Males
Flight like Mistle Thrush; eyecatching colour

Female (left)
Very narrow yellow bar on edge of wing

Oldest females are most yellow; no black between eye and bill

Juvenile
Black streaks below vary individually

Female, one year old
Note narrow yellow band on edge of wing; broader on male at all ages

Juveniles
Yellow rump, underwing, tail corners; compare Green Woodpecker

Nutcracker *Nucifraga caryocatactes*

T he Nutcracker is a remarkably handsome and fascinating bird of northern or high-altitude coniferous forests. Given a good view it is unmistakable, yet wishful thinking accounts for many reports based on misjudged Starlings or young thrushes!

FEEDING Nutcrackers do eat nuts (chiefly hazel), plus conifer seeds (especially Arolla pine), berries, and various insects. They bury large stores of food under leaf litter or moss, and these are essential for seeing the birds through each winter.

VOICE In summer they use harsh calls; in winter they are silent.

BREEDING Although they often live in flocks, pairs separate out even in winter, and they nest independently of their fellows. The nest is made against the trunk of a conifer; three or four eggs are incubated for 18 days and the young fly within a month.

MIGRATION Mostly resident, especially in the west of their range, Nutcrackers sometimes move west and south in autumn in search of food; few survive these 'irruptions' to return in spring.

LENGTH 32–33cm (12½–13in)

WHEN TO SEE All year; in west vagrants usually September to spring
WHERE FOUND S Scandinavia, Germany, and Alps eastwards, mostly in mountains

Sits on top of pine trees

A uniquely white-spotted, chocolate-brown bird with dark cap and wings; vivid white under tail and tail tip. Closely associated with pines, but turns up in unlikely places during irruptions. Much bigger than Starling

Broad wingtips, white bars under wing, white streaks on middle primaries; unique white-black-white undertail

Thin pale tips to primaries on adult (left); wider on juvenile (right)

White tail tip obvious from rear

Drops like a stone from perch

Eastern race
Thick-billed

Siberian race
Thin-billed; some difficult to separate

Bold white spots on body, black cap and wings and white splash under tail produce unique pattern

Jay *Garrulus glandarius*

Bold, noisy, beautiful and, in the main, unfairly persecuted, the Jay is an intriguing species. In most forests it is wild and shy, justly so as the gamekeeper is against it; in gardens and parks, however, it may become more approachable if it is left alone.

FEEDING The Jay eats nuts, seeds, berries, insects, and occasional small mammals or birds and their eggs. In autumn it collects huge numbers of acorns and buries them for future use, memorizing their location so it can retrieve them in late winter and spring.

DISPLAY & VOICE Males raise their crest and rump feathers in aggressive displays. Calls include a nasal *miaow* and, most typical, a loud, rasping, tearing screech, like *skairk!*

BREEDING Five to seven eggs are incubated for 16–17 days in a coarse twig nest in the fork of a tree.

MIGRATION Jays are resident in the west and south, but some birds from the north and east move south in search of food each winter, sometimes in sizeable flocks.

LENGTH 35cm (13¾in)

WHEN TO SEE All year
WHERE FOUND All Europe except for Iceland, extreme N Britain, N Norway, and Sweden, parts of interior Spain

Blue wing patch more or less conspicuous depending on view

Typical flight around treetop height except when moving long distances; wingbeat mostly below horizontal

White rump often raised in flight

A colourful, elusive, sometimes noisy bird, most obvious when collecting and transporting acorns in autumn

Glides down to feed or collect acorn

Crown raised in anger, alarm, or curiosity

Bold black moustache and white chin obvious

Broad black tail

Darker in west, greyer in north, pinker in south of Europe. Juveniles have less intense colours on the body

Big white rump obvious on ground and especially in flight

Moves on ground with leaping hops and sideways shuffles

Siberian Jay *Perisoreus infaustus*

The Siberian Jay favours dense tracts of unvarying, undisturbed forest, untouched by people. Yet in contrast with the Jay it is remarkably unafraid of humans when they appear in its remote forest home. It is a noted 'camp follower', quickly appearing beside tents and camp fires. It prefers areas of Norway spruce and Scots pine, but may also be found in larch and birch. Forest disturbance and logging have caused widespread declines in recent decades.

FEEDING Much more of a hunter than the Jay, it captures small mammals and birds, and eats nestlings and eggs; it also scavenges from dead animals. Nevertheless much of its food is seeds, berries, and insects, and it caches seed stores for use in winter.

DISPLAY & VOICE There is much aggression and calling when Siberian Jays are feeding, but the flocks move around silently. The song is a low, varied chattering; typical calls are harsh repetitions of *eee* or *eeer*.

BREEDING Three to four eggs are laid in a loose nest of twigs in a conifer, and hatch in 16–20 days.

MIGRATION Resident.

LENGTH 30cm (12in)

WHEN TO SEE All year
WHERE FOUND Norway, Sweden, Finland, N Russia

An orange and grey bird of the northern taiga forest, unlike any other European species; shy in summer, tame around forest camps in winter

Very orange below. May moult central tail feathers together, so tail looks all orange for short time

Juvenile
Darker, browner, duller than adult

Deep orange in wings and on tail sides

Extent of orange varies individually; some buff, others grey below

Short, broad wings, adept, agile flight

Adults
Dark cap, pale bristles over bill, pink patch under bill shows when throat pouch extended by food

Magpie *Pica pica*

Many people detest the Magpie because of its reputation for killing songbirds, yet it is a bold, intelligent, highly attractive bird with a talent for thriving in modern suburban conditions. In Britain it is now returning to the countryside after centuries of persecution.

FEEDING Insects, especially beetles, as well as berries, seeds, and all kinds of scraps form the bulk of a Magpie's diet. In spring it eats eggs and nestlings, and rarely small adult birds, but it prefers to eat insects whenever they are available.

DISPLAY & VOICE Groups of Magpies sometimes gather in mysterious communal displays or in pre-roost flocks. They communicate with their bold plumage and long tails and various loud, harsh calls, especially a staccato *cha-cha-cha-cha*.

BREEDING A roofed, mud-lined fortress nest of thick twigs is built in a tree or tall hedge. Five to seven eggs are incubated for three weeks.

MIGRATION Resident.

LENGTH 44–46cm (17–18in)

WHEN TO SEE All year
WHERE FOUND Throughout Europe except N Scandinavia, Iceland, extreme N Britain, high Alps and some Mediterranean island groups

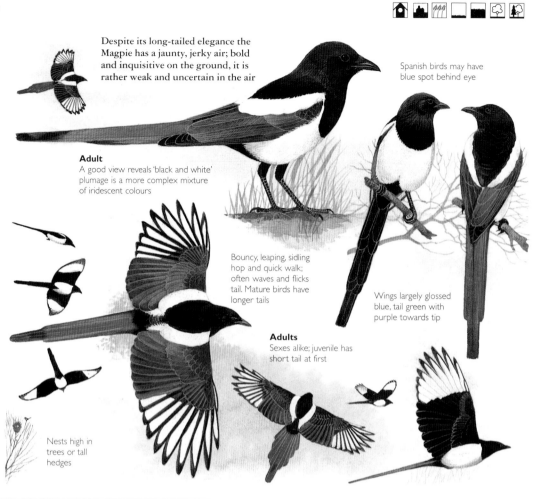

Despite its long-tailed elegance the Magpie has a jaunty, jerky air; bold and inquisitive on the ground, it is rather weak and uncertain in the air

Spanish birds may have blue spot behind eye

Adult
A good view reveals 'black and white' plumage is a more complex mixture of iridescent colours

Bouncy, leaping, sidling hop and quick walk; often waves and flicks tail. Mature birds have longer tails

Wings largely glossed blue, tail green with purple towards tip

Adults
Sexes alike; juvenile has short tail at first

Nests high in trees or tall hedges

Azure-winged Magpie *Cyanopica cyana*

This dramatic species lives in Spain and Portugal. A similar-looking species occurs in eastern Asia and Japan. It roams through the open forests, cork oak groves, and stone pine covered sand dunes in small flocks, looking and behaving like something between a Magpie and a Jay. Where it occupies plantations it seems to exclude otherwise locally abundant Magpies.

FEEDING It eats beetles, seeds, and fruits, mostly found on the ground; it stores acorns, olives, and pine seeds.

DISPLAY & VOICE After each breeding season family parties from the small breeding colonies form flocks; these defend large communal territories from other flocks. Calls are many and varied, typically a husky *schrie*.

BREEDING The nest is a bowl of twigs mixed with dung, mud, and roots, built in the top of a tree far out from the central crown. Five to seven eggs hatch after 15–16 days; the chicks fly after a further two weeks.

MIGRATION Resident.

LENGTH 34–35cm (13½–14in)

WHEN TO SEE All year
WHERE FOUND European range W, central and SW Spain, SW Portugal

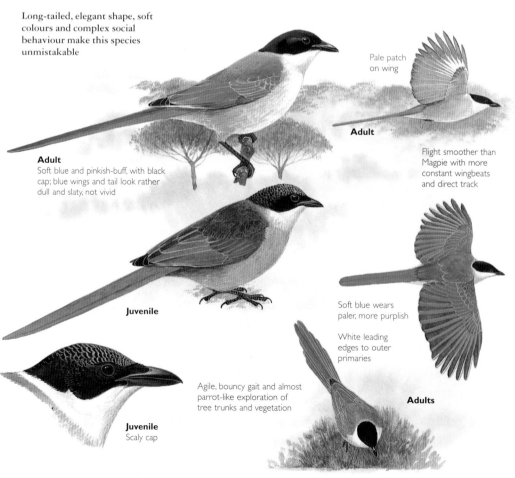

Long-tailed, elegant shape, soft colours and complex social behaviour make this species unmistakable

Pale patch on wing

Adult

Flight smoother than Magpie with more constant wingbeats and direct track

Adult
Soft blue and pinkish-buff, with black cap; blue wings and tail look rather dull and slaty, not vivid

Juvenile

Soft blue wears paler, more purplish

White leading edges to outer primaries

Juvenile
Scaly cap

Agile, bouncy gait and almost parrot-like exploration of tree trunks and vegetation

Adults

Chough *Pyrrhocorax pyrrhocorax*

Slim head and bill, unlike Jackdaw, which it often accompanies

Adult male (above)
Broader wings, shorter tail than female: compare in side view

A square-winged, square-tailed crow with fingered wingtips

Juvenile female
Up to year old: narrow wings, notched tail; bill dull orange at first

Adult female (above)
Narrower wings, longer tail than male: hard to see in flock, obvious in isolated pair

A glossy crow, lively and entertaining as it flirts its wings and tail, calls loudly, and flies with graceful but bounding, energetic swoops and undulations; red bill is diagnostic

Extravagant flight actions matched by explosive calls

Female

Flight direct, fast, or in long, swooping bounds; soars and dives

Male

Adult female
Wingtips equal tail

Adult male
Wingtips beyond tail; shaggy undertail coverts

Red legs, red bill distinctive

Of all the crows this is the most ebullient, lively, energetic, and graceful in all its actions. In Britain and Ireland it is mostly coastal, but elsewhere it inhabits inland cliffs and gorges, and mountain peaks. It needs areas of old, unfertilized turf preferably grazed by cattle or sheep all year.

FEEDING Ants are important, and various other insects found in or under animal dung or locally in mats of seaweed, especially in winter.

DISPLAY & VOICE Choughs display great agility in flight, revelling in their mastery of the air with exaggerated swoops and dives over or alongside cliffs. They call loudly: typically a yelping, explosive *pchi-oow!* or *keyaaa*.

BREEDING They build their nests in deep caves, quarries, mine shafts, under dark overhangs in cliffs, or in derelict buildings. Three to five eggs are incubated for 17–18 days.

MIGRATION Resident; almost unknown outside breeding areas.

LENGTH 39–40cm (15½–15¾in)

WHEN TO SEE All year
WHERE FOUND SW Scotland, Wales, W Ireland, extreme NW France, S France, Iberia, Sardinia, central Italy, Sicily, Balkans, and Greece

Alpine Chough *Pyrrhocorax graculus*

Males

Longer, rounder tail, rounder wings than Chough, but can be difficult at long range

Adult male
Longer tail, subtly more bulging wings than female

Two-tone underwing may be obvious

Huge, swirling, fast-moving flocks sweep across valleys

Easily overlooked with Choughs and Jackdaws; rounded wing and tail more Jackdaw-like

Adult female

Smooth, glossy, highly gregarious, a crow of high-altitude pastures and snowy peaks, distinguished by its rounded tail and yellow bill

Long, slim, tapered and small-headed

Often covers vast areas in huge mountain landscapes, but also tame around buildings, ski-lifts

Adult
Stubby yellow bill like big Blackbird, but legs red; very smooth, glossy, immaculate plumage

Juvenile

Adult

Its name betrays the restricted habitat of this bird: it lives in or around mountains, crags and nearby montane grassland, descending to meadows in high valleys mainly in winter. It is also frequent around ski lifts and high-altitude resorts. In the Alps it reaches 3000m (9800ft) above sea level.

FEEDING It forages for grasshoppers, leatherjackets, and other insect food in rough grass; it also eats refuse and scraps around ski resorts.

DISPLAY & VOICE The Alpine Chough is quite as acrobatic in its social displays as the Chough. Its calls are highly distinctive: a high, penetrating, far-carrying *chree* or *tree* and and more rippling, softer, *chirrish* or *zirrrr*.

BREEDING The nest is on a ledge in a cave, tunnel or mine shaft, often in darkness inside a deep cave, reached through a small entrance. Three to five eggs are incubated for three weeks.

MIGRATION Resident, but moves up and down mountains with changing weather conditions.

LENGTH 38cm (15in)

WHEN TO SEE All year
WHERE FOUND N Spain, Pyrenees, Alps, Corsica, Italy, Balkans, Greece

Jackdaw *Corvus monedula*

All crows are credited with more intelligence than most other birds, and the Jackdaw, in particular, is a real character, even among the crows. It is difficult to believe that it is not genuinely clever.

It is a bird of temperate regions, avoiding excessive heat or cold, yet it occupies a broad range of habitats from coastal cliffs to inland crags, from quiet cathedral closes to busy, noisy supermarket car parks, from old woods and parks to warm Mediterranean slopes. It is a social bird that roosts and nests in groups, and to thrive it needs plenty of holes in trees or buildings, or sheltered, overhung ledges; this requirement gives it a localized and patchy distribution.

FEEDING Jackdaws feed in pairs or small groups, often mixed with larger numbers of Rooks and Stock Doves. They take almost all their food from the ground, except for caterpillars when they are abundant in foliage. They eat acorns, but not from beneath oak trees in a wood; they prefer to forage on open fields, lawns, and derelict ground, finding insects, seeds, berries, and scraps. At the coast they often feed on the beach. Some Jackdaws develop a taste for eggs, including those of cliff-breeding seabirds. They do not store food for the winter so much as other crows.

DISPLAY & VOICE Flocks are often to be seen flying around crags or over trees, revelling in the wind, sometimes more or less synchronized in their movements. They call loudly. Pairs seem to come together through such behaviour, with little obvious display. Calls include a sharp, squeaky *kya*, or *kee-yak* ('Jack'); also a great variety of grating *kaarr* notes, yapping *ya!* or *yip* sounds, and clucks and hisses.

BREEDING They build their nests in a great variety of places, ranging from old chimneys (sometimes in use) and cavities in church towers or other buildings to holes in trees and rock faces. Rabbit holes are sometimes used, as are Black Woodpecker holes. Jackdaws may restrict hole-nesting species such as the Stock Dove by monopolizing suitable nesting sites. Four to six eggs hatch after 17–18 days' incubation; the chicks fly when 28–36 days old.

MIGRATION Northern birds move west to southwest in autumn; they migrate by day, often with Rooks. Continental Jackdaws reach Britain in October and November.

LENGTH 33–34cm (13–13½in)

WHEN TO SEE All year
WHERE FOUND Breeds in most of Europe, except for Iceland, NW Scotland, most of N and inland Norway and Sweden, and parts of N and W Iberia

A bold, noisy, agile crow, rather pigeon-like in outline and flight actions, with a distinctive black cap and pale nape. Flocks are full of nervous energy, flying off at great speed, soaring over cliffs or buildings or circling above woods; frequently mixes with Rooks

Typical flight shapes, with slightly rounded wings swept back, protruding head but small bill, short, slim tail

Wingbeats much quicker than Rook, with snappy, jerky action

Flocks often found in urban or suburban situations, around ruins, cathedrals, old houses with big chimneys, civic buildings

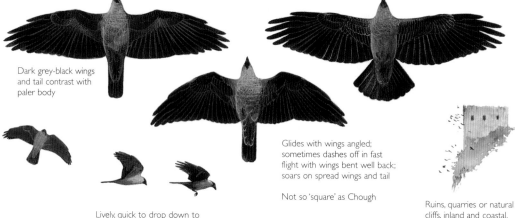

Dark grey-black wings and tail contrast with paler body

Glides with wings angled; sometimes dashes off in fast flight with wings bent well back; soars on spread wings and tail

Not so 'square' as Chough

Ruins, quarries or natural cliffs, inland and coastal, provide nesting places; Jackdaws exploit rising and swirling air currents in acrobatic flight

Lively, quick to drop down to investigate potential food; upright or forward-leaning on ground, with quick walk, jerky hops; flirts wings and tail

Adult
Shiny black cap, pale bluish-grey nape and pale eye unique; plumage wears duller in summer; sexes alike

Juvenile
Duller; less glossy, nape darker, eye greyer

Daurian Jackdaw
Vagrant from eastern Asia to northwestern Europe; much whiter neck and body, dark eye

Adult
In northern Europe often shows paler neck patch in fresh autumn plumage, but not always safely distinguishable from southern birds; wears duller and darker

Rook (above)
Long wings, rounder tail

Rook
Larger, longer-winged, longer-headed than Jackdaw

Jackdaw

Jackdaw

Raven   *Corvus corax*

A Buzzard-sized, all-black crow distinguished by a long, arched bill, long head and neck and a wedge- or diamond-shaped tail. In flight long head/neck and tail give more obvious cross-shape than other crows, while wings are long, fingered at the tips, often angled at the wrist

This is the world's biggest and most impressive crow. Seen on the ground at long range it is not always easy to separate from the Carrion Crow, but in flight its shape and actions are always distinctive, as are its calls. It is usually associated with wild and remote landscapes: mountains, crags, coastal cliffs, even deserts. Yet in many areas it lives quite happily on the fringes of towns and cities, flying over built-up areas quite regularly. It is also at home in 'softer', farmed areas with mixed landscapes of rolling fields and patchy or extensive woodlands.

FEEDING Compared to other crows the Raven is more capable of killing small animals such as rabbits, mountain hares, and medium-sized birds. It eats a great deal of dead meat, too, such as sheep or deer found dead on the open hill, rabbits killed by road traffic, or carcasses washed up on a beach. It also eats insects such as big beetles and fat caterpillars, as well as shellfish on coasts; in fact it eagerly devours almost anything edible.

DISPLAY & VOICE Non-breeders form flocks, but breeding pairs defend territories, mainly through aerial advertisement. Ravens regularly roll over in flight (a sideways roll with half-closed wings, then back again); other aerobatic and soaring flights help them communicate with each other. Calls are important too: even when far apart pairs stay in contact with loud calls that can be individually recognized. Typical calls are hoarse, full-throated and far-carrying, such as *prruk-prruk* or *cronk cronk*, with a barking quality. Others are more metallic, ringing notes: *tonk tonk*. A quiet song includes variations on these notes, together with a variety of clicks, rattles, and softer, more musical sounds.

BREEDING Raven nests are built up year after year in traditional sites, on ledges under overhangs on cliffs, in quarries, or in tall pines or oak trees. In undisturbed regions the birds may nest in lower situations. The nest is made of thick, gnarled sticks, lined with earth, dung, and roots, a layer of moss and grass, and a final lining of wool, hair, and lichens. Four to six eggs are laid in late winter or early in spring, and incubated for 20–21 days. The chicks fly after 45 days.

MIGRATION Resident; a few northern birds wander in winter, and immatures disperse from their native areas.

LENGTH 64cm (25in)

Long head/bill projection

Tail rounded or wedge-tipped (compare Rook)

Raven
With Carrion Crow (right) to same scale

Carrion Crow
Rather square with short, square tail

Feathers of crown and throat often raised, giving exaggerated large-headed effect

Ravens

Spread primaries create loud rasping sound in display flights

Raven has longer, more shapely wings than crow, longer head and neck, and longer tail with rounded tip when closed

Flight powerful, with deep, regular wingbeats, but also much soaring, gliding and aerobatics

Heavy arched bill most powerful of any crow's

Adult
Neat, all-black plumage, long wingtips and tail; tail may extend beyond wings (above) or not (below)

Wing shape of juvenile or full-feathered adult smooth and graceful; moulting adults often show notch on trailing edge, emphasising angle

Throat feathers pointed, may be raised to create 'beard', especially when calling

Carrion Crow
To same scale as Raven, far left

WHEN TO SEE All year
WHERE FOUND Breeds in most of Europe, but absent from large lowland regions including much of England, France, the Low Countries and parts of Central Europe

Carrion Crow *Corvus corone corone*

Its taste for dead meat has given the Carrion Crow a bad reputation, yet it is an undeniably impressive, even handsome bird. Its intense blackness, solid build, thick bill, and bright, intelligent eyes give it great character. Despite persecution it survives on farmland, at the edges of woods, and on coasts, often feeding on beaches.

FEEDING It takes mostly large insects and grain, supplemented by whatever small rodents, birds, and nestlings it can catch. It also eats eggs, dead fish, molluscs and scraps. Hundreds may feed together on recently manured fields and refuse tips.

DISPLAY & VOICE Both sexes, but mostly the male, call while bowing with wings raised above the fanned tail. Calls are harsh, deep, *kraaa* notes, falling in pitch, often repeated without variation. The 'songs' are rarely heard mixtures of soft calls and mimicry.

BREEDING Big stick nests in trees, or bushes in open areas, contain up to six eggs which hatch after 18–19 days.

MIGRATION Resident.

LENGTH 45–47cm (18–18½in)

WHEN TO SEE All year
WHERE FOUND Most of Britain, throughout Iberia, France and east to Germany, Austria, north to S Denmark

Squarer wings and tail than Rook or Raven

Deep wingbeats; glides with wings slightly drooped

Typical flight shapes: compare with Rook. Not easy to separate at long range

Big, black, broad-headed and thick-billed, tight-feathered and smooth; in flight square, short-headed, with fingered wings, quite heavy and deliberate, not so acrobatic as the Rook or Raven

Calls loudly with forward bowing action, from high perch

Adult Heavy and powerfully built; stout bill more arched than Rook's

Thigh feathers tighter than Rook's

Rook

Crow Note flat head

Hooded Crow *Corvus corone cornix*

The Hooded Crow is sometimes treated as a separate species, but it is usually considered a race of the Carrion Crow. Where the two meet they may hybridize, but the bulk of both populations breed only among themselves and remain pure.

FEEDING To a great extent Hooded Crows rely on refuse and offal in winter and insects in summer; they eat fewer eggs and kill far fewer small animals than is commonly believed. They forage on beaches, around animal feed, and on pastures with animal dung.

DISPLAY & VOICE Their behaviour and calls are much the same as those of the Carrion Crow. Some calls are perhaps slightly less harsh in character.

BREEDING The nests is like a Carrion Crow's, built of thick sticks lined with soil, moss, roots, wool, and feathers.

MIGRATION In winter many northern birds move south to the coasts of the Low Countries, fewer to Britain. Western birds are resident.

LENGTH 45–47cm (18–18½in)

WHEN TO SEE All year; migrants on coasts October to April
WHERE FOUND Breeds N Scotland, Isle of Man, Ireland, N Denmark, north and east through whole of Scandinavia, Russia; E Europe south to Italy, Corsica, Sardinia, east to Balkans and Turkey

Black head, wings and tail contrast with grey body, unmistakable

A striking, handsomely-patterned race of the Carrion Crow, identical in its shape and behaviour

Flight shape and actions like Carrion Crow; much bigger, paler than Jackdaw

Hybrid Carrion X Hooded Hybrids occur along borders of range; variable between pure extremes

Often in pairs or small groups, sometimes larger gatherings at rubbish tips or along coasts in winter

Adult Body grey, but variably tinged fawn, beige or pinkish, partly depending on light and surrounding colours; wings glossed green-blue

Rook *Corvus frugilegus*

Rooks are not everyone's favourite birds, but they are undervalued. They are surely inseparable from the typically British countryside of open parks with clumps of trees, spinneys, and copses surrounded by farmland, ploughed fields, and stubbles among old, dense hedgerows and churchyard limes. There will always be rooks in such places, calling with their lovely, rich voices, often in sharp counterpoint to the bright, squeaky calls of Jackdaws mixed with them. Yet Rooks are now equally likely to be seen feeding beside motorways, looking for insects dashed to the side by passing traffic, or even scrounging scraps of bread and biscuit in motorway service car parks, surprisingly tame and bold.

FEEDING Their staple diet for much of the year is earthworms and various large insects, especially beetles. Rooks forage on pasture, ploughed fields, and cropland: freshly turned earth is ideal for snapping up worms and grubs, while newly sprouted cereal fields and land fertilized with farmyard manure provide opportunities for Rooks to search for insects and seeds with their steady, rolling walk. They usually feed in flocks, almost always on the ground, only rarely taking caterpillars from foliage. At times they eat newly drilled grain and ripening cereals.

DISPLAY & VOICE Rooks often display on and around their treetop nests, with much bowing, lowering, or raising of half-opened wings and fanning of their raised tails. Their calls are varied, with frequent strangled, almost ringing, trumpeting calls mixed with rattles and churrs in a kind of song. Their usual call is rougher, flatter, and more open-ended than the Carrion Crow's: a more even *kaah kaah kaah*.

BREEDING The nests are mostly built high in treetops, rarely on an open side branch or near the trunk. They are substantial structures of sticks, lined with roots, moss, clay, feathers, and various rags or bits of paper. Pairs often steal material from neighbouring nests. Two to six eggs hatch after 16–18 days; the young fly when 30–36 days old.

MIGRATION Breeding birds from Asia and northeast Europe move south and west in winter, more obviously in cold winters. British and Irish Rooks are resident, and joined by many from the Baltic in winter, especially in the east.

LENGTH 44–46cm (17–18in)

Wingtip fingered when fully spread; tail slightly wedge-shaped or rounded at tip inviting confusion with Raven at long range

Carrion Crow
Wingtip slightly broader, squarer, head and bill slightly heavier

Rook
Wingtip rather tapered when angled backwards

Compare wingtip shape (more pointed) with squarer shape of Carrion Crow (below)

Noisy social behaviour around treetop nests is distinctive, with familiar croaks and far-carrying, strangled metallic notes

Rook

Tail closed in direct flight; wingtips outstretched, tail fanned out and rounded in soar

Carrion Crow

Rook

Small groups often soar in tight circles; capable of rising to considerable height in warm air or in wind against hillside

Adult male
Bare parchment buff/white face with flexible pouch beneath chin; steep forehead, long, pointed bill

Good views reveal bright purple-blue gloss on adults

A big, black crow with a strong, purplish-blue gloss. Its steep forehead, pointed bill and hanging underpart feathers give it a distinctive shape: more waddling, narrow-shouldered and broad-bodied than Carrion Crow on the ground, rounder-tailed and more pointed-winged in flight. Noisy and sociable, both feeding in fields and at rookeries

Adult female
Wingtip reaches tail tip, unlike male in which tail protrudes

Juvenile
Bill and face black; head and neck dull, rest of body more glossy

Juvenile Rook

Carrion Crow

Adults

WHEN TO SEE All year in Britain and Ireland; winter only in S Europe
WHERE FOUND All of Britain and Ireland except N Scotland; but absent from most of Scandinavia, S France (except in winter), Iberia and Italy; mostly only in winter in much of central and SE Europe

House Sparrow *Passer domesticus*

House Sparrows hop and chirrup their way through life in all kinds of places inhabited by people: from town parks and railway stations to suburban gardens and farmsteads. In Britain there is some evidence that House Sparrow numbers in gardens are declining, although in most places this remains a common bird.

FEEDING Adults eat seeds, and to a lesser extent shoots, buds, and berries; they feed their chicks on insects.

DISPLAY & VOICE A male will hop around females on the ground or on a roof, his head and tail raised, his wings slightly open and lowered. His song is a jumble of chirruping notes; calls include a bright *chirp, chweep, chrrup,* and *chirrup*.

BREEDING The nests are large, oval balls of grass, lined with feathers, and usually well-hidden. Three to five eggs are incubated for 11–14 days.

MIGRATION Virtually sedentary.

LENGTH 14–15cm (5½–6in)

WHEN TO SEE All year
WHERE FOUND Farmland with cereal fields and weedy stubbles, gardens, town parks, shrubberies, and hedgerows. All Europe except Iceland and high northern mountains

A busy, bustling, noisy bird with bright, chirrupy calls, streaky above but plain beneath. Female has a broad pale band above the eye, male has a grey cap and black bib. Their tails are plain, without the white sides or coloured patches of many buntings and finches

Sparrows often chase pigeons in flight

Male, winter Note plain tail, white wingbar

Slim when alert, often dumpy when feeding

Female Mid-brown; thin wingbar, broad buff line over eye

Female **Male**

Adults, winter Undersides entirely unstreaked on both sexes. Adult male's bib is at its smallest, least well-defined in winter, as shown below

Male, summer

Female, summer

Male (right) has longer body than female

Male has longer bib and cleaner head pattern in summer

Tree Sparrow *Passer montanus*

Tree Sparrows seem to have always undergone marked fluctuations in numbers and distribution, but recent declines in western Europe, including Britain and Ireland, seem especially severe. In some areas they have become rarities where once they were frequent.

FEEDING They take plant and animal foods according to their abundance, supplementing seeds – picked from both plant stems and the ground – buds, and a few berries with insects of all kinds from tiny springtails and thrips to grasshoppers and beetles.

DISPLAY & VOICE Like other sparrows, the male shows off his dark bib in stretching and bowing postures, raises and quivers his tail and droops his wings. The song is an excitable series of chirrups; calls include chirps and a particularly distinctive, deep *tek*.

BREEDING Tree Sparrows nest in holes in trees or walls; the 2–7 eggs hatch in 11–14 days.

MIGRATION Northeastern breeders move south in winter; birds breeding in the British Isles are resident.

LENGTH 14cm (5½in)

WHEN TO SEE All year
WHERE FOUND Deciduous woods, farmland. Absent from N Scandinavia, Iceland, parts of Scotland and Ireland

Both sexes much like the male House Sparrow, but slightly smaller, rounder, often with a cocked tail. Face pattern and brown cap are the best clues

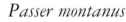

House Sparrow

Tree Sparrow

May look slim, but feathers fluffed up in cold weather (above), when it looks very round; tail often cocked

Two white wingbars; brighter, buffer rump than House Sparrow

Underwing warm orange-buff; cold grey on House Sparrow

Female Sexes alike in pattern: brown cap, black spot on white cheek

Male Tail slightly longer than female but difficult to distinguish

House Sparrow

All-black bill in summer (below), pale base in winter (below right); white neck ring distinctive

Tree Sparrows

Spanish Sparrow *Passer hispaniolensis*

A highly gregarious, lively sparrow that congregates in noisy flocks before roosting; contrasty summer males obvious, but dull winter males and other plumages less so; note colour of cap and streaked underparts

Bill heavier than that of House Sparrow

Summer male

Male, winter
Pale feather edges create a hoary, greyish or cold buff look with obscure black marks; grey mottles below

Female
Back sometimes more heavily marked; underparts softly marked with subtle streaks but these often obscure and match those of House Sparrow

Male, summer
Gradual wear of pale tips from winter to spring gives vivid breeding plumage with much intense black, including flank streaks

Male, summer
Rusty-brown cap, white marks near eye, black bib and bold white cheeks; extreme wear produces almost black back

A male Spanish Sparrow in spring is a superbly handsome bird, although its other plumages are less distinguished. It is associated with people, but far less so than House Sparrows in most areas, preferring trees and shrubs, often willow thickets, typically near lakes and marshes. It is more of a town bird where House Sparrows are absent.

FEEDING Groups eat insects and buds in bushes; large, dense flocks may gather to feed on grain and insects in fields.

DISPLAY & VOICE More gregarious than even House Sparrows, Spanish Sparrows live in flocks throughout the year and breed in colonies. Males sing at the nest to attract mates; their song is like that of a House Sparrow but more strident: *cheeli-cheeli-cheeli*. Calls are varied chirps.

BREEDING Breeding colonies may consist of thousands of nests: in trees or bushes, on pylons, in the 'basements' of White Stork nests, or in holes.

MIGRATION Mostly resident, but some eastern European populations migrate in dense flocks to the Middle East and Africa. A rare vagrant north of its range.

LENGTH 15cm (6in)

WHEN TO SEE	All year
WHERE FOUND	Scarce S and central Spain, E Portugal, Sardinia; commoner Balkans, especially Greece, Turkey

Italian Sparrow *Passer x italiae*

A stable hybrid form of sparrow, most like the House Sparrow but with some features resembling its other ancestor, the Spanish Sparrow

Males
Winter plumage (left) has pale tips obscuring crown colour and bib; summer pattern (right) revealed as tips wear away

Male, summer
Crown and nape rich chocolate brown, cheeks white; large black bib, but flanks obscurely marked at most; upperparts lightly marked

Male, summer

Female, winter
Dull, pale head; pale-based bill larger than that of House Sparrow

This is something of an enigma: apparently a long-established, self-perpetuating, stable hybrid between the Spanish Sparrow and the House Sparrow. It is more like the Spanish Sparrow in the south – almost purely Spanish in Western Sicily and Malta – but less so in the north. This is an unusual situation, as hybrids tend to be at a disadvantage and typically soon disappear unless interbreeding between the parent species takes place again.

FEEDING In much of Italy Italian Sparrows feed in towns, more like the House Sparrow than the Spanish.

DISPLAY & VOICE In courtship they behave more as the House Sparrow than the Spanish Sparrow, and have similar chirping calls.

BREEDING In many areas they nest in buildings, much like House Sparrows. Their nests are rough, domed structures of grass and straw. Four to six eggs hatch after 11–13 days.

MIGRATION Italian Sparrows are mostly resident, but there is some evidence of movements to the Middle East and north Africa in winter.

LENGTH 15cm (6in)

WHEN TO SEE	All year
WHERE FOUND	Italy, Corsica, Crete, Rhodes

Rock Sparrow *Petronia petronia*

In southern Europe nasal, twangy, cheery calls from rocky gullies, roadside cuttings, even the roofs of old, decrepit stone buildings, will often lead to a group of neat, streaky, pale birds: Rock Sparrows. They like sunny places, often exposed and barren, as well as sheer cliffs in sun-warmed gorges, but they also enjoy greener, cultivated places with fig trees, olives, and thickets. Ancient walls around towns and villages are often ideal.

FEEDING They eat seeds and berries all year, but feed protein-rich insects to their chicks.

DISPLAY & VOICE Males sing to attract two or three mates. The song is very simple: one, two, or three syllables based on the call, which is a nasal, piercing, far-carrying *pey-ee* or *peeyuee*. Calls are repeated for long periods.

BREEDING Nests are in rock crevices, or holes in buildings or earth banks. Four to seven eggs hatch in 11–14 days. The chicks fly at 16–21 days.

MIGRATION Resident, apart from some local dispersal in autumn.

LENGTH 14cm (5½in)

WHEN TO SEE All year
WHERE FOUND Widespread in Iberia, S France, Corsica, Sardinia, S Italy, S Balkans; very rare vagrant outside breeding range

A chunky, pale, sparrow-like bird of semi-arid, stony or rocky places, often heard before it is seen; undistinguished unless head stripes or tail spots are visible

Adult
Pale tertial tips and wingbars in fresh plumage

Tail from above (left) and below (right): size and shape of spots vary between individuals

Adult
Pale crown stripe and line behind eye distinctive; yellow breast spot often hard to see

Striped flanks, mottled undertail coverts often show well, unlike House Sparrow, but compare female Spanish Sparrow

Juvenile
Duller head; no yellow on chest; more buff than adult

White tail tip obvious from below; spots show from above when tail is spread

Very white underwing visible from side or below

Adult
Tertial tips and wingbars wear away on old feathers

Trumpeter Finch *Bucanetes githagineus*

This is essentially a bird of Middle Eastern and African desert fringes, even penetrating far into real, barren desert, especially where there are rocky outcrops or crags. A few Trumpeter Finches occur in Europe, where they have found a suitable niche in the 'desert' of southeast Spain.

FEEDING They pick seeds from the ground, occasionally directly from short herbs. They are inconspicuous when feeding, shuffling around or flitting short distances.

DISPLAY & VOICE Males sing in wide, circling, fast song flights, with short glides. They also sing from the ground. The song is a nasal, long-drawn-out, peculiar note, often compared with a tiny toy trumpet. Other calls are more abrupt, such as *chik*, *kek*, or *tset*.

BREEDING Four to six eggs are laid in a nest in the shade of a rock or tussock, and incubated for 13–14 days.

MIGRATION Although basically resident they make some nomadic movements, usually associated with their need for fresh water.

LENGTH 12.5cm (5in)

WHEN TO SEE All year
WHERE FOUND Extreme SE Spain; N Africa and Middle East. Extremely rare vagrant elsewhere

Adult female
Fresh plumage dull and brown; bill variable but dull, rump pale sandy-pink

A small, thickset, stub-billed finch that lives in arid and often stony places; usually inconspicuous, but betrayed by its call

Juvenile
Nondescript; dark eye in plain face, dark wing and tail tips

Immature male
October plumage shown: drab brownish, rump dull against blacker tail, bill already pink-orange

Juvenile

Adult male
Bright pink rump

Pale underwing, black tail

Adult male
Bright bill, plain greyish head with dark eye; pink/brown with black wingtips, pink rump. Wears paler overall

Juvenile

Hawfinch *Coccothraustes coccothraustes*

One of the larger, heavier finches, large-headed, big-billed and short-tailed. Perches upright in treetops, looking bull-necked and crossbill-like; also remains much more secretively within foliage, or on woodland floor; small groups fly up into trees when disturbed

Male, summer
Bold underwing pattern against dark body; bill marked with black in summer

Female
A one-year old

Bill is all-pale in winter

Juvenile/first-winter
Wing pattern dull, white parts streaked dark; bill yellowish

Adult, winter
Wings have strong white bars, easily seen in brief flight views; white tail tip can be obvious

Juvenile
Underside barred brown, chin pale, face dull

Female, summer
Richly coloured, with orange-brown crown against pale grey neck; grey secondaries behind white wing patch (black on male)

Male, summer
Blue-black on wings; broad, heavy head with deep, sharp-pointed bill give distinctive silhouette

Primaries
have unique billhook shape

Frequently in spindly twigs at top of trees; feeds inconspicuously on ground despite large size, flying up vertically when disturbed to perch half-hidden behind branch

Female

Hawfinches are enigmatic birds: they seem to be genuinely scarce in most places, even when woodland areas seem suitable for them to colonize. In other areas they are seen year after year in traditional spots, along particular avenues or beneath the same clumps of beech and hornbeam trees. Here they can be approached with great care and watched while they feed, but the least disturbance sees them off and away, high into the trees or even far across the treetops out of sight. Their chunky shapes and rather long, tapered wings with bold white or semi-translucent bands, combined with their fast, bounding flight, make them easy to identify – if only you can see them.

FEEDING Its muscular cheeks and broad, deep bill allow the Hawfinch to break larger seeds and nut kernels than other finches. It is famously fond of cherry stones (and capable of dealing with them), but is also associated with hornbeam, beech, elm, crab apple, and maple. It eats buds, too, and in summer caterpillars and other grubs. In late summer it turns to raspberries, rose hips, and other fruits.

DISPLAY & VOICE Males approach females with drooped wings dragged along the ground, swivelling from side to side to display their white shoulders. More rarely, they perform butterfly-like courtship flights. Their song is quiet: a broken series of sharp notes in no particular pattern. Their calls are sharp, Robin-like ticking notes: *tik* or *tzik*, becoming a more explosive *tzick!* in flight or a louder version in alarm.

BREEDING The nests are sited in old, gnarled oaks or fruit trees, well-hidden among tangled foliage or in the cover of ivy or honeysuckle. Often made of thin birch twigs strengthened by stiffer twigs of oak or bits of bark, they are lined with grass or lichen, never feathers. The three to five eggs are incubated for 11–13 days by the female only. The chicks fly after 12–13 days.

MIGRATION Most Hawfinches remain in the same area all year round, but northern populations are more migratory. Juveniles move farther than adults, and females more than males. British Hawfinches are apparently resident, but occasional ones and twos appear in unexpected places.

LENGTH 18cm. (7in)

WHEN TO SEE All year
WHERE FOUND Usually in open woodland, woodland clearings, mature avenues with shrubby understorey; especially of cherry and hornbeam. In S Europe in olives and almond orchards. Absent from Ireland, most of Scandinavia; sporadic and local in most of Britain and rest of Europe, but in S Europe more widespread in winter

Brambling *Fringilla montifringilla*

In summer Bramblings are birds of northern birch forests with open heathy clearings, or mixed birch and conifers with plenty of light, airy woodland edge. A few can be found in late spring singing in similar habitats much farther south, including heaths in Britain, but they very rarely stay to nest. In winter Brambling numbers are very variable in most areas, depending on the success of the breeding season and the availability of food. In some winters Chaffinch flocks feeding beneath beeches or in weedy fields may attract similar numbers of Bramblings, while in other winters they are few and far between. Some immense flocks have been recorded in Central Europe. Bramblings are often attracted to Chaffinches, and feeding Chaffinch flocks are often the best places to look for these more boldly patterned relatives. Males can be easy to spot but females and immature birds are much duller and surprisingly hard to find. Their mixture of black, white, and orange, rather than brown and pink with bold white wingbars, separates them from the Chaffinches.

FEEDING Bramblings feed mainly on insects in summer, but seeds are critically important to their survival in winter. They take most of their food from the ground, and may join Chaffinches gleaning seeds scattered on the ground beneath bird tables.

DISPLAY & VOICE Males in spring sing from high treetop perches. The song is a simple rattle between deep, nasal, monotonous *dzweee* notes recalling a Greenfinch. Their flight calls have a harder tone than a Chaffinch's, easily distinguished with practice: a *tchek* or *tch'k* rather than the Chaffinch's soft *tsup*. Another distinctive call, based on a typically finch theme, is a twangy, nasal *tsweek* or *tswairk*.

BREEDING Built in a tree or bush, the nest is a neatly constructed cup woven from grass and stems with various fibrous plant materials, lichens, and feathers. Typically five to seven eggs are laid and incubated for 13–14 days by the hen; the chicks fly when two weeks old.

MIGRATION They make irregular, large-scale, long-distance movements when food supplies fail in the north. Some remain in southern Scandinavia in mild winters, but normally many move south into central Europe while smaller numbers head west to Britain and Ireland and further south to Iberia.

LENGTH 14–16cm (5½–6¼in)

WHEN TO SEE In N Europe mostly April to October; elsewhere September to April or May

WHERE FOUND Breeds throughout Scandinavia and east into Russia; winters widely throughout Europe but absent from Iceland

A richly coloured, long-winged, short-legged finch; narrower wings and shorter tail than Chaffinch, but with obvious resemblance. Often found with Chaffinches: white rump and orange wing panels useful identification clues, but females difficult to pick out in mixed flock

Typical finch bounding flight with open-shut wing action

Orange-buff and white shoulder patch, buff wingbar

Long, narrow white rump patch

Male, autumn

Male, breeding
Solidly black head and back diagnostic; steely bill

Female, autumn
Broader wingtip than male

Male, breeding
Contrasted black, white, and buffy orange

Juvenile
Narrow rump has snaky look as bird rises

Female, winter
Yellowish underwing, black undertail and white belly, unlike Chaffinch

Male, spring (below)
Black head develops before pale feather edges wear off to reveal black back

Intensity of orange varies

Spotted rear flanks

Orange breast contrasts with white belly, even in head-on view, unlike any Chaffinch

Male, winter
Mostly yellow bill obvious, unlike any Chaffinch

Female, breeding
Spotted flanks; back may wear to plain brown

Female, winter
Pale nape and dark cheek surround; only small orange patch above bend of wing

Back feathers of male: broad pale edge in autumn (left), wears thinner and paler until April, then breaks off to produce black of summer

Wing coverts tipped orange, October, fade to white by spring

Chaffinch *Fringilla coelebs*

A common finch showing much white when it flies, but this may be hidden when standing. Large flocks are rather loose and less synchronized than smaller finches; frequently feeds on the ground under trees or in open fields

Female, summer
Dull olive and greenish, but white bars obvious

Male, summer
Belly darker and underwing whiter than Brambling

Male, first summer

Male

Upright stance, peaked head distinctive

Male, summer
Broad white band on forewing, narrow second bar; white tail sides; wings broader at tip than female

Wingbars striking, rump green, no white

White wingbars exposed in threat or display; may be hidden by overlapping feathers when feeding

Female

Male, spring
Clear blue cap, blue bill, rich pink underparts

Wing feather fringes worn narrow and whitish

Juvenile
Buff rump

Female, spring
Olive-brown, becoming greyer during summer

Female, autumn
Dark sides, pale centre to nape more subtle than on Brambling

Male, winter
Spring colours obscured by buff feather tips

Female, winter

Chaffinches are common and familiar birds in many areas, yet unaccountably scarce in some others. In many rural regions they are remarkably tame and bold around car parks and picnic sites, often hopping about looking for crumbs and even taking food from people's outstretched hands. They are also frequent visitors to gardens. Yet winter flocks in open fields are wary of any disturbance, and all too ready to fly up and move off to the nearest hedge or tall tree. These flocks generally lack the sudden movements and tight, coordinated flights of Greenfinches and Linnets. A male Chaffinch is a seemingly discordant mixture of colours – pink, blue, black, white, green, and reddish brown – yet the bird is not nearly so gaudy as such a list implies; the overall effect is soft and subdued. A bright male in spring is, nevertheless, a real treat. The song is a bonus: one of the most welcome sounds of late winter, and continuing into summer, it is a lively, energetic performance – if not the most musical.

FEEDING In summer Chaffinches take huge numbers of caterpillars and other insects from tree foliage. In winter seeds are much more important, mostly taken from the ground. Chaffinches hop about in fields gathering a variety of grass and herb seeds, and they also search for tree seeds, especially beechmast, on the ground in woods and parkland.

DISPLAY & VOICE A courting male displays his bold white wing markings, drooping one wing and tilting over towards a female. He also sings from prominent perches, using a simple, lively, rattling, and cheery phrase with a faster flourish at the end: *chip-ip-ip, cherry erry erry, chipip-tchewee-oo*. The length and complexity of the song varies individually. Calls include a far-carrying, sharp *fink* or *pink* much like the call of a Great Tit; a simple, slightly vibrant whistle; a rising *wheeet*; and sharp, fine *zee*. In flight a Chaffinch makes an abrupt but soft *tsup* or *yup*, repeated but not running into a trill: a frequently heard and easy clue.

BREEDING The nest is an immaculate little cup covered with moss and lichen, in a tree or tall bush. Four or five eggs hatch after 12–13 days, and the chicks fly at two weeks old.

MIGRATION Large numbers of Chaffinches move south and west from northern and eastern Europe in autumn; they are common migrants along North Sea coasts.

LENGTH 14.5cm (5¾in)

WHEN TO SEE All year except in N and NE Europe, where mostly April to October
WHERE FOUND Throughout Europe except for Iceland and extreme N Scandinavia

Greenfinch *Carduelis chloris*

There are smaller finches that are equally green and yellow, but none are so large and sturdy, or so plain and unstreaked as the Greenfinch. It is a bird of tall, overgrown, thorny hedgerows, orchards, old gardens, and parks, with plenty of trees and belts of tall, leafy trees such as limes and poplars. In winter Greenfinches move to open fields, the edges of saltmarshes and even lake shores where seeds are heaped up in the waterside drift by the wind. They often mix with Sparrows, Chaffinches and other seed-eaters such as Reed and Corn Buntings.

FEEDING A seed-eater, the Greenfinch likes large seeds such as cereal grains and the bunches of seeds inside rose hips, which are too tough and leathery for smaller-billed species. Rarely it feeds in small herbage, more usually in bushes and trees, or on the ground. It may jump up to seize the stem of a plant such as a dandelion in its bill, then hold it down under one foot. Greenfinches are also fond of peanuts and sunflower seeds taken from bird tables and hanging feeders.

DISPLAY & VOICE Males sing from a perch and in flight, using a strange, fluttery, bat-like flight action on widely-spread wings, looking as if they must fall from the sky at any moment but continuing in wide spirals at treetop height. Their song is a loud, staccato, trilling rattle varied with more musical notes and a droning, wheezy *dzweee*. The usual flight call is a chatter or trill, less hard than a redpoll's, but firmer than a Linnet's: *chichichichichichit*. Their many other calls include a looser trill: *chil il il il*, a loud, Crossbill-like *chup* and a twangy *diuwee*.

BREEDING The nest is a large one, made of twigs, roots, grass, and moss and lined with fine hair and plant down. It is usually built against the trunk of a hedgerow bush or tree, or in a strong fork. Conifers are preferred, especially early in the season when cover is otherwise sparse. Four to six eggs hatch after 11–15 days; the chicks fly after 14–18 days.

MIGRATION Many Greenfinches from northeast Europe move south and southwest in autumn, and others from the south and west of the range disperse to a greater or lesser extent. They spend the winter entirely within their breeding range, but numbers increase in Mediterranean countries.

LENGTH 15cm (6in)

WHEN TO SEE All year
WHERE FOUND Throughout Europe except for central upland Scandinavia, N Finland and N Russia

Flight shape chunky with long, pointed wings, short but deeply-forked tail

Yellow stripe on wing breaks into series of streaks in flight; yellow tail sides then more obvious

Adult male, breeding Brightest, with most yellow

Adult female Duller than male, less yellow, but unstreaked

Adult male Song flight on outstretched wings, bat-like fluttery beats

Crossbill may look equally green but has dark wings with no yellow

Siskin has yellow (and black) bar across wing instead of along its edge

A sturdy, sociable finch, marked by yellow streaks along (but not across) wings and tail, with a distinctive large, pale orange-pink bill. Feeding flocks fly up in dense, synchronized groups when disturbed

Dark face gives angry frown

Adult male, spring Wings largely grey with yellow patches

Adult female, spring

In Spain, yellow on belly

Adult male, winter Duller than summer bird

Adult female, winter

Male   Female

Juvenile female Brownest plumage, least yellow, most streaked

Siskin *Carduelis spinus*

A tiny, neat, contrasty finch of pine forest and mixed woodland, that visits gardens in late winter and spring; outside the breeding season it feeds in tight-knit, coordinated flocks

Distinctive black and yellow bands on wings and bright rump, yellowest on males

Male
Black cap in spring and summer; white below with fine streaks

Juvenile lacks yellow in tail

Adult male
Yellow wingbar broader, black narrower, than on female at all ages

Adult female
More streaked than male

Juvenile male
Yellow across base of primaries broader than female's of any age

Adult male, breeding
Distinctive black cap and chin; lime-green to yellow neck and chest, banded wings

Adult female, breeding
Heavy streaks on white underside; broad black and narrow yellow wingbars

Male, first winter
Black cap obscured by pale tips; breast pale, streaked

Juvenile

Juvenile
Brownest plumage but wings already distinctive with black and yellow

Small, active, agile, with deeply forked tail and long wings; sharp, slim bill for probing into cones

Adult male
Yellowest on rump; adult female (far right) more streaked, narrow yellow bar on wing

Adult female

In winter Siskins dash in and out of the tops of spruce, alder, and larch trees in tight, coordinated, busy-looking flocks. They are often mixed with redpolls, sometimes with Goldfinches: all of them tiny, delicate birds. Siskins visit gardens, especially in March and April, and a close view of one on a peanut basket reveals just how minute it really is: barely as big as a Blue Tit. Size alone is a good clue to its identity, especially combined with the green, yellow, and black patterns of a male, but against a grey sky in winter Siskins often appear as little more than silhouettes. Then their calls provide the best means of separating them from redpolls.

FEEDING Siskins feed mainly on the seeds of pine, spruce, alder, and birch, as well as some shorter herbaceous plants. In summer spruce or pine seeds are essential. Siskins are less likely to feed on the ground than redpolls, although they do take seeds washed up alongside rivers and pools beneath alders in late winter. A Siskin uses its slim bill to tease out seeds from cones, although its bill cannot penetrate so deeply as the larger Goldfinch's.

DISPLAY & VOICE Pairs are formed in winter flocks and occupy territories together when they return to breeding areas in spring. Males often sing close together and in wintering areas, suggesting that song is more important in pairing than territorial defence. The song is a lively, prolonged twittering, interspersed with chattering and nasal notes, and with a wheezy note towards the end. Calls are distinctive, typically with a ringing, twanging, metallic quality, such as a descending *teeyu* and a rising *tsooee*. Flocks make a fast, rattling twitter and short, hard *tet* or *tut* notes.

BREEDING The nest is usually high in a conifer, fixed to a hanging, outer twig. It is made of twigs, heather, grass, moss, and bark, lined with hair and plant down. Three to five eggs hatch after 12–13 days and the young leave the nest when 13–15 days old.

MIGRATION In northern Europe the Siskin is mainly a summer visitor. Elsewhere some individuals return year after year to the same wintering site; others visit various sites and may even change from country to country in different years. In the south and west many Siskins are resident.

LENGTH 12cm (4¾in)

WHEN TO SEE All year; in the north, mostly April to September
WHERE FOUND Almost the whole of Europe except for extreme N Norway and Sweden. Leaves most of Scandinavia and Russia in winter

Serin *Serinus serinus*

There are many serins in Africa and Asia, including the canaries, but the two on this page are the only ones that breed in Europe. The Serin is a tiny, lively bundle of colour and song, widespread in Europe but especially common in Mediterranean areas.

FEEDING Serins feed mainly on the ground and in low herbs, eating seeds and a small number of insects.

DISPLAY & VOICE Males sing from high perches, and in song flights over and beyond the boundaries of their territories. The song is a fast, jingling, or sizzling (glass-splintering) trill, higher, faster and more prolonged than a Corn Bunting's. Their calls include a rippling trill in flight, as well as a rising *tsooet*.

BREEDING The nests, tiny cups of stems and lichen lined with feathers, are usually in dense conifers; three or four eggs hatch within 12–13 days.

MIGRATION Northern breeders move south in autumn; southern ones are mostly resident.

LENGTH 11.5cm (4½in)

WHEN TO SEE All year in S Europe; in central Europe mostly March to October
WHERE FOUND Breeds widely across Europe south of Baltic; rare and sporadic in Britain

Young male
Note cheek pattern, pale spot under eye, dark ear patch

Adult female
Pale marks under eye, yellower throat

Adult male (left)
Yellow crown, pale under eye, whitish cheek patch, long-tailed

A tiny, fast-flying finch with oval, leaf-shaped wings, a tiny bill and, in males, a bright yellow forehead and rump; often makes constant jingling calls

Adult male (above)
Bold yellow front, white belly, white wingbars, fast twittering song, short-tailed

Adult female
Dull rump still catches the eye in dancing flight

Juvenile
Dull, plain rump, pale wingbars

Adult male
Yellow rump; fresh wingbars buff, wear whiter

Both sexes seem to exhibit long and short tail projections

Juvenile male
Dull, pale, streaked (broader streaks than Citril Finch)

Citril Finch *Serinus citrinella*

This is one of the few species essentially restricted to Alpine environments, preferring high woodlands with a good deal of spruce and clearings such as Alpine meadows, right up to the tree line. It can be elusive, but may be tame enough to allow excellent views once discovered.

FEEDING It eats seeds, especially grass seeds but often those of spruce and pine, plus insects in summer. It feeds mainly on the ground; it sometimes forages in trees, but is less agile than the Redpoll or Siskin.

DISPLAY & VOICE In spring males sing close together in small territories: the song begins with a few distinct notes followed by short, variable phrases with a buzzy or tinkling quality.

BREEDING A neat nest of grass, roots, and spiders' webs, lined with hair and feathers, is made in a conifer; four or five eggs are incubated for 13–14 days.

MIGRATION Resident, except for movements downhill in winter to avoid heavy snowfall.

LENGTH 12cm (4¾in)

WHEN TO SEE All year
WHERE FOUND Breeds in E France, Alps, Pyrenees and mountains of N Spain, Corsica, Sardinia

A small, neat finch of high-altitude forest edge, with unique green, grey and yellow plumage

Adult female
Dull, but with green-yellow rump, grey nape, pale bars on blacker wing

Juvenile
Streaky, but fine lines below; two pale wingbars

Corsican race
Brown back

Male
Some have pale yellow faces

Female (left)
Usual deeper yellow face

Male
Wingbars dull in autumn, wear brighter by spring

Amount of grey beneath variable

Male
Yellow bars on black wing, green wing panel; grey hood diagnostic

Corsican/Sardinian race
Brown back

Goldfinch *Carduelis carduelis*

Adult male, autumn
Flight and tail feathers have buff tips, which soon fade to white

Female has less intense black face patch, less extensive red than male

A small, delicate, boldly-patterned finch, gregarious and easily seen except when nesting secretively in the foliage of leafy trees

Quick, springy, bounding flight, with constant slurred, liquid calls

Adult male, spring
Wing and tail feathers lose pale tips with wear; during the spring the back becomes paler, less rich brown; cheeks get whiter, nape patch bigger, face glossier red, and underside slightly greyer

Adult, spring
Cinnamon to buff-brown breast patches; may join in bar across chest on female

Adults
Unique bold red, white, black head pattern and black wings with broad yellow band above

Adult, winter (right)
Pale tips make head duller, more buff; broad pale tips to flight feathers; rich buff flanks most extensive on female

Juvenile
Wings and tail as adult but broader, buffer feather tips; plain head with no red or black

Despite becoming a garden bird in places, and even learning to feed from hanging feeders, the Goldfinch is essentially restricted to places with plentiful seeds on tall herbs. It does not like 'clean' farmland with no weeds; it revels in untidiness and rough, overgrown places.

FEEDING Seeds of thistles and similar tall plants are essential, especially when soft, 'milky', and half ripe. In winter it also takes alder and pine seeds. It feeds acrobatically in small groups, directly from the seed heads, using its feet to manipulate stems.

DISPLAY & VOICE Gregarious, but separating into pairs in spring, Goldfinches defend small territories but feed elsewhere. The song is a long, rambling, twittering version of the call, which is distinctively liquid and slurred, and varies between pairs: *chwee, chlui, tutitee,* or *tuleep.*

BREEDING They nest in the outer twigs of tall leafy trees; four to six eggs hatch within 11–14 days.

MIGRATION Northern birds move south in winter to the Mediterranean.

LENGTH 12cm (4¾in)

WHEN TO SEE All year
WHERE FOUND From Britain and S Scandinavia south throughout Europe

Bullfinch *Pyrrhula pyrrhula*

Male, NW and W Europe
Smaller than northern race, less extensive white rump, duller breast (palest Britain, redder NW Europe, reddest Spain)

Male, N Europe
Large, heavy, with very wide white rump, deep, vivid pink underside, some washed pink above

Male

Female

White wrap-around rump and vent, and square, blue-black tail distinctive at all times

A thicket, rather slow-moving, heavy-looking but quite acrobatic finch with a strikingly broad white rump, often evident as it dives out of sight through a hedge or into a thicket

Juvenile
Like female except no black on head, browner wingbar. Black wings, white rump and black tail distinctive, separate it from bigger-billed Hawfinch, Brambling, and Chaffinch

Females
Black cap as male, pale grey hind neck and wingbars, big white rump, black tail

You might expect such a subtly but beautifully coloured bird to be easy to see, but it is often rather elusive, drawing attention to itself only by its low, fluted calls. It often feeds in pairs at the edges of woods or hedges, quietly slipping out of sight if approached.

FEEDING Bullfinches specialize in eating soft buds and green shoots, and nibbling small seeds from fruits on the twig: with their blunt, rounded bills they are unable to pick small seeds from the ground. Insects are vital in summer for feeding their young.

DISPLAY & VOICE The song is rarely noticed: a long-sustained, varied mixture of calls and whistles with a vibrant, reedy quality. The calls are simple, clear, pure whistled notes, typically *piew* or *phew,* but with hoarser variations.

BREEDING A loose nest of twigs in a thick bush or tree contains four or five eggs, incubated for 12–14 days.

MIGRATION Mostly resident, but northern birds move south in winter.

LENGTH 14.5–16.5cm (5¾–6½in)

WHEN TO SEE All year
WHERE FOUND Breeds throughout Europe except for high areas of N Scandinavia

269

Mealy Redpoll *Carduelis flammea*

Individual variations in redpolls have bedevilled their identification and classification. Here we accord full species status to the Mealy and Lesser Redpolls and split the 'Arctic' birds into the Arctic and Hoary Redpolls, on the basis of a suite of characters that include structure and plumage. We also treat a fifth group, breeding in Greenland, as a separate species. They remain an identification challenge. Icelandic birds require further research.

FEEDING Mealy Redpolls eat small seeds, including those of birch, alder, willow, and grasses.

VOICE Call like Lesser Redpoll's metallic, chattering, far-carrying *chut-chut-chut* that blurs into song with sharp, fast rattles between calls.

BREEDING Nests are usually in small willows, poplars, birches, or alders; four to five eggs hatch in 10–12 days.

MIGRATION Most Scandinavian birds move southeast in autumn, but in some years large numbers wander southwest and reach Britain.

LENGTH 13–15cm (5–6in)

WHEN TO SEE All year; in N Europe mostly April to September
WHERE FOUND Breeds in N Sweden, Norway, Finland, N Russia; range fluctuating

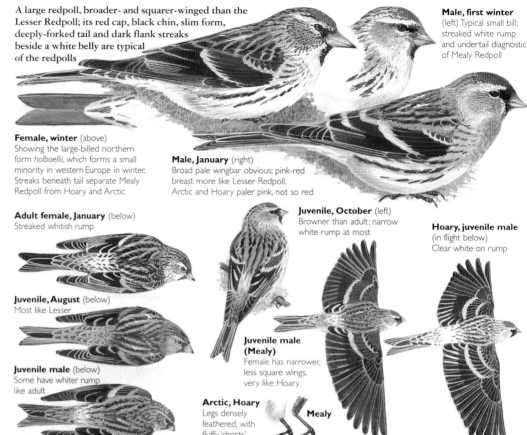

A large redpoll, broader- and squarer-winged than the Lesser Redpoll; its red cap, black chin, slim form, deeply-forked tail and dark flank streaks beside a white belly are typical of the redpolls

Male, first winter (left) Typical small bill; streaked white rump and undertail diagnostic of Mealy Redpoll

Female, winter (above) Showing the large-billed northern form *holboellii*, which forms a small minority in western Europe in winter. Streaks beneath tail separate Mealy Redpoll from Hoary and Arctic

Male, January (right) Broad pale wingbar obvious; pink-red breast more like Lesser Redpoll. Arctic and Hoary paler pink, not so red

Adult female, January (below) Streaked whitish rump

Juvenile, October (left) Browner than adult; narrow white rump at most

Hoary, juvenile male (in flight below) Clear white on rump

Juvenile, August (below) Most like Lesser

Juvenile male (below) Some have whiter rump like adult

Juvenile male (Mealy) Female has narrower, less square wings, very like Hoary

Arctic, Hoary Legs densely feathered, with fluffy 'shorts', unlike Mealy

Mealy

'Arctic' Redpolls *Carduelis hornemanni, C. exilipes & C. rostrata*

Redpolls from Arctic regions are treated here as three species: a dark Greenland one, *rostrata*, a north Canadian group, *hornemanni* (Arctic Redpoll), and a north Siberian group, *exilipes* (Hoary Redpoll). All three are rare visitors to northwest Europe, including the UK.

FEEDING They eat small seeds, such as those of birch, alder, willow, and grasses, along with insects in summer.

VOICE Their calls are very like those of Mealy and Lesser Redpolls, with a basic hard *chut-chut-chut* pattern, the notes perhaps a little slower or more well-spaced. They are quiet birds in winter.

BREEDING All three species nest low down in small trees or shrubs; four to five eggs hatch in 11–12 days.

MIGRATION Usually there are just short-distance movements, by part of the breeding population, but in some years larger numbers move south in Scandinavia and may reach Britain. Greenland breeders winter in Iceland, along with the resident Icelandic population.

LENGTH 13–15cm (5–6in)

WHEN TO SEE All year; in NW Europe November to March
WHERE FOUND Breed Finland and extreme N Norway; Greenland; Canadian Arctic; rare vagrants elsewhere

Two thick-feathered, round-headed, small-billed, white-rumped 'Arctic' redpolls and a large, dark, heavily marked, rather Twite-like form from Greenland, all with typical redpoll red caps and black chins

Hoary, juvenile female Smallest, but still substantial; unmarked white rump

Hoary, male (left) Whitest of all redpolls, like snowball when white rump is fluffed out

Tiny bill, wide head, bull neck

Hoary and Arctic both plain white beneath tail

Hoary, juvenile male (left) Bold white rump, small red cap

Arctic, winter male (above)

Arctic male (left and above) Bright buff head, dark wings, white belly; broad, square wings (Hoary narrower at tip)

Arctic (above) White bars on black wings; very long wingtips; very white below; big white rump; feathery 'shorts'; tiny bill

Greenland thickly streaked beneath tail

Adults are whiter on flanks but boldly striped

Bill rather deep; mostly tawny-brown, rump brownish

Greenland, juvenile males Broad-winged, long-bodied; dark, with three broad flank stripes, buff wingbar and throat recall Twite

Lesser Redpoll *Carduelis cabaret*

The smallest redpoll, lighter in bulk and narrower winged than the Mealy

First winter
Red cap, unlike autumn/winter Linnet

Flocks feed acrobatically in trees

Male, spring (above)
Deep red crown, extent of pink-red on breast and rump varies, some very eyecatching

Female, winter
Fresh feathers edged whitish; some white on rump

Wingbars, buff flanks, white belly recall Twite

Juvenile (below)
Black bib, no red cap; typical long, slender rear body and wingtips, long tail

Deeply forked tail

A tiny, quick-moving, acrobatic redpoll, rather dark brown and well streaked, with a black chin; flies in tight, coordinated flocks, often mixed with Siskins

Male

Dark bill in late spring

Female, autumn
Always duller than male, usually more buff. In summer, wears dark brown above and whitish below

Juvenile female
(left) Narrower wing than adult

Female, spring
Lacks pink-red breast of male

Lesser Redpolls have enjoyed decades of expansion followed by sudden declines. The increases were related to increased planting of conifers in Britain, and of birch and alder on dunes in the Low Countries, but the declines are puzzling. They became suburban birds for a time, but they are essentially birds of the northern woods.

FEEDING The staple food is tiny seeds, especially of birch, which they take from the trees or the ground below.

DISPLAY & VOICE The song, given in looping, undulating flights, is a fast, metallic, reeling trill interspersed with staccato flight calls: *tchuch-uch-uch-uch*; harder, less jingling than a Greenfinch. A nasal, twanging *tsoo-eee* is often used.

BREEDING A small, neat cup of twigs, bark, flower heads, and leaves, in a shrub or tree, contains four to six eggs; they hatch after 10–12 days.

MIGRATION Western birds move short distances, northern and eastern birds much farther, sometimes in widespread irruptions in search of food.

LENGTH 11.5–14.5cm (4½–5¾in)

WHEN TO SEE All year; in N Europe mostly in summer
WHERE FOUND Breeds N and central Europe south to France, Alps, Danube

Scarlet Rosefinch *Carpodacus erythrinus*

Juvenile (left)
Rounded bill; black eye in plain face; streaked chest

A slim-tailed but heavy-bodied, large-headed, fat-billed finch with a bold dark eye, dull in most plumages except for two wingbars

Juvenile

Immature male, spring
Two thin wingbars, greenish above, pale beneath, nondescript

Juvenile, autumn
Beady eye, two wingbars, streaked chest

Compare with buntings (most have white in tail, Corn Bunting is much bigger, more striped on head)

Adult male
Strawberry-red head, chest and rump of variable extent

Juvenile, September
Two wingbars, dark tail (no white)

Dull head, but dark eye and stubby, dark bill obvious

Adult female (left)
Soft breast streaks; only one strong wingbar

Adult male
Red rump, pinkish wingbars, deeply notched tail

A western representative of a chiefly Asiatic family, the rosefinch is a colourful bird in male breeding colours. The other plumages are dull and undistinguished. There has been a general westward spread and increase in its numbers in central Europe, with the beginnings of colonization in several western European countries.

FEEDING It uses its thick bill to open buds and soft or unripe seeds; it also eats soft fruit, shoots, and other vegetable matter, as well as insects.

VOICE The song consists of a variety of bright, whistling, or piping phrases with a marked rising and falling pattern. Calls include a short *zik* or *zit*.

BREEDING The nests are well hidden in thick scrub or herbage. Four to six eggs hatch after 11–12 days.

MIGRATION In autumn Rosefinches migrate to Pakistan, India, and east to China. Small numbers of immatures move west and may appear in western Europe, especially in coastal areas.

LENGTH 15cm (6in)

WHEN TO SEE All year; in W Europe mostly September/October, increasingly in late spring
WHERE FOUND Breeds S Norway, much of Sweden and east from Germany; more locally through central Europe and along North Sea coasts

Linnet *Carduelis cannabina*

One of several relatively featureless, small, brown finches, the Linnet is distinguished by the plumage of the spring male, which develops a beautiful flush of crimson. It is a bird of dry, open ground with abundant bushes and herbs. It breeds on open heaths, at the edges of higher moors, on farmland with uneven hedgerows, and high in the foothills of the Alps and Pyrenees where low hedges cross flowery green meadows. In winter Linnets are often found in flocks on open farmland, on saltmarshes and weed-grown shingle, and around freshwater marshes where seeds collect along the edges of pools and ditches.

FEEDING Linnets are essentially seed eaters, taking fewer insects than other finches, so they require 'waste' ground and are unable to survive in areas of weed-free agriculture. Less agile than the Redpoll and Twite, which gather seeds while clinging to plants, they feed mostly by standing on the ground and picking seeds from overhanging stems, or from the soil beneath.

DISPLAY & VOICE Males frequently sing from bush tops, even in late winter flocks. Their small territories are defined by singing: a rather quiet, musical, fast, repetitive medley of fluty whistles, warbles, chirrups, and trills. Calls include a typical small finch twitter, which is metallic, quick, dry, and lighter than the hard notes of a Redpoll: *chichichichit* or *tet-tet-terret*. Like other finches it also produces a plaintive *tsooeet*.

BREEDING Linnets are sociable even in summer, gathering where seeds are abundant. Several pairs can exploit small areas of plentiful food (unlike the Chaffinch, for example, which feeds its young on caterpillars and must defend a larger territory to ensure a sufficient supply). The nests are neat, tiny cups of twigs and roots, lined with hair and wool. Four to six eggs hatch after 12–14 days' incubation, and the chicks fly when 10–17 days old.

MIGRATION In autumn most Linnets move southwest to winter in the south of the breeding range, mainly around the Mediterranean. Many coastal areas, particularly, see straggling groups and sometimes larger flocks of Linnets on the move in autumn and spring. In countries such as Britain and France Linnets are residents, summer visitors, winter visitors, and passage migrants!

LENGTH 13.5cm (5¼in)

WHEN TO SEE All year; mostly summer in north and east of range
WHERE FOUND Breeds through most of Europe, except for Iceland, most of Norway and N Sweden; in winter mostly south from Britain, Denmark, and Germany to Mediterranean coast

Male, breeding
Variable amount of red on crown and chest; back unstreaked rusty-brown

Female, breeding
Warm brown with only fine streaks; pale marks above and below eye and on cheeks

Female

A slender, petite, gregarious finch with a light, dancing flight, that feeds on the ground beneath vegetation rather than on the stems and foliage. Warm colours with darker wings and tail, each marked with streaks of white, are distinctive

White sides to tail and streaks on wings a good clue, but compare Twite

Constant face pattern: pale around eye and on cheeks

Male, autumn
In fresh autumn plumage dull feather tips obscure red beneath; they gradually wear off to reveal brighter colours

Female, winter
Compared with Twite and Redpoll, Linnet is a plainer, redder brown above, brighter buff below, with greyer head and whiter throat

Juvenile
Dullest and streakiest plumage with hint of wingbar; compare with Twite

Juvenile

Female

Male
Rump wears paler and greyer

White on wing and tail breaks into separate streaks when spread, obvious in flight

Males

Twite *Carduelis flavirostris*

Winter flocks sweep round in tight, calling groups before dropping silently out of sight

Scandinavian bird, winter
Particularly buff

Bill grey in summer; yellow in winter

Female, breeding
Worn plumage dark, white on tail reduced, wingbar narrow; face more buff, overall less rust/ginger than Linnet

Juvenile male
Bright and buffy; wingbar broad buff; white streak along wing and obvious white tail side

Female, autumn
Yellow bill, broad orange-buff throat; wingbar like Redpoll, white streak like Linnet

While clearly closely related to the Linnet, the Twite often looks more like a Redpoll with its warm buffy-brown colour and pale wingbar

Male, October
Pink rump begins to show in September/October, brighter by spring

Female
Shorter tail

Pink rump of male becomes brighter as brown tips wear off

Compare tail pattern with Linnet

Juvenile
A 'ginger' bird in the field, with tawny throat

In some ways the Twite seems to lie half way between the Linnet and the Redpoll, but it is most closely allied to the Linnet. A bird of low vegetation or the ground, it is even more terrestrial than the Linnet. It breeds in more northerly or higher regions, where it is associated with upland farms and coastal crofts; it frequents saltmarsh in winter.

FEEDING Twites pick small seeds from the ground or herbs, and from the vegetation washed up along tidelines.

DISPLAY & VOICE Males circle with flapping wings and glides while singing; they also sing from perches. The song is Linnet-like but more twittering and metallic, less musical, with a nasal jangle or twang. Calls include a Redpoll-like *tup-up-up*, harder than a Linnet, and a nasal, twangy, almost rasping *twaa-eet*.

BREEDING Four to six eggs, laid in a nest on the ground in heather or other herbs, hatch after 12–13 days.

MIGRATION Upland breeders move to the coast in winter; northern birds head south to central Europe.

LENGTH 14cm (5½in)

WHEN TO SEE All year; April to September in N Europe
WHERE FOUND Breeds Norway, Ireland, N Britain; winters Sweden, Denmark, E England, Low Countries, central Europe

Pine Grosbeak *Pinicola enucleator*

First-winter male

Female, summer
Bronzy yellow; dark wings with thin white bars

Female
Shorter tail than male, slightly broader wings

Short fast bounds with closed wings create deeply undulating flight

Male
Striking raspberry-red head and breast with variable grey

First-winter female

A very large thrush-sized finch of the far north, shy in summer but remarkably tame in winter. Flocks may feed in suburban areas but rarely stray far south. Its size, deep bill, and black wings with white feather edges are distinctive

Adult female, winter

This remarkable bird lives in the forests of the far north, to the edge of the tundra, both in conifers and in birch woods. In winter some move into towns to find food.

FEEDING It takes buds, shoots, seeds, and fleshy berries both from trees and from the low shrubs beneath them, or at the forest edge. It is acrobatic when feeding, often hanging upside down almost like a small parrot or a Waxwing, but using its bill to cling on or to grasp berries like a Crossbill.

DISPLAY & VOICE Both sexes sing, males most loudly, with a short phrase of yodelling, fluty, rich whistles. Calls include a Bullfinch-like flute and soft, silky sounds; also a loud *tui-tui-tui*.

BREEDING The female builds a large nest of ragged twigs, lined with moss, lichen, and roots, against the trunk of a tree; three or four eggs hatch after an incubation of 14 days.

MIGRATION Mostly resident, but some migrate short distances; all are likely to move when food is short, Russian birds moving into northeast Europe.

LENGTH 18.5cm (7¼in)

WHEN TO SEE All year; around fringe of breeding range mostly August to April
WHERE FOUND Breeds locally Norway, Sweden, Finland, Russia; rare vagrant to south and southwest of breeding range

Parrot Crossbill *Loxia pytyopsittacus*

Crossbills worldwide have adapted to local conditions and appear in a range of forms, with different bill sizes, plumage intensities, and calls. In Europe this is the biggest, and feeds on the toughest seeds. It lives in tall, open pines in northern forests, less often in mixed coniferous woods.

FEEDING Parrot Crossbills feed in the canopy, extracting seeds from the cones of Scots pine, less often spruce. They use their feet and bills to manipulate the cones; falling scales and empty cones give a clue to the presence of birds feeding silently above. They also eat some insects in summer.

VOICE Calls may be deeper and louder than a Crossbill's, but some are indistinguishable: *kop kop*, *choop choop* and a very hard, deep *cherk cherk*.

BREEDING They nest high in conifers at the forest edge, laying three or four eggs very early in spring.

MIGRATION Normally resident, they sometimes wander in search of food, periodically irrupting in large numbers that may penetrate south of the Baltic.

LENGTH 17.5cm (7in)

WHEN TO SEE All year
WHERE FOUND Breeds Scandinavia, Baltic States, eastwards through Russia

A thickset, heavy-billed finch, remarkably similar to Crossbill and Scottish Crossbills and often difficult to identify, although typical, large-billed males are distinctive

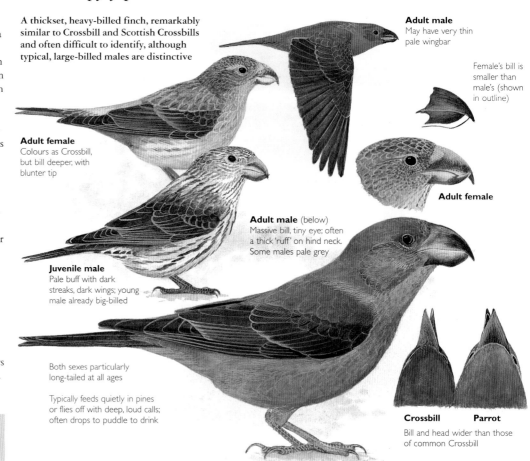

Adult male
May have very thin pale wingbar

Female's bill is smaller than male's (shown in outline)

Adult female

Adult female
Colours as Crossbill, but bill deeper, with blunter tip

Adult male (below)
Massive bill, tiny eye; often a thick 'ruff' on hind neck. Some males pale grey

Juvenile male
Pale buff with dark streaks, dark wings; young male already big-billed

Both sexes particularly long-tailed at all ages

Typically feeds quietly in pines or flies off with deep, loud calls; often drops to puddle to drink

Crossbill   **Parrot**
Bill and head wider than those of common Crossbill

Two-barred Crossbill *Loxia leucoptera*

A small, distinctive and bright crossbill, this is a bird of larch and spruce forest with a mixture of other trees. It prefers woodland edges in some areas, dense forest in others.

FEEDING It feeds mainly on larch and spruce seeds, taken from cones on the trees, but it may eat alder, birch, and other seeds. It also takes insects from pine needles in summer.

DISPLAY & VOICE The male sings within a small territory; the song is distinctively fast, with rattles, buzzy notes, trills, and musical whistles: more like a Redpoll or Canary than other crossbills. Calls are high, dry, and less metallic than the calls of other crossbills: *kip kip* or *tyip tyip*.

BREEDING Nests are made of dead twigs and stems, in spruce trees. Three to five eggs are incubated for 14–15 days and the chicks fly at 22 days old.

MIGRATION Usually resident, but like other crossbills it has to make local movements in some years to find food. Every few years larger numbers move much farther afield; some then reach Scandinavia, and rarely Britain.

LENGTH 15cm (6in)

WHEN TO SEE Mostly July to March
WHERE FOUND Mostly visits Finland, Norway, and Sweden from N Russia

Young male
Grey-brown, red on rump

Adult male

A slim, neat, small-billed crossbill with a distinct wing pattern, often seen with other crossbills

Note curved wingbars, broad at base (upper edge on closed wing)

Juvenile (above)
Greenish, streaked, wingbars already distinct

Some have heavier bills (lower mandible still slim)

Crossbill (above)
May have narrow wingbars of different shape

Tertial tips V-shaped or stepped, not smoothly curved as on Crossbill

Adult females

Adult female
Worn plumage, October

White tertial tips large and obvious

Adult male
Cherry-red to pink-red unlike Crossbill; blacker wings

Underwing of male buff in front (all grey on Crossbill); undertail white, some with dark streaks (all grey on Crossbill)

Crossbill *Loxia curvirostra* Scottish Crossbill *Loxia scotica*

All crossbills are very similar and difficult to identify: all males are red with dark wings, all females grey-green, and all have remarkable bills with crossed tips. They feed quietly in conifers, fly off noisily and frequently come to water to drink. Some populations are long-bodied, others short-bodied, giving a short- or long-tailed effect; bill size and calls also vary, but these variations do not seem to be related. Research is required on the relationship between primary tips, body length, bill shape and calls in populations. They are highly irruptive and populations may temporarily breed in areas not normally occupied

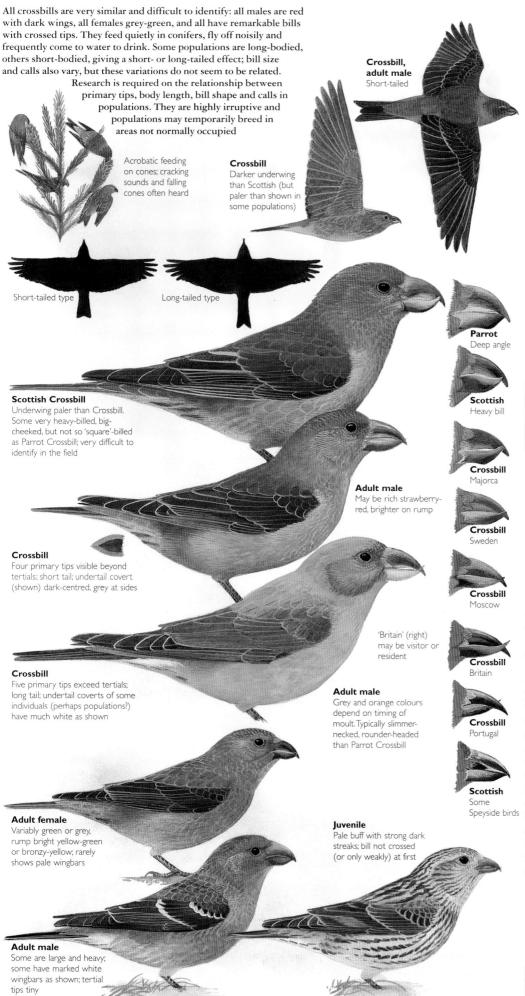

Acrobatic feeding on cones; cracking sounds and falling cones often heard

Crossbill
Darker underwing than Scottish (but paler than shown in some populations)

Crossbill, adult male
Short-tailed

Short-tailed type

Long-tailed type

Scottish Crossbill
Underwing paler than Crossbill. Some very heavy-billed, big-cheeked, but not so 'square'-billed as Parrot Crossbill; very difficult to identify in the field

Crossbill
Four primary tips visible beyond tertials; short tail; undertail covert (shown) dark-centred, grey at sides

Crossbill
Five primary tips exceed tertials; long tail; undertail coverts of some individuals (perhaps populations?) have much white as shown

Adult female
Variably green or grey, rump bright yellow-green or bronzy-yellow; rarely shows pale wingbars

Adult male
Some are large and heavy; some have marked white wingbars as shown; tertial tips tiny

Adult male
May be rich strawberry-red, brighter on rump

'Britain' (right) may be visitor or resident

Adult male
Grey and orange colours depend on timing of moult. Typically slimmer-necked, rounder-headed than Parrot Crossbill

Juvenile
Pale buff with strong dark streaks; bill not crossed (or only weakly) at first

Parrot
Deep angle

Scottish
Heavy bill

Crossbill
Majorca

Crossbill
Sweden

Crossbill
Moscow

Crossbill
Britain

Crossbill
Portugal

Scottish
Some Speyside birds

Wonderfully entertaining to watch, Crossbills feed quietly and inconspicuously in trees, now and then calling loudly before flying off.
FEEDING They prise the seeds of pine, spruce, and larch from cones, using their curved bills and tongues to extract the seeds while they manipulate the cones with both bill and feet in almost parrot-like fashion. They visit water to drink several times a day.
DISPLAY & VOICE Males sing from exposed, high perches or in a slow display flight: a hesitant, varied warble mixed with buzzy notes, calls and trills. Calls are distinctive, staccato, loud, and explosive: *chip chip* or *jip jip*.
BREEDING They nest in the tops of trees, laying their eggs very early in the year, but also in late summer depending on the cone crop. Three or four eggs hatch in 14–15 days.
MIGRATION Resident to dispersive, Crossbills sometimes move long distances to find food, turning up in some unexpected places in conifers.
LENGTH 16.5cm (6½in)

WHEN TO SEE All year; often late summer in areas outside breeding range
WHERE FOUND Local in Britain, Iberia, France, central and SE Europe; widespread N and E Europe

While common Crossbills are widespread in spruce, larch, and often Scots pine, and Parrot Crossbills are more northern birds of pine forest, the Scottish Crossbill is a more or less intermediate form found in the ancient Scots pine forests of northern Scotland: it is Britain's only unique species. Identification is a challenge, for bill size and calls are of limited use.
FEEDING It eats mostly Scots pine seeds, using typical crossbill technique.
DISPLAY & VOICE Like other crossbills, male Scottish Crossbills sing from perches in the nesting territory, but whole flocks may sing on cold, sunny days in winter or spring. Calls include a deep *chup* – distinguishable with experience but difficult for most people to recognize given the variation of Crossbill and Parrot Crossbill calls.
BREEDING The nest is typically high in a pine, in the centre or out on a wide branch, near a clearing. Three or four eggs are incubated for 12–14 days.
MIGRATION Resident, except for local movements when food is short.
LENGTH 16.5cm (6½in)

WHEN TO SEE All year
WHERE FOUND N Scotland only

Corn Bunting *Miliaria calandra*

The Corn Bunting has become scarce in intensively-farmed landscapes in recent years, after a period of increase and spread. Such population fluctuations are normal for many species, but birds such as the Corn Bunting have been hard hit by the increasing use of insecticides and herbicides, which make it very difficult for them to find sufficient insects to eat in summer, and seeds in winter. In southern Europe, however, the Corn Bunting is still a common bird; it is often seen from roadsides as it perches on wires, or on top of straggly bushes beside fields. While the brighter Crested Lark flies up from the roadside verge or runs about on bare places, the more sluggish Corn Bunting hops quietly on the ground and tends to be far less conspicuous when feeding. In winter, at dusk, Corn Buntings can sometimes be seen flying overhead in small groups towards their communal roosts – which may involve scores or hundreds of birds where they are still common – drawing attention with their distinctive flight calls.

FEEDING A ground feeder, the Corn Bunting finds seeds, shoots, and – especially in summer – insects on arable fields or grassy, bushy slopes. In autumn it gleans waste grain from the stubble of harvested cornfields. It is far less likely to visit farmyards and similar places than the Yellowhammer, except in the most severe weather.

DISPLAY & VOICE Males often pair with several females; they arrive on the nesting grounds earlier than females and sing, but after mating they have little to do with them. A male usually sings from an obvious perch, but sometimes from a low clod of earth or stone. The song is a brief, fast, jangling phrase, beginning with separate ticking notes and ending in a tuneless, metallic jingle (often likened to a quick shake of a bunch of keys, or breaking glass). The songs may be heard all day long, throughout the summer. Calls include a loud, slightly liquid, abrupt note: *quit*, *quick* or *plip* with an emphasis on the final 'click'.

BREEDING The female builds a loose structure of grass, green stems, and roots on the ground in grass or herbage, lays four to six eggs and incubates them for 12–14 days.

MIGRATION In some areas Corn Buntings are resident, in others they move short distances; smaller numbers migrate south into Mediterranean countries, including north Africa.

LENGTH 18cm (7in)

WHEN TO SEE All year
WHERE FOUND From England and Scotland, Denmark and Germany, south and east into Middle East and north Africa

Plain tail with no white sides, unlike Yellowhammer and other buntings, or Skylark

All pale tawny-brown with darker streaks; paler rump and plain tail with no white sides

A large, heavy-billed, fat-bodied bunting with no white in the tail; recalls Skylark, but typically perches on overhead wires, bush tops, hedgerows, and raised clumps of earth and does not walk for long periods over open ground

Male (left) has broader, rounder, outer wing than female (right)

Male, autumn
Fresh plumage in October/November

Female
Shorter body than male produces 'shorter' tail

May briefly dangle legs as it leaves a song perch

Streaks on chest often make dark central V-shape

Sings with head raised, held back, and bill wide open

Drooping tail and humped back may give untidy look on perch; often flicks tail

Longer flights are undulating and powerful, with bursts of beats between brief closures of wings

Bill from front

Large bill with S-shaped cutting edges; deep, broad shape unique among buntings; compare Skylark

Female
Short tail

Juvenile
Warmer buff

Male
Longer tail

Adult
Worn plumage, June/July

May be confusing when feeding quietly on ground: note large, pale yellow-brown bill, trace of pale moustache, dark-streaked chest

276

Ortolan Bunting *Emberiza hortulana*

A slim, sharp-faced bunting with a pinkish bill, yellowish line beneath the cheek, and fine pale eye-ring; typical of upland meadows and hot stony slopes with low bushes

Female, first winter
Female has shorter tail, blunter wings than male; note pale eye-ring

Male
Longer tail and more pointed wings than females; pale eye-ring, pink bill, green chest

Male, breeding
Green chest looks pale, but whole bird darkens with wear

Mostly white underside of tail shows well on perched bird

Female, breeding
Distinctive facial expression with sharp bill, flattish forehead, yellowish stripe under cheeks, but compare Cretzschmar's Bunting

Male

Two outer tail feathers have white beneath; rarely white spot on third

All have pale pink legs, quite long, pinkish bill with darker ridge

Male
Richly-coloured with yellow, green, and dull orange-rufous at close range but usually looks pale, with little contrast

Male, first winter
Adult colours, but obscured by streaks

Female, first winter
Facial characters distinct but require good view; clay-brown on back and rump but wing feathers edged with rufous; thin white upper wingbar; lacks yellow until autumn

Note shorter tail of female (above)

The Ortolan is a round-headed, longish-billed, plump, long-tailed bunting of open slopes and pastures with scattered bushes and trees or forest edge. In southern Europe it is perhaps most familiar on hillsides with a mixture of a few tall trees and many more low bushes and aromatic herbs, but it ascends to greener, softer regions with grassy fields and clumps of trees. Farther north it likes plantations and forests of pine and birch with clearings. There are a number of other small, neat European buntings with a similar pattern to the Ortolan, especially Cretzschmar's Bunting, with which it is easily confused. Changing farming methods have caused a widespread and serious decline in Ortolan Buntings, especially in the west but increasingly elsewhere as agriculture is intensified in eastern Europe. It seems that the removal of hedges, elimination of field weeds, and reduction in crop variety is to blame, with a consequent loss of nesting sites and food.

FEEDING The Ortolan feeds mainly on insects, with some seeds in autumn and winter. It picks caterpillars from trees and can even catch flying insects, but its long bill is best adapted to seizing insects and seeds on the ground and manipulating them between the sharp cutting edge and the tongue. This splits and peels seeds, and removes the legs or antennae of insects so the bird can swallow them more easily.

DISPLAY & VOICE Males sing to advertise their territories and to attract mates. They use the same perches repeatedly, mainly in bushes (often not quite at the top, so the singers can be hard to spot), in trees or on wires, but they also sing from the ground. The song is characteristic, tuneful, but short, with a clear, ringing quality. A simple phrase, descending at the end, is repeated several times, then again at a different pitch: *tsee-tsee-tsee-tsu-tsu-tsu*. Calls are rather abrupt, fuller than a Yellowhammer's: *tsip* or *twik* in flight, and a thinner *tsee-up* or *tseeu* in summer.

BREEDING The female builds a nest on the ground – often in cereals or potatoes, among thick grass or on a rough slope – using stalks and stems lined with finer grasses, roots, and hair. She incubates her four or five eggs for 11–12 days, and the chicks fly when 12–13 days old.

MIGRATION All European Ortolans migrate south in autumn; they spend the winter in Africa well south of the Sahara, mostly in the east.

LENGTH 16–17cm (6¼–6¾in)

WHEN TO SEE April to October
WHERE FOUND Breeds from Sweden and S Norway east through Finland to Russia and south to Germany and Poland; also from Iberia through S France and Italy to E Europe and the Balkans

Yellowhammer *Emberiza citrinella*

Few birds call in the heat of the afternoon on a summer's day, but the Yellowhammer sings his cheerful, repetitive song all day long, all summer through. A typical bunting, its long body, slender white-edged tail and flat-topped head – with a thin upper mandible and more bulbous lower one – distinguish it from all the finches and sparrows. Yellowhammers are characteristic birds of heathland with bushes and open grassy spaces, farmland with hedgerows between pastures, and grassy strips with mixed gorse bushes and bracken above coastal cliffs. In farmland areas they have declined with the loss of hedgerows, and especially the loss of winter food: stubble fields and stackyards are now rare, and seed-eating birds like the Yellowhammer are suffering as a result.

FEEDING In winter Yellowhammers eat seeds, shoots, spilled cattle food, and other scraps foraged from fields and under hedges. In summer they eat more insects. They feed on the ground, often in scattered flocks, and frequently with Chaffinches, Reed Buntings, and House and Tree Sparrows. If disturbed, they move to the nearest hedge or tall tree with a quick, jerky flight action, showing the extensive white sides of their flicked tails.

DISPLAY & VOICE The male usually sings from an exposed perch: a bush top or open branch, or a fence post or wire on more open ground. The song is somewhat variable but typically a short series of sharp, metallic notes, often repeated, with the penultimate or final one higher or lower than the rest: *tit-it-it-it-it-it-teeee-tip*. Call notes are also sharp and metallic, and distinctive once learned: *tswik* or *twitik* and a more rasping *dzu*.

BREEDING The nest is a rather bulky structure of grasses and straw, lined with finer grass and hair to form a soft, smooth cup. It is usually at the base of a hedge or close beside the roots of a bush, or in a low bank. Three to five eggs hatch after 12–14 days and the chicks fly when 11–13 days old.

MIGRATION Some northern European Yellowhammers reach Britain in winter, but most of the birds in Britain and Ireland are resident. Birds that breed in northern and eastern Europe move south to wintering areas in Spain, Italy, and Greece.

LENGTH 16–17cm (6¼–6¾in)

WHEN TO SEE All year; only winter in much of Spain
WHERE FOUND Farmland and grassy uplands with hedges, woodland edge. All Europe except N Scandinavia, Iberia and extreme SE in summer; general southward movement in winter

More elongated, sharper-faced than finches, the Yellowhammer is a slim, long-tailed bunting, often found in small groups and mixed with finches and sparrows outside the breeding season. In summer, males typically perch on bush tops or posts, repeating their simple, metallic songs

Female (left) has shorter tail and narrower wings than male (right)

Male
Rich rusty-red rump diagnostic of all ages, both sexes

Male, spring
Striped head wears to all-yellow by August; cheek stripes variable

Male, spring
More rufous variation, duskier below

Dull breast of winter male becomes bright yellow and rufous in spring

Yellow undertail coverts, but underside of tail mostly white

Adult female
Duller and less yellow than male; rump similar

Distinctive mixture of greenish-yellow and chestnut-brown with blacker streaks, yellower belly and streaked flanks; orange-rusty rump rules out Cirl Bunting

Female, breeding

Adult female, winter
Note fine streaks on crown and lower face, streaked chest, clear greenish-yellow belly

Male, first winter
Male long-bodied, with rump and tail extending farther beyond wingtips than female (below)

Female, breeding

Adult male
Some males more streaked beneath than others

Juvenile female
Wingtip/tail position indicate female; less white in tail than male, but still conspicuous; juvenile slightly less white than adult female

Tail pattern

278

Cirl Bunting *Emberiza cirlus*

Juvenile (left)
Like pale brown Yellowhammer but rump dull, not rusty, sharp streaks on buff below

Adult male
Rusty on wings, tertials, framing olive rump

Adult male
Head pattern obscured by pale feather edges in winter

Adult female
Dull rump; long tail with white on sides

A neat, slim bunting, with a distinctive olive rump against rusty back, yellowish below; males strongly patterned; frequent song and short, high, thin, elusive call note

Adult female, spring
(right) Looks like a pale-throated male in spring

Adult male (below)
Black, yellow, and green head and breast unique

Outer tail has limited white

Adult female
Sharp-faced, with flat crown, slightly more striped face than Yellowhammer, dull crown with no central stripe, rufous scapulars against duller wings

Cirl Buntings are typical of warm, lazy summer days in southern Europe, where sunshine bathes the bushy slopes or fills the orchards and vineyards with light. At the northern edge of their range they rely more on old meadows and bushy hedgerows in summer, and weedy stubbles with plentiful seeds in winter.

FEEDING They feed mainly on various seeds taken from the ground, but grasshoppers are important in summer.

DISPLAY & VOICE The song is the best clue to a Cirl Bunting's presence in summer: a simple, short, metallic trill, fast and 'dribbling' or slower, more of a rattle, on one note. It is harder than the trill of Bonelli's Warbler, and lacks the usual longer note at or near the end of a Yellowhammer's song. The call is frustratingly difficult to pinpoint: a short, high, soft *sip*, often repeated.

BREEDING Three or four eggs are laid in a well-hidden nest low in a bush or creeper. They hatch after 12–13 days.

MIGRATION Almost entirely resident.

LENGTH 16cm (6¼in)

WHEN TO SEE All year
WHERE FOUND Breeds extreme SW England, most of France, Spain, Portugal, Italy and Mediterranean islands, Balkans, Turkey and locally in NW Africa

Cretzschmar's Bunting *Emberiza caesia*

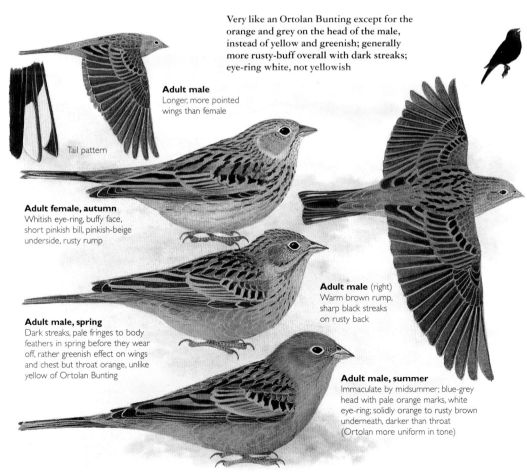

Very like an Ortolan Bunting except for the orange and grey on the head of the male, instead of yellow and greenish; generally more rusty-buff overall with dark streaks; eye-ring white, not yellowish

Adult male
Longer, more pointed wings than female

Tail pattern

Adult female, autumn
Whitish eye-ring, buffy face, short pinkish bill, pinkish-beige underside, rusty rump

Adult male, spring
Dark streaks, pale fringes to body feathers in spring before they wear off, rather greenish effect on wings and chest but throat orange, unlike yellow of Ortolan Bunting

Adult male (right)
Warm brown rump, sharp black streaks on rusty back

Adult male, summer
Immaculate by midsummer; blue-grey head with pale orange marks, white eye-ring; solidly orange to rusty brown underneath, darker than throat (Ortolan more uniform in tone)

A southeastern equivalent of the Ortolan Bunting, this is a colourful bunting of low, rocky places with scattered bushes, often near the coast or on islands. It seems to be intermediate between species such as the Ortolan and Cirl Buntings, which require more vegetation, and buntings of barren rock or desert farther south.

FEEDING Of all the buntings this is perhaps the most terrestrial, foraging entirely on the ground for small seeds and sluggish insects.

VOICE Males have a simple song, less ringing or musical than an Ortolan's; there are usually three or four notes, the last one longer. The usual call is a sharp *tchipp*.

BREEDING The nest is sheltered by tussocky vegetation and rocks, usually on a slope. Four or five eggs are laid; they hatch in 12–14 days.

MIGRATION In autumn Cretzschmar's Buntings move south via the Middle East to winter in Sudan and Eritrea.

LENGTH 16cm (6¼in)

WHEN TO SEE March to October
WHERE FOUND Breeds in most of Greece and some Aegean islands (but not Crete), Turkey, Cyprus and Middle East. Extremely rare vagrant farther north or west of this range

Black-headed Bunting *Emberiza melanocephala*

A large, bright bunting of high summer in southeast Europe, this is a rare early-summer visitor to the north. It likes open, airy places with warm sunshine penetrating open olive groves and vineyards, and orchards and fields with surrounding hedges, overgrown walls, and small copses.

FEEDING It eats insects in summer and seeds at other times, picked from the ground and from among leafy vegetation.

DISPLAY & VOICE Males sing from prominent perches at any height, all day long, and also sometimes while in flight. The song is short but develops into a full, throaty warble. Calls are short and hard, like *cheuh* or *chup*.

BREEDING It nests in a thorny bush or vine, laying four or five eggs which hatch after 14 days.

MIGRATION They migrate to India in early autumn, returning in late spring; a few overshoot to northwestern Europe in June.

LENGTH 16–17cm (6¼–6¾in)

WHEN TO SEE Mostly late May to August
WHERE FOUND Breeds locally in Italy, more continuously along Balkan coasts of Adriatic and through Greece, Turkey and Cyprus; rare vagrant elsewhere

A big, solid bunting, big-billed and long-bodied; males obvious, but females and juveniles require care in identification

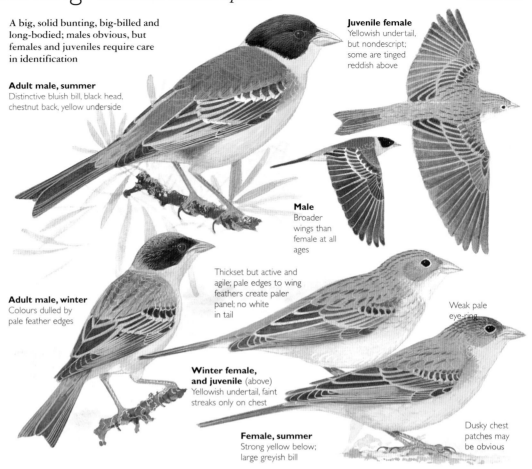

Adult male, summer
Distinctive bluish bill, black head, chestnut back, yellow underside

Juvenile female
Yellowish undertail, but nondescript; some are tinged reddish above

Male
Broader wings than female at all ages

Adult male, winter
Colours dulled by pale feather edges

Thickset but active and agile; pale edges to wing feathers create paler panel; no white in tail

Weak pale eye-ring

Winter female, and juvenile (above)
Yellowish undertail, faint streaks only on chest

Female, summer
Strong yellow below; large greyish bill

Dusky chest patches may be obvious

Yellow-breasted Bunting *Emberiza aureola*

Like the larger Black-headed Bunting, this is a bird that moves to Asia in winter, rather than Africa. It is a much more northerly breeding species, however, that is unfamiliar throughout most of Europe but occasionally encountered as a vagrant. In some places, such as Shetland, it is seen every year.

FEEDING It eats insects in summer, but otherwise this is a seed-eater, feeding mostly in or beneath long grasses.

DISPLAY & VOICE Pairs breed in small, loose groups, with nests sometimes very close together. Males sing from low bushes, with a melodious, jingling phrase; calls include short, sharp notes sounding like *tik*, *zip*, or *tzip*.

BREEDING The nests are built in grass tussocks or tree roots in wet areas, or on the ground where it is dry; four or five eggs hatch after 13–14 days.

MIGRATION In autumn an eastward, then southward, path takes them to southeast Asia; a few go 'the wrong way' to end up in northwest Europe.

LENGTH 14–15cm (5½–6in)

WHEN TO SEE Mostly late May to August
WHERE FOUND Breeds eastwards from Finland; vagrant in Britain, Scandinavia, Italy

Male, summer
Broader-winged than female

Male, year-old
Winter adult has all-yellow throat

Male, summer
Unique black face, yellow and chestnut breastbands, white wing patch

White underwing on young male (buff on female)

Juvenile female
Females narrow-winged

Some juveniles much paler, almost unstreaked below; a few intensely streaked

Juvenile female
Pale yellow over eye, on throat, thin pale centre line on crown; rump grey-brown, striped, unlike Yellowhammer

Yellow over eye, dark border to cheek, pale eye-ring on juvenile and female; two wingbars

Pink on bill

Tail pattern of female; some have white only on outer tail feather

Female, summer
Very worn wing and scapular feathers. Streaks on back recall House Sparrow

Pale centre line on crown

A slender, sharp-billed, streaky bunting with a flush of yellow on the face and underside; spring males are unmistakable

Little Bunting *Emberiza pusilla*

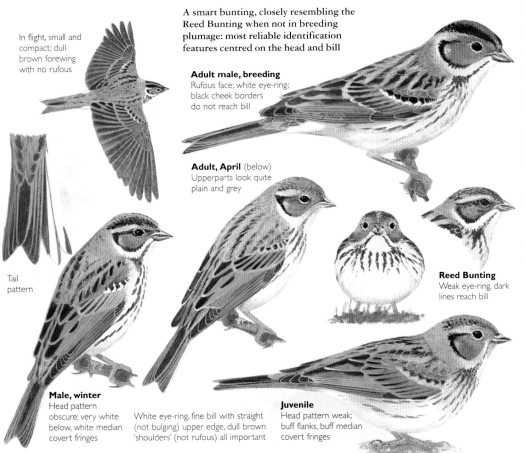

In flight, small and compact; dull brown forewing with no rufous

A smart bunting, closely resembling the Reed Bunting when not in breeding plumage: most reliable identification features centred on the head and bill

Adult male, breeding
Rufous face; white eye-ring; black cheek borders do not reach bill

Adult, April (below)
Upperparts look quite plain and grey

Tail pattern

Reed Bunting
Weak eye-ring, dark lines reach bill

Juvenile
Head pattern weak; buff flanks, buff median covert fringes

Male, winter
Head pattern obscure; very white below, white median covert fringes

White eye-ring, fine bill with straight (not bulging) upper edge, dull brown 'shoulders' (not rufous) all important

R are in western Europe, this small, neat bunting is a breeding bird of the far north. It likes moist, shrubby tundra in summer, rather than the more open spaces occupied by Lapland Buntings and the thicker woods preferred by Rustic Buntings.

FEEDING Although they take insects in summer, Little Buntings are usually seen feeding on seeds in crops, on ploughed earth or on footpaths.

DISPLAY & VOICE Males sing from treetops, with a variety of buzzy phrases and unmusical clicks. Calls are short, sharp, quiet clicks, unlike those of a Reed Bunting: *tik*, *zik*, *stip*, or *twit*.

BREEDING Four to six eggs are laid in a small, neat nest under the shelter of a grassy or mossy tussock, often in a thicket of willow, birch, or alder.

MIGRATION North European breeders migrate to southeast Russia and China; a few move westwards instead, reaching western Europe as vagrants.

LENGTH 13–14cm (5–5½in)

WHEN TO SEE Reaches N Finland end of May or early June, leaves by September; vagrants often seen late autumn or even into winter
WHERE FOUND Breeds eastwards from N Finland; vagrant Britain, Scandinavia, France, and the Low Countries

Rustic Bunting *Emberiza rustica*

A distinctive bunting in summer, but autumn migrants easily mistaken for Reed Bunting despite rusty rump and pale, peaked crown

Male, breeding
Boldly striped head; rufous streaks on white below, like no other bunting

Female, winter
Peaky crown; rufous flank streaks

Rufous rump recalls Yellowhammer

Adult, winter
Rufous breastband reduced to central mottled patch

Adult male, winter
Dull black stripes on rich buff face, pale cheek spot; flanks heavily marked rufous

Tail pattern

Juvenile female, September
Weakest head pattern; note peaked crown, black corners to cheeks with white spot; rufous flank streaks, pinkish legs

A breeding bird of northern woods, the Rustic Bunting prefers wet places with willow, birch or conifers growing from riversides or swampy ground. With a slightly less northerly range than Little or Yellow-breasted Buntings, it is more familiar in much of Sweden and Finland.

FEEDING It typically forages on the ground like other buntings, looking for seeds, but also takes many insects and spiders in summer.

DISPLAY & VOICE Males sing from high perches with a short but melodious, even mournful phrase. Calls are short, sharp and high: *zit* or *tik t'k*.

BREEDING Nests are on or near the ground, in tussocks or root tangles beneath bushes. Four or five eggs hatch within 11 days; the chicks leave the nest well before they can fly.

MIGRATION In autumn western breeders move east, then south, to spend the winter in China or Japan. A few move west instead, reaching western Europe in autumn.

LENGTH 15cm (6in)

WHEN TO SEE Mostly late May to August; vagrants September to November in west
WHERE FOUND Breeds Sweden, Finland, Russia; vagrant Britain, the Low Countries, France

Reed Bunting *Emberiza schoeniclus*

Male Reed Buntings in spring are unmistakable, but juveniles and females are sufficiently like several scarcer species to raise hopes of a more exciting find. Consequently, like other common buntings and finches, they are sometimes treated as the haystacks in which rarer needles might be discovered. Not that Reed Buntings are not interesting birds to watch in their own right. They like mixed fen, with sedges, irises, reedmace, and purple loosestrife mixed with reeds. Lines of willows beside rivers, or alongside flooded gravel pits, also make very acceptable habitats. In some areas they may breed in damp places on upland hillsides, with rushes and long grassy tussocks. In winter Reed Buntings remain close to wet places for the most part, but often feed in what stubbles they can find; they regularly visit gardens. They are frequently to be seen mixed with Yellowhammers, Corn Buntings, Chaffinches, and sparrows.

FEEDING They pick most of their food from the ground, often from among the stems of bushes and tall marsh plants. They eat mainly seeds and buds, but in summer they also take many insects and spiders.

DISPLAY & VOICE Males sing their short, jingly songs repeatedly from low perches in spring and summer. The typical Reed Bunting song is a short series of discrete notes followed by a trill; unpaired males have a faster song, while paired males have a slower, less interesting version with longer spaces between the notes. The usual call is a soft, quite full *seeoo* or *tseup*, very distinctive once it is learned. In spring they give a very thin, high *seee*. They do not give any of the ticking calls typical of other buntings.

BREEDING The nest is well hidden in a dense tussock of sedges or grass, or in the base of a bush growing from a damp marsh. Four or five eggs are incubated for 13 days, and the chicks fly when about 10–12 days old. They leave the nest three to five days earlier, to clamber about in nearby vegetation.

MIGRATION In spring small migrating parties often appear on grassy places beside freshwater pools or lakes on their way to higher or more northerly breeding areas, usually accompanying Meadow Pipits and Pied Wagtails. Scandinavia and eastern Europe are almost entirely vacated in autumn as the birds move south and west.

LENGTH 15–16.5cm (6–6½in)

WHEN TO SEE All year in W and central Europe; March to October in N Europe; October to April in most of S Europe
WHERE FOUND Breeds Britain and Ireland, mainland Europe south to central France, locally S France and Iberia; in winter, from Baltic south to Mediterranean coasts

A richly coloured bunting with much rufous-brown, cream, and black and a broadly white-sided tail; breeding male unmistakable, but other plumages need care

Male, winter
Tail has white sides; note much broader wings than female

Female, summer
Narrower wings than male

Rufous 'shoulder' patches

Male, breeding
Long-tailed bird; all pale tips worn off head

The difference in body size of males is a puzzle that has yet to be resolved

Male, autumn
Long-tailed individual

Male, spring
Short-tailed individual

Male, late summer
Very worn, dark above

Black and cream on back, more rufous on wings, becoming darker with wear

Female, breeding
Dark cap, cheeks, and malar stripe; pale over eye and under cheeks; dull eye-ring; compare with Little and Lapland Buntings. This is a long-tailed individual

Tail often flicked to reveal broad white sides

Female, winter
Two pale stripes on back; short-tailed individual

Darker legs than Little Bunting; bill thicker, more convex

Female

Juvenile

Lapland Bunting *Calcarius lapponicus*

Pale underwing coverts; lark-like shape, with long, straight outer primary

Tail dark with little white on edges

Long wings, forked tail; bounding flight

Male, winter Mottled black/grey forewing, rusty midwing panel, fine white wingbars

Female, first winter Tail of female looks longer than male's

Female (left) has broader wingtip than male (right)

Wings long and narrow compared to Reed Bunting

An inconspicuous bunting in most plumages; spring males are obvious but others are more difficult: blackish ear-covert corners, dark mottled stripes beside throat, mottled breast sides, rufous midwing panel are all helpful features; more terrestrial than Reed Bunting

Male, spring Pale crescent behind black face, black breast, black streaks on white flanks, bright rufous nape

Note long wingtip projection compared with stubby tip of Reed Bunting

Female, summer Bright nape; broad buff stripe over eye curves under dark-edged ear coverts; yellow bill unlike Reed Bunting

Female, winter Paler central crown; plain cheeks with black corners; mottled chest around white V

Juvenile female Dull; dark rufous wing panel edged white, heavy black striping below

Juvenile male Two pale back stripes join pale, curved wingbar; bright nape

Adult   Juvenile Adult tail has bright white, juvenile tail is dull white/grey on outer feathers

Juvenile Pale, buffy type most like Reed Bunting; note rufous wing panel

Superficially like a Reed Bunting, the Lapland Bunting also has a lot of the Snow Bunting's character about it. It is a similarly low-slung, short-legged, feathery-thighed bird of the far north, which visits low-lying coastal marshes and muddy tidelines in winter. It can be remarkably elusive in long, tussocky grass, but a close view is rewarding, especially of a well-marked male. A hint of the summer pattern often remains even in winter, and the colouring always has a pleasing richness and complexity. Wintering birds in eastern Europe are often far from the sea, but in western Europe they remain more or less coastal. In summer they avoid the rocky terrain favoured by Snow Buntings and breed in shrubby tundra with dwarf birch and willow, or mossy places with scattered stones and shallow pools.

FEEDING In midsummer an abundance of flies provides their main food. At other times they feed mainly on seeds. Lapland Buntings run on the ground, stopping to pick up seeds or shuffling up to tussocks of vegetation to search the stems for insects. They occasionally feed in low bushes, but rarely on really bare, open ground.

DISPLAY & VOICE The song flight is a pipit-like performance, with a steep, silent ascent followed by a wide, spiralling descent with full song. This is lark-like, full-throated, but short: *teeTOOree-tooree-treeoo*. The calls are worth learning, as they frequently draw attention to migrants and wintering birds: a bright, metallic *teeu* and a hard, drumming or stuttering rattle, tuneless and flat *t'k-r t'k-r t'k* or *tikitikitik-teu*.

BREEDING Nesting is timed so the birds can feed their young on the brief midsummer abundance of flies in the far north. They build their nest on the ground, in a hollow or sheltered by a tussock, frequently near water and often sheltered by an overhanging spray of birch or willow. Five or six eggs hatch after an incubation of 11–13 days. The chicks leave the nest before they can fly, which they do after just 9–10 days.

MIGRATION All European breeding birds move south in autumn, becoming rather scarce migrants and local winter visitors in eastern Europe and around the North Sea.

LENGTH 15–16cm (6–6½cm)

WHEN TO SEE May to August or September in breeding areas. Migrants in September/October on W European coasts; in wintering areas mostly October to April
WHERE FOUND Breeds arctic Russia, N Finland, N Sweden, Norway. Winters Denmark, S Baltic coasts, Netherlands, E Britain; also Hungary and Ukraine

Rock Bunting *Emberiza cia*

Often inconspicuous and detected only by its call, this sober little bunting reveals a neat pattern and rich colouring if seen clearly. It likes a mixture of bushes and rocks, where scrub meets open spaces such as alpine meadows and grassy slopes at the upper edges of forests. It is not, however, restricted to really high ground and often descends to the lowlands in winter.

FEEDING It eats seeds and buds all year, insects in summer. It feeds on the ground, standing on stems to bend them over to reach seeds, or in bushes.

VOICE The song is similar to that of a Dunnock or a short, weak Wren. The usual calls are a short, thin, elusive, yet penetrating *seee* and a harder *zit*.

BREEDING The nest is built in a crevice or below a bush growing from between boulders; the clutch of four or five eggs hatches after an incubation of 12–14 days.

MIGRATION Resident except for short downhill movements in winter.

LENGTH 16cm (6¼in)

WHEN TO SEE All year
WHERE FOUND Breeds SW Germany, S France, the Alps and Apennines, higher parts of the Balkans and E Europe, and most of Iberia. In winter more widely in lowland Italy, Greece

A richly coloured bunting with a unique head pattern, usually on or close to the ground and rather unobtrusive

Male, first winter

Female, spring

'Sinister' face

White coverts below; grey forewing above

Broad wings, long tail, rufous rump, grey and black bill in all plumages

Broad white outer tail feathers

Males, summer

Unique pale grey–rusty orange contrast

Male, winter
Whitish breast streaks

Juvenile
Greyish throat and chest, dull bill

Both male and female wear to duller colours when breeding

Grey, whitish, and black head stripes always distinctive

Rufous rump, white wing lining, grey forewing characteristic of species

Snow Finch *Montifringilla nivalis*

More sparrow than finch, this is a bird of alpine habitats, moving only a little lower in winter. It spends most of its time on the ground, on rocks, or on roofs. It breeds in exposed, often partly snow-covered areas, near grassy slopes above the tree line and on screes. In winter it hangs around high ski villages, the back yards of hotels and border stores, and farm buildings.

FEEDING Insects and spiders are most important in summer, seeds in winter.

DISPLAY & VOICE Winter flocks disperse in spring, breaking up into solitary breeding pairs. The males sing to defend their territories, both while perched and in flight. The song is a varied, sparrow-like, sometimes prolonged chirruping. A hoarse *szi* or *tseeh*, often repeated, is a frequent call.

BREEDING Nests are in cavities in rocks or banks. Four or five eggs are usual, hatching after 13–14 days.

MIGRATION Snow Finches make small movements to lower, milder altitudes in winter.

LENGTH 17cm (6¾in)

WHEN TO SEE All year
WHERE FOUND Breeds Pyrenees and NW Spain, Alps, locally central Italy, very locally on highest areas through the Balkans

A large, sparrow-like, thickset bird of high altitudes, with a lot of white in the wing

Adult, winter (below)
Pale face, yellow bill

Male, spring (left)
Black bill, dull black face and throat, reddish-brown back

Adult, summer
Back duller than in spring; white across primary coverts

Male, spring
Dusky black throat

Juvenile (below)
Streaks on hindwing; all black primary coverts

Juvenile

Often droops black inner coverts so white partially obscured

Adult, winter
Yellow bill, white throat, paler back; grey head always distinctive

Snow Bunting *Plectrophenax nivalis*

Flocks fly fast and low, wings swept back, with flickering jerky action

Wings long and pointed, tail short, forked

A long-bodied, short-legged, heavy bunting, starkly pied in summer, richly coloured in winter when it often shows little white until it flies

Male, winter
Maximum amount of white on wing

Female/juvenile (left)
much paler under wingtip than adult male (above)

Juvenile female, midwinter
More rufous in autumn, but wears to duller colour in winter

Back of male bright in autumn, duller from November until spring

Male
Some have dark rim to primary coverts

Females at all ages have dark-centred median coverts

Juvenile male
Median coverts all-white, creating white wingbar

Dark wing with broad white band (below) may indicate second-year female or a different race

Female, winter

Juvenile male

Female, breeding
Plain white beneath; Norwegian birds may wear much browner

Male, breeding (right)
Brown of winter plumage wears off to reveal smart black and white

Great variation in winter appearance may reflect area of origin

Female, winter
May lack breastband

Juvenile female (above)
Back may be more rufous or much greyer; note cheek patch, yellow bill, small black feet almost hidden, white on wing

Female
This plumage believed to be adult

Long black wingtips tight over tail, long body, tiny feet characteristic of species

Male, winter (right)
White forewing means male; complex rusty-orange head and breast pattern wears off in spring

Long, low-slung and short-legged, the Snow Bunting is quite different from the typical farmland buntings of the lowlands. In summer it is a mountain bird, but while some remain on the hills throughout the year others move to the coast, where lively, engaging flocks live on sand and shingle beaches and the saltmarshes just inland from the shore. These winter flocks feed inconspicuously, but may suddenly fly up and dash along the beach, flashing their white wing patches as they go; they then either double back or just dive back to the ground. They may seem to stop dead and disappear but, with care, it is possible to approach them and get a close view. Their rich colours and varied patterns are always fascinating. In summer Snow Buntings are different birds: they must be sought on the highest cliffs and screes in Scotland, where they are rare, in Scandinavia, or on bleak, rocky places beyond the tree line in Iceland and the remote Arctic islands.

FEEDING Snow Buntings search the ground intently for seeds, shuffling forward on their short legs. They avoid grassy fields, but in much of Europe they visit arable land with stubbles and ploughed fields. In northwest Europe seed-rich muddy and shingly patches beside saltmarshes and, less often, stony ploughed fields are typical feeding habitats. In summer they also eat insects; these and spiders form the sole diet of the chicks.

DISPLAY & VOICE Males attract mates and defend territories by singing. They sing from high boulders and in short, rising song-flights. Their song is loud and musical, with fluty two- or three-syllable notes like *turee-turee-turee* and *sweeto-swevee-seeetuta*. In winter two calls are distinctive: a loud, clear, full *too* or *tuu* and a silvery, rippling, twittering trill, *p-trrr-iririp*.

BREEDING The nest is located in a deep crevice between boulders, or on a scree slope. In Arctic areas nests are often built in buildings or other stone structures, or even in discarded tins or boxes. Four to six eggs are incubated for 12–13 days and the young are fed in the nest for a further 12–14 days.

MIGRATION In winter Snow Buntings vacate the northern parts of their breeding range, but elsewhere many birds remain in the breeding areas. Large numbers move south and west to lowlands and coasts.

LENGTH 16–17cm (6¼–6¾in)

WHEN TO SEE All year; in wintering areas, mostly October to March
WHERE FOUND Breeds Spitsbergen, Iceland, Norway, highest and northerly parts of Sweden, N Finland, N Scotland. In winter, hills and coasts of Britain, North Sea coasts, east through N and E Europe

Glossary

ABRASION The effect of wear, chiefly on feathers. It is especially marked on the pale parts that lack the dark pigment melanin, since this strengthens the feather. White tips or pale spots at feather edges may wear off, changing a plumage pattern quite markedly. Abrasion can make bright colours duller, but dull tips may also wear away to reveal brighter colours beneath.

ADULT A bird that has reached maturity and whose plumage no longer changes with age.

ALULA The small feathers on the 'thumb' or bastard wing, often prominent on birds of prey which use it to control the airflow over the wing, but visible on the folded wings of most species.

AXILLARIES A small group of feathers underneath the base of the wing, in the bird's 'wingpit'.

BAR A 'bar', or a barred pattern, refers to lines across a feather or plumage tract (as opposed to streaks or stripes, which are lengthwise). A Chaffinch, for example, has wingbars, and a Kestrel has a barred tail.

BILL The beak, made up of two parts, the upper and lower mandibles, each covered with a bony sheath.

BLEACHING The fading of feathers in sunlight. Combined with abrasion, this can radically alter the appearance of a bird without any change of feathers. For example, the blackish wing feathers of many immature gulls in autumn fade to brown by the following spring. More subtly, the grey feathers of an adult gull become tinged with beige when faded and worn. Some large birds of prey grow glossy black-brown feathers that fade to dull brown or even pale buff as they are bleached. 'Old' and 'new' feathers can often be detected like this, indicating the state of moult, but parts of feathers usually covered when the wing is folded remain darker than those constantly exposed.

BREEDING Pairing, laying, and incubating eggs, and rearing young.

BREEDING PLUMAGE The bright plumage in which birds display at rivals and court potential mates, typically in spring and summer but in some cases in winter prior to the breeding season. Male ducks, for example, are at their brightest in winter but become dull when the females are on eggs or tending young.

BROOD The young birds hatched from one set of eggs; a 'second brood' results from another set of eggs laid later during the same breeding season.

CALL Call notes are distinct from songs, and used in many situations: most calls are 'contact calls' used by social species to keep in touch, or alarm calls used to alert others to potential danger.

CLUTCH A set of eggs laid within a few days and incubated together.

COVERTS The short feathers that cover the leading edge of a bird's wing.

DIVING DUCK A type of duck that dives underwater to feed, unlike a 'surface feeder' which feeds either by filtering food from the shallows or up-ending to reach more deeply without submerging. Diving ducks always submerge from the surface while swimming, not by plunging from the air.

ECLIPSE The plumage acquired in early summer by male ducks (drakes), in which bright colours and patterns are lost so the birds resemble dark females. By this time drakes do not need to display, so they adopt better camouflage while they moult their wing feathers: a process that may make them flightless for a time.

EMARGINATION A marked narrowing of the web on the outer side of a feather. On many birds of prey emargination of each outer primary, together with a deep notch on the inner side of the adjacent feather, produces 'fingered' wingtips. On small birds such as warblers emargination can usually be examined only on a bird in the hand (or on a close-up photograph) but may be important in identification.

FERAL Wild birds derived from domestic or captive stock that has either escaped into the wild to form breeding populations, such as town pigeons, or been introduced, such as Greylag Geese in lowland Britain.

FIRST YEAR A bird in its first year of life: a term applied to plumages after 'juvenile'. In species with very distinct plumage sequences, such as larger gulls, the autumn and spring moults produce a sequence from juvenile to first winter, then first summer, second winter, second summer, and so on.

FLUSHED Startled from cover, usually by the close approach of a potential enemy.

FORM A variant or 'morph' within a 'polymorphic' species that occurs in two or more plumages, such as the Arctic Skua which has 'pale', 'intermediate', and 'dark' forms (sometimes called 'phases', which is misleading as each individual retains one plumage that does not change with time). Such forms occur together and interbreed freely; they are not races or subspecies.

GENUS See *Scientific name*.

GLIDE Flight without active wingbeats, either using momentum to maintain height and speed or losing height to gain forward movement.

GONYS The fusion of the two sides of the lower jaw near the tip of the bill; on gulls, for example, it may create a marked angle.

GORGET A band of colour or pattern around the chest.

HYBRID A cross between two species. Hybrids are usually infertile but wildfowl, in particular, may produce fertile hybrids that may be very difficult to identify, some looking confusingly like other species.

IMMATURE Not yet fully adult and sexually mature: implies that plumage will change (becoming closer to adult pattern) with increasing age, but not always so. Different species progress to adulthood over different lengths of time: for example, a Herring Gull may be visually distinguishable in its first, second, third, and sometimes even fourth year before becoming adult, after which its age cannot be judged by plumage pattern, but smaller gulls may become adult within a year.

IRRUPTION An irregular mass movement, usually caused by a food shortage, that results in birds occurring outside their usual range. Not to be confused with regular migration.

JUVENILE A young bird in its first set of feathers, in which it makes its first flight. Juvenile plumage may be short-lived before being replaced at the first moult.

LORE The area on a bird's head between its eye and bill.

MIGRATION Regular movement between geographical areas from season to season, for example between summer breeding areas in Europe and wintering areas in Africa. Some migrations are much shorter and may involve, for example, movement from inland hills to lowland areas on the coast. Species that migrate may be described as 'migrant' and individual birds seen during migration as 'migrants'.

MOULT The replacement of feathers. Birds moult in a strictly ordered fashion at specific times of the year, which in some cases vary between sexes and age categories. A moult may be partial (typically replacing head and body feathers, but not those of the wings and tail) or complete; complete moult may take place in a continual sequence or may be suspended for a period, such as during migration.

PAIR A male and a female that breed together. In many species, however, a single polygamous male may mate with several females; in fewer species the reverse occurs. In some polygamous species, such as harriers, a male may help rear the young of more than one mate, but usually a male that mates with several females takes no part in caring for the eggs or young.

PASSAGE MIGRANT A bird that appears in a certain area only while on passage during migration, in spring and/or in autumn, neither nesting nor spending the winter in the area. Some individuals of a species may be passage migrants while others of the same species may breed or winter in the area. Green Sandpipers, for example, appear in Britain as passage migrants in spring, very rarely as summer visitors, commonly as passage migrants in autumn, and regularly in smaller numbers as winter visitors – but none are strictly resident.

PLUMAGE The whole set of feathers on a bird; also used when describing birds that change according to age, season, or sex, for example juvenile plumage, summer plumage, or male and female plumage.

PRIMARY FEATHERS The long wingtip feathers; together with the secondaries, they form the flight feathers or remiges.

RACE A local variant of a species, also known as a subspecies, that breeds within a defined geographical area and has evolved a slightly different form, colours, or patterns from birds of the same species elsewhere. Most races are difficult to identify in the field, but others are well-marked. Particularly distinctive 'races' are often elevated to the status of separate species.

RESIDENT A bird or species found in the same area all year round.

ROOST To 'sleep'; also a gathering of birds that may come together at night, or for example at high tide when wading birds are displaced from mudflats or beaches.

SAILING Used to describe a bird of prey flying in a wind or updraft without wingbeats, with a rather different appearance from a similar bird gliding or soaring – but these three intergrade.

SCIENTIFIC NAME The name, typically based on Latin or Greek, printed in *italics* following the English name of the species in each major heading in this book. Two words are normally used, but the full name may consist of three. The first (always with a capital initial) is the generic name, or 'genus', while the second is the specific name; the two form a unique combination that defines a species. The third name, if any, identifies a subspecies or race. The scientific name is useful because the first name – the genus – is applied to a group of species that share similar characteristics, and which are closely related. For example, the Reed and Marsh Warblers of the genus *Acrocephalus* have much in common, but Savi's Warbler and the Garden Warbler (*Locustella* and *Sylvia* respectively) are quite different, both from *Acrocephalus* warblers and from each other.

SECONDARY FEATHERS The shorter flight feathers on the trailing edge of the wing, between the primaries and the tertials.

SOARING Flying with wings fully spread and not flapping, often on warm, rising air currents, typically circling and gaining height (unlike gliding, which is moving directly forwards without wingbeats).

SONG A particular vocal performance used to attract mates and/or announce an individual's presence and claim to a territory. The songs of different species are mostly very distinctive, and help in identification (for example, the simple repetition of a Chiffchaff compared with the flowing cadence of a Willow Warbler) but some species display marked variation between individual birds.

SPECIES A particular type of bird (or other organism) that interbreeds with others of the same type to produce fertile young. For example, the Song Thrush *Turdus philomelos* is a species, while the Mistle Thrush *Turdus viscivorus* is another species in the same genus. The precise definition of a species is, however, debatable and the status of several 'species' in this book is still unclear (see the smaller shearwaters, gulls, and crossbills). Hybrids between species are exceptional, and typically produce infertile young, but they are more frequent in some bird families, especially wildfowl.

STREAK A lengthwise mark *along* a feather or plumage tract, such as a dark streak along the back or flank (as opposed to the crosswise 'bar').

SUB-ADULT An immature bird, in a plumage that is neither juvenile nor adult (but, by implication, closer to an adult in appearance).

SUBSPECIES See *Race*.

SUMMER VISITOR A bird (or species) that visits an area in summer to breed (such as the Swallow, which moves to Europe in spring, breeds, then departs in autumn to spend the winter in Africa); also, therefore, a migrant.

TARSUS The lower part of the exposed leg, above the foot. It is actually the tarso-metatarsus, roughly equivalent to the human foot, while the 'foot' of a bird is equivalent to human toes. The tarsus is usually the most obvious part of a bird's leg, below the exposed joint.

TERTIAL FEATHERS The innermost set of trailing feathers on each wing, between the secondaries and the body.

VAGRANT An individual bird that has turned up well outside its usual range by accident, for example a North American warbler blown across the Atlantic in the autumn; popularly, a 'rarity'.

WADER A typically coastal or marsh bird that often feeds by wading in shallow water, known in North America as a 'shorebird'. Neither term is satisfactory as the families of 'waders' include some species that do not wade much or at all (such as the Dotterel) nor live by the shore for much of the year (Lapwings breed on fields, Curlews on moors). On the other hand, some birds that do habitually wade (such as the Grey Heron and Spoonbill) are not referred to as 'waders' in the sense used as a handy shorthand reference to plovers, sandpipers, and their allies.

WEAR See *Abrasion*.

WILDFOWL The group of birds that includes all the swans, geese, and ducks.

WING FORMULA The structure of the wing described according to the relative lengths of the primary feathers on the spread wing (rather like the relative lengths of fingers on a human hand) together with any emargination of those feathers. In the case of some difficult warblers, for example, the wing formula, which is practically constant within species, can be helpful in identification (see, for example, Willow Warbler and Chiffchaff, Melodious Warbler and Icterine Warbler).

WINTER VISITOR A migrant that appears in the non-breeding part of its range, for example the Fieldfare winters in England but breeds in Scandinavia and northern Russia.

Acknowledgements

As the book has reached the latter stages of its long production, we have been
delighted to see the high standards of proofs and production values achieved
by the publishers and printers. We feel confident that this book will be a
pleasure to own in this respect and offer our sincere thanks to all of those
involved in the project along the way, who have done all they can to
accommodate our requirements. Not least, we thank our long-suffering wives,
Dorothy and Marcella, for their patience, encouragement, and consideration.

WITHDRAWN